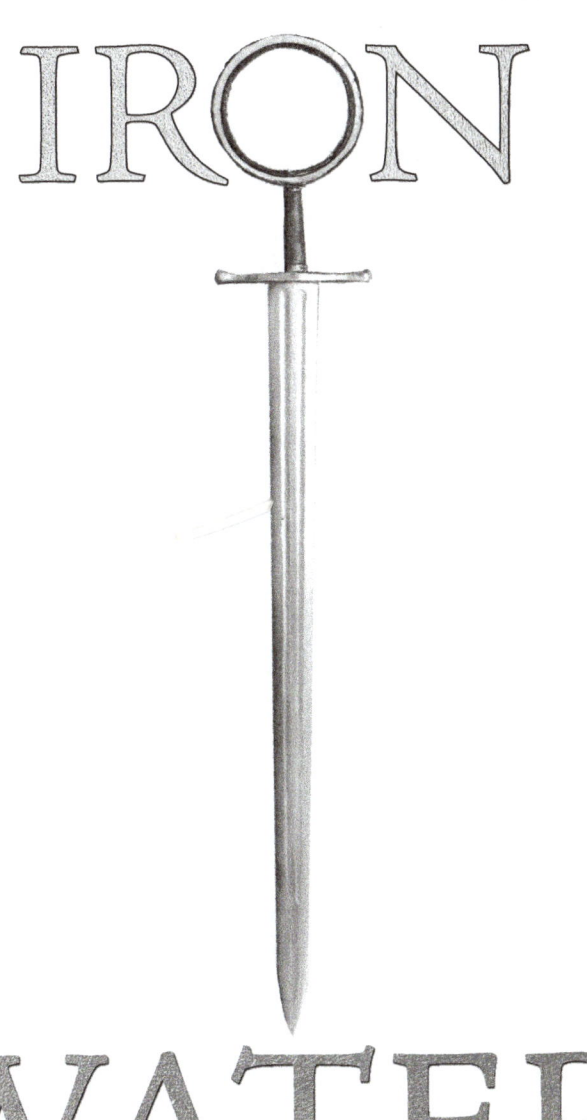

IRON

WATER

~ A Wetherill Mystery ~

IRON

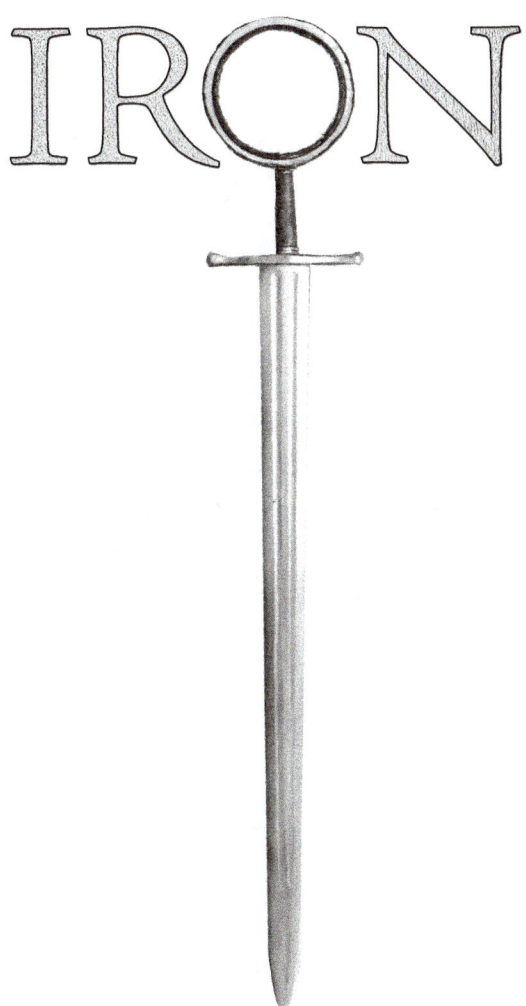

WATER

ᴓ Edward Robert Belding ᴔ

Iron Water
A Wetherill Mystery
© 2024 Edward Robert Belding

ISBN: 978-1-964335-06-3

Cover design and book layout: www.greatwriting.org

Dedication

Out of eleven siblings, five come to mind as worthy of inspiring and helping me to take the path less taken. Thanks to Jay, Duke, Tim, Sue, and Jen.

PROLOGUE... 10

GOOD NEWS AND BAD NEWS 14

THROUGH THE BARRENS 33

THREE HEROES IN ONE DAY 52

BIG TOM'S WELCOME... 71

A RENDEZVOUS OF SORTS 88

HAGER'S CHILD... 108

SQUABBLES AND STORMS 127

BAD NEWS AND NEAR DISASTERS 153

A STRANGE CONCOCTION AND ODD CONFRONTATION ..172

ESCORTS FOR A PRINCESS 191

A SUNDAY FEAST..202

A SEPARATE FEAST 235

TWO LETTERS READ, TWO LETTERS WRITTEN 249

THE IRON CAGE 264

THE THIRD CORPSE 275

AMANDA'S FIND... 291

ESCORT FOR A PRINCE 303

THE FIRES OF HIBERNIA 318

THE AMBUSH 333

THE RUSE 343

BLACKPOWDER 361

DEVILS AND WENCHES... 383

BAGGING A DEVIL..399

ALMOST HOME... 418

EPILOGUE.. 435

BACKGROUND NOTES 444

Ed. Belding lives in Kendall Park, N. J., with his wife, Florence, and two of eight grandchildren. He is a retired educator who graduated from Rutgers University with a B.A. in History and an M.A. + 30 in education. Belding has written two books and several manuscripts on the Revolutionary War in New Jersey. His Wetherill Mystery series is his latest foray into the time period. More than a thousand of his poems can be found on the "Ed. Belding, poetry collection" Word Press site. He is also an eclectic, self-taught artist whose paintings have appeared in several regional exhibits. He continues to employ all recycled materials in his works. Ed. Belding serves his community as the South Brunswick Township Historian.

Ed. is a retired softball pitcher who played in modified fast-pitch and slow-pitch leagues. He is presently conducting batting and fielding clinics for the South Brunswick Senior Citizens Center.

PROLOGUE
• • • • • • • • • •

At the Morris Town gallows, almost two-thousand folks witnessed the hanging of David Reynolds on Friday morning, September 17, 1773. The weather was ominously dry and unseasonably warm; thus, families brought forth food and drink to share. In the midst of such a communal good mood, the condemned man was led to the gallows to speak his last words. Women began to cry and a few men shouted the names of others who should feel the noose this day. After all, Reynolds was a lesser member of a notorious gang of Morris County counterfeiters and passers that included several gentleman types with connections to folks in high places. Some rumor mongers claimed this nefarious organization went as high as friends and business associates of William Alexander, the wealthiest man in these parts and the one who preferred to be called Lord Stirling. The good Lord William was, of course, untouchable as were all men closely connected to him. These were types who were well spoken for and ones who could afford good lawyers. The rest of the captured gang members belonged to well-respected families. They had relatives who rubbed shoulders with Lord Stirling's ilk. The folks in the hanging crowd knew all this. The other men accused would in time be set free, whereas poor Davey Reynolds would pay the price for all of them with his life. He had been caught lugging excellent plates and bundles of finely crafted twenty-pound East Jersey bills. His intentions were to sell the plates and pass the bills. To these crimes he confessed. The others captured had only confessed to passing counterfeit bills. However, under the law of the Jerseys, those who crafted, sold, or passed bogus Jersey money in the Colony were subject to capital punishment.

Thus, more folks joined in the call for the three men who had been given a last-minute stay of execution. Now the crowd was demanding that Benjamin Cooper be strung up besides Reynolds. They wanted Samuel Haynes on the other side of him. And they wanted Dr. Barnaby Budd to feel the noose. Even during Reynold's plea for all folks to be kind to and take pity on his wife and children, the riotous ones in the crowd continued to call out the names of the other three.

One young man in the crowd did not care either way. He was a rather coarse-looking fellow—an indentured stable man with unkempt curly hair of dirty gold under a torn castor cap. His dark brown eyes studied the most uncautious folks in the crowd. He cast furtive glances at the more affluent of these spectators. He made his way towards them with a noticeable limp, jostled into each one of them in turn, begged pardon each time, and slipped away quick as he could, even when a Constable bothered to keep an eye on him. He secreted his winnings into the deep pockets of his coat. This character was known to locals round Morris Town as the indentured stable boy of Samuel Haynes. Folks swore that he was good round the stage waggon horses, and Haynes told all of them that Jack Redmon was worth his keep. The boy had never tried to run away like his older brother had done. But what Jack Redmon did in his rare idle time was anybody's guess. He just disappeared, but always came back to chores.

Jack Redmon was damn good at thieving when he put his mind to it—good enough to never get caught. He had honed his pickpocket skills years ago before he left Dublin with his brother to try their luck in America. Redmon was still at his nefarious craft after he and his brother found work in Morris Town. Opportunites were slim in this rustic village, but he decided to stay. One of his legs was shorter than the other and walking at a brisk pace was difficult for him. When his brother decided to flee successfully on his last try, Jack refused to go because he did not want to slow his brother down. He never regretted his decision. Jack Redmon had big dreams for himself after he earned his freedom. Relieving this hanging crowd of some of its wealth was part of his plan to fulfill those dreams.

Nimble-fingered Jack was sure of one thing—he liked large crowds. Mobs like this one, caused by the hanging, was the largest gathering he had witnessed since being bought off a ship at Amboy by Mister Haynes. In quick time he worked the crowd and snitched real coin and several large bills. Before poor old Davey Reynolds was cut down, Jack Redmon was gimping off to the woods behind the tavern and stable barns owned by his master. Well he knew the way, for he had often disappeared from here during idle time to visit his secret haunt, and stash his stolen loot in a dark, dry place known only to himself.

The going grew difficult when the path turned miry and mean—not even a deer path, but a way just the same for its creator. Jack was surprised at how deep the muck and mush round his poor-shod feet felt as he progressed deeper and deeper into his hiding woods. The September drought appeared to have had no impact on this fetid place. He was leaving a trackable trail in the mud, but it did not worry him. No one would dare venture where he was going. Jack Redmon congratulated himself for being so clever. He thanked his master for the worn coat he wore. It had deep pockets and not one hole in any of them. He pushed a sharp branch away and carefully slid over the trunk of a massive fallen tree. He disappeared into the shadows of more foreboding ground.

Jack Redmon found his favorite hiding place long after the noon when the sun was starting to bow to the low mountains to the west. Long, impenetrable shadows were growing longer. Redmon tugged at the brush and small rocks piled against boulders pressed together over a crawl space. The ground cover here was tinder dry; so was the soil underneath. There was no evidence of the space having been used by beasts of any size. The place was just as Jack had left it. He got to his knees, removed his coat, and crawled on his belly. He pushed the coat, keeping it in front of his head as he eased into his secret lair. In the frail light that seeped in over his shoes, Jack found the sealskin pouch he had stolen from one of the stage waggons almost a year ago. He emptied the pockets of his coat, counted out his loot—more by touch than sight—and then deposited these latest winnings in the pouch. He shoved the pouch into a side crevice, then eased his way out feet first as he always did. He pulled his trusty coat after him. When he lifted his head to turn around in the spare sunlight, he was struck on the side of his skull just above his right ear. Then his throat was slit and his tongue was freed from its rightful place. Jack Redmon did not care either way . . .

1

GOOD NEWS AND BAD NEWS
· ·

*—at the Wetherill Plantation near Cross Roads,
Monday, September 20, 1773*

Colonial Assemblyman, John Wetherill, Esquire—the wealthiest man from the South Ward of Middlesex County in the Royal Division of East Jersey—stood at the large window of his study. He had left his morning coffee brew, which Sarah, his house slave, had brought to him an hour ago, untouched. John hated the aftertaste of the year's popular substitute for subsidized East India tea. Besides, his doctor had recommended a better substitute beverage. It would cost no more than it was worth. Mister Wetherill liked that idea. In fact, he had lived his long life with that motto in mind. People round here who voted for him over and over again called their representative a pinch-penny politician. They meant it and they were glad to call him that out of praise. He was their lion against King George's prerogatives, Parliament's unwanted over-reach, and a clever Governor William Franklin's machinations. Yes, old John Wetherill was proud to be known as frugal to a fault—a critic of the greedy practices of landed proprietors, a dissenter when it came to granting the King's agents more powers, and a rioter because he dared entertain the idea of independency. But, of late, he was slowed down by gout, headaches, and a riotous stomach. He was looking and feeling as old as he claimed to be, stooped at the shoulders, pale as scrimshaw.

At first, he blamed it on the exhaustive efforts to resolve that festering sore—the robbery of the Treasury of East Jersey, which occurred way back on July 21, 1768. To date, the monies had not been recovered; a gang of counterfeiters had been accused of the robbery—one poor fellow already hanged and three more men awaiting the same fate; the Treasurer, Stephen Skinner, was still holding on to his position thanks to the foolish stubborness of his good friend, the Governor; and, as a result of all this, a Legislature at loggerheads with the Governor over funding in various areas. Just thinking about all this caused John Wetherill's head to ache. He feared that he would not live to see the robbery solved. But he promised himself to die trying—Skinner must be forced to resign; the new Treasurer had to be chosen by the Assembly, as it was done in other colonies; the Governor had to be brought down a peg; the stolen money had to be found; and the true thieves brought to justice . . . ah, the new tasks of Hercules . . .

With hard hazel eyes, John Wetherill watched his friend, the good and fit Doctor Stites—up from the village of Cranberry to pay a brief visit and offer solicited advice—unhitch his Long Bridge sorrel, mount with a young man's agility, and trot down the apple orchard path from whence he came. The patient was not pleased with the outcome of the Doctor's visit. That is why John Wetherill stood stiff as an upstart boy before his favorite window, long after Hezekiah Stites had disappeared down George Rescarrick's Road. Old John tried to match the straight pose of the large lone oak that towered at the corner of the widower's beloved orchard. This majestic tree stood guard near the best scion branches on the pippins. He counted his prize graftings, whispering their names as if they were his children. He smiled. Nanna, his dear departed wife, would have been proud of his latest accomplishments in the soil. Then he sighed. His feet started to ache from standing too long, and his stomach complained about the large breakfast Sarah's mother—the slave cook, Fannie—had prepared for him. Maybe it was time to retire, give up on his quest to resolve the Treasury robbery scandal, sit for the rest of his days by the window, watch good things grow—perhaps even a grandchild prancing under the trees, and let his son, Vincent, run the plantation. After all, his brother, George, was allowing his son, Thomas, to run the tavern up Rescarrick's Road at Cross Roads. He might even convince George, now a Freeholder, to run for his seat in the Assembly.

John Wetherill took a deep breath and let it out slowly. His stomach growled in the process of taking its usual path of independency. He broke wind, then quickly eased away from his own stink like the gentleman farmer that he was. John returned to his finely polished mahogany secretary desk, took up the change Stites had left him, stuffed the crisp Jersey bills into the pocket of his snuff-colored waistcoat, sat down slowly on a spindly chair, and re-read the note the good Doctor had left there. He sat for a spell, scrutinizing the instructions from the one man he respected and feared in equal measure. The medicine in the tiny blue bottle on his desk was listed first, but it went by a name he could not pronounce. He was to take a drop or two a day in a cup of hot milk. The ingredients for a daily physic were listed next. John felt assured that Fannie, or one of his field slaves, could fetch each item in the spice garden and the swamp. He was to take two spoonfuls a day at least till the full moon ended October. During that time, he was to do light work only, avoid feasting on Fannie's richest foods, and take no lengthy sojourns. The trip allowed by the good Doctor would be the second sitting of the twenty-second Assembly in Burlington, which had been predicted for mid-November.

The note concluded with advice on employing a long-term tonic culled from boiling crushed sassafras leaves in iron water. The slaves could easily gather the bitter leaves, but finding good iron water would present a problem. The best source, way up on Schooley's Mountain, was a good distance removed from here— more than a day's journey. He had visited those highlands several summers ago, even taken baths in the spring pools there. That option was now out of the question. But acquiring good iron water would have to be done. Perhaps Vincent would tear himself away from his new bride of six months and make the necessary journey for him. His son had been planning to cart and sell barrels of true-aged apple brandy and cheap jack in Brunswick and Amboy this month. Perhaps his son might travel farther to ply his bounty. Doctor Stites claimed there was no need to rush on the tonic, but John Wetherill saw value in experimenting with the strange brew as soon as possible. The sassafras and iron water might just become John Wetherill's tea of choice. That would show the King what he felt about the hated imported stuff. John would pay little and enjoy every sip of the Doctor's rebel stimulant, even if it tasted like water from a shaving bowl.

That dour prospect forced John to think of ways to excite such a brew. The Assemblyman decided, then and there, to follow the good Doctor's regimen to the letter. John Wetherill was too important a man to entrust the running of the plantation to his son just yet, or let his brother take his place in the Assembly.

He had asked the Doctor for twenty more years, but was happy with Stites's guess of ten. There was still much to accomplish before laying claim to being the richest man moldering in a yet to-be-chosen cemetery. Folks called him the 'Keeper of the Public Purse,' and he intended to continue to be as tight with the people's money as he was with his own. In a way, the money stolen from the Treasury in 1768 was his money and the money of the people who had elected him. Skinner had been careless and lost over six thousand pounds of public funds. Wetherill wanted it back. He wanted those who were responsible for its loss to be dealt with properly. This had to be accomplished before he went to his grave.

John Wetherill turned the Doctor's note over, took quill in hand, dipped its point in char ink, and began listing all the maladies that were plaguing the Jerseys. At the top of his list was the interminable embarrassment caused by the Treasury robbery and the failure to make the Treasurer, Stephen Skinner, accountable for his carelessness. John, playing the role of a wise physician for the Colony, was about to write down the remedy when Fannie's man, Pharoah, tapped with his hoe on his master's favorite window. John struggled out of his chair, pen still in hand, and returned to his window to see what was the matter. His oldest and most trusted slave was pointing his hoe toward the orchard path and holding up two fingers with his free hand. Wetherill followed his slave's gesture and saw the dust cloud kicked up by teams of horses and the large wheels of two handsome carriages. The first he recognized as his own, driven by his stable slave, Boss. However, he could not identify the team and coach and driver following close behind. He had been expecting Boss to return by noon with his son, Vincent, and his daughter-in-law, Abigail, from Brunswick Town as planned; but whoever was in the second carriage was a mystery to him.

John Wetherill gave a quick glance skyward, gauged the sun's position, and determined that it was already past noon. He liked the warmth by the window, but not the quality of the air in his study. This was not the room for entertaining guests.

He decided to entertain them in the more spacious and less malodorous parlor room off the welcome hall. Quick as his old bones and goutish foot allowed, he sped to the adjoining front room.

He called for Sarah and she appeared instantly. A look of alarm spread across her bright-eyed, tawny face, but she was given no chance to speak.

"Sarah, my dear child, hurry to your mother," ordered John Wetherill with not a jot of patience in his voice. "Guests will be here in a minute. Tell Fannie to prepare suitable drink and treats . . . no tea . . . make it apple brandy and sweet cakes . . . you will serve them in this room."

Sarah gave a quick glance inspection of the parlor, frowned, then retreated to the warming kitchen to inform her mother of her master's instructions.

John Wetherill scanned the fine sea-blue room. He saw no need to fuss over its condition—too late for that. Instead, he gimped to the window, pulled the curtains wide, and raised the sash to a frugal six inches above the sill. A bit of fresh air on such a bright, sunny day might be all this room needs, thought John.

Before Wetherill could turn around, his son opened the door and strode in with his young, beautiful wife in tow. Vincent stood tall and erect as the guardian oak in the orchard. His brown eyes sparkled like amber jewels under thick brows. He was a young man of twenty-four, but possessed a confident countenance in the presence of peers and gentlemen much older than himself. He would make a fine militia officer some day, mused John. Vincent was already running the family business interests in Brunswick Town. He was trustworthy, honest in his dealings with associates, and, best of all, obedient to his father's wishes. Old John had no doubt as to who would take charge of his plantation when he no longer could. Abigail, his son's wife, was another matter altogether. She was frail as a dandelion in the wind and as shy as a field mouse. Abigail, or Little Abia as they preferred to call her, had so much to learn of wifely ways. In many respects she was still a child. But Abigail Lott Wetherill was strikingly beautiful—long flowing golden hair under a proper white bonnet; sparkling blue eyes wide with the fires of love and marital bliss. Her eyes burned with the same intensity as when she and Vincent wed in April. As John Wetherill was fond of saying: "The shine is still on their apples."

Little Abia stood close to Vincent's side, clutching his hand, posing with lips wavering between a pout and a smile. However, this time there was mischief aplenty behind the look. She was glowing in a special way. Somehow Abia appeared happier than when John had seen her last in late July. He could only guess the reason and wonder why he, an old widower, was so jealous of his son's good fortune. How John longed to wed again, preferably to a young woman who could bring joy to his day and outlive him.

"Good day to you, father," declared Vincent in a voice strong enough to jolt John Wetherill out of his moment of reverie, "How are you feeling?"

"The doctor visited today and offered up a foul-tasting recipe for success," answered John, as he eased from window to closest high-backed chair. He did not sit in it, but stood behind it holding on to its high knobs with both hands. "Now I can battle these devilish vapors that have plagued me all summer and look forward to a full recovery in a month's time . . . no need to fret over me."

John Wetherill invited Vincent and Abigail to sit in the cushioned settee, but they insisted on standing.

Vincent seemed unusually nervous as he spoke, "We are glad to hear such a promising report."

John scoffed, "Good news maybe, but at a handsome cost. I gave Doctor Stites a large bill of credit to cover expenses and he gave me but a few small bills in change."

"That's the spirit, father," said Vincent. "Your complaining about an overpayment is surely a first sign of your coming round."

John waved him off and ignored the fact that uninvited persons were standing in his hallway waiting to see him.

"Enough of this prattle about my health," said John. "Any good news from you and Abia?"

Vincent and Abigail smiled at each other.

"A yes to that," blushed Abia as she tugged at her skirts, curtsied, and exited the room in a rush.

"What's this about?" asked John amusedly.

"Little Abia is embarrassed to tell you, father," admitted Vincent, "so the task falls to me." Vincent beamed, "It may be too early to say, but my wife missed her monthly measure in August and now we wait another month to know for sure."

With that, Vincent rushed to his father, gave him a warm hug, and backed away so as not to smother the honorable Assemblyman.

John caught his breath. "Good news indeed," he declared, "by the fates, good news indeed."

Vincent coaxed his father into the straight-backed chair.

"That is enough news from us for now," said Vincent as he backed to the door. "I am taking up the time of important visitors who have gone out of their way to see you. Besides, I must go help Abia with the luggage and see her to my room."

"Make sure Boss helps you with your things," John insisted. "Use the master's bedroom, son. 'Tis where you were born. Your mother would like it so. It will bring you and Abia good luck. Besides, I sleep downstairs now since I've been troubled to walk."

"Thank you, father," answered Vincent. "Are you up to seeing these guests now?"

"Depends who they are and what they desire," said John. "I've a nap to take and I don't want it postponed."

"'Tis your cousin-in-law, Judge Dan Cooper, and Assemblyman Jacob Ford's son, who goes by the same name. They have business to tend to in Burlington, but, due to urgent news from their county of Morris, decided to discuss matters with you before heading down. They had stayed the night at the Indian Queen, where they told minehost of their desire to find you before heading to Burlington. They were informed of our presence in Brunswick and of our preparing to depart to care for you through the harvest season. Cooper and Ford found us just before Boss had loaded the last of the luggage bags on the coach, and they asked if they might follow us down to here."

"What is their news all about . . . good or bad?" asked John.

"Of that they gave no clue," said Vincent, "but I assume it to be important, since they have gone out of their way to have an audience with you."

John Wetherill waved his favored hand again, "By Jove's thunder, I'll listen to what these wasters have to say . . . but I do not have to like it . . . probably far from fair news . . . the kind meant to ruin the fine direction you and Abia have set me in . . . but it must be important . . . enough so, to cause them to alter their route . . . have them come in . . . you, Abia, and I will counsel about your promising news after our guests have departed . . . ah, and remember, before you leave on your little business venture tomorrow, I must go over the list of medical needs with you . . . don't forget, because I might . . ."

"Yes, father," said Vincent, as he was turning to open the door.

"Come join me if you can," added John, "in the parlor after your wife is set and satisfied . . . I will need someone to protect me from a pair of shrewd outlanders who are sure to talk my ears off . . . when you return, make sure you say something that signals the end of all discussion and the start of my nap, which Doctor Stites has ordered me to take every day."

Vincent smiled, nodded once more, and opened the door that led out into the hallway. He invited the two gentlemen into his father's parlor, introduced them by name, and excused himself in order to tend to what he described as personal matters.

John Wetherill summoned enough courtesy to welcome his unexpected guests, pointed to the settee and stuffed chair on which he wished them to sit, and described the refreshments Sarah brought in and placed on a small cherry wood table between chair and settee.

John addressed the older man first, "Cousin Dan, what brings you and your companion this far into the South Ward of Middlesex County?"

Judge Daniel Cooper, from Long Hill in the Passaic Valley, was related to John Wetherill by marriage. His first wife, Grace Runyon of Piscataway, was related to John's mother, Anne Susannah Runyon. Dan Cooper was a large man in all ways. He wore a fine peppery wig which neatly framed the jowls of his red face. His stern, dark eyes and his thin, tightly drawn lips broadcasted an air of superiority and self-importance. He was known for his adamant interpretations of the King's Law and a no-nonsense approach to justice in a backwoods county. He preferred to wear black, and this warm day was no exception—jet velvet jacket and black silk waistcoat with silver buttons in appropriate places. Locals, especially those who could not afford an expensive lawyer, knew full well not to bicker against him. By all outward appearances, the quick-tempered and robust judge was a righteous, honest, and stubborn fellow. But John Wetherill knew elsewise. The man had become a survivor full of bluff and bluster. In the strong winds of prevailing sentiment, during these hard times of scarce money and widespread debt, Cooper was more a willow than an oak. In the early years of Morris County, he had served as a feared, rather independent, constable of the peace; but, now, as part of the established order, he fell in line with the way his superiors got things done. From 1760 to the present, old Dan Cooper served as a well-respected magistrate. However, at the beck and call of a few who saw themselves as entitled to superiority, this Judge had learned to look the other way.

Dan Cooper took a polite sip of his host's apple brandy, then spoke: "We are the bearers of bad news, cousin John. We have come to you because you are a decision maker . . . a problem solver . . . you get things done . . . we need your help in resolving an indelicate matter."

Wetherill took a gulp of his best brandy and let it burn his throat sweetly. Such a fine eight-year-old batch, he thought . . . it will fetch a good price in this pre-winter market . . . good as a wife for warming on a cold night. He studied his half empty glass, then remembered that he had to respond to the Judge's gloom: "Out with it, Dan; you were never one to be shy. How bad can this news be?"

"There's been a murder in Morris Town," sighed Cooper, "and it comes on the heels of the hanging of that counterfeiter and passer, Davey Reynolds, whom I had condemned to death in my own court along with my own son and two others. I suspect this latest killing is connected somehow to the hanging. Someone is sending me a message I'd rather not receive."

John Wetherill was confused. He had heard about the hanging of David Reynolds, an innholder from Hacket's Town, who was caught with print plates and counterfeit bills of credit in his possession. Reynolds had also been found guilty of passing Jersey bills in his home colony. This warranted the capital punishment he received. However, Reynolds played a minor part in a loose network of tavern owners and stage waggon captains who were plying well-made false money in Morris County and beyond. Many felt the punishment for Reynolds was unduly extreme. From news accounts and word of mouth, John Wetherill also knew that three other underlings—Samuel Haynes, tavern owner in Morris Town; Doctor Barnaby Budd, just south of town; and Judge Cooper's own son, Benjamin, iron mine and furnace co-owner up around Hibernia—had received death sentences for like crimes.

However, their fate had been respited for some reason. Rumor had it that these three men, threatened with the rope, confessed to knowledge about the robbery of the Treasury back in 1768. To save their necks they were giving up the names of other members of the gang of counterfeiters, who had something to do with the robbery. The ringleader, Samuel Ford, Jr., of Hanover, who had printed the counterfeit tender, was the one they accused of masterminding the Treasury robbery. Unfortunately, Ford, and a few others who had been brought into custody, escaped gaol and fled to parts unknown. There were probably others who were involved in the counterfeiting and the robbery and who were never brought in. John Wetherill knew much about this matter, but he had heard nothing of the latest killing or its connection with the hanging. He did not really know how he could be of help to Morris County officials.

"Tell me what you know of this latest incident," said Wetherill, "and how you came to the conclusion that it is connected to the hanging of Dave Reynolds."

"Jacob knows more about the details than I," said Judge Cooper, as he gave a quick nod to his companion. "After he brings you up to date, you will have no choice but to draw the same conclusion."

"We'll see about that," said John Wetherill, who drained his glass of brandy with one more gulp. "I always like to have a few options."

Jacob Ford, Jr., cleared his throat. He had not touched the prize apple brandy, for he confessed that he did not drink spirits, but he had been nibbling on one of Fannie's tasty sweet cakes. This Jacob Ford was a younger version of Judge Cooper—taller than average, large boned, gangly and awkward in his fancy traveling outfit of red and brown velvet with prim lace at the throat. His complexion was darker than Cooper's and was crossed by some few pox scars. His own long black hair was tied back neatly with a lead gray ribband that did not match his outfit. But most striking about this fellow were his unreadable brown eyes that were set to a stare under thick black brows.

The man's look disturbed John Wetherill, but he politely kept his eyes on Ford's calloused hands. Here was a strapping, athletic backwoods version of a successful entrepreneur, capable of pulling off a shrewd business deal or pounding an opponent into submission with his fists. The younger Ford had come down from the iron mine on Horse Pound Mountain to run his ailing father's business interests in Morris Town. These included western land speculation, pig iron production and sales, plus grist, hemp, and powder mills. In addition to such business enterprises, Ford aspired to be a judge in Morris County. He had dabbled in law enforcement as an under-sheriff in the mountains, and he was now under the tutelage of Dan Cooper. The only mark against him, as far as John Wetherill knew, was that Samuel Ford, Jr.—the notorious counterfeiter and prime suspect in the Treasury robbery—was his cousin.

"The murder victim was one of Samuel Haynes's indentures," stated Jacob Ford, Jr., in a deep, somber voice, "a stable boy from Dublin, who went by the name, Jack Redmon. They say he was good around horses, and better at lifting things with his fingers. He had a brother who also worked for Haynes for a short time, but that one was accused of thievery and fled. Jack remained. locals suspected him of the same crime, but he was never caught at it. Folks remember seeing him last alive in the crowd gathered for the hanging. Some spectators thought it unusual for the boy to be wearing a heavy wilton coat in such warm weather—and a garment that had many pockets no doubt. After that, he disappeared till his corpse was found by another stable boy who went to change the straw in the far out-barn. In death's repose lay the body of Jack Redmon, just inside the entranceway . . . throat cut, ear to ear . . . mouth agape with tongue missing . . . in place of the tongue, a real johannes gold piece . . . and an ugly wound at the side of his skull, after his beaver hat had been removed . . ."

"I assume the other stable boy was the immediate suspect?" interjected the Assemblyman, as he steepled his fingers under his chin while listening intently. "Perhaps the two brawled and one was unlucky?"

"Of course the boy was interrogated at length by Constable Fairchild, who was first to be summoned by the tavern keep," replied Ford. "He was quickly dismissed as a suspect."

"How so?" asked the Assemblyman.

"The tavern keep, Henry Burnet, informed the Constable that the boy had accompanied Haynes's oldest drover in taking a provisions waggon down to Elizabeth Town the day before the murder. Those two did not get back till dawn. They missed the hanging and the murder. This other stable boy, whose name escapes me, led the team of horses back to the barn after helping to unload the provisions waggon. That's when he discovered the ruined Jack Redmon."

"Who else was questioned," asked John Wetherill, "and did anything come of it?"

"Nothing was learned," said Jacob Ford adamantly. "Constable Fairchild held audience separately with the rest of the indentured servants and slaves tied to the property of Sam Haynes. Each said they had neither heard nor seen anything. They covered for each other as to their whereabouts that night. The same goes for the hired help—those men and women who slept on the premises and those who did not."

"How about the travelers who had come in on a stage waggon and stayed over to enjoy accommodations at Haynes's establishment?" John Wetherill was casting a wide net with this line of questioning.

"There were five that I know of," responded Ford. "One who came in by horse fetched his own mount before midnight and took the east road to Hanover. The Constable is looking for that fellow. The other four stayed the night, were roused shortly after dawn, interrogated, and allowed to ride in the first coach waggon bound for Powles Hook."

"So nothing was learned from those four?"

"Nothing," said Ford in a crisp manner. "Two—a husband and wife—slept fitfully. I should say the wife slept fitfully. She heard dogs yelping, nothing more . . ."

"Let's return to poor Jack Redmon shall we?" asked John Wetherill impatiently.

"Of course," said Ford, as he cleared his throat again.

"What evidence did this murder victim offer to the authorities?"

"Certain interesting clues," contributed Jacob Ford, "but some of them merely allow speculation on my part . . ."

"And my part too," added Judge Cooper, who had drained his glass and requested more.

Sarah, who was standing by the open window glided silently over to the Judge and filled his glass.

Cooper thanked John Wetherill, not his slave. "Cousin, this is the best apple brandy I have tasted in years. You must make a cask or two available to me for purchase."

John offered a slight, sour look at the sudden change in the course of the discussion. The Judge's request jostled him off the track of his conversation with Jacob Ford. Yet, a chance to make a favorable business deal always seemed irresistibly inviting.

"My son, Vincent, is responsible for such transactions," admitted John. "He has a whole waggon load of barrels and rundlets to bring to market on the morrow. Vincent will gladly show you our orchards, press, and stills. He can easily set aside two casks of eight-year pippin brandy, either to accompany you or be delivered before the month expires."

"Such a delivery to Long Hill would be preferred," said the Judge. "To lug a pair of such prize spirit casks all the way to Burlington and back home would be risky."

"Our driver is more than fond of strong drink," offered Jacob Ford. "Younger jack or older pure is all the same to him."

The Judge roared in agreement, Ford chuckled, but John Wetherill merely offered a thin smile.

"And I have an idea for payment in kind," added the Assemblyman.

The Judge stopped laughing. He had been on the less preferred end of deals made with John Wetherill before. He knew his cousin-in-law as well as the Assemblyman knew him.

"Two casks of my best apple brandy for a full waggon of barrels filled with the best iron water from your blessed mountains," offered John.

Judge Cooper cast a look of perplexity, then chuckled at the deal presented by Wetherill. "My dear cousin, the barrels would be worth more than the finest spring water off Schooley's Mountain. It can be had for almost nothing."

John Wetherill rushed his words because he wanted to return

to the original discussion: "I shall return the barrels by next year if you desire them back. 'Tis the iron water I need to fulfill my Doctor's recommendations for a tonic. Besides, I have an idea for contriving a strong brew of my own using that very same water."

The Judge sighed, "You keep the barrels, which I pledge will be scoured clean and filled with the purest mountain water. Come next year you can sell me some of your own special tonic at some advantageous price to you."

"A wonderful transaction, indeed," boasted the Assemblyman, "one my son, Vincent, shall look forward to fulfilling each year for years to come."

The Judge sat back and began sipping his second glass of eight-year apple brandy. Cousin John had won again, but the Judge had not figured out how.

"My apologies, Mister Ford," said Wetherill. "Poor Jack Redmon lies cold and still and ignored by the likes of us. Please get back to him."

"Ah, yes," chirped Jacob Ford. Without skipping a beat, he continued, "First to examine the corpse was Constable Fairchild . . . second was the coroner—in this case, Doctor Inthill, who happened to have dropped by the tavern early in the morning to enquire about the well-being of the incarcerated Samuel Haynes. I was able to speak to both men . . . I concluded that their findings were in complete agreement."

"As were their speculations and yours?" asked John Wetherill.

"And mine also," chimed in Judge Cooper, as he answered for both himself and his companion.

"Not as I would hope," mused Wetherill, "but continue, Mister Ford."

"The corpse of Jack Redmon was parchment pale as if the boy had been startled by ghosts. Much blood had drained from the neck wound but little of it was on the Russia shirt or bearskin coat. Only a smear or two of his blood was found on the barn floor beneath him when he was rolled over. The assumption was made that Jack Redmon was dragged to the barn hours after being murdered . . ."

"And stripped and dressed in somebody else's clothes before ending up at the stable barn," interrupted John Wetherill.

"After much discussion between Constable and Coroner, that

opinion was agreed upon," admitted Ford.

"So whose clothes did the corpse wear?"

"The shirt and coat belong to Samuel Haynes," said Ford. "The boy's original clothes, including the coat he wore at the hanging, have not been found."

John Wetherill took another path: "I assume the blow to the head was not fatal, but intended to knock out the poor fellow?"

"Right you are," said Ford. "There was no blood at or around the knot on Jack's skull. He must have been out when his throat was cut and his tongue removed."

"Or vice versa," added Wetherill.

"How do you mean?" asked Judge Cooper between sips of his now favorite drink.

"Easier task to cut a man's tongue before cutting his throat," offered the Assemblyman, "and less of a mess in the long run. The trick is in prying the jaw open if the victim was not caught by surprise with his mouth agape."

"I do not think either man at the scene could tell," mused Ford. "Does it really matter in the end?"

"Depends on forthcoming events of a similar kind," said John Wetherill cryptically. "Let us hope this is the one and only killing that may have something to do with the hanging."

"I fear not," said Judge Cooper. "There is more to this. I fear that men of a higher station than poor Jack Redmon are in peril."

"What evidence do you have that points to such a view?" asked John Wetherill piquantly.

"The tongue," said Cooper.

Jacob Ford chimed in, "The boy's tongue was found in his fist. Someone had rolled it up in a fold of counterfeit bills and tied Jack's fingers round the roll. After the ribband had been unloosed, Constable Fairchild had to pry the stiff fingers apart in order to free the bundle of bills. After the roll was unfurled, a black tongue was found stuck to the innermost Jersey bill."

"None of Redmon's fingers were missing?" asked Wetherill.

"His hands were whole," admitted Ford. "Dirty with mud as if the boy had been digging with his hands . . . a scar across the back of his riding hand . . . it was an old scar."

"So he appears not to have been punished for pickpocketing?"

That is correct," responded Ford. "Neither a finger nor hand did Jack lose . . . just his life."

"And for what purpose I wonder?" asked the Assemblyman more to himself than to his guests.

The Judge rallied, "The indentured stable boy's death serves as a warning to those who did not hang alongside Davey Reynolds . . . someone does not like that Samuel Haynes avoided the noose on the day of the execution . . ."

"If that is the case," interrupted Wetherill, "then why was the boy's tongue cut out, either before or after he was dead?"

"'Tis not simply our decision to grant Haynes and his two fellow counterfeiters reprieves " opined the Judge. "It has to do with why the three, who did not evade the authorities, have decided to tell what they know of the Treasury robbery . . . I am sure of it."

"That is a great leap, cousin," said John Wetherill, "but not out of the realm of possibility. What say you, Jacob?"

Ford was slow to respond. It was as if he was juggling several options in his thoughts. "If you are correct, Judge, then not only is Samuel Haynes at the receiving end of a warning. Your son and Doctor Budd are in trouble too. The one, or perhaps more than one, who committed this murder, does not want the three men to talk. If they do, then they shall be murdered."

"This is worse than I originally thought," groaned Cooper, as he rubbed his forehead with his free hand. "The three men held must talk, whether they tell lies or truth, in order to be set free. If they do not talk, they shall be hanged. That is the deal in the works. Each of them has been vouched for by men of high station; and, other than serving as pawns in a counterfeiting game, each has been on the right side of the law. Reynolds was not vouched for to the same degree. He was also deeper into the game; so he's been silenced to serve as an example for the rest of us."

"So you do not believe the murderer, or murderers, simply desire eye-for-eye retribution for the hanging of Reynolds?" asked John Wetherill.

"I do not dismiss the thought," declared the Judge. "I saw the surly mob round the gallows, and I heard the names of the three called out. But this murder of Jack Redmon stinks stronger than backwoods 'Lex Talionis.'"

"At least Redmon has left enough clues to direct you on the path of motive," observed Wetherill. "It offers something to prove or disprove."

The Assemblyman's words evoked no response, so he plodded on: "Is there anything else you'd want me to know . . . is there any way I might be of help to you in this matter?"

"Only this," contributed Jacob Ford. "A knife of finest steel, clear of stain or blemish, was found on a cobbled rock at the sunniest corner of the barn."

"Perhaps it was used to slit Jack's throat?" asked John.

"The Constable and Coroner think not," replied Ford. "To them it was a brand new blade and not the one used for slaying Redmon. They showed it to Mister Burnet. He claimed the blade had been stolen from Mister Haynes a few months past, as were the clothes on the corpse."

"Which way was the blade pointing?" asked John Wetherill with a wink of his better eye.

Both the Judge and the entrepreneur stiffened at the question. They looked at each other with surprise and perplexity combined.

"Why do you ask?" said the Judge.

"Simply the curiosity of an old politician at play, gentlemen," confessed the Assemblyman, "and a hunch that you are closer to the truth than you are willing to admit. All you need to do is keep on the right path."

John Wetherill made a few suggestions for reaching some sort of resolution during the play of likely events in the next few weeks. He charged his guests and their law enforcement team with finding the murderer, or murderers, before a like killing was committed. The man who sped away on horseback before midnight had to be found and questioned. The source of the clothes that draped Jack Redmon's corpse had to be confirmed by Mister Haynes. The indentured servant's original clothes had to be found. The Assemblyman guessed that the boy's own garments had been discarded at his hiding place, the whereabouts of which was known only to the dead fellow and those who did him in. Wetherill suggested that hunting hounds be used to find the missing clothing and the hiding place. If successful in finding the latter, then more clues about the murder would probably be revealed in addition to all the loot stolen by Redmon.

"The corpse was stripped and dragged to the stable barn," opined Wetherill. "It must have been difficult going over a great length of rough terrain from hiding place to barn. I would guess the murderer had help. At the barn the scene was staged to appear as if the killing took place on Haynes's property. That means the boy's hiding place is beyond the acres Haynes owns. I would assume that the entire episode took hours . . . let's say it started after the hanging . . . and, obviously, ended before the body was discovered at dawn . . ."

"This must mean you favor our assumption that the murder serves as a warning to Haynes?" asked an anxious Judge Cooper.

"And a warning to the rest of the counterfeiters?" added Jacob Ford.

"Too early for me to commit to that," said John Wetherill. "I think you can eliminate an act of passionate rage against Jack Redmon by someone who simply did not like the fellow . . . you can eliminate retribution by some pickpocket victim who tracked the boy to his lair but forgot to retrieve the gold joe in his mouth and you can eliminate some uncautious fool's attempt to cover up an accidental slaying . . . and . . ."

"I see where this leads," interjected the Judge. "It leads us back to where we started from."

"There is another possibility," added John Wetherill, in a slow, sweet-brandied tone. "Suppose the perpetrators want to keep something hidden or want to find where something is hidden . . . something that goes beyond the mere counterfeiting game in your county . . . suppose they are also looking for the truth?"

Again, the Judge shot a glance over to Jacob Ford before responding. Then he spoke barely above a whisper, "What, pray tell, would they be searching for?"

"This is only conjecture on my part," admitted John Wetherill, "but something you might consider. A few clues at the staged murder scene seem to point to an attempt to warn certain parties to cease providing false testimony about the robbery of the Treasury."

Jacob Ford, Jr., remained as still as Sarah by the window, his eyes unreadable.

Judge Daniel Cooper squirmed, let loose a deep sigh, and whispered, "Pure speculation . . ."

"Give the thought time to ferment," said John Wetherill, as he lifted his empty glass up to the window light. He held his free hand up to stop Sarah from rushing over to refill the glass.

This gave the Judge enough time to rally and piece together his words hurriedly, "We all know my son and the other two who did not escape are lying to save their own necks . . . nothing will come of their testimonies . . . whether truth be told or not, they will be pardoned . . . no one else will be hung . . . the stolen money will never be found . . . Sam Ford will never be caught . . ."

"The murderers of Jack Redmon may not be interested in any of those things," declared John Wetherill, as his son entered the room noiselessly. "They may be concerned with administering their own brand of justice for an end we can only guess at . . . or they may be stirring up trouble for whatever can be gained from doing so . . . or . . ."

"Or both!" interjected Vincent with the exuberance of a young man who found need to change the subject.

2

THROUGH THE BARRENS
· ·

—on the way to Radford's Ferry Landing,
Tuesday, September 21, 1773

Vincent Wetherill figured he and Cutlope Hancock, the reliable waggoner known by folks between Cross Roads and Cranberry as just plain 'Cut,' were making good time. They used the plantation back path to get to Lawrie's Road, which ribboned north all the way to Radford's Landing. They made a brief stop at Rhode Hall to chat with a coach waggon driver and his passengers who were heading for Burlington. These travelers had stopped at Williamson's Inn for a respite before resuming their journey south. Vincent inquired about the status of Lawrie's Road up to the ferry landing. The coachman and passengers all agreed that the way was fast and clear with sparse traffic from farmers wending to market and not one horse rider of questionable repute. Vincent liked what he heard, thanked them for such positive news, and wished them all a good day. Upon moving out from Rhode Hall, he also wished himself a good day. His waggoner had plied this route often, but Vincent had not. His route of delivery had always been on Rescarrick's Road. Vincent hid his anxiety about cutting through the Barrens of Wickatunk. His childhood had been filled with scary tales of evil happenings there. Cut had been the author of the scariest ones.

He and Cut had six miles to go before reaching the Old Bridge that spanned the South River northeast of Spot's Woods. The dusty air was quickly warming as the sun climbed high in the near-cloudless sky. There was an abundance of birdsong emanating from the low branches of the stands of trees. There was the occasional chatter and skitter of hidden critters in the squat brush at the sides of the road. All living things were busy with the hustling which always heralded trenchant preparation for the onslaught of winter. It was not yet noon on the third day of what was shaping up to be another dry week. No stormy weather had been predicted. Other than the possibility of a forest fire or a smoldering swamp, there seemed nothing much to fear. John Wetherill's son was not familiar with the difficulties of this particular circuit route; however, Cut knew every inch of the way. Vincent figured the waggoner knew how to make it to the landing well before last year's time. Back then, Cut and two of his father's slaves, Boss and Pharoah, struggled through a driving rain. They did not reach Radford's till after dusk. This year's time for September was going to be better than last September's time. The more Vincent reflected on that prospect, the more he fell to liking the entire year. He had much to be thankful for. Helping others, like his father, in the months remaining of this year could only bring more good fortune.

"We've had good luck so far, hey Cut?" shouted Vincent, as he tugged the reins to signal his black Spanish barb to slow a bit so the waggoner and his team of bay Shires could catch up.

"Yup," responded Cut in a strong, deep well of a voice. He was a broad, barrel-chested man of fair German stock. Cutlope—a corruption of 'Gottlieb'—was a neighbor to John Wetherill, closer to Cranberry than to Cross Roads. At thirty-three years of age he was more a friend to Wetherill's son than to the Assemblyman. He ran his father's small farm and supplemented his income by working for John Wetherill at his apple press, stills, and as a teamster when needed. Cut, Vincent, and the nearby Carson brothers—Joseph and Charles—had recently formed the core of a local hunt club in the south county area above the Millstone River. They were men of humble station, save for Vincent who possessed a much higher status due to his father's wealth. He was the only one of them who could read and write. Thus, Vincent had been elected leader and spokesperson for a loose-knit brotherhood of rural freeman hunters that had yet to choose a name, build a hiding shelter or lodge, or come up with secret initiation rites or signs which many hunt clubs had.

Vincent might have been the leader, but he was not the most respected member of this particular collection of husbandmen who loved to hunt. Cut was the best shot. His father had given his son an heirloom German rifle at the age of twelve and showed him how to fire the weapon with keen accuracy. The Hancock family was never short of a good supply of fresh game. Cut's mother could do wonders in the kitchen with what he brought home. She was known as the best cook in the neighborhood with John Wetherill's Fannie running a close second. Be it a squirrel pie, a venison stew, or a boil of pigeons, no one bested Cut's mother. And no one enjoyed her efforts more than the members of the hunt club, who gathered monthly for feasting at Cut's humble farmstead. Cut's wife was an adept pupil of the senior mistress of the house, but she still had a long way to go before she was ready to take her mother-in-law's place. This observation came from Cut himself. He was never one to stray from the truth as he saw it.

Cut was stubborn and quite possessive of the few things of worth that he owned. His rifle was one of two prize possessions, equal in value to his portly, well-fardled wife—so he claimed. He kept the handsome piece wrapped in leather and always at his side. On this day, it was strapped to the board on which he sat. He was prepared to use the gun the instant a challenging shot came into view. Vincent was glad old Cut brought along the hunting rifle. He had merely a pistol at his belt—a small, puny piece that was only effective at close range. Indeed, Vincent was more than glad that his father had picked Cut to accompany him on this month's ride to the northernmost market. Cut and his rifle were two more reasons ensuring that this trip would be successful.

Most of the time, Cut kept his sparkling blue eyes on the rutty road ahead. With strong, muscular arms and large hands, he kept in strict command on the reins that controlled John Wetherill's pair of bay Shires. They were stout, dependable draft horses, but occasionally proved jittery over some slight disturbance. A sudden varmint come ascrabbling across the road could easily set the bays to panic. But Cut was the best at restoring order and keeping the Wetherill draft horses to the task at hand. He was all business on this trip, for he knew how valuable the apple brandy was to its owner.

Cut wore his green-checked wool cap low on his brow to keep the climbing sun out of his ever-watchful eyes. His straight sandy hair was close-cropped so that he did not have to worry about it getting in the way. His full face had been reddened by the September sun and the cool air of the morning had left him with a healthy glow. Cut's stout frame filled out his brown broad-cloth coat to where he had to keep it open and flapping in the gentle late morning breeze. This favorite hunting garment was frayed and patched in strategic areas, and on the verge of being worn one last time. Cut wore a green-dyed hunting shirt under his coat. It was thick and long, and lapped over his buff-colored buckskin trousers that were patched at the knees.

The trousers at the cuffs were tucked into black pegged boots that were strapped at ankle and calf. Cut was warmly dressed and ready for a long, arduous trip—one that just might stray into a little hunting along the way, or just plain trouble. But for now, he had only one thing on his mind and that was to make sure a waggon load of apple spirits got to its destination.

"Yup," repeated Cut in an even lower tone. "But we've got the Barrens to get through once we cross the bridge."

"Won't be any Indian ghost worries this time," declared Vincent with his usual confidence. "Isn't that true, Cut?"

Cut seemed not so sure: "Back in July, in the first dark hour, we heard a howling which started the horses. I had trouble controlling my team and got the wheels of the waggon mired in piney sand at the side of the road. We had to unload all barrels and rundlets to get the waggon free and rolling again." Cut concentrated on keeping his team of bay Shires, burdened waggon, and pair of quarter horses in tow to the middle of the road. "I'd say it was haints that caused such woe."

"Wish I'd been there to lend a hand," chided Vincent.

"Nein, you don't," said Cut with a trailing laugh. "You couldn't leave your wife so early, frail as she is and so much in love . . . it wouldn't have been right . . . besides, you're more afraid of haints than she is . . ."

"I am afraid of nothing," boasted Vincent with a nervous laugh. "I would have gone on the run, but it's not right to leave a woman when she's sick . . . at least that's what we thought at the time . . . but my woman is fit as a fiddle now."

"So is my mate," said Cut, "and it's great and good to get away from her for a few days at least . . . long as we don't run into no haints and no robbers ."

"Probably more than a few days," predicted Vincent, "and probably more than a few ghosts and villains."

"Haints or none of the sort," argued Cut, "the more time away, the better . . . that way my woman will appreciate me the more when I return to warm her toes."

Vincent chuckled at such wisdom. He wondered if it could be possible for his Abigail to love him more than she already did. Vincent was so glad his wife was convinced that she was with child, and gladder still that her desire for lovemaking had not diminished. Last night had been especially poignant with tears shed before and after. Abia did not want Vincent to leave her—not for a single day—but plans to do so had been made weeks before, after he had returned from August's sojourn to Burlington and Philadelphia. Vincent had brought her back such pretty things. That seemed to placate her. Now it was time for the traditional September jaunt that had to be accomplished before the rising of the harvest moon—the time for deliveries of prime apple brandy. The only difference this year was going to Amboy via the ferry at Radford's Landing, rather than to Brunswick. Boss was supposed to follow the Carson brothers up to Brunswick this time and make deliveries already paid for. Vincent had collected monies from clients during his last stay in Brunswick Town. Now his father had put him in charge of deliveries to Amboy and beyond. He looked forward to this responsibility. Vincent had promised Abia pretty things again, but also had to inform her that this trip would take longer than usual. He did not tell her why. News of a lengthier time of separation made Abia cry all the more. She wanted no gifts. She simply wanted him. Vincent insisted he would return before the harvest moon at the end of the month. Abia made her husband promise. He did so with all the earnestness he could muster, even though his promise was held erect by a guess. She kissed him deeply and whispered of ways she would like him to make love to her again. Vincent obliged her until sleep overcame them. He knew he had good reason to return to Abia as quickly as he could.

"Tell me again," blared Cut in a voice loud enough to rouse Vincent out of his pleasant daydream, "why we got a pair of old quarter horses in tow."

"My father's orders . . . they're part of his plan."

"We swapping two flea pouches for something of worth in a trade?"

"No, Cut," replied Vincent. "One's for the man we're supposed to meet up with at Johnny Rattoon's Tavern, and one's for the man we're supposed to meet up with across the Rariton in Amboy."

"Those two gentlemen going to eat 'em?" asked Cut. "'Cause that's all they're good for . . ."

"Nothing like that. We're supposed to convince the two men to ride with us all the way up and back. My father has kindly provided them with a means for making the journey."

"Depends on the journey's length," growled Cut. "I'll wager that closer to soon than to late our new companions end up carrying their mounts."

Vincent grinned at the prospect of that image. "My father has graciously offered to give the quarter horses to the men as long as they fulfill their obligations on the journey."

"Going to take more than two sway horses to do that," scoffed Cut indignantly.

"My father has seen to all that," said Vincent. "Both men owe him favors. He purchased the indenture papers for Ike Higgins from a foolish man who bet so much on the races at Powles Hook that he had no money left to pay off his last losing wager. My father was there and vouched for the man's debt of ten pounds. The man gave him Ike in return. The boy was fifteen at the time, and, as it turned out, no bargain. Ike was glad to trade masters, for the former had striped his back on more than one occasion, and once nicked his ear for stealing. However, instead of showing gratitude towards my father, the boy stayed lazy and frisky. In his first full year at the plantation, Ike did one thing well when he rescued me and Charley Carson from drowning under the ice on the mill pond."

"I remember that hellish event," interjected Cut as he tugged the reins to slow the team of horses at the approach to the stone bridge over the low and turgid South River. To and fro traffic was congregating there and folks were waiting for a turn to cross.

"It's the only reason my father kept Ike for another year," continued Vincent as the waggon in front of them came to a halt. "I considered Ike a hero for saving my life, but that deed was not enough to keep him. My father set him free with orders to find work elsewhere and pay back the ten pounds over time . . ."

"Your hero will never pay off his debt," declared Cut, who appeared irritated by the delay at the Old Bridge. "And he won't recognize you when you find him. If I'm right, old Ike will be in his cups or out cold after a brawly with a gloak twice his size."

"You might be true on all counts, Cut," mulled Vincent as he also grew impatient to cross over the bridge, plunge into the brooding gloom of the Barrens of Wickatonk, and eventually find who they were looking for. "Once I talk sense into Ike, he will remember me and remember that he still owes my father for his freedom."

"Ike's not worth a copper to us," scoffed Cut. "He's worth less than the quarter horse he'll get to ride. That one's trouble . . . you wait and see . . ."

"He's worked on and off at Radford's Landing, loading and unloading cargo, since sixty-three," said Vincent defensively.

"Most times off," guessed Cut, as the waggon in front of them started to roll. Cut set his team in motion to follow.

The two men ceased their idle conversation and concentrated on rattling and clomping across the bridge. The dust was high and thick here, sparkling in the golden sunlight whose source was now directly overhead and beating down, unopposed in a deep blue sky. Only the tallest twisted trees on the north side of the snaking river provided intervals of shade on this fine warming day. There was a heavy stink in the air, wafting up from the desiccating bogs in the Barrens. Gangs of insects attacked all sojourners with urgent fury. The choice was to swipe the air with a free hand whenever possible or simply ignore their presence. At such times, it was best to distract the mind with thoughts of more pleasant and pressing things beyond the disreputable Barrens.

Cut devoted time to scanning the sandy hills and stretches of marsh grass through which Lawrie's Road meandered. Above a wide length of treeless salt meadow, turkey vultures soared in circles, strategizing in the updrafts. Their shadows fluttered across the heartless landscape and signalled that a carcass of some unlucky beast, perhaps an old cow at its final grazing, was about to play host to a feasting. Prospects for shooting live game here did not look promising. The Barrens always reeked of things already dead.

Cut decided to break the silence: "If the quarter horses are meant for men we've yet to find, then, for sure, good John Wetherill reminded you about the one bay Shire meant for me."

"I wish it so, Cut," offered Vincent in as sincere a voice as he could muster, "but all that was said about you was the usual drover's fee, anything your hunting provides free and clear, and a barrel of four-year once our journey's done."

Cut swiped the air in front of his face with his free hand, and wiped his dry lips with the fingers of the same hand.

"Might be fair," mused Cut, "or might be not. Right now, it ain't . . . the only hunting prospects are my eyes, which these darn bugs are chasing . . . and I've a thirst one barrel of jack can't quell . . . tell me something to lighten my spirits, good Vincent, before I jump off this here waggon to go chase Wickatonk's haint and host my own party of vultures."

Vincent laughed at Cut's black sarcasm. "Plenty to look forward to, you cabbage head. There's all the days you'll be away from your wife . . . all the winnings you'll gain in Amboy, Elizabeth Town, and Powles Hook . . ."

"More the likes of losing the money your father has promised to pay me," retorted Cut. "I've never been good at cards, or dice, or picking a horse in a race."

"Not to worry, my good man," said Vincent with brimming confidence. "Ike Higgins will provide us in all games of chance . . . he has connections . . . he has clever ways of winning . . . and he is just plain lucky . . ."

"I heard he spends his winnings faster than he earns 'em," interrupted Cut "and only wins when he's sober, which is a rare event . . . and when he's moved by spirits, then he's a thief . . . remember this, he stole from my father and he stole from your father . . . not much to trust in that boy . . . he'll steal from us, too . . . you just wait and see."

"Last night, my father said that it takes a thief to catch one, and that's why Ike Higgins will join us."

"As I see it," said Cut with a long sigh of exasperation, "we're supposed to journey far out of our way into another county to help catch a murderer, not a thief."

"Probably a band of murdering thieves," reflected Vincent, as he remembered the gist of what his father had told him. "Ike's been suspected of murder as well as thievery. He has experience in realms that are foreign to us."

Now it was Cut's turn to laugh—a parched one at that: "This whole game old John's contrived, just to placate associates and strangers he don't particular like, is going to end bad for us . . . even bad for Ike and the other fellow . . . the onliest winners is going to be the murdering thieves we're looking for."

"Might prove to be the best hunting you've done in years," chided Vincent.

"Just keep Ike Higgins out of my sights, when I take aim at those devils," declared Cut. "If not, then that boy will lose both his pounders and his luck."

Vincent did not bother to respond. He knew that Cut's dislike for Ike Higgins went way back. There was no way to turn the German's thinking. He left Cut to his thoughts about what lay ahead. During the long stretch of road where it straightened and seemed endless, Vincent took the opportunity to reflect on all that had transpired since he had walked into his father's parlor and interrupted yesterday's conversation with the two gentlemen from Morris County.

Vincent had been filled in on the details about the murder of Jack Redmon and the larger picture, going as far back as the Treasury robbery of 1768. Possibilities, as to murderer and motive, were reviewed for Vincent's benefit. He confessed to knowing much about the robbery and little about the hanging of David Reynolds. He knew nothing about the slaying of the indentured servant. Vincent thanked the two visitors for bringing him up to date. The discussion eventually spun around to the requests made by Judge Daniel Cooper and Jacob Ford, Jr., to Vincent's father. Vincent listened politely and wondered what role he might play in the resolve.

All four men in the parlor room agreed that things might get terribly worse in Morris County. If the robbery, hanging, and murder were somehow interconnected, then the primary goal of those most concerned with bringing the Treasury robbery issue to resolution might be compromised. John Wetherill was convinced that Stephen Skinner, still the East Jersey Treasurer, had been derelict in securing the monies safely in his house. Jacob Ford took it a step further. He was adamant that Skinner had a hand in the scheme to rob the Treasury in order to pay off debts, which had accrued due to bad business deals. Many people knew about Skinner's financial situation. Judge Cooper was partial to his companion's opinion, but insisted that, before condemning a man of high station, a person was entitled to a fair trial. All three looked forward to the day when the Governor's darling resigned so that a trial could take place—the sooner the better. John Wetherill assured the others that Assemblyman James Kinsey of Burlington was spearheading the drive to oust Skinner and gain for the legislature the power to select the next Treasurer, as was the practice in neighboring colonies. All agreed that nothing should interfere with this effort, which would surely bring Governor Franklin down a peg.

The conversation finally boiled down to suggestions as to what should be done. John Wetherill listened to it all, even allowing his son a shilling's worth of opinion on the matter. However, at this time, the old Assemblyman did not let on that Vincent was to have a major role in the plan he was already formulating. The author of this plan was not physically able to carry it out; be that as it may, the author's son would do just fine.

Judge Cooper kept repeating his distrust of the enforcers of the King's law in his own county. He wanted an impartial company of investigators from another county to find out who was responsible for the murder, bring the wrongdoers to justice, and prevent more such incidents. He wanted his son and the two other counterfeiters to be free of reprisals in the aftermath of the hanging of Dave Reynolds. He did not want revenge by the mob to prevail. He also did not want his reputation as a fair judge besmirched by low-class hooliganism. John responded with a promise to form a team in Middlesex County—he already had decided who would be in this group, but he gave no names. He said that their identities would be known only to him and their methods of investigation would not interfere with what was already being done by authorities in Morris County. John Wetherill, however, promised no results. His men might find no further evidence and no murderer. They would not be able to prevent another murder; but he promised that his men would try. Judge Cooper seemed satisfied with that.

Jacob Ford, Jr., wanted more. He concurred on the idea of sending an outside team of investigators, but he wanted them to search for evidence that would clear his cousin of all charges relating to the Treasury robbery. He had no qualms about the counterfeiting allegations—everybody in Morris County knew Sam Ford, Jr., was guilty of making the best false bills and coins in the colony. Some folks considered him a sort of hero for his fine work. For this, he was known as the 'Treasurer of the Jerseys,' a skilled king of the counterfeit trade, and as charming as he was elusive. But Sam was no thief. Everybody in Morris County could vouch for that. The coaxed testimony of Haynes, Budd, and Cooper was seized upon by higher-ups as a play to quash the scandal raised by the Treasury robbery and get Stephen Skinner off the hook. This trick was all the doing of the Governor and his close advisors. Their effort to pin the robbery on Sam Ford and his gang of counterfeiters only vexed the Ford family's attempts to separate the counterfeiter from involvement in the robbery. Thus, Jacob Ford, Jr., was speaking on behalf of his distinguished father and his entire family. By clearing his cousin of the robbery charges, Jacob felt the Governor's scheme would fall apart, the testimony of the three being held by authorities would go unsubstantiated, and attention would, again, focus on Skinner.

Vincent warmed to Mister Ford's reasoning, but he could see that his father appeared bored by it. John Wetherill yawned. Perhaps it was a signal that the time had come for napping. His father stated that he would consider all requests and take action that would not interfere with the authorities in Morris County regarding the robbery investigation or the counterfeiting investigation. He promised nothing and he asked for nothing in return. There was no deal made, except that Jacob Ford, Jr., and his father would pay John Wetherill for all expenses accrued by the secret team. With that, the old Assemblyman struggled out of his chair and instructed Vincent to show the two guests around the near orchard, the cider press, and the stills. He also invited them to stay for Fannie's sumptuous midday meal, but they refused. Cooper and Ford had decided to take Lawrie's Road down to Randal's Tavern in Allen's

Town. They planned to spend the night there, then continue on to Burlington in the morning.

While John Wetherill was napping, his son gave Cooper and Ford a grand tour of the hallmark industry at the Wetherill plantation. The men were most impressed with the names that John had assigned to his precious fruit graftings, the size of his handsome press, and the ample storage facilities for the tuns of cider beyond the stills. Nothing further was said about the urgent issue which brought the men to the Wetherill plantation in the first place. By mid-afternoon, their coach-and-four was brought round and they boarded after making the usual deep-felt farewells. Judge Cooper offered that he and Mister Ford would return home from Burlington in four days at most, and that he would wait with great anticipation for the delivery of the two barrels of prime apple brandy. John Wetherill's son hinted that the barrels might get there before the Judge returned home, or, at the latest, prior to October's moon. With that said, the coachman hallood the team of jet black horses, and hooves and wheels kicked up a roiling dust cloud on the same path used to get to the Wetherill manse.

Later that evening, after a fine, light supper of boiled pork and roasted pigeon with peas and carrots—prepared by Fannie and served by Sarah—topics for discussion held to pleasantries, preparations for Vincent's imminent trip, and news that would not upset Abia. Talk gravitated towards her possible condition. She soldiered through the old man's barrage of questions without signs of her usual shyness or embarrassment. John Wetherill was pleased with her responses and toasted the probability of welcoming a new grandchild into his world. He already had five, but that was not enough for a wealthy man of his high standing. Vincent was even more pleased to raise a glass of Madeira, which his father had instructed Sarah to bring out for the occasion. Vincent was so very proud of little Abia for being forthcoming about their good news. Faces glowed warmly in the supper candlelight that night.

After consuming more wine than necessary, the conversation veered to the health of the master of the house and the role

Vincent's wife was to serve in his recovery, while he was away on business. Old John played down his condition and declared that in a month's time, according to the good Doctor Stites, he would be fit as a spring rooster. The wealthy duffer boasted that he would be ready for whatever Parliament or the Governor might sling at him. His head would be clear and his gut cleaned out before the next session of the legislature was called. In a month's time, he would be able to walk all the way to Burlington, once the prescribed diet and potion kicked in. Thus, John Wetherill insisted he wanted no one fussing over him. All he needed was for Abia to remind him when to take his required medicines; warn him of what he should, and should not, eat or drink; and assist him in preparing drafts of new bills he intended to introduce at the next Assembly. Abia declared in a soft, but firm, voice that she was up to these tasks. Her father-in-law was worth fussing over. She promised to do her best. All the while, Abia's beautiful sea-blue eyes were glaring at her husband. They flashed a clear demand. Vincent responded with an earnest promise to rush back from his journey as quickly as possible. It was all agreed that under Fannie, Sarah, and Abigail's care, John Wetherill was going to do just fine.

After a prize dessert of sippet pudding and pear brandy, Abia excused herself and retired to the master bedroom. Vincent and his father removed to the privacy of the study to review what the two visitors had said and formulate a strategy to deal with their request. What had to be discussed was not for Abia's ears. She was not to know that tomorrow's journey might be extended and consume more than the number of days Vincent had promised. Vincent would carry out the usual deliveries of apple brandy; however, a separate run would be made up to Long Hill to deliver a pair of rundlets to Judge Cooper. Vincent's father had decided that his in-law was not worth full barrels, and, therefore, he calculated that the smallish rundlets would suffice.

John Wetherill was not impressed by the two visitors. They had given much information about the murder of Jack Redmon, but the Assemblyman felt they had not revealed all they knew. Their speculations on who was responsible for the crime and possible motive came across as vague and evasive. Jacob Ford, Jr., especially, appeared to be holding back some crucial information.

The request for an outside investigative team seemed self serving. Vincent agreed that there was more at stake than saving Cooper's reputation and his son's hide. There was more to it than saving the Ford family name by clearing the counterfeiter of taking part in the Treasury robbery. Something was not quite right. On this, father and son were in complete agreement.

Vincent's father found the notes he had scribbled down after rising from his nap. He read them aloud to his son as the candlelight flickered eerily, casting dancing shadows on the mustard-yellow walls. His son listened carefully and set anything of import to memory. First came the clues at what John Wetherill concluded was a staged murder scene—a corpse redressed in a master's garments . . . might this mean the murderers posed the indentured servant as Samuel Haynes in order to send a message to the owner of the clothes? Slitting the boy's throat, cutting out his tongue, hiding the appendage in a fold of counterfeit bills, and placing a real johannes gold piece where the boy's tongue used to be—were these all warnings for Haynes and his compatriots to cease and desist providing testimony about the Treasury robbery and/or the counterfeiting activities? The Assemblyman saw such clues as sending a message about the robbery. Vincent was not sure. He admitted to himself that he was at a disadvantage because his father had served on the Legislators' investigative committee that heard from many witnesses and weighed all sorts of evidence in the Treasury robbery. His father had even gained an opportunity to visit the crime scene at Skinner's house in Perth Amboy. Unfortunately, that visit by a group of Assemblymen came years after the robbery was committed and nothing new came out of it.

Vincent did remember interrupting his father's reading of the notes only once. He asked about the disfigurement of the corpse.

"As I see it, son, the cut from ear to ear sends a message to someone to be silent . . . the tongue in fake bills is meant for a counterfeiter to stop talking . . . and the joe in the mouth has to do with showing what happens to anyone who offers testimony about the Treasury robbery . . . the message sent may be intended for more than three yappers . . ."

Vincent was not sure the gold piece had some connection to the Treasury robbery. He asked his father to elaborate on that point.

"Conjecture on my part," confessed John Wetherill, "but based on the High-Sheriff's audit of monies stolen from Skinner's house an the 21st of July in '68, all the coins filched that night were real and several of 'em were hard joes."

Vincent wondered if the coin in question was actually one of the stolen pieces.

"Doubt it much," mused John Wetherill. "No marked bill or coin has ever turned up . . . that loot is long gone . . . or hidden well . . . and I hope it stays unfound till after Stephen Skinner is removed from office . . . then I want it back . . . whatever you do, don't find the stolen money."

Vincent's father returned to his notes and began reading from them where he left off—the blow to Redmon's skull must have been the first wound. At the time he was brained, he must have been digging or crawling in the dirt, judging by what had been said about the filth on his hands. He had been surprised by his murderers. They may have followed him to his hiding place. He was rendered unconscious by a blunt instrument, yet to be found. He was sliced by a weapon, yet to be found. All this took place at a far distant murder scene. The corpse was stripped and the clothes were discarded at the bloody scene. His body was dragged a considerable distance over difficult terrain. It took more than one fellow to accomplish this.

Vincent could envision this scenario. He had no questions. It was quite possible that the weapons used were still in possession of the murderers. It was also possible that the stolen clothes used to dress the corpse had come from Redmon's stash of loot. Vincent kept these thoughts to himself and allowed his father to plow on.

John Wetherill admitted that the thing puzzling him most about the staged murder scene was the clean stolen knife set upon the stone by the out barn. His notes simply read: "pointing east."

Vincent asked his father how he came by that conclusion.

John replied guardedly, "Not a conclusion . . . simply mere conjecture based on testimony brought forth at the first Treasury robbery hearing. It was said by more than one inspector of the room in Skinner's house where the robbery took place that the master's unsheathed sword was laid out on the desk, which held the old key used to dub the money chest . . . the sword blade pointed to the open window out of which the public's money flew . . . that window sits on the east side of the house where the sun was streaming in and setting the sword afire, after the robbery had been discovered by Skinner's apprentice and slave . . . all this leads me to believe that the crime in '68 was staged . . . as was the recent murder, and perhaps incidents in between that we may have missed . . . as to the purpose behind these events, I know nothing."

Vincent was not convinced of the direction his father's line of thinking was taking. The events might not be connected at all . . . simply random, unrelated crimes separated by several years. He reminded his father of the surly attitude of the crowd at the hanging. The murder of the indentured servant might be the work of a disgruntled victim of pickpocketing . . . perhaps the stranger who rode away around midnight . . . or a few disgruntled supporters of revenge for what many believed was the unjust hanging of Dave Reynolds.

John Wetherill defended his stance: "I have not discounted the revenge motives, my son, but there are too many clues that reach beyond that point. No, this murder is the latest work of an organized group with an agenda that surpasses mere revenge. Too much planning went into this affair. I am afraid it is not over."

The discussion between father and son continued close to midnight. It concluded with instructions for what Vincent was to do in order to fulfill the Assemblyman's promise to Cooper and Ford. Vincent, accompanied by Cutlope Hancock, was to complete the planned deliveries of eight-year apple brandy in Amboy and beyond. Before crossing to the East Jersey capital, he was to locate Ike Higgins who was reported to still be working at Radford's Landing. Vincent was to convince the man to join what John Wetherill kept referring to as his 'investigative team.' The father convinced his son that Ike would gladly pay off a debt with a few days of easy work. John gave his reasons why Mister Higgins would prove his worth in this adventure. Vincent kept his doubts to himself and politely agreed to take Ike in. Next, John Wetherill told Vincent to cross to Amboy and locate former gaoler, William Jolly. John gave his son a letter to give to Mister Jolly. He explained why this veteran of law enforcement should be on the team. Vincent had no qualms about this choice. After all, Jolly had had a keen personal interest in the

Treasury robbery and was still tracking down leads on his own as to where the stolen monies might have gone. Mister Jolly would be most interested in exploring the connection John Wetherill had made between the old robbery and the recent murder. Besides, the former gaoler could keep an eye on that devious Ike Higgins. What could go awry?

The four men were to proceed up to Elizabeth Town and Powles Hook to complete deliveries and collect monies owed. That money could be used to cover expenses that were to eventually be paid for by the Fords. They would then head west to drop off Wetherill's gift to Judge Cooper.

"Spend as much time in Morris County," instructed John Wetherill, "as it takes for cousin Dan to return from Burlington and for him to acquire the iron water. That will be your excuse for the four of you to linger about and discover what you can about the murderers. Be cautious and careful, my son. You may be up against numbers greater than your team. Do not get in the way of Sheriff or Constable up there . . . do not look for trouble, nor stir it, nor stand in harm's way . . . don't bother looking for the stolen Treasury money . . . you won't find it. Keep your senses on the task of searching for the men responsible for the murder. See if you can find the purpose for their actions. Notify the authorities if you discover anything of import then return safely to your little Abia with a full waggon of iron water for me . . . and a few gifts for her, Sarah, and Fannie."

Funding, logistics, and arcane details were discussed at length. Strategies on how best to load the brandy waggon in the morning were covered. Eventually, Vincent helped his father to the downstairs bedroom and saw to it that John Wetherill was comfortable in his bed. When his son went to snuff out the candle standing guard above the night table, he noticed four bills smoothed out and laid separate on its shiny red surface.

"Father, what game is this?"

John Wetherill responded drowsily, "'Tis the change Doctor Stites offered in return for the large denomination I gave to pay for his visit . . ."

"Why lay them out like this?"

"To play a point, my son." The old Assemblyman yawned, "Turns out the good Doctor Stites is a passer and should be hung for doing so."

Vincent smiled at those words and picked up the four bills to examine each carefully.

His father continued, "I will be sure to notify the Constable on the morrow, right after you depart . . . my Doctor shall not go unpunished." John Wetherill chuckled at his own words which had been offered in mocking sincerity.

Vincent laughed also. "All four bills look fine to me." He placed them back down on the night table and positioned them as his father had left them.

The old Assemblyman pointed to where they lay. "Inspect the '63 Jersey bill again . . . extremely well done in signing and printing . . . turn it over . . . check the three crowns at the bottom of the sage leaf . . . the middle crown in a true bill should be smaller than the other two . . . the one you're holding has three crowns the same . . . someone took great pains to smoke and rub the bill to make it appear old as the other bills but the ink at the signatures appears still fresh and black . . . 'tis a fake or call me a damn fool."

Vincent confirmed what his father had described about the bill in question and dropped it on the night table. "You're no silly old fool father . . . you're quite right . . . but Doctor Stites surely did not know he was passing a counterfeit bill to you . . ."

"Of course not," scoffed John Wetherill, "but the courts don't know that till the accused comes to trial and his innocence is proved."

"And you'd be the first to vouch for his innocence," interjected Vincent.

"That I would," whispered John Wetherill. "So he'll never get the chance to clear his name because his misdeed dies with me. Now, wouldn't it be a marvel if the good Doctor's change, probably handed to him from a previous patient, contained a fine specimen of Sam Ford's best work?"

"Yes," surmised Vincent, "but it wouldn't prove anything beyond coincidence."

"No, you're right, but suppose these four bills stood for something . . . like cards of fate or clues laid before a certain barn . . . just suppose they stood for the four men who came to my plantation this day—you, the good doctor, Judge Cooper and Ford . . . two men I trust with my life . . . two I do not . . . one I trust less than the other . . . and that one I'd . . ."

Vincent noticed that his father was asleep. He pulled the gay quilt, which his mother had completed years ago, up to the old man's chin, snuffed out the candle at the night table, took up his own lamp, and quietly closed the oaken bedroom door behind him. Vincent slipped silently up the stairs and found Abia still awake and eager to make love more than once, before the morrow's journey would separate them for more than a few days . . . much more . . .

3

THREE HEROES IN ONE DAY

—at Rattoon's Tavern above Radford's Landing
Tuesday, September 21, 1773

Cut Hancock slowed the horse team and waggon, burdened with a half-dozen barrels of apple brandy, to a casual pace. They had reached the crown of the nearest of the roundabout hills and the place where the main road sloped down to John Rattoon's tavern. From this vantage point, he and Vincent Wetherill could hear and see a sudden commotion in front of the establishment where a large circle of spectators had gathered. The cursing of angry men and the clatter of weapon against weapon in the center of the action were not the usual sights and sounds of a welcoming party. Both horseman and teamster sensed that something fierce and wild was taking place where they had planned to stop.

"Let's halt," commanded the young Wetherill with his free hand raised in a fist. "No need to bring our goods into harm's way."

The efficient German pulled on the reins and clucked a command that brought the pair of dray horses and the waggon to a halt. The quarter horses, hitched behind the waggon were the only ones to complain. They whinnied in harmony and snorted with impatience.

"Looks like a bit of a brawly," observed Cut.

"A fight we should avoid," suggested Vincent with a nod. He was contemplating the landscape of squat hills, dusty fields, few houses and barns, stands of low trees, and crude fences all the way down to the landing dock where several boats vied for position in order to transfer cargo. Vincent finally pointed to a minor road— more a rutted path than a well-used road—that led to the nearest clay pits at the base of Swan Hill.

Cut peered in that easterly direction and scowled at the furrowed condition of the side road. "Nein, Mister Wetherill, I can't chance a cask exploding on such a bad road. Your father would never forgive me for wasting prime liquor on worms and snakes."

"What's to be done?" asked the impatient young Wetherill.

"We wait, is all . . . the Constable, here, and his finest men must have already been summoned by one of Rattoon's boys. They'll soon be on their way. Those randy brawlers will scatter . . . the slow stiffs will be nabbed and taken to gaol to sleep it off. Seen all this before in this knockabout town. Haven't been here once without some sort of fight breaking out at Rattoon's"

"No doubt these are boatmen come down the Rariton," interrupted Vincent, "with Radford's being their last stop before heading upriver with the incoming tide. They must consider this place their last chance at some fun."

Cut scoffed at what Vincent was saying, "Ain't boatmen causing the fuss . . . 'tis some upstart haulers, mostly redemptioners, from the back counties down here to unload the boats and have some fun till one of 'em gets hurt. Seen 'em here more 'n once."

Vincent Wetherill studied the ruckus down the hill, while Cut continued to opine about who was causing the trouble. The fight was intensifying with flying fists and hard kicks seemingly directed at one poor soul who fought with no weapon in his hand. Those few who had dared come to his aid were now sprawled out in the road not far from the steps of the establishment. One was a woman of large girth slumped by a hitch post and still clinging to it. The one man, still standing against the gang of rogues bent on killing him, sported a deep gash on his arm where his shirt sleeve had been torn away, and an assortment of ugly bruises about his head. Blood was dripping from his nose and mouth. No man of the law was in sight.

"I do not like the odds," shouted Vincent. "Let's even 'em up, Cut!"

With that, Vincent Wetherill drew his sword, spurred his Spanish barb, and galloped down the hill.

Cut grinned and shook his head. "Not like his old man," he muttered, as he snapped the reins and got the bay Shires to resume a slow, careful pace down the fairly steep incline. He kept the waggon to the shoulder of the road in order to proceed under the shade of trees casting their long shadows of late afternoon. In the process, he reached for the skin that encased his rifle and extricated the weapon for possible use at close range. Cut did not like easy targets. There was no challenge in that. But waving a sinister firearm was sometimes all that was needed to discourage most disorderly men. If he had to, Cut would be ready to wound the first one who made a move towards Mister Wetherill or the waggon. John's son could handle the rest.

Vincent Wetherill and his imposing horse charged at the circle of onlookers and scattered them along with most of the brawlers. A roil of dust shrouded the steps and ground in front of Rattoon's Tavern. The horse reared up on its hind legs. Its master brandished his sword above his head so that it caught a glint of sunlight shafting through the trees. This was demonstration enough to discourage most men from daring to approach his horse. However, a pair of brawlers were still pummeling the same poor fellow, who had finally slumped to the walkway stones. These two strapping characters were not moved by Vincent's display of superior might. One wheeled around and made a threatening gesture with a stout table leg. It was dripping with the blood of the man being bludgeoned. While his partner kicked the fallen man, this fellow charged at Vincent's horse, with his weapon poised to strike a fierce blow.

The crackling explosion of a well-aimed rifle shot and the splintering of the table leg left the charging man's hand torn and bleeding. Cut's one round of lead settled the whole affair. The last two adversaries scurried down the rest of the main road that yielded to the landing area. They were, most likely, headed to the boats they came in on. The spectators vanished as quickly as they had appeared. The men of the law were nowhere in sight. No citizen dared chase after the disturbers of the peace. Vincent was not even interested in galloping after the last two brutes. He dismounted and ran first to the woman who was struggling to stand.

John Wetherill's son offered a gentleman's hand and said, "May I help you get on your feet, my good woman."

The lady, so addressed, flopped down on the ground again, but she held fast to the ring on the hitch post. She offered an affirming round and red, sweaty face that could have been mistaken for a blush. Her wide grin revealed a large gap under a swollen lip where a front tooth had gone missing from some prior event. She took a deep breath and let it out slowly. Her ponderous breasts heaved when she did so. They were large enough to smother children or keep a lucky man warm on a winter night.

This woman, who had obviously been on the wrong end of blows from the men who had fled, spoke in a raspy voice: "Most of my customers call me good, kind sir, because I am damn good at all I do . . . even fightin'. To my favorites I am known as Good Mary Woods from Lancaster County. You might call me such . . ."

"And I am Vincent Wetherill, from Cross Roads," replied John's son with a slight bow and a tipping of his tricorn. "I have journeyed for miles through the Barrens to rescue a fair maid such as you."

Mary's bright cornflower blue eyes sparkled at such flattery and she chuckled: "Been so many years since a gentleman called me a maid, Mister Wetherill, sir. I'd say you was a tad late on that and a few hundred men behind. But don't let that stop you, for it sure as hell won't be stoppin' me." Mary paused to catch her breath again. "You, kind sir, is the second hero of my long day. You may, by all means, help me up, if you please . . . hurry on that . . . must tend to wounds on the man who defended my honor 'gainst those mamzers."

Before Mary Woods was finished explaining what she intended to do, Vincent eased her up to a standing position. She was as heavy as she appeared, but the young man was strong and up to the task. He was glad his little Abia was less than half the girth of 'Good Mary Woods' from Lancaster County.

Vincent and the large woman stepped over to where the groaning victim was sprawled face down on the path stones. The woman got to her knees and rolled the poor fellow over on his back to take inventory of the damage done. Vincent stood close by waiting to assist in any way.

"He's in a bad fix, Mistress Mary. I suggest you summon a good doctor quick as you can."

Mary Woods held up her blood-stained hand and waved it at Vincent as if to dismiss him. "No need for that, Mister Wetherill. Ike, here, has been through worse dousers than this'n. If I was to summon a good doctor for Ike, his repute as a brawler would be compromised. He'd surely beat me for doin' so. Besides, there ain't one good doctor at this landin . . . never was."

Vincent Wetherill stared down at the bruised and battered face of the moaning man he had failed to recognize until now. "So this gentleman of yours is none other than Ike Higgins?"

Mary Woods got up from her knees with the help of Vincent again. She looked him up and down while fussing with her scrambled hair and adjusting her precarious mobcap. She attempted to smooth her blood-stained apron. She quickly gave up on the idea of looking presentable. She clucked in frustration, then offered a smudged frown of suspicion.

"My Mister Higgins is more of a gentleman than you'll ever be," declared Mary Woods. "Though he looks a bit worse for wear today, 'tis his heart that counts the most. Now tell me how you came by his full name before I spoke of it?"

"My father granted Ike his freedom years ago," said Vincent proudly. "By fate's hand, my father has sent me to find your Mister Higgins to discuss a matter of important business."

Mary Woods formed a small oval of amazement with her wounded lips and flashed her bright, blue eyes. She whispered her words: "So you are the Vincent Wetherill my man has spoken so mightily of . . . as he has done so with your father's name."

"That is kind to say, my good woman," said Vincent with a genuine blush of his own. "I've always spoken highly of your Ike Higgins, for he once saved me from drowning."

"I heard that tale more often than I care to remember." Mary Woods turned her attention back to her first hero of the day. "Help lift Ike to the stairs. Let's get him into this fine public house and fixed so he can entertain this important business matter you have spoken of."

"He appears in no condition to be moved," advised Vincent as he bent to help Mary Woods with her singular purpose.

"Ike has no choice," she declared. "'Tis my way or none, and he knows it well."

A few onlookers had returned to the scene of the melee. Mary Woods recruited two of them to help her and Vincent get Ike Higgins into Rattoon's Tavern. In the process, Vincent called out to Cut to lead the horses and waggon back to the stable barn behind the tavern and remain there until he came to relieve Cut. The waggoner responded with a request for a strong drink to be sent out to him. Vincent promised that he would see to it. He then helped shoulder the fierce-beaten man up the few wooden steps that led to the scarred front door of the notorious establishment. With a noticeable limp from getting her foot stomped on during the fray, Mary Woods led the procession up and into the candlelit gloom of the main room of the tavern. One of her volunteers held the oaken door open wide as he could as Vincent and the other recruit entered with wobbly-legged Ike still scraping his boots on the floor.

The place was coarse and worn. It must have been older than the century's first Indian wars. Artifacts of the last war against the French hung from the walls and sat on the shelves. Amongst them were older, dustier items culled from the sea and donated by sailors who had marched up from the landing dock over the years and left their memories behind. Even the air reeked of sweaty working men and the cooking smells of good, honest food wafting from the warming kitchen. Today's odor was dominated by the boil of fish that had been purchased at the landing dock in the morning and was now being readied for the late afternoon fare. There was also the rival odor of poor man's rum clinging to the dark confines like mist round a bog. A good nose could also detect the faint rust-iron scent of blood on the boards of the floor. This was a place where trouble provided the entertainment.

Vincent saw little in the way of damage in the room where the most recent fight must have started. Manifest destruction was being attended to by the tavern master of the day—the absent John Rattoon's most trusted assistant and close relative of his and a hand of shy servants who had not been scared into hiding by the patrons' ruckus. Pieces of a broken table were being carted out back. A replacement was being brought in from another room. Overturned benches were being righted and the floor was being swept of debris.

The mocker-faced tavern master, fondly called 'Rat' by the steady customers, looked up from fussing over the broken shards of glass and red ware on the planks of the bar. He barked out further orders to the servants, then addressed his favorite serving maid: "Good

Mary, you can place Ike on the long table in the game room . . . just get 'im out of here."

"Don't you want to be knowin' how he fares, Rat?"

"I already know," said the tavern master blandly. "Like he always is after a brawl. I just don't want his arse in here. 'Tis near five of the clock and we have a meal to serve to our regulars . . . they should be comin' in right behind you . . . hurry to the back room with that bag of bones of yours. I'll need your help at the tables here."

"Ike comes first," blared Mary Woods. "Rattoon's comes second."

"Don't let Johnny Rattoon hear you say that," scolded the assistant tavern master with a laugh.

"Sober or not," countered Mary, "he's heard worse from my mouth . . . soon as Ike's fit to stand on his own, I'll be out."

Rat pointed to the game room: "Soon as Ike's able to understand you, tell him thanks for takin' his business to the street. He saved us a fierce bit of damage from this day's ruffians."

"Tell that to the Constable, if he ever gets here," said Mary as she motioned her helpers to follow her to the back room. "He'll be questionin' us all and blamin' Ike for what those pig irons started."

"You get back in this room quick," shouted Rat, "and I'll tell the good Constable just that."

"I'll try my best," promised Mary Woods, "but first I have to get Ike right for Constable Musgrave's questions. Don't let that man find Ike till he's ready to walk on his own."

"I'll keep Musgrave at bay," promised Rat in return, "but he may insist on talkin' to Ike and yourself right away."

"Stall the man," said Mary Woods, as she led the others into the dark back room. "You are good at the game."

Sparse light from the only window was making its way into the small, stuffy room used often for private games of chance. It revealed a large table against a back bare wall and a scattering of many chairs in no apparent arrangement. Mary started barking commands to a mulatto servant boy, who had followed her into the gloom. She called him "child o' mine" once and "little Ned" all other times. Vincent figured there was an interesting tale to tell in that. For now, there was no time for an explanation. Mary was all business. She demanded all three wall candles be lit. She called for a strong blaze in the room's humble fireplace, in which the embers sat long dead. She also wanted the overwhelmed boy to fetch a bucket of water to be put in a hearth pot for boiling, clean rags from the warming kitchen, and lye soap from the storage closet. In the midst of instructions to her boy, another servant—much older and bent at the waist from too many years of doing other people's bidding—brought in a jug of cheap Jersey lightning for Mary to use as an antiseptic.

"Compliments of Mister Rat," said the well-spoken old slave, who handed the prize to the self-proclaimed mistress of the house. He lingered for a moment in a permanent bow, then turned and scuttled back to his cleaning chores.

Mary placed the dark vessel of spirits on the window sill and then tried to pull the large, long table away from the wall. The oaken thing would not budge.

"Needs to move this horse to the center of the room so Ike can ride it and I can get round to all sides," said Mary mostly to herself, but loud enough to cause Vincent Wetherill to leave Ike standing and supported by one of the two volunteers Mary Woods had recruited. The other volunteer also responded to her implied request for help moving the table.

The three of them were able to scrape the heavy piece of furniture to the center of the room. Then Vincent helped the two volunteers lift poor Ike on to the smooth, hard boards of the table. The beaten man let out a boyish cry when his back and head pressed against the unyielding planks. He returned to moaning. His eyes remained shut. One lid was black and blue all around and shadowed by a sagging brow that sported a nasty cut above it. Ike's face was a map of similar lacerations and numerous bruises—islands of red, purple, and gray. Vincent feared that it would take several hours before Ike would be able to answer the Constable's questions. Worse than that, he feared old Ike would be in no condition on the morrow to make the crossing to Amboy. Things were not going quite the way his father had planned.

Mary finished pushing chairs out of the way and against the wall where the table had been. Then, with the jug of alcohol tucked under her arm, she rushed to the table to start working on her man.

"Everybody out, save Mister Wetherill. I thank you for your kind help . . . go fetch a drink on me . . . don't let Rat trick you into payin' . . . buy yourselves a fine meal of Rattoon's fish stew . . . make sure you tell your friends of Ike's victory today . . . don't want none of you goin' soft on his abilities."

The room emptied, save for Vincent who was ordered to remove his riding jacket, roll up the sleeves of his red flannel shirt, and be ready to assist when needed. Mary's boy scurried about like a mouse that landed on a coals pan. He rushed in with live embers, contained in such a device, which came from the hearth in the tap room. He piled slender faggots of starter wood over the coals. Instantly, a blaze started climbing its source in the fireplace. Then he ran for the items demanded by his mother. He returned in an instant with all she requested. Soon the pot he had filled, now hanging from a hook above the flames, was boiling. Mary praised the boy's alacrity and sent him in search of choice items for contriving a suitable tourniquet for Ike's worst wound.

Mary Woods returned to the task of stripping off Ike's torn nankeen shirt. As she cut the buff-colored, blood-stained fabric with a squat knife she had extracted from her apron pocket, Mary muttered and clucked to herself: "A mean stripe on the right forearm . . . still tricklin' blood down to the fingers . . . goin' to require a thorough cleanin' . . . a bloodstall to stop it from the seeps . . . rest of his damage sits on his face . . . more dirt there than blood . . . at least one fair sign on a luckless day for my Ike . . ."

"Any broken bones?" interposed Vincent.

"None I can find or feel," responded Mary Woods, as she poked and prodded her man from head to toe. "Bruises here 'n there from kicks 'n blows . . . a tooth broken off by half, at the forepart of his handsome smile."

Ike Higgins moaned at each touch from the strong woman. He turned his head in the direction of Mary's voice. This was taken as a promising sign. Next, he attempted to speak—something about needing a strong drink.

"Later, my love," cooed Mary Woods. "I've first to tend to your poor arm . . . be still."

She motioned to Vincent to lift up Ike's bloody arm, and showed him how to grip the limb firmly at elbow and wrist.

Then she went about cleaning the wound with soap on rags steeped in the boiling water. This made Ike grunt and growl, and demand a stiff drink all the more. Mary wound a long strip of linen, which her boy had found, around Ike's arm above the elbow across the bicep. To its ends she attached the handle of a broken awl and turned it until the tourniquet was tightly in place. She then instructed Vincent to hold the handle firmly. He did so gladly, for he wanted Ike to be whole as soon as possible.

"Now 'tis your turn, Mister Wetherill, to save the life of the man who saved yours."

"I have already done that out in the street, Mistress Mary," said Vincent, "with my waggoner's help, of course. This mending is all your doing. So far, your work is commendable."

Mary blushed, but kept her authoritative composure: "Just do as I say, young man, 'n I'll have old Ike ready to talk business with you afore midnight."

Little Ned rushed in with bread and herbs. His mother moistened her hands in the spirits she had poured into a small bowl. She rolled the bread and herbs in the palms of her large hands, then smeared the concoction along the length of the cut. She quickly stretched a length of linen cloth over the wound and laced it around the arm—three layers thick—before knotting the ends snugly at the elbow.

"Loosen the awl handle, Mister Wetherill," ordered Mary Woods with a sigh. "I thinks the bleedin' will cease 'n the healin' start."

Vincent did as he was told. He let the arm down gently, and noticed that Ike had opened one eye. The man was employing it to give Vincent the once-over.

Ike seemed to have forgotten about his request for a cup of comfort. He groused, "Don't need no darn doctor touchin' me, Mary . . . I told ye many times . . . no doctor."

Mary stifled Ike's complaint by putting a cool whiskeyed rag to his mouth and telling him to hush: "'Tis only a visitor who's come to help me get you up and off this table and back on your feet . . . claims to know you well . . . saved your arse this day . . . spared me the chance of buryin' you the next."

Ike pushed the sweet, tasty rag away from his mouth with his good hand. He squinted and spoke clear as he could: "Who might ye be?"

Before Vincent could respond, Ike did it for him: "By the stars, might ye be none other than old John Wetherill's son—the tadpole I onced pulled from a pond to keep ye from drownin' for sure?"

"Yes, Ike," admitted Vincent with a broad smile. "I'm one of two you saved that day."

"Well, I'll be damned," declared Ike as he tried to sit up, but Vincent held him by the shoulders while Mary finished cleaning his face.

"Too early to be up 'n ready for your next fight, my love," said Mary sternly. "Stay in place . . . get yourself a bit of rest before the Constable comes bargin' in to ask you a swat of embarrassin' questions . . . and Vincent, here, discusses business with you."

"I'll rest better with a full cup of Rat's best brew in me gut," begged Ike. "I've a need to clear me head."

"You'll have to sit up on your own for such as that," huffed Mary Woods disapprovingly, but resigned to let her man have his way sooner than later.

Vincent let go of Ike's shoulders after Mary Woods had signalled him to do so. As soon as he did, Ike turned on his good arm side and pushed himself up to a sitting position. He contemplated his bandaged arm, which hung slack yet showed no seep of blood through the cloth. He grinned at Mary's handiwork and said, "What have ye fetched for these thirsty lips o' mine, good woman?"

"A jug-near-full of Rat's best for you, my hero," said Mary with a wink at Vincent and a wide smile for Ike. She handed her man what was left of the liquor she had used on his wounds.

Ike grabbed the jug with his good hand and brought it to his swollen lips. He took a deep swallow, then another. "This here tastes o' cheap lightnin' to me," declared Ike, with his one good eye watering like a leaky barrel tap. "None the less, it sure tastes good."

The Irishman drank his fill, nearly draining the jug in the process. He then tried to slip down to plant his feet on the floor, but Vincent grabbed him and coaxed him back down on the table.

"Not so fast, my love," said Mary. "You're in need of a rest . . . you're half-dressed, besides . . . not yet presentable to the likes of Constable Musgrove."

"I've got nothin' to say to that fool," groused Ike.

"Mister Wetherill and some others besides me are here to vouch for your side of the story . . . now close that evil eye of yours and lay still."

Ike obeyed his woman. She whispered to Vincent that he was no longer needed and should step out of the room to see if the Constable had arrived. She also instructed him to get some of the fish stew before the regular customers had devoured it. Vincent gave a nod and a wink of compliance and exited the room. He now felt confident that Ike would make a remarkably speedy recovery and would be in good enough shape to join his team in the morning.

Constable Musgrave was, indeed, there in the main room, entertaining testimony from the tavern master and other eyewitnesses. Rat saw Vincent Wetherill emerge from the back room and called him over to share a drink with the Constable. After formalities were exchanged and Musgrove thanked Vincent for quelling the melee, he allowed the gentleman from Cross Roads to tell his version of the story. Vincent did so, and, in the process, vouched for Ike being the victim of an unfair fight. He justified Cut's single rifle shot, for it had evened the odds and scared off the last of the brawlers. Vincent confessed that he did not know how the fracas started nor who was to blame for starting it.

The Constable thanked Vincent for his candor and praised him for being the only witness of high status: "If this matter goes before the judge, I am sure the younger son of Assemblyman John Wetherill will lend much credence to Ike being innocent of any wrongdoing. As a matter of courtesy to Mister Higgins, who, I understand, is in a bad way, and my trust in your testimony, I find no reason to question poor Ike at this time. He is not one to admit guilt or make accusations anyway. Perhaps I shall, at a later date, question him, after we seize any of the wrongdoers."

"Any chance of catching them?" asked Vincent.

"Not till they return, if ever they do," confessed the Constable. "Those pig iron boys are a secret, surly lot from the back counties. 'Tis a different set of Satan's limbs each time. I've seen no more than a hand of the same men in the past six months. I've heard the mine owners and forge masters honor their workers by letting them take turns at a furlough to help transport the iron all the way down to here. Usually, any of them who end up in my gaol are put there for being too deep in their drink. Of late, however, they have turned to violence and destruction of property . . ."

"If you'd been here sooner," interrupted Rat, "you might of saved my table and nabbed the two ringleaders . . ."

The Constable flashed a simmering look, but kept his calm: "Sorry for the delay, Mister Rat, but me and my men were out beyond the clay pits using the hounds to track down the pair of runaway Africs which stole from widow McKnight, after raping her and leaving her for dead. I'd say that was more serious work, would you not?"

Rat admitted quickly that it was and Vincent Wetherill congratulated Constable Musgrove for doing so.

"Did you find 'em?" asked Vincent.

"Them and another pair who'd run away from a different master on the same day," boasted the Constable. "Seems to be a fine, dry season for runaways. Now I've got to decide which pair gets burned and which pair gets returned to their master."

With that, Musgrove finished his drink, failed to pay for it, bid his g'day, and exited Rattoon's busy, now peaceful, establishment.

Vincent ordered a large meal from Rat, but said it was not for himself. He would eat later. He was going to relieve his waggoner and send him in to eat. Rat thanked Vincent for his money in advance to cover the cost of two meals and an upper room for the night. While Vincent worked at finishing his drink, he asked how John Rattoon was faring during these rough financial times.

"Not so good," admitted Rat. "He's sinkin' in debt here 'n over in Amboy . . . creditors are snappin' at his tail . . . sure can't afford none of your father's prize apple brandy, not even a rundlet of your cheapest jack . . ."

Vincent Wetherill waved at Rat, as if swatting at a pesky fly, and laughed, "I'm not here to sell, if you're not buying. I just need to take that hero of yours off your hands for a few days."

Rat scoffed, "He ain't no hero of mine, more trouble than he's worth. If anything, Ike's only a hero to the likes of Mary Woods . . . she's the one to give permission not me . . ."

"Must be Mary's lucky day," interrupted Vincent. "She's gained three heroes in one day . . . and may lose 'em all, the next."

"She's entertained more 'n three on a good night," winked Rat. "I can vouch for that . . . even Ike can be replaced."

Vincent chuckled along with the tavern master. He then headed for the door and stepped out into the cooling pre-dusk air to locate Cut and to relieve himself behind the stable barn.

When Vincent Wetherill returned to the main room of Rattoon's Tavern, he sat alone at the replacement table. He was too late for the fish stew. It was the hour before midnight and earlier patrons had devoured the last of the prize dish of the day. Instead, Mary Woods served him a savory plate that started with raw oysters and smoked conners, and ended with boiled venison and hogs cheek. Vincent offered to pay for a refill on the house beer that came with the meal, but Mary refused to take his money. She returned with a full tankard and plunked it down on the clean table. Vincent noticed that she was sporting a clean apron and a striped over-dress of faded green and gray. Her outfit was an obvious second choice for her long day.

"Another drink for your kind services in the back room," whispered Mary. "I'd be hush about this, for I don't want my reg'lars to hear 'n be askin' for the same bargain."

Vincent whispered back, "I understand, nor do I want blue rumors to fly back to Cross Roads about the nature of those services I rendered on to you . . . especially don't want my wife to catch such gossip . . ."

"In ten years time, Mister Wetherill, you won't be so concerned 'bout what others say. Come back then," whispered Mary as she gave a playful wink, "and I'll find out what other services you might render on to me."

Vincent blushed with a mouthful of beer. He took a hard, fast gulp and was about to respond, when Mary Woods changed the subject. She looked around at the few other customers as she spoke in her normal abrasive voice: "My Ike will be comin' out soon to sit with you and entertain this proposition you've been hintin' at. He's changin' into clean britches and a shirt I found among the items certain of my customers forgot and left behind . . . should not take him long."

Indeed, Mary was correct on the timing of Ike's entrance. No sooner had Vincent taken a second helping of conners and a sip of his second house beer, than Mister Higgins limped into the main room. He acknowledged hussahs from two of his friends by waving his bandaged arm at them, but he did not delay in finding Vincent Wetherill at the new table. He pulled at the empty chair opposite the man he wanted to see and sat down with but a modicum of difficulty.

"Got kicked in the arse once'd too many times today," said Ike with a flutter of his only functioning eye. The other was still shut tight and more purple than before. "Thanks for helpin' me Mary with bringin' me back to life, Mister Wetherill. I owe ye one."

"We'll talk about who owes what a bit later, Ike. How about a good, warm meal at my expense?"

"Nah, Mister Wetherill, I ain't up to eatin' just yet." Ike paused to take a breath—neither long nor deep. "But I could use me an all out stingo, stronger than the one yer sippin.'"

Vincent called over the old servant who had brought alcohol to Mary Woods for her medical purposes hours ago. He instructed the bent fellow to tell the current bar master, who had relieved Mister Rat, to fill a tankard with the strongest beer in the place. The servant did as instructed and returned with the correct liquid treasure for Mister Higgins.

Ike thanked the young visitor for paying for a drink he could not afford. He took a few gulps of the warm amber brew and sighed, "Such is all the likes o' me needs till I break fast at dawn . . . then, I'm back to the boats comin' in."

"Maybe the morrow might start different for you," said Vincent cryptically. "No need to settle on the same old, dull fate."

"Each day's the same fer me, Mister Wetherill, ever since yer father gave me freedom." Ike paused to reflect on what to say next and drain away more of his beer. "I was s'posed to pay fer me freedom, but never did . . . soon I'll come into some luck at the races or dice table . . . then even accounts with yer father . . ."

"Not to worry on that," said Vincent, as he started on the sweet potato pudding, which Mary Woods demanded he save for last. She had made it herself before the fight broke out. The smooth pudding sure tasted good—the best part of a traveler's fine meal.

"So the matter of me debt to John Wetherill is not why ye came fer to visit?" asked Ike warily.

"That comes later. First, I want to know why Constable Musgrove did not hang around to interview you about the brawl."

"He's got better things to do than wait fer old me to come round."

Vincent was not satisfied with Ike's response, so he made another attempt: "The Constable swore you would never press charges against those who attacked you, and you never have in previous scrapes."

Ike started a grin and revealed his most recent broken tooth. "Most of them brawlies, I started meself 'n finished 'em too . . . most times charges was made 'gainst me 'n I ended up in the gaol . . . one time fer a killin' , which was no fault o' mine . . . 'n the judge claimed it manslaughter . . . had me hand branded 'n burned . . . then let me go."

"So you will not raise a complaint because you don't think Musgrove will believe you?"

"That," admitted Ike,"'n the fact of me bein' no coward with snitchin' bein' a coward's way . . . I defended me lady when she was taunted 'n teased by them pig irons right here at this place . . . took their blows like always, 'n I gives more 'n I takes . . . that's a hero's way in me book, though I'm a stranger to readin' 'n writin' both . . . but ye know'd all o' that, Mister Wetherill, so change the talk to why ye came so's I can close me sore jaw 'n get to sleep with me good Mary in the uppermost room, which'd I rent by half for protectin' this place from Mister Rattoon's foes."

"I would not want to keep you from that fine mistress of yours," confessed Vincent. "Where is she by the way?"

Might be up the stairs entertainin' a loyal customer," said Ike matter-of-factly, "or cleanin' up the kitchen 'n makin' sure her boy is safe by the hearth fer the night." Ike stared at his beer for a long moment, then took another gulp and saw that he was near finished. "She don't love none o' her customers, but she loves that half-breed Afric more 'n me."

Vincent signaled to the old servant idle at the bar. Another beer was brought to Ike.

"Got to be me last one, Mister Wetherill. When this one's drained, our conversin' is done . . . many thanks agin' . . ."

Vincent noticed that Ike was sipping this final drink of the night. It appeared that both of them wanted it to last for a time—hopefully until closing time.

"So tell me how the fight started," asked Vincent, in an attempt to gain some insight about a man his father thought could help the investigative team, but Cut felt was a rogue and a worthless tagalong. "I want to hear your side of the story. Then I'll tell you all about the proposition my father has for you in order to pay off your debt of freedom."

Ike perked up at the tail end of the young Wetherill's words. Even his bad eye fluttered open a bit as he began his account of what had transpired before Vincent and Cut came down the hill to rescue him.

"I was at the landin', chosen by the along-shore boss fer helpin' with loadin' sweet smellin' cedar logs, cut from the Barrens, into the belly o' the largest sloop at the shore. That's when me 'n the other lads, breakin' our backs 'n scrapin' our limbs, hear the pig iron crews on full Durhams come rushin' in to lighten their load and find somethin' to do while they waits fer the incomin' tide to send 'em back up the Rariton. Well, so far those cabbage heads 'n bog landers is all right to me . . . that is, till they finished unloadin' their bars 'n plates, stackin' 'em high for the smithy 'n merchant waggons just comin' in."

Ike paused to take one sip of his last brew, then he continued with all the seriousness of a key witness at a murderer's trial. "When these back county boys was asked to help load the waggons, they refused. Instead, they played about at a game of rounders with a rock 'n a puny cedar log which our boss had tossed aside. After tirin' o' such boyish fun, they started in with songs o' suns 'n swords 'n all such nonsense. They gets louder 'n louder, till I couldn't stand it no more. So I starts in with me own song 'bout sons o' bitches 'n bare fists. Those boys, chimin' so loud, stopped when they heard me singin' me own. They gave me the stares 'n the meanest o' looks, but me boss's crew o' along-shoremen far outnumbered them pig irons. They didn't like the odds. So me boss informs me to stifle me pipes, which I did. Right then, the Durham boys start headin' up to Johnny Rattoon's where we sit right now. I still had one hour to go, fer we couldn't stop with the cedar till no log was left on the landin'. Finally, we're done 'n I can go see me Good Mary Woods, who keeps me well fed 'n satisfied too."

"Were the iron men still at Rattoon's when you got there?" asked Vincent, who already knew the obvious answer.

"Sure they was," continued Ike, "and startin' in grizzlin' my woman by callin' her a wag-tail 'n such . . . then singin' them same old songs 'n repeatin' the name o' some mountain hero o' theirs . . . his name I'd never heard before . . . his name they hollered, but I forget . . . so when Mary slips out o' me sight, I takes me drink from the bar 'n finds the table once at this spot . . . I proceeds to start up me song 'bout bitches 'n fists . . . well, that invites a pair o' pig irons over to me, with one pointin' at his tattoo that took all the back o' his hand—a circle o' sorts with a sword at its heart . . . if I remember correct . . . so I open me left hand 'n show 'em me scar fixed on its palm, resultin' from the judge's burn fer me most serious crime . . . well, the other one, sportin' a like tattoo, reaches 'cross 'n pulls me up off me feet to throw me down on the table now broke . . . I crash through the boards 'n end on the floor as all sorts of brawlin' commences right here . . . reg'lars, I well know, took up sides favorin' me 'gainst the pig irons. I gets up fast as I can and runs out to save this place where me Mary makes a good livin' . . ."

"So you brought the fight outside to save Rattoon's?"

"That's it," said Ike proudly. "I've done so before . . . part o' me 'sponsibilities here . . . do it again if I have to . . . 'n that's the start o' how things ended . . . the brawlers, good 'n bad, all come tumblin' out 'n soon me side's down to one standin', which happens to be me gettin' a whippin' I don't deserve. . ."

"And that's when I and my waggoner evened the odds?"

"More 'n that, Mister Wetherill," insisted Ike Higgins. "You saved me life. Now we're squared an all accounts."

"Not so," said Vincent. "You still owe my father ten pounds, and you've stalled all these years since he let you go."

Ike stared for a long spell at John Wetherill's son. He appeared close t breaking into his favorite song again, but he did not. Instead, he spoke in a low, sad tone.

"I ain't never goin' to pay yer father. I makes close 'nough at the landin' each day to get through the day . . . no luck, save Mary, has ever come me way . . . never has 'n never will, since yer father let me go on me way . . . Mary's been me anchor since she ran away from her mate . . . she found work fer herself here 'n work fer me at the landin' . . . ain't much, but it's 'nough to get by . . . so there's no way I can pay back yer father, 'less I print me own bills or steal from folks . . .' "

"There's an honest way, Ike," said Vincent assuredly. "I'm here to show you how."

Ike looked up from his half-vanished brew. Both eyes were open now—one much wider than the other. However, there remained a furrow of doubt and suspicion weighing heavily on his swollen brow. He spoke with a tone of caution in his voice:

"So this business offer o' yers has to do with the debt I owe?"

"Yes," said Vincent. "Hear me out. If Good Mary will allow it, then we've got ourselves a deal."

"So this offer involves leavin' me love and this wondrous hole?" asked Ike with a shred of sarcasm.

"You are true on that," said Vincent. "I have a waggon of my father's best apple brandy to deliver all the way up to Powles Hook."

"So you need me fer rollin' barrels," assumed Ike, "'n drinkin' the profits."

"More than that, my friend. I need your help on a serious matter which occurred in Morris County after the hanging of Davey Reynolds . . ."

"I heard all 'bout his bein' singled out fer the counterfeitin', 'n his partners 'bout to be set free." Ike frowned at this, and Vincent took it to mean that the man was concerned about the matter. "Ain't it always, the poorest man gets the worst punishment . . . me brother faced the same charges Reynolds did 'n the same end of the rope . . . but he snuck on a ship . . . joined its crew . . . never returned to these parts."

"Some of the Morris County counterfeiters got away," added Vincent quickly, "but Reynolds and three others surrendered to authorities. They're all slated to hang."

"The three left alive are gentlemen just like ye, Mister Wetherill. They have as much a chance o' danglin' at the gallows as ye do."

"Their lives might still be in danger if and when they are set free."

"How so?"

"A murder took place in Morris Town right after the hanging," said Vincent in a low voice. "It's raised certain questions, which my father wants answered before another murder takes place. I intend to take a team of men up to Morris County, on the excuse of delivering the last of the brandy casks to Judge Cooper, and find some answers that will lead to the capture of the murderer, or murderers."

Ike offered as wide a grin as he could muster on his swollen and battered face. "This is all yer father's doin' . . . he wants the likes o' me on yer team 'cause I thinks like a murderer might . . . well, I've been accused of schemin' to kill a man . . . it was judged a mere accident . . . do I still qualify?"

"That is not why my father wants you to join Cut and me," lied Vincent. "He sees this venture as a means for you to pay off a longstanding debt by employing your expertise . . ."

"In dealin' with puggards and bad bargains," interjected Ike, "such as the kinds that barge into Rattoon's all the time?"

"I figure you and Cut Hancock can handle that chore nicely," answered Vincent.

"I don't need old Cut to help me with any mean fellers in Morris County," protested Ike. "I can do it by meself with these fists." Ike held up both arms and then corrected himself. "With one fist, till the other is fine 'n fit."

"Sounds like you're willing to join us,"

"Damn sure," voiced Ike with spirited confidence. "I might even get the chance to chase me a few tattooed pig irons up in those mountains."

"Better to have Cut's rifle protecting your back."

"I'll consider his help, Mister Wetherill. Now let me make for the bushes, then go tell Mary the news o' me leavin' on the morrow. The landin' boss will be pleased to learn he don't have to put up with me mischief fer a few days."

"Might be longer than a few," mused Vincent as he bent to the task of completing his ledger of expenses for the day.

"Don't matter to the likes o' me, Mister Wetherill. My luck's the same, here or there."

4

BIG TOM'S WELCOME
· · · · · · · · · · · · · · · · · · · ·

—arrival in Perth Amboy,
early Wednesday, September 22, 1773

The climb to the Long Ferry Tavern from the Amboy Landing
at the mouth of the Rariton River was an easy chore for John
Wetherill's bay Shires. Cutlope Hancock, sitting like royalty on the
seat board of the brandy waggon, leaned forward, snapped the
reins smartly, and cursed his charges but once all the way up the
path to the low porch on the sunny side of the old bay-weathered
tavern. He congratulated the pair on ascending the worn path and
called them by name—names their owner had given them upon
their purchase, when mere yearlings, for a pittance from John
Lawrence of the renowned Long Bridge Farm. The best studs in
the county resided there, and the pair of work horses now under
Cutlope Hancock's care were prize products of stud service at this
neighboring enterprise.

"Thor and Hercules," announced Cut proudly, "you've done
well during the river's cross in the fog at dawn . . . made it up this
steep bank. Praise to you both . . . but, in so doing, you leave me
vexed . . . which one of you to chose once'd this journey's complete?"

Cut thought it best to ignore the morning crowd waiting for
coaches to arrive. A few of these uppity folks on the porch of the
tavern shot curious glances at the newly arrived teamster. Most,
however, ignored his coming and continued their swapping of early
news and gossip. Cut did not offer any of them a customary "halloo"
or "g'day." They seemed not to care about a humble teamster and
what sort of brew he was delivering to the venerable Long Ferry
establishment. They were fair-dressed townsfolk and travelers
with soft hands—people of middling rank or better. Cut had no
patience with such time-wasters. They were not his kind. Let John

Wetherill's son deal with them. Hancock preferred the company of horses. For him, it was all about trust and understanding—both of which were hard to find in a river town like Amboy.

Cut glanced over his shoulder and squinted in the direction of the ferry landing. The fog had lifted. He could make out the low coast of Staten Island and the calm waters of the Rariton Bay to the south. The gray sky, which earlier had offered a tease of rain, was quickly tearing apart. Patches of blue were widening where the early sun was climbing its customary path. Cut had to assume it was going to be another dry, warm day. Too bad horses did not outnumber the people in it. Cut noticed that John Wetherill's son had finished bickering with the ferryman over crossing costs for five horses, a full waggon, and three men. Now Vincent Wetherill and that black deuce, Ike Higgins, were guiding their mounts up the path towards Cut's position under one of the few remaining locust trees which graced the tavern property. Cut smiled. Vincent was well in command of his handsome Spanish barb, but the bog lander might as well have been riding an untethered moose.

The two riders ascending made an unlikely pair—John Wetherill's son with his cocked black tricorn high above his brow and smart blue captain's coat with silver buttons down the front and at the sleeves. Under this short coat, he sported a shiny gray silk vest. He wore gray breeches and high black riding boots. Women on the porch gave him a second look. His sword, in a silver and black scabbard, slapped at his thigh, while its hilt caught glimmers of sunlight as he came closer to the gawkers assembled there.

Ike Higgins, however, encouraged no look of admiration. He provided a counter to the strapping young man who beat him up the path. The quarter horse, which Ike had selected, seemed not pleased to have been chosen by such a base man of questionable character. Ike even smelled of trouble. As a result, the beast wickered and snorted, started and stopped at its whim.

Once, on the way up the path, it turned full circle for no apparent reason other than to play ornery. Ike wrestled with the reins in all sorts of ways and cursed much bluer than Cut had done with the bays. A few of the women, coaxed by their escorts on the porch, retreated inside to the private room assigned for them. Meanwhile,

73

nothing Ike tried worked on the quarter horse. The remaining men and women on the porch were enjoying the show—pointing and laughing. One fellow went so far as to shout foul things about ragged Irishmen on poor horses. Ike refused to listen. He played his clod part well. He attempted to sit up straight in his frayed and torn broad-cloth coat. His linen trousers sported long patches at the knees. One of his shoes was split—a red-stockinged toe emerged like a hatchling from its nest. A red monmouth cap was perched precariously on his swollen and purpled head. To Cutlope Hancock, the Irishman looked like some forlorn exotic bird which had forgotten how to fly or had never learned. Ike attempted a smile, but it was still painful for him. Luckily, he failed to reveal his new crooked line of teeth crafted in yesterday's fight. At least the Irishman would have something to talk about once inside the confines of the Long Ferry Tavern.

Ike Higgins was saved by a piercing whistle offered by John Wetherill's son. The ears of the quarter horse stood erect. Then Vincent called the beast by name.

"Lord Corn!" shouted the spirited young man. "Come, Lord Corn!"

This got the crowd roaring with laughter again. The steed with the humorous name sped the rest of the way up the path. Ike grabbed at his cap with one hand and pulled the reins, tight as he could, with the hand attached to the bandaged arm. It hurt him severe, but Ike was never one to allow a show of pain. The sudden success of horse and rider received a rousing ovation from those still protected by the porch.

Ike slithered off his jittery mount and allowed a shadow-black stable boy, who came out of nowhere, to take the reins and lead the pitiful beast to the stables. Its rider took a bow, lifted his tattered coat, and revealed a broad patch Mary Woods had sewn on the backside of his linen trousers.

"My arse's worn out after ridin' old Lord Corn up from the landin'," bellowed Ike to the chuckling spectators. "should've picked the other one."

"Wouldn't of made a difference, cod snapper," retorted a squat, red-faced man in a green nankeen jacket—the man who had started the Irish insults.

Ike ignored him. He had something else on his mind: "Could use me a drink o' rum!"

"You've come to the best place for such," cried a lean gentleman dressed in a crisp brown velvet suit, fine lace at neck and wrist, and a tight, powdered wig mocking the white of snow. "That is, of course, if your master is willing to buy the first round for all us who can remember dear Lord Corn!"

That brought more laughter and a few hussahs from the porch gallery. Ike was not amused.

"I'm my own master!" shouted Ike, but he was drowned out by the hussahs of all the single men who saw the taproom door open and a giant of a man emerge from the darkness. His customers started their ritual climb and minehost began his traditional counting of heads.

This was Big Tom Carnes, standing larger than any other Perth Amboy man, at the top of his stairs—huge arms firmly clenched across his massive chest, and, from there down to his knees, a slightly blood-stained serving apron that billowed large as a soldier's tent. Mister Carnes, a hero from the last war against the French and a renowned brawler before, during, and after that event, stood six-foot-six-inches and weighed eighteen stone. No man ever beat him in a fair fight. All his regular patrons claimed no man existed who could ever beat Big Tom Carnes. If he had weaknesses, there were only two, which those who knew him well whispered about when he was not around. Carnes had one good eye with which to count those who were now slipping past him. The other, as a result of an unfortunate wound in the last war, was ruined and now hid behind a black patch. No one dared ask Mister Carnes about the particulars of how he came by such a wound. He never told a soul—not his dear departed wife or his four daughters. The daughters were his second weakness. They were raw-boned, coarse in looks and in speech, and taller than half the men who patronized Long Ferry Tavern. Big Tom had failed to marry off a single one of his daughters. They stayed with him and ran his business. He had little to do but keep order, act intimidating, and assist wherever and whenever needed.

When the customers were all inside and counted, Tom Carnes wiped his massive hands on his apron, then took a moment to stare at the three men still loitering in his yard—one handsome fellow mounted on a fine horse; one stout character, who looked familiar, sitting in a waggon; and one forlorn soul whom he knew well, standing in the dust.

"Two of you, I know," declared Mister Carnes finally with a blink of his one good eye. "One I still like 'cause he's honest and kind to my daughters . . . one I dislike 'cause he's always down on his luck and yearning to plug the holes in his empty pockets with bills of credit loaned by me . . . but the third before my eye is one I've never known."

Vincent dismounted, and, as soon as he did, another stable slave magically appeared and took the reins from him. John Wetherill's son fearlessly started to climb the stone stairs.

Before Vincent got half-the-way up, Cut called out: "Good to see you again, Mister Carnes. I am joined by none other than Assemblyman John Wetherill's son ..."

"I am part o' this," interrupted Ike Higgins, who dared take a tentative step towards the stairs.

Cut frowned, was going to say something, thought better of it, and held his tongue. Carnes ignored the Irishman's remark and held out his large-knuckled hand for Vincent Wetherill to grasp.

"So you must be old John's younger boy?" asked Big Tom warmly. "What name do you go by?"

Vincent took minehost's hand and felt a shock of pain shoot up the entire length of his right arm. He was glad his heart was on the sinister side. He struggled to speak: "Vincent, sir... and . . . and Cut and I have brought you a barrel of eight-year prime brandy for which, I understand, you paid for in advance last time Cut was here."

Big Tom Carnes was not ready to let go of the watery-eyed young man who stood before him. He responded, "I paid too much for it then. If I know your father, it'll cost more now . . . yes, I know your old man too well. Old John produces a fine, fine apple spirit, I must say. My customers like to sip it ever so slow . . . even when I cut it with good water from the Amboy spaw . . . my cutomers don't know the difference . . . so I turn myself a fair profit."

With that, Mister Carnes released Vincent's throbbing hand and let out a mighty laugh that made the other quarter horse jittery.

The only interruption clouding this merriment was provided by the cantankerous Irishman at the bottom of the stairs.

"Anybody far thirsty as me?" asked Ike, loud as he dared.

"Nary a one of my customers can drink as much as you, Ichabod Higgins," declared Big Tom Carnes, "and nary a one owes me as much as you."

"I'm with honest men this time, Mister Carnes. They'll vouch fer me 'n call me by the name I prefer."

"I bet they'll be paying for you too," retorted Carnes. "Remember, Ichabod, this here is my place and I'll call 'em who owes me what I wish."

Vincent spoke up: "My father has us on special assignment, Mister Carnes. He selected both Cut and Ike to join me on such after we've emptied the waggon."

Carnes scratched his clean-shaven chin with a squat finger and lowered his voice as if speaking in strict confidence: "I'd have sharp-eyed Cut Hancock in my company any day, but this Radford boy's another story. I don't know what Good Mary Woods sees in him."

Ike started up the stairs, keeping his bandaged arm close to his side. "Leave me woman out o' this, Mister Carnes. I got me ways to be useful to the Wetherills 'n good reasons too . . . now that I'm on their honest side."

Carnes stifled a rumbling guffaw. He decided to switch from riling Ike Higgins to playing the warm host: "Gentlemen, let's step inside my humble place and discuss business over that round young Vincent, here, has vowed to pay."

This Wetherill uttered no word of protest. After all, it was Jacob Ford who would be paying for this round and many more to come. He followed Big Tom Carnes and his shadow into the tap room. Ike Higgins was close behind.

Cut Hancock was glad to see Ike end up with Vincent rather than himself. He wanted no time alone with that fellow because he knew only something bad would come of it. The German clucked to his team of horses and guided them to the shadiest spot under the locust trees west of the tavern. Here, Cut allowed them and the other quarter horse to graze. He selected the largest tree, slumped to the base of its trunk, and stretched out on the dry ground to take a nap. He now had the eager daughters of Big Tom Carnes to dream about. Cut liked the idea of having four of minehost's girls to choose from. If Cut stayed too long at guarding a waggon, Mister Carnes always sent one of his daughters out with a fine ale and to see to the teamster's needs. Cut liked the idea of getting far away from his wife. He also liked the idea that none of minehost's four daughters had ever married. He liked all the possibilities conjured up in his dreams. Cut liked making easy choices.

❖

After concluding business with minehost, which involved advance payment for another barrel of eight-year and two barrels of jack to be delivered next month, Vincent had his horse brought round to the porch, and he departed from Long Ferry Tavern at noon. Arrangements for meals, drinks, and an upstairs room for the night had been made to the satisfaction of all—save for Ike, who was told by Big Tom to sleep under the waggon so that Cut could get a decent respite indoors, and so that nothing of value in the tavern went missing during the night. Vincent had no problem with Ike sharing guard duties with Cut; therefore, he endorsed minehost's idea. Of course, Ike protested. It was to no avail. He claimed he had rounds to make down on Water Street. Certain folks owed him gambling debts and he meant to collect at night when the gamers came out to play. Big Tom Carnes laughed at the Radford boy and told him to take care of all that before dusk.

"If you're late returning, my hard Paddy," instructed Carnes firmly, "then I'll take my mauleys to your hide and break that arm you seem to be favoring."

"I plan some honest work in the neighborhood," protested Ike, "which involves the likes o' me snoopin' at the Skinner house 'n market till I finds me some news . . . could take most o' the night . . ."

Carnes let out a roaring laugh and Vincent allowed himself a knowing smile.

"Always the sly boot," said Carnes as he slapped poor Ike on the back and caused him to choke on the free beer he was nursing.

Ike came up sputtering, "I—I know a servant or two by the Cove where the small boats come in . . . they can get me into places where secrets hide . . . may take till long after midnight."

Tom Carnes frowned. He cast his one good eye on John Wetherill's son. "This boy is wasting my time and yours. I say you let him off the leash till midnight. By then, he comes back here and relieves poor Cut in the yard. Ichabod, here, needs to learn to obey orders if he plans to stay on your honest side. This will be a good test for the boy. Let him take care of his business when you say so. Let him know who's boss. What say you, Vincent?"

The young man thought midnight was long enough for Ike to be snooping about. Thus, he instructed him to leave when he finished his pint and to get back at the appointed time.

"By the by," Carnes added, "Walk it, Ichabod, 'cause you will embarrass my stable boys if you ride that sorry quarter horse down Water Street. Tell not a soul 'bout where you plan to spend the night. I do not want my distinguished reputation tarnished by the likes of you snoozin' in my yard."

"I want no part o' the horse," admitted Ike. "Least there's one thing we agrees on, Mister Carnes. When I ride out from here on the morrow, my arse will be on the other one. No offense, Mister Vincent, but I've had it with Lord Corn."

"Not a problem, Ike, and no offense taken. You might have better luck with Mercury."

Ike drained the last of his beer and disappeared out the door. No one bothered to watch him depart. He vanished with the stealth of a fox. He was the perfect man to send to snoop around the haunts on Water Street. Besides, he did his best work when he went alone.

Vincent took another route into Amboy. He guided his horse through the commerce and confusion along High Street. As he made his way amidst the chaos, Vincent recalled the conversation he had had with Big Tom Carnes after Ike Higgins left them alone at the far-corner table where minehost kept his cautious eye on all his patrons. This was where Tom conducted his business while his handsome daughters conducted theirs. The Long Ferry Tavern was a well-run establishment—one that turned a fair profit each year and had a reputation for being orderly and clean. Big Tom took care of the former and his daughters and servants took care of the latter. No customer ever dared complain about the service at Long Ferry's. No one dared confront Big Tom Carnes about anything.

Vincent remembered Mister Carnes asking about the pitiful condition of Ike's face. The young man recounted the entire episode which occurred the day before in front of Rattoon's.

Big Tom shook his head. "That place is going under . . . the Rattoons are letting a bad crowd in . . . those pig irons need to be stopped at the door, not once they're inside. Old Ichabod and Mary can't do it all theirselves. Of recent, things have got worse with the likes of them luggers from out of county."

"Do you have trouble with them?" asked Vincent.

"Just last night, 'nother batch at our landing this side of the river came up the path to raise their brand of frolic under my locust trees . . . but my slaves are always quick to warn me of their coming. So I was at the top step outside the door and ready for 'em."

"What happened then?"

"Told 'em to go back whence they came . . . but two of 'em started to climb my stairs. I met 'em half-the-way, slammed their nobs together, and held on to 'em till the constables come to lock 'em away for the night in the gaol. Drunk and riotous would be the charges I'd prefer to lay on 'em."

"What about the others?"

"Scampered away like a herd of hunted bucks after the firing of a first musket round. I assume they returned to their boats or ended up killing time and their wages on Water Street. Your Mister Higgins will surely find out their fate."

"Anything strange about the two who challenged you?"

"Nothing worth recalling," sneered Big Tom Carnes, as if the two in question were not worth fighting. "They were a pair of your usual greasy pig irons . . . burly and bold and stinking too . . . called out something 'bout swords, of which they carried none . . . and they named some names of saints, or some such nonsense, which they seemed mighty proud of . . . so I took 'em as drunk . . . and I bet when they awaken this day, they'll not remember a thing."

Vincent thanked Carnes for his recollections of the night before, and then asked where he might find the former gaoler, William Jolly.

Minehost obliged him: "Old William's been keeping busy at assisting Sheriff Tom Skinner in some sort of capacity—special and secret, so I've heard. That one's a snooper for the law just as

Ichabod's a snooper for you. I don't know what title you'd give to Will Jolly, but I know for a fact he's now getting less pay than a constable."

Big Tom Carnes added that, if Vincent hoped to find Jolly, the first place to look would be the Courthouse. With that knowledge obtained, Vincent thanked minehost for the information, got up from the table of honor, and strode out to the steps down to where the stable boy waited to hand the reins of his mount to him.

Before he departed, to consume the middle hours of the day, he spotted Cut engaged in light conversation with a large-boned maid, who must have been one of Big Tom's daughters. Vincent saluted his waggoner, but did not go in their direction to interrupt whatever delightful progress was being made under the largest locust tree. Cut hoisted a tankard, which this good woman must have brought to him, and smiled broadly. Vincent was glad at least one of his men was enjoying what Perth Amboy had to offer.

Vincent found High Street to be wide and dusty dry. He made his way, quick as the commerce would allow, to the Public Square where horse apples were as plentiful as market hawkers. Horses in great numbers whinnied and wickered as they clopped along.

Those beasts pulling waggons caused a loud clatter. Merchants stood by their wares praising each item for customers passing to and fro. Many folks milled about, enjoying a moment of idleness and another brilliant day without rain. It had been this way since the two days of rain came on the skirt of a coastal hurricane back on August 26th and 27th. A Company of the King's Regulars marched by—their destination unknown, but their presence duly noted by busy folks and idle folks. Yes, there was a great deal more hustle and bustle here in the Province Capital, thought Vincent, as the soldiers in their bold red coats passed him. Amboy boasted a modest population for a capital town, but it attracted throngs of visitors and travelers each day. In addition, the seat of government for East Jersey housed scores of soldiers in the renovated Barracks far up North Dock Street on the outskirts of town. Those officers and soldiers, who could not be accommodated at the Barracks, were housed in private homes. Thus, an uncrowded town seemed always crowded.

Many residents did not like it that way—especially having to put up with quartering military personnel. Although over-crowded and in the midst of hurry-scurry each day, there was order and regimentation just the same. The town's flaws were hidden well. It wore its mask of prosperity proudly. Its citizens meant business— be it legal or not. The enforcers of the law in Amboy, bolstered by the presence of the King's military, meant to discourage the latter.

John Wetherill's son was able to maneuver his Spanish barb through the heart of the crowd and locate the Courthouse on the corner of Market and High streets. The two-story stone building stood behind four stately trees facing the Public Square. Vincent found a hitch post behind one of the trees, dismounted, and secured his mount's tether to the post. He stood before the Provincial Courthouse and paused for a moment to admire its facade and recall its significance. This was where his father was summoned to Assembly meetings when they were not held in the West Jersey capital of Burlington. The gaol had once been housed here as well, with William Jolly as one of the gaolers. It was here that John Wetherill met the law man, befriended him, and vouched for him when he was threatened by creditors.

That seemed so far in the past. It had been several years since the Assemblyman paid off Jolly's debts in order to have charges dropped. By doing so, the man avoided spending a length of time in his own gaol. To this day, however, Mister Jolly had not repaid Vincent's father. The son was here to correct that oversight.

There were two doors—one at each corner of the front of the building. Vincent selected the one not blocked by lawyers and clients. Once inside, he found a clerk who knew Mister Jolly well. However, the busy man did not know of his whereabouts. "Old Will is usually here at this time of day," said the clerk distractedly. "Something must have come up which tossed him off his schedule."

The sole Constable in the place—a short, squat fellow exuding self-importance—had been listening to what the clerk had been saying. He waddled over to confront Vincent.

"And who might ye be?" asked the Constable, looking up suspiciously at the tall, young stranger.

"Vincent Wetherill of Cross Roads, younger son of the Assemblyman who represents this county."

"Oh, I see," blushed the Constable as he took an exaggerated step back. "Begging your pardon, sir, but ye may find our Mister Jolly at the new gaol, investigating the escape of two gentlemen last night."

Vincent thanked the chagrined man for his information and asked for directions to the jail. Now the Constable appeared more than glad to give such particulars and send the well-connected visitor on his way. By all means, this fellow wanted to avoid any further embarrassment. The busy clerk was enjoying his associate's predicament. He paused from his work in order to take note of the Constable's next misstep. However, Vincent did not allow it to happen. He exited the building, mounted his steed, and headed north on Market Street. He found the jail on the corner of Back Street adjacent to a broad burial ground. The place was surrounded by harvested fields and few farmsteads. A cluster of buildings was located near the jail.

"What a fine place for a gallows," thought Vincent out loud to himself, as he approached the somber main building. He spotted a brace of men examining the ground between the jail and the nearest headstones. One man, by all appearances older than the others, was pointing north with a walking stick in his gloved hand.

Vincent approached on foot, with his Spanish barb in tow. "Which one of you gentlemen is William Jolly?" asked Vincent, as he reached into his vest pocket and brought forth a letter with his father's seal affixed to it.

"Who might be asking?" inquired the oldest man.

"I am Vincent Wetherill, son of Assemblyman John Wetherill of Middlesex County. I've a letter, here, to hand over to the right person—the contents of which is for his eyes only." Then Vincent, in an attempt to fill the silence, added, "The Constable at the Courthouse was kind enough to give me directions on where to find Mister William Jolly."

The oldest man directed his two companions to head back to the jail and wait for him. When the pair were out of hearing range, he turned to Vincent Wetherill and, using a gloved hand, took the letter from the young man. He broke the red seal, upon which the slender initials "JW" were affixed within the confines of a five-pointed star.

Mister Jolly's narrow brown eyes darted from word to word. He suddenly stopped reading the contents of the letter before finishing it. But he did not look up. "So an old friend sends his younger son to collect what is due him?" muttered the law man more to himself than to the messenger who stood patiently before him.

With a knowing grin on his face, the former gaoler resumed reading the letter. This gave Vincent an opportunity to size up the last person who was to join his investigative team. Jolly was a slim, almost gaunt, straight-backed fellow of middling height. His complexion was fair, but pale, with no evidence of the pox. There were deep crow's feet round his eyes and deeper worry creases spanning his forehead. His own nut-brown hair was thick and long over his ears, but the crown of his head was completely bald. The brilliant sun on this warming day was attacking there. Vincent wondered why Jolly did not wear a hat, which could have advertised position, status, or rank. The man sported no ribbon or badge on the shoulder or breast of his dull, brown coat. The outer garment was open, revealing an ill-fitting striped waistcoat of yellow and green, which must have been obtained at a cheap price. Knit buff breeches and yellow-stained long stockings completed the man's unimpressive outfit. His calfskin shoes with over-sized brass buckles were caked with dust. Vincent surmised that Mister Jolly had been busy plodding about the jail grounds and the cemetery looking for something important. What that was, he could not guess.

Jolly finished concentrating on the first page of the letter from John Wetherill. The thin-lipped smile he had been working on had vanished. Now the law man offered a stark frown. Reading the letter seemed to have made him suddenly weary, even sad.

"I shall not be able to accompany you," said William Jolly, as he tucked the letter into his waistcoat pocket.

"But my father assured me that you would be eager to join me," countered a perturbed Vincent Wetherill.

"Your father's offer to forgive my debt to him is most kind. However, my obligations for the forseeable future rest right here in Amboy. I am on assignment, answerable to the High Sheriff only. He, and those above him, still seek to prove the innocence of Stephen Skinner in the Treasury robbery. My job, these past few years, has been to clear that bastard's name by tracking down information which confirms that he had no part in the robbery. I've received a modest but steady pay for such a frustrating and futile cause. So far, I have found nothing to implicate or exonerate the man. So my hire for this assignment puts me on the opposite side of your father's wishes. The longer this Treasurer stays in office, the longer I keep my assignment."

"My views on the character of Stephen Skinner are not as strong as my father's," said Vincent, out of desperation in not knowing what to say.

Mister Jolly managed a knowing grin. He revealed crooked teeth—yellow as his stockings. "Mine are as strong as your father's, but I am getting paid to think the opposite."

Vincent was stunned. He struggled with what to say next. Here was a man, like his father, who wanted the current Treasurer out of office as soon as possible to face charges of negligence in securing the Treasury monies, yet he had been hired to find evidence that would keep Skinner in office and in the good graces of the Governor. What a cross-grained world.

Jolly picked up his conversation, which Vincent failed to interrupt: "Besides, I have other pressing obligations. A grievous crime was committed during the night, right here, and the perpetrators got away. This is the latest of interruptions which keep me from what I am supposed to concentrate on. Now, I must remain in town till repairs have been made on this gaol, inside and out. All the locks have to be replaced, if the keys are not found."

The former gaoler pointed his black walking stick at the edifice in question. Vincent caught the shimmer of sunlight off the silver affixed to the instrument. It was obviously the most expensive item in Mister Jolly's possession. The man handled it with such a flourish, as if it were a weapon. Then Vincent realized that it might very well be—inside a hard black scabbard, perhaps, lurked a long, thin blade. He was curious to find out for sure, but refrained from asking about the piece. Instead, Vincent inquired about the incident at the jail.

"Two jack fellow luggers were brought in last night," replied William Jolly in a bitter, leaden voice. "They'd been causing a row of some sort down at the Long Ferry Tavern . . ."

"I was told of the affair by Mister Carnes, himself," interrupted

Vincent. "I had business there, then decided to take a room at the place for this night before heading north on the morrow."

"So you know the details from the honest side," remarked Jolly, "but have you heard what happened to the pair who were brought in after resisting arrest?"

"Nothing good, I assume."

"Right you are . . . and embarrassed are we . . . those boys were locked secure in an upstairs room . . . the gaoler who took my place, Obediah King, put himself first at watch outside the door . . . the two luggers were loud at first, so I was told . . . singing queer songs and shouting odd chants. After a time, they quieted down, but Obediah could still hear their voices . . . 'twas the mere chatter and cursing of boys who did not particularly like being penned up for the night . . .'"

William Jolly started walking back to the jail. He ambled along with a noticeable limp and was in obvious need of his walking cane. Vincent coaxed his horse from its grazing and caught up with the law man on an ill-defined path which pretended to follow a crooked fence that fronted a stand of trees whose leaves were already turning golden. A pair of squirrels rustled about behind the barricade, busy with their own acts of thievery.

After pointing with his valuable cane to the upstairs room on the southeast corner of the jail, Jolly continued his account of the two incarcerated iron men. Vincent observed that damage had been done to the window below—panes of glass were missing and a shutter had been torn off its hinges. The shutter rested at the base of the east corner of the building. Someone must have propped it there for a purpose.

"An hour before Mister King was to be relieved by the midnight guard," continued Jolly, "a poor decision was made by the gaoler. The way King tells it, he decided to convince those two louts that joining the King's regiment would be better than facing charges Big Tom Carnes had against them. So Obediah, with lantern in hand, unlocks the door and peeks in. The boys are awake and willing to listen, at first, to the gaoler's plan, but they were all ruse and faking sincere . . . they agreed to join up with the Irish 26th Regiment of Foot already in town . . . so uncautious Mister King turns to go and he's jumped by the pair, who had plans of their own . . . they brained him . . . stole his keys."

"They could have burned this place down," opined Vincent, as he and Mister Jolly approached the damaged window.

"We were lucky in that," reflected Jolly. "Seems the two had escape in mind all along . . . so down the stairs they bounded . . . with all of the keys on Obediah's ring . . . past the first-floor guard, who'll be punished for sleeping at the worst time to choose . . . out the front door with only King's watch-hound taking notice from the neighboring yard."

Then Mister Jolly did a strange thing. He unsheathed the thin sword that Vincent had speculated was in the narrow, hollow chamber of the cane. With it, he traced lines that had been cut into the green shutter.

"Instead of bolting from here," reported Jolly, "the two puggards paused to rip this shutter off its hinges . . . use it to break the window, but quiet enough so as not to rouse the sleeping guard . . . then one of them must have taken up the largest shard of glass within reach and commenced to carve this here cross on the shutter . . . only thereafter do they run off through the cemetery, if I guess correctly . . . but they never dropped the keys . . . least ways, my men have yet to find them . . ."

"Not a cross," offered Vincent, as he glanced up at the sun, then focused on the symbol that had been carved on the shutter. "'Tis a sword."

Vincent spent a good part of the afternoon helping Jolly and his men search for the keys. They were unsuccessful. Finally, Mister Jolly called off the effort. The only thing positive that came out of the search time was that Vincent was able to convince Jolly to rendezvous at the Long Ferry Tavern after it got dark. The law man promised to get there after reporting his findings to Sheriff Thomas Skinner, after checking on Obadiah King's condition, and after sitting down with his wife for a late repast. In following a request made by John Wetherill in his letter, Jolly gave his word that at the rendezvous he would tell Vincent all he knew about the old Treasury robbery. He also planned to counsel Vincent on how to proceed with investigating the recent murder up in Morris County.

Jolly was aware of the hanging of the counterfeiter; however, he knew nothing about the slaying of the indentured servant until Vincent had given him the particulars about the crime. Jolly then opined that the authorities in Morris Town were keeping a lid on news spreading about it. He also thought the authorities considered the murder a matter of low priority, based on the meager status of the deceased and his reputation as a pickpocket. Jack Redmon, alive or dead, was not a topic worth talking about.

"Good riddance to poor dregs," surmised Jolly with the finality of a law man who had dealt with more than his share of miscreants. "But Redmon's murderer still has to be caught. I have some ideas to share on doing just that, Mister Wetherill. That will have to be later. It must wait till I tend to a few things."

With that said, Jolly gripped his special cane with both hands, slipped the secret blade out, and inspected it carefully. "The best weapon, Mister Wetherill, is the one unseen till it is too late."

"I do not disagree," said Vincent, as he kept his eyes fixed on the pristine blade.

"The same can be said for the sort of clues left behind by a good criminal . . . such clues are always there, but remain unseen . . . so it goes with the Treasury robbery . . . so it goes with the murder of Jack Redmon . . ."

"Perhaps with your robbery," said Vincent, as he looked Jolly in the eye, "but, I trust, not with my murder . . ."

"You'll find out soon enough," warned Jolly, as he sheathed his blade once more. He reached for Vincent's hand and shook it. He turned and headed for the door to the jail.

Vincent mounted his horse and headed back down Market Street to see if he could find Ike Higgins. He never did.

5

A RENDEZVOUS OF SORTS

· ·

—back at the Long Ferry Tavern,
late Wednesday, September 22, 1773

When Vincent Wetherill returned to the Long Ferry Tavern, the first thing he did was check on Cut. The man was busy exercising the horses within sight of old man Wetherill's waggon. He claimed he had been fed well and cared for by one of Big Tom's just-shy-of-handsome daughters. Cut needed nothing more. He was glad to learn from Vincent that Ike Higgins was going to relieve him at midnight.

"If you trust him, Mister Wetherill," said Cut with a sober glare, "then Ike's spelling me fits my plans good."

Vincent could not imagine what plans old Cut had in mind after midnight, but he dared not ask. There was more to Cutlope Hancock than the young Wetherill felt he knew. Vincent was still wondering about what Cut might be up to, when he ordered his first pint of ale from who must have been the tallest and oldest daughter of Big Tom Carnes. With drink in hand, Vincent found his way to minehost's far table. Carnes was not there. Mister Jolly was scheduled to arrive much later. So young Wetherill sat alone still wondering about what Cut was planning, what Ike Higgins was up to, and how he was going to convince Will Jolly to join his team. He had not even made it beyond Amboy and he was already having doubts about making sure his team stayed together and his father's idea came to fruition. He definitely needed Mister Jolly to make his plan work. That fellow was older. He had experience in law enforcement, and he was serious about catching criminals and bringing them to justice. Ike certainly was not. Cut seemed indifferent. When Vincent thought about it long enough, he did not really care either. Rather than achieving some projected outcome, this was more about fulfilling a son's duty to his father. Vincent had no goal other than to go through the motions—let events fall where they may. The outcome was of no concern to him. All that really mattered was getting back to Abia as soon as he could. Oh, how he missed her already. In the midst of loud voices exploring the issues of the day, Vincent imagined Abia sitting with him in the shadow of the darkest corner—laughing or crying, he could not tell which. To get his mind off her, young Wetherill reached for his tiny ledger in his vest pocket, took it out slowly, and, with a slender char stylus, updated his expenditures.

Vincent heard, but paid little attention to what the patrons were talking about. No gentleman in the main room of the tavern said a word about the Treasury robbery. It was old, stale news. However, Vincent heard Stephen Skinner's name more than once. It was uttered in anger followed by a few choice curses. This was a whiggish crowd. One amongst the gathering called for Skinner to resign. Another called for Governor Franklin to force him out. No one came to the defense of the proprietors' darling. One fellow called for Cortlandt Skinner, Stephen's brother, to step down as President of the Assembly, but others shouted down the loudmouth and called him a fool. They claimed all Skinners were not dishonest or incompetent. Cortlandt Skinner had represented Perth Amboy well. Even High Sheriff Thomas Skinner was doing an adequate job. No, there was only one Skinner to get rid of—that bumbling beef-wit, Stephen Skinner.

There were loud complaints about billeting soldiers in private homes—this had been going on for years and there seemed no resolution to the matter, even with recent renovations at the Barracks. Someone cursed the King over this, but the fellow was shouted down and a toast was made for George to live long and tax less. After a round was paid for by a rather distinguished looking gentleman dressed in fine burgundy velvet with a full fancy lace cravat at his throat, a toast was made to the Committees of Correspondence in Rhode Island, Connecticut, New Hampshire, South Carolina, and Virginia. A loud separate toast was raised to Massachusetts, followed by one to a future Committee for the Jerseys.

The strident voices then turned to complaints about the poor condition of the main roads; the failed lottery that was supposed to pay for road improvement; the cancelled horse races at Powles Hook; and the latest duties imposed by Parliament without consent of the Jersey Assembly. There were grumblings about restraints against iron mills. Opposition was voiced about having an English Bishop in the colonies. Someone cursed the East India Tea Company and yelled "up with coffee!" Calls were made for courage to the Assemblymen of Middlesex and for progress to be made at the next session. Vincent heard his father's name called out, followed by hearty cheers for the old man. Not one person in the room knew that John Wetherill's son was sitting in the shadows of the same room. Vincent preferred that it remain this way.

On went the grousing about such things as the cruel length of the season's dry spell, punctuated by cursing. However, there were occasional toasts to better times ahead, for it was that not all the rumors and news was gloom and doom. There were even a few things for this drinking crowd to be glad about. Toasts were raised for each one:

"To the boundary line 'tween New York and Jersey, finally fixed—may it hold for eternity."

"To the August visit by Governor William Franklin and the rumor of his coming to live in Amboy—may it ripen to fruition and bring great revenue to our town."

"To the marriage of little Billy Hoffmeister and his three-foot bride from Brunswick—may they enjoy the rewards of conjugal bliss and still have enough time to entertain audiences wherever they go."

Vincent was finally distracted from the tavern litany when the oldest Carnes daughter brought him a large bowl of thick stew and a round bannock loaf. She also brought him another ale and word that her father would be coming shortly. She left him alone before he could ask where Big Tom Carnes was coming from. It was none of his business anyway. Vincent was hungry.

He ripped off a piece of the warm oat bread and dipped it in the steaming stew. The din of the taproom crowd did not matter any more. His concerns about the viability of his investigative team could wait to be resolved. The whereabouts of minehost was of no import. What mattered now was enjoying good food and drink, and thinking about his five-foot bride.

❖

Big Tom Carnes emerged from the side room reserved for ladies and their escorts. He was greeted by cheers of recognition from many of his fawning patrons, who, by now, were heavily in their drink. Carnes paid them no mind and strode to his favorite table where young Mister Wetherill got up to make room for minehost.

"Sit your arse down, my honored guest." ordered Carnes. "Finish your meal and let's have another round of my heartwarming ale. Conversations go better with lubrication and fuel."

Vincent followed orders and agreed that one more house ale was in order. No sooner had he spoke and minehost snapped his fingers, than one of Big Tom's daughters rushed over with two pints of brew.

"'Scuse my absence," said Carnes, "but I was teaching the ladies a card game unknown to the likes of 'em . . . always like to teach the ladies new tricks . . . and new positions to play."

"What game is it?" asked Vincent between spoonfuls of the now less-than-warm stew.

"Quadrille," answered Carnes as if he were the only man in the room who was an expert at it. "A clever and complex game of forty cards . . . a good one for gambling . . . 'specially if you know the tricks and positions . . . more such and so if your opponents ain't wary. . ."

"I assume you have won your share at the game?"

"Always," confessed Big Tom unabashedly, "but the women don't play for money. They take their pleasures in other ways, if you catch my meaning."

With that, Big Tom slapped Vincent on the back, which caused John Wetherill's son to choke on the last of his stew. Minehost ordered Vincent to drink his ale to clear his throat. The guest quickly did as he was told. The golden brew burned as it went down, but it did the trick. Yet, when Vincent tried to speak, no words came out.

"So you're going to ask me if I heard 'bout the 'scape of the pair I'd sent to gaol," predicted Big Tom as he studied his large, weapon-like hands. "Yes, I did, but I'm none too happy 'bout it . . . least ways, I know them certain pig irons won't be visiting my place ever again."

Vincent finally recovered after another swig of ale: "Did you notice if the pair on your steps sported any tattoos?"

Carnes paused to recollect, took a gulp of his drink, and answered haltingly: "None do I recall . . . a scar or two, perhaps . . . maybe there was some mark or sign . . . can't say for sure."

"No sword or cross?"

"Don't recall," mulled Carnes while deep in what might be construed as thought. "Why are you asking?"

Vincent spoke of the tattoos Ike had seen on the hands of the men who thrashed him at Rattoon's and the sword carving in the shutter at the jail. He admitted considering it as mere coincidence, but, then again, possibly connected. At that moment, Vincent wondered why he was getting so concerned with a matter that had nothing to do with what his father wanted him to investigate. The pig irons were getting to be a distraction.

"The boys who visit Radford's Landing don't never cross over to Long Ferry," explained Big Tom Carnes. "They go upriver after a frolic over there. We get different crews, but made up of boys from the same forges and mines . . . mostly cod snappers and cabbage heads now . . . the ones causing recent troubles appears to be the mulers and luggers bringing the pig and plate to market . . . used to be an honor bestowed by mine foremen and forge masters on laborers chosen for such trips, but not so much in these restricted times . . . class and character of recent redemptioners has fallen in recent years . . . such pass through here, get broken in way upriver, and return to haunt these shores with their randy ways . . . if they was to rally themselves—miners, forge tenders, wood cutters, bloomers, charcoal makers, and such—then think of the woe they might cause."

Vincent agreed with Mister Carnes about that being an unpleasant. riotous prospect, but it was really no concern of his.

"With such ways the King restricts iron and steel making in Jersey, and the number of mine owners and furnace owners who are in debt," continued Big Tom, "'tis a matter of time afore something blows and we've a rebellion in the hills of the far counties . . . mark my words, Mister Wetherill, in a way, we're lucky to have the King's Reg'lars marching the streets of this town . . . 'tis one thing to have a band of well-to-do rousers talking riotous and such, 'specially up 'round Boston . . . 'tis another thing altogether when some louts and poor fish gets stirred up by a down-'n-out rouser. . . then 'tis real bad trouble for the King on down to us."

Again, Vincent could not disagree with minehost's speculations. The large man was crude in most ways, but knowledgeable and informed. Carnes was in a position to hear things first, put two-and-two together, and state an opinion grounded on a wealth of information.

"All those back county boys need," concluded minehost, "is a leader who can organize 'em . . . then it'll be Old Harry to pay . . . you heard it from my lips first."

As if by cue, William Jolly came through the main door and was following directions, given to him by one of minehost's daughters, to the table where Vincent and Carnes sat. No one cheered the former gaoler. He found the large shadow in the corner to his liking, since he seemed quite eager to go through unnoticed.

Big Tom Carnes gave Jolly a warm, though subdued, welcome.

He signaled for a spruce beer, which, he knew, the law man preferred. He enquired about the latest on the escapees.

Jolly had nothing new to report. The two pig irons were still at large. No keys had been found yet, even though his men spent the remainder of the day looking for them in and beyond the cemetery. He and minehost shared information about the men who had run away. Speculation about the carving on the shutter and whether the escapees may have had tattoos was touched upon, but not for long.

Vincent eventually admitted that he had matters of import to discuss with Mister Jolly and that the hour was getting late.

Big Tom suggested the two guests adjourn upstairs to the room he had assigned to Vincent earlier.

"The walls are thin, gentlemen," admitted Carnes, "but you will not have to put up with the awful din of clamor and cussing down here . . . besides, my youngest daughter, fair 'Becca, who has the night to herself, should be at sleep in her room next door . . . she snores 'loud, but that should not discourage you speaking in gentlemanly tones."

Vincent and Jolly agreed on Big Tom's suggestion and took their drinks with them up narrow stairs to the assigned room. A servant boy led the way with candle and key in hand. There were sounds behind the few doors they passed, but none resembled loud snoring. Perhaps the fair Rebecca would be quiet this night.

The servant boy unlocked the door to Vincent's room and went in first to light three wall candles with his own and raise a fire in the small hearth. While he fussed with mounding tinder just so and lighting it with his candle flame, Vincent inspected the room. The walls were close and gray, with the far wall sporting a low window tucked under a wide eve. The ceiling was slanted, but high enough to accommodate even Big Tom Carnes if he cared to slouch at his window. The corner bed was low to the floor and smallish for Vincent who was of above-average height. He wondered if any of minehost's long daughters would feel comfortable in such a bed. A plain table and two chairs dominated the center of the room. A washstand with a large water pitcher and an even larger chamber pot sat against the wall opposite the bed. High above the pitcher and pot was a board of pegs with but one gray cloth hanging from an end peg. There was nothing fancy about the room, but it was utilitarian; more importantly, it was clean.

Vincent was satisfied with it.

The servant boy departed after making sure a fair-sized piece of maple was catching flame in the fireplace. Vincent and Mister Jolly were already seated. The former gaoler had extracted the letter written by Vincent's father and placed it on the table. Vincent assumed Jolly meant to return the letter as a way of reiterating that nothing would convince him to join the investigative team. Vincent had to quickly decide what else to talk about. He wished Cutlope Hancock was here to participate, but it was not yet midnight and there was no guarantee Ike Higgins would return on time to relieve the German at guarding the brandy waggon. Vincent, most likely, would have to go it alone in attempting to convince William Jolly to join the team. It would not be wise to lead with that subject. Vincent struggled over what topic to choose.

Mister Jolly was pointing to the letter. "Your father wants me to tell you what I know about the Treasury robbery."

Vincent felt relieved from the burden of opening the conversation, but he did not show it. Stale news was a safe place to start. He decided to let Jolly lead in that direction. He gave the law man a nod in the affirmative.

"According to what your father wrote in his letter," said Jolly, as he opened the document on the table, smoothed its creases, laid his cane across it to keep it flat, and traced certain words with a thin, calloused finger, "you already know a great deal about the larceny committed by unknown folks on the night of July 21, 1768, at Stephen Skinner's manse on South Dock Street in this town. But you don't know everything. I intend to fix that."

Vincent was watching the man's finger on the letter. He looked up when Mister Jolly stopped talking. The law man was staring at him, or, more to the point, staring through him, as if he had seen something at the one window behind Vincent. Jolly was casting those same sad eyes again—the kind a law enforcer gains from witnessing too many villains getting away with crimes or simply getting away.

"Over six-thousand pounds was filched from an iron chest that night—Treasury monies meant to sustain the poor and other provincials, such as widows in need. They were mostly bills of credit—twenty to a bundle—plus several hundred Spanish dollars and a few gold half-johannes. What's most interesting here is that one-hundred-and-seventy pounds was left in the chest."

Mister Jolly paused to take a sip of his spruce beer, while Vincent pondered over the import of the sum of money left behind. Both of them remained silent for a moment as sounds of someone stirring next door came through the thin wall Big Tom Carnes had warned about. It was not a woman's snoring—just the quiet footsteps of someone pacing about . . . someone, perhaps, anticipating a visitor or the honest restlessness of a woman not yet ready for sleep.

The former gaoler broke the brief silence in Vincent's room: "First at the scene was Billy Campbell, one of Mister Skinner's apprentices, who intended to come round in the morning to grub a meal and break his fast. According to his original testimony, of which I learned later, he must have been the first to see the back room window with its shutter askew and a pane of glass shattered and laying about on the ground below the window. This Campbell takes a peek inside and realizes he's got his eye on the east room where the Treasury money was kept . . ."

Vincent interrupted Mister Jolly before the man could complete his information about the apprentice: "Did the boy find any symbol carved on the open shutter?"

Jolly laughed to hide his surprise and stole a quick, restorative sip of his beer. "None that the boy or anyone else, including myself, who got to examine the scene that day or days later. Don't try to make connections with what happened at gaol last night and what happened at Skinner's manse five years ago. That cross, or sword as your eyes see it, has got nothing to do with the Treasury robbery. That carving's the first one I've ever seen and the second one you know about. Hopefully, such marks are nothing more serious than the efforts of cod-headed boys attempting to be clever. I probably won't see that sign ever again in my life."

"I'm not so sure I have seen or heard the last of it, Mister Jolly."

"Think what you wish, Mister Wetherill, but I'll tell you this—the sign has nothing to do with the robbery. No prisoner at my gaol watch, for more than seven years past, ever carved your sword on anything nor tattooed himself with it. Next, you will be telling me sly Sam Ford sports such a scar on his body and he's scratching it on his latest plates."

It was Vincent's turn to chuckle. "That would make our work easier now, wouldn't it?"

"No," said Jolly adamantly, "much more complicated and quite perplexing. Now, let me get back to my account. This here Billy Campbell rushes to rouse the house slave, Bob, who's sleeping in the room next to where the Treasury money was kept. Black Bob, in turn, rushes upstairs to rouse Mister Skinner and tell his master the bad news. At first, that inept Skinner is far nervous with disbelief. Then, all three enter the violated room and see what I heard about later—sun shining brightly through a broken window; violated iron chest, nicked and dented, flush against the east wall and under the window; and, as your father claims in his letter and I confirm, the master's sword, unsheathed on his secretary desk and pointing to the window . . ."

"Quite similar to the murder scene at Morris Town, which I told you about," interrupted Vincent again.

"Five years is a long time to make such a leap, Mister Wetherill. Stealing money on a grand scale and slaying a servant are world's apart. I agree with your father on both crime scenes—they appear staged; but, after a close mulling on each, the comparisons scatter like dead leaves in a March wind. There is nothing worth comparing in what remains."

Vincent did not argue the point. He worked on his ale while Jolly paused to work on his spruce beer. Nothing was to be accomplished by challenging a man Vincent desperately wanted on his side. Mister Jolly was much older, much more experienced, and much more set in his ways. Vincent had to be cautious and careful in dealing with this one. Deferring to the man's opinions was a safe approach.

Jolly sought to conclude on what he knew about the Treasury robbery. The hour was creeping close to midnight and the spruce beer was making him too comfortable. The noises from the adjacent room suddenly turned louder after the opening and closing of a door. Two people were exchanging words, which were punctuated by taunts of laughter. Vincent guessed that a gentleman had come to pay a visit on the youngest daughter of Big Tom Carnes. Jolly was frowning. The law man had guessed the same.

"Let's get this done," he said with a slow monotone of determination. "So Mister Skinner sends Billy to fetch the Sheriff and whatever Constable could be found. Then, the fool orders Black Bob to start straightening up the ransacked room. This dutiful slave does his usual good job of ruining a chance at some clues. I was eventually called upon to guard Skinner's castle—to spell a Constable who'd been standing there all the first full day. My duty came as it was getting dark on the second day from when the deed was done. Thus, most of the facts I give you are second hand, but from reliable folks who came there before me. I had the honor to share most of it with your father years later. Now I share it again, and still there is no hope of recovering the stolen money . . . no hope of finding who took it . . . no hope of replacing that cork-brained Skinner, who is part responsible for me losing my gaoler's job."

Vincent did not want to go into Mister Jolly's employment history. He thought it wise to ask about suspects instead. However, the activity in the next room distracted the two men for a spell. There was much laughter followed by what sounded like a child being spanked by a strict parent. There were shouts and cries broken intermittently by more laughter. Finally, Vincent spoke above the din and asked his question:

"The thievery was committed by more than one man?"

"Of course," said Jolly without showing any sign of being distracted, "but it sure wasn't Sam Ford and his ram's horn gang of counterfeiters. Nobody clear in the head in Amboy or Morris Town believes such a gentle fox did it. I met the fellow when authorities brought him back from New York six years ago to face charges in his home county. This honorary treasurer of Jersey— as they branded Ford—stayed overnight in my gaol before his waggon ride in chains to the Morris Town gaol. He was a perfect gentleman . . . a descendant of one of the founding families of Morris County . . . close to forty in age . . . cheeks all red from good living . . . his own curled brown hair . . . remarkable dimple on his chin, as I remember . . . clever eyes and nervous twitch, be he serious or light . . . and a bigamist, so I hear, with a not-so-secret wife in Dublin and a devoted sow in Morris County . . ."

"But not a murderer or thief?" interjected Vincent.

"Doubt it much," responded Jolly. "Ford has a skill poor folks and debtors like me admire, and few detest. He has had no reason to murder or steal. Nothing in his history of counterfeiting, or managing the Hibernia furnaces and mines, gives indication of Sam Ford resorting to thievery or killing to get his way. The worst thing he ever did was make bills of poor quality when he first turned to counterfeiting in the middle sixties to get free of his debts. The way it was told to me, Ford sold off shares of his father's iron works, garnered more real money from selling his poor quality bills, and took his honest and ill-gotten gains to Ireland to pay for the best schooling in how to forge quality coin and print good false bills of credit. He returns, some few years later, a master at his craft and the envy of his peers in three counties. He thrives till caught in New York for dealing his plates and passing his best bills of credit. At the time of his capture, he was using a false name—Samuel Samson—but we knew who he was.

"When New York authorities were about to let him go for lack of evidence, he was picked up by Jersey agents. That's when he chanced to pass through us to face charges in his home county. Too many friends up there vouched for the fellow and charges against him were dropped. After that, Sam Ford floundered for a spell then returned to Dublin first and London second in 1771, to perfect his engraving and typemaking skills. Altogether, I estimate he spent close to six years 'cross the sea. For all I know, he may not have even been in the colonies when the Treasury robbery took place."

"Do you know this as truth?" Vincent had to raise his voice because the slapping sounds next door had produced moaning and deep sighs—the kind that reminded him of his last night with Abia.

"Not completely so, Mister Wetherill," admitted Jolly, who was seemingly unmoved by the intriguing sounds from next door, "but my sources are sure of the sum of years spent o'er the sea."

Vincent was not totally convinced of Ford's innocence regarding his possible involvement in the Treasury robbery. However, he said nothing more on the subject and Jolly continued to plow his furrow. After all, the music of passion was mounting on the other side of the slender wall with a bed now appearing to provide a rhythmic accompaniment. Thus, the law man merely raised his voice.

"Last year, Sam Ford's back at the business he knows best. In his own county, he sets up a ring of passers to distribute the best bill and coin ever seen in this Province. He reigns as king of his dark profession till this summer when fellow counterfeiters rat on him to save their own hides."

"Who might they be?" asked a partially attentive young man.

"Back in June, a counterfeiting tandem of Stephen Waterman and John Swan was brought in for questioning. They had been renting a house in Wood Bridge where they pretended to run a legal silver smith's trade. Instruments for making dollars out of milled pieces were found by authorities during a raid on the house. One thing led to another, as it always does with these snibbers. Other culprits were implicated, found, and dragged in for questioning. Far as I can recall, there was a Noah Colton, a Mister Hutchins, and a fellow named Boyd. All of them had bad reputations in the false money trade, but they found no gain in talking . . . that was till our High Sheriff brought them to this town, put them in gaol, and chatted with them separately."

"Did the strategy work?" asked Vincent, who now felt he could concentrate on what Jolly had to say, since the obvious lovers next door had found release and had gone silent.

"Not at first try," admitted the law man. "Two nights later, headway was made. You see, these men, or at least the leader, were from Rhode Island. They were members of a gang that was sundered in 1770. These few came down to East Jersey to set up shop again. So these rogues dragged in were seasoned criminals and they had nothing to gain by confessing anything. They had not coined any Jersey money, so they only faced a misdemeanor."

"Then how were they made to talk," asked a very curious Vincent Wetherill.

"I suggested to Sheriff Tom Skinner that they be told they would be shipped to New York to face felony charges for making and passing New York coin, which they had done. So Tom offered a choice—talk and face a misdemeanor charge in the Court of Oyer and Terminer in Middlesex County, or keep silent and, perhaps, face the death penalty in New York."

"That's all it took?"

"Nothing more. We only needed one to break and that was Mister Waterman. He chirps away about several gangs and the names of many men. Among those confessed was Sam Ford, Jr., Samuel Haynes, Benjamin Cooper, the Budd brothers, Davey Reynolds, two Captain Joes—Morris and Richardson—and one Justice of the Peace—John King. These are just some of the names of men associated with what turns out to be the Ford gang of counterfeiters in Morris County. So our Tom Skinner passes the names to his counterpart, High Sheriff Tom Kinney, up in Morris Town. You know the rest. A similar tactic is tried on the fellows captured up there, and, before the dust settles, both the Governor and the Treasurer have themselves a solution to the Treasury robbery."

"But you don't believe it?"

"Will Franklin and his Council do," responded Jolly. "Stephen Skinner has no choice but to believe it . . . same goes for all the thieving proprietors . . ."

"But you don't?" insisted Vincent.

"I'd put hard coin on Sam Ford having no direct hand in robbing our Treasury. On the night of the deed, Ford was not in town. He may have been across the sea learning his trade, or hiding in his swamp making more false money, or passing his kind in a neighboring colony. You can count on Sam Ford to have been mighty busy doing what he does best."

"Do you mean when you say 'no direct hand' that Mister Ford may have been in on the planning of it, but not actually in on carrying it out?"

"Not at all," scoffed Jolly. "You've got the wrong fag end of the deal. This is how I see it—there was no moon on the night of the robbery, as I recall. Shards of glass from the broken window were found outside on the ground, not inside on the floor. The old, rusty key that was found in the nearby desk was used to open the iron chest, after someone tried to force it open and failed. But no speck of rust was found on the money chest or near it. When the room was hastily tidied up on Skinner's orders, the old key was found and wiped clean by Black Bob. I was one of the few who bothered to examine the rag the boy used. There was plenty of rust smears on that rag."

"The way you put it," calculated Vincent, "sounds as if you favor someone from the inside carrying out the crime . . ."

"Yes," insisted Jolly, "and certain parties, in on the plan, outside the window waiting to receive the loot and run off with it, which they did."

"Who do you suspect?" Vincent had to raise his voice again. Sounds of passion were mounting on the other side of the wall. This time there was a muffled duet of feral grunts and groans, punctuated by sharp cries.

"Start with Skinner," said Jolly, who raised his voice also and ignored the noise from next door. "Work down from there. For some unknown reason, this robbery was staged. Skinner had much to gain by losing this money in order to get most of it back to line his own purse. He had the new key in his room that night. The violations to the iron box, the broken window, the sword on the desk, and the money left behind seem to me to be mere distractions. I doubt the apprentice, Willy Campbell, or the house slave, Black Bob, were clever enough, or brave enough, to carry out such a crime. But I've been wrong before. Same goes for the rest of the servants in the house—meek they are, but they know their way around in the dark."

"What about those you say must have been waiting outside the broken window—King's Regulars so I've heard?"

"Not soldiers . . . no way," insisted Jolly. "They would have gone on a spree the next day . . . gambling and such. There was no sign of such behavior in Amboy. Also, there were few desertions at around that time. It's convenient for certain rioters to blame the Regulars for everything going wrong then and now, but not in this case."

"Then who?"

"Half the folks in Amboy were capable of committing such a crime back then, and I'm not so sure about the other half. My best guess would point to a gang of bold-gall thieves with access to a skiff hidden in the Cove at the foot of Tower Hill between North and South Dock Streets. They gather the monies tossed out the window, scamper to their boat, and slip away on the waters of the Arthur Kull. They vanish and Skinner gets none of what's taken. Our Treasurer gets robbed twice in one day and all of us get robbed once . . ."

"If they were not members of Ford's gang, then which gang do you suspect?" As Vincent posed this question, there was a loud thump next door. It sounded as if someone of substantial girth had fallen out of bed and hit the floor hard. Then there was an exchange of heated words, followed by crying, followed by silence.

"Ford's gang was not yet strong, far as I know," mused Jolly, "Waterman and Swan were doing their dirty business up in Rhode Island at this time. This means you can eliminate them as suspects. That leaves me with two knots of rogues to choose from—the Hartwick boys from Brunswick or another band of Rhode Island counterfeiters led by Samuel Gustine and James Budd . . ."

"Is this Budd related to Doctor Budd from Morris Town?"

"Not likely," answered Jolly quickly. "These boys were neither scholars nor gentlemen. They were nasty brutes missing any chance of fair breeding. They were bastards from pure bastard stock. Well, anyway, the Hartwick brothers had the better alibi, since they left for Brunswick by boat the night before. They had witnesses for their leaving our landing and for arriving in Brunswick. So that leaves us with Gustine and Budd, or, should I say, them and the boys those two associated with. When they was caught and examined up in Rhode Island, they confessed little, but implicated other characters in all sorts of crimes from years past. One was a Mister Wills from Connecticut and another was a Mister Smith from New York who had boasted to Budd and Gustine about being in this fair town in July of sixty eight. They were intending to purchase counterfeit, but did not have enough real money to cover the cost. Wills tells Budd and Gustine about finding some way to get the real and purchase the counterfeit in New York. This Wills shows Budd and Gustine a roll of twenty he'd allegedly found in Amboy and a roll of false twenty purchased in New York. Neither could say the difference between the real and the false. Nor did they claim to know more of this tale."

"So Skinner has no chance to get back the Treasury money?"

"Nary a shilling," declared Jolly. "Soon as I heard this news, come down from Rhode Island, I knew the real money was gone complete. Wells and Smith have vanished. Budd and Gustine are not talking. So I got to thinking how our prime suspect, Samuel Ford, Jr., had his fingers in the pie. I figure it was his good counterfeit which was brought to and bought in New York. Our Treasury money, or some of it, was used in a purchase of Ford's best money. Ford must have used this real money and money gained from selling off the last shares of his forge and furnace to Lord Stirling, when he crossed over to Ireland."

"Ford might have hidden some of his loot," suggested Wetherill. "I've heard tales of mountain folks searching for it."

"So have I," admitted Jolly, "but such is a fool's search. I doubt your Mister Ford would squirrel away good money at a time when he needed it most. Even if he did hide the money we want back, he's clever enough to put it where no one can find it. We can't even find him. He, and a few members of his gang, escaped gaol and disappeared."

"Hard to believe all this you say could be true," sighed Vincent as sighs of another sort from a neighboring source found their way through a thin wall.

"I agree," stated Jolly. "Mine is mere speculation by a lowly ex-gaoler; but I stand by my account till I'm proved wrong. I still worry and wonder about this case. I want justice done, but I keep getting pulled away by drunken pig irons who steal keys. I'm getting too old to be bothering over stale crimes . . . too old to be chasing down suspects and clues."

"Not too old, as I see it," urged Vincent with the most serious tone he could summon. "Give it one more good try, Mister Jolly. Take my father's offer and erase the debt you owe him. He's even provided a horse for you."

The next-door rhythms of love and lust were mounting again, this time in a muted crescendo hinting of exhaustion about to seize the participants. Vincent was trying to imagine who the lucky guest of Big Tom's daughter might be. All the faces in the taproom paraded across his mind.

Jolly disturbed the inventory. "I possess my own steed, and a good one at that. Keep your horse for your own purposes." Jolly reached for his cane, but gripped it with one hand. "What am I to learn about the Treasury robbery by following a brandy waggon to God knows where?"

"There are possibilities," stressed Vincent in his most convincing voice. "First, you have surely heard of Samuel Ford's hideout being found, at the beginning of this month. A man with such knowledge of the robbery and such ability in sifting through clues might find something interesting in that swamp. Second, for all we know, the stories of Ford and certain members of his gang fleeing the colony and heading west may be untrue. The man you would like to seize and interrogate most of all may still be hiding in a cave or in an abandoned mine—near a forge, perhaps, around Hibernia. Third, you might easily gain the chance to question the three men in custody who most recently gave testimony about Ford's involvement in the Treasury robbery. Fourth, you might find something that can be used to drive your friend, Skinner, from office. If these reasons are not enough for you, then consider the possibility of ferreting out the men who stole your gaol keys. I have to scout around in Morris County to find out who killed a lowly stable boy. At the same time you could be looking for the men who ran off with your keys. We can help each other find thieves and murderers."

Jolly shook his head and slouched his shoulders. He slipped his hand from his prize cane and hid it under the table. He cast a discomforting frown and spoke skeptical words: "We'd have a better chance waiting for news to come to us rather than wasting time galloping over the rough roads of Morris County. Most folks up there are a strange and suspicious lot. They trust no stranger and they are none too generous with sharing information about their neighbors. The closer you get to those iron hills, the worse you'll be treated. Ford's a hero to most of those folks up there. Those that stole my keys are probably heroes already to their families and friends. Even the murderer of this boy, Jack Redmon, might be a hero to someone up there. Finding information about Ford, my keys, or the murderer has about the same chance as finding the stolen Treasury money."

"Maybe not the keys," offered Vincent, "but what about finding the pair who stole 'em? You could grab a feather for your cap if you brought 'em back in chains and locked 'em away for a spell."

Jolly scratched the stubble on his sagging chin. He was deep in thought. His shoulders were still hunched and his mouth turned down, but there was a glimmer in his brown eyes. He spoke guardedly: "Might be worth a try, Mister Wetherill . . . I'm not sure . . . I'd need to clear my going with Sheriff Tom Skinner . . . he would not let me go till the locks are changed and the gaol window is repaired . . . and I've the wife to deal with as far as permission goes . . ."

Vincent chuckled at Jolly's last statement and recalled how difficult it was to separate from Abia. "I know what you mean, Mister Jolly. Take a couple of days to set things right, then join us in Morris Town."

"Two days ought to be adequate," figured Jolly. "I could make it to Haynes Tavern by then . . . not the finest public house in Morris Town, but a logical place to meet and get started."

The two men stood and shook hands as if a crucial business transaction had taken place.

Vincent offered: "My men and I will complete our deliveries, then head to Morris Town with the gift of brandy for Judge Cooper. Such a journey should not take more than two days."

"Perfect," concluded Jolly, who was able to release his hand from Vincent's firm grip.

"By the way, all expenses you accrue shall be covered by the younger Jacob Ford. We are in his trust as long as we keep our purposes a secret."

"That may suit your purposes," counseled Jolly, "but may not favor mine. I am still under the employ of the High Sheriff of Middlesex County. My expenses can be taken care of by Tom Skinner."

"My father and I would rather have you reimbursed by a wealthy Morris County fellow than by the overburdened taxpayers of this county . . . what say you?"

This time, Jolly grabbed Vincent's hand and shook it. "I like the way you Wetherills have thought this thing out."

Vincent freed his hand from Jolly's clammy grip. "And I am fond of your final decision. T'wasn't hard to make after all, was it, Mister Jolly?"

"Not if I can shrug off a debt and seize a chance to gain favor with the Sheriff. Even if I find nothing, at least I can say that I tried."

"That's the spirit," concluded Vincent as he led Jolly to the door and opened it quickly. He had two letters to write for posting in the morning before leaving Amboy. It was already very late and he wanted to get to them as soon as possible. "I am approaching this adventure with the same attitude, Mister Jolly. We'll try our best and see what comes of it. Two days hence, I'll see you at Haynes Tavern then."

Jolly was about to answer in the affirmative, when the door to the adjacent room flew open and a half dressed, stout man rushed out. The door quickly slammed behind him. He brushed by the law man and beat him to the stairs. Even in the dim half-light of the narrow hallway, Vincent saw that the man looked familiar—broad and barrel-chested, close-cropped hair under a green cap, eyes down-turned and focused on the hallway floor, buckskin trousers held up to his waist by one large hand, brown coat clutched in the other, and a green hunting shirt with its tail flapping at his backside . . .

"So Ike returned early?" asked Vincent of the man.

Cutlope Hancock flashed a quick glance. In the next second, without stopping in his quest for the stairs, he exclaimed, "I must go check on that boy, afore he drinks all our profits, Mister Wetherill . . . see you in the morning!"

6

HAGER'S CHILD
• • • • • • • • • • • • • •

—on the outskirts of Morris Town,
Wednesday—Thursday night of September 22-23, 1773

Rachel saw herself as more than a negro wench. After all, her mother claimed she was a princess—said so to anyone who would listen. Her mother boasted that her Rachel descended from Afric royalty by half. The other half—her father's side—remained a mystery to her until just before she and her mother were sold by John Hager, the wealthiest man on Schooley's Mountain. Their new master was the overbearing Jacob Morrell, owner of a plantation southeast of Morristown in Chatham. Rachel was only ten years old at the time of the transaction, but already skilled in various domestic chores. She had been taught well by her mother during her last years in the Hager household. Rachel liked it there, especially the opportunities in summer to pick highland wildflowers and weave fanciful crowns out of them. She would play the queen and various farm animals and untamed creatures would serve as members of her court. Her mountain domain was vast and, in her imagination, rivaled even her master's holdings. However, neither her mother or herself ever found themselves in the good graces of master Hager's second wife. Rachel's mother was a favorite of the wealthy farmer, but he had not the fortitude or gumption to go against his young wife's wishes. After all, she was the youngest sister of his dear, departed first wife, and she possessed full knowledge of his weaknesses and his past indiscretions. She made her demand in November when Rachel turned ten, and, by the first of December, Rachel and her mother became the property of a brutish man.

Jacob Morrell was fond of referring to Rachel's mother as Hager's wench, and Rachel as Hager's child. Occasionally, he called Rachel a half-breed. She hated him for that. Such hatred grew from the start of the first full year under master Morrell. In January, Rachel's mother was accused of stealing food from the kitchen house. She was summarily whipped by Morrell. She died of pneumonia in February. Rachel blamed the new master for her mother's death and vowed that when she came of age, after summoning up enough courage, she would run away.

Hatred towards her master increased tenfold when she discovered that a runaway buck from Horseneck had been hiding for more than a month in Morrell's hay barn. This progger had been sneaking about in the middle of the night to raid the food stores in the kitchen house. He was discovered hiding in the loft of the barn by Morrell's foreman, Mister Tom Ward, and his rat-catcher mutt, two weeks after Rachel's mother had passed away. The thief confessed to stealing food and even more.

Ward whipped him so severe he could hardly walk. He was chained and carted off to jail, never to be seen again. Master Morrell allowed the boy to live in hopes the owner of this runaway would reclaim his property and pay expenses to Morrell for losses accrued during the boy's time in hiding. The runaway was fetched and Morrell was paid handsomely for his troubles.

There was not a word of regret from Morrell over his error in accusing Rachel's mother of stealing what someone else had stolen. An apology to Rachel never came. She never expected one from Morrell anyway. She never expected to be treated any better. Her master continued to call her Hager's child. Since her mother's passing, Morrell worked Rachel twice as hard. Thus, she had more reason for hating Jacob Morrell.

Rachel was now fifteen, near as she could reckon—almost a full-grown woman with a fine figure and budding breasts to prove it. She was acorn brown—much lighter than her mother, but not so pale and wan as other half-breeds she knew. Rachel was proud of her skin—more like her mother's than her father's. She had learned who her father was five winters ago at the bedside of her dying mother. He was John Hager. No wonder that wealthy man had treated her so kindly and his wives had treated her with such indifference. There was little wonder in why Hager had to get rid of Rachel and her mother. At least Rachel now had a surname to use once she stole her freedom. After all, she really was Hager's child—just as Morrell always called her. She would keep the 's' on the name to remind her of whom she belonged to by God's will. In freedom, therefore, she would be known as Rachel Hagers. However, Rachel did not wait for freedom's chance to come leaping, before telling anyone who would listen what her full name was and how she came by it. She boasted of being returned to her wealthy father some day. Folks laughed and told her she was wasting her words.

Freedom seemed to have less a chance of coming to fruition than returning to Schooley's Mountain. For that to happen, courage had to come from somewhere. A plan for escape had to be made. Rachel knew she needed help. She could not see herself sneaking away to a nearby farm, hiding in a barn, or stealing food from a kitchen in the middle of the night. She would not last a week on her own doing such things. She was so afraid of getting caught and dragged back to Morrell's farm to face a whipping more severe than what her mother had received. Rachel was a coward at heart. Someone would have to convince her to escape—run far away, never look back, never return. Someone would have to lead her, then she would follow.

Luckily, there was such a person—a newcomer to the Morris Town area and a stranger to Rachel up until three months ago. What a handsome and clever buck he was. Locals called him by several names—some fair, some foul. He preferred Mingo Tim. He was the newest field slave purchased for a scant price by Doctor Budd, who conducted a modest practice in Morris Town and the surrounding countryside. The good Doctor owned a small farm east of Morris Town in Hanover. He possessed few slaves.

Budd had lost a slave—one who disappeared some years ago. He always had a ready excuse for not replacing a runaway who also stole from him. Then, a few months ago, the Doctor took a chance on this Mingo Tim, because the price for the boy was cheap and even though he had once attempted to run away from his previous master. This slave already had many stripes across his back, but, after inspecting the fellow, Doctor Budd was not deterred. He counted out five pounds sterling of Sam Ford's best counterfeit on a clear, breezy day in June, and handed it over to Mingo Tim's previous master to complete the deal.

Mingo Tim did not become a favorite of any member of the Budd household, free or not. He was a shirker—slight of build and not much in favor of hard work. He sported a lazy eye which always seemed to be searching this way and that for a chance at mischief. He possessed a quick wit and a quicker tongue, which he employed often to charm the ladies regardless of their complexion. He also was spry with his fingers. Mingo Tim boasted of playing a fiddle better than anyone he knew in Rockaway, where he had been purchased by Doctor Budd. The new master took the boy up on his claim, and, for a promise to work harder through the harvest months, let him practice on an expensive fiddle which no member of the Budd family ever played or even knew how to play. It was an heirloom—rich in family lore and dust—the kind talked about, but never used.

When the self-taught Mingo Tim tuned up and applied bow to fiddle by the light of the kitchen hearth, toes instantly began tapping and voices began humming. In a week's time, on the third of July, Mingo Tim appeared as the entertainment at a Saturday frolic held at the plantation of Jacob Ford, Sr. This was where slaves from surrounding farms usually gathered for an evening of revelry before midnight, which heralded the Sabbath day. Slave masters sought to control such gatherings by limiting the hours and the number allowed to congregate in one place. Local foremen were recruited to police such affairs. Word spread quickly after Mingo Tim's first appearance that there was a very good reason to attend— Morris Town now had a fiddler who could even make a legless man dance.

Rachel loved to dance. By the middle of the summer, she heard the wild rumors about the handsome buck fiddler over at Budd's stead. She longed to go see for herself and get her feet tapping free as the wind. Her chance came under the first waning half-moon of August, when she found herself selected by Mister Ward, the foreman, to tag along with three older wenches and the eldest single buck owned by master Morrell. Permission had been granted for the five slaves to enjoy themselves at the latest gathering in the fallow field nearest the cattle barn owned by the Fords. Mister Ward had to attend this night. He allowed the five lucky servants to ride in his waggon all the way up to the Ford

IRON WATER

place. Rachel was ecstatic and forever grateful to the foreman. She told him so to his face and he blushed. The foreman, accompanied by his ever-faithful, rat catching cur, admitted that he also was looking forward to listening to the highly touted young fiddler and watching the Africs do their devil dancing. For the occasion, he wore a new snuff-colored nankeen shirt, but he still looked grimy as ever with flap-front baggy trousers and a dirty black cap pulled down to thick brows hovering nervously over a coarse pocked face and ever-suspicious eyes. Rumor had it that Ward had once been a soldier for the King, but somehow got involved with counterfeiters from a northern colony. Even though the fellow may have been a deserter and was probably on the run from the law, Morrell took the shy, rough man in, called him by the name he used, and put him to work as overseer of his slaves. Rachel never understood the worth of such a sad man. However, he did one thing well. Tom Ward treated all of Morrell's slaves firm and fair. That was more than what could be said for Morrell.

On previous occasions, the foreman only spoke of gaining a chance to drink with the other foremen. However, this time he not only got drunk, he got inspired.

The fiddler mounted a makeshift platform of boards over bales of hay fronted by a low barricade of split logs. Set firmly amongst the logs were long poles topped by torches snapping bright flames into the moonlit sky. Mingo Tim smiled as he counted the heads of those who came to hear him play his borrowed fiddle. He announced in a strong tenor voice that he was mighty glad to perform for so many pretty women. He confessed that he had yet to pick a wench for his own and had yet to sire a child. He offered a wide grin of good teeth and winked his lazy eye. Then he gave out a hearty laugh.

"When I'm done playin' for you all," he shouted, "my choice jus' might be made 'n my fust child started!"

Mingo Tim tucked his fiddle under his sharp black chin and flashed his bow in the torchlight. The instrument sparked like perfect tinder and suddenly flamed into a new frenzied tune no one in these parts had ever heard. There were gasps and shouts of glee, then the soft thunder of tapping feet smoldering on the dry grass. In the shadows, a negress of fifteen let her feet catch fire.

112

Folks nearest her moved back to give her leaping space. She did not disappoint. Mingo Tim caught her performance out of the corner of his roving lazy eye. He quickened the tempo. Rachel swirled. Others tried to keep up with her, but they could not.

Before Mingo Tim started up his second tune, he called for the girl in the shadows to step into the torchlight and lead the others in her dance. Rachel did not hesitate. The buck's second tune was as feverish as the first. Rachel's bare feet found the rhythm instantly. Mingo Tim led and Rachel followed. Through six more tunes this game was played—a give and take at breakneck pace—until Mingo Tim put down his fiddle and bow to take a rest. Rachel and the others close and far cried out for more. Some threw coins, plugs of tobacco, even pearly buttons and shells; however, all the buck fiddler asked for was a bowl of rum and a chance to talk to the dancing girl. He promised that, after he rested, he would play six more tunes before midnight came. The crowd allowed him to get his way on both counts.

Mingo Tim sipped slowly from a large red bowl brimming with cheap rum, as the girl who had caught his eye told everything about herself in response to his hundred questions. At certain intervals, he allowed Rachel to sip from the same bowl and ask as many questions about him as she desired. Their respite passed too quickly. A decision was made to meet again at the next gathering. Rachel sadly admitted that she could not promise such a thing. That was in the hands of her master. Mingo Tim made her promise anyway.

"Do whatever you must to see me agin," urged the fiddler. "I've great plans for the likes of you."

Rachel leaped from the hay bale she was sharing with Mingo Tim and started dancing away on her own without the accompaniment of a fiddle.

"Promise?" shouted Mingo Tim after her.

"Promise," she sang. "I promise so, more 'n anythin.'"

The buck fiddler smiled, stood up on the bales, and started in on his concluding set. The tunes were all happy ones. Rachel and the crowd responded enthusiastically. They did not let up with their dancing, singing, and hand clapping until Mingo Tim put down his bow. They wanted more—cheered for more, but curfew time had come. It was back to their miserable lives until the next get-together.

Rachel was able to see Mingo Tim perform twice more—once on the last Saturday of August before the second full moon of the month and once in September on the Saturday before the hanging of the counterfeiter, David Reynolds. On the night of August twenty-eighth, Rachel rode in foreman Ward's waggon to the Wick farm. The sky went black early and threatened rain. The crowd, gathered at Mister Wick's new barn, was much fewer in number than the throng at Ford's at the beginning of the month. Mingo Tim seemed not to care a lick about the turnout. He had made a secret deal with Mister Ward during the foreman's latest visit to the Budd farm. Rachel had been delivered to him and that set all things right. As soon as he started to play his fiddle under a candle lantern in a back stall of the spacious, sweet smelling barn, the skies opened up with a terrible pour. Slaves and free folk crowded in to escape the rain. This left meager space for the best dancers to prance and strut. The three foremen in attendance and the owner's son, Daniel Wick, shouted at the onlookers and pushed them back against the walls. This gave Rachel room to set her feet blazing and match the bright strains emanating from her buck's fiddle. Yes, Mingo Tim was Rachel's now. Folks could see it in her happy gaze and the fiddler's proud glances. The girl from Morrell's farm had become another instrument to be played by a talented man when she allowed him. Now she was ready to do anything for Mingo Tim—anything he asked.

During the break, the fiddler and dancer slipped out a midden door and stood under the long, low roof of a cob crib. Heavy rain tapped a tune of its own on the new cedar shingles. Lightning flashed from far away now and then. Thunder rolled, but kept its distance. Mingo Tim held Rachel close. His sudden warmth made her forget how cool the downpour had made the evening. She thrust her hips against him and wrapped her rain-moistened arms around his slim waist. They stood together for a long, seemingly endless, moment, enjoying the melodies of the storm. Then Mingo Tim kissed Rachel on the forehead below the fringe of her pale gray head scarf. She arched her neck, tried to stand taller than she was, and closed her eyes. The fiddler had no trouble finding her lips with his mouth. He offered a soft kiss—more a whisper and a tease. Rachel wanted more, but Mingo Tim had urgent things to tell her and little time to do so. He put his tongue near her right ear and let soft words spill over it as if he was a man at prayer.

"A month's time," he whispered slowly. "No more, 'n I be gettin' far from 'dis here county."

Rachel stiffened and attempted to struggle free—tried resisting the thought of losing the man she wanted—but the fiddler was too strong and held her tight.

"Hear me out, woman," Mingo Tim continued. "You follow . . . when dat right day come, be ready . . ."

"How will I know?" asked Rachel with wide, fear-filled eyes welling with tears.

"I be sendin' word to you by way of Mister Ward . . . you can trust dat man . . . he owes me . . . do what he say . . . promise?"

"Promise," swallowed Rachel with much difficulty.

Mingo Tim kissed her on the forehead again, said no more, and released her. They sloshed back to the barn in silence. Once inside, the fiddler was greeted with loud demands for more tunes. Mingo Tim snatched up his borrowed instrument and coaxed one of his best tunes from it. The dancing resumed and the drinking intensified. Rachel concentrated joyously on the former and ignored the latter. She now had someone to follow—follow to freedom.

The next meeting, again at the Ford plantation on the eleventh day of September, proved even more delightful for an eager Rachel Hagers. The air was smoky sweet, crisp and clear, with a touch of the fall season in the air. It was a night for shawls and jackets, but such garments were discarded soon after Mingo Tim started in with his first fiery tune. A bonfire was allowed in the middle of the fallow field. Dark bodies ringed the flaming logs. The swaying and gyrating of the dancers cast long, eerie shadows on the soft, dry grasses. Luckily, the soil had been turned earlier so that the fire was ringed by dirt. Large buckets of water guarded the blaze. Ford's foreman and his peers, on duty for these festivities, had taken no chances. The last rain had been in August and that rare pour had little effect on the current tinder-dry conditions of the season. The slaves at this latest gathering did not seem to care about current weather conditions. Mingo Tim had made them forget their worries and the dreadful work in store for them if a major conflagration visited these parts.

Rachel was one who did not care about all that. Mingo Tim had fetched her a small bowl of rum—a lady's cup, he called it—even before he started playing. He dared her to finish it before he took his break. She did—danced with the bowl in one hand . . . paused, now and then, to take sips . . . oh, it burned her throat so ...but it was good. Old man Ford sure had fine Jamaica rum. His slaves were darn lucky. Not one of them ever ran away from Jacob Ford, Sr. Though the world was now spinning faster than Rachel was and the stars in the cloudless sky were doing a blurry dance of their own, she knew this would not be a fair night to run away. Things were too perfect. Ford's magic was even working on her.

The break came, but Rachel remembered little of it. Practiced hands were all over her. A serpent's tongue was licking her flesh and probing the depths of her mouth. Teeth were biting her shoulders and neck. Fingers were stroking crevices and apertures that no man had ever explored. This was all done so suddenly, so quickly, so expertly, behind a barricade of logs and straw where Mingo Tim had led her. When she stumbled, due to the effects of consuming too much rum, the fiddler fell with her and resumed his delicious game. Rachel wanted more—so much more, but it ended much too soon. Mingo Tim pulled her up, helped her straighten her clothing, then held her close. He whispered instructions in her ear just as he had done the time before—only this time he was more serious and completely sober.

"You be set to run," said Mingo Tim, "eleven nights from now . . . gather what you will on de night of Wednesday . . . wait for Mister Tom to come fetch you . . . he goin' bring you here . . ."

"I'm afraid," whispered Rachel, as she trembled like a child in the arms of her man.

Mingo Tim gave her a fierce hug and spoke in a strong, low tone: "Nothin' to fear, my princess . . . jus' do as Mister Tom say . . . hide right here 'n wait for a tune I be whistlin' . . ."

The field slave started up with the tune he meant to start his second set with. Rachel recognized its refrain instantly, stopped shivering, and hummed along with Mingo Tim's whistling.

The two lovers started back towards the bonfire. They were greeted with the usual applause and calls for more grand music. Rachel suddenly felt a pang of loss—she would miss all the merriment of these Saturday gatherings. She wished every night was a Saturday. She wanted to dance to Mingo Tim's fiddle playing forever. Perhaps in freedom there might be more nights of spinning worlds and blurry stars . . . more nights of gentle, skillful hands exploring her body . . . more nights . . .

The ensuing days leading up to the twenty-second of September passed so agonizingly slow. Rachel fretted over what to steal and carry away of her master's possessions. She worried over what to wear—how many layers of petticoats and drab gowns. She dared not bring or wear anything that would attract undo attention—only essentials, worn or stuffed into one carry sack. After freedom was gained, Mingo Tim would get her all the fancy, gaudy things she ever dreamed of. He had promised her such. Anything she filched from Morrell had to be small, insignificant, not sorely missed.

Each day that passed was a day to gain confidence. Rachel did just that with few exceptions. The dread of Mingo Tim's plan failing flared worst on the day of David Reynold's execution. The slave gathering, scheduled for Saturday the eighteenth, had been cancelled. All festivities were scheduled for Friday, the execution day, instead. It was such a grand affair on the Morris Town green with over a thousand folks of various stripes and statuses in attendance. Farmers and their slaves came from miles around. Rachel saw Mingo Tim in the crowd, but a Constable was following him. Thus, she stayed close behind Mister Tom and his rat-catcher, which the foreman restrained with a short, thick rope. The dog was good for clearing a path through the spectators who were crowding in to gain a glimpse of the condemned Mister Reynolds. However, Mister Tom seemed more interested in weaving his way through the perimeter of the throng—stopping and staring occasionally, then resuming his search for something, or someone, Rachel did not venture to guess. She dutifully trailed the sad and swarthy man who was to be so instrumental in her gaining freedom. But now she was worried that all this commotion brought on by the hanging might ruin her dream, or, at best, postpone it.

At that moment, poor Mister Reynolds finished pleading with

the crowd to have mercy on his wife and children, and the noose was placed around his neck. Tom Ward handed Rachel the rat-catcher's rope and gave her orders.

"Head back to the waggon . . . keep my cur away from these folks . . . I'll soon return . . ."

With that, the foreman plunged into the pressing crowd as if hot on the trail of something important. Rachel had no time to respond. She watched her odd guardian disappear, then retreated with the dog, which struggled and strained to follow its master. She finally found the Morrell waggon and sat in the grass by one of its rickety wheels. As the festivities died down, other slaves of Morrell joined her. They brought her scraps of food and drink. One of her peers fetched a bowl of water for the rat-catcher. Rachel offered a few of her scraps to Ward's dog. The beast snapped them up greedily. Some of the slaves climbed into the waggon. Others hunched down by Rachel near the wheel. They waited for their foreman, but he did not return.

Before the sun was swallowed whole by the western Watchungs, Morrell's eldest buck came staggering toward the waggon. He was obviously drunk, but clear in his message from the foreman. Mister Ward had ordered him to drive the waggon and horse team back to the plantation. No reason was given for Ward's absence. Rachel feared the worst—something bad had happened between Tom Ward and her Mingo Tim. The plan of escape had been destroyed before it could be carried out. She did not know who to blame more—the foreman or the fiddler. More than likely, they got drunk, argued over some inconsequential event from the past, and fought over it. One, or both, was probably in gaol along with the three counterfeiters yet to be hanged.

The waggon lurched side to side under the awkward guiding hand of the eldest buck. The horses balked at his slurred commands. The sky was turning purple black—already brooding about what gloom and doom tomorrow would bring. Rachel pulled the rat-catcher close as she dared and scratched its ears. The scruffy black mutt nuzzled even closer and licked a few tears from her cheeks. Mister Tom, so it seemed to Rachel, was extremely important to them both.

As it turned out, the next day started as it always did. All the slaves went about their duties as if nothing out of the ordinary had occurred the day before. Foreman Ward was out in the nearest field overseeing the harvesters. The rat-catcher was happily chasing a rabbit nearby. When Rachel went out to fetch water from the well in the yard, she noticed Tom Ward leaning hard against a fence and yawning a great deal; other than that, he appeared his usual self. He was dressed in the same grimy clothes he wore to the hanging. She waved to him and he waved back. A crooked-tooth smile cracked his rutty face. All seemed back to normal. Rachel sighed and smiled back. The plan appeared to be holding.

And so it did. On the appointed day—a Wednesday to be exact—as the sun faded in a near cloudless sky, Mister Tom came around with his team and waggon. The rat-catcher was sitting proudly next to his master on the driver's board—tongue flapping from a drooling mouth and tail thumping the back board. In the waggon was a thick bed of straw upon which rested a few casks of salt pork, owed to Mister Wick for some debt Jacob Morrell had accrued.

The excuse for taking along Rachel Hagers was a flimsy one, but one Morrell agreed to. The young wench was one of the few slaves to whom the rat-catcher took a liking. The dog obeyed Rachel. Therefore, she was to tend to the dog while Tom Ward took care of the transaction at the Wick farm.

Morrell immediately saw the wisdom in his foreman's request: "That cur of yours sure knows good bloodlines when he smells 'em." The master paused to sneer at his own clever thought. "According to this wench's mother, she's a royal Afric princess. Can you believe such pack thread?"

Tom Ward nodded in the affirmative. He could believe it. He liked Rachel as much as his dog did.

"Can I trust you with such a precious possession?"

Tom Ward nodded again and added, "Sure as the days get shorter and the nights get longer."

"Good enough then," said Jacob Morrell, handing a piece of curled vellum over to his foreman. "Make sure you get Wick, or one of his sons, to sign this agreement which officially erases what I owe that bastard. If he claims I owe him more, offer the princess or the rat-catcher . . . but not both."

Ward grinned in disbelief. He blinked and picked at a pox scar on his cheek.

Jacob Morrell slapped his trusty foreman on the shoulder of his dirty coat. "I jest with you, my good man. If you broach the subject to old man Wick, he'll demand both for sure. Tell him to accept the three casks of salt pork or you'll bring 'em back. Now fetch the wench from the kitchen and be on your way."

Tom Ward bowed and retreated out back to find Rachel. As Morrell watched his foreman exit the waiting chamber, he wiped his hands clean with a lace kerchief. He still felt sorry for the chap. Back in 1767, Morrell's foreman was but a mere apprentice working under Barracks Master, Sam Sargent, in Perth Amboy. Back then, he was an upstart redemptioner from Ireland. He was filled with hope and vinegar about making his fortune in the New World. He went by the name of Billy Walsh. According to Sargent, this boy started out as a dependable, hard worker at the Barracks, but soon after got involved with some thieving Irish soldiers from Dublin, who were part of the Twenty Sixth Regiment stationed in Perth Amboy at the time. The Barracks Master caught young Billy at the thieving game. He turned the boy over to the Quarter Master to be punished. Billy was given the choice of the whip or joining up with the Twenty Sixth. Billy pledged to do the latter, but ran away in the night. He wandered north and found work cleaning horse stalls until early in 1768, when agents of the King picked up his trail. He took flight again—this time, heading west into the hills to find work in the mines. He changed his name in every forsaken place he worked, but he never got rid of the ugly dog that followed him everywhere since heading west. Billy's main problem was his inability to stay out of trouble and keep a job for any length of time. He could do neither. In one fateful incident, he was caught thieving at a meeting house in Black River, beaten severely by the locals who caught him, and hauled off to gaol in Morris Town. When questioned by the Sheriff, Billy spilled his whole story, filled by half with the truth told here and the rest as false as it was long.

In February of 1769, the Sheriff posted a public notice for the owner of the boy's papers to come forward, pay expenses, and claim him. However, at this time, Billy was a Tom whose surname was Ward. According to the wild side of his tale, Tom had been in the King's service both on land and at sea. After that, he had been involved in the smuggling trade, counterfeiting, and various robbery schemes. This Tom, or Billy, or whoever he was, claimed to have the marks, scars, and wounds to prove the worst of his inglorious past. None of it was taken as truth by the authorities. He was labelled a common thief with a drunken man's tongue.

The Sheriff spread word around Morris Town of the boy with the prattling mouth. He claimed Tom Ward would never be sought after, and could be purchased for gaol expenses. Jacob Morrell heard about the fellow and paid him a visit. The boy was, indeed, a forlorn sight—all bloodied and bruised, and filthy as a street beggar. However, Morrell needed a new foreman to work his slaves, since his previous one drowned under the ice at a nearby mill in January. Morrell had planned to wait until spring to replace the dead foreman, but the opportunity to purchase the services of a man so cheap was irresistable.

Tom Ward, in his own way, demonstrated gratitude for the opportunity to be gainfully employed and given a position of authority. He continued to drink heavily and ran his mouth on those occasions, but when he was sober he worked long and hard. He gained the trust of Morrell's slaves, because he was willing to learn from them as well as their master. He was shy with women, but respectful to them at all times. Morrell kept a close watch on his new foreman during the first year of his employ. No incident of thievery occurred. Ward kept mostly to himself, seldom spoke of his past, and continued to make sure the slaves worked long and hard like himself. Thus, he gained the full trust of Jacob Morrell.

All such coincidence favored the success of Mingo Tim's plan for Rachel and himself. Tom Ward was to serve as their angel—their accomplice in the scheme. It surely would not succeed without his help.

The first thing Tom Ward did was transport Rachel safely to the fallow field on the Ford plantation. A waxing half moon and a thousand stars provided barely enough light for the way going. Ward used the main road, to Morris Town, then headed east. He turned left on to the mill path paralleling the Whippannung River. Eventually, he had his waggon rumbling down to the rear acres of Ford's property where the ground was marshy and used mainly for grazing livestock. Ward managed to find his way to the logs and hay where Mingo Tim had performed so admirably weeks ago. He helped his passenger slip down off the waggon by offering Rachel a gloved hand, which she grasped eagerly.

"Stay put," instructed the foreman. "You know where to hide if you must. Mingo said he'd be comin' soon as he can."

"How will I know it's him?" asked Rachel, whose teeth were already chattering as the evening air cooled. "Somebody else might come about

"He'll be whistlin' one of his tunes . . . it's how you'll be knowin' . . . Mingo told me you knew 'bout it . . ."

"Yes, I remember."

Tom Ward climbed to the seat board of his waggon and snapped the reins. His two horses responded immediately and lurched up the troubled path which had been used to sneak on to Ford's property.

Ward called out to Rachel, "Got to deliver these casks of pork to the Wicks. Good luck, princess. I'll be tellin' your master a fanciful tale of how you was taken from me."

As he rolled away, Rachel could hear Tom Ward chuckling to himself. She wondered if that poor soul was clever enough to trick her master . . . probably not. By that time, however, she and Mingo Tim would be long gone.

The horses, waggon, foreman, and dog were gone. Rachel remained standing and listened for sounds—any sound that could scare her more than she was already scared, or any sound that heralded the approach of her lover. She heard a dog howl, but it was not the rat-catcher. It must have been one of Ford's renowned hunting dogs—those large ones often called upon to track down runaways. The thought of such beasts chasing her made her tremble all the more. Rachel heard tiny scurrying sounds in the hay and figured they were made by rodents emerging from their burrows to share the night with her. She stood for a long spell, keeping her arms close to her sides to fight the chill in her bones. The trembling refused to leave her. She shifted her heavy carry sack from hand to hand. Finally, she clutched it to her breast. She was expecting Mingo Tim any minute. She decided to let the sack slip to the straw at her feet. It was too heavy to hold for long. Rachel waited. Mingo Tim did not come.

Rachel started pacing around the logs that ringed the hay. She felt compelled to do this in order to keep warm. She gazed at the heavens and counted as many stars as she could. She was looking for a lucky one just as her mother used to do, but she could not tell which one was meant for her. After a time, she gave up. She and her fiddler would need more than one lucky star to succeed in running away—perhaps a dozen, at least.

Rachel grew hungry. She returned to the hay bales where she and Mingo Tim had once hid from the crowd, sat on a bale, and rummaged through her sack until she found two apples. She munched on one, then the other—down to seeds and core. She tossed the remains far from her in hopes of distracting the mice away from where she had positioned herself. Rachel had nothing to do but wait. Mingo Tim never came.

Rachel paced some more . . . wandered off once to lift her skirts, squat in the field, and pee. She returned to her castle of straw and hunkered down behind logs and bales. She leaned her back against the carry sack and promised herself to rest, but not fall asleep. She had to remain ever vigilant—ever hopeful that her man would come soon to fetch her . . .

Rachel did not hear the waggon approach. She was fast asleep and hiding well. She did not hear the tune which a man she knew was whistling—it was too soft, too slow to be recognized. The night breeze snatched it away. She did not hear the padding sounds of a dog snuffling about, picking up her scent, and following the circle of her trail until it came to where she lay. Then she awoke with a start. The rat-catcher was licking her face and planting its paws in her lap.

"By my lucky stars!" exclaimed Rachel, as she blinked wide-eyed at her rouser and pulled it close to give a hug and seize its warmth. "Have you returned with my man?"

Rachel looked up and saw the silhouette of a man, but he was not Mingo Tim.

"Change in plans," muttered Tom Ward in a low, sad voice.

"They caught him?" posed Rachel, as she pushed the foreman's dog away and scrambled to her feet.

Ward stepped closer as if to confide a secret he did not want anyone else to hear.

Rachel instinctively moved back, pressing herself against a stack of bales. Something was not right. She smelled liquor on the foreman's breath.

"Mingo was usin' the main road to here," offered the foreman, "ridin' Doctor Budd's prize gelding without saddle nor reins . . . the horse was in no mood to cooperate . . . threw your man to the ground."

"Was he hurt?"

"None which I know . . . but he was bein' chased by a few locals who spied him where he shouldn't of been on a Wednesday night . . . they was young lads out to give an Afric a scare."

"Did they catch him?"

"Punched on 'im 'n gave a beatin' afore I came 'long with my waggon empty 'n fast to see if you'd be gone."

"So you got to my man in time."

The foreman grinned at that comment, but Rachel could not see his face. "Course I did . . . took a few blows, but tore those lads off 'im . . . told 'em I'd take care of things 'n bring Mingo to where he belongs."

"Where is he, then?" Rachel looked beyond the silhouette of Tom Ward. She saw nobody else standing with him or behind him. Even the rat-catcher had vanished. She remembered that there were critters to chase. Rachel was alone with the wrong man. Something was definitely not right. She turned her back on the messenger.

"Not so fast, princess," said Tom Ward, as he pressed closer and placed his gloved hands on Rachel's trembling shoulders. "Those lads mounted their horses . . . sauntered off but a few paces to fetch Budd's gelding . . . said they would trail my waggon, 'case the Afric tried to jump out and run . . . not necessary was what I claimed, but they wouldn't budge . . . refused to let me hitch the gelding to my waggon . . . so I puts your Mingo on the straw 'n tied 'im down to stay . . . then I wheels 'bout 'n heads back to Budd's farm."

Rachel started to cry. She tried to struggle free of Ward's grasp, but he spun her around and would not let her go.

"Your Mingo won't never be comin' this way to fetch you," whispered the foreman grimly.

Rachel was sobbing now. The plan of escape was ruined. Now what would she do? Return to that wretched Morrell and spend the rest of her days as a wench in disfavor? And what were the foreman's intentions at such a sorrowful time? Did he realize that his grip was causing her pain?

Tom Ward let her free. Instead of backing away, Rachel came to him and put her arms around his waist. The rat-catcher suddenly reappeared, raised up, and ran its paws along the hem of her outermost skirt. She ignored the dog's intentions and placed her head on the foreman's chest. His coat and shirt reeked of a cross between rust and blood.

"Take me back, Mister Ward. I can't run away on my own . . . tell no one of this night. I'll wait till my man tries again."

"No need to be so hasty," said the foreman with an awkward rumble in his voice. He was not used to holding a woman so close. "After the lads went on their way 'n afore I could rouse Mistress Budd, your Mingo told me of his second plan . . . I listened careful . . . then, as I was promisin' to carry it out, he vanishes afore my eyes . . . but what I promised is goin' to take me till dawn to get back to Morrell's place . . ."

Rachel looked up and found Tom Ward's star-glistened eyes. "What is the new plan?" she said eagerly.

"I'm to take you to Mine Hill," confided the foreman. "Leave you with good Quakers your Mingo knows 'n I do too . . . kin to Abraham Sharp . . . nice folks who favor freedom for your kind, princess . . . they'll care for you till Mingo comes acallin' . . . he'll be walkin' the length by usin' no roads . . . don't expect your man too soon . . ."

"I'm afraid to do this alone," cried Rachel.

"Won't be alone," said Ward.

"What do you mean?"

"The rat-catcher wants to go with you."

Rachel looked for the nervous canine, but it had vanished again. "You'd part with your dog just for me?" she asked increduously, as she went back to staring at Ward's unreadable eyes.

"Till your man comes," whispered Ward. "I'll come fetch it from the Sharps by 'n by . . . just a favor in return . . .'"

Rachel pulled away. She did not like the tone in his voice. Fear welled in her throat.

"Just one favor," repeated the foreman, as he stepped back.

"What might it be?" asked Rachel suspiciously.

"Dance for me, princess." Tom Ward sat on the nearest bale of hay. "Dance for me, please. After I leave you with the Sharps at Mine Hill, I'll never see the likes of you no more, my princess . . . a dance is all I'm askin' . . . one dance . . ."

Rachel crossed her arms over the small buds that were her breasts. She shivered as she struggled to find the correct words to say. She had feared much worse a request from the sad and pitiful foreman. She scolded herself for thinking so poorly of the only person to save Mingo Tim from harm and the one man both her lover and she could count on. Of course, she would dance under the half-moon for Tom Ward.

"Whistle any song you like," suggested Rachel, "and I will dance on the straw for you."

The foreman removed his gloves, dropped them to the ground, stuffed his bare hands under the rope belt that held up his coarse trousers, and started whistling the tune he had attempted before— it was too soft, too slow, but it would have to do. . .

7

SQUABBLES AND STORMS

• •

—on to Powles Hook Thursday,
September 23, 1773

Vincent Wetherill spotted the post rider in the gray dawn light. The man was walking his fresh horse to the morning ferry bound for Radford's Landing. There was still time to catch the fellow before the ferry pulled away.

"Two letters for you, my good man!" shouted Vincent, as he galloped down the path to the landing and handed the post rider the pair of missives he had written and sealed after William Jolly had left the Long Ferry Tavern well past midnight.

"Who might be receivin' these?" asked the post rider, as he jerked the reins to prevent his mount from progressing on to the ferry.

"One's for my father, Assemblyman John Wetherill," said Vincent officiously, "and the other is for my wife, Abia Wetherill."

The post rider raised an eyebrow to demonstrate how impressed and honored he was to deliver such letters of high status. He tucked them into a leather pouch slung over his saddle.

"Their destination?" asked the post rider, as he accepted a more-than-adequate measure of coins from John Wetherill's son. "Rhode Hall or Cranberry?"

"A few days ago, I told my father to expect mail from me to be delivered at Cranberry. Doctor Hezekiah Stites, his good friend in town, can fetch the letters at the Inn and drop them off at the plantation when he makes his rounds."

"I shall tell minehost at the Inn to notify the good Doctor of mail for your father," said the post rider, as he touched the brim of his tricorn with a gloved finger. "I shall be honored to do so."

With that pronouncement, the honest-looking fellow led his

horse on to the planks of the flat vessel. Vincent watched and waited until the ferryman eased his boat out into the mouth of the Rariton River. He hoped the post rider's horse proved to be the fastest one on Lawrie's Road this day, and Doctor Stites would be quick to deliver the letters. There were key questions and important information in the one to his father. More importantly, there were heartfelt sentiments and sweet secrets for his wife in the letter for her. Vincent was already impatient to hear from them both. However, he would have to wait until he reached Morris Town. The place had been decided upon for sending and receiving letters. Vincent could not wait till then to send his first two. He was glad at the thought that his early correspondence would come as a surprise to his father and Abia.

Vincent turned his Spanish barb and sped past the Long Ferry Tavern to catch up with Cut and Ike. They had already set out north and east to find the Wood Bridge Road. He managed to get beyond Market Square by using High Street all the way to North Dock Street, which he took to get to Brunswick Road. It knifed between the jail and the barracks. Along the way, he kept a wary eye on the darkening sky. The clouds, rolling in from the west, were thick and low. No rain yet, but it felt inevitable on the day Vincent had chosen to make two deliveries before the last of the barrels were deposited at Powles Hook. A rain storm would make the roads impossible. This one-day trip of twenty miles might have to be stretched to two days.

Vincent cursed his luck. He coaxed his mount into quickening the pace. Up ahead, on the straight road in the gray, vague distance, he spotted the brandy waggon. He could see Cut sitting erect and attentive on the drover's seat. Lagging behind by several lengths was Ike, who was slouched in the saddle on the quarter-horse, Mercury. The cantankerous Lord Corn was up to his usual straining against its waggon tether. Vincent wished at that moment for Mister Jolly to be leading his team. That was not the case. The team was not yet whole. Jolly was to remain in Amboy until the jail had its locks restored and the broken window had been repaired. Jolly would not join the team for at least two days. Vincent was not at ease with this arrangement, but he had failed to convince Jolly to accompany him to Powles Hook. All the decision-making had to be done by one young man. All squabbles between the German and the Irishman had to be stifled and snuffed out by him. The strong chance of foul weather ahead would make things worse. Vincent might have to contend with both squabbles and storms all the way to Powles Hook.

His mount finally sauntered up alongside Ike's quarter horse, which was plodding along at a faltering pace. Ike paid his superior no mind, because he was in the midst of a heated argument with Cut Hancock.

"I'm s'posed to lead this here train when Mister Wetherill ain't 'bout."

Cut glanced back and saw that Vincent had caught up with them. He shouted, "Too late now, you prat. Since I'm second in command, you'll do as I say when he's not here. So keep to the rear and stay there!"

"Since when are ye second 'n I'm third?" snapped Ike in an angry shout.

Cut looked back again with a wide quarter-moon grin on his face. He shouted again, "You are not even third, my good ale captain. Old Lord Corn is third, 'cause he's sense enough to keep a lout like you off his back!"

"I should be second," maintained Ike, "fer I can prove it so with me fists in a fight 'gainst the likes of ye, fair or not!"

Cut laughed. He did not bother to turn his head. On the right, under a thickening mist, the Wood Bridge Road lay ahead. The waggoner was more concerned with ruts at the turn than the Irishman's prattle. It was important not to jostle the valuable contents on his vehicle. However, he managed one final boast: "I hold the rifle, and you don't!"

Vincent decided to enter the fray before fists and lead started flying. He had not yet taken his command position ahead of the bays, but he felt he had to quell this fuss. Vincent spoke loud enough for both men to hear: "Mister Jolly is my second-in-command. I want to make this perfectly clear before he joins us in Morris Town . . ."

"He ain't here now," piped Ike.

"Whether he is or not," bellowed Cut, as he guided the bay Shires through the turn, "You're still last, bog lander!"

"I'll get me turn to lead this here adventure," clamored Ike with finality. "Me time is comin'."

"I won't be driving this waggon when your time comes," said Cut. "Don't want to see any part of you in front of my eyes . . . neither lumpy head nor patched arse. Stay behind me and out of sight, or I'll quit this game."

Vincent knew he had missed the start of this spat. Maybe it was too late to repair the damage to morale, but, at least, he could find out the cause and seek to avoid it flaring up the next time.

"What is this nonsense all about?"

There was no response from either man.

"I'm in charge," proclaimed Vincent. "My horse leads the way. One man is responsible for waggon and its team—Cut is that one. One man is responsible for guarding flanks and rear—Ike is that one. 'Tis the way we started and the way we'll finish . . . enough said."

Cut kept his thoughts to himself and nodded in agreement.

Ike, however, was not yet ready to let go of his desire to lead: "What if ye fall, Mister Wetherill? What if ye ain't able to lead? What if Mister Jolly never shows in Morris Town? Who leads then?"

"Then the game is off, my good man," declared Vincent with conviction. "Without a complete team, there will be no need to carry on. You and Cut can go your separate ways . . . return home if you like . . ."

"I still owes yer father?"

"For certain."

"Then ye mustn't fall, Mister Wetherill," insisted Ike, "'n Jolly has to get to Morris Town."

"Right you are, Ike, on both counts. I intend to neither fall or fail. I have the law man's word—he will get to Morris Town two days hence. So do your job. Do it well, then you will have much to boast about after we return you to Good Mary."

"Lookin' forward to such, Mister Wetherill. I've got lots fer to boast 'bout already . . . more 'n better me news than the German's exploits with Big Tom's youngest girl . . ."

Cut turned his head quickly and snarled, "Keep Rebecca off your choice of words, cod snapper, or I've a rifle round to share with you."

Vincent cut in, "Our drover's business is his own, Ike. Let him be."

Ike went silent, though brooding was its form.

Vincent tactfully sought to change the subject. "I'm most interested in what you gained down on Market Street. Tell me now."

Ike raised his leg, held it straight out, and showed off his new footwear. "Won me this here pair o' new English shoes with one roll o' the dice in a game o' hazard."

Vincent took notice of the fine doubled-sole footwear, sporting pinch-beck carved buckles. He complimented his flanker on such a handsome acquisition.

The two of them had pulled up close behind the waggon after the turn was negotiated. Cut could hear every word loud-mouthed Ike said. The German could not resist an opportunity to rile the Irishman.

"Ike must have pulled them off a dead drunk gentleman," chided Cut.

"Won 'em honest 'n fair," countered Ike, as he jiggled the pouch at his belt, "'n all this here coin too!"

Cut sneered, said nothing more, and concentrated on the wide winding road leading to the bridge over Papiack Creek.

Ike relaxed his leg and studied the sky. He was searching for a sign of clearing. There was none to be found.

"I should've won me a great coat."

"Not to worry, Ike," said Vincent. "I've two cloaks in the storage box on the waggon."

"Never wore a gentleman's cloak afore," confessed Ike, with a squinting of his sore eye and a slight smile on his still swollen lips. "Ye certain the Craut won't look black upon me wearin' such?"

"Cut's all set for foul weather. He's got his hunting gear on. Besides, old Cut would never deign to wear gentleman's clothing. He won't complain, but he will make you the fool."

Cut heard everything, but said nothing. He did not bother to turn his head. He pretended he had heard not a word.

"I'd rather get a soak, if the sky comes 'round to rain," said Ike resignedly, even though he liked the idea of wearing a Wetherill cloak. It would make him feel like he actually was second-in-command.

"If it pours strong enough, my good man, you'll be glad to borrow every inch of the cloak."

"We'll see 'bout it, Mister Wetherill. But, if the rain be strong, I'm fer borrowin' the shelter o' any tavern 'long the way 'n sittin' out the storm fer its length."

"Wish we could do so," said Vincent, "but our only stops are the Wheat Sheaf Tavern north of Spank Town and the Nag's Head in Elizabeth Town. After crossing Round Creek at the half-the-way point, all I'll be concerned about is the condition of the road over to the Hook."

"A long stretch without no stoppin'," mused Ike.

"Much longer in time and trouble if the weather turns against us," added Vincent. "I don't intend to stop for any purpose. I've got good reason to get this journey behind us as soon as possible. We must get you back to Mary, get Cut back to his wife, and me back to Abia."

"At least two of us will agree on yer plan," snorted Ike with his good eye spearing in the direction of the waggoner. "But that one has a jileen in ev'ry town we pass."

"The man's a hunter," remarked Vincent with a wry smile, "and good with his gun."

"Problem is, Mister Wetherill," said Ike in a low voice of confidentiality, "he smells worse 'n me. Some women like such a strength in a man. Good Mary don't care one way or t'other."

"Abia cares," admitted Vincent wistfully. He felt a shiver in his shoulders, and shook his head. "Enough of this prattle. Tell me about your findings in Amboy, then I will get to the front of this waggon where a true leader is supposed to be."

Ike quickly recounted his experiences down on Market Street all the way to the Cove. After more bragging about his winnings and a near fight against a boatman, who called Ike out for cheating at pharo in Hull's Tavern, the Irishman spoke of a certain scullery maid with whom he flirted for a time at the Dock Street Market.

"She was a slight jileen with a heavy sack to be luggin' back to Skinner's castle. So, the gentleman which is me, I offers to lug the load fer her. She blushes red as ripe berries and obliges me all the way to the rear o' the house 'n into the kitchen itself. With few 'round, save fer servants 'n such, she gives me a tour without me askin'. So I gets to see certain rooms where the smell is of brimstone 'n the shadows appear ghosts to me. She knew little o' events here in sixty-eight, 'cause she was too young 'n not in the service o' the Skinners back then. I asked, I sure did, but learned nothin' from inside the place."

"So you never got into the room where the Treasury box was once stored?"

"Wouldn't have know'd which room was which, Mister Wetherill. This partic'lar maid led me to few 'n most was locked secure. She claimed this was how it had to be with Skinner bein' away, which'd he was. Sorry to say there's nothin' to be learned from snoopin' there now. The place is clean 'cept fer the smell . . . like death's been done there . . . or soon might be . . ."

Ignoring the subject of death and the implication of the presence of ghosts at Skinner's place, Vincent changed the subject: "Did you learn anything from your associates on Water Street?"

"Not so quick, Mister Wetherill. There's more which occurs at Skinner's fancy abode. Me 'n the scullery maid spent some o' the day strollin' out 'round the house afore she's back at her cleanin' chores. We pass close on the corners 'n under the windows—all closed tight in fine repair. Off to me right is a patch where the soil's been turned 'n I'm askin' this jileen what's it 'bout. So she's tellin' me 'bout a coin which was found there some few days ago 'n her master ordered the finder to dig 'round fer more . . ."

"Did she mention the name of who found the coin and who was told to dig?"

"One 'n the same," said Ike, as he held his good hand out to catch a few of the first drops of rain. "The maid tells me a certain Billy Campbell—on his own after servin' out his apprenticeship, but one who comes 'round fer to flirt with Skinner's maids 'n feager a free meal—found the coin half in the ground 'n glimmerin' like the sun on the eastern side o' the house."

"A gold piece then?"

"A Spanish guinea fer certain, so she says," answered Ike. "Billy was showin' it to all the servants, includin' herself, 'n tellin' where he found it. She claims a house slave, named Bob, runs 'n tells Skinner hisself 'n the master comes rushin' to take the gold piece from this Billy 'n warns all present to speak to no one 'bout this find."

"But the scullery maid told you?"

"'Cause I asked 'bout the pile o' dirt," said Ike with a grin. "I did so with the charm 'n guile o' a suitor . . . plus, she ain't one to pass on a chance to gossip . . . I found this out quick 'n then fer too long."

"'Tis a wonder she did not invite you to dig for a spell?"

"I thought the same, but no tool was left fer me to be diggin' with—just the head 'n half a tail of what looked to me the best part o' a broken spoon. So I escorts the maid to her chores 'n I starts back to Water Street to find some more gold on me own."

"I wonder why Billy Campbell would be digging with a spoon?" asked Vincent more to himself than to Ike.

"Prob'ly used it for siftin' soil so as not to miss a mite," said Ike, as he slipped a hand into the pouch at his belt, fumbled and felt around a bit, then extracted a metal object that did, indeed, look like a broken spoon. "After I left the dear jileen, I returned to the diggin' patch 'n retrieved this here piece o' brass. I figger'd nobody'd be lookin' fer the likes o' it."

Ike handed the piece of brass to Vincent. The young man held it up in his free hand and let the fine mist falling bejewel the dirty brass. This was no ordinary spoon—its head was too flat and narrow to have been used as an eating spoon. Vincent examined the brief length of the broken arm of the thing. He saw three dark grooves evenly spaced an inch or so apart on the limb.

Vincent returned Ike's treasure to him. "I know not what that thing is or its purpose, but it is a curious find. Hold on to it. It may be worth something to someone."

Ike tucked the broken spoon back into his pouch. "Sorry to say, there ain't no more to tell o' me visit to Skinner's palace. Other than me winnin's down on Water Street, I gained nothin' new— nothin' 'bout the robbery, the murder, nor the pig irons which'd Big Tom chased away . . ."

"You did the best you could, Ike," said Vincent, as he coaxed his mount to speed up and skirt around the waggon in order to take the lead position.

"Once'd we stop to unload a barrel, meant fer the Wheat Sheaf 'stablishment, I'll take ye up on yer offer."

"Which one?" called out Vincent without looking back.

"The gentleman's cloak, o' course!"

❖

The rest of the trip to Powles Hook was conducted in variations on the theme of precipitation. A cool, misty rain continued all the way through Spank Town, over the Raway River, and beyond the Wheat Sheaf Tavern. The road remained tolerable up to the Nag's Head Inn by the old mill in Elizabeth Town.

Vincent was pleased with the progress being made. However, he was not happy with the squabbling that intensified between Cut and Ike. The latter seemed emboldened after putting on Vincent's spare cloak. He also had found a dandy blue scarf in the waggon box. He wore it over his red monmouth cap to cover his ears and tie around his neck. When they stopped for refreshment and other needs, old Ike strutted about like a rooster free of its pen. He boasted loud and long about how warm and dry he was, and what a gentleman he would have made. Cut called him a fool and worse—called him a bastard and born to his fate. Ike countered with accusations of philandering on Cut's part. Things almost came to blows at the wooden bridge over Round Creek, when the sky darkened and rain began to pour. As the waggon rattled across the narrow span, the two adversaries were going at each other like fighting dogs held apart by flimsy tethers. The road on the other side of the bridge was a miserable maze of rut pools and slow-paced congestion. The way through Newark and on to the First River proved to be a waggon team's hell. Cut's vehicle kept slipping to one side of the road or the other. Vincent rode close to the bay Shires to encourage them and keep them to the center of the road. Ike, however, shouted out advice and commands from his position at the rear. He then blamed Cut for not following his wisdom. Cut cursed the Irishman, the horses, and the awful road. He kept doing what he thought was best.

After crossing the Passaic River by ferry, the three men kept to a bad road cutting through Barbadoes Neck. This way led to the ferry landing on the Hackensack River. It was already getting dark and the landing was not yet in sight. However, Vincent did not want to stop. They were less than five miles from Powles Hook. Just as Vincent was about to call out his intentions to push on, the waggon lurched sharply to the right shoulder of the miserable road and stopped dead. The front right wheel was stuck fast in a deep, water-filled hole. Cut cursed his luck. He hollered at his horses and they strained at their halters, but the brandy waggon would not budge. Vincent turned his horse around and sped back to assess the situation. Ike was already at the right flank, peering down at the wheel in the hole and offering advice which Cut did not want to hear.

"Ain't goin' to budge this old wheel on a night like this," shouted Ike, as he adjusted his scarf to make sure the back of his neck was covered. "I say me 'n the boss head to the ferry house fer the night 'n return in the mornin' to fetch you, Cut . . ."

"I say to hell with you and your bones, bog lander! You're not leaving me to camp under this cart while you're off drinking the night away by a warm fire. Get off your horse and help me unload this waggon."

Cut scrambled from his seat. His boots slapped the mud near the hole that held the wheel. Vincent had already dismounted and was sloshing towards the focus of their attention. Ike remained on his horse. He did not want to get his new shoes ruined by the fouled road. He repeated what he had advised before, but the other two ignored him.

"We will all help to unload the barrels," ordered Vincent, "then we will all help to free the wheel."

"Can't use me arm," protested Ike, as he held up the still bandaged limb that had been lacerated in the fight at Rattoon's.

The waggoner stomped over to Ike's mount, grabbed a fistful of the Irishman's borrowed cloak, and yanked him to the ground. There was a splash and a groan followed by the slap of handfuls of mud being thrown at a barely discernable target—a slowly moving target, trying to get to its feet . . . trying to get away from an infuriated beast.

Vincent rushed over and grabbed Cut. "Let the boy be . . . ignore his goading . . . he will do as I say."

Cut retreated. He wiped his mud-caked gloves on the sides of his thick hunting coat, then walked slowly to the rear of the waggon to find the roll boards.

Vincent hurried over to the pitiful pile that was Ike and pulled him up out of his mire of humiliation. He barked out specific orders: "You're not to go near the barrels. Cut and I will loosen the straps and roll them down the boards. You tend to the horse team and guide them, when Cut and I are pushing the emptied waggon free of the hole. If the plan does not work, you unhitch the team and we will roll the waggon back out of the hole."

"I'm feelin' water in me shoes," groused Ike. "Me new shoes is ruined!"

"Forget your losses, Ike. My riding boots are standing in the same mud as your shoes."

"Don't makes me feel no better."

"You'll be leading us, Ike. No need to complain upon gaining your first chance to do so. Now go stand with the Shires and be ready to lead 'em forward when I give the command."

Ike said nothing more than, "Sure will, Mister Wetherill." He limped to his suspect favored position, making an emphatic squish and clomp with every step he took.

Vincent hurried to help Cut roll the barrels off the waggon. When that was accomplished, the two men put shoulders to the moving task. Vincent shouted out commands to Ike, while he and Cut applied all their strength to freeing the vehicle from its trap. The horses started forward and to the left at Ike's coaxing. On the very first try the wheel emerged from the hole. The waggon sat safe from harm in the center of the road.

Vincent and Cut congratulated each other on their quick success. They reloaded the waggon with the barrels which seemed twice as heavy, and strapped them in place. Cut slipped the roll boards into position, secured the rear latch, and jostled the right front wheel to feel for any damage done.

"No break here, Mister Wetherill," announced Cut. "Axle is whole. We're sure lucky this time 'round."

"Lucky twice in not losing much time," added Vincent, who had remounted his Spanish barb. "Filthy and soaked to the bone are we, but lucky just the same."

Cut agreed with a nod and finished hitching the riderless quarter horse to the back of the waggon.

Ike had already mounted his favored quarter horse and was heading back around to take his usual position behind the waggon. He had no more advice to give. He was filthy and soaked to the bone also. Furthermore, he, too, felt lucky. By leading the dray horses and waggon out of the hole, Ike had gained a small victory. There was no need to say more,

Verdine Elsworth's one-story ferry house at Powles Hook was usually a noisy gamesome place, offering mostly legal entertainment for travelers passing to and from New York. Exotic liquors from all over the world could be had at a steep price in the spacious taproom of this establishment. The rude cost, even for common rum and beer, did not discourage the paying customers from consuming great quantities. Fine and fancy eatables, again at a handsome price, were being served in the two large dining areas—one which allowed women, one which did not. A stay overnight in Powles Hook was, indeed, an expensive proposition. The two large buildings closest to the ferry house rented rooms to travelers. The closer one was preferred by gentlemen in good standing and women with escorts married or not. The one farther up the road was for men of a lower stripe. A trio of whores ran this place. They charged the same for a room as the more dignified place did. In addition, a night of pleasure with one of these three women cost much more. There was no lack of willing customers.

The most experienced, voracious gamblers flocked to Powles Hook. They could be found in fair numbers on any given night in the game rooms of the ferry house. Buying into a game of risk and chance came at a very steep price here. The best at their game were always glad to free a traveler of whatever amount he wished to lose and, quite possibly, teach him a lesson in the process. Yet, Elsworth's place was equally known as an excellent venue for sharing news and gossip. This was the only thing offered and exchanged for free.

On this dreary Thursday night, there was less than the usual number of patrons who had crossed from Manhattan and Staten Island in order to find a seat on a stage waggon leaving at dawn. Some were planning to travel west or north into Jersey, but most were bound for Philadelphia to the south. These urbane travelers saw themselves as an elegant, genteel lot—though, at all times, loud and demanding. However, they passed through Powles Hook with good New York money. Captain Elsworth, himself a shrewd New Yorker and popular hero of the last war, was glad to extract their lucre from them . . . so were the gamblers waiting in the low-ceilinged rooms beyond the taproom . . . so were the three whores waiting up the road. Unfortunately, this would not be a good night for such a harvest . . . the rain was all about discouraging travel.

A small number of Jersey folk from the west had arrived on what locals at the Hook referred to as flying machines. They were late in coming due to delays caused by the unexpected heavy rains. These travelers meant to stay at Elsworth's until seats became available on small passenger boats crossing the Hudson River to New York. They were thirsty, hungry, tired and sore from rumbly rides over horrible roads. They had slight interest in gamblers or whores; however, they were gladly up to buying a pint or two, swapping tales, and partaking of a warm meal if time permitted.

Joining these late sojourners were three soaked and forlorn fellows up from Perth Amboy with half a waggon load of barrels of brandy—one barrel destined to be consumed here at Elsworth's Ferry House and the last two sold by the Captain at a much higher price in New York. After unloading the waggon at the storage barn on the far side of the ferry road, a short distance from the new, not quite completed, wharf, the three men brought their horses and waggon to the largest of the stable barns. This airy structure was newly completed and the latest pride of Captain Verdine Elsworth. This was where he kept his prize racing stallions. Here, Cut unhitched the bay Shires and led them into the barn. Vincent followed with his Spanish barb, and Ike struggled in with the pair of quarter horses. All of them were glad to get out of the rain. They saw to it that their charges would be properly groomed, fed, and secured in available stalls for the night. Then, it was back out into the rain to pull the waggon to a far corner of the yard and secure the remaining two rundlets of apple brandy under the driver's bench. They covered the diminuitive barrels and bench with a canvas tarp, which they secured with leather straps. Satisfied with the progress made, the three men sloshed through the rain and mud across the broad, dark yard. They found the long porch under the Dutch roof and broad eve of the ferry house. Before entering the establishment, they shook the rain from headgear and outer garments. They stomped their feet and kicked mud from their shoes. They still looked soaked and forlorn.

Once inside, the trio breathed in warm, smoky air wafting over the sparse crowd in the taproom. Vincent removed his cloak and tricorn before a dutiful uniformed slave could reach him. Ike removed his wet scarf, but kept his cap on his head. Cut removed nothing. While Ike wrung out his borrowed scarf, the other two were content with inspecting the few windy, blatant men gathered at the bar. Another group was huddled at tables in the shadows. Although meager in number, it was a motley gathering of loud wayfarers bent on enjoying their liquid spirits, tasty food, and boistrous conversation.

A servant, who finally reached Vincent, bowed deeply and relieved the young gentleman of his foul-weather garment and hat. The slave's appearance spoke well of the master's attention to detail. A white wig crowned his kettle-black head. He wore a shiny silk waistcoat of peacock green with large gold buttons down the front and at the sleeves. This impressively costumed greeter was about to open his mouth, when Vincent cut him off.

"Here to see your master, Captain Verdine Elsworth, on a business matter. He knows of my coming. I am Vincent Wetherill, son of Assemblyman John Wetherill of Middlesex County. My men and I have had a rough time of it in the storm. First, we would like to dry out by a good fire, warm our toes, and partake of your finest fare and strongest ale. Then, we trust you will gain for us an audience with your master."

The natty servant bowed again. He came up with a condescending look on his face, which he directed at Vincent. He frowned noticeably when he deigned to inspect the two men in Vincent's shadow. These were obviously not two men worthy of an audience with the distinguished Captain Elsworth, such a decorated military officer and champion of the horse races in these parts.

Vincent had to admit that Ike did look like a drowning rat, which had just escaped a watery grave. Cut looked almost as bad, but more sinister. His prize rifle, in its waterproof wrap, was slung over his shoulder. He flashed the desperate eyes of a hunter down on his luck. No, it would not have been productive to introduce this pair to Captain Elsworth.

Vincent caught the servant's frown and quickly corrected himself: "I need to speak to the master of this establishment. My companions will tend to their needs, then take turns keeping watch on our horses and waggon throughout the night at the racers' barn."

"Not necessary, Mister Wetherill, on a night such as this," said the well-spoken, finely dressed house servant. "You and your men enjoy your time safe and dry in here. Rest assured, your property and possessions will be safe under the watchful eye of my master's stable foreman. He will guard your steeds as well as he does the Captain's stallions."

The servant spoke with sincerity. It was as if a free man stood before Vincent and was sharing a confidence worthy of trust. He must have cost Elsworth a fortune, thought Wetherill.

"By what name does your master call you?" asked Vincent cooly, without adding the customary "boy" at the end of his question.

"Kersey, sir."

"Kersey, I shall take your word for truth and hold you responsible if anything untoward happens to beast or cart."

The servant offered a tight smile and bowed slightly.

"Now, please direct us to a free table near your closest hearth," requested Vincent.

The green-jacketed slave turned on his heels like a soldier, glided past the patrons at the bar, and pointed to an empty bench and table against the far corner closest to a cavernous hearth. The three guests quickly followed him there. The fire was blazing. It was being fed and tended by two slaves who were readying it for a cool night. Other patrons shied away from its heat; thus, there was plenty of room for Vincent and his two companions to stretch out and relax.

Kersey hung Vincent's tricorn and cloak on pegs at the lip of the hearth. He offered to do the same for Ike and Cut. They both declined. Cut sat down with Vincent at the table. He propped his rifle against the wall behind the bench. Ike located a three-legged stool, which one of the slaves had been using, and sat on it as close to the fire as he dared. He was careful to keep the ends of his borrowed scarf and fringe of the cloak shy of the sparks from the blaze. He proceeded to remove his soaked and muddied new shoes and prop them against hearth irons to dry. He studied them sadly. He kept his thoughts to himself. Steam wafted delicately from the moist cap on his head and from where the cloak draped his shoulders. Ike appeared to be smoldering, as if about to catch on fire—more like a ghost from hell, and a thirsty one for sure.

A red-cheeked serving maid, with bounteous breasts quivering like a pair of jostled pompions in a lace bag, came round with frothy pints of warmed ale. Ike's prayer was answered. Cut's was also. Both were half done with their brews before fine victuals were brought to the table by servants marching to commands from Kersey. Cut set upon the meal like a vulture; however, Ike did not get up from the stool. He kept to the company of his diminished pint, held firmly in his hands. He did not want to sit at the feasting table. He wanted to keep a safe distance from the German. Ike was not interested in breaking bread with a man who thought so little of him—a man who did not care whether he lived or died. Better to keep his eyes on the pint, say nothing, and listen to the rain drumming on the roof. He planned to eat later, after doubling the wealth in his pouch by gambling in one of the back rooms. As he dried out, his confidence of winning big seeped back into his bones and coiled round his heart.

First to be devoured by Cut and Vincent was a pompion soup served in large, steaming wooden bowls. Both men wielded their pewter spoons and attacked the milky brew lustily. They dipped chunks of cornbread into their bowls and sopped up the dregs.

Next came a platter of roasted meats—beef, lamb, and various fowls, accompanied by bowls of carrots and potatoes seasoned with cinnamon and pepper. Cut chose what he wanted by employing knife and spoon. Vincent preferred the more gentlemanly tandem of knife and fork. The two men consumed as much as they dared and waded through three pints of ale each before reaching the end of their late evening repast, which concluded with shattucks, cracknels, and quince in cream.

Before they were finished, Ike had disappeared. He had remained by the fire long enough to count the money in his pouch, struggle with putting on his shrivelled shoes, and devise a clever strategy to be employed at the card playing. With a bit of his winnings, he would buy his own sumptuous meal, enjoy it without Cut being present, then head back to the racers' stable where Vincent wanted him to take the first watch. The two men feasting took no notice of Ike's leaving. They knew where he would end up and that some sort of trouble would find him before they did. For the moment, Vincent and Cut simply wanted to savor the bounteous meal.

"Ford's vittles taste better than what you'd pay on your own," quipped Cut as he plunked down his third pint for the last time. "Wouldn't you say as much, Mister Wetherill?"

Vincent nodded in agreement. "No need to spend your own coin on essentials, Ike. My ledger book speaks for all such costs on this trip. 'Tis Jacob Ford's concern, not ours."

Cut finally got around to divulging his plan for the evening. It was neither startling nor new: "I'm in need of some rest, Mister Wetherill . . . so, if you do not need me, I'm heading up the road to occupy an empty space."

Vincent caught the wink his waggoner broadcast to him. "Go right ahead, Cut. I'll be settling accounts on this fine meal, renting a room next door if one's available, and attempting to find Captain Elsworth before he retires for the evening."

Cut arose from the table. He bumped the sleeping man at the bench to his left and behind him. His gun sack grazed the fellow's shoulder but he did not move. He noticed that the man just continued snoring softly.

"Must of had a worse trip than ours, Mister Wetherill, wouldn't you say?"

Vincent looked over at the sleeping man Cut was referring to. He appeared well set and of middling age . . . bald at the crown with a halo of brown hair curling over his ears . . . a swarthy complexion with evidence of the pox. A soiled castor hat sat by his calloused right hand. He wore a long pedestrian coat of bluish-gray and bearskin trousers. His mud-caked boots sported brass side-buckles. There was nothing outstanding about this man or his apparel. Vincent guessed the man to be a coach driver.

"You're probably right, Cut," opined Vincent. "He must have been on a longer and more difficult road than ours. He must be exhausted. Leave him alone to travel in his dreams. I hope his fate and ours improve on the morrow."

"Doubt it much, Mister Wetherill," said Cut as he turned and strode toward the door.

Vincent found himself standing alone—a safe distance from the nearest patron—the sleeping stranger. He communed with the brilliant hearth flames. Young Wetherill wished at that moment to be the man with his head on the table—an average, unassuming chap who probably had little responsibility and few cares . . . a man who could sleep anywhere at any time . . . one who could not be easily roused out of pleasant dreams . . .

"Captain Elsworth will see you now!" came the jolting words from Kersey, the uniformed servant—words which forced Vincent out of his standing reverie.

The young Wetherill rallied instantly and fumbled in his vest pocket for some bills of credit. "O yes, Kersey, but I must settle accounts for meal and drink . . . and pay in advance for a room next door to use this night."

The servant in the green jacket smiled broadly and revealed a pair of protruding front teeth. "All has been taken care of by the generosity of my master. He has not forgotten the great lengths your father took to support the financing of the Delaware River outposts during the Indian wars. Now the time has come for you to gain my master's favor. He will see you now."

Vincent followed Kersey, who strutted at a lively pace down a long corridor of dove gray walls, red pine wainscoting, and very little candlelight. Most transient customers were not allowed here. Only special guests were permitted to visit the very private and very wealthy Verdine Elsworth. He was a man who plied power and influence in two colonies. He did so, better than anyone who competed against him. The only man at Powles Hook who was more powerful than Elsworth was his partner, Faddy Van Vorst, the one who had built the popular one-mile circular racing course out on the flats. Van Vorst ran the lucrative ferry service across the Hudson River while Elsworth ran the Ferry House Tavern. They were a most successful team at making money and investing it wisely. The two men had few true friends and many enemies. Elsworth trusted no one, save his partner and his Kersey, who had been his batman during the last war. He dealt with all associates in a cool, businesslike manner—never letting his guard down and always ready to reveal a quick temper. He preferred to do important business in his private room at the end of the long, dark hallway. Everything was designed to show that Captain Elsworth was in control.

Kersey rapped a brass horse-head knocker against a thick metal plate affixed to an oaken door. He waited for a command from the other side. It came sharp and clear. The servant turned the latch and ushered Vincent into a modest, low-ceilinged room subtlely lit by a warm, low fire in a broad hearth and strategically positioned bayberry candles. The room was smoky, but it was a pleasant kind of closeness that reminded Vincent of a green spring season rather than a dry and dusty fall. The walls were the same soft gray as in the hall, but, the wainscoating, shelves, and beams overhead were all thick, dark oak. Burgundy velvet curtains shrouded windows from ceiling to floor. Large paintings of idyllic scenes featuring horses and hounds, framed in gold, hung from the wall spaces between the curtains. This was, indeed, a gentleman's quarters.

"Mister Vincent Wetherill, son of Assemblyman John Wetherill, to see you, sir," announced Kersey with a flourishing bow. "He claims he has business matters to discuss . . ."

"Ah, yes, young Vincent," exclaimed Verdine Elsworth, as he put down his long clay pipe and stood up from his high-backed chair, bent over his desk to shake the visitor's hand, and pointed to a comfortable leather chair.

"Will you require anything, sir?" asked Kersey, who remained by the open door.

"Nothing for now," said Elsworth with a wave of his lace-draped hand that signalled the dismissal of his chief servant. He put his hand gently on his desk and propped himself up with it. "On second thought, fetch Mister Jarlman for me in an hour's time. I've some ugly news from Morris Town to go over with him. He is back from making his rounds isn't he?"

"Yes, and taking a snooze in the main room. He shall be roused in time, sir," said Kersey, as he bowed and departed, shutting the door quietly behind him.

Verdine Elsworth waited for his guest to get comfortable in the leather chair. He offered Vincent a glass of claret, but the young man raised an open hand in protest and admitted to downing three pints of the host's best ale. He was in need of finding a privy in order to relieve himself, but that would have to be postponed until his business with the Captain was finished. He thanked the Captain for the meal and drink.

The host took one proper sip of his wine. With stern brown eyes under thick black brows, he studied the young guest. Vincent was casting eyes about the room, mostly focusing on the painting of a gray stallion, and waiting for Elsworth to start the first topic of conversation. Finally, he caught the Captain's stare and noticed a twitch on the left side of the host's face where a saber scar coursed from brow to cheek. The rest of Elsworth's features—the full red lips, prominent nose, and jutting chin—all spoke of confidence and getting one's way. He was dressed in a full-length, shiny black sateen evening coat with intricate silver and gray embroidery at his collar. His silk vest sported scarlet and gray stripes. White lace flowered from his cravat and ample sleeves. A perfect wig crowned his large head and rivaled the sheen of his lace. Besides confidence, Elsworth's apparel exuded wealth. Everything about him and his lair spoke of being a man in control—one not to be trifled with.

Finally, Elsworth reassumed his seat and placed his elbows firmly on the desk. He clenched large red hands before the scar on his face, as if attempting to hide some badge not worthy of attention.

"How fares your father?" opened Elsworth with genuine concern. "I understand he is not well."

"Recovering nicely," claimed Vincent, "under the care of the competent Doctor Stites of Cranberry."

"Good news, indeed," said Elsworth, taking another sip of his wine. "I expect your father to be in fair health by the time of the next Assembly session. Parliament's indifference must be countered by the likes of staunch representatives such as your father. We need more like him. I'm being taxed out of my profits while our Governor and our King turn a deaf ear to pleas. Those two can take turns kissing my arse. When they are done with me, I trust your father will convince Will Franklin to strangle George with his Bishop's entrails! But before the execution takes place, I want your father to finally convince our Governor to get rid of that weasel of a Treasurer. Justice has taken too long. The Sons of Liberty are right to organize and parade about. Their day and mine are coming, young man, quicker than late, if your father and his peers do not take action by peaceful means."

Vincent agreed with the latter half of the Captain's rambling rant. Many people, including himself, were growing impatient with the arbitrariness of laws and policies imposed by a King and his Parliament across the sea without any representation from the duly elected legislators in the colonies. Vincent was among those losing patience, but he would not go so far as to wish for the demise of the ruler and his Bishop. He wished the topic of conversation had not taken such a vitriolic turn. Young Wetherill did not know what to say.

Elsworth saw the disaffection in Vincent's eyes and apologized. "Ah, but you did not come all this way to discuss politics with a disgruntled entrepreneur caught between the rules and regulations of two rival colonies. Let me just conclude and say that there is much work to be done. Your father is one who must get back to such work "

"He will not disappoint you. If you are lucky, the Representatives from your county shall do the same . . ."

"Stick to what you know, lad. The Dutchmen up here are a wavering lot." The Captain paused to take another gentlemanly sip of his merlot. "Now, let's get down to business."

Vincent pulled his small ledger book out of his vest pocket at the same time Verdine Elsworth reached for the large bound ledger on his desk. Both men opened their books and studied their scribblings for a moment before the older man fumbled for his quill and prepared it for making an entry.

Vincent spoke first: "Three barrels we've brought for you. My men and I already unloaded 'em and secured 'em in the storage barn by Faddy's wharf."

"Kersey already informed me of your movements," announced Elsworth, as he made an entry in his ledger and slammed it shut. "One head for me and two for Anthony at the King's Arms . . . he will gladly pay twice as much as what I am going to pay you, young man."

With that said, the Captain bent down and unlocked a drawer in his desk. He extracted an ornate box, opened it cautiously, and extracted a small pouch with the Wetherill name sewn on its front.

Elsworth handed it to Vincent and barked an order: "Count the contents. See if it matches the amount owed in your ledger. It is all good Jersey bills of credit . . . no counterfeit, all old bills without Skinner's signature on nary a one."

"This will please my father," said Vincent, as he pulled out the bills and counted them. When he was done, had tucked the money into his pouch at his belt, and placed the Captain's pouch back on the desk, he declared, "Paid in full."

"You should have brought me more barrels, lad. The demand for your father's brandy is strong across the river . . . a fine brew, indeed . . . bring me twice as much next time . . . make it soon . . . and don't forget, I've empty barrels for you to cart back . . ."

"Not this time around," interrupted Vincent. "Me and my men are headed over to Morris Town. We've two rundlets for Judge Cooper . . ."

"Sell 'em to me, lad," said Captain Elsworth decisively. "I'll pay double the price your father is asking,"

"Not for sale," insisted Vincent with a bargainer's smile. "A gift is a gift and priceless indeed . . ."

"Nothing is priceless, lad," countered Elsworth, "not even a man's life . . . 'tis always a question of how much one is willing to pay."

"The brandy for Cooper is actually a trade already spelled out," confessed Vincent. "The Judge has promised to have barrels of iron water ready for us to load on our waggon soon after we arrive at his place. We give him two eight-year rundlets and he gives us some barrels of iron water."

The Captain offered a hearty laugh and slammed a lacy fist down on his desk. Items jumped at the blow and he caught one before it rolled to the floor. "What a waste of prime brandy," exclaimed Elsworth. "Iron water is foul tasting stuff . . . even if you boil, it tastes like sweat off a stallion's pounders . . . what in the Lord's name is your father going to do with so much of it?"

"Doctor Stites recommended it as a base for a tonic, which my father must take in order to keep fit."

"Those barrels of such bane will last John Wetherill for the rest of his life . . . one swig of the stuff and I bet he tosses the rest away."

"My father intends to experiment with the iron water," explained

Vincent, "brew it with secret ingredients, and make a fine elixir in the process. He wants to profit from his efforts."

"We all do, lad," admitted Elsworth with a frown, "but there are times we end up with other fools on a fool's path. Your father has as much of a chance turning iron water into molten gold as making a palatable brew. I can't wish him enough luck on such a venture."

"Once my father has found the new elixir to his liking, I'll bring you a barrel of the stuff."

"If I know your father right, he will charge me exceedingly for it."

"It will be a gift," joked Vincent in a loud voice of confidence, "and, if you gag on first sip, you can always sell the rest across the river."

Captain Elsworth roared with laughter and slammed his fist against the top of his desk again. Things leaped and some rolled. This time he did not bother to retrieve them. They plunked and plinked on the floor boards.

"I like your way of thinking, lad. I could use your kind around here to revive the horse racing and bring in good money for me. When you complete your rounds, why not tell your father of your plan to work for me?"

Vincent blushed. "Your words are most kind and encouraging, Captain Elsworth, but I know little about the racing business and less about raising a crowd for any event . . ."

"Easier than a baby coaxing milk from a portly mother's breast . . . quite easy for a man of your caliber. I fired my last hawker, Mister Jarlman, when he failed to rouse enough interest for races at Faddy's mile-long circle course out on the flats. As you may know, the runs this fall have been cancelled. All my man had to do was interest three other owners to run their capital horses for saddle, bridle, and whip. However, he is a lazy fellow . . . lacks direction, if not told what to do . . . does not inspire others . . . unlike you in any case . . ."

The Captain paused to sip his wine and reflect on what could have been.

He completed his thought: "This means my bay champion, Cyrus, will be consuming my hay and oats, and not paying his keep. The bettors are losing interest in the horses. I'm losing money. I need a sharp young man like you, lad, to bring the races back to glory. I need you now."

Vincent failed to blush this time. He spoke firmly and with conviction. "I have priorities Captain Elsworth, and obligations to fulfill. My father's health and business interests come first. Till things are back to the way they were, I am splitting my time between Brunswick and Cross Roads. My wife is with child. She is not in the best of health. I must hasten to Morris Town and rush back to her . . ."

"So it's duty to family and devotion to loved ones which are going to doom what might have been a lucrative partnership," sighed Elsworth. "I knew all along you'd be too honest a man to trick into working for me. How about the men you've brought with you? Either of them worth their weight? Can they be trusted around horses?"

"The better one is trustworthy, but a mere farmer who happens to be a good shot with a hunting rifle. He does have skill in managing a team of horses. The lesser one has yet to be trusted around man or beast. He is fond of gambling and taking risks. Neither of my men is an organizer, leader, or sharp in business matters. Surely, you must have a good local man in mind to run the races. How about this Jarlman fellow you mentioned?"

"He's the one I fired," said Elsworth, "and hired again as my fetch hound to chase down a thief rumored to be hiding in Morris Town—hiding in plain sight and using another name. I sent that faithful dog up there at the time of the hanging in order to snoop around and collar this thief who once worked for me as a stable tender years ago."

"What did he steal from you?"

"A brood mare and a rat-catcher . . . disappeared in the night . . . same night Billy Walsh vanished . . . must have been five, maybe six, years ago when the boy ran off with an expensive dame and a worthless dog . . ."

"After so many years have passed, how did you learn of this Billy Walsh being in the Morris Town area?"

"A long tale," admitted the Captain, with a deep scowl descending from his brow, "but I'll cut it quick. The mare was found loose and free in the cornfield of a Rockaway farmer. A young slave from a neighboring farm actually found my horse and rode it in bareback. I never got the boy's name—never gained a chance to reward him. The farmer, who received my horse and identified the mark on the dame's ear, was paid handsomely."

"How did the farmer know the mare was yours?"

"A simple coincidence of the finder of the mark being a patron of the races. Often, he has visited our circle course. My mark is burned into many a board there. It is well known in this province. So, on his next visit, the farmer brings my horse back. I find the mare none the worse for wear. Thus, I cover the man's expenses and reward him with a fine purse of silver coins."

"What if the farmer returned without your horse, but with the rat-catcher?"

"You play with me, lad. I am trying to be serious here, because this discussion will lead to news which is guaranteed to put you in no mood to play. I've decided to let you stay for my session with Mister Jarlman and let you hear what he has to say."

"I remain serious on all matters of import," said Vincent. "I am simply curious about the fate of the dog."

Elsworth peered at his guest skeptically. The scowl was still firmly balanced on his brow. "If the farmer brought me the unmarked cur, then he would have also brought me the thief— those two were inseparable . . . slept together in my old racers' stable . . . so long ago, I can't remember when the cur came here or where it came from . . . probably born under the causeway which leads to here . . . could have waltzed out of the marsh in search of a free meal . . . an abandoned pup . . . much like Billy Walsh himself . . . may have happened at the same time Billy appeared."

Verdine Elsworth paused to finish his glass of wine. He smacked his lips, then concluded his thought: "I will catch them both . . . pay the captor nothing for the cur . . . have it bagged and drowned in the river . . . pay the captor for Billy . . . have him bagged and drowned the same . . ."

"Are you so sure they will be caught?"

"I always accomplish what I set out to do, even if it takes years. I have Mister Jarlman to blame if the Walsh boy is not found. However, I know he will succeed. He is at least good at finding lost things. If he finds the thief, I will be a happy man. Such a game takes patience, lad. After all these years, I still possess but a small measure of it. When my patience runs out, I will turn my wrath on Jarlman once again."

A long silence followed Elsworth's rancor. He was definitely not a man to be trifled with—a character who always got his way. Vincent felt sorry for Billy Walsh. He also felt sorry for Mister Jarlman. However, he felt worse for the rat-catcher.

8

BAD NEWS AND NEAR

DISASTERS
· · · · · · · · · ·

—at Elsworth's Tavern, Powles Hook,
late Thursday, September 23, 1773

At exactly one hour after Kersey had introduced Vincent to Captain Elsworth, the same green-jacketed servant rapped the brass knocker sharply against the oaken door. He did not wait for his master's voice. Kersey opened the door and entered Elsworth's private room, followed by the man who had been sleeping near the hearth in the taproom. This was not a stage waggon driver. Vincent guessed him to be Mister Jarlman—a rumpled fellow, who was probably used to sleeping in his workaday clothes. The man was well set but somewhat stooped at the shoulders. Under his long, loose-fitting coat, he wore a checked woolen shirt tucked whimsically into wide bearskin trousers. Jarlman held his castor hat with both hands in front of him. His gray-green eyes darted about his boss's elegantly understated room until finally finding Vincent, who was studying him intently. Jarlman lifted a hand and used it to swipe at a lock of bowl-cropped hair that had vanished long ago. This brought attention to a deap red scar running above his left brow. He was not a handsome man, probably never was, and much drinking had placed grog blossoms on his nose. One ruddy cheek was sagging and much larger than the other—no doubt caused by entertaining a wad of snuff for many years. The stubble of a careless man grew thickly on his jaw and chin. Most outstanding, however, was a strong odor which Vincent could not quite place. It had wafted in when Jarlman made his entrance—strong as the acrid scent of a chap who missed more than a few monthly baths and now smelled like horse dung dipped in a tanning vat. Jarlman could not have been a married man.

"Beggin' yer pardon, Mister Elsworth, sir," offered Jarlman in a thick accent laden with Jersey Dutch undertones, "but mine bad news can wait if yer yet to be done wit' such a fine young gentleman . . ."

"Right on time, Anse," declared Verdine Elsworth with a profound slap of a hand upon his desk. "I like that in a footman who's been given a second chance. Don't you, Mister Wetherill?"

Before Vincent could respond, Elsworth was introducing the two men to each other and ordering his employee to get on with his bad news. He did not bother to invite Jarlman to take a seat next to Vincent.

Jarlman stood with his hat in his hands behind a comfortable looking, empty leather chair. He studied this stately piece of furniture, which he would never get to own or sit in, as he began his account of doings to the west.

"Burnet's flyin' machine come in two hours late from Morris Town . . . close to an hour ago . . . wit' but two passengers bound for to cross at dawn . . ."

"Besides a little lateness due to rotten weather, what's so foul about such news?" asked the Captain. "'Tis a blessing for business to be receiving at least a traveling pair who won't be able to cross till morn. May they spend good money here tonight and lots of it!"

"They will," added Jarlman. "They're country pikers come down from the hills wit' purses of hard money. Once'd off their waggon, they headed straight to yer nearest game room, Mister Elsworth . . ."

"So what's your bad news?"

"Comes from the waggoner who brought the pair in. Mister Barnet, hisself, sat wit' me by the fire . . . woke me, in fact . . . shared news, a few pints, and a meal . . . all of his account bad, and some of it included mine own self . . ."

"What trouble have you gotten yourself into now, Anse?"

"You remember when you sent mineself to Morris Town at the time of the hangin' to check on rumors 'bout that boy, Billy Walsh, workin in the area?"

"Yes," mused Elsworth sourly, "and you returned empty-handed with but a possible sighting of the rat-catcher in the company of a slave girl . . ."

"I got to the hangin' late, Mister Elsworth."

"My guest and I do not want to hear excuses, Anse. Give us the bad news and be done with it."

"Of course, Mister Elsworth . . . I'll be quick as I can. Well, after the hangin', I followed a rumor to a tavern—the Haynes place, as I remember . . . inquired 'bout this Billy Walsh which'd no worker nor patron there ever heard of . . . stayed late, did I, consumin' much time wit' mine interrogations. I galloped off from there 'round midnight with intentions of makin' the Hook by dawn."

"Which you did," confirmed Elsworth, "and delivered a tale void of what I wanted to hear. So far, Anse, you have told us old news and nothing bad. Get on with it."

"Whatever you say, Mister Elsworth," said Ansel Jarlman, as he continued to worry the brim of his hat with nervous fingers. "After I'd left, so I just learned, folks at the tavern were questioned by authorities and spoke of mineself as a suspicious character which should be found and questioned regarding the murder of a stable boy . . . 'cordin' to the waggoner, just come in, the Morris County Sheriff is lookin' for old Anse Jarlman but not knowin' mine name, but by witnesses to mine face."

"Still not even close to bad news," declared the Captain, as he slapped a palm on his desk. "All I have to do is send you right back up there to look again for Billy Walsh. This time, you will find the Sheriff and answer his questions. You've nothing to hide, unless there's something about the murder you have never told me?"

"Had nothin' to do wit' it, Mister Elsworth . . . never killed a man nor mistreated a horse."

"Good then," said Elsworth. "I'll send you to Morris Town on the morrow. You will accompany Mister Wetherill and his team. They have some brandy to deliver to Judge Cooper up there. You can serve as their guide and escort. I will charge the Wetherills nothing for your services."

Verdine Elsworth laughed at his own joke. The younger Wetherill did not follow suit.

"Might be the same foul weather for the next day or two," offered Vincent. "Perhaps Mister Jarlman should wait till Monday." His words came at a strong, slow pace, because he wanted to make sure the Captain heard him loud and clear—he did not want Jarlman tagging along with his team. The man seemed to be an inept bungler; besides, he was wanted for questioning about the murder. Vincent was supposed to be investigating without anybody, except Ike and Cut, knowing he was. If at all possible, he wanted to stay clear of authorities. Jarlman would bring undue attention to his team.

"Not a chance," declared Elsworth. "My bones don't ache. This rare rain will end before the sun is one hour high. Clear skies and another dry spell will follow this pour. I insist my man accompany you on Friday. Besides, you are a gentleman of fine lineage who can vouch for the upstanding character of my man."

"I know him not," said Vincent firmly.

"You will get to know him in a short journey's time," insisted Elsworth. "Besides, I will put quill to parchment and write of Ansel's attributes and trustworthiness. You will deliver it to Sheriff Stiles for me and vouch for my man at the same time."

"Sounds like an order, Captain."

"It is—one filled with resolve and conviction."

"Consider it done," said Vincent, although he still wanted no part in Elsworth's plan; however, he did not want to irritate a man who was one of his father's best customers.

"Good then," concluded the Captain, as he returned his attention to the bearer of alleged bad news. "Anything else to report, Anse, about doings in that devil's nest called Morris Town?"

"'Nother murder," replied Jarlman dully.

"I knew it," exclaimed Elsworth, as he slammed his fist down hard on his desk and quickly got up out of his chair. He proceeded to pace in a tight circle around his chair. He kept his head bowed and his eyes fixed on his brilliantly polished shoes. "Any details provided by this waggoner you talked to?"

"Plenty of 'em, and none to implicate mineself."

"Nothing more obvious, Anse. You've been right here under my feet ever since you returned after the hanging."

There was an uncomfortable silence which followed Elsworth's admission of an alibi for his man. Jarlman said nothing. The Captain continued tracing his circle while deep in thought. Vincent had nothing better to do than count the seconds of quiet. Finally, Elsworth continued the conversation.

"Are you telling me this most recent murder is somehow connected to the first?"

"That I am," stated Jarlman assuredly. "Accordin' to Windy Burnet, no sooner had they buried the stable boy than another boy was found murdered. The second murder was done by the one who committed the first murder. Least ways, Windy says the Sheriff up there is thinkin' such. So the one they're lookin' for sure ain't mine self . . . no way . . ."

"Give me the details," demanded Elsworth. "After you are through, instruct Kersey to find Mister Burnet and bring him to me. I want to hear his version on top of yours."

"'Course, Mister Elsworth," said Jarlman with a perplexed look on his face. "The man's heavy into his drink after drivin' such a rough road with hard customers, but it's a fair thing to be doing since I might of lost a detail or two in the chore of rememberin' and thinkin' . . ."

"Just tell me what you know," said Elsworth tersely, "and be quick about the telling. At the pace you are going, old Windy will have passed out by the time Kersey reaches him."

"An Afric was found dead on the main road where it passes Doctor Barnaby Budd's property . . . face down he was . . . stripped naked . . . a fiddle bow stickin' out of his arse . . . in addition to old stripes at his back, a fresh-carved cross was tricklin' blood . . ."

"A sword," interjected Vincent.

"Sword or knife for the cutting of the poor fellow," countered Elsworth, "what does it matter?"

"You misunderstood me, Captain. What I meant to say is that the boy had the image of a sword carved on his back, not a cross. . ."

"How do you know such a thing, young man?" asked Elsworth under a furrowed brow of skepticism.

"The rest of your man's telling will most likely prove I am right. This has to do with all I know about the first murder." At this juncture, Vincent was reluctant to tell Elsworth or Jarlman all he had learned about the first murder. He did not want to give away his main reason for heading up to Morris Town.

Elsworth turned again to Jarlman. "Tell the rest, Anse."

"The more Burnet swims in his cup, the more he talks to me, includin' him bein' the one who found the corpse, long before dawn on this day . . . his coach was full and he's frettin' 'bout gettin' to Dickerson's house on time . . . but his team of horses suddenly shy and slow to a halt on their own. Somethin' frightened 'em sure . . . Windy Jumps down and walks ahead till he steps on what turns out to be a fiddle in the road . . . he laughs at that bein' what gave his horses a fright, till he trips over a corpse face down not far from the instrument. He returns to his waggon to inform his passengers and keep 'em calm . . . one volunteer runs back up the road to the nearest house which'd happens to be Budd's and rousts whoever he can. The good Doctor ain't there, but his mistress is and she sends her most trusted pair of servants wit' lanterns to find out the fuss. These two Africs see who's been slain and know right away he's Budd's own buck fiddler, who's been entertainin' of late at the slave frolics 'round Morris Town. Goes by the name or Mingo Tim . . ."

"Never heard or him," said Elsworth, as he stopped pacing and sat down cumbrously in his favorite chair.

"Neither have I," said Vincent, "but it fits that this poor fellow is Doctor Budd's property."

"How so?" asked Elsworth.

"The murdered stable boy belongs to Samuel Haynes. The murdered slave belongs to Barnaby Budd. There might just be a connection, don't you think?"

"Haynes and Budd, along with Benjamin Cooper, are accomplices of the counterfeiter, Sam Ford—are they not?"

"Right you are, Captain," said Vincent with conviction. "This latest slaying could be another warning given by the murderer."

"So you're saying Judge Cooper's son will be next to receive a deadly warning?"

"I would not wish such a fate on anyone, Captain, but it sure looks like the pattern my father predicted is already playing out."

"Anything else, Anse?" asked Elsworth.

"I know nothin' 'bout no pattern," confessed Jarlman, "but I'm glad of hearin' of it, for it clears mineself of bein' accused of such crimes."

"That's already been determined," instructed the Captain in a fatherly tone. "Just give us the rest of what you have learned."

Jarlman twirled his hat and nodded. "So Burnet orders the two slaves to guard the corpse till the Sheriff is rousted by him when he reaches the Green, and rides back wit' him to the murder scene. But the slaves are tremblin' wit' fear, sayin they might be next. They're wantin' to run 'n hide."

"I don't blame them," said the Captain. "Bad news and disasters, near or complete, almost always happen before the dawn."

Vincent was surprised by Elsworth's support of such superstition. He would never have thought the man would justify cowardice from anyone. Vincent held his tongue and kept his thoughts to himself. He wanted to hear more from Jarlman.

"So the waggon master saw it the same. He got one of his passengers to stay behind—the same one who had fetched the slaves from Budd's stead. A promise was made to this brave fellow, who happened to carry a small pistol at his belt, that an extra horse would be brought for the ride back to town. Wit' such an agreement made, Budd's servants were coaxed into remainin' wit' the volunteer . . . they promised to stay till the Sheriff arrived. He showed up later wit' but one Constable and Windy Burnet."

"What did the Sheriff deduce from what he saw?" asked Elsworth impatiently.

"I'll get to such in time," said Jarlman. "To the Constable went the first task of pluckin' the bow stick from the arse of the corpse . . . to the pair of slaves and the Constable went the second task of rollin' the buck fiddler on his back . . . the slaves confirmed who he might be . . . to the Sheriff went the third task of inspectin' the wounds— throat slit ear-to-ear and tongue found in the buck's fist . . ."

"Was the tongue rolled in bills of credit?" asked Vincent.

"Wasn't told of such," responded Jarlman quickly.

"Does the Sheriff have any suspects in mind for this latest carnage?" asked Elsworth.

"There's talk goin' 'round, accordin' to Burnet, of a negro wench who ran away from Jacob Morrell's place on the same night the buck fiddler was dispatched . . . he and the girl were sweet on each other. There are rumors flyin' 'bout her carrying his first child . . . also a rumor of the buck already a sire from whence he came before Doctor Budd purchased him . . . and a rumor of him havin' three wenches wit' child at the same time! So the Sheriff is thinkin' a jealous woman took the buck fiddler's life . . . his prime suspect bein' the one who's run away."

"I wonder if this negress killed both—the stable boy of Haynes and the field slave of the Doctor?" ruminated Elsworth pliantly.

"Doubt it much," suggested Vincent. "There's more to these two murders than the jealousy of a young woman."

"The sheriff is thinkin' otherwise," countered Jarlman.

"That's because he has nothing else to go on," offered Vincent. "He wants a quick end to what has now gotten out of hand. Things may get much worse."

"I agree," declared the Captain, as he slapped his desk with finality. "The longer such devil's work goes unsolved, the worse it is for sojourners and business. I do not like where this mess is headed."

"Don't like it neither," chimed Jarlman, "but Burnet told me the Sheriff has his mind set on keepin' Mingo Tim unburied till the runaway wench is found. He's going to make her walk by the corpse to prove her innocence or guilt . . . if the boy bleeds or moves when she's forced to touch him, then she's the one who kilt him . . ."

"That's preposterous!" exclaimed Elsworth, as he leaped out of his chair, slapped his hands together, and proceeded to pace in a tight circle again. "Such backwoods barbarians up there, still believing in the bier right. I thought such customs were long dead . . . this is surely the devil's . . ."

Captain Verdine Elsworth was unable to finish his diatribe against the law of the bier and backwoods justice in general. Without the usual knock of courtesy, the thick oaken door to Elsworth's chamber was flung open by his faithful servant, Kersey. There was no time for a bow of respect. The slave was no longer nattily attired. He stood before the Captain and his two guests disheveled, mud-stained, and soaking wet from having come in out of the rain. He struggled to catch his breath as he propped himself up against the doorframe. He cried out as best he could:

"Racers barn! Fire in the racers barn!"

"The devil be damned!" ejaculated the Captain, as he leaped out of his chair and followed Kersey out the door and down the long hallway with Vincent Wetherill and Ansel Jarlman close behind. Elsworth's string of curses echoed in the hall.

The taproom was empty. Most folks crowded together under the broad eve of the porch. All eyes were on the billowing smoke and a few hissing flames emanating from the new barn. A light, but steady, rain was falling from a pitch-black sky and challenging the progress of the fire. Captain Elsworth broke through the crowd and led others who answered his call to help those already leading his prize horses out of the barn and away from harm.

With arms flailing and fingers pointing, the ferry house master barked out commands: "To the old stable out back with my racers! Account for each one! Hurry now, no time to waste! Visiting steeds to the storage barn! A handsome prize to the man who pulls the last horse out!"

Smoke was now billowing from the crown of the wide entrance and the open gable above it. Smoke was also emanating from most of the airy apertures on the east side of the roof line. The fire must have reached the hayloft, because juvenal flames were snapping at the sky from the vent holes in the cupola. A faint trail of smoke suddenly started escaping out the half-open Dutch door around back. The new roof shielded the conflageration spreading under it. This prevented the rain from dousing the fire. Only when the roof collapsed would the blaze succumb to a watery fate.

Captain Elsworth could not wait on such a tragedy. He considered such an option to be a defeat. So far he was winning— most of his horses had bean rescued from the smoldering inferno. His liveliest stallions—Macaroni and Cyrus—had been coaxed out first, plunging and fighting against their tethers held by the strongest stable boys. Now, locals, other slaves, and even a hand of travelers—all brave enough to enter the burning barn—were fetching the rest of the horses from smoke-filled stalls, where the bedding hay had not yet burst into flame.

Even young Wetherill and Mister Jarlman rushed in, crept low under the choking, blinding smoke, and found a bay mare kicking out the boards of her stall. Jarlman climbed into the stall. The mare stung him on the shoulder with a blow from her forehoof. He fell to one knee, but was up instantly. The shabby man called out soothingly to the frantic horse and dropped two lines over her head. He tossed one line to Vincent and called to him to open the stall gate. In an instant the kicking mare burst from her stall and followed the two running men to safety.

Similar heroic acts were repeated by those willing to sacrifice life and limb on such a terrible night. Only two horses—an iron-gray gelding and a Musgrove Arabian—broke free once outside the barn. They sped off in different directions—one toward the marshes, and the other to the road which led to the causeway. Captain Elsworth was generous in granting praise where it was due. He was quick to send teams of men out into the storm to find and fetch the runaway steeds. He was quicker to organize a bucket line from the nearest marsh creek. His battle plan was to defeat the fire before the roof collapsed.

The Captain cried out, "No fire set by the minions from Hell is going to defeat me!"

Men nearest the barn rushed to its entrance and flung water from filled buckets at the nearest flames. It appeared to be a futile effort from the start. The foremost men handed back empty buckets and took hold of filled ones. They repeated their tosses, refusing to stop until Elsworth gave the word. Vincent and Ansel Jarlman joined the line up close to the ones being spurred on by the Captain. Both men could see that the owner's plan was failing. Flames had reached the loft bales and were scorching the beams which held the roof. In a short time, the roof would smolder and crack. Flames would cut through seams and weaknesses, spit and hiss at the night sky, and burn wherever the rain allowed until the roof did, indeed, collapse.

Smoke became the worst enemy. If any man or beast was still inside the barn, there was but an angel's chance of getting out now. The smoke shrouded the entire entrance. It was thick, billowing, and climbing fast against the rain. The battle appeared lost.

The Captain stood resolutely before his ill-fated barn. He saw the men on the bucket line slowing the pace—their arms weary, their backs aching, their legs wobbly, their feet struggling against the sucking mud. A few fell to their knees and did not get up. They stared vacant-eyed at the victor, which was consuming the barn from within. Others decided to curse the rain. If it had been a dry, clear night, the barn would have flared like a tar-pitch torch and burned to the ground before a good bucket line could have been formed. However, the rain was delaying that inevitability. It had given time for rescuers to pull out all sorts of horses—from Arabian, a descendant of England's best stallion and Elsworth's finest racer, to Mercury, a plodding quarter horse of questionable lineage and one of Assemblyman John Wetherill's visiting horses. Vincent assumed the latter horse was the last one out. He had overheard Kersey, who was standing next to his master, account for all the visitors' horses which had been taken to the vacant storage building near the wharf. The unruffled slave described Vincent's Spanish barb, the two bay Shires, and a gentle quarter horse, whose name he knew not, as last out.

Vincent assumed the other quarter horse had been overlooked in Kersey's count. He also wondered about Cut and Ike. They were probably at the storage building tending to his father's horses. They must be doing what they were supposed to do and quite fortunate to have avoided a position on the Captain's bucket line.

Vincent turned his attention to the action swirling around the Captain. Verdine Elsworth was not one to recognize any cause as lost. He was a battler and a winner. He was made of the stuff that would be sorely needed if things got worse in dealing with the King and Parliament. He inspired others with his resolute spirit, just as he was doing in his strategy against the fire. His stoutest devotee, positioned in the forefront of the line, was about to throw another bucket of water against flame and smoke, when out charged a char-streaked man in a smoldering hunting coat. He was pulling a taut, short tether fixed to a white-eyed quarter horse, all sooty and singed like a failed burnt offering to old gods. Damned if it wasn't old Cut and the cantankerous Lord Corn heading down the bucket line as if it was a gauntlet.

"Soak us!" cried Cutlope Hancock in a raspy voice. "Soak us now!"

The line came alive with cheers and the tossing of water from the last full buckets. Cut did not stop. He wanted to get as far from the blaze as possible. He kept the tether low in order to force the wild-eyed horse to keep its head down. With his free hand in a burnt glove, Cut attempted to shield Lord Corn's eyes from the mad scene that surrounded them. He succeeded in moving far from harm's way, but behind him the cheers from the men in the line had turned to groans. At the end of a long, long rope, trailing from the neck of the quarter horse, a blackened lump of a fellow was being dragged through pools of mud. The man's torn clothes and naked limbs were actually steaming in the fitful light from the flames atop the stable barn. No one witnessing this sight could venture a guess as to who this chap was or whether this last man out was alive or dead.

Cut stopped running. He gasped for breath as he struggled to loosen the rope around Lord Corn's neck. The horse fought against him. However, Cut succeeded and let the rope fall to the ground. His intentions were to set the quarter horse free, and he did. Cut watched the troublemaker gallop off into the night towards the salt meadows, kicking its hind legs as if being chased by wasps. That bastard would probably be found in the morning, thought Cut. The rescuer turned his attention to what the horse had dragged out of the barn.

Someone had already severed the line and called for a doctor to be summoned. Several men crowded close to the bound body, still trussed expertly under the arms and around the waist. Vincent broke through the circle of men and knelt beside the poor fellow Cut had pulled from the burning barn. Ansel Jarlman was right behind Vincent with a bucket of water and some rags culled from an unknown source. As Vincent worked to untie the knots in Cut's rope, Jarlman started wiping the char and soot from the poor man's face. This fellow had lost his cap.

The borrowed scarf was gone. What few hairs he had on his head were burned off. As the grime was removed from his face, scarlet blisters and old, unhealed wounds were revealed on his nose, chin, and cheeks. His eyes were shut tight as Skinner's locked rooms, but his blistered mouth was open. Vincent put his ear to the man's lips and felt a shallow whisper emanating from a far-thirsty source. He guessed right—he knew the name of the burnt man. . .

"Give Ike something to drink," ordered Vincent to nobody in particular. "Make it purer than brook water and stronger too."

A man in the circle reached into his coat pocket and pulled out a fair-sized green bottle. "Try this," said the man, as he promptly handed it to Jarlman. It was then handed to Vincent.

"What might this be?" asked Vincient, as he cradled Ike's head with one arm, lifted him slightly, and brought the uncorked bottle to the burnt man's lips.

"Jersey Lightning," boasted the man, "and a pinch of musket powder . . . guaranteed to bring a dead boss back to life . . . me wifey dear swears by the stuff."

That comment brought gales of laughter from the men in the circle. It made them forget the tragedy of the burning barn for a moment. It made them focus on the last man out and reflect on the possibility that any one of them could have been Ike this night.

Vincent poured the smart brew and Ike swallowed. The Irishman's eyes fluttered open and looked around for something to recognize. He could not see—not at the moment. He needed tears, but he could raise none. Ike could not cry. He tried lifting his gashed arm. The bandage had been burned away. The exposed limb was red and raw. Fingertips were burnt and bleeding. He let the arm fall uselessly to his side.

Vincent decided poor Ike had taken enough of the brew in the bottle. He handed the vessel back to Jarlman and let Ike's head down gently. What a pitiful sight he was. Most of the rest of the borrowed cape had been sacrificed to the flames—a ring of its fabric at the neck and a tattered tail at his back was all that was left of it. His broad-cloth coat was gone, as was his shirt. His linen trousers were so filthy one could not differentiate patch from original cloth. His one remaining English boot was char-blackened and mud-caked. It smelled like branded hide. Every prideful thing in Ike's possession was either lost or ruined. Yet, he had made it out alive from his latest hell—thanks to Cut and Lord Corn. He suddenly realized he had one good arm and no burnt fingers at the end of it. Ike made a fist and raised it to wave in the direction of the new cheers from all the men who wished him to live. He saw not a soul, but he could hear them . . . and he knew he could speak to the nearest ones . . . barely . . .

"Bring me Good Mary," called out Ike in a voice not much greater than a whisper. "She will nurse me back to health, so's I can swaddle the pair which'd left me fer dead."

Only Vincent could make out what Ike was trying to say. However, young Wetherill misinterpretted what was being said. It appeared to Vincent to be a rehashing of old, bad news; however, Ike was not referring to the two pig irons who felled him in front of Rattoon's. He was talking about the two gamblers from Morris Town who had accused him of cheating at cards. They had taken more than a full measure of revenge . . . had run off . . . disappeared . . . like the gelding and the Arabian . . . like Lord Corn . . .

Vincent sought to reassure his flanker: "We'll find those pig irons, Ike. Soon as you are fit . . . soon as you can ride a horse . . ."

❖

Ike Higgins had been placed on the same table in Verdine Elsworth's establishment where Vincent Wetherill and Cutlope Hancock had had their late meal. Rain was still tapping on the roof, but faintly now. The patrons, who had come in from the porch, were quiet now. They mingled with the rescuers to catch a glimpse of the last man out. A sleepy-eyed Doctor, who had been found by Kersey, was dabbing a pungent salve on Ike's burns. When the task was completed to his satisfaction, he began to wrap the Irishman's old arm wound and newly mangled hand with a linen bandage.

"He will live," pronounced the slow-moving Doctor, who happened to be staying overnight at the house for gentlemen adjacent to the tavern. "I've put collyrium drops in his desiccated eyes . . . he will see again; but I will not venture a guess as to how keen his sight will be . . . whoever tends to him, make sure you keep this blindfold on till morn. I shall leave this bottle of drops to be administered then and at dusk. Keep his worse limb wrapped for a week's time. The tip of one of his fingers has been burned away . . . could very well putrify if not covered properly. The rest of his wounds, old and new, make him look worse off than he is. He's lucky to be alive . . ."

Expressions of agreement rippled through the crowd, gathered near the table by the hearth.

"Now who will pay for my services, so that I may sleep comfortably through the rest of this horrid night?" The Doctor was staring directly at the man across the table from him—the one who had listened most attentively to the instructions.

"Ike is my man," said Vincent, as he fished for his fold of bills of credit. "How much do you require?"

The Doctor did not respond with an amount. He was returning various items to a small black bag, then he pulled a squat bottle from his waistcoat pocket.

"I will accept only coin . . . gold preferred . . . a pair of joes will do . . . and I will throw in this humble vessel of my own brew guaranteed to get your man back on his feet by Monday. . . "

Vincent was about to confess that he had no gold on his person and state that he wanted no part of this Doctor's magic brew. He also felt this man was overcharging for the basic treatment Ike had received.

Another voice beat Vincent to it. "Ike will pay for his own care, once'd we find his pouch of winnings," declared Cut ominously from where he sat at the chair nearest the fire. He sat close as he dared to the flames to let his body, and the clothes he had not stripped off, dry out. He had taken off his outer garments. They were hanging on hooks to dry. Cut simply stared at the flames and took an occasional sip from a bowl of rum. His back was turned to the table that held Ike and the attention of all the others. The German showed no interest in Ike's well-being or what the haggling Doctor did or said. "Once'd the fire is out, I'll be searching for what's left behind, mein Doctor . . . if you live to see the morrow, then you'll get paid . . ."

Vincent showed the physician his bills of credit, but the man held up a hand of refusal.

"I shall return at dawn," said the Doctor tersely. With his medicinal bag in hand, he headed for the door.

"That one should be paid in brass spoons," snapped Cut for few to hear. "Gold is too good for the likes of him, and the patient ain't worth the fee."

Vincent turned his attention from the fitfully sleeping Ike to his sour waggoner. "Tell me, Cut, how you found the courage to rescue such a worthless man."

"And a worthless horse," added Cut, who was in no mood for lengthy conversation. He never was; however, he knew, if he said his piece once, Mister Wetherill would not ask him again. "I've rescued two bastards this day—one with four legs and one with two. I recall being late to the fire after pulling out of the fun at the low house . . . took me longer to reach the barn, since I was farther down the road. When I approached the blaze, I saw little harm done at the rear, so I plunged into the smoke 'scaping from an open riddler's door to see if anyone needed help. I heard a horse's whinny and the panicked beat of hooves against the boards of a stall. I rushed to such sounds and tripped over a man who'd been trussed to a rail. The smoke made it blinding dark, so I knew not who this fellow might be. Yet, I knew which'd horse was left behind—old John Wetherill's worst quarter horse. Quick as I could, I set a tether and line to the beast and the man . . . rushed 'em out of the burning stable . . ."

"So you did not know it was Ike you saved?"

"Only when the rescued man was freed from the rope did I realize I had saved the bog lander. If I had known earlier, there'd of been no need to fetch the chiseling Doctor. Strange how fire 'n smoke can turn fate. I wonder what hand set the blaze? Careless Ike, hisself, might've done the deed . . . it'd be my luck . . ."

Just then, Verdine Elsworth burst into his own establishment with a disheveled Kersey, Ansel Jarlman, the same Doctor, and several locals in tow.

"Rum for everyone!" roared the host. "I am proud to announce no horse nor man perished in the fire this night!"

His words were greeted by cheers from the crowd, which suddenly started breaking away from the table that held Ike. The majority of patrons rushed to the bar.

The Captain had more to boast about: "The frame of my barn still stands . . . rain has doused the last of the flames . . . most roof boards and shakes remain in place . . . a victory over the devil tonight!"

More and louder cheers followed Elsworth's announcement of the details of his moral victory. Toasts to his good fortune were made. Toasts were made to individuals who participated in saving the horses from what could have been the most tragic event at the Hook since several boat passengers fell into the Hudson River and drowned near Faddy's wharf.

Captain Elsworth raised his near-empty tankard to give the final toast. "To the fellow who saved the last horse out and pulled a man from sure death . . . may he live long to be a hero many times over!"

Cheers rang out and merry eyes looked around to find the man so honored by the host.

"Where is this valiant of the stable fire?" roared Elsworth.

A voice in the crowd shouted, "Wetherill's drover sits by the fire!"

The Captain and his entourage started making their way through the drinking patrons in order to reach the man of the hour. Happy noise and friendly jostling ensued, as men and a few women crowded close to gain a favored view of Elsworth's little ceremony.

Vincent turned to Cut, who was still concentrating on the dance of the flames in the hearth. He poked the German on a grimy, damp shoulder of his green hunting shirt, then used all fingers to shake him gently. Cut did not bother to look up. He was content to remain seated. However, he did place his empty rum bowl on a hearth stone.

Suddenly, Cutlope Hancock was the center of attention. Vincent, Captain Elsworth, and Kersey were so close to him now. He could not stand up even if he wanted to. The only major player not with this group was Ansel Jarlman, who remained at the bar with the lingering Doctor, counting heads and taking note of who was missing. He was ignored by the crowd, as folks pressed even closer to see what the Captain was going to do and what he had to say.

This was the last place Cut wanted to be—the center of attention and no chance of escape. He would rather be back at the low house in an over-priced room with an expensive whore. He regretted ever having the desire to satisfy his curiosity and see what all the commotion was about on the stable side of the tavern. He also regretted charging into the burning barn and rescuing what turned out to be two worthless creatures not fit to live. Now that pair had made him a hero—something he never wanted or needed. All Cut craved was to be left alone.

"So, Mister Wetherill," started the proud Captain, who kept his eyes fixed on the silent, filthy man sitting by the warm blaze, "this is your brave lad who saved your quarter horse and the poor Irishman on my table?"

"Yes, kind host," answered Vincent just as proudly. "Cutlope Hancock is my teamster and the one who snatched Ike Higgins, my flanker, from the clutches of certain death. I am as fortunate to still have them with me as they are to be alive."

"For certain," blustered Elsworth, "but the luckiest man this night is the one I intend to reward. Isn't that right, Kersey?"

The house slave, who had lost his pristine wig in battling the fire and soiled his green uniform in stumbling and falling in the mud when attempting to find a doctor in the pitch dark, handed a leather pouch to his master. Verdine Elsworth took the bag, shook it until its contents jangled, then turned it over and allowed ten gold Spanish dollars to spill into Kersey's cupped hands.

The crowd gasped in unison, then cheered the good fortune of the humble German farmer. Hussahs erupted in favor of praise for the host's generosity and his unflagging habit of always keeping his word. Hussahs followed for the Wetherill team—Cutlope Hancock, first; Vincent Wetherill, second; and the sleeping Ike Higgins, third.

As Kersey slipped the radiant coins back into the leather pouch and handed the prize to Cut, his master continued with his ceremony.

"Is there anything else you desire?"

"Nein."

"Surely there is more I can do for you, Mister Hancock?"

Cut took a deep breath and let it out slowly. He finally spoke: "Offer the Doctor, which'd fixed Ike, a choice—one of my Spanish dollars now or what remains in Ike's pouch at the scene of the fire . . ."

Kersey and his master scanned the crowd. They spotted him standing next to Ansel Jarlman, who had finished his inventory of the missing and his drink at the bar. The Doctor was still nursing his drink. Word of the offer was passed to the Captain's fetch hound, who in turn relayed it to the inattentive Doctor. The subject of money turned him away from his study of the pompous breasts of the serving maid. He quickly flashed one thumb up to signal his decision.

Kersey informed Cut of the Doctor's response. The German extracted a gleaming gold coin from the pouch and handed it over to the slave.

"Tell the good Doctor he made the right choice," said Cut, "'cause

Ike's pouch was prob'ly taken from him and may never be found."

Kersey bowed and slipped through the crowd in order to get to the Doctor.

"Anything else?" asked the Captain with finality.

"A soak," admitted Cut. "A soak in a tub."

Elsworth roared with laughter and slammed his hand down on the table that held Ike. The Irishman did not roll off or wake up. He was the only one who missed the merriment of the moment. Folks around him joined in the Captain's laughter and a toast was made about the merits of a warm bath.

"You and your clothes could well use a soak in my kitchen tub," announced the Captain merrily, "but a soak in it will cost you nine Spanish dollars!"

Elsworth roared again with laughter and slammed the nearest table with a fist this time. His followers and guests contributed another measure of outrageous laughter. The free round of rum had obviously worked its magic. The ruined stable barn was forgotten in that moment. Only Cut wanted to run and hide in the smoldering building.

The Captain was not finished with the waggoner. "I've changed my mind about the cost of your soak, Mister Hancock. Before I have Kersey escort you to your sorely needed oblation, I wish you'd tell me whom you suspect of starting the blaze in my barn—accident or crime, would you say? Your answer for a free bath."

The crowd behind Elsworth hushed to hear Cut's response.

"Ask Higgins when he's able," said Cut in the strongest voice he could muster. "When I found him trussed and burned, he was moaning of pikers who swagged his purse. When he's ready, old Ike'll tell you more 'n you'll ever want to know."

9

A STRANGE CONCOCTION AND

ODD CONFRONTATION
· ·

—on the road from Snake Hill to Book Town
Friday, September 24, 1773

Abrassy mid-morning sun was busy chasing away the last of the night's storm clouds, when Vincent Wetherill spied Snake Hill—the humped guardian of the Bergen Meadows. Surrounding the singular promontory was a brooding, dismal expanse of misty marshes and sluggish creeks. It was pierced by a less-than-adequate road, bolstered in the dankest stretches by beds of cedar logs. The Dutch had attempted to tame this wild place by draining many acres and growing salt hay suitable for their grazing livestock. But no man ever reigned here. From the rocky promontory, another kind of beast ruled, and had done so centuries before the Dutch even dared. This was the domain of the common black snake— villain in many a tale and harbinger of all sorts of misfortune.

Vincent had never passed this way before; however, when he was a mere boy with wonder swimming in his eyes, his father told him tales of hapless Dutchmen, African runaways, and Irish brigands who ventured too close to the rocks that made Snake Hill. Every man who did so met with a horrible end. Vincent was older now and not much afraid of the devil's minions. He was more afraid of delays. With his back against the invitingly warm sun, he scanned the bland horizon and saw nothing worthy of scaring him. He was about to embark on what he thought would be the last leg of the out-going part of his journey—delivering the brandy to Judge Cooper and handing over Captain Elsworth's letter to Sheriff Stiles. The only thing he looked forward to, after fulfilling his obligations, was starting back to Little Abia. He wondered what she would think of him if she could see him now. His clothes were dry, but stained and soiled. Worse was the burnt smell on them from last night's near-tragic fire. However, things could have turned out much worse. He could have been injured like Ike Higgins, even killed in the stable barn blaze. Vincent closed his eyes for a moment, then shook his head furiously to chase away such dark contemplations.

Vincent should have waited to stop at New Bridge where the Hackensack River narrowed, but that crossing point was miles away and he and his team had gotten off to a late start anyway. Mister Barnet's flying machine had left Powles Hook at dawn and was well on its way to Morris Town before Vincent's team was ready to depart. Poor Ike was the reason for the delay. Vincent wanted to stop now to check on the stubborn Irishman—make sure he was taking in adequate drink and not disturbing his bandages. The rousted Doctor back at Powles Hook had not been pleased with Ike's refusal to be left behind in order to mend properly. It was finally decided to let Ike ride on fresh straw in the back of the near-empty waggon until he was fit to ride his Mercury, which was again tethered behind the waggon. He had promised to drink from a jug of watered-down spirits concocted by the Doctor, after arguing long and loud for something straight and strong. The medicinal brew was laced with foul-smelling wormwood. Ike refused to take such stuff on his own. He declared that he preferred to endure the flare of pain from his burns every time he moved, rather than drink that devil's rot. He cursed everyone who came close to him, until the pain became unbearable and he allowed a brave soul to put the jug to his lips. In a lucid moment, which followed the first administration from the detested jug, Ike did swear not to tamper with the wraps over his wounds. He promised to keep them clean for a week. Everyone who knew Ike Higgins was sure such an oath would be broken in a day. However, Vincent meant to ensure that the good Doctor's orders were kept and Ike held to his word.

All such bickering and haggling destroyed any chance of Vincent's team following Burnet at dawn. They would be lucky to reach Morris Town before dark.

Vincent commanded Cut to halt. The German reined in the bay Shires. The leader dismounted and climbed into the waggon. Cut did not bother asking why they had stopped. He knew the reason and he did not care. He freed his rifle from its pouch, slipped down from his perch, and strolled to the side of the road to relieve himself behind a lone white cedar. He then scanned the meadow marsh for worthy prey and walked away.

Ike appeared to be sleeping. Both eyes were shut and his limbs were limp and crossed like a corpse readied for burial. But he was breathing through his mouth, loud and strong in his usual rumbly way. His ever-questing tongue—a tiny sentinel, alert for a taste of good brew—was peering out of the battered side of his mouth. However, such a prospect was not to be found in Bergen Meadows.

Vincent knelt close to his indisposed flanker. The iron reek of blood still emanated from Ike's latest wounds. He inspected the bandage on Ike's hand. He found it firm and relatively clean. There was minimal seepage and stain. Next, he examined the bound, shoeless foot, which had lost a precious prize in the stable barn fire. The Irishman had not tampered with the bandage there. Satisfied with the condition of the wrappings, Vincent reached for the small medicinal jug which had not been moved from Ike's side since the first dose was administered in front of Verdine Elsworth's establishment about two hours ago. At that time, Ike spit out most of the foul liquid, letting it dribble down his tatter of cloak, borrowed from Vincent, and the worn shirt Kersey had found for him to wear. Ike was such a sorry sight, and so were the remnants of the clothes that had given him such pride. However, old Ike still had a stalwart heart beating strong and lungs rattling like forge bellows. Vincent meant to restore Ike to a semblance of usefulness.

John Wetherill's son pinched Ike's nose. A pair of rheumy eyes under singed brows flickered, then opened wide in amazement. Ike noticed it was Vincent disturbing his reverie. He struggled to get to a sitting position. He got as far as propping himself up at the elbows. Vincent placed a firm hand at Ike's back and pushed him the rest of the way.

"I needs a strong drink, Mister Wetherill," declared Ike. "I needs one bad."

"Got one poured for you in my own cup," answered Vincent, as he reached for the wooden vessel with his free hand.

Ike spotted the sinister jug next to where the cup had rested. He raised the bandaged hand in protest. "Nah," he exclaimed, "I ain't botherin' with cat piss, no way . . ."

"You took it once," said Vincent, as he brought the half-filled cup to Ike's lips. "You can do it again."

Ike made a face which would have scared any innocent child. "I spit out the Doctor's brew once'd, 'n I'll do it all over."

"No you won't, not this time," insisted Vincent, as he pressed the rim of the cup against Ike's swollen lower lip. "You are useless to me in this state. If you don't do as the Doctor and Captain Elsworth told you, I shall allow Cut to haul your carcass up on Snake Hill and leave you there with only this jug."

"You wouldn't be so cruel to the likes o' me, now would you, Mister Wetherill? Least you could do is leave me with a barrel o' eight-year."

"I feel there's trouble ahead, Ike. You're no good to anyone as you are. At our going, I thought you'd come 'round and cooperate, but you've gotten worse than stubborn. If you won't obey me, then I have no choice but to leave you behind. The Doctor promised that his brew will trick you into feeling fit in a full day's time . . . so you can't refuse it . . . can't just stare at it . . . can't spit it out. You've got to down it in a swallow, or your arse shall be perched on yonder hill."

"None o' this was me fault," moaned Ike. "Why am I bein' punished fer what two roysters did to the likes o' me? Me 'n me partner beat 'em fair in a game o' five 'n forty . . . they claimed I cheated 'em with a jack on a double bid . . . which'd I swear on me mother's stone, I did not do . . . then they chase after me hide with a pan o' coals from the Captain's warmin' kitchen after they followed me there. I was fixin' to pay fer me own warm bath in the company room . . . a clean soak I never got."

"What a pity," interrupted Vincent, still holding the medicinal cup close to Ike's face. "Cut was rewarded with such a bath after he rescued you from the fire. I took one in Captain Elsworth's own tub this morn before we carried you to the waggon. I also used the Captain's shaving blade. Too bad you lost out on all such fun."

Ike glared at the spot of plaster which Vincent had applied to a shaving cut on his chin. "I've had neither bath nor shave . . . no reward fer scarin' off them two scoundrels which'd chased me from kitchen to barn. They beat me severe . . . tied me up . . . were fixin' to burn me fingers off, but I kicked 'em with both me English shoes 'n Gaelic feets . . . knocked 'em both down 'n sent the pan o' coals flyin'. When they spied the flames at the hay, they ran like the cowards they is . . . left me to die 'long with the steeds. Now I'm left bruised 'n burned . . . stink like a polecat . . . hairs on me head 'n cheeks all stiff 'n singed . . . even Good Mary wouldn't know me."

"If you drink this brew, she will," urged Vincent, who had decided to let Ike talk himself out to the point of exhaustion. With Cut's help, he would then force the liquid down Ike's throat. "This is your chance to prove you want to continue on the journey. Take this cup before Cut returns. The sun is growing strong. The black snakes will soon be abandoning their lairs to bask in the noon light. Cut wants to drag you to them . . ."

"You wouldn't dare permit 'im, Mister Wetherill," whispered Ike in disbelief. "Yer father wouldn't 'low it neither."

"He's not with us, is he? However, I'm glad you conjured up his name. Since you refuse to take what you must to get fit to ride with us, you can't work off the debt you owe my father. So, of what use are you to me or John Wetherill?"

Ike attempted to use the bandaged hand to push the awful cup away from his face, but he only swiped air when Vincent raised the vessel over his head. Ike's arm fell uselessly to his side. He stared at the appendage for a moment, gathering his thoughts and hoping to somehow restore his strength.

"I recall what's been told me by those two roysters from Morris Town, where we be headin' . . . their news is worth more to ye 'n yer father—more 'n the purse they stole from me afore they set 'bout to burn me nimbles off. You 'n Cut leave me on that there hill, 'n I never say what's been learned 'n you'll be up 'gainst somethin' worse 'n snakes."

Vincent possessed the patience to play Ike's game. He knew he would defeat the Irishman after all was said and done. The medicine would be administered properly. Ike was already weary and starting to slouch from sitting up too long. Furthermore, Ike just might have learned something from the two bastards from Morris Town. What he learned might be relevant to making sense of the mayhem occurring there. It was worth a listen.

"Go on," said Vincent. "Tell me something new you did not already pass on to Elsworth and Jarlman."

"Did Mister Jarlman find 'em 'n me winnin's yet?"

"Not up to our leaving, when you were asleep in the waggon. We left him searching with a band of local volunteers. Nary a sign of those two. Seems they disappeared, as did our Lord Corn. I was told that Jarlman was intending to post broadsides in public places. Those two rogues can't get very far. Neither of them crossed the Hudson. Neither plied the causeway. The watchers have not spotted them at the crossing places. I guess we will discover their fate when Jarlmen is free to find us in Morris Town."

"Them two left me fer dead without a pence in me pocket fer to place on me eye at burial time . . . even took the brass spoon I found at Skinner's place. Hope those two drowns in the marsh . . ."

"So tell me what of import you learned from those two," asked a curious Vincent, "then I'll consider what to do with you."

"Just a sip from the eight-year, promised to the Judge, 'n I'll tell all I know."

"Ike, you know the rundlets of brandy under Cut's bench are a gift to Judge Cooper. They are not to be tampered with. What would my father say to your request?"

"He ain't here," said Ike with a quivering smile. "What's a missin' sip or two to a man who's son is next on a murderer's list? The Judge has much worse to worry 'bout than a squib of good apple brandy."

"Tell me what you know," said Vincent with mounting impatience souring his usually calm voice. "After you drink down a fair measure of the Doctor's brew, I'll give you a tot of rum from my private store."

"Best do it afore Cut returns," warned Ike with anticipatory eyes.

"Not till you share your news."

"Well, it ain't much worth to the likes o' me, but it could be so to ye, Mister Wetherill." Ike cleared his throat and spat in the straw beyond his bandaged foot. "This pair, fresh from Morris Town, was impartin' fanciful tales while at the business o' cards, 'n losin' what they started with. They was tellin' all they know'd 'bout the latest slayin' up there . . . all 'bout the buck fiddler 'n the wench Sheriff Jonathan Stiles is chasin' after . . ."

"I heard all that from Ansel Jarlman," interjected Vincent. "He told me and Captain Elsworth all about it just before the fire. Jarlman got his information from a stage driver down from Morris Town."

"I must of got the same 'n more from the pair who later sought to do me in."

"So tell me the more and skip the same," insisted Vincent. "Let's get this done."

Ike gave a nod and delivered his news: "A sign, shaped as a sword was carved on the boy's back 'cordin' to both . . . they seen the body when it was brought in, 'n afore it was declared 'n put in the cold cellar at Arnold's Tavern . . . not just any sword, mind ye, but one they claimed held a large ring at its hilt . . . like the ones I seen tattooed on the hands of the pig irons which'd beat me at Rattoon's."

"Like the one I saw carved on the window shutter at the gaol in Perth Amboy," mused Vincent. "Did you speak of your knowledge of the sword?"

"Nary a word," boasted Ike. "I kept busy beatin' 'em with each card dealt . . . they was talkin' 'n I was winnin'."

"Anything else?"

"They said Sheriff Stiles was wrong in thinkin' some runaway wench kilt the buck fiddler . . . both never challenged 'im . . . called him a muddlehead 'n worse, but not to his face . . . they boasted to me 'n me partner at cards o' knowin' somethin' 'bout the sword 'n the men behind it. They speculated on this 'n that, but never told all o' it, far as I recollect."

"Tell me what you can remember, Ike."

"Seems this pair, intendin' harm to me last night, ran into a gang o' these tattooed rascals a few months ago . . . June to be exact . . . while on a hunt for conies up in the minin' hills way north o' Morris Town. Might o' been well past Rockaway or thereabouts . . . can't remember fer sure where they said . . . anyway, this here gang o' eight tattooed rascals claimed they was a newly formed hunt club . . . claimed to be at huntin' too . . . but they lugged no carcass nor hide . . . most o' 'em was on the far side o' drunk, which'd I longs to be . . . 'n one was carvin' a such 'n same sword on the stump o' a large, felled tree."

"Interesting stuff," encouraged Vincent. "Tell me more."

"What started friendly, with an offer to share a jug, soon turned sour with a threat to carve a like image o' that same sword on their backs if they did not hand over their string o' conies, their firin' pieces, their huntin' caps 'n shirts, 'n their handsome boots. They was surrounded by these mean luggers—each sportin' a primed musket, pistol, or blade—so they had no choice but to comply. Stripped they was 'n left to find their way back to Rockaway, which'd they did."

"Did this pair report the crime?"

"To none . . . they was shamed by the incident. Seems, at the time, they was not on the Sheriff's good side . . . so they claimed some Delaware squaws stole their garments 'n game."

"I suppose these nymphs were armed with muskets and pistols also?"

"None such, as I was told," admitted Ike, who took Vincent's question as a serious one. "This pair claimed to be takin' a swim in the river when the squaws appeared 'long the bank. They took to pointin' 'n laughin' at the pale-arsed pair, then ran off with certain possessions."

"But these dusky maidens were kind enough to leave behind trousers?"

"'Cordin' to the source at such a tale."

"Don't you find the gamblers' entire account a bit far-fetched?"

"Half o' it, yes, Mister Wetherill, 'cause they admitted to makin' up the butt end o' it . . . yet, the first half rings true as a church bell, if ye match it with what we know."

"So these two scoundrels, who almost did you in, contend that the Sheriff should be looking for a gang of mountain boys, pretending to be members of some secret hunting club, who enjoy carving swords on stumps or flesh?"

"I'm thinkin' the same," insisted Ike. "The Sheriff's wastin' his time trackin' down a runaway wench. From what I'm hearin' 'bout Stiles, he's stubborn as a stump . . . 'n he's goin' to keep his nose to the Afric's trail . . ."

"This bodes well for us, Ike."

"How so, Mister Wetherill?"

"While the Sheriff is about his business, we shall be about ours. Maybe our paths will not cross while we are attempting to solve the same crimes."

Ike attempted a smile, but it hurt too much to complete the task. He spoke in the middle of his grin: "So this means ye plan to keep me on?"

Vincent was about to give his answer, when he spotted Cutlope Hancock approaching. The hunter was empty-handed and appeared none too happy. When he reached the waggon, Cut addressed his boss in a somber tone: "Have you decided the fate of this useless bog lander, Mister Wetherill?"

"I surely have, Cut. Soon as Ike complies and takes his medicine, we're off to crossing the Hackensack and Passaic streams, then it's on to Horseneck."

"What if this calf-lolly don't take his gulps?"

"Then we stick to the plan you suggested before we stopped. We leave him behind on Snake Hill, then we go on our way."

"I like my plan whether he takes his medicine or he don't, Mister Wetherill. We left Lord Corn behind with no fuss nor feathers . . . we can do the same for our bad luck boy."

"Ye ain't leavin' me arse behind!" erupted Ike with all the strength he could muster. He used both hands to grab the cup from his boss. He drained it in two magnificent swallows. He smacked his lips loudly. "Best o' all brew I've tasted in a year. A prayer and praise to the finest damn Doctor at Powles Hook!"

South of the serpentine arch of the meandering Passaic River, and west of Aquakinunk, the landscape became a parade of handsome hills and valleys, forests of fading green, with hints of seasonal gold, red, and brown here and there, bordered farm fields which splayed out in irregular patterns that spoke of man's meager victories against great odds. The land was less yielding here, heralding greater challenges which lay to the west. The eventuality of mountains loomed far to the north and west—their vague, brooding shapes masked by a lingering haze under an intermittent sun. Alabaster clouds were rolling in from the lands beyond the mountains. They sought to replace the storm clouds of the previous day. It was a good time for tracking beasts and hunting game, but Cutlope Hancock had given up on that idea. He was back to concentrating on a rutty, narrow road leading to Horseneck and a second crossing north of the source of the Passaic River. He was back to following orders.

Vincent Wetherill led the way. His horse trotted proudly ahead of the steady-paced bay Shires. The air was crisp and cool—a beautiful and fair day for journeying on a peaceful road, which brought Vincent's team into and out of the sleepy village of Horseneck without incident. All he and his two men caught were a few stares from residents noted for being suspicious of outsiders. This was not a friendly place. Vincent knew of its reputation and expected a rude welcome. This was where the land riots started several years ago between the illiterate settlers, flaunting their Indian deeds, and the well-educated proprietors, insisting from a safe distance away that the King's Law was on their side. It was, and trouble started when the King's agents threatened action. Things were peaceful now, thanks to the legislative efforts of colonial leaders such as John Wetherill. However, bitter memories remained like smoldering embers, ready to ignite again at the slightest excuse. The authorities were not trusted here. They might as well have been strangers too.

A bit more than a mile outside of Horseneck, Vincent and his team reached the stout bridge across the rapid, north-flowing length of the Passaic River. This stream was swollen to its banks by the latest rainstorm, but the sturdy bridge was high-arched and, though narrow, accommodating. The horses and waggon had no trouble crossing to the other side. On a rise above the riverbank on the Book Town side, a party of three mounted men and a rather sullen-looking waggoner were waiting to greet all who plied the bridge.

"Halt right there!" came the sharp command from a short, red-faced fellow who was attempting to sit as tall as he could on the back of a handsome, white-socked sorrel. The man was dressed as fine as his horse looked. He wore a forrest green saggathy coat over a scarlet vest. A black neckcloth hung loose and long under his clean-shaven chin. His cheeks were pitted with pox scars, but adequately masked by a powder which speckled his face. His dark brown eyes smoldered with suspicion. His thin lips neither leaned towards a smile nor a frown. It was obvious he wanted to give the impression that he was in charge.

Cut did not care one way or the other about following orders. He clucked to the Shires and snapped the reins until he had the waggon turned to the left and had found the shade of a tall oak to his liking. Only then did he pull the reins taut. The waggon came to a halt. The quarter horse strained at its tether and showed interest in going down to the riverbank. Cut decided to ignore the horse as well as the officious man. He was none to happy with the delay.

The rest of the team was equally reticent to obey the well-dressed man in charge. From a sitting position inside the waggon, Ike peered over the sideboard for a second, then slumped to his usual sleeping position on the bed of hay. He felt it was as good a time as any to offer the pretense of a snooze. Vincent, on the other hand, was not as quick as Ike in reacting to the rude welcomer's command. He took his time coaxing his mount forward rather than stopping. He did so until the two men in faded blue duffel coats, who accompanied the man in charge, raised muskets and pointed them at Vincent's heart. In the same instant, the man in charge reached for his sword. Cut slid his gloved hand along the seat board until he found the sealskin case that held his precious hunting rifle. He knew trouble when he smelled it—the odor of impending death hung in the air.

"Far enough, young man!" barked the welcomer. "Instruct your driver to grip his reins with both hands—up above his knees in open sight where my constables can see them. There will be no bloodshed here, long as you and your driver abide by my rules and the King's Law."

Vincent gave a quick glance and nod to Cut. He noticed the German already had both hands on the taut reins. He turned his attention back to the man in charge.

"I assume you are the King's Law 'round here?"

"In the County of Morris, yes," said the short, gruff man. "I intend to keep it that way for a term or two. My name is Jonathan Stiles and I am the Sheriff in these parts. Two constables and a waggoner, on loan from Mister Morrell, accompany me on this assignment. I trust things will go smoothly. I will commence asking the questions. You and your men will commence providing honest answers."

"No trouble from me or my men, Sheriff Stiles."

The Sheriff called back to the glum man in Morrell's waggon, "Ever seen these men before?"

"Can't say I have," replied the waggoner in a raspy voice.

The Sheriff returned his attention to Vincent. "Well then, you do not appear to be the three men we are looking for, so who might you be?"

"I am Vincent Wetherill, son of Assemblyman John Wetherill of Middlesex County. We have come this far bearing a gift of apple brandy for Judge Daniel Cooper of Long Hill—a gift from my father to his favorite in-law."

"Nothing more?" asked the Sheriff with a skeptical frown. "I was informed by Mister Burnet, who recently returned from the Hook with his flying machine 'bout noon, that you'd more than likely be crossing the Passaic with a particular fellow I wish to question about an unsavory crime committed 'round the time of the hanging."

"That would be Ansel Jarlman, trusted agent of Verdine Elsworth at Powles Hook," responded Vincent quickly.

"None of that racetrack crowd, including Mister Elsworth, is to be trusted," declared Stiles adamantly. "Why is this Jarlman fellow not riding with you? Don't tell me he is the pitiful looking creature who was peeking o'er the boards of your waggon just a moment ago?"

The Sheriff motioned to one of his constables to advance to the waggon and inspect its contents. The duffel coat on the Sheriff's right spurred his horse forward, approached the side of the visitor's waggon in quick time, and pointed his musket at the pitiful fellow contained therein. Ike tried very hard to continue pretending to be asleep. The Constable used his weapon to give Ike a hard prod. The Irishman groaned, rolled over, and lay face down.

"Let my flanker be," insisted Vincent. "He was burned in a barn fire at the Hook and is recovering from his wounds. Leave him be. He is not the man you are looking for."

The Sheriff growled, then ordered his blue-coated underling to move around to the rear of the waggon and be alert for anyone else approaching the bridge. Stiles then guided his horse forward. His other duffel coat followed like a shadow. Nearby, his waggoner remained in the dark shade of a stout oak tree which guarded a corner of a burying yard.

Stiles stopped a sword's length from young Wetherill and eyed him warily. "Where is this Mister Jarlman I need to interrogate?"

"He was slated to accompany us and act as our guide," admitted Vincent, "but Captain Elsworth changed his mind and ordered his agent to hunt for the Morris Town gamblers responsible for the stable fire and the botched attempt on my man's life. By all accounts, that pair is still hiding somewhere on the Hook."

"The two mamzers you speak of are not from my county . . . they're vagabonds . . . just passing through . . . from the north, from what I gather . . . from the border mountains 'tween Jersey and York . . . skilled at stealing miners blind . . . till things got too hot . . . then they drift down to here to try their luck in Morris Town. Caught cheating at the Haynes place . . . caught up with 'em and ordered 'em to board the next stage waggon out. Good to hear they ended up at the Hook . . . an ideal place for the likes of 'em . . . hope they stay there."

"They'll be found," affirmed Vincent with conviction. "Captain Elsworth will administer a full and fair measure of punishment on their hides."

"Full, I have no doubt," mused Stiles, "but I have my doubts about fair."

"I have been assured by the Captain that Mister Jarlman will be headed this way once the gamblers are caught." Vincent fumbled in his pouch and extracted the missive intended for the Sheriff. He handed it to Stiles. "This letter from Captain Elsworth explains the purpose for his agent's visit at the time of the hanging and his whereabouts after that."

The Sheriff did not bother to break the seal on Elsworth's letter. He had no intention of reading it now or later. He stuffed it into his coat pocket. "I still need to question this Jarlman fellow, sooner the better. I consider him a possible suspect in the murder of Jack Redmon . . ."

"But not a suspect in the murder of the Doctor's slave?" inserted Vincent.

"How did you know about the recent buck fiddler's death?" hissed Stiles through clenched teeth framed by a suddenly reddening face.

"According to Mister Jarlman, your Dan Burnet is quite a talker, if the brew is flowing. Most folks at the Hook know about both murders, thanks to Burnet's yapping and the boastings of the two gamblers. Folks down there are now thinking the two gamblers had a hand in the slayings."

"Not a chance," protested Stiles. "Those two arrived in town together after the first slaying. They were seen by many, gambling at the Haynes place, the night of the second murder. We've a prime suspect for the fresher killing, and she may be responsible for the first. However, this is not to say Mister Jarlman is in the clear. I still need to question him. I plan to do a thorough job of that."

"As I've said, Elsworth's agent will find us in a day or two. Jarlman has nothing to hide. He will be glad to answer any questions you have for him."

"We'll see about that," groused Stiles.

"How goes the search for your prime suspect?" asked Vincent innocently.

"None of your damn business," scolded Stiles. "I have many a brave and loyal lad out searching for the pregnant bitch right now . . . won't be long . . . I've even employed the elder Jacob Ford's best hounds—the ones used by the Sons of Dawn hunting club . . . won't be long . . ."

"I wish you luck in finding your suspect," offered Vincent in a calm voice. "Now please allow us to pass and be on our way. We've got to get to Long Hill before dark . . ."

"Not so easy to let you pass so soon in these troubled times," said the Sheriff, as he glanced past young Wetherill and studied Cut. "I feel I can trust the likes of you in my county, but I am not so sure I can trust your traveling companions. I need to question your waggoner."

"Cutlope Hancock is a neighbor of mine and a stellar member of our hunting club back home. He comes from humble, law abiding German stock—farmers for generations . . ."

"You don't say?" asked Stiles with derision swimming in his voice. "I am sure you are itching to tell me that your man is a better shot than any member of the elder Ford's hunting club . . . even better than Lord Stirling himself?

"Perhaps," said Vincent cautiously.

"Why of course!" exclaimed the Sheriff. "I immediately took

your man for a refined gentleman of noble lineage the first time I laid eyes on him. I bet he is of royalty . . . if we trace far back enough. How about the other fellow—your flanker snoozing in the waggon? I bet he is royalty also . . ."

Vincent hesitated and cast his eyes to the side.

The Sheriff caught the weak glance and smiled. "So the wounded one may have questionable blood coursing through his veins . . . a fugitive perhaps . . . a bastard rogue whom authorities are looking for . . ."

"Nothing of the kind, Sheriff. Ichabod Higgins is a true Irishman—fond of drink and guilty of enjoying a brawl now and then, nothing more. Old Ike is employed as an alongshore man down at Radford's Landing. He is working off a debt to my father by accompanying me . . ."

"Hmpf," said Stiles in a disbelieving tone. "We must query your pair of cracked groats, then I may consider letting you pass."

The Sheriff signalled his waggoner to abandon the shade and draw his vehicle close to the Wetherill waggon. He and the second Constable joined the other law man at the sideboard which shielded Ike. They peered in, taking inventory of the Irishman's bandages and his unprotected cuts and bruises. Vincent positioned himself on the opposite side of the waggon and studied what was left of Ike. His man was still pretending to be asleep.

"This Higgins boy appears dead," opined Stiles sarcasticly. "He already possesses the stink of death . . . there be penalties to pay for transporting a corpse into my county, Mister Wetherill . . . you must know of such . . ."

Before Vincent could respond, Ike rolled over and lifted his head slightly. He squinted at the Sheriff with his one good eye. "Ain't dead yet . . . jus' comin' out a' me snooze 'n happy to be welcome here." Ike put his head back down on the straw and sighed loudly, "Jus' happy to survive such a rumbly trip with nary a proper drink . . ."

"You'll be happy if I don't throw you in Mister Morrell's waggon and cart you to gaol for a few dry days," said the Sheriff in his best voice of authority. "I've a few questions for you and the same for the cabbage-head waggoner, which will determine the transportation for the rest of your journey."

"Fine with the likes o' me," said Ike. "Ask away . . . any question, I'll answer. How 'bout ye, Cut?"

"Yup," was all Cut bothered to say.

"Good then," continued Stiles in his same stern voice. "Let's get on with this. May I assume no man here ever spent a day in gaol, save for my own waggoner."

All eyes, except for Cut's, turned to stare at the odd fellow holding the reins of the other waggon. Vincent saw that the man was bruised and battered around the eyes. His lower lip was swollen. This one had obviously been set upon recently. His eyes were darting here and there in an attempt to avoid the stares directed at him. He surely did not want to be the object of everybody's attention. Vincent felt sorry for this chap and wondered how and why he had fallen into the Sheriff's company.

"Tom Ward, here, saw the error of his ways," said the Sheriff proudly. "He turned himself into an upstanding citizen. He has good reason to volunteer his services to me . . . looking forward to hauling suspects and fugitives back to gaol . . . especially any of the rowdy boys who waylaid him on one of my better roads the other night."

The Sheriff did not bother with supplying details of the waggoner's misadventure, nor did he give any reason for drawing attention to this Ward fellow in the first place. Vincent dared not ask.

"What have you to tell me of your past, gentlemen?" asked the Sheriff finally.

Vincent spoke first in order to deflect attention from his men. "I descend from men of honor—a well-respected Assemblyman and a Captain in the last war. The latter ventured forth from the troubled Piscataqua settlement in Hampshire long ago. Far as I've been told, the bloodline before Captain Tom flourished in Massachusetts . . . and before that, there were the English Wetherills whose progenitor was the honorable Gyles Wetherill, Mayor of Stockton on Tees in old Durham . . . and further back . . ."

"Stop!" commanded Sheriff Stiles. "Fine stuff and most entertaining, Mister Wetherill, but unnecessary. I do not need to hear about you and your ancestors. The reputations of you and your father are unimpeachable. Be still. Allow me to hear from the company you keep."

"Tell the Sheriff, Cut," ordered Vincent.

"Nothing worth the telling," mumbled Cut. He was in no mood to play the Sheriff's lineage game.

"Ever in gaol?" asked Stiles.

"Nein."

"What of your ancestors?"

"Fishers 'n farmers all the way back."

"No debtors, no drunks?"

"Nein."

"You'll swear to it, then?"

"I'll swear t' nothin', if nothin' ain't there."

"Not even to keeping a mistress now and then?"

Ike interrupted the Sheriff's line of questioning before Cut had a chance to respond. "The German ain't like me, kind sir. 'Tis me who's spent time in gaol, bein' blamed fer slayin' a man, then let go with but a brand on me bandaged hand." Ike held up the hand which held the old branding scar. "'Tis me accused o' brawlin' in public 'n cheatin' at cards, but never hauled in fer such slights. 'Tis me which keeps a mistress down at Rattoon's 'n she sure makes me proud."

"So I can presume you descend from a long line of bandits and rogues?" interjected Stiles.

"Contrary to such is me," protested Ike as he struggled to a sitting position and aimed his one good eye at the Sheriff. "Yer lookin' at royalty pure as can be."

The Sheriff and both constables laughed heartily at Ike's contention. Vincent managed a tight smile. Both waggoners remained silent and solemn.

"Explain yourself, Mister Higgins," urged the Sheriff with an amused look on his face.

"I've more royal blood in me veins 'n any o' ye starin' at what's left o' me bones . . . 'tis a fact worth tellin' 'bout the O'Higgins clan as a branch o' the O'Neill tree. I'm speakin' 'bout a certain grandson who's none other 'n the great Niall o' Nine Hostages, fourth King o' dear Ireland . . . the one who started the Higgins line with the help o' fierce Vikin's . . . 'n the Barons o' Ballynary which'd ensued . . ."

"Enough, proud noble of Eire!" shouted the Sheriff over the resumed laughter of his men. "We are honored to have such refined blood pay a visit to our humble, backwoods county. May your stay here be a peaceful and rewarding one."

Vincent kept a smile in place and stared at his flanker with awe and disbelief. He did not know how much Ike had made up and how much was truth. Vincent was proud of him. The Irishman had succeeded in deflecting attention from Cut's improprieties and entertaining the law men of Morris County with his account of a suspect lineage.

"By what title shall we address thee, kind noble?" asked Stiles in mocking fashion.

"Lord Ike, Baron o' Radford's Landin', suits the likes o' me fine."

"Ah, a worthy rival to our Lord Stirling?"

"Never met the man, but I hear tell his wealth near matches mine."

Laughter again exploded from the three enforcers of the law in Morris County. Even Vincent had to chuckle at the haughtiness of his flanker. Ike had succeeded in changing the Sheriff's mood and avoiding a dour confrontation.

"I am going to let you and your team pass, Mister Wetherill," said Sheriff Stiles with finality. "However, make sure your waggoner and your flanker stay out of trouble and out of my way. I've a murderer to find as well as the usual assortment of horse thieves, counterfeiters, runaways, and sly-boot tricksters. There's no room on my plate for a Middlesex sod skipper and a mischievous tavern baron."

"No trouble will you find with us," promised Vincent. "We are pledged to deliver the brandy to Judge Cooper and wait for our waggon to be filled with barrels of iron water from Schooley's Mountain. Then we shall be an our way."

"What are you intending to use that foul-tasting iron water for?" asked the Sheriff.

"My father's idea," responded Vincent. "His purpose has to do with a tonic prescribed by a local doctor. My father is not well. The iron water mixed with certain ingredients will help to restore his health."

"Does John Wetherill need a full waggon of such stuff?"

"He intends to produce his own tonic—one that tastes favorable—and sell it at reasonable price."

"Your father will need the ingredient of luck," advised Stiles, "and lots of it. I wish him well in health and business. We're going to need more of his kind to face the troubles which lie ahead."

"I will pass your kind words along in my next letter to him."

"Now be on your way, Mister Wetherill. Enjoy your stay in my county. Perhaps before you leave, my men will have caught the murdering negress, and you can spread the news of our ending this killing spree."

Vincent knew better, but he kept his thoughts to himself. "Fair luck in finding your killer."

With that, the young Wetherill signalled to Cut to stir the Shires into pressing forward on the narrow road through Book Town. The waggon pulled away at a brisk pace. Ike remained in a sitting position, firmly planted on a throne of straw in his noble coach. With his good hand on the sideboard, he steadied himself. With the bandaged hand, he waved to the glum waggoner who had volunteered his services to Sheriff Stiles. The man simply stared at the Irishman as he passed. There was something sinister in his gaze—a look Vincent did not like, though he had no understanding of its import. Tom Ward looked as Irish as the man he was staring at . . . almost as battered looking . . . almost as filthy—from his greasy black cap down to his baggy, patched trousers. Perhaps this character was merely jealous of the attention old Ike had garnered from the overbearing Sheriff Stiles . . . or was it something else?

10

ESCORTS FOR A PRINCESS

· ·

—at a Quaker farm near Mine Hill,
Saturday, September 25, 1773

Rachel Hagers climbed up the pyramid of hay bales directly under the cupola atop the Sharp's cow barn where she hid. She and Amanda, one of the Sharp girls who lived here, had piled the bales just so, during the first full day of her clandestine visit. Rachel stood on the highest bale. She peered out through the narrow vent slats of the cupola. Warm, sweet air was escaping here and filling her nostrils with the heavy aromas wafting up from the ground floor. Rachel felt dizzy. She pressed five fingers in a tight grip against the base wood of the cupola. From this position, she took in the marvelously placid scene of shimmering farm fields, dark forested hills, and darker low mountains to the west. There was ample evidence of a hot, dry summer—fields were gold and brown . . . wind breaks of bushes, thickets, and cedars had failed to close ranks, but still stood defiantly green . . . stands of stately trees sported leaves already turning early seasonal hues . . . the iron mountains beyond seemed to be smoldering as the sun made its descent to rendezvous with the earth at dusk. The year was preparing to don its subtle shades of death. Along with the soft golden glow were the deeper, lengthening shadows striping a beautiful land. Winter and lost opportunities seemed not so far away.

The runaway slave turned slowly in a tight circle, being cautious and careful not to lose her balance. Rachel used both hands now to hold on to the criss-cross of beams supporting the cupola. She took in all the sights visible around the humble farm of the Sharp family. She spotted Elder Sharp coaxing a horse and cart over a small stream bridged by stout logs. Two of his sons, sporting broad-brim hats same as their father sat on a pile of apples in the back of the cart. They appeared to be heading back to their house to wait for the rest of the males in the large family to come in for their early supper. Off to the east far beyond a sweet water creek, the Elder Sharp's two eldest sons were bringing in the cows. Rachel studied the dust cloud they were kicking up and gauged that the livestock would not be in the barn any time soon. She still had plenty of time to get ready.

Rachel hopped down the bales like a playful child. The rat-catcher eagerly awaited her return—wagging its tail furiously and standing on its hind legs until she reached down to pet its head. She ordered the coarse-haired dog to go sit by the hay loft aperture and warn her of anyone's approach. The rat-catcher obeyed and Rachel returned to her bed of straw. Her fear of being on the run and having to hide alone in strange places had subsided, thanks to the warm hospitality of the Sharp Quakers and the constant companionship of Tom Ward's dog. When the time came to leave this place, it would not be so easy to do. She felt safe here. However, staying was not an option.

Rachel removed everything from her tattered carry sack and took inventory of what she had brought with her when Tom Ward delivered her to the Sharp's farm on the outskirts of Mine Hill. That frightening, but uneventful, waggon ride during the night seemed so long ago. Time had slowed to a worm's crawl since being so graciously welcomed by early-to-rise Quakers, on Thursday, September twenty-third. Now it was late Saturday, almost dusk, and still no sign or mention of Mingo Tim; yet, Rachel knew her man would come for her . . . just as he had promised and according to good Tom Ward. Furthermore, Master Morrell's foreman said her dear Mingo would have to walk the entire distance north from Morris Town, using no main roads and hiding during daylight hours. It might take him several days. Rachel sighed, folded once more the scarves and petticoats she had stolen from her master, and placed them in a large, quilted bag Amanda had given her on the second day of her stay. She would have to be more patient. Her man would come . . . perhaps this night would be the night. Friday's rains had passed. This night would be clear and starry and promising . . . a waxing half moon would rise to guide all wanderers . . . Mingo Tim would be one of them.

The rat catcher, aroused suddenly by a sound Rachel did not hear, stood at the lip of the hayloft aperture, where a stout wooden ladder led down to the earthen floor below. The dog's ears were erect and its nose was twitching in anticipation of something, or someone, stirring below. It allowed a throaty growl, but not a bark. Rachel remembered that it was close to the dinner hour for the Sharp family. The rat-catcher must have sensed that feeding time was imminent. Its tail began wagging furiously, again. Drool was spilling from its grinning mouth. Now, there was none of the usual defensive growling which always signalled the approach of a stranger. Someone familiar was coming. Rachel was glad to have nothing to fear with the ever-alert rat-catcher at her side in the loft of the Sharp's cow barn. Such a loyal guardian was Tom Ward's dog—a gift from a humble man and a godsend at such a crucial time. Elder Sharp had thought it best for Rachel and the dog to be hidden in the barn instead of the house. His large family had many visitors—mostly Friends of the faith, always dropping by to be neighborly and share concerns over the current matters of their society. Since these Quakers had no slaves, the hiding of a negress on Quaker property would have whipped the gossipers into a frenzy. Thus, Rachel and the rat-catcher were led to the cow barn and up the sturdy ladder to the loft soon after Tom Ward said his farewells and wished Rachel the best. Since then, Rachel was very careful in choosing when to exit the barn to relieve herself and get exercise along with the dog. When she did so, Rachel adhered to instructions never to leave the barn for very long and to wait until dark if at all possible.

Rachel quickly finished stuffing items in the quilted bag. She tied it at its neck and put it aside. She scooped up the half-empty bowl of suppawn pudding and the drained noggin which once held sweet cider. She dropped them into a small wooden box, which Amanda, the oldest daughter in the Sharp family, left near the hayloft ladder at breakfast time. Rachel had spent most of the day worrying—worrying about her man's well-being. She had lost her appetite. At least she was drinking all that Amanda brought to her. Rachel did not want to stay here. She wanted to leave. She was safe here, but she was sad here. Eating was not a priority. The food was simple here, but grand and good. Rachel did not want to appear rude by not eating all she was given. It was just that she couldn't. She was so confused.

Rachel found herself crouching now by the rat-catcher in anticipation of Amanda's coming. The plump girl in drab clothing would be bringing another box of vittles for the late-day meal. However, there was no sound of someone approaching—no shadow striking the ladder. Something else must have spooked the dog. She patted the rat-catcher on the head and scratched its ears.

"Be it puddin' or pie, my guardian," said Rachel softly, "I will share this last sup here with you."

The dog looked up with questioning eyes.

"My man will be comin' for me and for you. This will be the night . . . I jus' know it."

The dog seemed as interested in Mingo Tim and Rachel's prediction as it had been with the leftover suppawn. Someone was approaching, and that someone had to be bringing tastier scraps of food. The rat-catcher leaned forward, pointing its twitching nose over the hayloft portal, sniffing the air so wealthy with barnyard aromas, and seeking out the important scents of warm food and the odor of the usual bearer of glorious vittles.

Sure enough, Amanda's broad shadow danced across the barn floor and found the ladder. Suddenly, the shadow's owner came into view, whispered something Rachel could not decipher, and started climbing the ladder. The struggling Quaker lass held no vittle box under her arm this time. Instead, she carried a large leather pouch with its drawstring tied like a belt over her apron. The rat-catcher was not impressed. Amanda ascended cautiously, as she always did—not because she was afraid of the dog or the ladder. It was simply her great fear of heights. She was a shy and timid soul in all endeavors—neither beautiful, nor handsome. She was short and round—fond of cooking and sampling what she cooked. She hid most of her golden hair under a white round-the-ears cap, thus keeping her best feature a secret. Her nose was too red and too large for her face. The same could be said for her lips. Gray was her favorite color for a plain short gown worn over a pale Dutch petticoat. Stockings were gray, and her wooden shoes were squared and unpolished. Everything about Amanda spoke of reticence and last-to-be-noticed. However, she had a Quaker's heart and had become Rachel's dear friend right from the start. Every chance she could, Amanda came to the barn to visit Rachel, to bring her things, and to serve as a lookout when Rachel came down the ladder to go outside, or simply linger in the loft to chat and share a few meager experiences. The young host was a better listener—she had fewer experiences to share. She especially enjoyed Rachel's tale of royal lineage.

"I am not the least hungry, Miss Amanda," declared Rachel in what could only be considered a rude welcome.

Amanda struggled to reach the top of the ladder, held it firmly with both hands, and frowned at the amount of corn porridge remaining in the breakfast bowl.

"What bothers thee, my Princess?" asked the Quaker girl breathlessly as she waited for Rachel to grab her arm and help her up off the ladder.

"Nothin'," answered Rachel, "nothin' at all."

Amanda thanked Rachel once again for assisting her off the long ladder. She stood before the secret guest and loosened the drawstring at her waist. She handed the leather bag to Rachel, then sat down on the nearest bale to catch her breath and wipe her sweaty face with a corner of her apron.

"I've brought some traveling vittles for thee," said Amanda rather sadly, "Thy man hath finally sent waggon and escorts for thee. What hath been wished for hath come true. Best to get ready."

Rachel dropped the leather pouch and ran to her newest friend, pulled her off the bale, and gave her a warm hug. She added a gentle kiss on Amanda's cheek. The rat-catcher got busy sniffing the leather pouch for anything worth tasting.

Rachel pulled away from Amanda and clambered quickly up the bales to peer out from the cupola.

"Such good news you bring, Miss Amanda," exclaimed Rachel as a tear explored her cheek. She wiped it away. "But I do not see waggon nor men in the yard. Are you playin' a cruel game with me?"

"Wish that I was, dearest friend, but I shall lose thee today to truth. Men and horses wait for thee under trees by our road. I was chosen to fetch thee."

Rachel hopped down from the bales and looked around frantically. "I must gather my things."

"No time to waste," interjected Amanda, as she reached out to take hold of Rachel. "Men who have come for thee gave strict orders—bring nothing, save a pouch which holds vittles. My dear father had to bargain with them even to allow such fare I'd already boxed for thee. They deemed boxes too cumbersome. My father suggested a pouch would be easier to lug about."

"This means I'm not to bring the fancy things in the quilted bag you gave me?"

"No, Rachel," sighed Amanda, "those men forbid such. They say to bring only what is worn. Leave thy finery with me. I will keep it safe till I see thee again."

"Use 'em as you wish, Miss Amanda. I can do without. Besides, I might never see you again."

"Do not say such a thing," protested the Sharp girl.

The runaway slave and the shy Quaker embraced one last time. The rat-catcher took it all in with a wagging tail, questioning eyes, and a cocked ear. It was trying hard to figure out what all the fuss was about. The dog waited by the loft portal wondering when Rachel was going to carry him down the ladder for an overdue run and a chance to chase down a live meal. The event was supposed to happen before the cows returned to the barn. Something was causing a delay . . . something was wrong . . .

Amanda freed herself from Rachel's embrace. They stood for a brief, silent moment—eyes fixed on eyes, hands holding hands. Then Amanda whispered the worst news.

"Thy dog must stay."

Rachel pulled away. Her look of surprise turned to anger. "The rat-catcher is mine to keep. Tom Ward willed it so. My little companion has helped me conquer my fear of sleepin' in this barn. I don't care what my escorts say."

Amanda turned her eyes to the leather pouch which Rachel had discarded on the bed of straw. "These men who wait by that road forbid thee bringing anything but food I've prepared. They told my father of Tom Ward returning for his cur. Thy rescuer must have had a change of heart . . . misses his dog so . . ."

"I don't believe them," snapped Rachel angrily. "The rat-catcher comes with me, or I will not go. Mingo Tim can fetch me hisself. I can wait one more day."

Amanda was still staring at the pouch she had lugged up the ladder. "These men who wait for thee will not leave without thee. They are a mean lot—fierce in countenance and short on patience, according to my father. He warned his sons to keep a fair distance from such fallen men. They are not men of God, but men of blood and backwoods justice. They claim to work for one who hides thy man and they have orders to fetch thee by any means necessary. There is no choice to make, my dear princess. Time has come to go with them."

"I will not depart from here without the rat-catcher."

Amanda counted the air holes she had cut into the neck of the pouch before hurrying to the barn. She was pleased with the modest total of her handiwork.

"The dog will leave with thee . . ."

Rachel wished the cloak of night, with its myriad count of sparkling, silent stars and bold leering moon, was warmer. She was not dressed for the cool of the evening. She regretted not donning more layers of clothing when she had the chance back at the Quaker barn. Amanda Sharp had rushed her, hurried her down the ladder, and ran with her to greet the men who were supposed to take her to Mingo Tim. Without a word exchanged, Rachel climbed into the small waggon and was whisked away before she could say her goodbyes. She shivered at the thought of never seeing the Sharps again . . . especially Amanda.

Rachel was getting more uncomfortable every mile of the journey. There was no straw to sit on—just cold, hard planks. With one hand, she held tight to a sideboard. With the other, she clutched the warm leather pouch to her breast. It was downright chilly. If the pouch had been large enough, Rachel would have crawled into it and shared the rat-catcher's warmth. Such a dream, however, did not warm her. She was thankful for the lace cap round her ears, but the striped lindsey short gown and single petticoat were proving inadequate for a night journey. She wished for a cloak—one with bright stars on it. Rachel knew this was going to be a difficult ride; yet, if it meant reuniting with Mingo Tim at journey's end, then it would be all worth it.

At the start of the journey, the reinsman for the one-horse waggon glanced only once over his shoulder. He offered a wink from his good eye. The other eye, if he had another, was covered by a dirty red rag. The man mumbled something in German, which Rachel did not understand. She was afraid to interpret the wide grin on his ugly face as he spoke. He was gaunt, gangly, and unkempt. A strong reek of sweat and rawhide came drifting back from his clothing as soon as a command was given by the lead horseman, whom the others referred to as 'Leutinger.' The reinsman clucked to his horse, which broke into a canter down the lane past the humble Sharp house of logs and stone. Long shadows pointed the way along the winding Quaker Church Road. Rachel glanced back at her pleasant refuge, but the house and barns were now hidden by thick stands of trees guarding the westering road. The sun, at the time of the journey's birth, was blocked by foliage. Soon thereafter, the air turned cool and darkness fell . . . soon thereafter, Rachel felt things were not quite right . . .

The contents of the leather pouch stirred. Rachel felt the slight movement at her arms. However, the rat-catcher made no sound. She was glad the dog was so well-behaved. She whispered to it and spoke of trust and patience. This was all she had left to rely on, and she meant to share her conviction with the one who gave her courage. Rachel wondered how miserable she would have been if she had left the rat-catcher behind. The thought made her shiver even more.

It appeared to Rachel that her escorts were heading up into the hills where the Dickerson mine was located. She guessed they were going to take the difficult miner's road up to Rockaway and, perhaps, go as far north as Hibernia. Mingo Tim had talked about all the secret lairs for hiding between those two places. Yes, her man must be hiding somewhere up there, thought Rachel—such a long way off, such a hard journey, such a test of endurance. She wondered if these grim men planned to stop along the way. She had forgotten to relieve herself or let the dog run behind the Quaker barn before rushing to the waggon. She had to pee so badly . . .

The nearest mountains had swallowed the sun. The purple sky had turned to black. A night wind was sighing. A low moon and high stars provided meager light over the hiding hills. All the horsemen and the reinsman took a rough road which pointed in a northerly direction. They galloped at a pace normally used during the light of day. Rachel assumed these men had used this way to get to the Sharp farm. They appeared to know it well. The miner's road was narrow, winding, and rutty. The axles of the small waggon groaned and creaked over every impediment. Even the Rockaway River, where fresh logs had been recently laid, was forded in quick time. Rachel still held tight to the sideboard. She wished she had two hands free for the task. There was nothing under her to cushion the raw, splintery boards slapping her backside at every jump and jolt. She wanted to cry out for the one-eyed reinsman to slow the pace, but she dared not. She wanted the men to halt so she could pee. She wanted the same for the rat-catcher, but she had not the courage to request it. Rachel doubted that she could hold on much longer. The dog squirmed noticeably in the pouch.

Along the western bank of the Rockaway River, far above the crossing point, but some few miles short of Alten, the lead horseman halted. His followers did the same. The man in charge gave orders, but Rachel did not understand them. Her heart leaped. She wondered if this was the rendezvous point selected by Mingo Tim. The waggon came to a stop under a pitch-black canopy of trees. The turning leaves were whispering, but they were revealing no secrets. No starlight penetrated such a dense barrier. The only illumination came from the moonlight reflected off the nearby Rockaway River. This provided enough light for Rachel to observe the cluster of horsemen gathered at the river bank. They were discussing some matter of import in low, somber tones. Their accents were thick—a mixture of German and English. Rachel had difficulty discerning what was being said. Suddenly, their leader raised his voice and spoke sternly to the others. Even the reinsman, who was using the stop time for a quick nap, snapped to attention when the leader spoke. This time the words were all in English.

"There'll be no more, my brothers . . . time's been wasted down from the hiding cave . . . more time's been wasted coming back. We haggled too long with Meekers over the princess. We must be faithful to our commander's orders . . . his righteous cause is our cause . . . must return before dawn to prepare for the ritual. Water your horses here . . . then, it's on to Hibernia. No more stops for us or it's the cage for the likes of you and worse for me."

Rachel tried hard to comprehend all that the Leutinger had said, but she could not. She gathered that she would not be meeting Mingo Tim here. The rendezvous with her man appeared to be a long way off—the most difficult leg of the journey probably lay ahead. But for now, she only wanted permission to relieve herself. She did not want to do it on the floor boards of the waggon. Rachel suddenly realized the reinsman was staring at her again. He was also pointing to a thicket just beyond the canopy of trees. He spit once and gave a hasty command.

"Be quick 'bout yer business, me lady . . . 'n don't give a thought to outrunnin' the horses."

Rachel offered a quick "God bless you" and scrambled off the waggon. She still clutched Amanda's clever pouch and carried it all the way to the thicket. With trembling fingers she untangled the drawstring and let her companion free to tend to nature's call. Rachel squatted low to do the same. Not far away, the horse riders were at the bank of the river. They were tending to similar matters as well as watering their steeds. The rat-catcher growled once, but came to Rachel at her whispered command. It crawled obediently into the pouch.

When Rachel got back to the waggon, she saw that the reinsman was not perched on his fore board. She looked behind her and saw him limping towards his vehicle as fast as he could. He was chuckling to himself as he approached.

"Had to 'tend to sim'lar business, me lady . . . all in God's plan . . . with me havin' to keep an eye on yer bones at all times . . ."

The reeking man ventured closer and gave out a strong, malodorous laugh. Rachel put her free hand up to her face to ward off the stench of his foul breath.

"You are most kind," said Rachel, who was at a loss for words of protest or anger.

"Saw nothin' I'd never seen before," said the reinsman, as he turned his head to the side and spat again. "'Twas too dark fer details if you know what I mean . . . but I did make out the furry creature you caught in the bag . . . a fine catch, indeed."

"I've scarves and petticoats in this pouch," declared Rachel, "nothin else."

The reinsman chuckled as he struggled to lift himself up to his seat.

"Git into the waggon, me lady . . . I'll n'er tell. Yer secret's in me heart . . . might serve well to have a companion in yer cage."

11

A SUNDAY FEAST
. . . .
—at Daniel Cooper's Long Hill estate in the Passaic Valley,
Sunday, September 26, 1773

Guests on fine horses and guests with their women, riding in fine carriages, were still arriving at Judge Daniel Cooper's palladian door in the late afternoon on a pristine September day. There was a breezy chill in the air. Falling leaves were busy crab dancing across Cooper's impeccably landscaped grounds. All moving things seemed to be hurrying to prepare for the first signs of winter. Church services had long been concluded and circuit preachers were already starting their journeys back to their homes. Those using the main road through the Passaic Valley were always invited by the ostentatious Judge to stop by to share a bountiful repast with local dignitaries and notables who came from near and far. It had become a tradition to visit the Cooper estate on certain Sundays—to pay respects to a most honorable and influential man. Men of the cloth were especially welcome on these occasions.

Among the few preachers who wended up the gravel path flanked by broad yards, fading flower beds, and stately trees in motley seasonal garb, was a salt-of-the-earth Baptist minister. He was known as the right Reverend Heaton—Samuel Heaton, a former forge master and once reknowned for various feats of strength. He had most recently come down from Schooley's Mountain to assist an ailing peer in tending to a flock of shy and slacking worshippers at a little log church in the Black River Valley. From there, Reverend Heaton journeyed east to visit an old friend, Ellis Cook of Hanover, for a few days. Cook had been a worthy adversary in wrestling matches held at summer fairs. That was long ago, before Heaton was blinded by the fire of faith. However, the itinerant minister never forgot that he won the majority of contests. During his visit, he made sure Cook had not forgotten either. On Saturday, he guided his trusty gelding south to Chatham to assist in the next day's services at the Anabaptist meeting house there. The turnout of true believers was discouragingly meager. Most were passive, dull-eyed, and unchallenging folks, who displayed no outward response to his thundering sermon. He meant to scare them into hope, but he could see he had failed miserably . . . maybe next time. There was always a next time in faith . . . always hope.

However, one congregant summoned enough courage to praise Heaton for chasing the devil from his heart. The man was eager to unburden that same organ of troublesome news he had been carrying for these last few weeks. He had traveled quite far down from the north and needed to tell someone in a position of authority what had to be told. Although Heaton would be delayed in his leaving, the minister took the man aside and listened to his grave concern. In doing so, Reverend Heaton arrived at Judge Cooper's manse late and in a glum mood. The weight of bad news always made him droop his broad shoulders.

He was not at his Sunday best—neither in mind nor appearance. He wondered if it would do any good to share what he had learned with anyone at such a festive gathering. It was probably not the proper time or place for spreading news, which might have been more rumor than fact.

The circuit preacher planned to drop in, pay his respects to the host, be talked into partaking of the feast and staying overnight in a comfortable goose feather bed, just like the last time he was here. He was weary from his circuitous journey—too many days away from his wife and children, too many hours counseling others about their trouble and woe, and too many miles of difficult roads on horseback. This huge and humble man of the cloth, ordinarily filled with pious energy, had but one good deed left to do. His friend, Ellis Cook—a former renowned blacksmith along the Whippannung and now proprietor of the most popular tavern in Hanover—had asked him to deliver two letters which had been dropped off by a post rider—a pair of letters intended for the son of Assemblyman John Wetherill. Mister Cook had told his dear friend all about the respected political leader and the man's mistrust of certain parties in Morris Town, where he had originally intended to drop off the letters meant for his son's eyes only. The post rider had delivered this sentiment to Ellis Cook, the one Whig old John could trust explicitly. The Assemblyman's friendship with Cook spanned more years than the warm association between Cook and Heaton. The tavern master made sure the Reverend knew everything about John Wetherill worth knowing.

Finding the son of John Wetherill was proving to be an easy task. Word of Vincent's visit to Judge Cooper's place had reached Ellis Cook's ears via Sheriff Stiles. The good Sheriff and his men had stopped in Hanover at Cook's tavern before heading back to Morris Town. Stiles spoke of no luck in finding the she-slave, whom he suspected of slaying the buck fiddler, nor the rogues who had thrashed Mister Morrell's foreman. However, he did mention confronting Vincent Wetherill and his team at the county border bridge, and being told of their purpose in dropping off a gift of apple brandy at Judge Cooper's place in return for a waggonload of barrels of near worthless iron water. A good laugh was shared over John Wetherill's scheme to turn unpalatable iron water into a tasty tonic. Reverend Heaton remembered Ellis Coak telling him that, if anybody was foolish enough to attempt and succeed at such a trick, it would be old John Wetherill.

"The man's an alchemist when it comes to brewing," declared Mister Cook. "He's the second man, known to us, who would dare turn water into wine . . . and iron water at that!"

The tavern master and the wayfaring minister garnered a hearty laugh over that comment. Cook's words echoed in Heaton's head as he stepped between stately columns, removed his wide-brimmed hat, and entered the crowded welcoming parlor. Judge Cooper's wife was the first to greet him. Heaton bowed politely. The hostess courtsied with difficulty. Her ponderous, towering wig was precariously perched upon her smallish head. Her tight-fitting pink and blue gown, hiding several petticoats, restricted her slightest movement. Even her hand gestures were cautious and labored. However, her eyes twinkled with a what-do-you-think-of-me expression, rather than the customary so-glad-of-you-to bless-our-home-with-your-presence look. In sum, her face was a mask of secrets under pink rouge, with an obvious diamond-shaped patch hiding a pox scar on one cheek. Below a long pale neck—

by far, her best feature—a scalloped flowered bodice revealed a modest measure of adequate breasts. Heaton praised the Lord for that. Under all the restrictive camouflage, there was either a plain or beautiful woman. The holy man from Schooley's Mountain was not experienced enough to tell. He was left to wonder why women of wealth went to such lengths to masquerade as ornate clowns.

Heaton was glad his wife dressed within her means and shunned attempts to paint her face. Her beauty was her own. He loved her for what she was. It was important that he and his wife looked like the folks he ministered to. He and his wife had come from poor stock and they knew hardship. This helped them to know where they were needed most. Heaton had little tolerance for those who put on airs of superiority, yet he felt no malice toward high folks. Many of those he ministered to did, but he did not. He felt sorry for those who flaunted their pelf and equally sorry for those who were envious of the wealthy.

Both types would have trouble getting past the gates of Heaven. The folks of humble means and honest hearts—for certain, the ones he preached to—would have no trouble at all.

As Reverend Heaton moved down the line of greeters and went through the motions of introductions to noteworthy folks who had not yet partaken of the sumptuous buffet, he kept thinking about those who would have the easiest time finding hell. Upon each introduction, Heaton smiled carefully and said the appropriate things one is supposed to say to folks of high station. His thoughts now drifted to the words of the congregant who had made him late to Cooper's Sunday feast. The sad fellow spoke of a rogue preacher, come down from the north mountains to rile the laborers at various mines and forges. Apparently, this character was having some success recruiting followers from the Hibernia works, which were now completely owned and operated by Lord Stirling. This self-proclaimed preacher was rumored to be all about gaining revenge for injustices perpetrated by titled nobility and the wealthy. His answer was resorting to violence against all enemies. Thus, his faithful were into thievery, kidnaping, and worse. All honest, hard-working hill folk lived in fear of these boys. They had become nothing more than land pirates, bent on robbing wayfarers and raiding homesteads and hamlets. They hid in caves and abandoned mines by day, and did their best work in the middle of the night. No wonder the innocent were terrified of this rogue preacher's minions.

The man, who informed Heaton about this, said he was certain he saw a gang of such boys escorting a waggon to the main road where it passed a Quaker farm—the Sharp's farm to be exact—late on the previous day.

"Nasty 'n mean they appeared," said the worried man, "with but a fear-eyed negress ridin' in their cart. I was startled by the sight 'n concerned for her well-bein', so I paid a visit to my neighbor, Elder Sharp. I 'quired 'bout what I seen. Sharp voiced similar concerns for the Afric wench 'n 'greed with me on who those boys might be. Yet, he refused to say more 'n claimed God would care for the likes of her, 'n deal with the likes of her escorts . . ."

Heaton reassured the far-traveled congregant that he would pray for the negress and the hill folks. He warned the man to be ever-vigilant and go to the authorities if he learned anything more about the untoward land pirates and their leader. The man seemed relieved after sharing his concern and receiving some assurance that God was looking out for the innocent. Heaton, on the other hand, departed from Chatham without the same trust in his own words. Something evil had been unleashed in the iron hills.

Heaton knew nothing about the negress; but, after remembering his conversation with Ellis Cook over Sheriff Stiles's failure to find his runaway suspect, he had an idea who had been taken from the Sharp farm. How she got there, he did not know. Heaton also remembered something that might be connected to the men who had come for the negress. There was a far-fetched tale circulating up in the hills around Schooley's Mountain of a band of violent characters heading south and west in search of loot. They had been described in similar terms used by the worried man who visited the Sharps. In addition, Heaton remembered his mountain neighbors claimed these rogues were scarred with crude tattoos. The symbol they wore, they also carved on surfaces wherever they brought woe. Their leader was also rumored to be a self-proclaimed preacher— some prophet of salvation . . . a leader of a new order . . . a leader of a band of soldiers preparing for war . . . a peasants' war. Reverend

Heaton was sure he knew this leader . . . he knew Johnny Spolden all too well . . .

At the end of the greeting line by a table of seasonal flowers in the far corner of the welcoming parlor, stood two men of the cloth that Heaton knew well. One was a Presbyterian pastor from Morris Town with the fire of his morning sermon still burning in his eyes. He seemed to be preoccupied with staring covertly at the younger women in the gathering—the younger, the better. The other was an Episcopalian priest, still in his robes and flashing condescending looks at all the sinners who ignored him. Both men welcomed the Baptist preacher coldly and showed no interest in what he had to say. Heaton left them to their own selfish machinations and headed for the spacious social room with its high-beamed ceiling, tall windows, and chandeliers twinkling with new lit candles. Here was where guests found sumptuous food and stately fiddle music, performed by three musicians on a raised platform. Heaton did not care for the secular melodies, but he was hungry. He had had little to eat since leaving his friend's tavern in Hanover. It was best to fill his belly before attempting to save a soul in a place like this, reasoned Heaton. He held little hope of accomplishing more than postponing starvation and delivering two letters to Mister Wetherill. Thus, he toyed with the idea of leaving right after accomplishing these two things. Let the other men of the cloth, here, save the souls of such haughty types. He had no stomach for it. At least, the Lord had been shown some respect by the fiddlers not playing any backwoods tunes and no guest daring to dance to the music on a Sunday.

A steaming flank of beef, recently brought in from the kitchen hearth spit by sweating slaves, was the center of attention at this buffet feast. It was surrounded by roasted turkeys, smoked hams, boiled fish, and bowls of exotic spices. Everything was positioned neatly on a long table near the warm fireplace. The blazing wood therein discouraged any drafts from getting beyond the welcoming parlor, where the main door continued to be opened and closed to allow more late guests in. Reverend Heaton was drawn to the warmth and the table of fancy eats and wondrous smells. He took up a large pewter plate, and knife and spoon. He selected helpings of whatever caught his eye. He passed over the tempting desserts arrayed splendidly on a separate table, and the wines and brandies being poured by an eager servant. No devil's fork would he ever use and no devil's brew would he ever consume. Any dessert was a temptation bordering on gluttony. He chose a small bowl of apple cider and then searched for a place to sit.

Heaton found an empty chair at a small table dominated by a few elderly matrons dressed nearly as fine as the hostess. They seemed happy to gain a minister's company and invited him to sit and eat with them. Their table was the one nearest the fireplace. They were quite eager and glad to share such warmth with a man. In the midst of their twitters, chirps, and giggles they all confessed that their husbands were meeting in secret session with the host, Judge Cooper, himself.

"Our husbands have rejoined with the host in his library study to share a fine Wetherill brandy—just come in—and discuss plans for the next gentlemen's hunt," said the obviously oldest queen in the bunch. With her eyes crinkling at the corners with crow's-feet, she explained further. "We must await their decision on the date so that we can set a good and proper time for the harvest ball."

"Ahah!" exclaimed Heaton with a feigned show of sincerity and surprise. "So that is why I have seen so few men on the welcoming line and at the feast table."

"Yes," continued the eldest matron, as she worried the lace closest to her withered breasts. "The members of the Sons of Dawn abandon us every chance they get to play their silly secret games. They love to lose themselves in a hunt in the far hills . . . any excuse, and they disappear."

This declaration was followed by more twitters, chirps, and giggles from the eldress's peers.

"I am grateful you have told me of their purpose, madam," said Heaton, as he worked on his bounty of food then paused to take a sip of the pedestrian cider. "I am even more grateful of your telling me where I might find them. Thank you much, for I need to find the Wetherill who brought the brandy to Judge Cooper."

"'Tis odd, indeed, Reverend Heaton," said the dominant eldress, "but you will find John Wetherill's son in attendance at the same secret meeting I have mentioned. How that handsome young man weaseled his way into a session for members only, and the King's visiting mining agents did not, is beyond me."

The twittering which followed the old woman's words was entangled with whispers and comments about how handsome this special guest was.

"Perhaps, your men like his brandy much more than they like what the agents are offering. They simply mean to honor the lad and ignore trouble," surmised the preacher, as he proceeded to sweep his plate with oat bread and drain his cider bowl.

"I suspect there is more to breaking their silly rules this time," opined one of the other women at the table.

The eldress concurred, but offered a glance of annoyance. She obviously felt she was the only person in the group worthy of conversing with a man of the cloth—a rugged, sandy-haired, and handsome man at that.

"If this young Mister Wetherill succeeded in breaking the rules, then I must give it a try. I shall deliver the letters, then be on my way." With that, Reverend Heaton arose, made a polite attempt at a leg, blessed the ladies for their hospitality, and asked for directions to the Judge's library study.

Twitters, chirps, and giggles followed him out of the social room at the same time the musicians paused between secular, but still safe, songs. Heaton took the women's noise as a compliment and the musicians' music as a compromise in the eyes of the Lord. He felt better now. Perhaps it was simply that the food had done the trick. His belly was full. Now, he knew where to find young Wetherill. His visit was near half over. Praise the Lord for speeding things along.

The blue-gray hallway to the study was deserted save for a husky, armed man guarding the far door. Light was allowed in through two small windows on one side, but the guardian of the sanctuary for the Sons of Dawn was mostly in shadow. Before Heaton could reach him, the man spoke forcefully:

"You've taken a wrong turn, mate. Best you go back the way you came."

"My apologies, good man," answered Heaton, "but I have urgent business with Mister Wetherill, who, I've been informed, attends the hunt club meeting."

"You'll wait till it's over," insisted the guard. "Go fetch a plate of vittles 'n entertain yourself in the social room."

Reverend Heaton dared approach the armed guard and share the shadow with him. The man did, indeed, sport a mean look, but he appeared shorter now and his pistol seemed such a puny thing. The former forge master knew he could take the man if he wanted to . . . in a former time, when he was as young as this man appeared . . . in a former time, when he was not yet a man of the cloth. . .

"Put your weapon in your belt, my good man," advised Heaton calmly. "I am a shepherd of the Baptist faith. I pose no threat to you in coming to deliver a pair of letters to Mister Wetherill, a guest of honor to Judge Cooper. Let me complete my mission, then I shall go on my way."

"Don't care what stripe you be nor the business you're about," declared the guard, who gripped the pistol in his hand even tighter. "Mister Ford pays me 'n he tells me what to do. In these troubled times, my job is to stand here 'n protect both Fords—the elder 'n the younger—'n their companions as well. I've been ordered to let nobody disturb the Sons of Dawn . . . not even the likes of you. When their meeting is over, I'll be relieved by another fellow 'n I can retreat to the kitchen house to join my kind in a separate feast. I am looking forward to such 'n you're not going to cause a disturbance on my watch, nor spoil my fun."

"Wouldn't dare, my good man," said Heaton calmly. "Honest work deserves its own reward."

"Mister Ford rewards me fine for my services, preacher man. I need no blessing nor compliment from you."

"Perhaps a gift then . . . perhaps you require a mere laying on of hands to come round to the Lord's way of thinking."

The stubborn guard was not able to finish a repeat of his command for the preacher to return to the social room. A mighty hand gripped the fist which held the pistol. The other hand tightened around the guard's throat. In an instant, his head was pounded against the door he was supposed to be guarding. This pounding was repeated until the gun fell from his grip and everything before his eyes went black. He crumpled in a heap on the floor. The door opened behind him and he heard vaguely familiar voices swapping expressions of concern and surprise. The words made no sense to him. He felt the cold floor with hands and knees, began to crawl toward the nearest window, but collapsed and passed out. He dreamed of being carried to a huge white mansion by a giant of a man—so strong he was, but gentle was his voice. So soft the man's words, repeating and repeating, "Honest work deserves its own reward . . . honest work . . ."

"A little misunderstanding 'twas all," said the second non-member of the Sons of Dawn hunt club to enter the gentlemen's sanctuary, ripe with the welcoming smells of polished oak, pipe smoke, dusty books, and animal heads. "No need to apologize, Judge Cooper. Your man was only doing his job."

"He's my man," interrupted Jacob Ford, Sr., the only club member who failed to rise from a comfortable chair and put down a glass of brandy when Reverend Heaton strode into the library study. "He's my loyal batter bull and a fine one at that. I trust him more than any fellow who replaces him at the door."

"He is a determined lad," confessed Heaton, as he scanned the room to figure out which man was John Wetherill's son. It proved an easy task, for the youngest gentleman was standing over by a window. He was dressed in ill-fitting, obviously borrowed clothes. He was flashing alert, curious eyes framed in a face as handsome as described by the elderly ladies in the social room. Reverend Heaton decided, then and there, that the young Mister Wetherill was the only one in the room he could trust.

Judge Cooper completed his apologetic welcome before the elder Ford could demand an apology. He was dressed in a long velvet coat burdened with intricate silver and cream embroidery at his lofty collar, and maroon silk vest accentuated by cascades of frost-white lace at his slender neck and thin wrists.

"My sympathies, just the same," declared the Judge in his usual bombastic voice. "We Sons of the Dawn Sword have completed plans for the upcoming harvest hunt. I was about to terminate this session and dismiss the majority of gentlemen gathered here. There is but a small matter to discuss with a few members who will remain, along with my honored guest who came to my door rather late Friday night, but is now well rested . . ."

"Please, I don't mean to interrupt anything," offered Heaton, as he extracted two letters from his bible pouch. "I simply have to deliver this pair of missives from Assemblyman Wetherill to his son and then I shall be on my way."

The younger Jacob Ford, standing behind his father's heavy chair, pointed to Vincent Wetherill. Heaton walked over to the young man and handed him the letters without saying a word. He turned as if to go.

"Won't you join the members about to leave for the feasting?" asked Judge Cooper in a forced tone of politeness.

Heaton bowed slightly. "Already have, kind sir. Your fare was excellent and I've taken my fill."

"Then, please stay the night." insisted Cooper. "You have such a long journey back to Schooley's Mountain and the hour is late. I've a room for you just like the last time."

"Your generosity is most kind, sir, but I promised my wife and children I would return before Monday's dawn. There is trouble brewing in our hills, and my kin are sore afraid. It is best for them that I go now."

Judge Cooper kept a startled look on his face much too long. Heaton noticed and so did Vincent Wetherill.

"Stay for but a moment, please, begged the Judge, as he was pointing to various club members and motioning them to leave the room. Those asked to leave were the ones who had said their piece about whether or not to have the annual harvest hunt before the moon was gone. They did not vote to postpone it till November, nor did they vote to cancel it. The majority voted as expected. This hunt was to honor the club's most renowned member, William Alexander of Baskeridge. He had been unable to attend the meeting, but had sent word favoring the holding of the hunt as usual. He also indicated that he would abide by the decision of the majority of the members of the club. His desire to carry out plans as usual, regardless of the local murders and mayhem plaguing the area, swayed enough members to vote as Lord Stirling wished. Those in the minority, who voted to postpone or cancel the hunt, were the ones Judge Cooper asked to stay.

"Mister Wetherill, please take a seat once more," instructed the Judge. He was pointing to the chair Vincent had been sitting in before Reverend Heaton employed a man's skull to knock on the door.

After most of the club members had exited the room in search of wives, food, and festivities, Judge Cooper resumed his seat at his desk. He started to reach for his brandy glass which contained a wonderful bit of the gift from John Wetherill, then pulled his hand back when he remembered that Reverend Heaton was close by. The preacher had taken a seat next to Vincent by the window and was observing Cooper's every move. The Judge decided to count those who remained. The elder Jacob Ford was still in his chair, looking sour as a lemon peel and waiting for an apology from the rude Reverend Heaton. His son, wearing no wig, but looking dapper with curls cascading over his ears and braided with a green silk bow in the back, had taken a seat next to his father. His outfit was the equal of his father's, but his waistcoat was a deep crimson with garish gold buttons at the front and on the sleeves, instead of the father's understated genteel silver. The elder Ford posed as a lean hawk; the son, a stout peacock. To Judge Cooper, these two birds were indispensable. He knew he was the same to them. All three protected secrets known only to themselves. Heaton already suspected as much. Until they acknowledged their sins, they were of little use to him. Whether they did, or not, Heaton would always remain of little use to them. At least, that was what Cooper was thinking at the moment.

Jacob Morrell and Daniel Wick were also in the room. During the hunt club session neither would look at the other. Morrell still owed Wick a tidy sum and had failed to have his man deliver the promised casks of salt pork in order to pay off the debt. Wick did not want to hear Morrell's excuses. He did not feel the least sorry for Morrell'a predicament—a young female slave running off, his foremen accosted by highwaymen, and the salt pork lost to such thieves. Wick decided to ignore the debtor. Morrell decided to stare out the window behind young Wetherill and the broad-shouldered minister. The last hour of daylight streaming in was providing a halo effect on the two guests in the room. Morrell was content with trying to figure out the import of such a sign.

"Now, Reverend Heaton," announced Judge Cooper finally, "Please tell us about the pending trouble up on Schooley's Mountain. I was planning to send two of my men up there with a barrel waggon to fetch iron water for Mister Wetherill. Shall it be safe to send them at the dawn?"

The elder Ford decided not to allow the minister to respond to the Judge's question. "Why are we being detained for what appears to be a private matter between you and this rude man who comes barging in on a secret meeting after waylaying my watch-keep? I demand an apology from him, then an explanation from you for our purpose in being kept from the festivities."

Before Judge Cooper could explain his purpose, Reverend Heaton offered an apology of sorts: "The Lord is pleased to bless those who do a job well. I was simply demonstrating to your man that he was not adequately prepared to carry out his responsibilities. His weapon was not primed. He held it for show and made no effort to employ it. In attempting to free himself from my instructive grip on his gun hand, he left himself exposed to an attack on his own person. His focus was entirely on rescuing his useless pistol. This allowed me to grip his throat and use his noggin to announce my intentions. I was merely showing him how to be resourceful—use what God hath given thee. Your man has learned a valuable lesson, Mister Ford. He will not make the same mistake again, praise the Lord. I would expect no word of gratitude from you, nor would I anticipate such after your man has had a real occasion to protect your person from harm. My apologies, if I caused your man any injuries."

Daniel Wick sniffed the tense, silent air. Jacob Morrell fingered the lace at his cuff and kept his eyes busy with the task of searching for dust on the floor of a well-swept room. Judge Cooper waited politely for the elder Ford's response. It did not come.

Ford's son spoke in his stead: "We thank you for instructing our ward so that he may learn the proper way to perform his duties. I am sure he will do better now in protecting us against harm. Your apology, Reverend Heaton, is accepted."

"Good then," beamed Judge Cooper, now confident that progress could be made. "Let's get on with the matters at hand. This trouble Reverend Heaton alluded to may have some bearing on our troubles down here 'round Morris Town."

"Doubt it much," groused the ever-sour elder Ford.

"Give the preacher a chance," piped Mister Morrell.

"Make his quick," countered Mister Wick. "I'm hungry as a black bear, and twice as angry my brothers in the club voted against my proposal to cancel the hunt. I'm in no mood to receive more bad news."

Judge Cooper ignored Wick's complaint and kept his eyes on Heaton. He offered an open-handed gesture to the newest visitor and said, "You have our undivided attention."

Reverend Heaton decided to stand in the sunlight and address these influential, strong-willed entepreneurs of the hinterlands. He was intrigued by Judge Cooper's hint at a possible connection between events in Morris Town and Schooley's Mountain. Heaton had learned little about the murders of the stable boy and the fiddling slave. He knew less of the ongoing investigation. More than likely, he felt he would learn more than he wanted to about such crimes before leaving to return home—more than he intended to tell these men about the anticipated woe coming to plague the folks on Schooley's Mountain. For now, he saw no connection between what he was about to say and the local troubles vexing these men. However, he would allow for his perception to change.

"Rumor has it," began Heaton with his most serious Old Testament voice, "a prodigal son of the darkest sort is planning to return to our peaceful highlands. Folks there remember him as a dabbler in the divination of astrology, a free thinker, one enamored with the anarchos of Zeno . . . with Burke's idea of abolishing government. He left our mountain to raise a following—an army of rioters in favor of bloody revolution. He promised to return as the messiah of a new order . . . to baptise his followers in awful waters . . . to loose a sacred stone in the mountain, meant to crush and sunder the old order. He sees himself as God's necessary instrument, sent to fulfill what is prophesied in Hosea, Chapter thirteen, Verse eleven: 'In His rage, God hath given the world lords and princes, and in His exasperation He will do away with them again.' He believes these cruel times are ripe for overthrowing nobles and persons of great wealth . . . for raising the poor and downtrodden to equal status. This man is promising the low ones, who follow him, all the amenities of a comfortable life . . . the wealthy must pay to make this promise come true. I am told he stirs many souls north of here. He has been especially successful among disenchanted mine and forge laborers. Some men have abandoned their jobs to join this black cause. They now favor hiding in caves and abandoned mines by day and marauding by night. They have spread in all directions, intent on robbing innocent folk—wealthy or poor. They pose a new threat to all. Recent tales about them speak of kidnapings, cagings, maimings, even beheadings. How much of it is exaggerated, or downright untrue, is open to conjecture. All their foul deeds are done to honor their leader, to whom they sing impious songs and toast his name with roaring shouts . . ."

"Who is this apostate, riding on depravity's path?" asked Jacob Morrell with feigned concern and amazement at how animated the preacher had become.

"Jack Spolden is his name . . . a former apprentice at my forge . . . of Irish and German parentage, so he claims. . . came into my care in sixty-seven—a mere wandering orphan of sixteen, who demonstrated an eagerness to learn the forge tender's trade. He is a sharp one—quick to get things right and quick with his tongue. He speaks several languages . . . could read and write better than any man under me. While he was with me, he developed a keen interest in religion . . . or, should I say, all religions . . . especially the origins of sects and faiths, even those which ended poorly. My first mistake was encouraging Jack to read books on the Christian faith, for, at the time, I was starting on my journey as a shepherd for the Lord and leaving most matters of the forge in my brothers' hands. I saw no harm in the boy reading, though he favored obscure and controversial texts from my vast collection. I tried to steer him away from aberrant teachings by suggesting safer tomes, but he liked choosing of his own free will. His questions to me were deep and dark. They centered 'round righteous justice for those who bow and scrape . . . those treated harshly by arrogant betters . . ."

Jacob Morrell made a rumbling attempt to clear his throat. He swallowed hard. The two Fords looked at each other with uncomfortable eyes. Judge Cooper steepled his fingers in front of his mouth. Daniel Wick scratched an ear and yawned. Vincent Wetherill remained politely still and silent. Heaton was helping him make invaluable connections for the first time. Vincent could not wait to be alone to read the recently delivered letters, and write again to his father and Abia. There was so much to report since he and his team had departed from Amboy.

Reverend Heaton was satisfied that he had made the wealthy locals uncomfortable. He made eye contact with each one of them and decided to plow on: "All was fine and dandy between Jack Spolden and me till last year when I loaned him a difficult book given to me by Reverend John Gano of Hopewell. It is a translation of Kerssenbruck's history of the riotous Anabaptists and the Munster affair of two centuries ago. Long forgotten are the details of the horrors which befell the folk in the northern reaches of Germanic land. However, my Jack memorized every word and told me of his odd interpretation of the 'Deutscher Baumkrieg' in old Westphalia. He came to admire the ways of radical Anabaptists . . . the teachings of Jan Matthias. With inspired eyes set aflame by the rhetoric of long dead revolutionaries, Spolden announced to others his plan to set things right in the New World. Another Peasant War had to be waged. Only by the sword would his revolution succeed. Good would accrue from breaking the peace and causing enmity among the wealthy factions in power. He intends to bring down the old order and raise up a new order. I tried to discourage him . . . lead him back to the true and virtuous path of the dutiful, humble Christian. It was too late. Spolden claimed he had already started writing a scurrilous gospel . . . had already started recruiting others by making all sorts of ugly flouts against the likes of wealthy John Hager, Lord Stirling, and others of great means and influence, and had already started fomenting strife between those faithful to the King and Parliament and those protesting colonial policies. I saw no evidence of progress on his part, other than a few scribblings of bombast which he allowed me to see. All his efforts seemed to be mere farts in the wind—the rantings of an intense young man who saw himself as the second Thomas Muntzer come to save the world. Members of my flock could not tolerate such apostasy; thus, Spolden was disowned from the true faith by unanimous vote. On the night of the decision, he vanished along with two other laborers of mine, three stout horses, and a Kerssenbruck volume . . ."

"Where does this troublemaker hide—near, or far from here?" asked Judge Cooper with fingers still at his lips.

"I know of Jack Spolden's whereabouts only by way of rumors harvested as I make my rounds," confessed Heaton. "They say he got as far as the Half-Jacks at the New York border and hid out with them for a few months. He must have learned only bad things from their ilk. That tribe will borrow your scalp if you look cross at them, and cut off your cock 'n bells with the same knife if you don't. Thereafter, they say he returned south, hiding in caves and abandoned mines along the way. His following, at the start, was but a hand of men already into thieving when they wished and stealing from backwoods folk what they wanted. Fearsome tales of Spolden's gang must have started from these early victims. They were first to call the leader, Black Jake. Authorities got word of this menace, but they have yet to corner this elusive gang. Since venturing south, Spolden's kind has expanded. Several separate haufen gangs and a number of rogue individuals now claim an association with Spolden's cause. There is a fresh rumor that a large gang of land pirates joined up with Jack Spolden— an alliance of sorts among evil men who share a similar lust for disrupting the old order. Their kind appears to be gathering momentum—rapidly expanding in lucrative directions, yet not taken seriously by the King's law men. I am told their behavior will one day rival the Paxton boys of the previous decade or the rioters over in Horseneck. For all I know, Spolden's men may be headed this way . . ."

"They won't dare plague us," offered the younger Ford. "Our Sheriff and his men are on high alert since the murders followed the hanging. Your Jack Spolden would be a fool to meddle down here. As far as I know, we have lost not one laborer to his cause—if such a cause actually exists. I, for one, think the rumors about the man and the deeds of his followers are woefully exaggerated—the stuff of tall tales from the woodlands . . . the kind contrived to scare women and children."

"I hope you are right, Mister Ford," said Heaton. "However, I know Jack Spolden is real and that he has good reason to turn south. My home and hearth is where he started. He means to fulfill a prophecy he made last year to lay claim to Schooley's Mountain as a sacred place and baptize members, old and new, into his unseemly faith."

"At the iron water springs, no doubt," muttered Judge Cooper with skepticism clinging to his words.

Reverend Heaton nodded his head in agreement, fell silent for a moment to let the import of his message sink in, then he turned to address the young Wetherill: "I have been informed by Ellis Cook of Hanover—my friend who graciously received the letters you hold—that your father plans to put our mountain water to good purpose. I trust a man of his caliber shall succeed in such an endeavor. Yet, for every man who seeks to do good in this world there is always one who strives to do evil with the same device. My followers fear the spawn of the devil shall rise from the pools of iron water when, and if, Jack Spolden returns. I dread the day it happens."

Vincent, so addressed, felt compelled to speak for the first time since acknowledging the graciousness of his host, Judge Cooper, and the praise for his father's brandy, which came from all those who had gathered for the secret meeting in Cooper's library study. He wished to say as little as possible, for he did not want to give away anything he knew or suspected.

"I am astounded to learn of this agent of the devil, Reverend Heaton. Let us hope rumors about Black Jake remain as such."

"My sources tell me otherwise," said Heaton. "The threat is real."

"I do have one question," asked Vincent politely. "How do we know his kind? Do his men share any signal, symbol, or password?"

"I know of none," stated Heaton tersely. "Their ways are secret as are their haunts . . . like the ways of all ungodly fraternal orders."

"Have you heard of any tattoo Spolden's men might be sporting?"

"I do not know, Mister Wetherill. It is possible. No one I have spoken to has mentioned a tattoo."

The elder Ford squirmed in his chair. He lacked the patience to listen to conjecture. "I feel confident this ghost of a fellow will dare not venture far from his hiding cave. If he does, the authorities will catch him and bring him to justice. I know my men at the mines and forge are loyal to my son and me. They guard our holdings well. I fear not the wrath of this sudden devil."

"He hasn't been caught yet, Jacob," challenged Daniel Wick, as he dared test the self-important man's confidence. "From what Reverend Heaton has told us, this man and his minions have already committed serious crimes in a short time. As far as I know, no law man 'round here is out looking for the cur."

"We are wasting our time," countered Mister Morrell with a squint and a frown directed at Wick. "Jack Spolden has nothing to do with us. We have more important matters to contend with. Let the preacher be on his way. Let us squeeze some joy from the remainder of this fast-souring day."

The Fords demonstrated agreement by rising from their comfortable chairs in imitation of Mister Morrell. Judge Cooper was about to adjourn his ad hoc meeting of those who had voted against the harvest hunt, when Daniel Wick tossed out a final question:

"Did you not tell me, Mister Morrell, that a gang of banditti accosted your foreman and got away with my barrels of salted pork?"

"According to my man, Tom Ward, they were young locals," responded Morrell defensively, as he glowered down at the man who refused to rise from his chair. "They beat him severe, scared off my slave wench who has yet to return, and took my horse, waggon, and barrels. You have no claim to any of this property, Mister Wick, since my man never made it to your place that night, it is not yours till you receive it."

"Are you sure your foremen is telling the truth?"

Morrell took a threatening step towards Wick's chair. "He showed me his bruises and scars . . . such wounds convinced me of his speaking the truth."

Wick was not finished baiting the man who had failed to settle an outstanding debt: "I do not care a jot over the condition of your foreman. He appears to have recovered quickly from his beating. The tale of thieves attacking him bothers me . . . moreso, since hearing Reverend Heaton's news . . ."

"Are you saying my man lied?"

"I am saying he may be mistaken. Perhaps, the men who pounced on him were not young locals but some of Spolden's men come down to start trouble?"

"Nonsense," declared Morrell.

"To date, your foreman has not been able to identify any of the men who attacked him. How does he know for certain they are young locals?"

"My man was surprised by the scoundrels in the pitch black of night. He did not get a good look at them . . ."

"My point exactly, Mister Morrell . . . perhaps the Sheriff has been encouraged to look in the wrong corner?"

"Are you accusing me and my man of making up a story in order to delay the settling of a debt?"

"Nothing of the sort, Mister Morrell. I am offended that you would even think such a thing."

Now Wick was out of his chair and waving his cane in Morrell's direction. The latter took another step forward and swiped at the cane.

"Now, now, gentlemen," scolded Judge Cooper, as he arose and sped around his desk to stand between the two adversaries. "Please respect the presence of a man of the cloth in our midst. This is no time to open old wounds and pick at each other. Events of these past few days have put us all on edge."

The Judge pointed to empty chairs and scurried back to his chair at the desk.

"Come sit . . . everybody sit . . . let us air our views on what has transpired here. Let us finish our business on a note of some accord. The food will taste better after we do . . . come sit . . ."

The Judge sat down with a heavy sigh. Morrell scuttled back to his chair, but kept his eyes averted from Wick. The Fords returned with a flourish to their comfortable chairs. Vincent had never moved from his chair. Heaton was anxious to leave, but he dared not offend the host. He returned to his chair warmed by the sunlight piercing the window.

"Reverend Heaton has been kind enough to linger long to share his news of a possible threat. It is only right for us to reciprocate with our take on the local murders."

"You are most gracious, Judge Cooper," said Heaton with a slight bow of his sandy mane, "but if I remain any longer I will have to accept your invitation to stay the night."

"I shall be honored to have you," said Cooper with a nod. "My waggoners, charged with fetching the iron water in the morning, can serve as your escort. I will make sure they are heavily armed."

"Much appreciated," offered Heaton, "but the Lord supplies all the protection I require. Just the same, I will accept the invitation to accompany your men. My wife will be put at ease when she sees my escorts are carrying weapons."

"My men can linger for a day or two at Schooley's if Mister Wetherill is in no rush to return home after transferring the barrels of iron water to his waggon. What say you, Mister Wetherill?"

Vincent was jolted to attention by Judge Cooper's words. The sun at his neck had lulled him into a moment of inattentiveness. He arched his back and shook his shoulders. His thoughts had wandered elsewhere, but he heard enough to respond to the Judge's question.

"I can spare another day or two at most," calculated Vincent honestly. "I am needed at home by my frail wife and my ailing father. I had promised to return by the full of the harvest moon."

"Good then," affirmed the Judge. "Reverend Heaton shall stay the night and Mister Wetherill will complete his business in two days. Now let's conclude our discussion of foul matters . . . purge all the bad vapors out of our systems. . . then join the others for what remains of the merriment. Who wishes to speak first?"

The younger Ford did not wait to ask. He went over all the details of the first murder, as he had done for John Wetherill a week ago. Then he plowed into the details surrounding the murder of Mingo Tim. He concluded with his take on who might be the next victim.

"You and yours shall not be next," opined the Judge. "I thank you for bringing your own bodyguards to my house, for, if the murderer holds true to form, my son's kind, or my own, is next. I am the one most in need of a bodyguard this evening. That is why a constable has been loaned to me."

"After the third murder." interjected the elder Ford, "whose property and kin do you think the evil doer will go after?"

Daniel Wick chimed in to stoke the fire: "The kin and kind of Sam Ford."

"Right you are, Mister Wick," declared the elder Ford. "All the evidence leads back to us. It was my cousin who started the counterfeiting ring. He disgraced the Ford family and made us many enemies. Now he has fled to parts unknown—a fugitive from the law. We are left to face the wrath of some avenging killer—a mad one, I must say, who plays a cruel game to get to me and my son . . ."

"We are all potential victims here, one way or another," added the Judge. "We waste our breath worrying about who will be next. The murderer must be caught before he brings any more notoriety upon our families. We should be thinking about how we can help the Sheriff find the murderer . . . any suggestions?"

Jacob Morrell was first to chime in: "Stiles does not see a pattern so obvious to us. He's convinced himself that my missing wench killed the buck fiddler and had something to do with the fate of Jack Redmon. My negress is afraid of her own shadow. When the authorities find her and return her to me, it won't stop the killing. Mark my words, our job is to put Stiles on another path. At least, so I hear, he's been convinced to bury the buck fiddler's corpse on the morrow. Now we have to convince him to go after the real killer, or killers."

There were rumblings of agreement. Even Vincent Wetherill voiced approval of this strategy. However, he was concerned that Stiles might stumble on to the path he wanted to take. In his heart, he felt it would be better to keep quiet and let these locals come to their own resolve. The next one to speak rescued the guest from Middlesex County.

"I say the Sheriff should be keeping his eye on the kinfolk and friends of Davey Reynolds," offered the younger Ford.

"I can be convinced to favor such a path," stated the Judge officiously. "The problem is to get Stiles to come 'round to our way of thinking."

"If not, we must do it ourselves with the resources we have," added the elder Ford, "but do it without bringing anymore attention to ourselves."

"Are we all in agreement?" asked the Judge with finality.

There was no objection. The men arose from their chairs and headed for the door. The elder Ford muttered something about having to relieve himself. He exited the room first, followed by Mister Wick, Reverend Heaton, and Mister Morrell. The younger Ford reached the door, said something to the second guard, and closed it. He turned to face the two men still in the room.

"We've matters to discuss, gentlemen, before joining the others . . . secret matters known only to ourselves."

Judge Cooper and Vincent Wetherill were tired of sitting. They remained standing while getting on with the business at hand.

"So your father has sent you and two characters of questionable repute as the investigating team?" began the younger Ford.

"Right on that," said Vincent.

"Not quite what the Judge and I had in mind."

"Don't forget that Mister Jolly, in service as an agent of the Sheriff in Perth Amboy, will be joining our team shortly. Also, I understand Mister Jarlman, whom I mentioned to you earlier, may assist in our efforts."

"The former I can trust, though he is a bit long in the tooth," said the younger Ford. "However, he has yet to arrive. The latter is here, but is being detained by Sheriff Stiles at gaol in Morris Town. Even if he is set free, I have doubts about his worth to us."

"So that leaves us, for the time being, with an inexperienced young gentleman and two louts to investigate a most serious matter," assessed the Judge, who went back to stroking his chin with his fingers.

"Is this the best your father could do, Vincent?" asked Ford in a somber tone.

"My men and I have learned much along the way here, gentlemen. After this session with Reverend Heaton, I am sure my team is on the right path."

"Reverend Heaton never mentioned the Reynolds family," said Ford. "He knows them not . . ."

"Not the path I'm interested in," countered Vincent. "I shall leave that furrow for you and your cronies to plow. In doing so, however, you may not be prepared for what is to come."

"What way interests you the most, Mister Wetherill?" asked Judge Cooper.

"The way to the leader of the Sons of the Dawn Sword."

The Judge took a deep breath and placed his fingers in front of his mouth. His face turned red. He exhaled noisily. The younger Ford took a step toward Vincent in the same menacing way Mister Morrell had done a short while ago. He turned his angry face to give a quick glance at the door to make sure it was latched properly. Then he cast narrow, smoldering eyes at Vincent and whispered:

"We do not call our hunting club by the old name anymore."

Vincent glared back at Ford: "Judge Cooper used just such a name minutes ago."

"A-a slip of the tongue," confessed Cooper. "I meant to say our true and proper name—the Sons of Dawn."

"Let's not get into this, Daniel," barked Ford with a dismissive wave of his lacy hand. "It has absolutely no bearing on the threat to us and our keep."

"Yes it does," insisted Vincent, "and I mean to get to the bottom of this."

"Then you shall not be paid," declared Ford. "You are terminated from service to us. You may wait here for your iron water, then be on your way back to your father. He has tricked us by sending incompetents with wild imaginations."

There was silence. Ford went to the window, hands clenched behind his back. He stared intensely at the well-organized bucolic scene, but he focused on no detail. Judge Cooper bowed his head like a tutored boy who had been caught committing a grievous error in judgment. Vincent scanned the bound volumes on the uppermost shelf and waited for tempers to cool and reason to set in. He had struck a nerve and was proud of it. Incompetent he was not. He knew he was on the right path. He could not wait to write to his father and congratulate him on the accuracy of his speculation.

Judge Cooper finally broke the silence by clearing his throat. He was hungry in his own house and wanted all secret meetings to end.

"We will pay you for expenses up to this point. To earn twice as much, we simply insist that your team help keep an eye on the Reynolds clan. Work with us on this and you shall be handsomely rewarded."

"I'd rather work for nothing, avoid a dead end in this investigation, and follow my own wits to solve these recent crimes."

"We can't let you do it," retorted Ford with anger clinging to his words. "You will bring unwarranted attention to us . . . perhaps, even blame for crimes we had no part in . . . old wounds may be opened . . . you do not realize the far-reaching woe which might be stirred up . . ."

"Better to lay low, Vincent," added the Judge. "Keep out of this boil . . . till it's time for you to go."

"I've a hunter and a risk-taker with me," said Vincent confidently. "I've all I need to find your murderer, or murderers. I plan to complete the task in two days."

Ford scoffed and returned to the window. Ravens stealing in a distant field caught his eye. The Judge kept his gaze on the stoic young man. He reached for his chin and applied stout fingers to ample flesh.

"Suppose Mister Ford tells you why he does not want you plying the path you insist on following. Will you tell us, then, that you will cease and desist in your independency?"

"I cannot promise such at this juncture," said Vincent, "but I may consider it after the telling."

"How say you, Mister Ford?" asked the Judge.

"Let's do it and leave our secrets in this room," responded Ford, as he returned to a standing position by the chair he had vacated. He put one hand on it to steady himself and then he began: "Several years ago my father and a few other illustrious gentlemen of lower Morris County formed a hunt club. It had no name at first, no hiding lodge in the forest, no secret signs, oaths, or passwords. It was just as you have told us about your fledgling club in south Middlesex County. Ours developed from a horsemen's society, which occasionally featured a chase 'round here in the valley or up in the highlands. For each event a different locale was chosen. For each event a different beast was featured—be it deer, fox, wolf, wild shoat, or bear. As the club expanded, members would recruit more and more volunteers as bush beaters, hound and horse tenders, equipment bearers, game trackers, and so on. These men came from the ranks of menial laborers at our mines and forges. Others were our estate laborers and trusted slaves. It was an honor for each of them to be chosen to participate in the hunt . . ."

"When was the name for the hunt club decided upon?" interrupted Vincent.

Judge Cooper answered, "Around the time Lord Stirling joined us."

"Correct," said Ford. "The founders of the club were early rousers—always up before dawn and eager to hunt when the sun appeared. Whether in tents the night before or in one of their secret lairs, all members were ready to battle the forces of nature."

"No matter how late the revelers lasted the night before or how much liquor was consumed," added Cooper, "we were ready. As you have seen, the current members still hold to that original zeal. The majority of them voted to schedule another hunt regardless of the recent terrible events and the dire prospect of a hurricane heading up the coast."

Vincent was growing impatient. These two gentlemen were telling him little. He attempted again to learn what he wanted to know: "Exactly when did the name come into use and why that particular name?"

The younger Ford served up a ready answer: "Lord Stirling, himself, suggested it—a man of rare lineage offering a noble name for our hunt club to use. Do you remember when the name was first used, Daniel?"

"Can't say as I do . . . early sixties, perhaps . . . sixty two, sixty-three . . . I do remember particulars about the origins . . . remember Lord William explaining that the Dawn Sword was an ancient symbol of a wending tribe of conquerors, who swept across Europe . . . inspired several tribes to conquer Roman Britain . . . such tribes also carved the sacred symbol everywhere they went. According to Lord William, the large ring at the hilt was used to capture the sun at its rising and steal its power against the challenges of each day . . . powerful, indeed, and a symbol well-suited for our hunting club."

The younger Ford tempered the explanation Cooper had started: "Whether Stirling's account be true or not, the club members liked his story and like the symbol more. Thus, the Sons of the Dawn Sword came into being. Over time the name was deemed awkward. It was shortened by new members like myself. We now prefer 'the Sons of Dawn.'"

Vincent broke in, "That's all there is?"

Cooper obliged, "There's more."

Ford continued, "Unfortunately, there is always more to tell . . . difficult for me to speak about the rest, especially after what Reverend Heaton has told us. I will plow on, if you promise to tell no one else . . . not even your father."

"Hard to promise not telling my father," said Vincent. "I can promise no other, except my father, will hear of it."

"Fair enough, then," piped Cooper, a bit too loud. "Get on with the telling, Jacob. I'm starving."

Ford hesitated. He seemed to be struggling with how to begin. He sat down, gathered his composure, and somehow found a way to start: "Many years ago at the tavern nearest my father's forge, a child was born to an Irish serving maid who worked there. She was a young and healthy woman—strong as she was beautiful, and a favorite with all the men who worked at the forge. None knew who the father of her child was and the mother never spoke of it. She gave her son her surname, Fagan, and the first name, Dan. The boy grew into a well-built lad—strong and tall, hearty and good-humored. He made friends easily and developed a fondness for drink early on. After his mother perished in a fire that consumed the old tavern, my father hired her son as a ditcher and wood gatherer at the forge. However, the lad no longer possessed a fair disposition. His tongue was whittled sharp against authority. He developed a fierce and mean disposition in quick time. When I took over the business, I meant to let this fellow go. However, my father insisted I keep him on. He gave no reason and I gave no argument. In the summer of sixty-seven, Dan Fagan and a pair of his drinking companions ran away—vanished without a trace and took with them tools and instruments used in the mining trade. I posted notice of his leaving and the things he stole, but nothing came of it. He and the other two were gone and soon forgotten by everyone save my father. He still asks upon occasion where Fagan has gone . . ."

"In some ways," interrupted Vincent, "your tale sounds similar to the Reverend's account of Jack Spolden's behavior?"

"Similar, yes, on several counts," continued Ford, "but different in many ways. The devil takes on many guises—as many as the reasons why I am reluctant to talk about our Mister Fagan. I don't want us Fords blamed for anymore trouble around here. We've gone through enough embarrassment with Sam Ford's counterfeiting shenanigans. We can't face more threats and ridicule. My father's reputation is at stake. Another scandal would blacken his name for sure—end his days as an Assemblyman for this county. Folks would look elsewhere for a less tarnished leader."

Judge Cooper added to the plight: "My reputation would suffer as well, for I know what young Jacob knows and my tenure as Judge is tied to old Jacob's tenure as Assemblyman. My reputation has already been tarnished by my decision on the fate of Reynolds and the fate of my own son. One more dark incident involving another wayward son and I am done as a Judge in this county."

The silence in the room was as ominous as it was long. Vincent's head was filled with swirling thoughts and possibilities. The full truth had almost wiggled out into the light. His next question had to be carefully shaped. At last, he had it primed and ready:

"I sense your concern over the reputations of good men. To lose such a tenacious Assemblyman and stalwart Judge in such sore days would be a serious blow indeed. However, I fail to understand how a menial laborer at one forge, who disappeared years ago, has any bearing on the present situation . . . unless, you have held from me the reason for your father's undying interest in the fate of Dan Fagan. Please help me on this small matter."

"'Tis no small matter, Mister Wetherill," grumbled Jacob Ford in a low, hesitant tone. "My father did not merely lose a poor employee . . . he lost a prodigal son."

In the silence, the younger Ford faced the window and peered out on the pre-dusk scene. Not much had changed—the birds were still committing petty crimes in the pristine fields. The sun was lower, but still shining brightly. Shadows were lengthening and growing deeper. It was still a nice day for revealing the truth. Jacob Ford finally broke his silence:

"When Fagan was initially in service to me, I had no idea he was my half-brother. However, I am sure he knew early on who I was to him."

"How did you come to this conclusion?" asked Vincent.

"The way he acted when I came 'round . . . his leering grin . . . eyes, yes, his eyes always staring defiantly at me . . . his slowness in obeying my commands . . . words he employed when he knew I was still within earshot . . . he was jealous of my station and quite upset about my taking over from my father . . . his father."

"Perhaps his mother had told her Dan early on about the Fords?" asked Vincent.

"Perhaps," echoed the younger Ford. "He sure did look like me . . . stouter and stronger, but features which caused some of the men at the forge to call him 'Little Jake' instead of Dan Fagan . . . those who teased him with the name felt his wrath at the receiving end of foul words and fists. It got much worse when I took charge."

"I wonder why Fagan's mother decided on the name, Daniel, in the first place," mused Vincent.

Judge Cooper cleared his throat and reached for a bit more of the Wetherill brandy in an ornate vessel. He spoke as he fussed with the pouring: "Jacob was already taken. The bitch took the name of the man who'd been drinking with old Jacob at the Sign of the Raven on the night her only child was conceived. That drunken soul happened to be me. I knew all about this way before young Jacob found out, but I was sworn to secrecy. I've maintained it till now."

"Gentlemen, I appreciate your trusting me with such secrets," said Vincent, "but I do not see how Dan Fagan is connected with my purposes for being here. Are you asking me to do nothing, because your reputations may be compromised if I find out anything about this Fagan character? Are you now asking me to go look for him instead of spying on the kin of Reynolds? What is it going to be?"

"We are simply trying to show you how dangerous this whole mess has become, since Reverend Heaton announced his concerns about Jack Spolden." Judge Cooper was spilling his words now, as easily as he was spilling his brandy. He sopped up the droplets with the lace on his sleeve, as he continued, "There may be a connection between Spolden and Fagan—a connection of dire consequences for us, if word gets out that the latter is the Assemblyman's bastard son."

"Another blight on the Ford family," interjected young Jacob. "I will not allow it. I am sure my father has not made the connection which the Judge and I have made. He still longs for his wayward son to return and for all to be forgiven. This will never happen. I wish Fagan dead."

"My team was not hired to slay anyone," specified Vincent.

"Nor are we asking you to do such a thing," countered the Judge. "We simply want you to know about Fagan, since Heaton has obviously inspired you with his tale. In whatever you do, Mister Wetherill, while you are with us, you might happen to find out something of Dan Fagan's fate."

"Whether he's alive or dead is all we need to know," said the younger Ford. "We will take it from there."

"Since I'll be snooping about on my own without pay," remarked Vincent sarcastically, "I will make it a point to find out little about Dan Fagan. He is worth nothing to me. Still, it might be good to be adequately forewarned about him. Why not tell me the circumstances in how he came to leave your employ at the forge and what possible connection he has with Heaton's rioter? You have made me curious, and I figure the more I know the better to shape my strategy."

The younger Ford did not hesitate. He had said too much already. A bit more information on the man he hated most would not hurt anything: "While Fagan was in service to me, I entrusted him with tending a pair of hounds during our club hunts. He so looked forward to the event each season, for it provided an opportunity for him to demonstrate his skill in tracking. In his last year with us, he came up with the idea to allow my most trusted laborers and servants to go on informal local hunts of their own, every now and then. At the time, we members of the Sons of Dawn thought it a grand idea to allow our boys to hone their hunting skills. From the start, Dan Fagan and his cronies began calling themselves the Sons of the Sword."

"We thought nothing of it," chirped Cooper. "What harm was there in low men mocking our secret organization?"

"No harm at all," continued Ford, "till things got out of hand. News got back to certain members of our club—Lord Stirling among them—that boys in the Sons of the Sword were often heavily into their cups and causing trouble for innocent folks here and there. Rumors of brawling, thieving, and worse started to circulate. I confronted my workers and servants, who were members of the Sons of the Sword, and I insisted that their informal hunts cease and desist till I decided otherwise. Their leader, Dan Fagan, deemed my decision unfair because the hunts for the Sons of Dawn were not postponed. I failed to see his logic in this. I stood resolute. Fagan backed down when I threatened lashes for any man of mine who could be identified by the victims of hunters' crimes. Fagan sulked and shirked for weeks then ran away with two other Sons of the Sword. The tools they took with them allowed me to assume they were headed for the iron mines . . . most likely ones far from here."

"They stole nothing else?" asked Vincent.

"Nothing that was brought to my attention."

Cooper contributed, "They did steal something else."

"What do you mean?" asked Ford.

"The name . . . the name of their hunt club . . . they took it with them."

"Ah, of course, Daniel . . . I know what you mean. I was not considering the taking of their name as a theft, but you're right in a way."

Vincent was intrigued by the direction he thought this conversation was heading. Perhaps this Dan Fagan was worth knowing about after all. "So what you are telling me is that Fagan disappeared, but the name of the low men's hunt club did not die when you ordered the informal hunts be discontinued. The Sons of the Sword are still around today?"

"Right you are," affirmed the younger Ford. "The name crops up now and then when trouble is reported up in the far hills. Their symbol, a tattoo of a sword in a circle, is whispered about now and then by certain victims. The tattoo is nothing new. Miners and forgemen have worn such from the days before I cancelled the informal hunts. The sign is now worn by younger men who never participated in a hunt and had no association with Fagan. They know nothing about my half-brother's fate. He is dead to them as much as he is to me."

Vincent shared some of his experience regarding rowdy pig irons and the tattoo they sported: "I witnessed the same on the limbs of iron haulers down at Radford's Ferry and heard of the same while in Amboy."

"'Tis a popular, harmless sign on good people," offered Ford, "but quite the opposite on the limb of a black jobber."

"Quite strange to know Lord Stirling introduced the symbol to the Sons of the Dawn Sword," posed Vincent, "but the lowbred end up with such a sign on their flesh."

Judge Cooper pointed to the wall space between shelves filled with books. A faded banner hung there. "The Dawn Sword is emblazoned on gold cloth—the image sewn by my first wife, bless her soul. None of us sports a like tattoo. Such branding is beneath a gentleman's stature. All we have is our not-so-secret sign on cloth."

"'Tis a wonder your Dan Fagan did not steal the banner too," chided Vincent.

"If I guess right," said Ford, "I think Fagan did use the sign as well as the name after he left his position at our forge. Some months after he departed, a band of mountain men raided our northernmost mine. They got away with weapons and foodstuffs, but little more. I wasn't there at the time of the raid, but when I returned and inspected the damage done, one of my foremen pointed out a carving on a mine entrance post."

"A Dawn Sword, no doubt," guessed Vincent, "and pointing east."

"Right you are," answered Ford, with a perplexed look on his face. "And the name carved below the blade?"

"Little Jake," responded Vincent facetiously.

"You play with me, Wetherill. 'Fagan' was carved there."

"This gang ever visit again?"

"Not our mine, but the site seven miles away where the Sign of the Raven establishment had burned down. My men speak of gatherings there of mountain men drinking hard around campfires and singing rousty songs . . ."

"The same place where Dan Fagan was conceived and raised," interjected Cooper.

"Any sighting of Fagan there?" asked Vincent.

"Not a one," said Ford, "and none anywhere else. However, my thinking's changed since Reverend Heaton told his tale. I have a bad feeling Fagan's gang, if he ever had one, has been welcomed into Jack Spolden's fold . . . criminals joined with zealots . . . a bad combination . . ."

"I need to know the whereabouts of this tavern you have spoken of," asked Vincent, "the one which burned down."

"The Sign of the Raven fell to ashes so many years ago," lamented Cooper. "The fire was of dubious origin. The owner, two of his slaves, and Fagan's mother perished in the blaze. Dan, himself, was not there at the time. There were no witnesses. Locals speak of seeing ghosts dancing about, but they are probably the few drunken men who gather now and then . . ."

The younger Ford was more direct in answering Vincent's question, after cutting off the Judge: "The ruins of the tavern are four miles west of the Hibernia forge along the old mine road . . . nothing there but a chimney of stone and a pile of rubble."

Vincent rushed an odd request: "Judge Cooper, will you have any empty barrels left after your men have loaded their waggon for the run to Schooley's Mountain?"

"I imagine so," said Cooper, with a puzzled look on his face. He glanced at his brandy glass which was empty again. "At least a dozen or more . . . why do you ask?"

"I have a plan. I shall require at least four standard-size barrels. Lend me these and I shall demand no more pay for expenses."

The younger Ford stepped in: "For what purpose?"

"The purpose shall be known to those who journey with me on the morrow to an abandoned site—a tavern which burned to the ground long ago. In this way I will occupy my time for two days and be out of your way. I will not be able to interfere with anything transpiring around here."

Judge Cooper held up his empty glass, neither to toast Vincent's idea or surrender to it. He simply asked, "And what shall we say is contained in these barrels, if anyone may ask?"

"Iron water," said Vincent, "pure iron water . . ."

12

A SEPARATE FEAST
· · · · · · · · · · · · · · · · · ·

—at Daniel Cooper's Kitchen House,
first floor Sunday, September 26, 1773

Two tables had been set up in the storage room of Judge Cooper's two-up-and-two-down kitchen house of goodly size. One was small and squarish. The other was long and stout. Cooper's kitchen servants had pushed stores aside and arranged the room in anticipation of men assigned to various menial tasks by the lofty visitors at the mansion. Such common men were scheduled to eat in shifts, each taking a turn when an empty bench became available. Foodstuffs—some in containers of various sizes, some fresh from the autumn harvest—had been pushed to the walls. The room was dark, with but one small window providing meager light. There was no fireplace . . . no candles . . . no lantern hanging from a hook. The air was heavy with the dominant and excessive aromas of the produce in the room and the odors and noise wafting in from the hearth room next door. Three men were seated at the long table, nursing their drinks and waiting for the kitchen servants to bring them their food.

Tom Ward entered the storage room and ignored the three men. They did not bother to give him a glance. He pulled a stool to the small, unoccupied table, took off his heavy oznabrig coat, hung it on a peg under the window, and sat by himself in anticipation of the hearty fare earlier men had come away boasting about. He had nothing better to do than study the men sitting on short benches at the other table. He'd seen one of them often. That one was the brother of the barkeep at Haynes Tavern. Most folks called him Windy Burnet, because he could talk long and loud to anyone who had no choice but to listen. Ward had met the other two only once. He knew little about them and cared less. In sum, he wished he had never met any of them. They were doing an excellent job of ignoring him. Usually that would not bother him so, but this time he liked it. He could enjoy a good meal, stay out of their conversation, and leave without being noticed.

Ward recollected all the times he had seen Windy Burnet run his flying machine on the main road to and from Morris Town. He had been warned at the Haynes place, even by Windy's brother, to avoid the man. Windy had a taste for gossip and a propensity for spinning wild tales. He was doing his best, right now, by trying to capture the attention of the two men who sat on the other side of the long table. Ward noticed that Burnet had brought his own jug of 'Kemble's Thunder,' a local brand of apple jack, more commonly referred to as 'Jersey Lightning.' He was close to finishing off his first cup of the potent stuff. For some reason, unknown to Ward, the waggon captain was not sharing. The other two seemed resigned to bowls of house cider. Burnet was talking loudly to them—something about news harvested from a recent run to Powles Hook and back. He was asking one of the two for confirmation of what he was saying. That one was nodding his head occasionally and starring at the jug of apple jack. After Burnet had emptied his cup, he became loud enough for Ward to hear the man's every word. Ward learned that two gamblers had burned down a horse barn near the racing oval at the Hook. After that kernel of plausible truth, the stage driver's exaggerations and lies mounted. Ward wished his food and drink would come soon. He did not like truth or lies about a place that reminded him of the miserable days of his life he had wasted there. He wished the whole place had burned down.

Ward decided to concentrate on the other two men at the long table. They were separated by one empty bench, not interacting with each other, nor much concerned with what Burnet had to say. The one in the brown hunting coat glanced up at the talker rarely, but when he did so, offered empty eyes. This chap showed no interest or emotion over any of the details in the coachman's story. Ward remembered seeing this burly fellow at the bridge near Book Town two days ago. The man was the waggoner for Cooper's guest of honor, Vincent Wetherill. This one seemed a rough character—one to avoid. The poor chap near him—the one bandaged and bruised—had possibilities. This one was half-listening to Burnet's account. He kept turning his head to stare at the jug of blue lightning. Ward recalled that this was the one who had been hiding in the near-empty waggon at the bridge on Friday—the same one who prattled on about his noble lineage. Such a tale had amused Sheriff Stiles at the time. It had interested Tom Ward greatly. Morrell's foreman wondered if this fellow Irishman's account was true or as exaggerated as Burnet's account was becoming. Ward promised himself to find out when he got the chance. He had much to gain if the battered chap's boast was true.

Burnet's news was interrupted by a pair of ebony servants—actually children of one of the cooks—who swept into the storage room with boards and bowls of steaming fare—heaps of boiled beef, potatoes, carrots, and onions. They also brought in a large tray of buns and scones for sopping the gravy. It was such a plain meal, when compared to the fancy treats being served in Cooper's house, but it was piping hot and in large quantity. It roused no complaints. Another pitcher of hot cider was brought in by one of the serving boys on his second trip. By then, the other boy had filled a wood bowl and plate for Tom Ward and brought it to him. Morrell's foreman accepted the ample fare without uttering a word of gratitude, because the slave-child failed to bow to him. The boy retreated to help his brother attending to the other table. Ward wanted to call the insolent Afric back, scold him, and demand a bowl of hot cider, but he was suddenly distracted by the next person to interrupt Burnet's chatter. Ward decided it would be best not to draw attention to himself, since a law man he knew well had just entered the storage room. Ward would deal with Cooper's charge later.

Zachariah Fairchild, a local Constable of questionable repute, stomped in noisily and approached Burnet's bench. His eyes were on the food just brought in.

"Not too late, I see," said Fairchild with gusto. "This fare looks right rummy."

"Sit," ordered Burnet. "Come join us, sit next to me, and fill your belly afore you get back to work."

Fairchild did not bother to remove his voluminous blue duffel coat. He sat down on Burnet's side and instantly started filling his plate. As he did so, he made an apology of sorts:

"I have not even put in my first hour at guarding the Judge and his family. Business at gaol set me late in coming to relieve the early man."

"The poor fellow remains standing by the guest entrance," chuckled Burnet. "He won't mind another hour. His sore feet can't get much worse. Besides, I need a man of experience to lend an ear to the rest of my news from the Hook. I need someone who knows better than most which words sound best. It appears you are the lucky one, Fairchild. Hear me out, then listen to what these two gentlemen across the table have to add . . . should take less than an hour."

The law man raised an eyebrow and frowned. He had caught Burnet's implication about having experience. However, he said nothing, bobbed his head in agreement, and took his first mouthful of boiled beef. It was best to keep silent and comply in the presence of a man like Burnet. Windy knew all about Fairchild having 'crossed the road' to become a law man. In a former time, he had been quite a slippery fellow—a runner for Samuel Ford in the early years of the counterfeiting business. However, when Fairchild was finally caught, he gave testimony cross to Ford and his gang. This led to Ford's first arrest. At the time, the charges against Sam Ford did not stick and he was let go to resume his illegal trade. At the same time, the elder Jacob Ford vouched for Fairchild's character in the most positive terms and earned the man a full pardon. A short few months after being pardoned, Zachariah Fairchild was appointed a Constable. Since he knew the ways and wiles of criminals, he became an invaluable snitch and hound for the authorities. Burnet was itching to drudge up every aspect, both good and bad, of Fairchild's history and share it with his two listeners.

However, he knew Fairchild was a quiet man and a good listener—just the kind old wag-tongue Burnet did not want to offend or embarrass at this point in time. Windy had to finish his exaggerated tale of doings at the Hook, and now he had three men to enthrall. The one sitting by his lonesome did not count. Burnet never liked Morrell's foreman. There was something about the man not to trust. Tom Ward had an unreadable face, worse now since being battered and bruised from a confrontation with local toughs, according to what Burnet had found out on his own, and now truly believed. The immutable Ward looked almost as bad as the Irishman on Mister Wetherill's team. At least the fellow, introduced as Ike Higgins, was somewhat attentive to Windy's wild version of the stable fire. The teller was pleased. Three out of four captives would do just fine for his audience of fiction.

"Allow me to pour you a cup of Kemble's brew, Constable," said Burnet, as he set about doing so before Fairchild could respond.

"No Jersey lightning for me," protested the Constable with a wave of his spoon. "I've a hard case of the gravels . . . got to stay sober for a full night's responsibilities . . . never know what may happen next 'round here . . . been a bloody cock up in these hills ever since the hanging. Forces a man of my station to remain sober."

Burnet pushed the full cup of lightning over to the Constable anyway. Ike Higgins paid close attention to the gesture. If the brew was offered to him, he would accept it gladly and avoid the hot cider entirely. However, upon entering the kitchen house, Cut Hancock had announced to anyone who bothered to listen that no man was to give Ike any strong drink as long as he was on his medicine. Nobody questioned the stout German waggoner who shouldered a handsome musket-rifle. The weapon was now propped against the table and out of its pouch. Cut meant to clean it before going on his own hunt in the morning. Mister Burnet wanted no part in challenging such a brute or bringing attention to the weapon. The man could do anything he wished. Burnet wanted things to remain just as they were. The Irishman's attention remained on the cup filled with strong drink. The German and the Constable were busy eating. All was quiet, save for the sounds of chewing and gulping. The three men, at least, could be counted upon to half-listen. Burnet was glad for that and continued his overweening narrative.

Even Tom Ward bothered to listen. He perked up and flashed wary eyes each time Burnet mentioned Verdine Elsworth or Ansel Jarlman. The two names brought back memories—all of them bad. Morrell's foreman forced himself to return to concentrating on the movements of the two visitors. Their backs were to him and they seldom turned their heads. They had yet to turn around to acknowledge his presence in the room. That often happened to Tom Ward. On the one hand, he took it as an advantage and liked its potential; on the other, he took it as a slight, and it filled him with a rage which had to be satiated. He had to find a way. The more he thought about it, the more he considered the vulnerability of the wounded Irishman. The poor fellow had played the coward in the waggon back at the bridge. He probably had exaggerated the truth about his noble lineage—more than likely, an out-and-out lie. He obviously had a weakness for strong drink. This was just the kind of fellow Ward could handle. If this Ike Higgins could be separated from the German, then Ward could do what he had to do. After a few strong drinks, the Irish noble would be his . . .

Windy Burnet concluded his account of the fire at the Hook, asked for confirmation of his take on the subject from Cut and Ike, and, when he received mere grunts of agreement, turned to Constable Fairchild.

"Anything new to report from gaol?"

The law man kept hold of knife and spoon when he picked up the conversation: "The Jarlman fellow was brought in this noon. The Sheriff and myself escorted him down from Book Town without incident . . . most cooperative he was and willing to answer any questions . . . said he had nothing to do with either murder and his alibi appeared strong for the second one, but the Sheriff is not sure on the first one, since this Jarlman was at the Haynes place on the night of the murder of Jack Redmon . . . claims he knows nothing about it . . . says he did not stay the night, in order to return to the Hook by dawn the next day . . . says he came to these parts at his boss's behest, looking for a runaway fellow named Billy Walsh . . ."

A choking sound from the other table interrupted Fairchild's banter. All heads turned to have a look at Morrell's foreman. Now the poor man was getting the undivided attention of everybody in the room. Tom Ward was doubled over and struggling mightily to clear his throat. Burnet noticed that the man in distress had no drink at his table. He reached for the cup of Jersey lightning Ike coveted so dearly.

"Constable, please rush this cup over to Mister Ward's table . . . hurry!"

Fairchild dropped his utensils and leaped to the task. He

brought the potent brew to the victim of a bad memory. Ward was coughing fitfully and struggling to sit up straight.

"Sip this here brew, Billy," whispered the Constable in a brotherly fashion. "This'll quell your bark and keep you at your game."

The foreman grimaced and grabbed the cup and drank deeply. He stopped his coughing, but he failed to thank Fairchild for bringing the cup to him. Instead, he gave him a sour look.

"Must've been eatin' too fast," muttered Ward, "'n tryin' too hard to figure out your game, Zachariah."

"Listening to Windy's tale is what did it," joked Fairchild in his usual loud voice. "Mind what you're gnawing on."

The foreman glowered at the law man he trusted the least, and went back to finishing his meal as quickly as he could.

Fairchild returned to the long table to face Burnet's questions.

"So the Sheriff now has two suspects—one for the first murder and one for the murder of Mingo Tim?"

"Not as clean as that," offered Fairchild. "Looks like the Sheriff still feels the buck fiddler's girl had a hand in both murders. Problem with Jarlman is that the man admitted he found out the authorities were looking for him, but he did not return to Morris Town soon as he knew. Jarlman admitted to the search business for the two gamblers who burnt down Elsworth's barn. The search ate up his time . . . appears the Captain would not let him go till those boys were found. So the Sheriff is angry at Elsworth—not Jarlman. To get even, Stiles is keeping our latest visitor in gaol for a day or more . . ."

"For further questioning, I presume?" surmised Burnet, as he chomped on his latest mouthful.

"A safe guess," affirmed the Constable. "The Sheriff is not going to learn more even if he keeps Jarlman as long as he's kept the three counterfeiters."

"Pardon me askin'," said Ike Higgins all of a sudden, and sober and serious, "but do ye know the fate o' them two gamblers ye speaks 'bout?"

Constable Fairchild gave the bandaged man a condescending glance, then looked to Cut Hancock, as if waiting for permission to speak to the Irishman who had interrupted him. The German was concentrating on eating. He never lifted his eyes to acknowledge

Fairchild. He knew Ike was itching to tell his version of the story of the barn fire and outdo old Windy Burnet in the process. Cut did not care about any of this. He reached for a scone.

"Reason I'm askin'," added Ike, "'cause I'm out me fortune due to the thievin' o' the pair which'd Mister Burnet know'd little 'bout. I was near fair ruined by 'em . . . robbed 'n burned . . . survived . . . 'n I ain't ready fer no angels to piss on me grave . . . I 'spect back what'd be mine."

"So you're the one Mister Jarlman asked me to deliver a certain poke to, after he learned where Mister Wetherill was being entertained and I was supposed to be headed?"

With that said, the Constable stood up again, reached under his duffel coat, and extracted a fagged leather pouch. He tossed it on the table. Ike grabbed for it with his good hand.

"The way Jarlman tells it," continued the Constable, "his team of trackers and hounds found two of the Captain's horses early on, then, much later, the bodies of the two gamblers. They were discovered in the high salt grass beyond the far side of the racing oval. They also found a quarter horse grazing nearby . . ."

"Me winnin's is missin'," grumbled Ike, as he turned his pouch upside down, shook it, and let a broken piece of brass fall to the table. He fixed his good eye on the worthless piece of metal.

"Oh," breathed Fairchild innocently, "Jarlman said he found your poke not far from the fellow who caught a pistol round through his eye. The other man was close by . . ."

"How'd he die?" asked Windy Burnet, with his mouth near to full.

"Pierced near the heart by the other fellow's sword . . . bled to death, 'cording to Jarlman's guess," reported Fairchild. "The assumption's been made of an argument over who should get what from this man's bounty. This led to one being stabbed and the other being shot. The latter died instantly . . . the former staggered and fell . . . eventually bled to death . . . with the quarter horse being the only witness and none too talkative . . ."

"So what'd be the fate o' me coins?" asked Ike sadly.

"I know nothing about 'em," confessed Fairchild. "Jarlman simply told me to deliver the poke to its rightful owner. I've done so. When the Sheriff releases Elsworth's agent, you can ask the fetchman yourself."

"I plan to," muttered Ike angrily, "'n get me winnin's back 'fore we finish our converance work."

"You may have to return to the Hook for such," advised Burnet, as he poured himself another cup of Jersey Lightning.

"I'll be up fer a journey or a fight jus' fer fun come mornin' . . . soon as I loose the knots in me limbs," boasted Ike. "Almost to the end o' the Doctor's potion . . . feelin' fit already . . . while me friend, Cut, is at his huntin' game, I'm thinkin' I'll do some sniffin' 'round fer coins buried by them counterfeiters I been hearin' lots 'bout . . ."

Burnet laughed. Fairchild joined in. Cut remained silent, but managed a frown. Tom Ward was busy finishing his meal and keeping silent, save for an occasional cough. However, he did perk up when the Irishman announced his plans for the morrow. It was near to the perfect time to get up and go.

"Where are you fixing to search?" asked Fairchild, feigning concern over a visitor snooping in the barrens of the area.

"I takes me quarter horse to the edge o' Sam Ford's swamp up 'round Hanover 'n seeks out his hidin' place which'd I learnt 'bout jus' this day," responded Ike with confidence. "I ain't 'fraid o' nothin' . . . jus' wants to replenish me pouch."

Burnet chuckled this time, but Fairchild only managed a grin: "We picked Sam Ford's island clean days ago . . . found his press . . . found his plates . . . found some few folds of bills . . . found nary a coin—true or fake . . . all the way to Black Brook."

"Perhaps you missed lookin' in certain right places," suggested Ike.

"Perhaps the Sheriff will not like you snooping 'round where you don't belong," countered the Constable.

Just then, a pair of unexpected things occurred. A man known only to Burnet and Fairchild came limping into the storage room. He was rubbing the back of his head with one hand and clutching the pistol at his belt with the other. He said nothing, quickly surveyed the prospects for a seat at either of the two tables, and then sidled over to the bench between Cut and Ike.

Burnet played his self-appointed role as host: "Jimmy Hornbeck, you old muler, glad to have you come sit with us. Please tell us how the rich man's feast is going. Then we will forget them, for our feast is fair and fine enough. There are still plenty of vittles here for a hungry fellow like you coming off your duties."

The fellow so addressed was still rubbing his head. He responded in a blue tone, "A drink's all I need."

Burnet poured another cup of his precious thunder and passed it across to Hornbeck.

"Looks like you've been kicked by one of your trail mules," said Fairchild. "I didn't know of any such beasts being invited to Judge Cooper's Sunday feast."

"'Twas no mule," groused Hornbeck, as he proceeded to take a handsome gulp of Burnet's brew. "A damn gospel preacher dared slam my noggin 'gainst Cooper's door, I was guardin', in order to gain entrance."

"You stopped him, of course?" asked Fairchild.

"Don't want to talk 'bout it. Let me clear my head 'n get to eatin'. I'm sure Burnet 'n you got more importin' things to talk 'bout with these gentlemen."

"Why, yes we do," said Burnet as diplomatically as possible. "Mister Higgins, on your right, was just talking about his plans for the morrow and the Constable was giving him some advice."

"A warning," added Fairchild.

Jimmy Hornbeck seemed not the least bit interested. He finished his drink and was involved in filling a plate with less-than-warm victuals. Words meant nothing to him now. His ears were still ringing from the pounding his head had suffered.

The second unexpected thing came on the heels of Fairchild's last words. Tom Ward was standing at Ike's end of the table—very close and looming over the seated men. He was staring down at the survivor of the stable blaze. In approaching the long table, Ward had noticed that Ike was unshod.

"I've spare boots in my waggon," offered Morrell's foreman, as he reached for the piece of ruined brass on the table and snatched it up. "Perhaps they be too big for you, but suitable for your hunt."

"Right kind of ye, me good man," said Ike, who had followed the ascent of his precious piece of brass. "Yer timin' fer off'rin' such is good . . . 'course I'll needs good shoes fer me feets, if I'm to be snoopin' 'round the dismals. Thanks mostly fer such a kindness, but I ain't givin' up me brass ye hold fer nothin' . . . 'tis a find holdin' secrets I've yet to figure on . . . could be a key to a myst'ry o' sorts . . ."

Tom Ward waved the piece at Jimmy Hornbeck and got the man's attention.

"Ain't no key," said the latest guest. "Ain't worth no pair of boots, neither."

"What is it, then?" asked Windy Burnet, who was ready to mine a tall tale out of anything.

"That there is a muddin' spoon, or least ways half a spoon," said Hornbeck with a wink of a knowing eye projected at the man holding the thing. "I knows its use for slippin' a measure of explosives so many inches into a hole careful and cautious like.... a miner's tool for keepin' alive . . ."

"So that's the purpose o' them equal grooves on the arm o' the thing?" ruminated Ike.

"The few what's left indicates such," said Hornbeck. "The thing ain't worth its weight 'cause most of the arm's been broke off. 'Twas probably used for to pry open something locked tight. Whoever failed with it probably tossed it away."

Tom Ward dropped the broken miner's spoon on the table. Ike snatched it up before it stopped rolling. He examined it as if it were a jewel.

"Yer tellin' a plausible, Mister Horn," said Ike in the clearest dry voice he could muster. "Where I found this piece is a place fer tossin' such away . . . 'n nearby was once'd a window 'n a chest worth bothrin' to pry open. What I'm holdin' here could be the key clue to a treasure which'd disappeared. I better hold on to it."

"You've been listening too long to Windy's tales," chided Fairchild. The Constable glanced up at Tom Ward. "Does this mean your fellow mick here don't get the boots?"

"My offer stands, with or without the brass," snapped Ward nervously. "Won't be a bother come the mornin'. My boss is stayin' the night 'n I'll be in charge of guardin' his person 'n his wife for the night. On the morrow, my boss is all about business of some sort with the Judge and the Fords. In the mornin' I'll be free to use my own waggon as I wish . . . probably sleep in it till noon . . . not expected to leave with Mister Morrell till way past noon.

"You've a kind boss, Tom Ward," opined Constable Fairchild.

Windy Burnet agreed by contributing a humming sound, but

his mind was focused on trying to figure out what treasure Ike Higgins was talking about. There was a fair tale to be mined in that.

"Kind enough to me," responded Ward, as he fidgeted and shuffled his feet. He gave every indication that he wanted to depart.

"Not most others," added Windy.

Ward ignored the slight and attempted to wrap up the conversation and leave. "Since I have to be up the night, which I prefer, I asked my boss for the favor of a wee bit of time to meself. He would not of granted such if I did not ask."

Morrell's foreman turned to go.

Constable Fairchild's words stopped Ward before he reached the door: "Murders 'round here are all happening in the night. Be careful, Mister Ward. Don't take advantage of Morrell's rare kindness."

Tom Ward glared at the Constable, but said nothing.

"'Tis the kindness o' Mister Ward I'd like to toast afore he leaves," interjected Ike, as he secreted away his odd piece of brass in his empty pouch. "After I do, when do I gets to try on them boots, Mister Ward?"

"I'll bring my waggon 'round to yours at dawn," said Ward, "and, besides, I've one offer to make 'bout your search plans."

"I'm list'nin', careful as can be," said Ike, as he leaned in the direction Ward had taken to get to the door.

"The Constable is right 'bout Sam Ford's hidin' place bein' picked clean," said Ward. "No need to bother yourself there . . . might I suggest, in its stead, a search for Jack Redmon's trove . . ."

"It's never been found," added Fairchild quickly.

Tom Ward decided to walk back to where he had been standing by the long table. The conversation had shifted from drawing attention to him to the subject of Redmon's treasure.

"The Haynes boy stole from all of us," contributed Burnet. "Whoever finds Redmon's hiding place will gain a heap of coins."

"Chances are slight to none," observed the Constable. "The first victim of the murderer we seek was a sly-boot when he was out and about in a crowd. We never caught him at his trade. He would vanish for long spells—far from the Haynes place, so I've been told . . . no telling where he stashed his pickings."

"I'm up fer findin' what no person yet's been able to find," boasted Ike. "Point me in the right direction, Mister Ward. I'll find Redmon's trove afore ye have to follow yer master back home."

Tom Ward placed his large hands on his hips and stood as straight as he could. A hint of a smile formed on his swollen lips. "Good for you, Mister Higgins. Soon as the sun's up, I'll take you in my waggon so's you don't have to ride . . . we'll get to where I'm guessin' the poor boy met his end. I'll sleep there in my waggon while you're out on your hunt."

"We searched the stable," offered Fairchild. "Ain't nothing there which shouldn't be."

"Tom's not talking 'bout where Redman's corpse was found," scolded Burnet. "He's talking 'bout what many believe—the boy was murdered elsewhere and dragged to the Haynes barn. Ain't that right, Tom?"

"I've heard such a rumor," mumbled Ward awkwardly, "'n I believe it. Redmon was carted in from somewhere . . . more 'n likely near his hidin' place."

"Still leaves you with a guess, and only a guess," chided Fairchild. "No one's going to find Redmon's stash of loot."

"I will," insisted Ike, "'n when I returns I may even give some o' it back to right deservin' owners."

When Burnet, Fairchild, and Hornbeck started laughing at the Irishman's boast, Tom Ward donned his grimy cap and left the storage room. A slight grin was still on his face.

Cutlope Hancock was the only one who bothered to watch Morrell's foreman depart. He saw no reason to laugh or smile.

"Don't trust him," muttered Cut to himself.

"Nor do I," whispered Hornbeck, as he reached for another helping of boiled beef. "I trust him much less than any man in Cooper's house, including, most of all, the preacher who tricked me today . . ."

"Why is that?" asked Cut in a low voice only Hornbeck could hear. His eyes were on Fairchild, who abruptly got up and left.

"Ward ain't who he says he is," answered Hornbeck.

"I suspected as such," concluded Cut.

"I know'd him from the mines afore he came down here . . . used to be known as Billy Walsh back then . . . a fugitive from the law . . . no different from most men at the mines. Always keeps to hisself . . . slippery as a black snake. Moved from mine to mine . . . one step ahead of the law."

"Mister Jarlman would like to know all that," whispered Cut.

"The one brought to gaol?" asked Hornbeck too loudly between mouthfuls.

"Yup," said Cut.

13

TWO LETTERS READ,

TWO LETTERS WRITTEN
· ·

—at Cooper's manse, second floor guest room late Sunday, September26, 1773

22nd Day of September

Dearest Vincent

    My love and my life, you have been gone from my side but two Days and I miss you so. Your Absence has caused such a great longing in my Heart. With each empty Hour passing, it aches more without you here by my side to soften the moments in our Marriage, just six months young. Promise you will hasten back soon as you can. I will tolerate no Delay. I long for you to hold me close—the moreso, since Nights grow cool. I long to be calmed by your Voice. I long to feel the warmth of your Kisses on my skin. Your presence makes me strong, gives me the Reassurance that all is safe and well. I know I am with Child—I just know it. All the more reason for you to Return in haste—Quick as you can, before the harvest Moon if at all possible. I shall depend on you to get me safely through these precious Months ahead. You are my faithful, affectionate, and trustworthy Attendant in our journey. I am likewise yours for all time—the Reason you must hasten back. We must be together at this blessed Time.

As a Consequence of our being apart, I have taken ill. It is nothing to worry over—simply a Melancholy and a touch of the Vapors, which I intend to bring to Doctor Stites's attention when he pays his next Visit on Monday morning. My condition has left me Nauseous and light-headed. Fannie has brewed a fine Elixir for me—a splendid home Remedy culled from her secret sources. Sarah serves it to me at each Meal. Notwithstanding its bitter taste,

Fannie's concoction is well worth the taking till, and if, the good Doctor recommends something better.

Fannie and her Daughter fuss over me so. You would think I am the patient around here, and not your Father. They tend to my every need. Not one of my Requests to them is treated lightly. Please remember them in your quest for Niceties you promised to bring back with you. I will be so cross if you Remember me but forget pretty things for them.

The other Soul around here, who fusses so over me, is your Father. He is more concerned about my Health than his own. He pampers me. He treats me like a Child. Your Father offers advice on all subjects having to do with good Health, raising Children, drinking Coffee instead of Tea, and the Responsibilities which attend people of high Station. Fortunately, all his fussing and imparting of paternal Wisdom seems to get his mind off his own Ills. Since the last Visit by Doctor Stites, your Father has been doing much better. I make sure to remind him to take the prescribed Remedies regularly, eat and drink in moderation, and take his Nap each day at the recommended time. He gives me no Argument on all counts. Most of his hours are spent on Reading his favorite Histories or preparing Drafts of new Bills for the anticipated Assembly in November. I have helped him with the latter by writing legible Drafts. His skill in this area has Deteriorated with age—his letters tend to crowd together like Pigs in a Sty at feeding time.

I hope this letter finds you well and out of Harm's way. I shall look forward to reading of your Adventures in your first Letter to me, if it ever Arrives before you return. May the Roads you choose be smooth as Slates and the Skies above be Shining bright. May your Deliveries conclude without a hitch.

I pray to the Lord, you will experience no Delays. Hasten back, for my Love is waiting to be shared with only you.

Your sweetest Joy,

Abia

Sept. 26th Day

Dear Sweet Abia I am sad to learn you are not feeling well. I blame Myself for not following the ways of the Heart instead of Obedience to one's Parent. Your well-being comes first, and here I am far from your side in another County enjoying all the grand comforts of a most gracious Host.

I should be at your side administering to your needs and nursing you back to Health. I miss you so. Nary an Hour passes that I do not think of you and your Love for me. All that I can promise is to hasten back soon as I can, when I am done with Business here in Morris County. My Team and I are waiting for Judge Cooper to fulfill his Promise to my Father to provide us with the agreed upon number of Barrels of iron water. His Waggoners will be heading out on the Morrow at Dawn with orders to fill the Barrels at the Schooley's Mountain springs. They are scheduled to return the following Day, or shortly thereafter. Soon as we load our Waggon with same, we shall head home. My Hope and Prayer, my dear Abia, is that I make it home in time to share the harvest Moon with you—to share all the Kisses I have saved up for you.

There is no Reason to be discomfited till I return to your side. It is good to seek the advice of Doctor Stites. However, I am saddened to learn that he will not be paying a visit till Monday. He will be bringing my first Letter to you—later than I expected and too late to cheer you. There is no telling when these Words will reach you—probably after I return. In any case, I know you will listen to what the good Doctor tells you and follow his advice. I know I can trust you to do the same for your own Sake and the Sake of our first precious Child.

I am glad to hear that Fannie and Sarah are taking good care of you. Next to Doctor Stites, old Fannie and young Sarah are the best healers in the South Ward. They shall be rewarded with fine Gifts, soon as I return. I promise not to forget them whilst I complete Business here.

Good to learn that my father is showing concern and assisting in your return to good Health. He can be difficult and stubborn as a Boulder in the Road. Fortunately, he is so fond of you. Now that he knows you carry our Child, he will do nothing or say anything which may upset you. Together, you two can Accomplish a great deal before my return. You may even get him to improve his Handwriting.

As for my Status, there is nothing to worry over. I am weary from the Journey, but was able to rest yesterday and enjoy fine food and high Company today. Judge Cooper and his Wife are splendid hosts. They have treated me to all the Luxuries which attend a Guest of honor. I think it is the apple Brandy that convinced them to put me in such high regard. They insisted, when I arrived, to remove all my soiled traveling Garb and don the finest apparel Judge Cooper had on hand for choice Visitors. He is a large man and his Clothing hangs loose on me, but I dare not complain. In the interim, my traveling Garb is being cleaned and mended by his Servants. I should get my Clothes back on the morrow.

How my Garments got so tattered and dirty is not worth a fret. Actually, in sum, the Journey to here was a swift and safe one. In my first Letter, which you have yet to receive, I told you of the initial, uneventful leg from the Plantation to Radford's Landing and the warm and boisterous reception at Rattoon's Tavern, where Cut and I found Ike Higgins. I also told you about our safe crossing to Amboy and our success in convincing Mister Jolly to join us later. He has yet to arrive. What is new has to do with the rest of the Journey and our various Adventures. On the way to Powles Hook, the Skies started to pour. We completed all our Deliveries and got stuck in the mud but once. We were warmly received by Captain Elsworth at the Hook, and we assisted in dousing a stable fire there. Neither Man nor Horse was lost to the flames, not one Scar or Bruise did we receive, but soiled and smudged were all of us. From there, we headed out to find two River crossings and Judge Cooper's estate at Long Hill. We completed such in good time—safe and sound, save for our Uniforms.

As you can see, there is no need for Concern over my Safety. I have come through this Adventure with nary a Scratch—a button missing, a torn sleeve on my Jacket—nothing more. I shall look forward to likewise Luck all the way back to you. I long to hold you in my arms and keep you warm all through the cruelest Months. There shall be no more Journeys for me till long after our little One is born—an easy Promise to make and keep, for it is my Promise to you, my Sharer of sweet Secrets.

Your Love forever,
Vincent

❖

22nd Sept., 1773
Dear Son:
Here it is two days out since you departed with old Cut and a Waggon of my best Brandy, and I already have the itch to write my first Letter to you. I have good Reason, and I intend to reveal such in this Missive. Firstly, with this writing, I seek to test the post Rider out of Brunswick who crosses the Raritan at Middle Brook and gallops the Circuit from Veal Town to Morris Town, Chatham and Springfield, all the way back in two days. I am trusting no one in Morris Town, so I have given Instructions to your cousin Thomas, who leaves Cross Roads on Business in Brunswick at noon, that my Letter and little Abia's missive be delivered by the post Rider to my dear friend, Ellis Cook, in Hanover. I predict that our Letters will be in Mister Cook's hands by Friday and that he will somehow get them to you soon thereafter. I will assume your receiving them on Saturday, the day I predict you will have reached my cousin Daniel's place. Please indicate in your letter to me that this past Schedule has worked out, for I should judge our Correspondence necessary and frequent and drawn out due to the mysterious Depredations afoot in the back County of Morris.

I trust all went well with the Deliveries and your Journey across County lines to Morris Town. Boss and the Carson brothers will accompany Thomas all the way to Brunswick. Their Deliveries should be done by the morrow. I trust you succeeded in your Pursuance of our plan to recruit a certain Ichabod Higgins and a certain William Jolly for your investigative Team.

I assume all members of the Team are at the Judge's place and eagerly looking forward to carrying out their clandestine Activities. I will not tolerate Failure. Allow your men to employ any Measures necessary to succeed—simply remember not to cross the Authorities or get caught carrying out your Enterprise. Soon as you find out something of Significance, get Word to me quick as you can. I expect to be better informed on this matter than the Coopers or the Fords.

As you can tell by my Enthusiasm over getting to the bottom of this Matter we have been dragged into, I am feeling better and recovering rapidly. Hezekiah's remedies are working splendidly, Fannie's cooking never tasted better, and Sarah and your little Abia tend to my every Need. I feel like a Turk with a dutiful Harem. Royalty is not treated more considerately than I am. The Attention to detail by my three Sisters of Fate has left me quite tranquil of Mind. They have raised my Spirits and given me Energy I thought I had lost long ago. My feet do not ache, nor does my head; but my Bowels remain often riotous. I must start looking for a young Woman to call my own—not too late to Wed again. However, such is a future Consideration—a trifling Concern right now, but a Concern nonetheless. There are more pressing Matters to attend to. By the Fates, I now have the Energy to deal with them.

For the most part, all round here has been peaceful and uneventful since you departed. Your cousin Thomas came calling yesterday and stayed over the Night in advance of his leaving on his jaunt to Brunswick Town. He reminded me to do something about the incident Wednesday last when two bucks from the Long Bridge farm came to gather up bruised apples for the horses.

These two, as you know, have done this Chore before, and I allow them to do so as a Courtesy to a trusted Neighbor. We cannot use the bruisers for our Brandy, so their Fate is with Shoats and Horses. I allow them to take only the ones which have fallen to the Ground—always enough to fill their dray Cart. All went well till the pair took pause from their Labors and bothered Fannie at the kitchen. Seems they did not beg for food, but an audience with her Daughter. My good Fannie denied their request, declaring Sarah too young for the likes of them and too good for boys who smell like Horse shyte.

The Long Bridge pair did not take kindly to Fannie's remarks and cursed her out. Pharoah heard the noise and came running with Axe in hand. Unkind words were exchanged, with the Lord's name taken in vain. Threats were made, till Boss came along and evened the odds. The rude Visitors backed off, turned their half-filled Cart round, and headed up Rescarrick's road. Sarah's honor was maintained and no one was hurt.

Your cousin Thomas is concerned about Punishment for all

Slaves involved in the incident. He plans to talk to the chief Overseer at Long Bridge when he returns from Brunswick. He has indicated the number of Lashings he will recommend be administered to the Backs of the two apple Pickers. This is his call till the Lawrences return from Philadelphia in the Spring, for he remains in charge of Long Bridge till then. He wants me to have a talk with the Lawrences about the low Behavior of many of their Slaves. I intend to do just that in the Spring, for I have other concerns, such as the Rowdiness of their Slaves at the monthly Gatherings. The Lawrences have too many Servants and too few Overseers. Things up on the Ridge are out of control. All they need is one buck Leader to rally them and there will be Trouble indeed. We have a growing Problem and the festering, I fear, will get much worse.

Thomas also asked me the nature of Punishments I have in store for Boss and Pharoah. I felt chipper enough to tell him to mind his own Business. There will be no Punishment for either of mine. Defending the Honor of a young Maiden and her Mother is an act to be rewarded. You and I will discuss a suitable Prize for the both of them upon your return.

Enough said on the doings round here. I have spent much Time working with little Abia on preparing Bills for the upcoming Assembly. Her script is much better than mine, so I let her toil on the final Drafts and read them back to me. We make a splendid Team. Too bad she is a Woman, for Abia would make a fine Legislator after she raises all the little ones the Fates will bless you with. She has contributed worthy Suggestions on several points and has enhanced the Clarity of what I meant to say. I shall look forward to presenting our ideas at the upcoming Session, if the Governor allows. I have heard from reliable Sources that Franklin is planning to open the Session, slated for mid-November, with a Speech on closing the Treasury Robbery case once and for all. I still do not know whether the Assembly will convene in Burling Town or Amboy. Regardless of location, I must be fit to travel and prepared for a lengthy Session. If the Governor intends to close the case, keep Skinner as Treasurer, and pardon Cooper, Haynes, and Budd, then he is in for a Fight. My Peers intend to push for the power to appoint the next Treasurer and demand the dismissal of Skinner so that we can exercise such Power. Closing the Robbery case and exonerating the three Men in Morris County must include the Resignation of the current Treasurer—anything less spells Trouble.

Thus, I need for you to find out what you can about the Treasury Robbery, as well as the Murder of Jack Redmon. Do not desist in your Efforts. I need to be armed with as much information as possible before I begin my Journey to the Assembly Session. I am counting on you and your Team to go beyond the wishes of Daniel Cooper and Jacob Ford. Take all measures necessary and discover what Secrets hide under what Rocks up there. We can agree on the Risk. Be most careful and conduct yourself well. In so doing, none of your Actions will leave me with Remorse.

No matter how I try, I cannot rid my thoughts or my dreams of some Connection between the Murder of the stable boy and the Treasury Robbery. I know the idea seems absurd, but I keep bumping into the associative Facts—bills of Credit, real or otherwise, left behind at the Scene; premises of the Crimes made to look staged; and Blades carefully placed and pointing East. There is more that plagues me, but I choose not to bore you with what you already know. Your job may be to prove there is no Connection between Robbery and Murder. I hope you prove me wrong.

To find any Person responsible for either Crime would earn an eagle's feather for your cap. We might have to assume that some fellow, or perhaps more than one, has played with Authorities for years. Murderers and Thieves are all about gammon—they play at Crime in order to experience the Thrill of not getting caught. Our Murderer enjoys his game too much. He intends to remain Elusive—no doubts on this. He silenced one who must have discovered something about him—something that must remain Secret. He will strike again for the same Reason.

I sense our Perpetrator has been imitating a man he so admires— to gain favor, praise perhaps, or recognition as an equal in foul Deeds. This means our man might be aspiring to join a Band of men— Counterfeiters, perhaps, or Banditti. He may already be a member of some fraternal Order up to no good, or worse. You may laugh at my Speculations on this, call me an old fool who has succumbed to Hallucinations born of strong Medicine, but you may find it advisable to search for a Group of men to which our

Murderer associates. If I am correct in my Assessment of Cooper and Ford at the time of their visit, they know of this secret Group. Why they did not bother to inform us of such is beyond me.

I do remember the elder Ford boasting to me several years ago of organizing a club for Gentlemen hunters up in Morris County. The reason I remember this now has to do with his fascination over a certain ancient Sword—a Symbol he drew at an early Session we both attended. Old Jacob intended to name his hunting Club after this Symbol. How odd to remember, after all these Years, that his drawing on a scrap of Vellum had his precious Blade pointing to the Right—not north, south or west, but East. This may mean nothing in your Efforts to find out the Truth up there. However it turns out, your findings may help me clear my Head of the trifling Thoughts of an old man.

There is no need to worry overmuch about solving a Murder which has little to do with us. Whatever you find about the Treasury Robbery is more important to me. If you can somehow definitely connect that scoundrel, Sam Ford, to the Robbery, that would really be something. I have my Doubts on it, and I have my Doubts about the three men who have traded Evidence for a possible Pardon. I might have better luck interrogating Doctor Stites about the source of the Counterfeit bill he passed to me the other Day. His suspect is probably as guilty of the Treasury Robbery as Sam Ford is.

To get my mind off this unsolveable Maze, I have turned to reading a few Volumes the good Doctor loaned me at his last Visit. The first is William Whiston's version of The Works of Josephus. I find the ancient Histories fascinating, and this one is definitely so. I am through the first of it—all about the Jewish War, in which Josephus, himself, participated and survived, though all his Comrades perished in an odds out sort of way. Before I return it to Hezekiah, you must read it, Vincent. I know you will find it as captivating as I have. We can learn much from this Revolt against a mighty Empire—learn how to avoid the Mistakes made by the ancient Revolutionaries. Such Knowledge may come in handy in the future. I wonder if we have the Courage to fight Tyranny and choose Death rather than surrender. I wonder who among us will be clever enough or coward enough to survive. I wonder.

Enough of the Maunderings of an old fool, who has but a Decade to accomplish something more than Graftings on an apple Tree. Be safe and be well, my Son. Do what you can, then hurry Home with my Iron Water. There is somebody here who longs to have you back more than I do—plus aegri ex abitu viri, quam ex adventu voluptatis cepi—Plautius, Amphitruo 634.

Your proud father,

J.W.

❖

Sept.— 26th Day

Dear Father —

Your letter and Abia's letter were delivered to me today by the Reverend, Samuel Heaton, of Schooley's Mountain. He is a circuit Minister of the Baptist faith and a good friend of your good friend, Ellis Cook. Perhaps you know this strong and honest man. I have grown to trust him in a very short time. Reverend Heaton paid a visit to Cook's tavern some few days ago and graciously responded to Mister Cook's request to find me and hand over two letters delivered by a post Rider on Friday. Heaton was told I could be found at Judge Cooper's estate at Long Hill. Since he had decided to stop here and pay his Respects before returning home, delivering the letters to me was no problem. I am glad a Minister took on the chore. Who better to trust than a Man of the Cloth—at least most of them. Thus, your worry over my receiving the letters is unfounded. The success can be determined by your choosing Mister Cook to receive them and your friend's decision to let a Minister deliver them. You were correct from the start on this, as correct as you are an all things.

I arrived with my Team and the gift of Brandy at Judge Cooper's place late Friday evening. We were exhausted from our Journey up from Powles Hook and rested all Saturday. I thought it best to write my second letters to you and Abia after receiving your first letters. Reverend Heaton handed them over in the midst of a secret Meeting called by the Judge. This was followed by Sunday feasting, which had been interrupted by the hastily called Meeting. Needless to say, I did not get to your letters till I was alone and splendidly ensconced in a fine, cozy Room on the second floor. Your Cousin-in-law tells me this Room was his Son's when he was a child—none other than Benjamin Cooper, one of the three whom you predict will soon be pardoned by the Governor. Your prediction is more than a strong Rumor up here. Many take it as Truth. As I write this letter to you, I recall that Reverend Heaton pulled me aside at the feasting and spoke to me at length about the Hanging and the aftermath. He waxed eloquently about the power of Forgiveness and the pardoning of Sinners who demonstrate Remorse for foul Deeds done. In Heaton's eyes the three condemned men—Haynes, Budd, and Cooper—should be absolved of any wrongdoing. He knows they will be anyway, because their high Station not only allows them to live but also ensures their freedom. In their case, Heaton doubts that Remorse will be a factor in the Governor's decision. The Reverend whispered to me, when we finally sat down and he watched me eat, that poor Reynolds should have been allowed to live to be pardoned. He did not deem it Fair for a man of lesser Station be chosen for the Gallows and three of higher Station never feel the Rope. He saw Reynolds as the truly remorseful one of the lot. I agree with Heaton on this flawed Habit of the King's Law. It must change. Perhaps, if those for Independency get their way, a chance for equal Justice for all free men may occur.

For what Reverend Heaton shared with me this day, and for many other Reasons, I have come to like this man. I sense he may be a valuable source of Information about the doings in Morris County. He has taken a liking to me and has offered to assist me for as long as he remains here. He was talked into staying the Night and plans to start back Home to Schooley's Mountain in the morning. As coincidence would have it, he intends to accompany Cooper's waggoners—the pair assigned to fetch your Iron Water. They will probably leave at the Dawn. I am going to attempt to rise much earlier than that, continue my discussion with the Reverend, and see the three men off.

I have been informed by your Cousin-in-law that his men have been ordered to return no later than Wednesday. This means I will not make it back till the harvest Moon begins to wane. Please reassure little Abia of the Moon still rising when I return—at the least, half the Moon will be better than none. This will give me enough time to ferret about and accomplish something.

Things have been complicated by Happenstance, as far as my Team is concerned, and by the Vicissitudes of those who asked for our Assistance. Let me start with the latter group. Judge Cooper and the younger Ford are not enamored with the Team. They consider me inexperienced. They have doubts about the Trustworthiness of Ike and Cut. Mister Jolly was detained in Amboy and has yet to join us, as he promised. There is a Mister Jarlman, an Agent who works for Verdine Elsworth. He arrived soon after us, but has been detained by Sheriff Stiles for questioning about the Murder of Jack Redmon. I do not have enough Ink to explain all about Mister Jarlman—suffice to say he comes highly recommended by Captain Elsworth, but he is useless to me as long as he remains in the clutches of the Sheriff. Thus, our Clients have quitted the idea of paying us for Expenses beyond this date, if we fail to confine our Investigation to members of the Reynolds clan. Notwithstanding their strict prohibitions, I advised Cooper and Ford that such an Endeavor would be a waste of our Time and that I would complete my Investigation the way I thought best without a penny more from them. They warned me not to and spoke of the Trouble I might cause. I insisted on going my own way and finding out the Truth before I left here. With that, our contrary Clients caved in and told me what they had held from us when they visited the Plantation. You are correct about Cooper and Ford having Knowledge of a secret Group, or, should I say, secret Groups.

The way the younger Ford tells it, his father and other distinguished Gentlemen, including Lord Stirling, formed a hunting Club in this area. They first called themselves, Sons of the Dawn Sword. Their symbol is the same as what the elder Ford showed you some time ago. They recruited mine and forge Laborers, among others, to attend to the menial tasks associated with a successful Hunt. All went well for years—that is, till a certain Indenture, named Fagan absconded with tools and a Name for a gang of Thieves he was forming. By the time this Fagan ran away, the Gentlemen's hunting Club had shortened the Name to Sons of Dawn. So Fagan took what was left and called his gang, Sons of the Sword. According to the younger Ford, the Fagan gang is still operating up north of here in the mining Hills. Among its slew of Crimes, this gang keeps busy at raiding iron Mines and forge Stations, stealing what they wish and extorting Coin of the Realm in return for a Promise not to raid again. Mister Ford paid them off when they visited his Mine and that was the last he saw of the men sporting a Sword tattoo.

Mister Ford knows of a place these Louts may still gather at, and I am considering a visit to such when my Team is whole. I plan to head up to Hibernia, and, from there, find this gathering place. Those fellows in the gang may know a thing or two about recent Crimes around here, may know about Sam Ford's activities up to the time he disappeared from these Hills, and even a thing or two about the Treasury Robbery. I have nothing to lose in the trying and I will not be interfering with whatever is going on around Morris Town.

My reasons for taking a Path out and away are tied to certain Revelations since I wrote to you last. I've already told you about the tattooed pig irons who attacked Ike at Rattoons. I've also mentioned the Sign of the Sword left by the men who escaped from the Amboy gaol. Mention of like tattoos and the Carving of such a Sign cropped up again at Powles Hook. That is where further Knowledge was gained and our Troubles began. All went well, and with alacrity, on our jaunt from Amboy to the Hook, save for when a spell of Rain mired us down. We stopped at the Wheat Sheaf and acknowledged a Request for two Barrels next time and empty Barrels to be returned. At the Nag's Head, we took order for the same Quantity of one next time and noted the empty Barrel was damaged and not worth repairing. At Powles Hook, all went well with Captain Elsworth, who sends his Regards. He wants six Barrels next time and has several Barrels to return.

The darkest incident of our entire Journey was a stable fire at the Hook, which almost got Ike killed. After he was pulled from the Blaze by Cut, and all Horses were accounted for, Ike came around and recounted what two Pikers had told him at the game Table before the Fire broke out. This pair was at hunting in the Hills near Rockaway, back a spell, and ran into a Gang claiming to be at the same Purpose. They were described as wearing a like Tattoo of a Sword. One of these Rogues busied himself with the carving of such a Sword on a Stump. Soon thereafter, these two were robbed of everything they possessed. They were embarrassed by such Misfortune and never reported it to the Authorities when they returned to Rockaway. This is another place I plan to visit on my way up to Hibernia.

These two, along with the coach Captain who brought them to the Hook, were also privy to information about the murder of one of Doctor Budd's slaves. I heard about this latest slaying from two sources—Ike's reporting of what the two Gamblers told him, and Mister Jarlman's account which was garnered from the coach Captain, named Burnet. Jarlman reported to his Boss in my presence what he had found out. In some ways the Murder was similar to Redman's demise—Throat cut ear-to-ear and Tongue clutched in the slave's Fist. No Blade was found near the Victim, but the image of a Sword was carved on the boy's Back. If I was to bet Money on it, I would guess the position of the Body had the Blade of the Sword pointing East. Neither source mentioned such.

The Sheriff, whom we ran into upon crossing the Passaic River into Morris County, is convinced that a runaway Wench, rumored to be the second victim's Girl, is the prime Suspect. Stiles, who, by the way, wishes you well in Health, Business, and Political matters, also believes the Wench has something to do with the first Murder. He has his men out looking for her. That is good for my Team, because we shall be looking elsewhere and avoiding the Sheriff and his kind.

At the time we first ran into the Sheriff, he had with him a certain Waggoner who works as a slave Foreman for Mister Jacob Morrell, a member of the Gentlemen's hunting Club started by the elder Ford. The man's reason for being with the Sheriff was to identify the Gang of locals who accosted him on the same Night Doctor Budd's slave was murdered. The man was volunteered by Mister Morrell to cart back to Gaol any suspects caught by the Sheriff and his Constables. After a good deal of Rumination this Night, I got to thinking that the Gang of so-called locals is actually a faction of the Sons of the Sword and somehow responsible for the Murder of Doctor Budd's slave as well as the beating suffered by Morrell's foreman. If I am right, then it is possible to pin the Murder of Redmon on this Gang as well.

What convinces me most that I am on the right path is what

the Reverend Heaton told Cooper and Ford after the majority of members of the hunting Club left the room. He spoke of a former Apprentice of his who ran away—a fellow named Jack Spolden. He is rumored to be hiding in Caves and abandoned Mines up north, and preaching his own twisted version of God's Word to other Runaways and disenchanted Workers from the Mines and forges. I hear the most recent Desertions occurred at the Hibernia furnace this summer, soon after Lord Stirling became the sole owner of the Works formerly owned by Sam Ford. I am planning to visit that forge if time allows. Such recent Deserters joined other followers and have organized themselves into a loose network of marauding Gangs, which prey on innocent Hill dwellers. It is worth noting there may, or may not, be some sort of confederation between Spolden's following and Fagan's gang. This apostate Brotherhood appears to have a singular Purpose. They mean to slay all Persons of wealth and nobility, destroy the established Order, and wage War till a new Order arises. The good Reverend is afraid this new menace is spreading, growing in strength, and will eventually venture down from the Hills. I suspect some of its members have already done so, or, at least, Fagan's kind has.

The mastermind, Jack Spolden, a Rioter of the worst stripe, may have already sent disciples down from his latest Lair. According to Reverend Heaton, Spolden has intentions of returning to Schooley's Mountain with a large Following. Rumor has it, he means to baptize his Faithful in the Springs found there. This is the same source Cooper's men will be drawing from for your Purposes. Reverend Heaton doubts the Day of Baptism is imminent, but eventual. This means I have time to intercept this Devil and his Followers. What I do after that is still undecided. At times such as these, I wish you were here to assist me in crafting a clever Plan. All I have now, and for such a brief time, is the Counsel of Reverend Heaton. After he departs for Home, I am on my own.

Keep me in your Prayers.

Your loving and obedient son,

Vincent

14

THE IRON CAGE

- - - - - - - - - - - - - - -

*—at the Old Johnson Mine on Horse Pound Mountain
early Monday, September 27, 1773*

Wild horses thundered by on the seldom-used mule path as
they skirted around the mouth of the abandoned Johnson
Mine. Something must have frightened them up in the highlands
above the great rock ledge that hid the old mine entrance—a
black bear on a midnight prowl perhaps, or a pack of gray wolves
up to no good, or a knot of drunken rogues returning noisily over
the mountain from a successful raid on innocent folks. Maybe
it was simply time for the free stallions to lead their mares and
their offspring to warmer climes down in the valleys. For whatever
reason, the wild horses were on the move and making enough of a
rumble to wake the dead.

A young black woman and a mongrel dog, suspended in an
iron cage above the path, were awakened by the roaring herd. Two
pitch torches, still aglow at the entrance to the played-out mine,
provided enough light for the naked woman to make out the
ghostly, glistening shapes—swift beasts and their giant shadows
stampeding down the narrow mountain path in search of safety
and freedom before the dawn.

Rachel Hagers struggled to a sitting position. Her stiff limbs
twitched convulsively. The biting cold of the pre-dawn air made her
shiver violently. Fingers were numb . . . bones ached . . . no feeling
in her feet. Panic swam in her eyes. She had been rudely awakened
from a troubling dream only to find herself in a nightmare of noise
and dust raised by the galloping parade beneath her. She was
choking and her eyes were stinging, but there was no way to move
away from it. She felt for the rat-catcher, pulled it to her breast,
and held the dog tightly. Her sole companion in the cramped, cold

iron cage was too weak to yelp at the horses. It was trembling worse than Rachel was, offering a whimper and a whine that was quickly lost in the rolling noise below. The proud negress attempted to speak, but managed only a whisper. She was hampered by an iron collar, with prongs facing out, snugly encompassing her neck. A long, heavy chain hung from it and snaked to one of the vertical bars behind her. The collar and the roiling dust made her mouth and throat too parched to raise a decent voice for her words. She wanted to cry out, but she could not even cry. A pathetic whisper to her loyal companion would have to do.

"By the morrow, we gonna chase the horses . . . follow them to freedom, my li'l friend . . . freedom one way or t'other . . . 'live or dead."

Rachel rocked back and forth. She tried singing a sweet lullaby Mingo Tim used to sing to her. It, too, came as a whisper—a ghost of a song from the lips of a young woman close to gaunt and nearly a ghost herself. Rachel stopped trying to sing. It was not warming her. There was no need to bother. Even hope was starting to taste bad.

Suddenly, it was still again. The wild horses had disappeared as swiftly as they had come. The rat-catcher stopped trembling. It was licking Rachel's arm, waiting patiently for her to figure out just how freedom could be attained. The one-eyed guard at the entrance to the mine was nowhere in sight. She and the dog were completely alone, save for the few birds now chirping in the darkness. Rachel had no idea what hour it was. She had a vague recollection of her first full day in captivity. The partial moon was still drifting laterally at the horizon—near to half and boldly bright. Many stars were still competing for attention. Rachel hoped the dawn and warmer temperatures were not far off.

A cool breeze started up again, wafting through the cage and causing all warm-blooded creatures to shiver once more. Rachel knew she could not endure another night of such misery. She had to get out of the cage. How? There seemed no solution. It would be easier to contemplate death . . . so much easier . . .

To keep her mind off the inevitable choice, Rachel decided to rake over what had happened to her on the previous day. She remembered being hauled to this spot, arriving in an unforgiving waggon driven by the reinsman who was supposed to be guarding her now. So sore and stiff she was . . . and bent as an old field slave. She was yanked from the waggon by rough hands—not by the one-eyed fellow, but by two of the horse riders who took orders from the Leutinger. He was the one who commanded the pair to strip her down and wrest Amanda's clever pouch from her grasp. Shortly after the two men accomplished what they had been ordered to do, Rachel broke free from the one holding her and lunged at the other. This man held the pouch and was peering into it, trying to figure out the source of the growling inside. The man did not see fingers with nails sharp as talons seeking to rip at his eyes. Rachel's weapons found his flesh—tore into the man's cheek, narrowly missing his right eye. The other man and the Leutinger were quick to react and came to the rescue. The leader and the underling pounced on the wild negress. She was screaming the name of the only one who could save her . . . but Mingo Tim was not there. He would not be coming . . . not now . . . not later . . . not ever . . .

Rachel struggled against the holds administered by the two men. It was useless to try, but try she did. She let out another scream and demanded they give her back her prize possession. The man left bleeding from her attack finally opened the pouch, reached in, and was promptly bitten by the scruffy devil contained therein.

The last thing Rachel remembered that night was giving out a vindictive laugh, then being struck on the head by the haft end of the Leutinger's knife. When she awoke to daylight on Sunday, she found herself in an iron cage suspended from a thick chain coiled over a stout tree limb. There she was ten feet above the ground, her head throbbing with pain, and her vision blurred. The rat-catcher had been incarcerated with her. She and the dog had no choice but to bear witness to the odd scene below. A gang of men were scurrying about, making preparations for leaving. Each had a horse to tend to. However, the men took turns staring up at their caged princess, pointing to her nakedness, flashing insidious eyes, and saluting her with obscene gestures. The only one to call out to Rachel was the Leutinger. He was waving the same knife he had used on her in the early morning hours of her first day of captivity.

"Hail to our princess . . . the fruit of Afric royal blood! May you live long . . . long enough to see who reigns with you in the next cage we raise!"

There were cheers from his underlings, but Rachel did not understand what all the fuss was about. She was a slave, and she felt she would always be a slave. How did these men know about her mother's boasts—about the noble blood in her veins. It was doing her no good now. Her head hurt so bad. She did not feel up to pondering her situation or fate. Her first priority was to find a way to chase the chill she awoke with. It loitered in her bones like an unwanted guest. She was thirsty and hungry. A nauseous feeling kept haunting her gut, causing it to complain with a rumble. Rachel recalled that her captivity had really begun on Saturday when she was taken from the kind Quakers back at Mine Hill. Recollections of the members of the Sharp family were vague, but they were all she had to warm her. It seemed so long ago that Rachel hid in the safe confines of their barn loft. Oh how she longed to be imprisoned there instead of here. How she longed to wait for dear Amanda to struggle up the ladder with another fine steaming hot meal. Rachel promised herself, if she ever got the chance, to finish every morsel of suppawn pudding or anything else from the Sharp kitchen. She promised to save ample scraps for the rat-catcher. However, a dark, empty feeling always returned—none of what she hoped for was going to happen. The noise of the men leaving shook her from her wakeful dream. They mounted their horses and followed the Leutinger down the mule path. They had left her nothing, save a bag of shells dangling from a corner bar of the cage. Rachel had tried sucking on one of the shells, but it made her stomach complain even more. She knew not the import of the bag of shells in this mad game, nor did she want to. The guard, who was left behind, ignored her every plea; now, even he had disappeared. There was no bucket on a rope, for drink or victuals, to pull up to the cage. No scraps of food were tossed up to her. She was given nothing but the bag of shells. Rachel knew her captors meant for her to die. For whatever reason, she could not fathom.

There was nothing Rachel could do to remedy her plight.

She had pulled and tugged each metal bar of her strongly wrought cage, searching for a weakness. There was none. The new cage had been soundly crafted by skilled hands. Two other cages sat on the ground. She guessed they were waiting for victims. Rachel toyed and twisted the handsome lock on the cage door many times. It too was new, well-made, and unyielding. There was not a speck of rust on the lock or the bars of the cage. All parts of this ungodly contraption were dark, strong, and cold . . . and mercifully glistening wet at dawn. It was the only time Rachel could gain sustenance—the only time to lick moisture from the bars. The last thing of note was a wooden placard someone had hung by wire on the outside of the cage. Rachel could not see all the letters which had been burned into the wood, for its message faced out for others to see. She figured it spelled something about death.

There was no need to do anything when the sun went down. Rachel held the rat-catcher close as she could and curled up on the floor bars of the cage. She cursed the men for not giving her any straw to lay on. The cold iron bit into her flesh. After the first hour in darkness, she did not care. She was determined to sleep until the sun came up. A pleasant dream would come—a dream of climbing up the pyramid of hay in the Sharp's barn . . . of loosening a few stays that held the cupola in place . . . flinging such an impediment aside and wiggling out to stand on the roof of the barn . . . gazing at the wending geese overhead . . . deciding to mock them and fly away . . . feeling torn about leaving the rat-catcher behind . . .

At dawn, a one-eyed man with a noticeable limp emerged from the mouth of the old Johnson Mine. He was dressed in a sweat-stained hunting shirt and patched, mud-stained trousers. He spied a familiar horse rider approaching and raised his spout lantern. He waved it twice over his carbuncled head to signal his friend that all was well, and it was safe to proceed. While still holding the unnecessary light source high, the one-eyed man peered up at the iron cage dangling from the nearest of three stout trees that loomed over the mine entrance and the stones piled here and there in front of it. He could see one dark, naked shape curled in repose on the floor bars of the cage. He could not see the dog, but it had to be in there. Nothing could ever escape from a cage he helped to craft. The first captive of royal blood was probably asleep with the dog held close and not in sight . . . or was she and the dog already dead? The guardian of the cage and mine decided this was a good time to wager a bet with the man approaching cautiously up the mule path. It was also time to rekindle the fire by the large ceremonial ring of stones and prepare a hot meal. The dawn sun was heralding what might add up to a warm, busy day—one which might include the burial of a princess and her dog.

By the time the horse rider had made it up the path, dismounted, and finished tending to his charge's needs, the one-eyed guard had raised a warm welcoming fire and had a pot simmering above the flames.

"What's aboilin', old man?" asked the horse rider, as he neared the fire and rubbed his hands together in its curling smoke. The man wore a faded sailor's jacket and black, baggy trousers. A wool hat bound with black ferret crowned his full face. He was red-lipped and snag-toothed, and far from handsome. The fresh scratches and dried blood still on his cheek did not help either.

"A fav'rite o' yers, Fahnrich," said the one-eyed man with a near-toothless grin of welcome on his whiskery face. "'Tis a squirrel soup I'm readyin' fer the likes o' you 'n me . . . found four grays in me traps afore dawn 'n skinned 'em soon aft' fer to keep 'em fresh in this here pot o' brook water. Their meat's all cleaned 'n cut from their wee li'l bones 'n mingled real nice wit' some secrets o' mine . . . might e'en rub some o' it on yer wounds which'd the negress 'n her dog gave you yest'day."

As the horse rider looked on, the guardian took the long knife he was holding, leaned over the steaming pot, and stirred its contents gently with the mean-looking instrument.

"Your secrets reek of goose fat and onions," sniped the horse rider, as he picked at the dried blood on his cheek and stared up at the cage. "Might not be worth a taste, much less considered as a salve . . ."

"Lots o' good things in this brew, which'd we've borrowed from the klompdraggers 'n local farmers 'round here . . ."

"Whether they was willing or not," scoffed the horse rider with a proud grin.

"Anythin' new be gained by the boys who went down in the valley yest'day?"

"I was sent back here too soon to know," said the horse rider who held the rank of Ensign in the gang. He found a rock by the fire and sat on it. "Seems Black Jake and Little Jake got into quite a boil down at the Smultz place . . . plans for our band to raid Hibernia was delayed."

"What was the Prophet 'n the Gen'ral bickerin' 'bout?"

"Seems Little Jake is for fattening up the princess nymph and selling her off."

"The Prophet will have none o' that," surmised old one-eye.

"I know . . . we all know," added the Ensign.

"He wants her down to bones 'long with the same to the cur, long afore the final battle 'tween God 'n Satan."

"'Tis the reason our Leutinger sent me back."

"Fer to tell me o' a decision we could have eas'ly guessed," scoffed the one-eyed man in disbelief.

"Some of that 'n more, old man."

"Look at her," suggested the reinsman as he pointed his stirring knife at the suspended cage. "She's near to dead. Too late to waste vittles on her now."

"How long you think she has left?"

"Without food nor water since Saturday late, I'd say the negress will be but a sack o' bones by the morrow. I'll wager on it."

"I say she strangles the dog before the morrow and survives off the meat for days . . . I'll wager on that."

"Yer a fool to think she'd do harm to the onliest dear thing she's left wit'," argued the older man, as he stirred his squirrel soup one last time. "Yer money is better put on the dog eatin' her 'n livin' till the first snow."

"Least we agree one of the pair is going to survive the other."

"Guess we could bet on it," advanced the reinsman. "Chances is slight they'll both be stiff on the same hour."

"Then I say the dog goes first," declared the Ensign with his sinister hand extended for an exchange of good luck. The sleeve of his short sailor's jacket was pulled back and a tattoo of a short sword in a ring was revealed on his arm just above the wrist.

The one-eyed man reciprocated, all the while keeping his stirring knife in his right hand.

After the amount of the bet was decided upon, the pot was

removed from the flames. The older man employed iron tongs to do the task and continued to use them to pour the broth into two large bowls warmed on a flat rock by the fire. With his knife he scooped out equal measures of squirrel meat and bits of onions and the secret ingredients he had added to the mix.

The Ensign took up his bowl with both hands and held it close to his face. He let the steam of the reinsman's magic redden his face and bring healing moisture to the fresh scratches on his cheek.

The reinsman was already attacking the contents of his bowl with a long wooden spoon. He was sucking on a piece of squirrel meat when he decided to break the silence and speak:

"You didn't come all the way back here early jus' to wager a bet, Fahnrich. Why was you sent?"

"To see if you found Sam Ford's trove of stolen coins yet," joked the horseman, as he started to sip the hot broth. "Black Jake and Little Jake want you to remember to give 'em each a fair share."

The reinsman was grinning. "If'n I do find any belongin' to the wayward counterfeiter, it stays where I find it till those two are long gone."

"Find anything yet?"

The older man gave a feigned look of astonishment. "Now why would I bother meself with lookin' fer somethin' which'd can't be found? Whate'er o' value Sam Ford lugged up to these parts, he took wit' 'im when he fled west. His coin 'n such are buried under an Ind'an's tree close by where the Mississip' flows . . . 'tis what's been told me 'n 'tis what's to believe."

"You mean to tell me you've been left up here to your lonesome and you never gets the itch to snoop around in this mine once owned by Sam Ford?" asked the horseman in disbelief. "You know as well as me, Ford couched away more gold and silver 'round here than he could carry with him when he departed. Ford's trove has to be somewhere . . . somewhere close . . ."

"The Leutinger ordered me to keep me one good eye on the princess in her cage, 'n I do jus' that . . . night 'n day."

"She ain't going nowhere," judged the Ensign. "All she's got left to do is suck on the shells the Prophet gave her, then die. What you've got is a great deal of time on your hands. I bet you spent most of the night crawling 'round in this old mine."

"So you wants to wager on me nightly habits, do you, Fahnrich?"

"No need to," said the horseman with a confident smacking of his lips. "By the looks of the stains on your breeks, I'd say you were knelt down digging in some mud, and it sure wasn't gained at your traps on dry ground."

The one-eyed man looked down at his damp and soiled trousers. He realized he had lost a chance at another bet.

"So I poked 'round a bit . . . 'tis no crime . . . nothin' was found 'n nothin' was lost . . . you'd do the same if left to yer lonesome up here with nothin' but wild horses and a near-dead wench."

After another small stretch of silence, the Ensign picked up the thread of the conversation. "The Leutinger did not send me back to see what you were up to . . . he trusts you, much as I do, old man. He was told by Black Jake to send someone back to tell you not to lower the cage when you find the princess is dead . . . not to bury the corpse nor bother with the dog. The Prophet wants her to rot in the cage . . . has to do with giving the next royal captive something to ponder in the next cage to be raised."

"Thought 'bout buryin' the negress," mused the reinsman, "'specially if the stench got too bad. . ."

"'Tis against the Prophet's ways to bury royal blood," explained the Ensign soberly. "Such flesh will taint our holy ground. No matter how bad she reeks, you're not to lower what is left of her."

"'Tis a waste o' good iron," groused the reinsman, then he promised he would do as told and went about finishing his bowl of soup. He speared the last pieces of squirrel meat with his knife and brought them to his lips, then he lifted the bowl to his mouth and gulped down the dregs.

The horseman was not as fast. He preferred to savor each morsel of meat and sip the remaining hot liquid in his bowl. He paused and rested his vessel on a flat rock.

"Got some jack hidden somewhere?" asked the Ensign. "I feel like drinking till my legs cause insurrection . . ."

"You'll find it in the mine shaft where I perched a jug o' lightning on top of a heap of Ford's coins," chuckled the one-eyed man. "Left it there to celebrate me find . . . got to get me some more jugs to mark the other heaps as mine."

The horseman joined in on the joke with a hearty laugh and a retort of his own: "Don't need your silver, old man . . . just fetch me some of that jack of yours . . . we'll steal more jugs later after the Leutinger returns."

The reinsman got up and disappeared in the mine. He returned in an instant with the aforementioned jug of hard cider and plunked it down on the flat rock where the horseman's bowl of soup rested.

The Ensign picked up the large vessel and drank directly from it. He smacked his lips and put down the jug.

"Now that's better, old man," declared the horseman. "'Tis the best way to break the fast and greet the day."

The reinsman was not paying attention to the man with whom he was sharing his morning meal. Something was stirring in the cage and the movement caught his eye. It was the little dog which was crawling out from under the clutches of the sleeping princess. The black thing tried to stretch on spindly legs. It shivered and shook its hindquarters, then staggered a step to the bag of shells to see if it had magically turned into something to eat. The dog sniffed the air and caught the scent of the soup. It sauntered to the side of the cage closest to the reinsman's fire and peered down— mouth open and dry tongue out and drooping to one side.

"Look, Fahnrich, one o' 'em's stirrin'!"

"The other one might be dead."

"Not a chance," countered the reinsman. "She's a battler, that one."

"I know it better than most, old man," said the horseman, as he touched his scored cheek gingerly with his hand. "There ain't nothing noble in her blood . . . that negress fell from a devil's loins."

"Look," exclaimed the reinsman, pointing his knife at the iron cage. "The princess is risin' . . . she lives 'nother day!"

Rachel attempted to stand but her limbs would not respond. They were too stiff and ached to the bone. She turned to the side closest to the men's fire and stared out at the two of them with wide, hungry eyes. The older one was pointing a knife at her and saying something about her, but she could not catch all the words. Rachel concentrated, instead, on the wonderful aromas swirling up from the fire. She sniffed the warming air and caught the scent of squirrel skins drying on a rock by the flames. She also spotted small, white bones with bits of flesh still attached to them, basking in a tiny pile on the same flat rock. Oh, how she longed to gather them up, gnaw the bones down to nothing, and scrape the skins clean with her teeth . . . and share a few remains with the rat-catcher.

Rachel reached for the clumsy lock on the cage door and rattled it as best she could against the bars at the frame. She used all the might she could muster to sound a pitiful alarm. The result was a slow clicking—metal against metal—as if a morning breeze was teasing the lock on the cage.

"She's tryin' to 'scape," continued the reinsman.

"Want to bet on her chances?"

"Rather bet on our chances o' findin' Sam Ford's coins—real or not," muttered the reinsman.

"Sounds like similar wagers, old man," surmised the horseman after taking a decent swig of Jersey Lightning. "You ain't never going to find Ford's treasure and your princess ain't never going to gain her freedom."

"Would be sure on one, Fahnrich, but not so on both . . ."

15

THE THIRD CORPSE
· · · · · · · · · · · · · · · · · · ·

—on Judge Cooper's estate early Monday,
September 27, 1773

Cutlope Hancock had the storage room all to himself. The
feasting by low men was over. The two tables had been cleaned
off by the serving boys. Only the large table remained in the room
where stores and supplies had been put back in place. Before the
last boy left the room, Cut asked him to fetch another candle so that
he had enough light by which to clean his prize musket-rifle. The
cook's boy obliged him then ran from the room to join his brother
in whatever mischief they had planned after toiling so hard in the
kitchen house. Now Cut sat alone, under the flames of two stout
candles. He enjoyed these occasions when he could work on his
weapon and conjure up visions of the beasts he might slay after the
sun came up. The best part of it was gaining the chance to clean his
firearm without being disturbed by pesky Ike, or distracted by one
of Windy Burnet's boring tales. The only thing he regretted was
spending another night alone—another night without a woman to
please him and keep him warm. His last moment of pleasure had
been interrupted by that damn fire at the Hook. Opportunity was
mostly luck and his seemed to have turned as empty as Ike's pouch.

A tall, husky Afric woman, dark as midnight, poked her scarf-
wrapped head into the storage room and addressed Cut in a strong
voice of concern:

"Seen my boys, Neb 'n Bale, missa?"

"The pair who served such a fine meal?" asked Cut in response.

"De same two," the woman replied, flashing long yellow teeth
stained by snuff, "'n a heap o' tanks fo' likin' my fare . . . so, you's
seen my boys?"

"They finished up in here 'bout an hour ago," said Cut slowly, as he continued to work on the firelock of his gun. "The last one out was the shorter one. He fetched me this here candle, then he skipped from here fast as a rabbit . . ."

"Dat's my youngest, alright," said the bold negress, as she stepped into the room and eased toward the table. "Dat'd be li'l Neb . . . de other's slow 'n can't never speak."

"I didn't get a chance to thank either of 'em," apologized Cut, even though he felt he did not need to.

"You's already gives 'nough by praisin' de meal, missa," replied the cook, as she placed her large hands on her ample hips. The shadow she cast took up most of the wall behind her. "Guess I gives up de search fo' dem boys . . . prob'ly out playin' hide 'n seek game in de dark . . . guess I gets to see 'em in de mornin'. Neb'll lead Bale back to me . . . he always do."

"Gives you a chance to sleep with your man, and not be disturbed by your little ones," offered Cut rather boldly.

The slave woman let out a deep, husky laugh and spat on the floor. "My man's been playin' hide 'n seek in 'nether county fo' years . . . ain't neva comin' back . . . neva. I's swore off men long 'go . . . jus' turned down an offer by de Cons'able an hour 'go, when he was snoopin' 'round . . ."

Cut placed his weapon gently on the long table and reached into the deep inside pocket his wife had sewn into his hunting coat. He found what he was looking for. He pulled out a shiny gold coin—one of the Dutch johannes Captain Elsworth had awarded him after the fire at the Hook. The German placed the coin on the table, but kept his hand on top of it.

"'Tis not good to sleep alone, woman," said Cut softly. "I meant to reward you for feeding me well . . . now I'm considering this as a reward for allowing me in your empty bed."

"Got my reasons double so fo' not lettin' such a han'same debble as you nex' to my black arse in my straw bed."

"I intend you no harm, my good lady."

"'Tain't none o' dat worries me," declared the slave cook with a wink and another smile. "I can take care a' mineself fo' free or fo' gold, no matter how fierce you's be in de bed . . ."

"Then what can be the bother?"

"My younger sister's in my bed up de stairs . . . already

'sleep . . . already snorin' good, since it be pas' midnight. She's God-fearin' . . . ain't neva had no chile 'n don't want none."

Cut produced a throaty chuckle and also spat on the floor to show he was about to give up on his generous offer of gold in order to sleep with an excellent cook. "I will behave . . . keep you warm on your cold side . . . and be gone afore you or your sister rise . . ."

"'Nother reason's mo' impo'tent den my sister's honor, missa huntin' man," retorted the slave woman, as she shifted her feet and scratched a mole on her chin. "Don't want a half-jack tearin' 'round de kitchen 'n forcin' me to ansa all de queries. Two boys is 'nough fo' me 'n all's I needs to love 'n hold dear . . . don't needs a poke from yo' cob 'n a half-jack to fall outta me . . ."

"There are ways to keep a cob where it's safe to go," offered Cut, as he stood up and started putting his musket-rifle in its sealskin pouch, and his tools and vial of grease in a much smaller pouch. He looked around the room to see if there was a suitable place to hide his prize possession and a place to sleep. "There are ways men have learned to be tame 'n fair."

"I knows all 'bout de back porch, missa huntin' man. By de way, what should I be callin' you's?"

"Mein friends call me, Cut, 'n you can do the same. If you share your name with me . . ."

"Miss Nettie," snapped the black cook without hesitation. "Least ways, my own kind calls me dat. De Coopers calls me, Net. So you's can calls me each or not."

"I will call you, Miss Nettie, for I've taken a liking to you. I respect your fine cooking first, and your honest reasons for not sleeping with me second."

With that said, Cut bowed low, as if he was at Cooper's feast and stood before one of the Judge's honored female guests.

Nettie put a lardy hand to her mouth and winked again—this time, embarrassed . . . also amused.

"Might jus' go fo' a taste o' dat cob, missa Cut . . . right here at yo' bench be as good a place as any . . . 'n don't puts away dat gun slick jus' yet . . . I gots some plans fo' dat."

The German held out his calloused hand, as if he was again at Cooper's feast and inviting an honored lady to join him for a genteel dance before the musicians playing a safe, secular tune.

Nettie reached eagerly for Cut's large hand and allowed herself to be escorted to the bench by the long table. She sat, keeping one eye on Cut, who was fussing with the broad belt that kept up his trousers, and the other eye on the gold coin gleaming under the tall candle.

"I'd feel more so at ease," whispered Nettie, "if you's lock up de door to my storage room 'n took dat gun o' yours offa de table."

"More than honored to fulfill your requests, Miss Nettie," offered Cut, as he rushed to the door and latched it from the inside. He returned to his work table, removed the sealskin pouch and its contents, and hung it from a peg over the window. He returned to his quarry and fussed, once more, over his belt.

"Hurry, missa Cut, ole Nettie's gettin' hungry fo' some cob . . ."

Cut stretched and yawned under the bright eye of the dawn sun. A good morning for hunting, he thought, as he slipped the skin which held his weapon over his shoulder and ambled toward Wetherill's waggon. He passed three men who were busy inspecting the axle of a waggon piled with empty barrels. The one wearing a preacher's broadbrim looked none too happy. He was listening, intently to an explanation, by one of Cooper's men, of the repairs which had to be done. Cut ignored them. Their plight had nothing to do with him. Also, Cut had not been assigned to guard anyone. He had no real part in Cooper's festivities. Vincent Wetherill had insisted on taking care of himself. All Cut had to do was make sure Ike swallowed the last of his medicine and refrained from consuming any alcohol. Those responsibilities were accomplished before Cut led Ike to the waggon after the feasting and made sure the poor fellow was safely ensconced in the vehicle, on a bed of fresh straw provided by Cooper's stable boys. Cut left Ike there to sleep under the stars, and, hopefully, awake a new man at the dawn. He left Ike with a warning not to go with that glum foreman, Tom Ward. Ike did promise that he would stay in the waggon. However, Cut did not believe him.

Although Cut had gotten little sleep in the storage room, he felt like a new man. He blamed Nettie for his condition, and he blamed her for the broad smile on his face. Cut walked up to the waggon under his charge, peered over the sideboard, and saw the impression in the hay where Ike had slept. The Irishman was gone. He probably took off with Morrell's foreman, thought Cut—more than likely, pursuing his dream of finding the pickpocket's hiding place. Cut shook his head. His eye caught sight of a cracked apple jack jug by the rear wheel of the waggon. He bent down and saw that little of its contents slicked the grass. Ike must have consumed near to a full jug, surmised Cut. There was nothing he could do for Ike. Thus, Cut headed for Cooper's stable to check on the bay Shires. After doing so, Cut found himself free to hunt on his own all morning . . . maybe bring some fresh kill back to give to Nettie . . .

The copse wood at the edge of Cooper's marsh seemed a fair place to do some tracking. Cut already had a long string of rabbits and a turkey hen, but he wanted more. The ground was moist and it held the impressions of a horse's hoof prints followed by a pair of cart wheel tracks. Cut followed the impressions, which he calculated to have been pressed into the spongy soil several hours earlier. The sun was almost above the trees. Everything was either brilliant green or the bright reds, golds, and burnished browns of the season. There was no horse or vehicle in sight—not a chance of anyone scaring off potential kill. Cut removed his rifle and string of kill from his shoulder, propped his weapon against his leg, and checked the skin tied around his waist. Then he primed his piece. He stood, silent for a long moment, and scanned the area, looking for the slightest movement . . . nothing yet, just the glint of insects in the sunlight and a pair of turkey vultures circling overhead.

Cut walked slowly towards the nearest tree, keeping to the wheel and hoof tracks. He knew he was about to get lucky. Something had died . . . it may have attracted a scavenger of some sort . . . something better than a stinking carrion bird . . . something worth bringing back to Nettie.

In the shade of the tree, flies were swarming over what was left of little Neb—on his back, with eyes staring at the leaves and branches overhead. Sure enough, a scavenger beast had gotten to the boy's entrails. However, some evil thing had done the boy in before any scavenger had come along. Evidence pointed to a killer of the human kind. Cut bent over the corpse, touched the dried, black blood where the throat had been sliced ear to ear. The boy's mouth was agape and the tongue was missing—many flies appeared to be searching for it. Cut found the tongue grasp firmly in the fist of Neb's left hand. There were no bills wrapped around the shriveled, black thing. Cut looked about for a blade or sharp tool—something pointing east, as he had heard Vincent Wetherill mention on a few occasions. There was nothing in the grass . . . nothing resting on the corpse . . . nothing carved in the boy's flesh.

The dreaded sign had to be somewhere. This was the third corpse—poor Nettie's child killed by the same man who killed Jack Redmon and Mingo Tim . . . had to be, thought Cut. What could be the reason for such senseless killings?

Cut stood up, wiped a rare tear from his eye with the sleeve of his hunting coat, and walked slowly over to the trunk of the tree. Sunlight dappled the bark on the east face of the modest sized oak. There it was, plain as day, a crudely shaped carving—a circle with a sword blade piercing it!

The successful hunter returned to the corpse. He pondered his next move. Cut thought of lugging the remains back to Nettie, then decided against it. Instead, he bent down and closed the dead boy's eyes with his gloved hand. One lid refused to close all the way. It seemed little Neb was not quite ready to accept death. Cut felt the boy was watching him, waiting for his rescuer to make everything right again. All Cut could promise in a whisper was to gain revenge. Cut freed the sealskin pouch from his waist and placed it gently over the boy's face. He removed his hunting coat and spread it over the length of the corpse. Then he snatched up his musket-rifle, which he had left propped up under the carving on the trunk of the tree, and retraced his steps that joined the cart tracks to higher ground. Cut decided to run back to Judge Cooper's kitchen house. All the way, he kept promising himself that his next prey would be the killer, or killers, of little Neb. No amount of gold coin would bring the boy back. Nothing of wealth would make Nettie happy. The death of Neb's killer might . . .

❖

Vincent was preparing to shave when the head house servant, who had brought him a bowl of hot water from the warming kitchen, came rushing back to pound a fist against the door of the guest room. The servant was also calling out Vincent's name:

"Mister Wetherill, sir, come quick! Your man found a corpse! He's out by the kitchen house . . . come quick!"

Vincent hastened to the door—his borrowed banyan fluttering at the ankles as he sped across the cold floor. When he opened the door, the head servant, a well-spoken redemptioner from Dublin, lowered his fist, but not his voice:

"Hurry, sir, a third murder's been done . . . close by . . . near the marsh on Master Cooper's downs. Your man is asking for you . . . come quick."

"I'll be coming, soon as I dress," said Vincent.

"Shall I help you, sir?"

"Not this time, my good man," declared Vincent, as he turned to pull down his cleaned and mended clothes from the wall pegs. "I am faster at it on my own."

He suddenly remembered the letters he had written at the midnight hour. Vincent reached for them on the table, checked the seals, and handed them to the head servant.

"My good Timothy Brown, anyone trustworthy, leaving this morn? I am hoping a good soul is headed to Hanover, or might be stopping there?"

"The three widows from Whippany will be leaving shortly, soon as their coach 'n four's brought around," reported Timothy Brown. "I know their driver well . . . trust him like a brother."

"Good then," barked Vincent hurriedly. "Tell your brother to deliver these letters to Cook's Tavern in Hanover. They are for Ellis Cook's eyes only." Vincent reached into his vest pocket and pulled out a few coins of modest value. "Give the man you trust this humble remuneration for his troubles and wish him God's speed."

"Don't you want to know his name, Mister Wetherill?"

"I know yours," shouted Vincent, as he grabbed his captain's jacket and rushed down the stairs.

Vincent cursed the missed opportunity to apply a welcome

measure of warm water and mild lather to his face, and apply one of Cooper's sharp, cool blades against his skin. He also regretted the missed opportunity to apply some of Cooper's expensive spikenard to a smooth chin and cheeks. If he ever got the chance to return to the guest room, the water would have turned cold and the time would have been too late in the day to shave. Vincent cursed again—this time for being angry over such a trifle. Ike, or Cut, had found a murder victim. Maybe the finder had discovered evidence that would lead to a killer. This reason for rushing was much more important than the desire to harvest some stubble.

Vincent realized he had not finished dressing. He slipped his other arm in the sleeve of his cleaned and mended captain's jacket as he exited through a side door and ran down a wide cobbled path which led to the nearby kitchen house. Judge Cooper and a few of his guests, along with their bodyguards, were already there. The focus of their attention was a black woman, sitting on a bench and wailing. Vincent glanced back at the large house he had come from. Men, women, and servants were staring out the windows. The two Fords were at one window, squinting at possible trouble and staying safely indoors. They were flashing questioning eyes and mouthing words of curiosity. Something terrible must have happened—something too close for comfort.

Vincent turned his attention to the two horsemen and waggoner who were heading out from Cooper's stable towards his dismal acres. The waggoner was pressing his pair of steeds into a lively trot and the two horsemen were following close behind. The horseman, wearing a blue duffel coat, looked familiar, but Vincent could not recall where he had seen the man. Identifying the waggoner was much easier—there was Cutlope Hancock snapping the reins over the backs of the bay Shires and guiding the Wetherill waggon over unkempt ground. The German appeared intent on getting somewhere fast. So did the two riders flanking him. In quick time, all three vanished from view.

"Bad news indeed," came the voice of someone who was tugging on Vincent's sleeve. Vincent turned back to what the gathering was focusing on. Mister Morrell was the one drawing Vincent closer to the bench by the wide Dutch door of the kitchen house.

"What has happened?" asked Vincent in a soft voice of concern, as he slipped closer to the bench.

"One of Judge Cooper's boys has been murdered," whispered Morrell. "You know what the import of such means to us, Mister Wetherill . . . don't you?"

"Yes," answered Vincent, as he struggled with what to say next.

"Your man returned from his hunting just minutes ago," continued Morrell in a voice louder than he intended. Two other men close to him turned to listen as intently as Vincent was listening. "Your man rushed to the kitchen house to tell the Judge's cook of what he found near the bog . . . her younger boy . . . so I just learned . . . little Neb, they call him . . . Nebuchadnezzar, his full Christian name . . ."

"So my man has taken my waggon and team to retrieve the body?" interrupted Vincent, as he focused on the poor, distraught woman on the bench. She was being consoled by a younger wench who closely resembled the grieving woman.

"Right you are," said Morrell. "Your man fetched and harnessed the horses without being told to do so. Constable Fairchild, the Judge's bodyguard, wants to hold your man here for questioning till Sheriff Stiles arrives, but the fellow will not hear of it. He is bent on retrieving the body and bringing it to the mother. She, of course, is beside herself with grief. She has called for her other boy, but he has yet to be found. We expect the worst . . ."

"The other one will turn up," opined Vincent, as he moved to separate himself from the spectators and join Cooper and Heaton, who stood over the wailing woman on the bench. They were still trying to calm her down when Vincent approached. The other woman had wrapped her arms around the disconsolate mother and was weeping also. Both women remained seated as they rocked back and forth. Vincent was about to announce his presence to the host and master, but he held his tongue so as not to interrupt the Judge.

"We will catch the malfeaser who dispatched your Nebuchadnezzar," said Judge Cooper in a firm, calculating voice. "The murderer will pay dearly for this horrible deed."

"Damn his soul!" screamed Nettie. "I wants dat man dead!"

"My dear Net," said Cooper calmly, "Sheriff Stiles was summoned away from Morris Town last night. I've sent Jimmy Hornbeck to find him. Constable Fairchild is with the man who insists he knows where little Neb lies. Soon as they return with the body and the Sheriff arrives, interrogations can begin and the hunt for the killer can commence in earnest. Let justice prevail in this . . ."

"Only one kind a' justice, massa Cooper," growled Nettie between sobs, "'in dat's de Lord's will 'n de Debble's hand . . . now I'm favorin' de hand 'n I don' care if'n I uses my own or someone else do kill de bas'ard . . . I wants de man dead!"

"The Lord will have the final say," interposed Reverend Heaton, who acknowledged with a hand gesture that Vincent had arrived. "First thing is to grieve our loss properly. I suggest prayer. Don't you agree, Mister Wetherill?"

The question caught Vincent by surprise. All eyes, including Judge Cooper's nearsighted ones, were fixed on him.

"For certain," said Vincent quickly. "By all means, a prayer and a reading from the Holy Script is in order, Reverend Heaton."

"And a proper Christian burial for Nebuchadnezzar," added Judge Cooper, as he grabbed Vincent's arm and pulled him to the side.

Reverend Heaton was left to console the grieving Nettie. He had pulled his Bible from his pouch and was reading scripture to her. She continued to sob and moan uncontrollably.

"Your waggoner is under suspicion for this crime," shared Cooper in a soft voice, so that no one else but Vincent could hear him. "Constable Fairchild wants to hold your man till the Sheriff gets here . . . bring him back to gaol and interrogate him there."

"Cut must have an explanation for his whereabouts since yesterday's feasting," pondered Vincent. "Why would he bother to discover the body, return to tell the boy's mother, and take the waggon to fetch the corpse? Cut may be none too cooperative, but he's no murderer."

"I must say, Fairchild was harsh with your man, when he confronted Mister Hancock in my stable where he was preparing the bays for a hasty jaunt," explained Cooper. "Your man refused to answer any questions . . . simply told the Constable to talk to Net . . ."

"Seems impossible for anyone to talk to that grieving wench right now."

"You're correct on that," agreed the Judge. "My poor girl has lost a son and the other one is missing. I've sent most servants out to look for Balthazar, but no luck yet. I'm afraid her older boy's been taken."

"Not in the cards," said Vincent. "The one who killed the boy is playing his game of eye-for-an-eye. You and your kind were to be the third victim, and it has come to pass."

"Then the Fords are next," sighed Cooper.

"Maybe, maybe not," offered Vincent. "I think the man is done with his devilish game. He may want to move on to bigger things, or he may have been scared off . . . probably long gone and far from here."

"How could you possibly know all this, young man?"

"Let's just say a letter from a man much wiser than myself has put me on a ripe path. I plan to keep to it and get results."

"I don't understand you," breathed the perplexed Judge. "You can't go anywhere without your team. Your waggoner is now a suspect who refuses to say anything. That is why Fairchild and my overseer followed him to find the corpse. The Constable wanted to subdue your man . . . restrain him till the Sheriff arrives . . . but he is afraid of your man . . . so is my man. Thus, Fairchild decided to shadow your Mister Hancock wherever he goes . . . keep a safe distance from the brute."

Vincent was smiling to himself. "If Cut so desires, he will find a man's heart up to two-hundred yards away with his rifle. Fairchild better keep a farther distance behind."

"I know your man won't take off," said Cooper. "He's intent on bringing the boy's body back to Net."

"And I know my Cut will cause no trouble in the doing," emphasized Vincent. "I hope the Sheriff will not detain Cut like what's been done to Mister Jarlman. I'll be sore angry if I have to stay here another day and not be headed up to Hibernia like I planned."

"I can't speak for Stiles," confessed the Judge, "but I'll put in a good word and vouch for your man. The Fords and I want you and your team far from here for as long as it takes my men to bring back the iron water, load your waggon, and bid you well on your journey back home."

"At least we agree on such," said Vincent. "Now let's make sure my leaving happens before noon."

"Can't promise anything till the Sheriff gets here."

"Stiles might be too late in . . ."

Vincent did not finish his words. The folks standing back aways were pointing and shouting. They had sighted a waggon flanked by two horsemen returning from their mission. The three nearest Nettie turned in time to watch Cut bring the waggon in. Nettie's sister let go of her blood kin and stood to greet the worst prospect of her young life. Nettie leaned forward, but did not stand. She placed her elbows on her knees and pressed the palms of her large hands against her eyes. She did not want to see what was coming.

"Where's my Bale?" she cried. "Where's my livin' son?"

Nobody had an answer yet. Most folks assembled there thought they never would.

Cut jumped down from his seat board. He left his prize weapon and the sealskin case, now bloodied and flecked with gore, up on the seat. He ran around to the back of the waggon. One of Cooper's stable slaves came to unhitch the bay Shires and lead them back to the barn, but Vincent stopped the boy and told him to keep them just as they were. He wanted to be ready to depart as soon as possible.

Meanwhile, the German put his arms under his coat, which held Neb's remains. He cradled the corpse in his arms and brought it to Nettie. There were gasps and cries from the throats of the onlookers. There were tears streaming down from the eyes of Nettie's sister. Cut knelt before Cooper's cook and placed the dead child at the mother's feet. Reverend Heaton put a strong, but gentle, hand on Nettie's shoulder and whispered the Lord's Prayer. Nettie stopped crying. She slipped one hand from her left eye, studied the remains for a few seconds, then put her hand back in place.

"Slay de bas'ard, missa Cut," growled Nettie. "Use dat gun o' yours 'n do it slow . . . leg"im fust . . . make 'im crawl . . . den put 'im down like a lame dog worth nothin'. Promise me, missa Cut . . . promise . . ."

Cut stood up and leaned over Nettie. He whispered something in her ear. She did not remove her hands from her eyes, but she gave a sigh and nodded her head.

Judge Cooper stepped forward. He sought to take charge of the situation. He ordered two of his servants to lug the remains into the storage room of the kitchen house and stay with the corpse until the Sheriff arrived to inspect it.

Cut spoke up: "I want my hunting coat . . . uncleaned . . . just as it is."

That got the onlookers murmuring again. The day was warming unusually fast and the waggoner was wearing a heavy green hunting shirt. These uppity folks knew he would not need such a coat until long after the sun went down. There was plenty of time for Judge Cooper's servants to clean it.

However, Cooper did not insist on sprucing up the filthy garment or offer to provide a substitute. He ordered his servants, who were already on the way in, to lay the remains on empty sacks on the cool floor away from window light, and send out the coat with a kitchen slave. They disappeared. In an instant, a slave appeared with the befouled garment held at arm's length. Cut snatched it, checked the pockets, then flung it up on the seat board where it covered the musket-rifle. Flies immediately attacked it.

All the while, Judge Cooper was counseling with the Constable about getting permission to bury Neb's remains as soon as possible.

"I'm in no position to make such a decision," objected Fairchild. "My job is to keep the corpse and the suspect around till the Sheriff gets here. 'Tis Stiles who will make the call on both counts."

Vincent wanted to get to Cut, who was still hovering over Nettie along with Nettie's sister and Reverend Heaton. They were trying to get Nettie to go inside and lay down for a spell.

"I'm havin' none o' dat," Nettie growled. "I'm sittin' right here till my Bale's brought to me . . . 'live or dead."

"Your master has several of his boys out looking, Miss Nettie," explained the Reverend as respectfully as he could.

"How come you all ain't lookin' fo' Bale?" she asked angrily. "Seems like mo' folks is standin' 'round than lookin'."

Cut knew she was right. He patted her on the shoulder and turned to go back to the waggon.

The Constable broke away from the Judge and stepped in front of Cut. He brandished a pistol, and so did Cooper's foreman who stood behind him. The German was about to shove Fairchild aside when Vincent caught the sleeve of Cut's hunting shirt. His quick fingers held it firmly.

"You ain't going nowhere, Mister Hancock, till the Sheriff gets to question you," commanded Fairchild.

"Got to look for Bale," was all Cut bothered to say.

"Can't allow it," said Fairchild. "You're already a suspect for one . . . 'n you might've done in the others . . ."

Cut tried to raise his free fist and slam it into the Constable's face, but Reverend Heaton had hold of Cut's other arm. The limb wasn't going anywhere.

"Now, now, gentlemen," declared the Judge, as he came between the hunter and the law man. "There'll be no more trouble on my property. Let us reason this out. Perhaps we might even clear up a few things before the Sheriff gets here. We should all be looking for Balthazar. He was probably frightened off by what he saw and is hiding . . . scared out of his wits. My guess would be the bog beyond the copse wood. We must find him for Net's sake, and the fact that he may be the only witness to the murder. If we find Balthazar, then it will be the first time in three murders that we have a witness."

The Judge had talked long enough to calm things down. Fairchild and the foreman put their pistols in their belts. Vincent and Heaton still held Cut by the arms. Most of the guests, who had come out to gape and gawk, retreated inside.

Constable Fairchild broke the silence first. "This one refuses to give us any information. He was free all the night to slink about. He says nothing when I ask him where he went and what he was doing after we left the storage room. Was he to guard anyone?"

"My flanker was to watch my waggon," said Vincent. "My waggoner was to guard me, but I refused his services. Cut was free to do what he wished. He is no murderer. By the looks of the way the boy was mutilated, I'd say the one who did in Jack Redmon and the buck fiddler also did in Nettie's child. My man was in another county when the earlier slayings occurred. Cut did nothing wrong."

"I don't care what you think, Mister Wetherill," chirped Fairchild, with no hint of respect for a man of high social status. "If your man won't talk and there are no persons about who can vouch for where he went last night and what he was up to, then I can't let him go till Stiles gets here. When the Sheriff gets here, your man may be detained for questioning for a long spell."

Vincent could not afford to lose Cut for a length of time . . . Ike perhaps . . . not his waggoner. He also did not want to lose face in front of a haughty Constable of low upbringing. Vincent was beginning to dislike the man.

"Why don't you tell the Constable your whereabouts last night, Cut?"

"Not my call," muttered Cut.

"You mean to say you were with someone who could vouch for you?" continued Vincent.

"Yup."

"Who might that be, son?" posed the Judge.

Cut said nothing, but gave a nod toward the bench.

Vincent, in an incredulous whisper, guessed wrong: "Nettie's sister?"

Cut shook his head.

Vincent let go of Cut's sleeve. The Reverend grasped it with his free hand.

"Come with me, Constable," said Vincent. "Judge, you come too. Let's get to the bottom of this and find out what transpired here last night,"

Nettie's sister was back to sitting and holding the one she loved the most. The one who had lost her son was sitting up now, watching a crow in the tree that stood between her house and the master's house.

"The Constable needs to ask you some questions, Net," implored the Judge gently. "Are you up for it?"

"If'n it bring back my boy, Bale, den I'm fine wit' it."

"What you say may free us here to go look for your boy," encouraged Vincent.

"What's you wants to know?"

"Where were you last night after finishing your chores in the kitchen?"

"Went lookin' fo' my chilluns, 'n havin' no luck, I's went to bed . . . slept next to my sister till morn . . ."

Nettie's sister offered a frown, but said nothing.

Fairchild caught the look and took advantage of it: "I've been told otherwise, Net."

"I search long 'n hard fo' dem boys . . . must'a got back real late . . . search all ways 'n ev'rywheres . . ."

Vincent chimed in: "Did you see my man, Cut, at any time in your search?"

"Saw him by his lonesome, cleanin' his gun careful like, when I peeks in on him in de store room. I asks 'bout my boys, but he know'd nothin'."

"Was he still there when you got back from your search?" asked Fairchild.

"Never left de room," muttered Nettie.

"How do you know that?" asked Vincent softly.

"'Cause I never left de room," sighed Nettie. She looked at the interrogators with sad, confessional eyes. "Now go looks fo' my son . . . please go!"

It was unnecessary for any of the men at the kitchen house to join the search for Bale. One of the stable slaves, who had been out searching on horseback, was returning at a gallop. Seated behind him and holding on for dear life was Nettie's older boy. Vincent knew right then and there the identity of the murderer was close at hand, but he had already guessed who to track down . . . Cut did also.

16

AMANDA'S FIND

· · · · · · · · · · · · · · ·

—from Cooper's estate to Sharp's farm Monday,
September 27, 1773

It was getting close to noon. Vincent was more than anxious to depart. Morrell's foreman had not returned with Ike. Sheriff Stiles had yet to appear. To make matters worse, the cook's son, Balthazar, was terrified each time any white man came near him. He sat in Nettie's lap on the bench in front of the Cooper's kitchen house, and buried his eyes between his mother's ponderous breasts. The woman shooed away all those who frightened her boy by scolding them for not understanding that her Bale was mute and would be of no use in answering their questions. Finally, she retreated into the kitchen house with Bale to dress her dead son for burial in the slave's graveyard up behind Cooper's stable.

Constable Fairchild appeared satisfied with Nettie's explanation of why her living son was useless to him. He was also satisfied with her explanation of where Cutlope Hancock had spent the night. Based on Nettie's word, the Constable let Cut rejoin Vincent to make preparations for their sojourn up to Hibernia. In surprise fashion, he even encouraged it. Actually, Fairchild had no choice. He dared not question the word of a grieving mother who had just lost a son. He was also glad to be rid of the responsibility of detaining the German brute. If Cut wanted to accompany Mister Wetherill, then he was going to do as he pleased. Nothing short of a pistol round was going to stop Cut. Sheriff Stiles would have to be placated later. Fairchild was good at making up excuses and lies—better than his aim with a pistol.

Vincent stood with Constable Fairchild, close to where Cut was supervising six of Judge Cooper's slaves in loading barrels of creek water into the Wetherill waggon. Also helping in the process was the foreman who had driven Cooper's waggon to and from the creek. He made sure the slaves wasted no time in filling the barrels and rolling them on and off the waggon. The entire operation was going smoothly and efficiently. Cut directed the slaves with the authority of a stern master. They responded well—more out of fear of the man than anything else.

"What's your purpose in all this?" asked Fairchild of Vincent.

"A courtesy to Judge Cooper," rejoined John Wetherill's son.

"I have been asked to deliver water barrels up to Lord Stirling's forge, while I wait for a fresh supply of iron water to be brought in by his men who have yet to leave for Schooley's Mountain . . ."

"Seems like a waste of time 'n horses, if you ask me," said Fairchild, as he spat on the ground.

"My going, or Cooper's men going?"

"Both, Mister Wetherill. Iron water never lives up to its claims. Might as well bring creek water to the sick 'n the lame."

Vincent gave a quick glance at Fairchild's eyes, but they were unreadable. Maybe the Constable knew some more about the ruse Vincent was planning. Who would have told him? He thought it best not to ask.

"Soon as my waggoner checks the bindings and stays," said Vincent, "we'll be going . . . can't wait any longer for my flanker. Cut and I will have to manage the rough roads north. Let Ike rest here at Cooper's . . . await our return, then we'll take him safely back to his woman."

"If your second man ever does come back," sighed the Constable, as he searched the trees for crows but saw none.

"What do you mean, Fairchild?"

"I assume your waggoner told you the whole story 'bout Morrell's foreman offering your flanker a pair of boots 'n an opportunity to ride his waggon in search of Redmon's treasure?"

"Cut did fill me in on what transpired at your feasting in the kitchen house," confirmed Vincent. "Yes, he told me who was there and the order you guests came and went . . ."

Fairchild chuckled more to himself than to Vincent. "Your man was, indeed, the lucky one last night—first to arrive, along with your flanker . . . 'bout the same time Windy Burnet came by, so I've been told . . . 'n the last to leave."

Vincent ignored the implication. He felt uncomfortable around the Constable. There was something not to trust about the man—not simply that he had 'crossed over,' but that he always seemed to know more than anyone . . . always one step ahead of everyone else. Vincent felt glad about leaving Fairchild behind. Maybe the Constable would catch the murderer before anyone else did. Certainly this man was more clever and cunning than the bumbling, often invisible, Sheriff.

"So what do you have to say about my flanker having gone off with Morrell's foreman? I understand mister Morrell expects his man back shortly."

"Morrell can anticipate his man's return all he wants, Mister Wetherill. It will not happen today or any other day. The one you know as Tom Ward will not be coming back . . . neither will your flanker. Both of 'em are up to no good 'n headed to parts unknown."

"How do you know?" interrupted Vincent, with noticeable irritation in his voice.

"'Cause I followed Ward out after the feasting 'n found 'im in the kitchen conversing with Nettie's sister 'bout having to go find his mongrel dog, which Morrell's negress had run off with. The man was asking the Afric if she had heard where the buck fiddler's girl had gone. She claimed to know nothing 'n turned to get back to her work. That's when Mister Ward grabbed her arm 'n I stepped in to instruct Ward to leave the wench alone 'n be on his way."

"I wonder if you, or the negress, might have made Morrell's foreman mad enough to slay the cook's son?"

"I'd go along with such opinion, Mister Wetherill. Don't think I won't bring it up with Sheriff Stiles. You see, I already figured out who this Mister Ward really is . . . got what I needed to know from who's being detained by my boss."

"You're talking about Ansel Jarlman?"

"Yes, indeed," admitted Fairchild. "Captain Elsworth's man gave a full enough description of the man he is looking for—called him Billy Walsh, a piker of ill-repute who comes 'round, stays, then leaves when his true identity is revealed. Soon as Jarlman finished his description, I knew who he is looking for . . . but I kept such knowledge to meself . . ."

"The man known around here as Tom Ward, the slave foreman for Mister Morrell?"

"None other, Mister Wetherill," boasted Fairchild, "'n no more. The boy's gone 'n he convinced your man to go with him. They've gone to find a worthless dog and a pickpocket's treasure. Such was the story given to your man at the feasting. I would bet there was a promise of strong drink thrown in before the dawn . . . seems your man was thirsting for such at Windy's table."

"Sounds like something my Ike would fall for," mused Vincent, as he noticed Cut pulling away from inspecting the waggon and walking towards him and the Constable. At the same time, he noticed Reverend Heaton returning on horseback from the site for little Neb's grave. He wondered why the preacher was headed towards him. Vincent rushed his words to conclude his conversation with the Constable. "Those two characters could not have gotten far from here in their searching. . ."

"I disagree," said Fairchild. "Billy Walsh wants nothing to do with being cornered by Captain Elsworth's man. He does not want to be dragged back to Powles Hook. Billy is far from here. My guess is he's headed back to the mines whence he came from . . . 'n your man has been convinced of vast wealth hiding in the hills up yonder."

With that, the Constable sauntered away and Cut took his place.

"Waggon's ready . . . horses too," said Cut. "Waiting on your word, Mister Wetherill."

At that moment Reverend Heaton reached the two men, but did not dismount. "I see you are ready to depart."

"Yes," said Vincent. "I cannot wait any longer for my flanker. Mister Jolly never came around. Mister Jarlman is still in gaol. I am left with Mister Hancock and no one else . . ."

"Well, I wish I could depart same time as you," sighed Heaton, "But I keep being delayed from leaving Judge Cooper's place. First, his waggoners find their axle cracked after loading the vehicle with empty barrels, mind you . . . then they can find no spare waggon that can hold the weight of the barrels full . . . so they have to unload the barrels in order to allow the wright to mend the waggon. The man's still at it, so I've been told . . ."

"Any word as to when Cooper's men will be ready to leave?"

asked Vincent, who was anxious to get going himself.

"Not a clue," said Heaton. "In the interim, Judge Cooper invited me to preside at the burial of Nettie's son. I graciously declined, of course, because Sheriff Stiles has not yet arrived to inspect the corpse and release it for burial. The slothfulness of the wright and Cooper's waggoners have given me enough time to bury three Nebuchadnezzars!"

Vincent motioned to Cut to climb on the Wetherill waggon. After Vincent had mounted his horse, he bid farewell to the preacher: "I wish you well in your journey to your home, Reverend. I thank you for your information on Jack Spolden. It may come in handy."

Vincent clicked a command to his well-rested Spanish barb and urged the eager horse forward.

Reverend Heaton fell in at his side. The gelding also seemed eager to get going.

"I've decided, Mister Wetherill, that you are going to need all the help you can muster. If you're intending to meet up with the Devil, be he in the guise of Spolden, Fagan, or both, you are going to need a man of the cloth at your side. Besides, I've been longing to come face-to-face with Old Harry and tell him a thing or two. I've told the waggoners to inform my wife that I have been detained by God's work and will be home when the moon is full."

Vincent smiled at that remark, and then he laughed. "You are more than welcome, Reverend, to join my team—a Presbyterian, a non-believer, and now a Baptist . . ."

"Before we're done, there'll be three Baptists returning!"

Vincent laughed again at Heaton's humor. "If we don't, there may be three non-believers sleeping for eternity in the hills . . ."

"Have faith, Mister Wetherill. I have evened the odds for you. Remember, I can turn your creek water into wine if I so choose . . ."

Vincent laughed a third time. "Iron water will do, Reverend."

"Which way, Mister Wetherill," called out Cut, as the three men were approaching a fork in the road where Cooper's property ended. One of the Judge's slaves was there, mounted, but not armed. Vincent asked the servant guard about the two roads. The one to the right would take them down to the river. The one to the left snaked around the Great Swamp.

Reverend Heaton interjected his idea: "I say we head to Mount

Kemble, keep to the road north which slips around Morris Town, then head for Mine Hill. Let's pay Elder Sharp a visit and find out what he can tell us about the negress taken from them by a suspect gang the other day. I am curious to confirm what their pious neighbor told me and find out if anything new has occurred since I was first informed."

"Can we get to Hibernia from Mine Hill?" asked Vincent.

"Easy as a muler's train making it down to the nearest forge, my son . . . even easier with the fine Shires under your waggoner's command. I'd say less than ten miles . . . trust me on this."

"I do," shouted Vincent, as he turned to Cooper's slave and told him to inform the Judge of the new plan to stop at Mine Hill first.

The slave promised that he would relay the message. He watched the hasty team veer left and disappear beyond the tall trees which guarded the road to Morris Town.

Amanda Sharp was busy plucking acorns from the reachable branches of the large oak down by Quaker Church Road. She wanted to beat the squirrels to the best ones, just for fun. She planned to pierce the unblemished, plumpest ones with her father's awl and string them together to make a necklace for herself. The late afternoon meal was over and done with. Her cleanup chores had been completed. Now she was treating herself to an hour of solitary amusement before the sun went down. She also had another reason for venturing down near the by road.

It had been a rather strange and terrifying day at the Sharp farm. Just before noon, the man who had brought poor Rachel Hagers to the Sharps on Thursday returned in a rush up the cart path with his horse team and waggon. This coarse man indignantly called out for Amanda's father to hasten out to him and answer his questions. All the Sharp men, however, were in the far fields tending to harvest chores. Amanda's mother went to the Dutch door, flung open the top half, and glared at the rude man whom she recognized immediately. The Eldress Sharp's daughters, including Amanda, were right behind her, peering out at the unexpected guest who sat, with whip in hand, on the seat board of the waggon.

"I come to fetch what's mine," declared Morrell's foreman.

"Thy slave child is not abiding with us, Mister Ward," said the eldress firmly. "Men came for her on Saturday and took her away."

"Not here to fetch the princess," said Ward, as he put down the whip and climbed down from the waggon. "I've come for me dog is all . . . where do you keep 'im?"

"Not here, Mister Ward."

"What do you mean, woman?" asked Ward in a sharp, demanding tone, as he proceeded to the back of the waggon to fetch a water bucket. He walked to the rain barrel at the corner of the log house porch. Without seeking permission, he drew water from the barrel. As he did so, Ward asked again: "Are you speaking truth, Miss Sharp?"

"Thy dog is with thee slave child. She took thee little beast with her . . ."

"I don't helieve you," growled Ward, as he brought a full bucket to the horses to water them. "I gave specific orders to the princess and to your husband that I would return for my dog, I don't give a damn 'bout the Afric wench . . . I just want my rat-catcher . . ."

"Somehow this princess hid thee animal on her person, that night rude men took her away," explained Amanda's mother.

"You don't sound so sure of yourself, woman," snapped Ward. "If I had the time to spare, I'd take a look 'bout this place, but I've a sick man in my waggon 'n I've got to get 'im to where he belongs . . ."

"Let us help, Mister Ward," offered the Sharp woman. "My daughters and I might be able to nurse him back to good health."

Ward gave out a hearty laugh, as he climbed back to his seat board and gave a glance at the bound and gagged man in the back of the waggon. "Ain't no cure for that one, Miss Sharp. He suffers from royal blood in his veins 'n it will prove the death of 'im . . . just needs to isolate this fellow so's he don't taint the rest of us."

With that, Ward turned the waggon around in the side yard and guided his horse team back on to the cart path. The Eldress Sharp and her daughters, save for Amanda, retreated from the door. The plump girl felt a pang of guilt for abetting Rachel in her scheme to steal the man's dog. Perhaps she had been an unwitting accomplice in sin—an accessory to the Devil's work. Amanda knew she would have to pray—pray hard to have God keep unwanted guests from the Sharp farm . . . pray for forgiveness . . . pray for Rachel's well-being. Suddenly, Amanda saw a man's hand arc above the sideboard of Mister Ward's waggon. She caught the glint of a lump of something tossed from the vehicle before the hand disappeared from sight. Amanda would swear that what she saw was real, but then she thought her folks would not listen to a girl's imaginings. Maybe her eyes were playing tricks on her.

When the waggon disappeared from view, Amanda flung open the lower portion of the Dutch door, ran down the cart path, and started searching for whatever had been tossed out of Mister Ward's waggon. The grass was high and thick on both sides of the wheel ruts. It refused to yield any secrets other than insects taking flight in the warm noon sun. Amanda was having no luck in her search. Her mother called her to return to help prepare the late afternoon meal for the men. Amanda abandoned her search and ran back to the house. She promised herself to return after her chores were done, and resume her search. For some reason, she could not get it out of her head that whatever had been tossed out of the waggon was something important—a sign of import to someone.

Upon returning to the site late in the day, Amanda was glad she had used the excuse of going to hunt for acorns. She had not lied, because the pockets of her apron were soon filled with the best she could find. At the bottom of one pocket was also the prize that had been tossed from the waggon at noon— a hefty lump of brass that appeared to be the better half of a broken spoon. Amanda had no idea what the purpose of such a thing might be or its import. It would be hers to secret away until the poor, sick fellow, who tossed it out, returned to retrieve it. The man never would, thought Amanda. If he lived, he would disappear and never return . . . just like dear Rachel and the rat-catcher.

The birds, settling in the branches above, suddenly took flight. Something must have disturbed them. Amanda looked about, but saw no beast lurking in the grass. However, in the distance, she spied dust kicked up by two horseriders and a waggoner in charge of a stout pair of bay Shires. They were approaching at a quick pace on the seldom-used road. More trouble was coming, thought Amanda. This time it would be worse than what happened some few hours ago.

Amanda lifted her drab, homespun gown and ran as fast as she could up the cart path towards the house. The weight of the treasures in her apron pockets slowed her down, but she dashed up the wheel rut faster than at any time in her life. She had to warn all family members in the house. At least her father and her brothers were there this time. Amanda's squat legs were working well until her toe snagged the end of her drooping apron and caused her to fall face down. Acorns spilled from her pockets. She managed to get to her knees, but, instead of picking herself up and running the rest of the way to the door, she went about retrieving the wayward acorns and putting them back in her pockets. It was too late to run anyway. The horsemen and waggoner had swiftly followed Amanda up the path. They halted so as not to run her over.

A large, handsome man with a wide-brimmed hat, similar to her father's, dismounted, came to Amanda, and lifted her up.

"We did not mean to frighten you, miss," said the strong-voiced man, who towered over Amanda. "Are you hurt?"

"If I possessed pride, kind sir, that would be all to be hurtin' me," said Amanda, as she dusted off her gray gown and adjusted her apron.

"We come in peace, my dear, to speak with Elder Sharp, whose neighbor down the road I have had some acquaintance with. He mentioned Elder Sharp in a recent conversation and his words have encouraged me to follow with a visit."

"Thee speaks of my good father, sir," said Amanda. "Whom should I say comes acalling?"

"Reverend Samuel Heaton from Schooley's Mountain and two gentlemen from Middlesex."

"And what shall I say is thy business with my father?"

"In all honesty, a serious matter not intended for your young ears, my dear. Please tell your father it concerns a matter of saving someone's life."

Amanda turned quickly and rushed to the door. She called out to her father and he emerged without his hat or his farmer's smock. He looked wizened and small without his customary garments. However, his blue eyes were keen and filled with an honest man's fire. With them, wide opened and unblinking, he measured the second guests of the day and stepped forward to greet them without any show of fear. Amanda stood at the door, wishing her father had been around to greet the noon waggoner. These new guests did not seem threatening. She had no reason to be leery of them, especially the one who had kindly lifted her off the ground. Still and all, she was glad to see her father handle this situation. Her sisters and one brother stood behind her on the other side of the Dutch door.

There was suspicion in their innocent eyes. They did not share the confidence their oldest sister possessed.

"Welcome to my humble estate," announced Elder Sharp to the three unexpected guests. "What is mine is thine in all things . . . we have fine vittles to share . . . my sons will tend to thy steeds, while thee partake of a warm meal . . . and, God willing, join my flock in humble evening prayer . . ."

"Much obliged," bowed Reverend Heaton, after removing his hat. "You are most gracious, Elder Sharp. My companions and I are in a rush and we have to make it to the Hibernia forge before midnight."

"One needs lanterns for such a jaunt . . . torches at least," advised Sharp. "'Tis a rough going over to that main road north . . . should take thee a good few hours to complete the six . . ."

"We have two lanterns in the waggon," called out Vincent Wetherill, who remained on his horse and close to Cutlope Hancock sitting atop the waggon.

"I insist all allow time for a meal," prodded the Quaker. "My sons will water thine horses and fetch two stout torches dipped in pitch and thirsting for a flame."

Reverend Heaton gave a glance at Vincent and waited for his nod of approval. He got it and bowed again to the kind host. "We accept your hospitality, kind sir, but we must do so with alacrity. Let me introduce myself and my companions. I am Reverend Samuel Heaton of the Baptist faith. My companions are Vincent Wetherill, son of Aseamblyman John Wetherill of Middlesex County, and of the Presbyterian faith. His waggoner is Cutlope Hancock, a husbandman from the like county, and a man of discernment on his path to faith."

"Welcome one and all," announced Elder Sharp. "Come inside and sit at my table, join us in a brief blessing before partaking of good food. I would be most honored, Reverend, if thou might lead us in prayer."

"Most kind of you, Elder Sharp. After my benediction, there is a matter of utmost urgency Mister Wetherill and I must discuss with you."

"Yes, yes, of course," said Elder Sharp, half-listening, as he gimped to his door, opened it, shooed Amanda in, and motioned the guests to enter.

A prayer was given and the victuals were blessed. The meal was quickly devoured. The eminent matter was discussed. Vincent asked about Rachel Hagers. Elder Sharp went over all that he knew about her and the man who brouht her to the Sharps. He also mentioned about the men who took Rachel away. Sharp described them as best he could, but turned to his wife and asked her to provide more details. She did her best to describe what had transpired only hours ago between her and the man who came to retrieve his dog—the same man who had brought Rachel to them. The Eldress Sharp was a shy woman especially with strange men on the wrong side of her door. She struggled with her description of the coarse man who had been so rude to her.

"He was none too joyed to learn poor Rachel had taken thee little beast," said Eldress Sharp. "That man kept calling her a princess, but claimed he cared nothing about her . . . he was only concerned about his dog."

"Did he mention where he was destined?" asked Vincent.

"He claimed to be transporting a sick man in his waggon, but he said not the destination . . ."

"Did you see the chap in the waggon?"

"I saw little, Mister Wetherill. There was a trussed body in that waggon—stiff and still . . . could have been a corpse . . . may thee Lord bless his soul."

"He lives!" blurted Amanda.

"Be still, child," scolded Elder Sharp. "Thou shall not predict what only God knows."

"Please let your daughter speak, kind host," interjected Reverend Heaton, "Mister Wetherill is not insulted by your daughter's enthusiasm. She may know something of import."

The Elder Sharp frowned, but signaled Amanda to speak to the men.

"Tell us what you know, my dear," said Reverend Heaton in a soothing, encouraging voice.

"I stayed at thee door . . . saw a man in thee waggon toss something . . ."

"Could you tell what it was?" asked Vincent eagerly.

"No," confessed Amanda, as she reached into the pocket of her apron, raked through the acorns until her fingers found the metal object she was looking for. She pulled it free and placed it on the table in front of her father.

Cut snatched it up and held it close to the candlelight. He exclaimed, "Ike lives!" He quickly slipped the broken utensil into the secret pocket of his coat. He extracted a gold coin from the same source and plunked it down on the same spot where Amanda had placed her find. "A trade, Miss . . . gold for brass . . . 'n a thanks for confirming a sly dog lives . . . 'though he ain't deserving of it . . ."

17

ESCORT FOR A PRINCE

· ·

*—at the Old Johnson Mine on Horse Pound Mountain
late afternoon Monday, September 27, 1773*

With the sun at his back, Billy Walsh—known to his pursuers as Tom Ward—snapped his whip over the pair of Morrell's horses pulling a filched waggon. He had pushed the steeds hard ever since leaving the Sharp farm at Mine Hill, but the most challenging leg of the journey lay ahead. A low mountain loomed in the distance. The sky was a cold blue with few clouds to break its beautiful monotony. This had turned out to be an unusually warm day. Insects were swarming, to the delight of the meadow birds. All living creatures seemed in a rush to get things done. Billy was one of them. He knew he should rest the horses before climbing the mule path up the western face of the mountain in order to get to the other side. He thought of stopping by the winding creek at the base of the mountain to water the horses, check on the trussed captive in the back of the waggon, and chat with the watchkeep who was always on duty there. Maybe the fellow might have jack or rum to share. Billy had wasted all his liquor on getting Ike Higgins muddled enough to subdue. The man drank so much at Cooper's place that he passed out. This made hogtying the Irishman an easy chore. However, Billy was left with nothing to drink except some rain barrel water back at the Sharp's place.

Billy was parched and angry. He cursed at the horses he had stolen and he cursed the name of Rachel Hagers. She had tricked him after he had tricked her into believing she was being taken to her lover, Mingo Tim. In a sinister way, Billy Walsh had been truthful to the Afric princess. She would be eventually reunited with her man . . . in death. However, Billy had not planned on the wench stealing his dog. The theft was not part of the deal. Now it became the main reason for conquering the back trail to the Old Johnson Mine in record time. Now he needed to coax his team all the way to the ridge and down to where Rachel Hagers was probably caged by now. Hopefully, the Afric trickster was alive and able to account for the rat-catcher. However, Walsh refused to let go of the possibility that the Sharps had lied about his dog and had hidden the animal from him. He would find out soon enough who was keeping his dear mutt. Yet, the darkest thought of all suddenly crept into his mind—old One-Eye, the crippled codger who did all sorts of menial chores for the Prophet, could have taken the dog and made a meal out of the poor critter. Such a dread made Billy all the more irate. There would be no time to rest the horses or steal a drink from the creek. There would be no stopping for any reason. The brooding man figured on at least a half hour's time to make the ridge. He would have to settle for nothing better.

The back way to the played-out Johnson Mine, last owned and operated by the elder Jacob Ford, was seldom used by any law-abiding colonist. It was presently void of wayfarers who might have puzzled over a trussed man in the back of a racing waggon. Billy Walsh was glad for that. He was also glad to see evidence of the last ones to use the path—wild horses. They had trampled the grass and widened the way. Insects attacking the dung also made the trail easy to follow. Instead of expressing his gratitude in a joyous way, Walsh cursed wild horses and insects alike. He was jealous of them . . . jealous of all wild creatures . . . jealous of the freedom to come and go as they pleased . . . do whatever they desired. Billy craved such freedom. All his life he had taken orders from uppity folks and done their dirty work for little or no pay. Only Jack Spolden rewarded him handsomely, and for mad purposes he did not have the ability to comprehend. At least., he had never been called upon to murder anyone, like others, hired by Spolden and Fagan, had been ordered to do. Billy was simply a secret bounty hunter of sorts for crazy 'Black Jake' Spolden.

Billy was charged with bringing in alive three individuals who claimed to have royal blood coursing through their veins—simply kidnap three haughty souls and be rewarded with great wealth. With the capture of Ike Higgins, Billy was more than half-the-way there. He was that much closer to gaining riches, freedom, and respect. He was almost ready to discard his former miserable life, assume another identity, and move on. However, he was not there yet. The first two kidnappings proved easier than he ever imagined. The main reason for his good fortune was that the Prophet had no one in particular in mind, save for the third victim. The choosing of the first two victims was up to Billy. The third victim was a different matter. That challenge lay ahead. Additional aspirants had been challenged by the Prophet to go after the same nobleman. Billy knew he would have skilled rivals vying for the same prize—William Alexander, known more commonly as Lord Stirling, Scottish Earl of Menstrie from the County of Clackmannan and a well-respected Proprietor in Jersey. The highest bounty prize would go to the man who brought in this gilt-edged man. The way to ultimate success was clear to Billy Walsh; however, his first priority had to be getting his dog back.

Morrell's ex-foreman cracked his whip over the slacking team and got them to pick up the pace. The path ahead revealed no impediments. Billy thought it odd not to see smoke from a watchkeep's fire, spiraling up from the lookout ledge. Maybe the Prophet was getting careless . . . maybe the strange man had become over-confident . . .

The one-eyed reinsman was tired of guarding the entrance to the mine. He limped about in a circle for a spell, then spat on the ground before leaning against a large rock which shadowed the morning cooking fire he had raised. Back then, he had only Fahnrich and the Princess in her cage to contend with. Now, there were the Prophet, his bodyguards, and a score of new recruits busy at initiation rites in the mine. Old One-Eye yawned, tugged at the fringe of his sweat-stained shirt, and picked at a spot of mud at the knee of his damp trousers. He wondered why the secret ceremony was taking so long in a secret chamber, which was no secret to him. He had explored every nook and cranny of the played-out mine—the one the Prophet had predicted held great treasure. However, it was the reinsman who discovered exactly where Sam Ford hid a trove of hard coin—real and sham. No one else knew of its location, save for Sam Ford, himself, and, possibly, a few of his cronies who fled with him into the hinterlands. Old One-Eye knew the counterfeiters would never get the opportunity to return to the Johnson Mine. They had become hunted fugitives with a Governor's bounty on their heads. Their treasure was his to keep and never tell a soul about—not even the Prophet. Fahnrich, the ever-inquisitive scout for Spolden, seemed overly curious about the location of Sam Ford's coins. However, the horseman appeared rather ignorant of the history behind the trove. He asked all his questions, but pried no answers out of old One-Eye. The Ensign, based on the Prophet's prediction, guessed right that it was Sam Ford's hoard hidden in the mine—all the coins the fugitive could not carry with him when he fled. Neither Fahnrich nor Spolden would ever find the hard money hidden at the bottom of the water-filled chamber deep within the Johnson Mine. The reinsmen was sure of it, because neither of them could swim or dare dive down deep to retrieve a single sack of coins at a time. Old One-Eys smiled to himself. His secret was safe. He was a wealthy man, patiently waiting for the Prophet to move on or witness the man's revolution falling apart. All the reinsman had to do was outlast the movement—one he did not really believe in. Spolden was attracting desperate, gullible men who yearned to be worth something to somebody before they died. Months ago, the reinsman, himself, had been desperate enough to fall for Spolden's malarky. Back then, he was promised by the Prophet that sight would be restored to his ruined eye. However, a miracle healing was never attempted. The signs were never propitious. His duties were always menial tasks. Never once was the hobbled, one-eyed fellow invited to participate in a raid. He was always left behind, except when a waggoner was needed to haul loot, supplies, and, most recently, to fetch a suspect princess for one of the Prophet's cages. What a waste of iron, he thought. What could be the Prophet's purpose? Surely, Black Jake was rummy in his head. The reinsman paused to stare at the naked prisoner trapped behind the iron bars he helped to shape. If she lived long enough, promised the reinsman to himself, and no one was about, he would lower the cage, spring the lock, and set her free. He planned to explain to the Prophet that the Afric escaped while he slept with his one good eye shut. He would insist that if he had had two good eyes, she would not have been able to escape, either by magic or miracle. Old One-Eye laughed out loud at a joke he would never dare tell the Prophet. He would think of some believable excuse more palatable to a humorless man.

The princess stirred in her cage, but it was not the reinsman's laugh that roused her now, nor the warm sun that found her. Loud, raucous men, stripped to the waist, were emerging from the mine and streaming past the reinsman. They were led by two stalwart men, who had been appointed officers of the Prophet's newest secret cell. After all the new men had passed, Spolden emerged with his bodyguards. The reinsman decided to stand at attention as best he could. It did not matter. No one bothered to acknowledge his existence. No one bothered to pester him about his recent, secret discovery either. He needed no recognition from any of them— not even from the one who claimed to be immortal . . . claimed to possess messianic powers . . . claimed to divine the future from crystals and stars . . . claimed to have visions of the perfect world to come. Yet, even this seer could claim no knowledge of exactly where Sam Ford's treasure was hidden. The self-anointed holy one, who mesmerized all followers with gibberish about the New Zion, had not located a single coin. All the Prophet's gleaming words about overturning the old order and establishing a new one were vapor and mist, worth less than Ford's worst counterfeit. Old One-Eye smiled again, after the confident entourage had passed. He knew who would own the future and have the final laugh . . .

The mountain's shadow was poised to swallow the largest and tallest flat stone marking the easternmost point of the ring of stones and tailings. All the initiates had received their distinctive tattoos. The young, fair-skinned man, dressed in a tawny robe and crowned with a red Spanish cap, stood motionless atop the commanding stone. The brilliant sun made his copper eyes sparkle, as he surveyed his newest recruits and decided to conclude the ceremony of initiation. The shirtless men in the sacred circle were now branded the same—a fresh tattoo of a sword and ring. Their backs had been scored by whips and glistened red raw—the result of a ceremonial lashing by the newly-appointed officers, who would lead them against their enemies. Such ritual punishment was deemed necessary by the Prophet in order to drive disobedience and cowardice out of the new soldiers going into battle. The pair, who administered the lashings, were called the Schultheiss Marshals of the new cell. They were charged with maintaining order during the ceremony and commanding the new recruits on their first raid. Each stood on either side of the robed man. Martinets still dangled from their fists. The Prophet's bodyguards stood outside the ring, each striking a taciturn pose. One of the Marshals called for silence and ordered the latest score of the Sons of the Sword to kneel before the exalted Prophet of the New Zion. They fell to their knees eagerly. Most of them avoided the searing gaze of the one whom the veteran members called Black Jake, behind his back. Half of them stared at the naked woman squatting in the suspended cage. She was staring back at them, keeping still and holding a lifeless dog. The men, who bothered to give her a look, had a difficult time seeing her as the enemy. The letters burned into the dangling wooden sign on her cage read: 'Princess of Axum.' The gazers and gawkers knew nothing about this caged noble—never heard of her. However, they had been told she was the spawn of the Devil—a vile consort of the 'grosse hansen,' so the Prophet called her. If Black Jake said the Afric wench was of nobility, then noble she must be. If their leader claimed she had to die, then so be it. Few bothered to question why the woman had to experience a slow death. God and Black Jake were working in mysterious ways . . .

The rest of the initiates kept their eyes on the Prophet's sword. The double-edged, broad blade was flecked with blood and rust. The weapon was obviously old, but not well-cared for. Nobody dared question Black Jake about the condition of his ceremonial sword. Despite the rust, the thing appeared sharp and functional. The stains of blood indicated that it had been used recently. A few of the new men in the circle speculated about the sword's last deed. They did not have to wonder for long.

"By the exalted blade God's angels forged for me," commenced the robed Jack Spolden, standing tall on his prominent rock, "I invite you to follow it into battle against the grosse hansen—those of noble blood and commoners of wealth who plague our virgin land. Help me and my sword to rid these hills of snakes and eels . . . to eliminate those who are at cross purposes to our own . . . to separate heads from the shoulders of corrupters and cowards, as was recently done by the blade I wield . . . and to prepare the way for the great baptism of all Sons of the Sword. Only then shall we be ready in heart and mind for the final battle between God and Satan. Brothers, before you came along, have already started on Gideon's path—have already begun their search for the inner word by employing the outer weapon. When I raise this avenging sword—my singular obrigkeit—I invite you to recite with me the names of the secret cells already fighting to free the oppressed . . . do so at my command!"

Spolden raised the heavy sword above his head—kept it aloft by holding its large ring haft with both hands. He gave the command and led the recitation of the names of the existing cells: "Peasants of Melchior! Avengers of Zwickau! Angels of Muhlhausen! Miners of Mansfield! Covenanters of Allstedt! Refugees of Albermarle! Ravens of Munster!"

After the chant of the current bands of the Sons of the Sword, Spolden lowered the ceremonial blade to his shoulder. He made sure the tip was pointing behind him—pointing east, where the movement he had conjured in his mind started.

"Remember where you came from, my brothers, and know where you are headed." The Prophet paused to make sure all the new members of his movement were listening. Eyes were focused on his, but they were dull glass and empty of understanding. Jack Spolden, ever the enthraller in his own mind, offered a smile of satisfaction and addressed the new ones with his stentorian voice: "You shall henceforth be called the Palatines of Leyden!"

Cheers rang out in the ceremonial circle. Nary a one knew what a Palatine was or the significance of a place called Leyden. Their name, however, spoke of strength and honor; thus, the name was raucously cheered and unanimously accepted.

The two officers restored order by shouting down the new Palatines. When they were quiet, the Prophet made his concluding remarks: "My righteous brothers, the days of being flayed and fleeced by the royals and the wealthy are numbered. The time has come for you to prey on them . . . turn things 'round . . . destroy their apish game . . . start anew."

Cheers rang out again in the circle. The two officers, for a second time, had to raise shouts of their own to quell the enthusiasm. One of the officers had to employ his whip to silence a rather boisterous fellow. The raucous noise caused the rat-catcher to tremble . . . so did Rachel Hagers, but she was gladdened by it because she had proof the dog had not accepted death. She watched the loud men being stirred by the strange young man who wielded a great sword. Her head was spinning with possibilities of what those men might do to her and the dog. She might be raped by the spirited initiates . . . impaled on a stake . . . beheaded by the ritual sword . . . tossed on a pyre of sacrifice . . . or, worst of all, simply ignored and left to die in the slowest way. Rachel could not decide which manner of torture and eventual death she would prefer. Strangling the dog with her own hands and cutting her wrists with a jagged piece of broken shell seemed the only option. Such deeds would take courage she did not possess. If only Mingo Tim or Tom Ward might return for her . . . if only someone cared . . .

Order was finally restored and Jack Spolden plowed on: "Things failed to go as planned on our latest raid. Our General employed too few men against the forge at Charlotteburg. We gained little and lost face. One overman did not follow the General's orders during the attempt to surround the forge master's house where the pay chest was secured. One man's foolery placed the entire raiding party in harm's way. This one Captain paid dearly for his indiscretion. You will find his head riding a post at the Sign of the Raven. Remember this, my brothers, failure and misdeeds will not be tolerated . . . no shirking of duty . . . no cowardice . . . no act of disobediance . . . no act counter to God's will shall ruin our plans."

Spolden paused to allow his message of unity of purpose through fear to sink in. He read their eyes. The Prophet knew he was good at this—as good as his ability to read the stars. Most of these men cast their usual dull stare. A few pairs of eyes sparkled with a modicum of intelligence. Thus, the majority would be loyal soldiers—easily led and willing to die for the cause. The bright-eyed minority would prove to be the dangerous ones—potential officers in a new movement of revolution, but also possible rivals capable of ruining the order of things to come. Spolden knew he could stay in power as long as the feared Dan Fagan was his co-leader in mayhem. The Prophet could continue to inspire and unite all followers in common purpose. The General could threaten and intimidate in order to keep the sentient ones in line. The Palatines of Leyden appeared ready to be turned over to Little Jake. He would test them quickly and severely.

"I send you and your officers with a trusted guide to the colliery where the General awaits you. From there, you will march to the Sign of the Raven to await the arrival of the Leutinger's band. You will be part of a large raiding party which will attack the Adventure forge at Hibernia, and regain the glory lost at Charlotteburg. If our plan to wreak havoc succeeds in drawing our arch-foe, Lord Stirling, there, then you shall be rewarded handsomely. I want that noble captured at his ruined place . . . I want him dragged here in chains from his forge . . . I want him tossed in the third cage, hoisted between two of his peers . . . I want him left to rot!"

Cheers climbed like flames from a staked fire. The Prophet had succeeded in challanging the Palatines of Leyden. He watched them prepare noisily for their rendezvous with Dan Fagan at the Smultz colliery. Those with horses fell in behind the guide and the officers. They were followed by a waggon filled with Palatines who possessed no mounts. The vehicle was driven by an initiate who had volunteered his own waggon and a team of horses. After Spolden had inspected the line of loyal brigands and saw that the men were ready to move out, he gave one final command to the horseman in the lead:

"Fahnrich, waste no time in reaching the colliery. The General is an impatient man, as you know."

"Not to fret, my Prophet."

"After the Palatines have been welcomed by the General, press on to Hibernia to scout the area," instructed Spolden. "See if any preparations have been made in anticipation of a raid. Find the weaknesses. Evaluate our prospects, then hasten to the Sign of the Raven and counsel with the General. Do all I ask of you, and, if the raid on Hibernia proves successful, then I will grant you an advancement in rank."

"To serve you is honor enough, sir."

"If this raid succeeds in capturing the Earl of Menstrie, then I shall make you Feldweibel."

"Such a glorious day," said the Ensign, "to accomplish, so soon, what you divined at the summer solstice . . . and such an honor you hold for me."

"Divining the future is an easy trick with God on one's side, my faithful messenger . . . elevating you in rank is even easier . . . now be on your way!"

The horseman saluted with a raised fist, spurred his mount, and trotted off in the direction the wild horses had taken the previous day. The Palatines on horseback and the ones in the waggon followed at a lively pace. They were singing a German Anabaptist hymn Spolden had taught them.

The Prophet smiled as he watched his new charges disappear from view. The setback at Charlotteburg was an aberration, soon to be forgotten. Things were going well once more. The stars held great promise. Fortunately, Dan Fagan truly believed Jack Spolden could read them . . . luckily, the General was a superstitious fool . . .

The sun still danced above Horse Pound Mountain when Billy Walsh guided the waggon and horses down the steep mule path, which snaked from ridge to mine entrance. Several men, at their leisure around a small cooking fire rose to greet him. Two did not—the one-eyed man stirring a bubbling pot of bear's paw and the robed man holding an amber crystal up to the sun.

"Billy, Billy," shouted the first man to reach the waggon, "what prince have you brung us this time?"

"Second half of the bargain," announced Walsh, as he swung his legs over the seat board and planted his feet next to his latest captive. He noticed the bound fellow had freed his good arm from the tethers and that he was gripping his precious pouch with the free hand. Walsh saw no harm in Ike's minor success against the restraints. It was too late to trifle over its significance.

"I've got here the Baron of Ballynary," boasted Walsh, "a direct descendant from the old kings of Ireland. Afore you help me lift these princely bones out of me waggon and I turn this proud and jaggered Baron, who's downed all me jack 'n rum, over to you, I've three requests to make."

By this time, all men, save for the one-eyed cook, had sauntered over to the waggon to see what they had gained. Even the Prophet seemed curious. He spoke for all:

"Ask away, Mister Walsh. Besides the usual bounty for a noble captive, what can we do for you?"

"I've been hard on Morrell's horses," replied Walsh. "See to it they gets proper care. I mean to keep 'em fit for a spell 'n somebody fetch me a steel-nose drink!"

The Prophet snapped his fingers and two of his guards jumped to the task of unhitching the horses and leading them away. Another retreated to the cooking fire and fetched a jug of One-Eye's rum.

"What else?" asked Spolden.

"I mean to speak to the princess," stated Walsh boldly, after he had taken a deep gulp from the jug. "I see she swings in her cage . . . she looks to be livin'."

All eyes turned to inspect Rachel, whose back was turned to her captors. She was close enough to hear their conversation, but she showed no sign of interest in it. Hidden from view was the rat-catcher. She cradled the creature in her arms, as if sensing death was near.

"The princess is not long for this world," said Spolden. "She's kept herself alive for to see the prince you have brought her. Soon as we remove this alleged Irish noble from your waggon, strip him down, and prepare him for a stay in the far cage, we'll see if the Baron's presence animates her. She has gone silent on us . . ."

"I've no interest in the wench's condition, nor her fate," interrupted Walsh, as he put down the jug and wrestled with the dead weight of Ike's stiff and lifeless body. This prince was faking sleep, or death again, for purposes known only to himself. Walsh kicked Ike in the ribs and the blow caused the Irishman to moan.

"I need to ask the Afric wench 'bout me dog . . . want to know what she's done with it."

With that said, Billy Walsh lifted Ike over the side of the waggon. Two of Spolden's guards grabbed the bound man and lowered him rudely to the ground where Jack Spolden stood. He studied his latest trophy and waited for the captive to open his eyes. Ike did not cooperate.

"This strange duck looks like he's been on the losing end of a few brawls," mused Spolden. "He might give us trouble."

One of the guards suggested that Ike remain bound and clothed in the cage—simply toss the fellow in and raise him as he lay.

"Not as I have prophesied," scolded Spolden. "Lug this prince to his cage, take a few of your kind with you to help strip him down and toss in the cage. Do not raise the device till old One-Eye has burned the noble's full title on a placard of wood. Whichever one of you reads and writes, stay with our cook and help him with the letters."

"What's this one to be called again?" asked the one guard, who admitted he was literate.

"The Mute of Barley Corn, from the looks of 'im," joked another guard.

"He's the Baron of Ballynary," snarled an emboldened Billy Walsh, as he tossed the emptied jug aside, jumped out of the waggon, and stepped too close to the Prophet. A guard stepped forward to restrain the audacious hunter of nobles. Spolden waved him off.

"Wouldn't doubt his title, if you claim it so, Billy," said the Prophet calmly.

"Even if I'd come here with no name for this bastard, you'd of come up with a name . . . you're good at this darn game you're playin' . . . so burn the man's proper title in the wood 'n be done with it . . . 'tis over for the likes of me. I'm through fetchin' warm bodies for the likes of you . . . lost a good, honest job 'cause of you. Now I'm suspected of murders I'd never done . . . 'n lost me dog. I must talk to the Princess 'n collect me bounty on this man. I'll be on me way soon as the horses are rested . . . could use 'nother drink . . ."

A broad grin creased Spolden's boyish face. He responded in a soft, fatherly voice: "You have performed adequate service, Billy . . . provided two stone-roasted excuses for nobility, suited to sit in cages on either side of the Scottish Earl of Menstrie. When we catch Lord Stirling, and I predict it will be soon, my prophecy of three nobles in a year's span shall stand complete. The noble

Proprietor, who surrounds himself with such stiff rumps of power and influence, will be pleased and honored to be flanked by a Prince and a Princess, Billy . . . and to think, you brought them to me for your own lecherous gain."

"Also for certain secrets kept 'tween you 'n me," added Walsh, who had completely missed the Prophet's sarcasm.

"Stay with us, Billy," coaxed Spolden with all the sincerity he could muster. "I need one more officer for my newest cell— the Palatines of Leyden. I have sent them to join Little Jake at Smultz's colliery. They intend to participate in the raid against Stirling's Adventure forge at Hibernia."

"You know full well I don't get 'long with Dan Fagan, even afore the alliance was formed. He suspects I know'd somethin' 'bout who started the fire at the Sign of the Raven."

"And that is why you do my bidding, and Fagan relies on the other fellow down in Morris Town."

"I scare up nobles for your odd-rum purposes, 'n the other one scares Ford's wealthy friends for whatever murderous game Fagan is playin' . . ."

"So it shall remain, Billy. Continue doing what you are doing for me, while I continue to reward you well and keep a lid on those secrets. I intend to lead my holy cause for ninety-nine years. God has willed it so. During my time here, I wield the power to choose who shall live as long as I do . . . long as they remain in my service . . . long as they continue to serve me and do as I wish . . . there will be many more hungry cages to fill . . ."

"The last one at this forgotten place is reserved for Lord Stirling's bones. How am I s'posed to bring him in on me own with folks lookin' to catch meself for certain crimes I didn't commit. The way things are goin', I'll be dead afore the year's out."

"You are best on your own, Billy," confided Spolden. "You prefer nobody bothering you. I have always honored such. However, to bring in Lord Stirling it will take several wolves, not just one. I will have others, besides you, hunting for our Mister Alexander. Whoever bags the bastard will garner the highest prize. If you are not the one, you shall still be rewarded for trying . . ."

"I want me dog back," demanded Walsh, "then I'll decide to keep with you or not. I was plannin' to fetch the rat-catcher 'n head north, since I can't return to Morrell . . . too dangerous . . . can't do you no good, Spolden . . . no way me arse will be gettin' close to Lord Stirling."

"Assume another name, my servant of God," encouraged the Prophet. "Find the noble Proprietor where he must go—Burlington, Amboy, perhaps Manhattan—places where you are unknown, or, at least, have been forgotten. Do this one final mission for me, Billy."

"The dog first," insisted Walsh, "me decision second."

"You can ask the Princess all you want," allowed Spolden, "but you will not like her answer. Best to leave such things in God's hands."

Walsh ignored the robed man, who always talked such gibberish and played such cruel games. He swept past the one-eyed man and the literate guard, busy at burning letters on a pine board. He paid no bother to the guards wrestling the clothes off Ike. The newest captive had come out of his false slumber and was flailing away with his one good arm. He was trying to hold on to his empty pouch with his injured, and still bandaged, arm. That piece of leather was quickly ripped away from his grasp. The poor Irishman was left with nothing more than new bumps and bruises caused by resisting, and the singular prospect of spending the rest of his life in an iron cage. He cursed the guards and he cursed the captor passing by . . . he wished Tom Ward dead.

Billy Walsh approached the suspended cage which sported the sign, 'Princess of Axum.' The letters held no special meaning for him—no letters did, for he could not read. He gave the placard nothing more than a glance. Instead, he fixed his eyes on the one he knew as Rachel Hagers. Her back was to him, swaying a bit and holding something close to her—something Billy could not see. He circled around the perimeter of the cage, glancing down so as to be careful not to step in the offal under it. When he reached the eastern side of the cage, he had to shield his eyes from the virulent sun above the ridge. What he saw made him sick. The Afric wench with dim eyes was staring at sky. Her mouth was open, but she uttered no sound. Behind her hands and shielding her breasts was the limp body of the rat-catcher.

"Unlock this cage, Spolden, unlock it now!" roared Billy Walsh.

Neither Rachel nor the rat-catcher were stirred by a voice they should have recognized immediately. They remained unmoved. However, the Prophet heard Walsh's command loud and clear. He lifted his robe and extracted a fine dueling pistol from his belt. He readied it for one well-aimed shot.

"I cannot undo what the Lord commands, Billy."

With that, a pistol shot echoed against the ridge face of the mountain. Billy Walsh, who had gone to the chain holding up the cage, fell to his knees. His gloved hands were still clutching the links of iron. Blood seeped from a hole in his skull just below the rim of his greasy cap.

The Prophet strode proudly to the victim of his expertly placed round. He gave the kneeling body a swift kick. Billy's gloves slipped from the thick chain and his corpse toppled face-first to the ground.

"One-Eye!" shouted Spolden. "When you complete the Irish noble's placard, cut out Billy's eight eyes and feed them to your fire. Bind his bones with the tethers he used on the Baron of Ballynary, and drag what's left of him to the sacred cave."

"What shaft had you in mind, sir?" asked the reinsman, who paused from his work. "He'll sure to be stinkin' by morn."

"Drag him deep into the mine . . . to where the water has seeped in . . . weigh him down with some handsome stones . . . toss him in . . . no one bothers to venture there . . ."

"Yer speakin' the truth, sir," chuckled old One-Eye, as he went back to his work on the sign for Ike's cage.

18

THE FIRES OF HIBERNIA
· ·

*—at Lord Stirling's Adventure Forge. before midnight
on Monday, September 27, 1773*

The drumming thunder of six-hundred-pound hammers at the Adventure Forge in Hibernia echoed against a looming backdrop of mining hills. It rumbled down the Carriage Road out of Rockaway. The constant thud-thud-thud could be heard by wayfarers, even those who had not yet made it to the Mill Creek Bridge. Though it was dark, close to nine, and bats owned the night air, the eighteen-hour laborers were still at their toil . . . furnace men, forge tenders, drawing men, casting house men, top loaders, and the rest were still busy turning molten iron into pigs, bars, rods, and practical shapes allowed by royal edict. There was greed's reason for such hard-working men laboring so long and so late—not for themselves, but for their bosses, the investors, and the King. British demand for quality iron was up, though colonial profit margin was down. Thus, production volume served as the solution and the cause for the constant thunder. There was an urgency in the effort, for only two months remained until the forge wheels were seized by frost and ice clogged the streams.

The three wayfarers, fast-approaching, knew all this, but they were not used to the roar of such a pulsing hell. The closer they got, the louder the rhythms of such industry became. The sounds came as a warning to keep a safe distance—a warning to turn back. However, these determined men and their steeds pressed on to the wooden bridge which spanned a modest creek. The music of the forge destroyed the muffled melody of water spilling over boulders and tailings. It was here that the grim trio caught sight of the infernal glow of three fires emanating from blast furnace portals, brightened by huge bellows. A shining also came from rivulets of molten iron running in search of mold forms. It was a scene a sensible man should run from. Many a slave and redemptioner had . . . others escaped through hard drinking and breaking the law. Rare was the man who lingered too long at the fires on the fringe of hell.

At the bridge, Vincent Wetherill decided that the torch he carried was no longer needed. The bright, near-to-full moon, squatting low in the sky, and the in-blast furnaces of Lord Stirling's forge provided ample light. He tossed the torch into the low creek. Reverend Samuel Heaton, who followed Vincent across the span, held on to his. He brandished it like a weapon—the only one he carried, since the Elder Sharp's boys had fashioned it for him at Mine Hill. Last to rattle across the worn bridge was Cutlope Hancock and his team, pulling the waggon and its four barrels of creek water. The men and their horses veered to the right, off the main road, and headed straight toward the forge entrance gate.

What lay ahead was Lord Stirling's recent purchase of a ten-thousand acre complex of furnaces, mills, mines hidden in the hills to the north, a manor house, crew bosses' houses, work men's cottages, charcoal huts, powder magazines, a school house, church, and store. Here was an entire plantation village, missing but one thing—a tavern. This was due to the Ordinance of 1769, which forbade any drinking establishment from being closer than four miles from the forge. The Sign of the Raven had been the nearest and most popular watering hole for the Hibernia laborers, until the day it burned to the ground. The employees at Stirling's complex now had to travel farther out to find a public house, or they had to wait for an itinerant peddler—unconcerned about legal distances, ten shilling fines, or banned spirits—to pass by with a waggon of wares, which happened to include a profitable, clandestine measure of apple jack or rum. Such peddlers knew, however, not to come too close to Lord Stirling's operations. His guards were gruff and would not hesitate to fire a round or two at a peddler who ventured too close. On the rare occasions peddlers came, the Hibernian men knew to meet them on neutral ground. They jokingly boasted of being the soberest iron laborers in the colony. Their forge master, Hard Joe Hoff, boasted of the same thing . . . but not jokingly.

Two very sober and ill-humored armed guards, dressed in the usual forgeman's garb of black trousers and shirts, trimmed in red, stopped the trio before they reached the entrance gate. The man with the torch held it high to make sure the guards saw his preacher's wide-brimmed hat, and to show he and his two companions had nothing to hide. Heaton was upset with Vincent for having discarded his torch. In the short time the preacher knew young Wetherill, he felt the Assemblyman's son was rather hasty in his actions, but one who managed to hide his fears and lack of experience well. He saw Vincent as a potential leader of men, but one who still needed a man of experience and mature wisdom by his side. Hence, Reverend Heaton was keenly aware of his role on this venture against evil. He meant to serve as Vincent's shield, and to make sure the lad got through this ordeal unscathed . . . some folks were worth saving.

"What might two gloaks 'n a preacher be peddlin' at such a late hour?" challenged the larger of the two guards. He employed a booming voice and was wielding a nasty-looking pike.

"Hope it's rum in them barrels," joked the lesser man, who stood behind the other, with a musket primed and raised.

"Nothing to sell here," snapped Vincent in as loud a voice as he could muster. "Neither rum nor anything useful for the likes of you."

"Then I'm callin' ye lost . . . declarin' ye trespassers, 'n orderin' ye to turn the waggon 'round." The challenger pointed his pike toward the bridge which the trio had just crossed over.

The other guard aimed his weapon at Cut for some unknown reason. The German had not even reached for his firing piece. He knew better this time. He sensed the guard was mere show and no substance. Cut kept still, reins in hand, and fixed his stare in the direction of the nearest furnace. Sounds of the iron-making industry fascinated him. He could watch and listen all day and not be bothered by its madness. He knew he could be entertained by it, even with a gun pointed at his heart. Cut was not worried—Vincent and the Reverend would work things out. The waggoner simply did not want the delicate negotiations to take long. Cut had a killer to find and bring down with his own weapon. He was so glad Heaton had talked Vincent into visiting the Sharps, and doubly glad that the Elder Sharp's well-fardled daughter had found the mud spoon which Ike had left behind to show he was still alive. All Cut had to do was find the kidnapped negress who stole the killer's dog. Initially, the task appeared impossible. The choices of where to look had narrowed dramatically since the visit to Mine Hill. They were about to narrow even more.

"Now, now, gentlemen," intervened Heaton, as he dismounted and strolled confidently over to the guard with the musket. He held his flaming torch high above his head and invited the guard to point his weapon at it. Instead, the fellow stepped back a pace and aimed at the minister's heart. Heaton ignored the guard's move. He kept his eyes focused on the other man and addressed him. "We come in peace, bearing good tidings from Judge Daniel Cooper, Jacob Ford and his son. Our sponsors have sent us to warn your superiors of possible trouble from a rogue band of thieves and murderers."

"We also wish to ascertain directions to the Sign of the Raven," added Vincent.

Both guards let out laughs which rivaled the wheezing furnace bellows and pounding forge hammers. The larger of the two paused to catch his breath and hurl a curt retort:

"The boss ain't here, preacher man . . . out recruitin' woodcutters 'n ditchers for quellin' some trouble we might be havin' with the same such land pirates ye come all this way to warn us 'bout what we already know'd well. Tell your companion here of ye also bein' late on the Sign of the Raven, 'since it burnt down long ago. Way I heard, some farmer was at burnin' trees for ashes to liven his soil . . . but winds held other ideas 'n the tavern was in the way. Ain't nothin' but rubble to visit four miles out . . . nobody but ghosts there now."

"We've heard certain parties still meet there," insinuated Vincent.

More laughter followed his comment.

"For no legal purpose we knows of," answered the guard with the pike. "I'd advise ye all to avoid the place . . . trouble's brewin' 'round here . . . bandits was causin' woe up at Charlotteburg most recently . . . not a good time for the likes of a preacher 'n an uppity gentleman to be wanderin' 'bout these hills. I suggest, preacher man, ye step away from my man's firin' piece 'n head back down to Rockaway. I suggest ye do so now."

"My uppity friend happens to be the son of Assemblyman John Wetherill of Middlesex County. He has been hired by Judge Cooper and the Fords to find a man who is suspected of killing three folks in Morris Town. We think he may be in league with the banditti you speak of. Mister Wetherill is accompanied by his capable waggoner, Cutlope Hancock. I am Reverend Samuel Heaton of Schooley's Mountain. Please allow us to pass in order to counsel with whomever is in charge this night and obtain directions to the Sign of the Raven."

"I don't give a pig's fart who ye might be travelin' with or where ye might be goin', preacher man . . . wastin' precious time searchin' for a tavern no longer there. Turn the waggon 'round 'n head back where ye come from. Me 'n my lads will take care of business 'round here."

Neither Reverend Heaton nor Vincent Wetherill got the chance to respond to the head guard's rude command. All heads turned to watch a score of men approaching on the march from the northern leg of the Carriage Road. A short man on a stout horse led them. He sported a cocked hat of beaver felt and a dark blue coat of coarse wool. He held a modest torch in a gloved hand. The other horseman, who trailed the marchers, was coaxing them by cursing at them. It was too dark to make out any of his features. A few of the men on foot were hurling curses back at the second mounted man. Their din rivaled the storm of noise from the forge.

"Looks like your business with brigands, piker, has come a bit early!" shouted Cut, who ignored the guard with the gun and reached for his own weapon.

"Make way for the Forge Master, ye cheap-jacks," shouted the head guard, as he pointed his pike at Cut and ordered him to move his team of horses and the waggon to the shoulder of the road. Cut slipped his piece back into its pouch and did as he was told. Vincent and the preacher joined him. They were now in partial shadow provided by humped beeches and hornbeam. Heaton's torch had gone out. Only the two waggon lanterns provided meager light. They were forgotten by the bullying guards, who rushed to greet their boss and report that all was well under their watch.

The lead horseman was not paying much attention to the pair. He seemed distracted. He caught sight of the three wayfarers and halted. The men on foot behind his horse did the same; however, they continued cursing, and started griping about not being fed.

"Shut your gobs, you wood jacks 'n ditchers," bellowed the stubby, red-faced man in the blue coat. "This night, I've promised you vittles worth dying for . . . on the morrow, barrels of rum, after you succeed 'gainst the scarlets headed our way."

"What if they be cowards 'n never appear?" shouted a hungry ditcher standing with the men behind the Forge Master.

The leader did not turn his head to single out the impudent laborer. He preferred to fix his eyes on the barrels in the waggon at the side of the entrance road. "Look over there!" exclaimed Hard Joe Hoff. He was pointing both his torch and a flogging birch at Cut's waggon. "See the barrels brim full of rum 'n just come in . . . all for the likes of you whether you bring down the rogues on the morrow or not t'all."

"They ain't acomin'!" shouted another laborer.

"Let's drink it now!" bellowed a third.

Now the Forge Master turned and cast angry eyes on the motley recruits he had managed to gather together to defend Lord Stirling's complex. Their number was not nearly enough, but it was the best he could do. They were all brawlers, just for the fun of it. They were all hunters, and dangerously good shots with company muskets in their hands. Hoff knew they would perform well. The promise of more pay, come Saturday, had not moved them. However, the promise of good food and lots of rum cemented the deal.

When the men quieted down and their grumbling ceased, the Forge Master addressed them calmly, but with the same booming voice: "We made a deal, my filthy kinchins, 'n you dare not call me Hard Joe Hoff for nothing. I made you an offer 'n you 'cepted it—vittles 'fore the fray 'n rum after. Once'd I've said what's been said, I stick hard by it. Any man dare question my word or cross my plan, then he gets a taste of my thrashing stick instead of the vittles 'n rum."

There was a bit of grousing, but it could not be heard above the pounding of the forge. Hard Joe Hoff took it as silence from his men, and it left him grinning at them.

"Good then . . . we all agree . . . now get to the kitchen house for some feasting. My pike man will lead you 'n keep an eye on you. Pray a bit this night 'n get some sleep . . . we're up 'fore dawn to carry out my intercept plan, you filthy kinchins. Be ready to earn your rum!"

Cheers followed Mister Hoff's words. The men rushed past him and followed the pike man to the forge complex. The other horseman joined the Forge Master. They approached the three spectators waiting in the shadows.

Hoff addressed them: "Gentlemen, I count four barrels on your waggon . . . not 'nough for my thirsty men. I ordered six . . ."

"Sorry to disappoint you, sir," piped Vincent, loud as he could without appearing out of sorts, "but we carry no rum. There is creek water in our barrels. You must have us mistaken for someone else."

Hard Joe Hoff let fly a roaring laugh which turned his face a deeper shade of red in his own torchlight. The man of many curses, accompanying Hoff, was silent now. He gave no sign of emotion. His face was an unreadable mask, save for deep scratches on his cheek. Some beast must have attacked him recently— maybe that is what made the man so grim.

Hoff stopped laughing, wiped some spittle from the side of his mouth with the back of his hand, then directed his question to Vincent: "Who in the devil comes riding 'bout in the pitch of night with a waggon of common creek water? Are you intent on dousing my furnace fire with the likes of it? You wouldn't be the advance marauders my boys are preparing for, would you?"

The Forge Master was at his laughing again—brief this time, but just as loud.

"None of the sort," said Vincent seriously. He introduced himself and his two companions, and then explained, "We intend the water as a ruse against the same rogues you are after."

"On my side, then," said Hoff, with a trace of suspicion in his voice. "A politician's son, a preacher man, and a stout waggoner . . . poorly armed, but of possible use just the same. You would've been of better use to me with a waggon of rum or blasting powder for the morrow . . . guess I'll be waiting longer for such to roll in. So who sent you for the fun?"

"We were originally in the service of Judge Daniel Cooper and the Jacob Fords of Morris Town—an investigative team charged with finding the murderer of three folks down there . . . now we're on our own."

"I heard of one slaying," interrupted Hoff. "Don't tell me there's been more?"

"Doctor Budd lost a field slave and Judge Cooper's cook lost her younger boy just last night. The latest victim was found by Mister Hancock this morning. We have suspicion that the murderer is connected somehow with the outlaw band pestering folks in these hills . . . we aim to track him down."

Hard Joe Hoff scoffed at the idea. "We aim to slay as many scarlets as we can . . . the ones we capture are due for hanging where we find 'em . . . ain't going to be none left to ask, young man. I'm the law up here in these hills, 'n what I do with vermin I catch is my business . . . 'tis eye for an eye up here, long as the King is looking the other way."

Hoff winked at the horseman who was alongside him. Vincent took no notice of it, but his waggoner did. All this time, Cut was wondering about the deep scratches on the horseman's face. The fellow had been obviously in a recent tussle—perhaps the handiwork of an enraged woman, thought Cut . . .

"Allow us to interrogate your captives before you do them in," beseeched Vincent with a bit of urgency in his voice.

"Won't do you no good," advised the Forge Master, as he grabbed his reins and turned his horse. "A man 'bout to be hung will tell you anything you want to know . . . you ask a dozen captives if your suspect is the killer, they'd be all saying whatever it takes for their lives to be spared. Best bet is for us to slay your murderer 'n end the killing down in Morris Town."

"Let us join your vigil band, Mister Hoff," interjected Reverend Heaton. "Each of us is armed and skilled in singular ways. There is room in our waggon for explosives and supplies to haul wherever your intercept plan is meant to be carried out. If you succeed, please allow Mister Wetherill a few moments with the captives."

"We'll see, preacher man," responded Hoff, with a wary glance at the horseman in his shadow. "Need all the help I can get . . . rumor has it, the brigands gathering for a raid on my place may number three score or more. I'll be lucky to lead half of that 'gainst 'em. Too bad there ain't more of your kind . . ."

"There is a slight chance of a few more men following us," offered Vincent.

"The more, the better . . . 'specially if they be armed better than this here preacher man," shouted Hoff, as he spurred his horse toward the forge entrance. "Follow me, gentleman. You shall be my guests for the evening at my humble cottage. We've lots to chew on . . . sustenance, reputations, histories, 'n plans . . all 'fore the dawn . . ."

The Forge Master's house had originally been a workman's cottage, but built on to and greatly expanded. It sat a few furlongs beyond an open common surrounded by true cottages for the free labor-ers. The two-story Hoff house, nestled among a ring of giant ever-greens, was fronted by a row of guardian shrubs. A modest garden for flowers and herbs sat on the sunny, cleared side and allowed for an unencumbered view of the low hills to the north. This hand-some place stood far from the furnaces and forge, but the ceaseless pounding of the hammers could still be heard loud and clear. Once inside Hard Joe Hoff's abode, however, the pounding became mut-ed. Thick stone walls and shuttered windows helped muffle the noise. The host and his three guests did not have to raise their voic-es to be heard. The air in the place was heavy with cooking smells and undertones of iron and rust. This was a true forge house, and quite suitable for convening a meeting of import—a place good as any for establishing a measure of trust, sharing information about tomorrow's enemy, and discussing the best strategy for being successful against a formidable foe. The participants sat in heavy wrought iron chairs, outfitted with deerskin cushions. They were close to flames flickering around a large log in a huge fireplace. A broad triptych of iron, positioned behind the log, caught and cast heat into the room, making the place warmer than necessary. There was no need for waistcoat or vest by this hearth. A comfort-able glow pervaded Hoff's sitting room—from the dancing checker pattern of the floor tiles, to the soft blue walls with buttermilk trim, to the iron and glass storm lanterns lit and hanging from chains attached to ceiling hooks in the corners of the room. Secrets found it difficult to hide in Hard Joe Hoff's sitting room. Guests were put at ease here. The host wanted to make sure anyone invited in held nothing back from his knowing. Hard Joe always got his way. This time would be no different.

So far, things had gone well. His mistress had been able to be abed at her usual two hours before midnight. Hoff and his guests had been fed well by then—a redolent fish chowder served in bowls of fine steel, accompanied by loaves of next day's bread still warm from the kitchen hearth. The cider, served with the meal, had passed as acceptable—less sweet than preferred, but adequate when warmed. After the repast, Hoff led his guests to the sitting room. Servants were left behind to clean up in the dining room, and Cut was dismissed to check on the bay Shires and the waggon. After a brief exchange of pleasantries, Vincent completed the telling of his journey from his father's plantation and his purposes for doing so. He purposely mentioned nothing about the Treasury robbery or Sam Ford, because he figured both subjects were stale news. Reverend Heaton followed with his telling of what he knew about the Prophet, Jack Spolden, and what fears his people on Schooley's Mountain had about the man. The horseman, who had accompanied Hoff and had been introduced at the start of the meal as his fetchman, said nothing. He sat closest to the fire, by the bucket of sand meant to quell sparks and stray flames. Yet, he was listening intently to the guests.

Hard Joe Hoff was also listening intently. With large, calloused hands, he gripped the arms of his iron chair. He meant to make no distracting moves when others spoke. His claret-hued vest had been removed and draped over the back of his chair. His underblouse was open at the neck. It allowed his broad chest and ample belly a bit of freedom. What made him short were his bowlegs. He still wore his riding boots, which nearly came up to his knees. They covered half the length of his black forgeman's trousers. Hoff slouched some, in order to have his boots touch his checker floor.

Reverend Heaton, with eyes burning bright, made his concluding remarks: "The infernal Jack Spolden is the head of the snake we seek to destroy, gentlemen. We must not be distracted from God's intent. His will has brought us together. 'Tis not simply fate calling us to counsel. We must plan well for His triumph over depravity. We are the Lord's knights—His instruments—in this matter. The supremacy of virtue must abide in plan and action. If we fail, the arch enemy prevails. We must cut the head from the snake at the first opportunity . . ."

"I disagree," said the host. "The one bothering mineself is Dan Fagan. He's the hellion leading brigands on raids 'round here, abusing folks in these hills, 'n pestering mines 'n forges. The other snake head talks nonsense, so I'm told. He hides from view like a coward. Black Jake ain't a threat to my kind. I've been invited to an iron masters' meeting next month 'n I plan to bring with me good news 'bout dispersing the likes of Fagan, Balcock, Steel, my own brother, Charlie Hoff, 'n others linked to the Sons of the Sword . . . lost sev'ral 'demptioners 'n slaves who ran away after Lord Stirling took over . . . most of 'em, so I'm told, joined up with Fagan."

"What about the murderer from Morris Town who's run off with my flanker?" asked Vincent.

"Know nothing 'bout such a fellow," admitted Hoff with a dismissive sigh, "nor do I wish to be bothered by such. I've recruited men for going after one partic'lar ruffin 'n that's all . . . can't waste time nor bodies chasing a murderer, kidnapper, or holy hermit. What say you, Mister Bruder?"

The horse rider in the travel-worn sailor's jacket, who was sitting by the sand bucket, seemed surprised to be called upon to address Hoff's guests. However, he was quick to respond:

"Can I trust you two to keep secret what I say? My life depends on your doin' so . . ."

"You have my word," said Heaton without hesitatiom.

"Mine too," said Vincent.

"Good then," continued the horseman, as he picked at a scratch on his face. "Allow me to introduce myself, gentlemen. I am Karl Bruder, and I have more important duties than servin' as Mister Hoff's fetchman—such is the cover for my real responsibilities in these parts. I answer to certain investors 'cross the sea. They originally hired me to investigate the poor quality of iron once produced by the forge workers and superintendents under a certain schemer by the name of Peter Hasenclever . . . seems he was sendin' high-quality samples, gainin' lofty praise and great demand for his product, then turnin' out inferior stuff at high volume. I discovered what he was up to and my report led to him bein' forced out of the business. The same investors asked me to remain to keep an eye on those who replaced Hasenclever and his cohorts. Most recent, they asked me to infiltrate a certain gang of banditti, who have been lurin' laborers from the mines and forges. I was able to join up with Dan Fagan's gang and was soon accepted as a fullfledged member."

Bruder stopped talking in order to roll up the left sleeve of his jacket and show the tattoo above his wrist.

"The sword inside a ring!" exclaimed Vincent.

"Correct," said Bruder. "The same as you described on the pig iron haulers, the shutter at the Amboy jail, and at the three murder scenes."

"So you became one of the Sons of the Sword?" asked Reverend Heaton guardedly.

"A price I had to pay and I'm still payin'," confessed the horseman, "in order to gain the chance to help destroy a new and growin' threat . . ."

"Bruder knows 'bout both heads on your snake, preacher man," interjected Hoff with a chuckle, "'n he may know something 'bout your murderer, Mister Wetherill."

"I know too much 'bout too many things," remarked Bruder, as worry lines deepened above his shaggy brows. He cast dark, piercing eyes at the fire. "If I'm found out, I'm to lose my head and other choice parts. This is accordin' to rules written down in Jack Spolden's gospel. I've seen the worst work of him and Fagan—even took part in it, so as not to be discovered."

"Care to share any misdeeds with us?" invited Hoff with a wink and a grin.

"None, now or later," emphasized Bruder, "not even after the damnable pair's been dispatched. However, I will share my intentions in order to reach that end. At first, I thought the best way to slay a two-headed snake was to cause dissension between Fagan and Spolden. It did not work. They already distrusted each other and still do. Their alliance is formed out of necessity, not loyalty or friendship. My efforts only put me in danger; however, I was singled out for my knowledge of the area and my horse ridin' ability. The Prophet took me in for service as a scout and messenger, much to the dismay of the General. I was elevated to the rank of Fahnrich in a secret cell, named by Spolden as the Ravens of Munster. Later, I learned the reason for the promotion—the Prophet deemed me too smart to waste as a mere soldier under his General. So he took me in and shared secrets I would, otherwise, have never learned. Most recently, I have been ordered to spy on the General and report directly to the Prophet. This works fine for me. All the while, neither rogue knows I am workin' for a wealthy group of investors, which includes several of noble lineage—the kind Fagan and Spolden despise the most."

"Anything about the croaker we are after?" asked Vincent impatiently.

"The Prophet has his agents—'angels of righteousness' he calls 'em," said Bruder in a low voice. "These are individuals recruited by Spolden to stir up trouble among the wealthy folks in the colony. I've met some of 'em. They report in now and then to boast of their deeds and get paid. Fagan likes to imitate the Prophet every way he can, so he has hired his own agents to boil up his own mischief and mayhem. He prefers to call his kind, 'devils of mercy'. Their main responsibility is to seek out good places to raid. At this moment, I am servin' both men in such a capacity. I'm supposed to be scoutin' 'round Hibernia, avoidin' the guards, probin' for weaknesses, reportin' back to Fagan, first, before he leads his men to join up with another cell at the Sign of the Raven . . . then I'm supposed to head back to the Johnson Mine to report to Jack Spolden . . ."

"So you are saying the murderer we seek may be one of Spolden's so-called angels?" queried Vincent.

"Or one of Fagan's devils," countered Bruder. "I do know the negress you have spoken of hangs in a cage at the Johnson site. The Prophet has accepted her as royalty though she is but a slave. One of Spolden's agents, who, I've heard, operates 'round Morris Town, has been given credit for her capture. I've never met the bugger, but I'm told his mission is to bring in nobles—live ones, not dead ones. I doubt if he's your man. The last time I was up on Horse

Pound Mountain, the rumor goin' 'round has this same agent due to be bringin' in a second noble any day. The Prophet has predicted such. He's takin' it as a sign that the capture of Lord Stirlin' will soon follow."

"The sinner we're looking for has to be the same fella who's run off with Mister Higgins," opined Reverend Heaton. "He is the slayer of three innocents."

"Perhaps," said Bruder. "All I know is the second captive is to be brought to Spolden. The agent will get paid and be on his way."

"Then we must hasten to the Johnson Mine to rescue Mister Higgins," urged Heaton. "In the process, we will take care of this so-called Prophet by luring him out of hiding with iron water as the ruse."

"If we're lucky," added Vincent, "we can chase the killer back to Morris Town, after we've dealt with Spolden and saved Ike."

"Going to need more than luck 'n iron water 'gainst the likes of Spolden," advised the Forge Master, who had been listening politely to the banter of his guests. "Soon as you start on your separate way to the failed mine at Horse Pound, Fagan will get wind of your approach 'n cut you down . . . got to deal with one head first . . . then Spolden's second . . . no way 'round it."

Karl Bruder seconded that opinion. He spoke of the necessity to bring down the General first. Fagan was to leave the Smultz colliery at dawn and head to the ruins at the Sign of the Raven. He was going to wait there for the third cell to join with his and the Palatines. They were going to wait until nightfall then head out for Hibernia, which was a mere four miles from the ruined tavern site. Fagan would not move out from the colliery until Bruder told him the route was clear all the way to the Mill Creek Bridge. Based on complete trust in Bruder's word, Fagan would suspect nothing was amiss.

"I favor the plan to set up an ambush at the Sign of the Raven," concluded Bruder. "If you leave here at dawn, you will have plenty of time to position your men."

"We will be outnumbered three to one," grumbled Hoff, "but I like such odds . . . 'n with a preacher man on my flank, I see our chances as playing even . . ."

"Let us have as much faith in the plan," reasoned Bruder.

"A surprise ambush should do the trick. Remember this—the Palatines are raw recruits and will be easily scared off. The late-arriving cell consists of men who caused the failure at Charlotteburg . . . they are not to be feared. The meanest ones are 'round Fagan . . . worry 'bout them. Make quick work of downin' the General and you will succeed. Don't give the local authorities time to get involved."

"I plan to arm all my men with new hunting muskets," boasted the Forge Master. "Each of my kinchins was chosen for their 'bility to bring down fresh kill at seventy yards . . . half of 'em Jersey Dutch . . . the others, near-sober Gaels . . ."

"I can do as well," added Vincent, "and Cut can do better."

"Amen," said Heaton.

19

THE AMBUSH
• • • • • • • • • • • •

*—at the Sign of the Raven,
on the morning of Tuesday, September 28, 1773*

It was a bright, rummy day for an ambush. Hard Joe Hoff, Forge Master of the Hibernia iron works, and each of the ambushers under his command sported a scarlet ribband, affixed to their hats and caps. Thus, in the heat of the anticipated skirmish against Dan Fagan's following, they would be able to tell friend from foe. Hoff had also ordered his score of wood cutters and ditchers to precisely spaced positions along a barricade of their own making. Their work on mounding ramparts of earth and topping them with felled trees had started as soon as Hard Joe marched them down from the abandoned farmhouse adjacent to the ruins of the Sign of the Raven. Hoff's team had arrived at the run-down farmhouse shortly after the sun came up. Each man carried his own tools and two muskets. The muskets had been hauled to the site in a company waggon and distributed to those entrusted to use them well. The well-outfitted team left ten horses and three waggons behind— well-hidden between the farmhouse and largest barn. Also left behind to guard what had to be hidden were two waggoners from the forge. The third vehicle was also hidden from sight, but it was unattended. It contained four small barrels of suspect liquid, a spare barrel of quality blackpowder, and a number of sundry tools and spare firing pieces. Its waggoner had been sent by Hoff on a special assignment, along with Vincent Wetherill, Reverend Heaton, one Adventure foreman, and two slaves. They, too, felt it was a bright, rummy day for an ambush.

Hard Joe Hoff had given these men extraordinary roles to play in the ambush plan. He was sure they would come through splendidly. He had ordered his foreman and pair of slaves to cart one of the barrels of blackpowder from the farmhouse to the standing chimney at the site of the Sign of the Raven. The foreman, once a miner with skill at drilling rock and filling holes with proper measures of powder, led the way across an unkempt field, over a broken rail fence, and through an unruly copse wood in order to get to the chimney. Hoff's three guests followed with cumbersome gear and heavy weapons. Reverend Heaton refused to carry a firing piece. Instead, he lugged the ember box and other equipment to be used to set fuses. Vincent hefted two muskets, as well as his customary sword and pistol, which marked him as the man in charge. Cut balked at the order to carry another musket, but Vincent talked him into it. Vincent explained the Forge Master's reason for each man carrying a pair of guns. Cut still did not like the idea, said so, but finally complied out of respect for his boss.

Upon arrival at the tavern site, Hoff's special unit paused to stare at the severed head crowning a post at the center of the ruins. Crows had taken liberties with the eyes and most of the flesh. Insects were taking care of the rest. Reverend Heaton offered a quick prayer for the restless soul of a wayward man who had met a bad end. After a brace of hasty amens, the six men set about doing what they had been ordered to do. They split into two groups of three.

Vincent, Cut, and the preacher piled liftable materials around a depression in the soil close to the main road and as far as possible from the chimney. According to Hoff's orders, their position had to face the terminus of the by-road and Mine Hill Road. They left openings on the side facing the roads, and placed charred beams and long boards over their construction in order to protect themselves from stray pieces of the doomed chimney. While the three guests were working on their masterpiece, the foreman and two slaves were busy with their stout hammers and chisels. They loosened stones and mortar at the base of the far side of the chimney, tore stones free, tossed them aside, and poured measures of blackpowder into the resultant pockets and crevices. They shaped a fuse trail. Finally, they practiced their retreat route to the remains of the second chimney, which was close to where Vincent, Cut, and Heaton hid. One slave climbed the highest pile of rocks and sat on the uppermost ones. He watched the by-road and the northerning main road, waiting to signal the arrival of the foe. The foreman and the other slave hid behind the lookout pile, waiting for the signal and gauging which way the chimney stones would fall. When their primary task of firing the fuses was completed, they were supposed to scramble to the safety of the hiding place.

According to Hoff's instructions, Vincent, Cut, and the foreman would fire muskets at the brigands who came closest to their position. Reverend Heaton and the two slaves would crouch behind the shooters and trade spent muskets for ones already primed. Thus, according to the Forge Master's way of thinking, more rounds could be fired in less time. Cut took exception to Hoff's idea, for he did not like having someone else handling his prize weapon. Reverend Heaton, who refused to fire any piece, talked Cut into trusting him to handle the gun with care. Cut grudgingly agreed to comply with Hoff's strategy.

Meanwhile, the main group under Hoff's direct command had settled down behind their barricade in anticipation of a long wait. The rampart stood approximately forty paces from the by-road and was about the same in length. It stretched west from where the by-road met Mine Hill Road. From the same point of origin another barricade parallelled the broader main road. The armed men under Hoff's command were prepared to shift to the other wing of the ramparts if the enemy happened to approach the Sign of the Raven by using Mine Hill Road rather than the by-road. Hoff made sure his men had practiced the shift several times before deciding to settle in behind the barricade facing the road Fagan would most likely use. It was a gamble, but one based on solid information from Karl Bruder.

After repeating salient points of strategy while waving a pistol in one hand and sword in the other, Hard Joe finally told his men about the signal to fire: "My 'venture foreman 'n two of my most trustworthy Africs have set a decent charge of black powder in the standing chimney 'cross the way. They will fire the charge soon as the first of Fagan's gang crosses Mine Hill Road . . . soon as you kinchins hear the explosion, fire in unison . . . drop your first musket darn quick . . . waste no bother reloading yet . . . fetch up your second piece already primed . . . fire 'gain . . . shoot to kill . . ."

Hoff's men voiced approval of his strategy. They liked the

idea of pretending to be a larger force than they actually were. The double-volley tactic with quality muskets might just do the trick. They were all for succeeding, because victory meant grand drinking back at the deserted farmhouse, where barrels of rum in the forge waggons waited. Luckily, this rum had been delivered just before they departed from Hibernia. The men were thirsty then and doubly thirsty now. They wanted the dangerous chore of skirmishing to be over and done quickly. Good rum was waiting— at least a mile's trot across the main road and farm field to the waggons. Every man under Hoff's command expected to survive the pending fray. Every man longed to scramble over the rotting post and rail fence and run to the farmhouse to enjoy the fruits of their labor—raise their vessels of rum and toast the likes of Lord Stirling, Hard Joe Hoff, and, perhaps, even the King . . .

Dan Fagan was in a foul mood. Every time he had to visit the place where his mother had perished in a tragic fire, sour memories swirled in his thoughts. They made his head ache. However, the Prophet's darling, Karl Bruder, more recently referred to as the Fahnrich, had advised taking the by-road up from the Smultz colliery to the Sign of the Raven in order to join with the hapless Covenanters of Allstedt. This cell had been charged with the task of stealing horses to be used in the raid. They would straggle in late, of course, from the north on the main road. Excuses for lateness would be many and varied. The count of steeds would be insufficient. These characters would be led by an upstart—the one who recently replaced the Captain blamed for the failure at Charlotteburg. Neither man was worth his weight in any situation. Fagan never liked the dead one, whose head guarded the rendezvous site, and he did not trust the young fellow who replaced him. The promotion was Spolden's idea, not his. Fagan dreaded the idea of raiding the Hibernia forge with the likes of the Covenanters and the Palatines—proven bunglers and untested initiates. Fagan had to admit to himself that Black Jake was making poor decisions of late. Perhaps, the Prophet was misreading the stars, or being tricked by his crystals. Maybe God was looking the other way. For whatever reason, Little Jake was not liking the results of recent actions tak-en. His men were growing restless and hungry for loot. They had been promised much at Charlotteburg, but gained little. There was more to be seized at Hibernia, but the place was guarded well and would prove a challenge. His men felt the same as he did—leave all bunglers and inexperienced novices behind. They should have left the colliery before the Fahnrich arrived with instructions from the Prophet. They should have ridden directly to Hibernia and raided the place on their own. Fagan was sure his men would like to re-turn to operating on their own. He secretly wanted the same. How-ever, things had changed and a greater force led by a greater leader was needed for what had to come. Miserable and bitter though he was, Dan Fagan knew he had to be subservient to the greater good. It was still the best way to get back at the wealthy types he so despised. Only he knew the lengths he was taking on his own to bring down the gelt-mongers—especially the Fords. At least, he could take great pleasure in the success of his personal devil agent in Morris Town . . . at least, he had this one secret thing to brighten his mood.

The by-road was narrow. Each side was shaded by mature trees. The late morning sun was rarely able to dapple the way. Dan Fagan, on a favorite purloined horse, was accompanied by the Leutinger. The rest of the General's men followed two-by-two, mounted on quality steeds obtained in the same way their leader acquired his. Most of these men had been with Fagan from the start. They were fierce, grim men who had sworn to defend their leader to the death. They did not care much for Jack Spolden's nonsense, but, as long as Little Jake fell for it, then it was tolerated by them. Fagan's men were more concerned with loot garnered from raids rather than turning the order of things upside down. They did not care about revolution; instead, they worried about what could be stolen today. Tomorrow was not worth the bother, until it came. Thus, they followed in silence—their eyes hungry and their throats parched.

The Palatines in the waggon behind Fagan's men and their brothers on horseback, bringing up the rear, were another story altogether. They were still drunk on the inspiring words of the Prophet. They sang his hymns with sharp, clear voices. They recited his names for the secret cells, but saved the Palatines of Leyden for last. They made all sorts of boasts about their bravery. Such merriment lasted until Fagan sent the Leutinger back to quiet them down. The column of villains was approaching the final bend in the by-road. From then on, the way was straight as a spear and a short distance from Mine Hill Road. Fagan did not want to attract the attention of a rare traveler plying these roads. He heard the Leutinger cursing at the raw recruits and then he heard silence. The General took a measure of satisfaction in knowing the Palatines were afraid of the Leutinger. It meant they were afraid of him. Fagan smiled for the first time since leaving the colliery.

Things, indeed, grew quiet as the column approached the main road—too quiet, thought Fagan. There was no breeze taunting the leaves overhead . . . no birds reporting on their harvest progress . . . nary a crow boasting about the remains on the head which the Prophet had planted on a stake in the tavern yard. Surely, there must have been a morsel or two remaining for a carrion bird, mused Fagan as he guided his horse on the last forty yards of the by-road. The General noticed that foresters must have been felling trees near the shoulder of the by-road. How odd such fellows left so much timber behind and piled so far in from the road. Fagan hoped they would not return for the wood until after his party had moved on to Hibernia. The timing would depend on how quickly the Covenanters reached the Sign of the Raven with the stolen horses. Fagan was not optimistic about their arrival occurring before dark. Upon reflecting about their performance in the last raid, the General lost his smile.

Little Jake could see the chimney and the remains of the tavern now. Someone had moved stones about, but for no purpose he could discern. Perhaps the woodcutters had spent the previous night there, feasting on fresh kill and raising vessels of rum to toast the Captain's head. Fagan liked the idea. At least someone had found a purpose for the gruesome trophy.

The General and the Leutinger started to cross Mine Hill Road. The Leutinger proceeded, but the General hesitated. He glanced to his right and caught sight of three horse riders kicking up dust a great distance away. They were approaching on the main road, but at a cautious pace. He wondered who they might be and the nature of their purpose. Fagan did not have to wonder for long. A deafening explosion captured the attention of every man approaching the Sign of the Raven. Chimney rocks flew in all directions. In a breath's span, the structure was reduced to rubble and a roiling cloud of dust. Horses reared, men cursed and shouted, and a thundering volley of muskets was followed by another thundering volley. Fagan felt the sear and sting of a musket ball in his right arm and a worse pain in his side below his heart. He noticed that the Leutinger fared worse. His favorite underling had been thrown from his horse. The man lay in the ditch at the side of the main road, face up, mouth agape, and a ball hole in his eye socket.

With great difficulty and all the strength he could muster, Fagan turned his horse. He scanned the chaos and carnage behind him. A number of his own men had been thrown from their mounts. Three were dead on the ground. Steeds, alive with panic, lurched about madly, then galloped off in various directions. The waggon of Palatines had veered off the shoulder of the by-road and toppled on its side. Frightened, wild-eyed passengers tumbled from the vehicle and scrambled for cover. The raw recruits on horseback, who brought up the rear, turned tail and were galloping back down the by-road. Most of Fagan's following, seasoned or not, were scampering into the woods on the side of the by-road opposite from where the musket smoke was billowing. In the next instant, Fagan made up his mind. The game was over. Someone had tricked him. However, he was still alive and had not been captured. There was good reason not to surrender. He waved his spent pistol and shouted out to his own horse riders—those who had not fallen or fled—to follow him up the northerning length of Mine Hill Road. His horse lurched forward, causing a stab of pain in his side. Fagan leaned forward and, with his good arm, clung to the mane of his mount. A dozen others followed him. Only their General knew their destination . . . only their General knew their singular purpose—revenge. After a third musket volley, there was dead silence. It was broken by a stentorian behest from Hard Joe Hoff: "Surrender, you mamzers! Toss aside your weapons and march out to the road . . . arms outstretched 'n palms showing . . . do as I say or it's death to those who disobey!"

Again there was silence, disrupted only by the sound of the hooves of three horses approaching the by-road terminus. Their riders looked strangely familiar to Vincent Wetherill, who had emerged from the covered rampart along with his compatriots. One of the riders called out to him and waved his black walking stick. William Jolly, Ansel Jarlman, and their guide, Jimmy Hornbeck, had finally arrived. At the same time, Hard Joe Hoff came down from his hiding place, after ordering his men to cross the by-road and search for any villains hiding in the woods. The Forge Master recognized only one of the three men on horseback. He addressed Hornbeck before Vincent got the chance to introduce the other two.

"Well, if it ain't Jimmy Hornbeck come for a visit to my party . . . a slight bit late as usual."

"Looks like you didn't need the likes of me 'n my new friends, Mister Hoff . . . seems like you scared 'em off by your lonesome."

"Not hardly," chortled Hoff, as he surveyed the damage done and counted the bodies in the road. "I had me some help from too few kinchins . . . could've used some help from you 'n your new friends . . . 'n could use you now, if you numbered more 'n three on horseback." Hard Joe used his sword to point north to Mine Hill Road. "Seems the leader of these scarlets got away with more following him than the likes of you could ever handle."

"Who might their leader be?" asked Hornbeck.

"Dan Fagan, the one called the General to his face 'n the one called Little Jake behind his back," answered Hoff. "He's the one been causing the most trouble in these hills. The gloak I really wanted to bag . . . would have you 'n your companions chase after him, but I counted a dozen sons of white hens joining him on horseback. You wouldn't stand a chance."

"Not so sure I would agree," interrupted Vincent, as he stepped forward and flashed a smile of recognition at the three mounted men. "I have been expecting Mister Hornbeck's so-called friends for some time. I must thank Jimmy for serving as their guide. 'Tis a welcome sight, indeed, to meet up again with William Jolly, retired gaoler and special agent to the High Sheriff in Amboy, and Ansel Jarlman, private agent for Verdine Elsworth of Powles Hook." Vincent turned to Hard Joe Hoff to complete his introduction of the pair he was very glad to see. "Mister Jolly means to retrieve gaol keys stolen by pig irons who sport the same tattoo Fagan's men wear. Mister Jarlman seeks to find the same fellow I mean to catch. Unfortunately, he was rudely detained by the Sheriff in Morris Town. That is why my associates are late in finding me, Mister Hoff. 'Tis also the reason they want to make up for lost time and help any way they can . . . even if it means chasing down the General."

"I'd allow it," chuckled Hoff, "if I thought Fagan's kind wouldn't detain your hides permanently . . . let's forget 'em 'n celebrate our victory here. You newcomers are welcome to join us."

The three late men dismounted and exchanged the usual manly greetings and news. Hard Joe Hoff filled the three in on what they had missed. He heaped praise on his foreman for his exemplary work in toppling the chimney. He ordered the foreman and the pair of slaves to return to the hidden waggons and prepare for the return of his thirsty men and the guests. Hoff, then, turned his attention to the slain man at the shoulder of the road.

"Could this be the jack-fellow you 'n your friends are looking for, Mister Wetherill?" Hard Joe poked the corpse of the Leutinger with his sword. "Whoever put him out of his misery made a masterful shot."

"Nein," snapped Cut. "That one came closest first, so I shot him dead with my own piece . . . thought he was the General . . ."

"He ain't Fagan," said Hoff decisively.

"He ain't who we're looking for neither," affirmed Cut.

Ansel Jarlman was the only one who could support the German's contention. He gave a complete description of the murderer they were looking for.

"So who might this one be?" asked Vincent.

"You're looking at a high-ranking piece of shyte in Fagan's gang . . . going way back . . . one who was disowned by his fam'ly years ago. Now I gets the honor of burying his bones in the tavern yard . . ."

"Does he have a Christian name?" asked Reverend Heaton innocently.

"Won't do him no good now," said the Forge Master, "where he's bound for."

"I must pray for his soul, regardless," insisted the preacher. "By what name shall I call him?"

"Charlie," hissed the Forge Master. "Call him Charlie Hoff, my own brother . . ."

20

THE RUSE
· · · · · · · · ·

Vincent Wetherill decided to let his men rest their horses. It had been an arduous, roundabout journey from the farmstead, adjacent to the Sign of the Raven, to the start of the mule path west of Horse Pound Mountain. They had made good progress, but a difficult climb lay ahead. Vincent decided to use this time to go over plans for what was to come once his team reached the mountain ridge. After the horses had been watered at a nearby stream and tethered for grazing in a pristine meadow, Vincent called his team together.

The men gathered along the stream bank where their leader was sitting on a rock. He was impatient to begin. He counted five men under his command, but he would have preferred six.

Jimmy Hornbeck was a welcome addition; however, Ike Higgins was still missing. Cut Hancock had been with him from the beginning. Reverend Heaton had quickly become a reliable mentor. The late arrival of Ansel Jarlman and William Jolly completed the team. Vincent was not sure that Karl Bruder had made it to the Old Johnson Mine. Thus, he had to settle for his definite five and strategize accordingly.

A bright, warm autumn sun in the late afternoon was at Vincent's back. Although his audience reclined in the partial shade of the willow closest to the stream bank, all the men shielded their eyes from the intrusive sun. Ansel Jarlman pulled his soiled castor hat lower over his brow. Reverend Heaton tilted his wide-brim. Cut used his large hand to shade his eyes. When the men had quieted down, Vincent began to review the details of his plan.

"Our primary goal is to rescue Ike Higgins. We must assume

our Tom Doodle is still alive and kept secure under strong guard, either in the mine or close by it. The Reverend and I will stick to using the barrels of iron water as a ruse to gain admittance to the Prophet's sacred place. It will serve as a distraction, while we figure out how to free my flanker. The other reasons we have for coming here are important, but secondary. We've been told Ike's captor, and prime suspect in three murders, is already headed back to Morris Town or parts unknown. Our chances of having to deal with Tom Ward, alias Billy Walsh, at the Johnson Mine are slight at best. If he happens to be there, then any one of us has good cause to take him down. We would prefer to capture him alive, but we would be glad to see him dead. It matters not to me. If the Afric wench is still alive, then rescuing her is also a possibility. We've been told she swings in a cage near the mine entrance. If we get a chance to size up the mad contraption, then we can decide how to free the poor girl. We might get lucky and find that Dan Fagan made it to the Prophet's headquarters. How splendid it would be if we captured both rogues in the same place. I'd settle for one. My money is on seizing Jack Spolden. If Fagan has made it to the mine, then a dozen of his followers are with him. This will make our chances doubly hard. Those of you, whom I send over the ridge to the ledge above the mine entrance, will have some fun picking off Fagan's men and Spolden's guards. I'm counting on you four— Cut, Jimmy, Will, and Ansel—to aim straight and fire steady. Our last reason for climbing this mountain, for the time being, is best forgotten. The mine used to be one of Sam Ford's hiding places, so I've been told. Another rumor has it that he hid his trove at the Smultz Cabin. However, he could have just as easily hid his loot in, or near, the Johnson Mine. I have a feeling Sam Ford is too clever for us. His wealth—counterfeit or not—is in neither place. So let's not concern ourselves with treasure hunting. We've lives to save and devils to bring to justice. Let's get to work."

"'Tis God's work we must complete," added Reverend Heaton, "and 'tis nothing close to easy. We must be resolute against Satan's legions. Let us finish the task."

"We have good reason to succeed," continued Vincent, after giving Heaton a nod and a look to indicate that he was definitely in charge. "First, we have to climb the mule path, get to the mountain ridge, and split apart. Reverend Heaton will continue with me in the waggon carrying only four barrels of Judge Cooper's creek water and one barrel of Forge Master Hoff's black powder. All borrowed muskets and other equipment must be taken off the waggon and carried by the rest of you. Cut, Jolly, and Jarlman will follow Mister Hornbeck over the ridge and down to the rock-bound ledge. Jimmy has worked this mine. He tells me the ledge is the best vantage point for picking off rogues below. Heed his advice and things should go in our favor."

"This is all cart before the horse," complained William Jolly, who fidgeted with his black walking stick. He was not looking forward to climbing among mountain rocks, and he said so. This was the second time he voiced opposition to his assigned role. The first time was close to noon after the four captives had been interrogated during the Forge Master's celebratory merriment at the rum waggon. Back then, Jolly was talked into joining the shooters below the ridge. However, after sizing up the mountain looming in the distance, he had second thoughts. "You are forgetting what may lie ahead before we even make the ridge."

"What do you mean?" asked Vincent, who shot a glance at the sun in order to gauge how much time remained before dusk.

"Surely the rear approach to the mine is guarded," insisted the retired gaoler, pointing his walking stick in the direction of the mountain. "Ought you not send someone ahead to make sure the way is guarded or not?"

Vincent responded with Jolly's own words mingled with his own: "Good idea to send someone ahead—someone who knows this land."

"That'd be me," chimed Jimmy Hornbeck, who got to his feet and started toward the meadow to retrieve his horse. "I'll be on me way to the ridge . . . meet you all there if the way is clear . . . shall return if I sees a watchkeep."

"Remember how I showed you to use your hands against those who stand in your way," advised Reverend Heaton.

Hornbeck turned his head, grinned, and replied: "A knife's goin' to be in me hand 'n preferrin' a silent kill with nary a word exchanged."

"God's speed, Jimmy," offered the preacher with finality.

Vincent watched Ford's man mount his horse and head up the steepening mule path. He was glad to have Hornbeck on his team. Though rough around the edges, Hornbeck was proving to be a most valuable asset. He knew the lay of the land, knew how to handle explosives, and how to fire a musket. However, Vincent wondered if the man had volunteered to guide Jolly and Jarlman, or had been ordered to do so by one of the Fords. He assumed Jimmy Hornbeck was trustworthy, even though he might have been sent by the Fords to carry out their agenda and keep an eye on Vincent's moves. Nevertheless, Reverend Heaton vouched for Hornbeck and declared him steadfast to a fault. The preacher's endorsement was good enough for Vincent. Now, he simply had to deal with the reluctant member of his team.

"Anything else bothering you, Mister Jolly?"

"One thing only, Mister Wetherill. My bad leg is acting up . . . ever since Mister Jarlman and I left Morris Town. Mighten I serve you best by staying behind to keep an eye on this here mule path?"

"I was counting on your ability with a musket, Mister Jolly," said Vincent with a frown. "We may be sorely outnumbered, even if Dan Fagan fails to make it to the mine."

"I'm afraid a climb o'er the ridge will do me in," groused Jolly.

"Waste of a man down here," opined Ansel Jarlman, who busied himself with picking at a grog blossom on his nose. "Why not have Mister Jolly guard our backs 'n our horses up near the ridge? Looks to mine own self like one can get a grand view of the waypath from there. Such a rear guard will not be far from the rest of us, gone o'er the ridge. Mister Jolly might toss a few stones to warn us if anythin's amiss."

"Good thought, Mister Jarlman," praised Vincent. "Any among us for or against having Mister Jolly remain behind near the ridge?"

There was silence.

Reverend Heaton broke it: "Your decision, Mister Wetherill . . . you are in charge here."

"Very well then," said Vincent without hesitation. "Jolly, you will remain at the watch to guard our rear. You shall tend to the horses and any equipment left behind. Keep to your position as long as you can defend it. Wait for one of us to come fetch you. Do not come searching for us. We will tell you when the fun is over. If you have to warn the three men below your position, do as Mister Jarlman has suggested—a few tossed stones will not alert our adversaries."

"Fine with me," said Jolly halfheartedly. He was not looking forward to climbing the mule path on horseback. He dreaded the thought of having to dismount and walk any difficult stretches. He did not like the idea of waiting alone for woe to find him at the top of the mountain. He regretted ever having promised to join young Wetherill. Jolly had grave doubts he would gain any information about the things that concerned him. He made the trip up from Perth Amboy because he had promised the young Wetherill and out of respect for the elder Wetherill. So far, he had learned nothing new about the Treasury robbery, or any connection Sam Ford had with it—merely, all the same rumors heard many times before. Mostly, the former gaoler learned much about the prime suspect in the three murders around Morris Town, after he helped convince Sheriff Stiles to release Captain Elsworth's man. He also learned a few things about the sword-and-ring tattoos. This resulted from his participation in the questioning of Hoff's captives. Unfortunately, Jolly felt the fugitive everyone wanted captured and the leaders of the so-called Sons of the Sword had nothing to do with the Treasury robbery. He was wasting his time up here in the hills. He wanted to return to Amboy where he had recently stumbled upon new information about certain Irish soldiers who had deserted their posts at the Barracks in sixty-eight. Their disappearance coincided with the night of the Treasury robbery, and, in the days following, made them immediate suspects in the crime. Jolly needed to talk more with the retired Mister Sergent, who had served as Barracks Master in Perth Amboy through most of the previous decade. This man visited the Long Ferry Tavern two nights ago and shared a few schooners of warm ale with Jolly. It was then that the former gaoler was able to garner the names of a couple of suspects and a rather detailed description of one of the deserters. There was one named Welsh, or Walsh, but Sargent could not remember the soldier's first name. It would be a long shot, indeed, if this fellow was the Billy Walsh, alias Tom Ward, everybody was looking for. Jolly did not feel that lucky.

Mister Sergent described another bog jumper—a rather short

fellow . . . walked with a limp—one leg shorter than the other . . . lost an eye in a tavern fight in Amboy . . . relegated to repairing and making locks for the King's facilities in the city. Sergent went on to say the fellow was skilled in several ways but seldom trusted. He had the reputation of being a sneak thief and was watched closely. He often bragged of finding great wealth some day. The man's surname, according to the half-drunk Mister Sargent, was Parrot, or something of the sort. Sargent swore to it, but, again, he could not remember a first name.

"We all called him by his nickname," confided Mister Sargent in a slur. "We called him One-Eye."

Ike Higgins realized that the best way to be ignored by his captors was to pipe down. All afternoon, he had been beating two thin iron rods, which had been left in his cage for some inexplicable reason, against the bars. He clicked and clanged with them as he shouted out to be freed, clamored to be fed, and demanded his clothing be returned. Ike was cold, sore, and hungry. But, most of all, he was angry—enraged at his captors for stripping him of everything he possessed, even the bandage he had worn on his bad arm. He was angry over being tossed into a narrow, hard cage and hoisted high above the ground to sway in the wind—all for the amusement of a strange robed fellow and several armed characters who jumped at their leader's every command. Ike was angry for one other reason—in a suspended cage just like his, but closer to a ring of stones and a cooking fire, was the motionless body of a dusky woman. She lay still, clutching something furry—something as dormant as she was, and more than likely dead. Ike was angry at himself for not being able to do something for the woman. However, he was also angry at her for reminding him that his fate was going to be the same as hers. Thus, he raised the loudest ruckus he could—sang sweet songs to the woman; insulting songs, laced with the most vile sailor's curses, to the guards below; and lusty drinking songs to himself. If anything, Ike proved to one and all that he was not going to die easily. He was trying with all his might to fight death for Good Mary's sake. After all, he was from hardy stock—a descendant of Irish nobility, according to relatives who enjoyed a strong drink more than he did. The placard on his cage confirmed it. The robed man declared it so. Ike was unable to read the placard, but he heard others joke about what it spelled out. This made him all the more irate and more determined than ever to stay alive. He would show his captors what a true thatch-head was made of.

And so, Ike raged on with his noise until his throat grew parched and failed him. With his last drinking song but a raspy whisper, Ike decided to set another goal for himself. He would escape.

The trick was to be patient, wait for the head man to return to the confines of his lair, and count those who followed the odd one into the mine and those who remained outside. The guards, to a man, seemed bored and lax. At first, they found Ike's noisy antics amusing. A few of them tossed stones at his cage and called him worse names than he called them. They soon tired of their taunting game and ignored the latest captive, even though he continued to rattle and roar for a long spell.

Several of the Prophet's wardens turned to the entertainment provided by a crippled fellow with a rag over one eye, who kept to a cooking fire for most of the day. These guards gathered there to watch him cut up the corpse of Tom Ward—the bastard who duped Ike, bribed him with a pair of boots, got him sorely drunk, bound and gagged him, and brought him to a worse bastard. Ike was glad Morrell's foreman had been shot dead by the latter. However, being a witness to the dismemberment of his kidnaper sickened him. The one-eyed fellow was slow and deliberate with his knife. He seemed to enjoy his work and having an audience for the gruesome task, which the robed one had instructed him to do. First, he separated Ward's head from the body and tossed it into the fire. The thing popped and sizzled much to the delight of the tattooed sentries. The spectators reminded Ike of the pig irons who beat him up outside of Rattoon's. He vowed to get revenge against these brothers of the ones who thrashed him . . . he vowed to get revenge against them all.

Ike started formulating his plan of escape as soon as the one-eyed man completed the removal of Tom Ward's privates and a few other gobbets of flesh, and tossed the cuttings into the fire. Ike had a fair amount of time to decide on what means to take to extricate himself from the cage. The cutting ritual was followed by a lengthy round of chanting and drinking. Finally, the one-eyed man, assisted by three guards, dragged what was left of Ward's torso to the mine entrance. There, an argument ensued over who was to accompany the corpse to its burial place and who was to stay behind. Ike could not imagine what horrors might take place in the mine during the burial ceremony. He wondered how many bodies had been deposited in the mine and what else was hidden in there. He was determined to make sure his plan of escape would prevent these fiends from hiding his bones in a mine shaft. Ike was determined to make his getaway at the first opportunity.

Luckily, as it turned out, all sentries and the one-eyed man at the mine entrance were summoned in by their leader, who had emerged to inspect the carvings on the corpse. He approved of the knife-wielder's efforts and ordered all men standing there to help lower the torso into the mine. As soon as the burial party and the robed leader disappeared from sight, Ike counted those who remained in daylight. Three guards were near and about—two at the cooking fire and one keeping watch at the mule path. None of them bothered to give quiet Ike a glance. Thus, Vincent's naked flanker got down to work.

Ike estimated the length of heavy chain, which ran from his iron neck collar to a stout frame bar at the north corner of his cage. It appeared to be about four feet long. He examined each link and found none of them flawed. Two links were gapped slightly—one near his neck collar and one half-the-way down. He decided to work on the latter. If he could widen the gap on that link, he could free up at least three feet of chain for dangling from the cage in order to drop down. Ike had often used rods and bars for prying and loosening chores at Radford's Landing. Gapping a chain link with two thin rods seemed easy work. The Irishman set about positioning the rods in the holes of two adjacent links—one already-gapped, and its neighbor not. He pulled the chain taut on the floor and pushed the rods down against the opposite sides of one of the floor bars. Ike positioned himself so that he could pry the rods apart, first with his hands until his bad arm hurt, then with a foot and his good arm. He was silent as a cat. Neither guard at the cooking fire paid any attention to his game. In the span of a few breaths, the rods came far apart and slightly bent. Ike released his grip on them and examined the targeted link.

Its gap had widened enough to set free most of the chain. However, Ike kept it whole and rolled noiselessly to the placard which spelled out his noble title. He worked some wire free from where it was used to hold the placard to the cage. He straightened two pieces of wire and slipped over to the large lock on the cage door. The lock was a new one. It faced out, away from Ike's nimble fingers. He knew his bad arm would tire easily, so he worked quickly on springing the lock. This was something he had done often when necessary. His efforts were usually met with success. The trick, this once, was working backwards to tumble the well-made lock. But Ike was up to the task. He had great desire and keen purpose, as well as consummate skill. In little time the lock yielded. All was set for an escape.

Ike studied the scene below. The sentry at the mule path was distracted by something or someone approaching from the valley below. Both men at the cooking fire appeared to be snoozing. The moment was perfect. Ike separated the chain at the gapped link. He crow-hopped to the cage door, slipped the lock from its position, and gently placed it on the cage floor. He swung the door open, making sure to do it slowly so that it did not sing with a squeak. It was not oiled, yet it made no grating sound. Ike grabbed the rods and tossed them to the ground, making sure they fell far apart from each other. Each made a thudding sound, but not loud enough to arouse suspicion. Next, Ike lowered the short length of chain still anchored to the frame bar, and used it to descend. He swung down, let go of the chain, and fell to the ground. Ike retrieved both rods. He flung one in the direction of lower ground. He grasped the other, with intentions of using it as a weapon. He held the length of chain still attached to his neck collar taut as he could to keep it from jangling. Ike bolted for a stand of trees which stood on higher ground far below the ore-streaked ridge. He scrambled among slippery, moss-covered rocks and jagged tailings, cutting his feet as he ran. He did not care. It felt good to acquire a few fresh wounds—badges of freedom gained. As he made his way to higher ground, Ike held but one regret—there had been no time nor opportunity to save the dark women from the fate they were destined to share. He slipped into the black, cool shade of the stubborn mountain trees. There, once hidden completely from sight, Ike resolved to return to fetch the Afric. He had to do it. Good Mary would expect nothing less.

❖

Two riders, their horses kicking up dust on the mule path, ascended speedily toward the lone sentry at his station rock a hundred yards from the entrance to the Johnson Mine. The sun was in their eyes and close to caressing the mountain ridge. They spurred their horses to full gallop, appearing to have no intention of stopping to identify themselves or reveal their business. The sentry raised his musket and ordered them to halt, but they sped by as if he was invisible. He wanted to fire a warning shot over their heads in order to stop them, but he was afraid to do so. He knew these two men to be favorites of the General. It was not wise to rile any of Fagan's men. By the wild-eyed look on their sweaty faces, the sentry sensed something had gone wrong. He decided to abandon his post and run after the pair of riders. By the time he caught up with them, they had roused his two comrades at the cooking fire and were demanding the Fahnrich be turned over to them.

"Where's the Prophet hidin' that bastard scout o' his?" growled one of the horsemen.

"Ain't here," gasped the sentry, who struggled to catch his breath after a long run to the cooking fire. "The Prophet ordered him to return the way he came to check on progress made."

"We ain't seen his stinkin' hide on our way up here," scoffed the rider who had initiated the conversation. "An', besides all that, there ain't goin' to be no progress made." The angry man spat on the ground and frowned at the bloody bandage on his left hand. "We was led straight to slaughter this here morn by followin' the advice of the Fahnrich as to the when 'n where of his plan."

"The Prophet will not be pleased to hear of your failure," said the sentry boldly.

The same angry horseman spat in the direction of the vocal guard, but missed him. "Keep yer tongue in yer mouth, taffy, or I might be forced to cut it out with me knife 'n while I'm at it, the tongues of yer two mates here. Ain't us who's to blame fer no raid on the Adventure works this time 'round . . . thank the Prophet's darlin' fer the failure. We've been ordered to escort him back to the colliery. Fagan wants to question the bastard . . . put his head on a stake."

"The Fahnrich passed my post 'bout an hour ago," explained the winded sentry. "He departed on a fresh horse with orders to find out if the Covenanters of Allstedt arrived with mounts for the Palatines. The man's likely half-the-way there . . . took the mule path down."

"No he didn't," insisted the rider with bitterness painting his words. He spat again and used his tongue to shift the snuff in his mouth. "An' there ain't no reason fer to go to the Sign of the Raven . . . the bastard knows none of the livin' is there. We scattered like leaves in a wind . . . even the chimney's gone . . . toppled by the smiters who ambushed us. Our game's 'bout done . . . yers too . . . no reason fer any of us goin' there now. The Fahnrich must've gone somewheres else."

The sentry insisted that Karl Bruder went where he was told to go, then he reiterated his original opinion: "The Prophet will not be pleased to hear your account."

"Where might yer Black Jake be hidin' while we're out there riskin' lives fer him?" asked the horseman with a look of disdain on his face.

"At the rituals in the mine," answered the sentry. "He gave orders not to be disturbed, for he mourns the loss of the agent of righteousness who fetched him two nobles for the cages."

Both horsemen turned their heads in the direction of the two suspended contraptions. They were not impressed.

"Seems you've lost one of yer lords," remarked the rider, who was pointing his bandaged hand at Ike's vacant cage.

The guards at the cooking fire leaped to their feet and ran to the empty cage. The mule path sentry ran to the mine entrance to alert those inside that one of the captives had escaped.

The horsemen turned their steeds and trotted briskly down to the mule path. They wanted no part in the hunt for the escapee—a clever fox, who vanished right under the noses of the Prophet's elite guards. They had another clever fox, named Karl Bruder, to find and bring back to the colliery where their General was licking his wounds. The two riders coaxed their horses into a full gallop. They were laughing now—glad to share a spate of bad luck with the other half of a doomed movement. They knew their time of service was almost done. Fagan was near death. With his passing, the two riders would be on their own to form a new gang of banditti. Unfortunately, they would fail to fulfill the General's last wish—the resumption of their search for the Fahnrich was headed in the wrong direction.

Fagan's horsemen were out of sight before the Prophet emerged from the mine and ordered most of his men to search for the Baron of Ballynary. He instructed the three guards who were at their watch when Ike Higgins escaped, to stay put. He also told the one-eyed reinsman and three guards, who had been with him in the mine, to remain behind. When the searchers were out of sight, Black Jake sent One-Eye back into the mine to fetch the ceremonial sword. The trio of negligent guards were disarmed by their peers and ordered to kneel in the sacred ring. They were advised to pray for forgiveness. They were about to lose more than their tongues.

Spolden's search party found an iron rod in the brush east of the cage, which had held Ike Higgins. The searchers descended into the valley of the wild horses, thinking that was where they would find the escapee. Meanwhile, Karl Bruder was approaching Mister Jolly's position near the mountain ridge. At the same time, there happened to be more than one fox climbing Horse Pound Mountain—more than one man eager to join Vincent's team.

The sun was squatting on the crown of the mountain by the time the Wetherill bay Shires and waggon came into view. At first, all men at the cooking fire and ceremonial circle ignored the latest visitors. It had been a busy day and three headless bodies had to be attended to. The pair in the waggon emerged from deep, dark shadows cloaking the mule path. The man who held the reins kept his father's horses to a deliberate pace. The man in the broad-brimmed hat, next to the driver, gripped both seat and sideboard with his large hands. He quickly realized the way down to the mine entrance was steep and uneven—well worth a prayer, uttered softly.

Reverend Heaton was, of course, unarmed. Vincent Wetherill had his pistol well-hidden in his clothing trunk under the seat board. His sword and dagger were squirreled away in the same place. They intended to approach as innocent, unarmed men, bearing a precious gift for a holy man of the mountains. How generous their effort to share in God's bounty, thought Heaton. He also considered how foolish of his companion to think the ruse would work.

One of the three spared guards ran to intercept the latest unanticipated visitors before they got too close to the ceremonial ring. He was armed with musket in hand, and pistol and knife at his belt. By the sour look on his face, he appeared in no mood to exchange pleasantries with strangers.

"No need stoppin' here, you buncers," announced the grim sentry, who took the pair to be itinerant peddlers. "There'll be no buyin' nor sellin' on this sacred ground. Be on your way and make quick work of it."

"My good man," offered Vincent with a beaming smile and an open hand raised high. "My assistant, the good Reverend Heaton of Schooley's Mountain and I bear a precious gift of four barrels of iron water. They are meant for the baptism of holy men 'round these parts. Consider the precious barrels as an offering to the one fondly called the Prophet."

"And who might you be in your fancy Captain's jacket and shiny boots?" challenged the surly guard, as he looked in the waggon and counted five barrels.

"My name is Johnny Rattoon," replied Vincent in the most honest voice he could muster, "a tavern master at Radford's Landing now and an Indian fighter before that . . ."

"Don't see no scars on that pretty face of yours, Mister Rattoon, and your mauleys are lookin' soft to me," sneered the guard. "Besides, I count five barrels, not four . . ."

Vincent gave a chuckle and Heaton grinned assuredly. "Oh that," said Vincent. "The fifth barrel is meant for the one they call the General up here—a gift we shall deliver after unloading the iron water meant for your leader's sacred purposes."

The sentry was perplexed. He lowered his musket, cradled it in one hand, and scratched his ear with the other. Finally he said, "Wait here. I will bring word to the Prophet and let him decide." With that said, he turned sharply and jogged back to the cooking fire where Jack Spolden was chanting prayers over the body parts which his reinsman was tossing into the flames. The guard stood silently behind Spolden and waited for his leader to complete the gross work.

Vincent took advantage of the lull by pretending to gauge how much daylight remained. He looked skyward above the mine entrance and scanned the ridge. He saw no sign of his men up there—they were either hiding well or had not yet made their descent to the ledge. He noticed that very little of the sun remained above the mountain's crown. Time to take action was running out.

The guard returned and climbed into the back of the waggon. He inspected the barrels. He poked at the clothing trunk with his musket, but did not open it. He came up behind the two men and frisked them for weapons. After he was satisfied, he finally spoke:

"No weapons, I see . . . when I say so, you will proceed to the sacred ring of stones . . . I will tell you when and where to halt. The Prophet is eager to counsel with the preacher man, but not you, Rattoon . . . you will remain in the waggon . . . make no false move. When we halt, Reverend Heaton, you will step down and proceed to the center of the ring. The Prophet will be there to greet you . . . kneel before the Prophet and speak only when spoken to. Your time with the holy one shall be brief. Have you any doubts about proceedin'?"

"None," said Vincent, who was eager to get this confrontation over with.

"How 'bout you, preacher man?" asked the guard almost politely.

"One question only," posed Heaton. "I am unarmed. I see your Prophet wields a cumbersome sword. Shall it accompany him in the ring of stones?"

"Of course," scoffed the guard, stifling a derisive laugh, "'tis an ancient sword with powers beyond your comprehension . . . do not question the manner in which the Prophet employs the blade. A man of piety, such as you, should harbor no fear of such a thing . . ."

"Fear is not the issue," expressed Heaton rather pedanticaly. "'Tis the odds which concern me."

The guard ignored the minister's comment. It was not a question so he felt no compulsion to respond. After all, the man's fate had already been decided. The fate of Mister Rattoon had been decided as well. The Prophet suggested that the guard plant a musket ball in the stranger's back as soon as the preacher was decapitated. Thus, two more bodies would have to be dismembered. Two more torsos would have to be prepared for burial in the watery mine shaft. It was going to be a long night . . .

"Proceed, Mister Rattoon," ordered the guard, "and be quick at it!"

Cut was bored. He yawned and attempted to stretch out a kink in his leg. He had been crouching behind a stunted tree and ridge boulder for too long, waiting for something to happen. Shadows were deepening now and it was difficult to make out what was going on below. He could still see two men standing a safe distance apart in a ring of stones. A robed fellow was balancing a two-handed sword on his shoulder. Cut assumed this one was none other than Jack Spolden, the Prophet. The larger man in the ring, wearing a wide-brim hat, was Reverend Heaton. Cut was sure of it. These two appeared to be exchanging words in a civil manner. No trouble there.

Cut, however, did not like to see the preacher separated so far from his boss. Mister Wetherill was sitting patiently in the waggon at the far side of the cooking fire. One of the Prophet's sentries was standing behind Vincent. He was armed with a musket. There was no way Cut could bring down the guard and the Prophet in good time. He had an extra musket, but, still and all, events below might happen faster than the span of two rounds in a double volley. Cut decided to concentrate on the sentry behind his boss. Heaton would have to rely on the Lord.

Something to his left and a fair distance below caught his eye—a creature of some sort was scrambling up, but using the cover of large trees and huge boulders in the ascent. Cut caught a glimpse of the thing before it disappeared from view— a bear perhaps, or a bobcat, maybe a wolf . . . such bad luck to have game approaching at a time when all rounds had to be reserved for humans. Cut cursed to himself and gave a hand signal to Ansel Jarlman on his left. He alerted the man that something was climbing close to his position. Cut gathered a handful of stones just in case. For practice, he cooly tossed a stone in the direction of the beast, which was inching closer to Jarlman's hiding place. Cut tossed another. It clicked against a boulder. He waited for the thing to slip out from behind the struck rock. The German had no intention of firing his weapon at the thing. Such an act would ruin whatever negotiations were going on below. Perhaps, the tossing of stones and the sight of a man behind the gesture would be enough to frighten the creature away.

However, the thing that came into view was no slinking beast. It was moon pale, wild-eyed, with hands open and held high . . . plus, it was fast approaching. The thing was none other than a naked Ike Higgins. Cut dropped his clutch of stones and clambered down to inspect what was left of the hapless flanker. Ike collapsed in his arms. Cut lowered Ike to a sitting position and crouched close to him. The Irishman was tattooed with cuts and scrapes obviously gained from climbing the steep face of the mountain. He was in bad shape, but his eyes were bright with spirit. He grasped his collar chain with a quivering hand.

"Fancy meetin' up wit' the likes o' ye, cabbage head," said Ike, as he struggled to sit up. "One strong drink's all I needs 'n that fine musket o' yers to fire at them bastards below."

Cut offered a rare smile and replied: "Looks like you could use mein hunting coat as well, bog lander." The German stood up removed his favorite garment, which was stained with Little Neb's blood, and draped it over Ike's shoulders.

"You'll find a pint flask of rum in the chest pocket 'n various treasures in other pockets."

With the dexterity of a pickpocket, Ike found the magic vessel, gulped down its contents, and smacked his lips loudly. "Much better," sighed Ike. He sniffed the air and wrinkled his nose, "'cept fer the coat . . . reeks o' death . . ."

Cut grinned again. "I'd take it back, bog lander, but it's all I got to offer. Besides, if you button the coat full down, you'll not be scaring the ladies with your dangling chain.

"No needs to worry 'bout such up here," countered Ike. "The stink o' yer garment will scare 'em away afore I unbuttons the thing."

"Wear it with pride," stressed Cut. "I used mein coat to cover the body of a boy slain by the same bugger who kidnaped you . . . never bothered to clean it . . . want to be reminded of the man I have to bring back to the boy's mother—dead or alive. You'll find your good luck spoon in the inside pocket 'long with the coins I won from saving your arse down at Powles Hook."

Ike felt for the prize and made a jingling sound with the coins as he did so.

"Don't filch no gold while you're at finding your brass spoon," warned Cut.

"Wouldn't think o' such, cabbage head," shot back Ike, as he pulled out the object which meant so much to him.

"The thing was found by the Obadiah's daughter right where you tossed it," explained Cut. "Lucky for you she did. I purchased it off her for a coin of mine . . . so your spoon is worth something now."

"Priceless to the likes o' me 'n the onliest treasure I've found so far," concluded Ike, who got to his knees, put the spoon back in the pocket which held the coins, and buttoned the coat. "Glad ye saw the spoon as mine, cabbage head, 'n rushed up this way to rescue the likes o' me . . ."

"Not as plain as all that, bog lander," interrupted Cut. "After paying a visit to the Sharps, your boss 'n a preacher man headed for Stirling's forge where we was volunteered to fight 'gainst a robber gang." Cut pointed to the red ribband still affixed to his green-checked wool cap. "'Tis where I earned this badge for bringing down an outrider. After some success, we headed to this here Godforsaken place to carry out your boss's plan 'n rescue you . . ."

"I saved meself from certain mad folks down there, which'd were tryin' to keep me caged till me own death," bragged Ike. "Didn't needs no help fer escapin', but I could use a wee bit a' help with revenge."

"Got no boots nor drawers for you to wear," quipped Cut, "nor tools to free you from that iron collar 'round your neck . . . but I've a spare firing piece to lend . . . we can use 'nother man up here."

The two men scrambled up to Cut's original position. When they got there, the German reached for one of Hoff's muskets and paraphernalia necessary for loading the weapon. Ike accepted the hardware eagerly and started priming the piece at the same time Cut was readying his German rifle. With nimble fingers, Ike poured a measure of powder down the barrel of the musket. He then shoved a patched lead ball down the barrel in imitation of Cut's moves. Lastly, Ike used a powder horn containing prime-grade powder for the pan. He pulled back the hammer and made sure the frizzen was closed.

"Take your time, bog lander," warned Cut. "No one up here fires till Mister Wetherill gives the signal."

"Ain't got that long to wait," countered Ike. He pointed the borrowed musket at the cage which held Rachel Hagers and the rat-catcher. "See the black jileen behind them iron bars."

Cut acknowledged that he was aware of her plight.

"She's been swingin' there longer 'n me," growled Ike. "Sure to be near death . . . ain't got no time fer no damn signal."

Ike swung the musket and took aim at the robed figure standing over the preacher, who appeared to be kneeling before him. Cut had no time to snatch the weapon from the vengeful flanker. There was a brilliant flash and a sharp roar echoing off the mountain ridge. Another flash and roar came from Cut's weapon. The guard behind Vincent tumbled out of the waggon. Cut's well-aimed shot was followed by a crackling response from the muskets held by Ansel Jarlman and Jimmy Hornbeck. The peaceful negotiations had come to an abrupt end . . .

21

BLACKPOWDER
• • • • • • • • • • • • •

—at the Old Johnson Mine on Horse Pound Mountain close to nightfall on Tuesday, September 28, 1773

"Your day is done, Johnny Spolden," said Reverend Heaton evenly, as he assumed the crouching position of a cat about to pounce. "Your cause was doomed from the start . . . your General lies mortally wounded . . . your followers flee to parts unknown . . . even the Devil has abandoned you. A revolution is coming, but it won't be yours."

"How dare you blaspheme the seer of God's plan," parried Black Jake Spolden with anger boiling under his words. "I am the Lord's instrument, yet you continue to utter falsehoods during our brief and last encounter. Shame on your soul, Samuel. I am just beginning my campaign of fierce righteousness. There is no room for your kind in my movement. You were instructed to kneel before me . . . to show respect . . . yet you do so half-the-way—just as I remember your preaching to be . . ."

"You were a good listener back then, Johnny," said Heaton with a soft gaze meant to distract the mad one, "but a poor interpreter of God's word . . ."

"On your knees, defender of the old order and ape's game," insisted the Prophet. "On your knees!"

The robed one lifted his sacred sword confidently above his head. As he did so, Heaton lunged at him—one large hand at Spolden's neck and one pushing hard against the hilt of the sword. Heaton placed a heavy boot behind Spolden's unshod foot. Thus, he started his maneuver for toppling the dangerous man to the ground. At the same time, the roar of a musket and the buzz of a musket ball cut through the air above his head. Both men went down—preacher atop prophet.

A second shot followed immediately after the first. This round found its mark. The guard with the rock-hard frame and steely limbs—the one standing behind Vincent—toppled out of the Wetherill waggon. His musket flew out of his clumsy, mauly hands. He was dead before he hit the ground. The bay Shires whinnied and turned on their own after being startled by the masterful second shot. In the next instant, the wheels of the waggon rolled over the dead guard. Vincent was unable to get the horses under control until the panic-struck steeds reached the tallest rocks that made the ring. By this time, shots were flying from other muskets up on the ledge above the mine entrance. A sentry by the cooking fire went down with a ball against bone at his knee. He shrieked in pain and began a slow, agonizing crawl to the mine entrance. The other guard at the flames stood and fired his musket just as Vincent rolled over the seat board and tumbled into the back of the waggon. The shot was high and it pinged off a tall rock. Vincent crawled to his clothing chest, extracted his weapons, leaped out of the vehicle, and took shelter behind the rock Jack Spolden preferred to stand upon when addressing his followers.

From this vantage point, Vincent spotted two men abandoning the cooking fire and slinking past the three decapitated corpses in order to make their way towards the center of the ring of stones. One held a spent musket and the other, a large knife. Vincent quickly realized the pair meant to strike Heaton and rescue the Prophet. He readied his pistol, got off a round, and legged the man with the musket. With cutlass in hand, Vincent leaped into the ring of stones to save his pious mentor. At the same time, the knife-wielder was gimping, fast as he could, towards the two men wrestling on the ground.

It was really no contest. Heaton insisted on subduing Spolden with a choke hold. The man had already let go of his unwieldy blade and was flailing his arms in an attempt to tear at Heaton's face. The preacher lost his wide-brim in the process. Spolden found a fistful of Heaton's long, sandy hair and held on for dear life. He pulled with all his might and attempted to roll Heaton off him. Spolden unexpectedly succeeded, but did so with some assistance.

The one-eyed knife-wielder meant to plunge his blade into the preacher's back. He missed, but sliced the man's shoulder instead.

Heaton groaned and let go of the Prophet's throat. With his good arm, he swiped at the knife-wielder. He struck the stinking man with a rock-hard fist and sent him reeling head over heels. The filthy rag, covering where the struck man's eye used to be, flew off and fluttered to the ground. By this time, Vincent had made it to Reverend Heaton, who was standing and clutching his shoulder where blood began seeping through his fingers. He was staring in the direction of the mine entrance. The robed man was running to it, sword in hand, and suddenly out of sight. The guard, shot in the leg by Vincent, limped in after Spolden disappeared.

"May God have pity on his soul," sighed Reverend Heaton. "Poor Johnny Spolden, I fear, cannot be saved."

"We almost had him," snapped Vincent, as he kicked the unconscious, one-eyed man's knife away and placed a boot on his chest. "And this miserable snibbler almost had you."

Heaton scanned the black-streaked ridge and the narrow ledge where the musket fire had originated from. All was quiet once again. The sun had been completely swallowed by the mountain. Reds and purples crowned it. Its shadow dominated the landscape below

"One of your lads fired too soon, Mister Wetherill," observed the preacher stoically, "and came mighty close to striking me dead."

"T'wasn't Cut," offered Vincent. "Either Ansel Jarlman or Jimmy Hornbeck must have grown impatient for my signal. I'm betting the man who almost cut you down is Ford's bodyguard."

"Don't lay the blame just yet," admonished Heaton. "Call them down, Mister Wetherill. We need to address the problem of the few roysters who are hiding in the mine. We have to figure out how to free the precious maiden from that confounded cage. What happened, by the way, to your Mister Higgins? And where are all of Spolden's guards, and Fagan's men that Mister Bruder warned us about?"

"None of those things matter at this moment," Vincent said with some urgency. "You need to get your stab wound tended to."

"'Tis a scratch," scoffed Heaton, as he shuffled to the edge of the ring of stones and sat down heavily. "My wife'll be more concerned with the tear in my coat."

"Soon as Mister Jolly joins us," confided Vincent, "I'll have him take a look at your shoulder. He has some experience in mending such wounds—experience gained from quelling fights and cleaning up after them, during the years he served at gaol."

"Summon your men, Mister Wetherill," groaned Heaton. "Do it now. We may have precious little time left till more adversaries appear."

Vincent agreed and called out to Cut. He shouted, loud as he could, to Jimmy Hornbeck to fetch Mister Jolly and the horses. No acknowledgement came from the latter, but Cut replied with a trilling whistle. The signaling back and forth caused someone at the mine entrance to fire a musket round. This was followed by an eerie silence, broken only by a falling rock allowed by one of the men climbing down from the ledge.

In the growing darkness, broken weakly by the rising moon, the glow of the crackling cooking fire, and a sputtering torch at the mine entrance, three men came into view. They had made their way successfully down the mountain face. Two were expected— Cutlope Hancock in his green hunting shirt and Ansel Jarlman under his castor hat. The third man, wearing Cut's coat, was a welcome surprise. Emerging from the shadows and stepping into dim light was a ghostly figure. He sported an iron collar and a length of chain dangling outside of Cut's filthy, broad-cloth coat. Nothing else. Vincent took his foot off the unconscious knife-wielder and ran to greet the half naked, unshod, barely recognizable fellow who stood beside Cut.

"Ike Higgins, great to see you alive!" Vincent exclaimed, as he embraced the Irishman. Young Wetherill released him quickly when he realized the foul odor emanating from Cut's garment was now on his clothing. He made a hopeless attempt to wipe it away with his hand. Vincent was still trying when he asked how Ike had escaped.

"Least important thing right now, Mister Wetherill," said Ike, as he shifted a borrowed company musket from one shoulder to the other. "I'll save me tale o' escape 'n climb fer the first tavern we find. Fer now, 'tis all 'bout savin' the Afric jileen who lays as did meself in a cage. Me 'n Cut will tend to the chore."

The two men were already scrambling to the chains at the tree which held Rachel's cage, when Vincent shouted out in support of the action: "Get her down, men! Save the wench if you can! Hurry! See if there are tools about, to work the lock and chain."

Ansel Jarlman was standing idly by, catching his breath after the difficult climb down from the ledge in the dusky shadows. He spoke up: "Should I assist 'em, Mister Wetherill?"

"No," Vincent said decisively. "I need you to approach the mine entrance, close as you can behind rocks and tailings. Make sure none of the three ruffins, who went in attempt to get out. Answer with your musket if you are fired upon."

"With pleasure, Mister Wetherill," saluted Jarlman. He slinked off and took up a position behind a heap of tailings to the left of the cooking fire.

Next, Vincent checked on Reverend Heaton and found him to be cogent and alert. He reassured the preacher that Mister Jolly would be coming soon. He ripped the lace cravat from his neck and gave it to Heaton to staunch the bleeding at the shoulder wound. The preacher thanked Vincent and reminded him to restrain the one-eyed fellow who knifed him. Vincent said he would, but he had already formulated another plan for the knife-wielder.

Vincent found the fellow still on his back. He was holding a blood-stained hand over his empty eye socket and moaning to himself. Vincent placed the tip of his cutlass blade on the man's chest and let him feel the weight of the deadly instrument. It rose and fell with the rhythm of his breathing.

The strange-looking man opened his one good eye, blinked, and caught sight of the weapon perched on his chest and the person holding it. He groaned some more and finally spoke: "Careful wit' that thing, Mister . . . Mister Rattoon is it?"

Vincent flashed a look of surprise at the man who uttered his false name. He parried with recent information Mister Jolly had given him: "How'd you come by my name, Mister Parrot?"

"The watchkeep who stopped you 'n come rushin' to me cookin' fire spoke o' yer name 'n that preacher man I meant to slay, aft' you first arrived wit' yer waggon o' iron water . . . caught the Prophet unawares, I must say . . . first time I ever seen Black Jake hesitate in decidin' what to do . . . t'was either the preacher man's name or the water which'd threw 'im . . ."

"T'was both," Vincent said proudly.

"Closest strangers ever got to 'im . . ."

"We almost had him, Mister Parrot," countered Vincent, "but you and your knife got in the way."

The one-eyed man flashed a weak smile which revealed few teeth—the ones remaining were wayward and stained. He then spoke in a low tone, as if confiding a secret: "Folks 'round here calls me One-Eye fer the obvious reasons, Mister Rattoon . . . but yer callin' me by me given name, which'd you got near right . . . 'tis Barrett . . . 'n how'd you come by me long-lost name, I've not used in years?"

Vincent lifted his sword from the man's chest, but held it at the ready in case the so-called One-Eye made a false move. "A mere guess based on information from a gaoler down in Amboy who was talking recently with the former Barracks Master in that town. Their conversation was all about some Irish Regulars who deserted their posts in sixty-eight and disappeared into the night . . . the same night of the Treasury robbery. Mister Sargent recalled that one deserter was named Parrot, and another bog jumper as Walsh. Remember anything about that night, Mister Barrett?"

"Nothin'," grinned One-Eye, more widely than before. "Never heard o' yer Mister Sargent, nor Mister Parrot, 'n knows nothin' 'bout no Mister Walsh . . ."

"Surely you heard of the Treasury robbery," Vincent asked in an attempt to try a divergent path of questioning.

"Heard little," One-Eye admitted, " 'n most all o' it 'bout Sam Ford, hisself, who used to own the Hibernia works . . . heard 'bout his gains in real coin from that haul, which'd he traded fer by usin' much o' his counterfeit to gain it . . . folks is still lookin' fer where he hides it . . ."

"Would those folks include you, Mister Barrett?"

"I ain't sayin' yes, nor is I sayin' no, Mister Rattoon, but it seems to me yer askin' very hard 'n could be up here lookin' fer it yer ownself . . ."

"Perhaps I am, Mister Barrett, but other matters come first. How successful I am this night depends on your help. How cooperative you are determines whether you live or die."

The grin vanished from One-Eye's face. His hand slipped from his vacant eye socket. "Fetch me patch rag, Mister Rattoon, 'n I'll consider yer deal . . . fer me, 'tis either die by yer blade or the Prophet's blade . . . his has been mighty quick 'n overused of late . . . yers is lookin' mighty clean."

"Your Prophet's been busy," Vincent observed. "I see the headless bodies near your fire and their heads perched on rocks nearby. What transgressions did these men commit?"

"They was to keep an eye on things," said Barrett, who seemed strangely relaxed for a man so close to being dispatched, "while the rest o' us was at the burial o' the Prophet's fallen angel—the one whose black nob lies in me cookin' fire awaitin' the others. While we was dumpin' a nob 'n snatcher's bones in a watery shaft, the three keepin' watch failed to notice the Baron o' Ballynary escapin' from me lock 'n cage. That sneaky one got clear away . . . headed to the valley with all keeps followin', 'cept fer the three ye was shootin' at. The Prophet gave orders to chase down the escapee 'n don't come back without 'im . . . 'n when they return, ye 'n yer preacher friend is goin' to end up kilt the same way as the three you see layin' by me fire . . . but ye won't get a proper burial . . . yer parts'll be fed to the rats in the mine.

Vincent leaned close over his blade and tried to read the foul man's whiskery face. The look was calm, bland, and unreadable. However, Vincent was sure that One-Eye knew much more than he was voluntarily revealing. He decided to change the subject again.

"Hold on, Barrett," Vincent said sharply. "Back up a bit. You mean to tell me Tom Ward, a murderer three times over, has been slain?"

"Weren't no murderer, Mister Rattoon," blurted One-Eye, who offered the sincerity of a man taking a stab at telling the truth for once. "The Prophet hired 'im fer kidnapin' nobles fer the cages, not fer murderin' folks. Lord Stirlin' hisself is to be slated fer the third cage . . . but Tom Coward, as he should be named, wanted out . . . he'd had 'nough 'n was soured on the Prophet's scheme. So Black Jake honored the shy-cock's request 'n gave 'im a right proper burial . . ."

"How can you be so sure Tom Ward is no murderer?" Vincent asked.

"Know'd 'im from way back, when we both worked the mines," replied Barrett, "'n even afore that. I seen 'im in fights 'n such where he could've easily killed a bloak . . . always pulled back 'n walked away . . . even when I lost me eye, he was there 'n had a chance to slay the bugger who thumb-cored me . . . but he played it like an old woman . . . left all killin' to others, Mister Rattoon. Cross Tom Coward off yer list . . . don't have to worry 'bout 'im no more . . . he's dead."

"Did you know him to go by any other name?" Vincent asked.

"Many a name he's used," answered One-Eye, "but I don't care to remember 'em all . . ."

"How about the name, Billy Walsh?"

"Used such long ago, Mister Rattoon, but I can't remember 'xactly where or when . . . know'd a few men who borrowed such a name . . . all his names can't help Tom Coward now . . . he ain't comin' back to borrow 'nother one . . . missed his chance to get baptized on Schooley's Mountain, soon as the Prophet finds what he's been lookin' fer here. The only one bein' brought back to this place will live out his few days in the cage he's 'scaped from . . . the Prophet's keep will see to it . . ."

"The last man you speak of has returned on his own," chuckled Vincent. "He climbed down from the mountain, determined to free the Afric wench from her cage. He and his friend have already lowered the contraption and picked the lock."

"Yer playin' with me, Mister Rattoon."

"See for yourself!" Vincent demanded, as he grabbed the filthy man and stood him up. He turned One-Eye to face the frenzied activity at the cage. Cut was holding a torch he had found and fired at the cooking blaze. He also held some tools, which he had found at the same place, to be used to free Rachel and Ike from their collars and chains. He kept the torch high so Ike, who had crawled into the cage, could see what had to be done.

"She needs drink!" Ike shouted.

Vincent shook Barrett violently and said, "What have you got for the girl?"

"Bowl of her finder's black blood by me fire," joked Barrett. "Plenty left after I spiced it up 'n the Prophet took his fill . . ."

With the flat of his cutlass blade, Vincent cuffed the man by his ear. "No time left for you to be cruel or queer, you one-eyed cod. Answer me true and quick, or I'll use the sharp edge of this blade on your reeking hide!"

"Jug o' sweet water 'n jug o' rum beside the blood bowl, Mister Rattoon." rushed One-Eye, rubbing his head where he had been struck a second time. "Have the Baron mix 'em half-to-half for the Princess . . . should be some potato 'n bacon soup left in the boilin' pot . . . yer welcome to it all."

Vincent called out to Cut with instructions on where to find suitable drink and how to water down the rum for the girl. Cut jumped to the task and rushed the two jugs and an empty bowl back to the cage.

"There's a cur in with the woman," hollered Cut, as he ran past Vincent and the one-eyed man. "Appears the little beast is dead!"

"I'll be losin' me bet," muttered One-Eye sadly.

Vincent did not understand what the man was saying. He threw the alleged Mister Barrett to the ground and pressed his sword point against the man's throat.

"You're going to lose everything in a minute if you do not help me with my last priority," Vincent demanded. "Ike Higgins has returned. Morrell's servant has been rescued. You've told me the kidnaper is dead . . . and I'm telling you the guards in the search party are not coming back."

"What's left fer the doin'?" asked Barrett in a whisper.

"I need to lure your Prophet out of the mine."

"He ain't comin' out," insisted Barrett. "Nobody's ne'er close to catchin' the likes o' 'im . . . he's livin' on his own terms fer ninety-nine, whether yer likin' it or not . . . promised me to live as long . . ."

"Neither one of you shall live a day more, if you don't do as I say," stressed Vincent, still holding the tip of his weapon firmly against the wrinkled flesh of the man's neck. "Your boss is cornered in his own lair. You must enter the mine and convince him to come out. Do this final task well, and I will set you free to hunt for Sam Ford's trove or follow whatever dream fits your fancy."

"Don't needs to be huntin' no more," wheezed Barrett. "Where I go is where treasure lies . . . 'tis where I plans to be fer the rest o' me days . . ."

"Fine with me," said Vincent, who again misread the strange man. "But before I let you go, you must fetch the Prophet."

"I'll be squattin' at both ends o' yer bargain, Mister Rattoon," said Barrett cryptically, "but yer never gettin' the Prophet to cooperate wit' yer plan. I'm the onliest one who might come close to convincin' 'im, 'cause he can't slay me. He suspects I know'd what he don't . . . but close in convincin' ain't goin' to bring 'im out . . ."

Vincent was baffled by One-Eye's jibberish, but he knew the man was his best hope for drawing the Prophet peacefully out of the mine. He was all for giving a person one more chance. It was a lesson learned from Reverend Heaton—a difficult lesson, when dealing with such devilish types as Dan Fagan and Jack Spolden. The task at hand was to get Spolden's faithful fetchman to cooperate. Vincent had no choice but to make the decision easy for Mister Barrett. Young Wetherill raised his cutlass as if poised to slash the man's throat.

Barrett slipped both hands up to his eye, took a deep breath, held it for as long as he could, then let it go. He whispered what he feared might be his final words: "Fetch me rag 'n I'll do as yer sayin' . . . must look me best when facin' the Prophet . . . must make 'im proud o' me."

Vincent sheathed his sword. He searched around for the filthy cloth which was so important to the one-eyed man. He found it and brought the thing to Barrett. Vincent helped the man to his feet and handed him the greasy cloth. Barrett snatched it up and quickly wrapped it around his head. He slipped it down over the scarred flesh where an eye once sat. He looked straight at Vincent for approval, but received none.

"Fetch me knife, Mister Rattoon," requested Barrett. "'Tis precious to me."

"Can't do it, Mister Barrett," replied Vincent sharply. "You used it once on my new friend . . . can't take a chance you might use it again,"

"Needs to defend meself in the mine if things don't go as planned . . .

"Trust in yourself, Mister Barrett, and the kindness and mercy of your leader. You've gotten this far and you're still alive. Besides, you said yourself that the Prophet would never slay you."

Vincent grabbed One-Eye by his rawhide collar and pulled him towards the position Ansel Jarlman had taken behind tailings. The man did not resist.

"Hope yer words ring true on such, Mister Rattoon," sighed Barrett. "Do I gets me knife back when this plan o' yers is o'er?"

"Depends on what you bring me from the mine, Mister Barrett."

"Ain't never goin' to be the coins yer lookin' fer, Mister Rattoon . . . never . . ."

"I'll settle for the Prophet," concluded Vincent, "then the deal is done . . . his hide for your freedom . . ."

"'N me knife?"

"If the Baron of Ballynary takes no fancy to your blade," Vincent said, "then it'll be yours to keep."

The one-eyed man pushed Vincent's hand off his collar. He limped on his own towards the mine entrance. No shot rang out. Barrett hesitated for a moment, stumbled a bit, seeming to debate whether or not to enter the darkness of the old, played-out mine, which had been abandoned to a mad man, ghosts, and Sam Ford's secret. In the next instant, the so-called Mister Barrett was gone. Vincent Wetherill and the members of his team would never see One-Eye again.

The silence of the wait that followed Barrett's disappearance was broken by the sound of hoofbeats on the mule path. First to appear was Karl Bruder with Reverend Heaton's gelding in tow. Then came Jimmy Hornbeck with Vincent's Spanish barb on a short tether. Bringing up the rear was William Jolly with Ansel Jarlman's mount. The parade was headed toward the cooking fire, which put these men in line to be fired upon by anyone at the mine entrance. Vincent, who was busy at the fire extracting Tom Ward's blackened skull from the bed of embers, lifted the long flaming stick he was using and waved it in the direction of the bay Shires and the waggon. Bruder caught the signal and turned his horse. He led the others to a safe position behind tailings and tall rocks. A shot was, indeed, fired from the mine entrance, but it was late and wayward. It whizzed harmlessly over the head of William Jolly.

Vincent returned to his task at hand. He poked his smoldering stick into an empty eye socket of the skull, raised the thing from its fiery resting place, and brought it to Ansel Jarlman. Vincent informed Captain Elsworth's agent that this was all that remained of the man they were looking for. Jarlman asked if he could keep the skull to show his boss. Vincent acquiesced. He advised Jarlman that the skull would be better proof than the carcass of the rat-catcher. Jarlman agreed with a nod, and Vincent left him alone to continue the vigil chore.

With the torch, which he had re-ignited at the cooking fire, in hand, Vincent retreated across the ring in order to reach his waggon. When he got there, he saw that Ike and Cut had carried Rachel Hagers to the Wetherill vehicle. She was sitting up with her tawny back pressed against the Prophet's favorite rock. She cast a confused look—dazed was more like it. With shivering hands, she attempted to hide her nakedness. She was not even wearing an iron collar or chain. Ike had also lost his collar and chain, thanks to Cut's skill with the proper tools and his strength.

The unfettered Irishman was holding a small bowl up to Rachel's lips. She took a few sips of watery rum, as if it was a curious tea created by her dear friend, Amanda Sharp. She took the bowl from Ike, held it firmly, and stared at its contents. Ike busied himself with a few stale scones he had found in one of Cut's coat pockets. He tore them into bits and offered them to Rachel. She took one, then another, then she paused to watch Cut, who was trying to revive the rat-catcher. The German was using his finger and the mud spoon to slip drops of straight rum down the rat-catcher's throat. The dog accepted the brew in the same manner Ike Higgins always did—lustily and impatient for the next round. Cut followed the spoonful of rum with a measure of water. With a slobbering tongue. the dog fought against it. The rum was preferred.

"Mister Hornbeck," instructed Vincent, who decided to take command of the situation, "dismount, grab a musket, and trace the stones at the ring to Mister Jarlman's position. Assist him in making sure those in the mine stay put."

Hornbeck immediately jumped to the task. He seemed eager to participate and see more action.

"Mister Jolly," called Vincent, "you will find Reverend Heaton has a wound which needs your attention. He sits at the far edge of the ring. Go to him. See what you can do to ease his discomfort."

Jolly slipped from his horse, stepped gingerly between two mounds of tailings, and hobbled off into the purple shadows to find the preacher. He was more than glad to demonstrate skills the others on Wetherill's team lacked. He had gained another chance to show he could be useful.

Vincent took note of the responsiveness of his team members. He was satisfied with the progress being made. However, the positive feeling was short-lived. Karl Bruder, who was still mounted, was frowning at the proceedings. He appeared none to happy with Vincent's operation.

"We've priorities here, Mister Wetherill," needled Bruder, as Vincent inspected the progress Ike and Cut were making. "We've a foeman to bring down. My sponsors are eagerly waiting to hear of his demise."

Vincent chose to ignore the prattling man. He preferred to concentrate on the rescued pair, whom his waggoner and flanker were treating. His own priorities came first.

"Cut, let the cur be," directed Vincent. "It'll run right to the girl. Climb into the waggon and fetch garments out of my chest. Make sure the girl gets my cloak to stay warm. Too bad I've no boots or shoes for Ike."

"He can steal 'em off the guard I shot," said Cut, ". . . the one who meant to put a hole in your back."

The German put down the rat-catcher after a second spoonful of rum. It wobbled on shaky legs, but went straight to Rachel's lap. Cut snatched up his torch and climbed into the waggon. In the sparse light from Vincent's torch and his own, he went to work selecting suitable things for the naked ones to wear.

"We're wasting precious time, Mister Wetherill," objected Bruder. "We've more important things to do than bother dressing a slave and a barley captain . . ."

"You have your priorities, Mister Bruder, and I have mine," retorted Vincent in a firm voice. "I heed advice from Reverend Heaton, not you . . ."

"I'm not giving you opinions or advice, Wetherill," corrected Bruder. "I'm giving orders."

"Give them to your team, Fahnrich," snapped Vincent, "and I'll give orders to mine."

Cut tossed selected articles of clothing out of the waggon. Vincent, who had planted his torch in the ground, caught the garments and brought them to Ike and Rachel. He gave instructions to Ike to dress the slave as best he could and to make sure Rachel got the cloak. Ike nodded that he understood and put up no fuss. Vincent turned his back on the pair, but Bruder, now seething, was watching their every move.

Mister Jolly suddenly appeared with Reverend Heaton. The former gaoler shouldered the larger man. Neither one was sure on his feet. Jolly called for assistance in getting Heaton through the narrow space between the mounds of tailings. Vincent lent a hand.

"We'll sit Reverend Heaton next to the wench," ordered Vincent. "They can keep each other awake by swopping tales of what they've experienced these last few days, while we attend to other matters . . ."

"A splendid idea, Wetherill," sneered the impatient Bruder. "Your first good one."

Vincent ignored the man again and addressed Cut instead: "After we deal with drawing the Prophet out of his lair, you, Ike, and Mister Jolly may escort our patients to the cooking fire . . . they can warm themselves there."

"Back to another wasteful idea, Wetherill," opined the annoying mining agent. "Jack Spolden is not coming out . . . neither are any of those who went in with him. They mean to wait you out and trust the search guards return soon from the valley."

"Not going to happen, Mister Bruder," insisted Vincent. "The searchers have been scared away by their own leader. I say we all move close as we can to the mine entrance . . . use our muskets only if fired upon . . . convince Spolden to surrender . . ."

"Devils don't surrender, Wetherill . . . neither do moon struck men," posited Bruder. "I say we put the Prophet out of his misery. I say we do it now with the blackpowder, which I instructed the Forge Master to give to you. Just make sure you employ the correct barrel. Your iron water is useless now . . . so is your idea of luring the Prophet from his hiding place."

"The water allowed us to get this close," said Vincent defensively.

"The blackpowder will allow us to leave with a claim of victory," Bruder countered.

Reverend Heaton was listening patiently to the debate between the two men—one struggling to seize command of the situation and one struggling against losing it. He finally spoke up and used the strongest voice he could muster.

"Gentlemen, gentlemen, we have a dilemma on our hands and no easy choice to make. There have been many lives lost in this clandestine affair. The killing must end. To allow Johnny Spolden to live may mean more deaths will follow—so far, the dead have come from the ranks of the humble folks he purports to free from tyranny. He has succeeded in doing so only by slaying them—no other way. The Prophet, to his own following, is either mad or a fool, drunk on his own perverted wisdom. However, any sinner deserves a last chance to surrender his sins to a forgiving God. I say you give him a final chance."

"The bastard don't deserve another chance," insisted Bruder. "We're wasting time here . . ."

"What if we give Black Jake one more opportunity to surrender and he fails to comply, Reverend?" asked Vincent.

"Then he invites the wrath of a judgmental God," reasoned Heaton. "Johnny wields a double-edged sword. I witnessed his blade close up. God's weapon is also double-edged—one side merciful, one side not. The time has come to witness which sword is mightier and which sword will prevail. You must serve as God's instruments in this contest. I suggest you get started . . ."

Cut leaped from the waggon and unhitched the bay Shires. A near fully dressed Ike Higgins led them, and the other horses, to the safety of a fenced pen behind two outlying sheds. He returned in time to help unload the useless barrels of creek water, and turn the vehicle around. Vincent ordered the able members of his team to pull and push the waggon close to Ansel Jarlman's position. Vincent, himself, as well as Cut, Ike, and Mister Jolly, put their limbs to the task. Bruder had dismounted, but he did not help move the waggon. Instead, he walked behind it. Reverend Heaton was left behind to watch Rachel and feed the last scraps of the scones to the rat-catcher. They were flanked by the two torches, which had to be left behind.

When the waggon was in position, Vincent ordered his men to fan out on either side of Ansel Jarlman. They took up safe positions behind the waggon, tailings, and large stones. He ordered that no man was to fire a weapon unless fired upon. Vincent and Bruder crouched behind the same impediment Jarlman was using. Elsworth's agent reported that nothing out of the ordinary had occurred—other than two rounds fired, since he took up his position. Also, he reported that one of the two torches at the mine entrance had gone out on its own.

"Your move, Wetherill," whispered Bruder, as he checked the finer powder in the pan of his musket. "Who are you sending to negotiate with the Devil?"

"I thought you might enjoy the honor, Mister Bruder."

"Can't let Spolden see me," said Bruder quickly. "He spots me and I'm a dead man . . . wouldn't make it three paces . . . I'd be shot . . ."

"Because you betrayed the Prophet?" asked Vincent.

"Betrayed his trust," offered Bruder. "'Tis the worst sin in Spolden's book . . . so it won't be me walkin' near the mine entrance."

"I can't expect any of my men to put themselves in harm's way," admitted Vincent. "I will go myself."

"Suit your fancy, Wetherill," said Bruder curtly. "'Tis a waste of a good man—a gentleman at that . . ."

Vincent propped his borrowed musket against a rock and handed Jarlman his cutlass. He tucked his knife in his boot and slipped his pistol under his belt. These were inadequate moves, he figured, but they gave him a measure of confidence. It was better than nothing. Now he was ready. Vincent decided against walking directly toward the mine entrance. Instead, he circled to his left, away from the light provided by One-Eye's cooking fire and the solitary torch. Under cover of deep shadows, he made his way silently to the twin boulders standing like mute sentries on either side of the cleft in the mountain that was the entrance. He crouched low under the spent torch, grabbed a few pebbles, and tossed them against the nearest boulder on the opposite side of the entrance where the lit torch stood.

Nothing.

No response from within.

Vincent tried the trick again. He garnered the same results. He pulled the pistol from his belt and worked on priming it. At last, he called out to the Prophet: "The game's been played, Mister Spolden. I offer you an opportunity to surrender honorably . . . avoid a cruel fate . . . allow justice to prevail."

There was a long, dull silence, disturbed but once by a bat flitting in the night sky near the mine entrance. Vincent watched its progress above the torch until it vanished into the darkness of the moon shadows. He decided not to repeat his message. His attempt to carry out Reverend Heaton's wish had failed. Vincent was not about to stand in the open and call out to Spolden, nor was he going to enter the mine and attempt to negotiate with the man. It was time to acquiesce to Karl Bruder's demands.

Vincent started to back away into the safety of deep shadows. He meant to retrace his steps all the way to Jarlman's position, but he did not get far. One of the Prophet's guards suddenly emerged from the mine, took aim with his musket, and fired at Vincent. The shot, meant for his back, went high—grazing his temple and tearing off a bit of his left ear. He also lost his tricorn in the process. Vincent fell to his knees . . . stunned . . . but he spun about and fired his pistol blindly at the moving shadow about to disappear into the mine. Vincent's shot also went high and ricocheted off the boulder illumined by the torch. Vincent's men took the musket and pistol shots as a signal to start firing. A withering volley echoed off the face of the mountain. The guard, who had surprised Vincent, went down. Invisible hands pulled the wounded fellow into the mine. No shots followed the volley. Again, there was an eerie silence, which marked the end of the attempt at negotiations. All that had been accomplished was the wounding of two more men. It was time to stop the bloodshed.

Cut and Ike managed to get to their boss and carry him back to the waggon. Vincent was dazed and disoriented. He was also bleeding profusely from the wound at his ear. Mister Jolly was summoned from his position at the far right in order to assess Vincent's condition and determine what should be done to stop the bleeding.

"Mister Wetherill, you're a lucky man," opined Jolly. "You came close to getting brained."

There was no response from Vincent.

"Lost his hat," offered Ike, "which'd we failed to find in the shadows."

"A trifle in the scheme of things," said Jolly. "Fetch me some linens from your boss's trunk . . . rip them into broad strips. I mean to staunch the bleeding and bind his head. If there be any rum left, make sure your boss gets his fill."

Ike jumped to the fetching task. Cut, meanwhile, used his strength to lift Vincent and prop him against a wheel of the waggon. Jimmy Hornbeck was sent back to see if there was any rum left to cleanse Vincent's wound and clear his head. He returned with a near-empty bowl and word that the rat-catcher had lapped up most of it.

"This will have to do," surmised Jolly, who went to work immediately on his latest patient.

"Ye could o' been a doctor 'stead o' a gaoler," observed Ike, who gave his boss three sips of the rum then finished the dregs in the bowl himself.

"Most of my patients would've died in my care, jug-biter," said Jolly, as he wound the linen strips tightly over the remains of Vincent's left ear and around his head. He made sure the cloth arched high over Vincent's eyes so he could see.

"All folks die soon or late, dependin' on luck 'n chance taken," mused Ike. "Doctors 'n such jus' delay the soon 'n stretch the late . . ."

"Enough of this talk of delays!" barked Bruder suddenly, as he emerged from his hiding place. Ansel Jarlman was right behind him. "Mister Wetherill almost got himself killed tryin' to carry out his plan . . . time to get to work on a better plan . . . my plan. When we're done, we must leave the God awful place to its rightful owners—ghosts of the dead and devils in robes. Time to get to work . . ."

Vincent was left in Mister Jolly's care. Neither man was fit to participate in the agent's dangerous plan. Bruder deemed the rest of the men suitable to participate. Cut and Ike were eager to comply—the former, to get the madness over with; the latter, to gain revenge. After setting the loading planks in place, they scrambled into the waggon and rolled the barrel of blackpowder to the ground. Jimmy Hornback was put in charge of setting the explosives above the mine entrance. He and Ike rolled the barrel along the route Vincent had used. Cut and Ansel Jarlman, armed with their barkers, flanked the barrel rollers. Karl Bruder, carrying a lit waggon lantern, followed and kept a safe distance behind the others. He carried the necessary gear for setting charges and laying fuses. He was confident that his plan would succeed. He did not care whose side God was on and he did not care who lived or died in the execution of his plan. Fagan had been neutralized, if not killed. Now it was Spolden who had to be destroyed. No one knew better than Bruder how evil the Prophet was. The investors' agent had seen the acts of depravity with his own eyes—unbelievable crimes against innocent folk, and even his own followers. Many of Black Jake's deeds would not be believed by Bruder's sponsors. Much of it would not appear in his report to the committee of investors. Black Jake was to meet with an unfortunate accident, while searching for Sam Ford's treasure in a played-out mine. No bodies would be recovered. No authorities would be notified. No person who assisted Bruder would be mentioned in his report; it would be plain and simple—Black Jake did himself in.

In a way, the Devil's advocate was sealing his own fate. This was reason enough for Bruder to go along with Reverend Heaton's insistence on giving Black Jake one more chance to gain mercy, and the upstart Wetherill to have had an opportunity to carry out his foolish plan. Attempts at negotiating with the enemy almost got them both killed. Whether they lived or died did not matter to Bruder. It looked like Heaton and Wetherill would live to die another day—probably sooner than later, predicted the agent. He felt the same about the others. They were all humble men who did not count for much in the grand scheme of things . . . even Reverend Heaton. Such types did the dirty work—the bidding of those of high station. Bruder knew this, because he was one of the lesser ones—at the service of superiors who couldn't care less who perished in order to get the job done. However, he was a survivor who knew how to get out of harm's way. He could get others to carry out the dangerous work. Bruder would simply instruct them and remain in the shadows. He even considered the possibility that he might be the only one to survive this adventure—all the better for his report. No one would be left to challenge his word. All praise would be reserved for him.

Bruder instructed Hornbeck and Higgins to fill satchels with blackpowder from the barrel. These two had been chosen to climb to the ledge with the satchels, set them in place above the mine entrance, and run a fuse trail to the crest of the ridge. They were to raise a fire there by employing a strike stone and blade. Bruder told them to wait to ignite the fuse trail with a flaming stick until Hancock or Jarlmen fired their muskets at the torch planted at the far side of the mine entrance. This would give ample time for the participants below the ledge a fair chance to escape the anticipated avalanche meant to seal off the old mine once and for all.

Ike had one request: "I wants me mud spoon fer this chore."

"Don't need one," chided Hornbeck. "We want to destroy the ledge, not cut a hole in it."

"Ain't a care 'bout none o' that," said Ike. "Jus' wants me mud spoon fer good luck 'n a chance to put it to its proper use afore I lays content."

"Where's this useless tool?" demanded Bruder impatiently. "I want the both of you climbing now, not at dawn."

"The cabbage head's got it in his stinkin' coat," said Ike. "Me spoon is sleepin' with his winnin's."

Cut reached into his secret pocket, sifted through his coins, and pulled out the broken piece of brass. He held it up to the moon and then tossed it to the man he rescued more than once.

"May the spoon bring you luck again, bog lander," whispered Cut. "You're going to need it."

"'Tis all the luck I needs," said Ike too loudly, as he shoved the spoon into the pocket of the borrowed lacy shirt he had gained from Vincent's clothing chest. Ike grabbed two full satchels of blackpowder and joined Jimmy Hornbeck for the difficult climb in the moonlight. The pair quickly disappeared into the high shadows.

While the two men were at their dangerous climb over slippery, moss-covered rocks, Bruder directed Cut and Ansel Jarlman in the placement of the rest of the blackpowder as close to the near side of the mine entrance as they dared get. These two were swift and silent in the doing. No shot was fired from the mine entrance. No sound of any kind came from the bowels of the Johnson Mine. Cut paused from his work every now and then. He was hoping for one of the Prophet's guards to appear at the entrance. He wanted to bag another one of them with his lineal rifle—wanted to gain revenge for the wounding of his boss. However, nobody appeared.

Cut had to settle for the planting and firing of the blackpowder. This effort would finally complete an awful adventure. Cut was glad agent Bruder was so decisive in his actions—never hesitating, never tolerating delays, always so assured in his convictions. The German wished his boss might acquire such traits in future adventures. Worry over right and wrong always led to costly delays, mused Cut. That was not the case now. .. not since Bruder took charge.

The two men finished setting a fuse trail. It snaked back to the waggon where Vincent was being tended to by Mister Jolly. Young Wetherill was up on his feet, but keeping a hand on Jolly's shoulder to steady himself. Bruder ordered Vincent to climb into the waggon. At first, Wetherill's son protested and insisted he could walk on his own. Cut talked his boss into complying with the agent. He helped Jolly lift Vincent into the vehicle. Bruder ordered the fit men to move the waggon out of harm's way. It was pulled back to where Reverend Heaton and Rachel were hiding behind the tallest stone. Bruder sent Jarlman to fetch a pan of embers from the cooking fire. He ordered Cut to return to his former position to prepare to fire off a signal round at the torch still licking at the foul draft emanating from the mine entrance.

The wait was long. Patience was required, but Bruder had little of it. However, he kept his emotions to himself. He was not satisfied with the performance of young Wetherill's men—they followed orders, but they were bumbling and slow. Bruder seemed to be the only one who feared the odds shifting if the Prophet's searchers returned before the fuse trails were fired. He did not put any faith in young Wetherill's prediction that the searchers had been scared off by the execution of three of their peers. He knew Black Jake well. The man had a hold on his followers which could not be explained. The guards would likely return—alarmed by the musket fire, which had echoed down to the valley. They were returning on the run in order to save their beloved leader. Bruder was damn sure of it. But he had to wait. The two men on the ridge needed ample time to set their charges. Bruder wished he could have completed the task himself, but such work was beneath him. He had to learn to be patient with lesser men.

In an hour's span, a pine torch flamed at the crown of the ridge.

Bruder whistled to Mister Hancock. The German fired his weapon and split the torch shaft in two. Bruder called out to Ansel Jarlman, who was nearby, to drop embers on the fuse trail. He figured he had given Hornbeck and Higgins ample time to set their trail and scramble back to the other side of the ridge. It was then Bruder noticed that Jarlman had not yet ignited the fuse trail.

"Drop your pan!" barked the agent excitedly.

Jarlman let the embers fall, and, in less than a minute, one mighty explosion was followed by another. Huge boulders and jagged rocks came thundering down. A plume of thick, choking dust rose in the air. Uprooted trees rolled down in all directions. One-Eye's cooking fire was obliterated, as was the closer half of the Prophet's sacred ring. The heads and other body parts of the executed guards were buried under rubble. Best of all, the mine entrance was no more—it was sealed under tons of rock and debris.

When the cloud of dust followed a southerly breeze and allowed the waxing moon to shine near full once more, Karl Bruder finally smiled. The men who had retreated with him, behind the Wetherill waggon, cheered. When they stopped, they could hear Ike singing, loud as he could, at the top of the ridge. It was a lusty song, which he had entertained the Prophet's guards with when he was confined to his cage. Reverend Heaton frowned. He did not approve of any verse of Ike's song. He apologized to the Princess of Axum for her rescuer's rudeness. Rachel smiled politely and held the rat-catcher close.

"The song is beautiful, preacher man," sighed Rachel, "even better the second time 'round . . . even better."

22

DEVILS AND WENCHES
• •

—from Horse Pound Mountain to the Smultz Cabin
after midnight on Wednesday, September 29, 1773

"None of this ever happened," declared Karl Bruder emphatically as he mounted his horse, which he had fetched from the far distant horse pen along with one of Jack Spolden's steeds. "Say what you wish, Wetherill, 'cept the truth . . . be careful with your words. The report to my sponsors will contain what I want 'em to know . . . do the same towards the ones you represent. A terrible accident befell certain parties here . . . you and I survived, and live to tell 'bout it. That's all there is to it . . ."

Vincent stood nearby, but he was ignoring the man in the none-the-worse-for-wear sailor's jacket and unstained trousers. Bruder seemed in a terrible rush to leave before anyone else was ready. He was in no mood to help Vincent's team in the completion of the leaving tasks. On the other hand, Vincent was in no mood to be distracted from directing his men in what had to be done. While Bruder rattled on, Vincent surveyed the visible ruins caused by the twin explosions of blackpowder. He wondered where his tricorn lay buried in the rubble, never to be found. A trifle loss, he thought . . .

Vincent's head still hurt from where a musket shot grazed his skull. The pain worsened after the explosions and had not subsided. Luckily, the bleeding at his ear had stopped. He had Mister Jolly to thank for staunching the flow and binding his head so expertly. Vincent would have a great deal of explaining to do when Little Abia saw him. He hoped he would be still alive to explain himself. Oh how he missed her . . .

A near-perfect full moon and a convention of brilliant stars in a cloudless sky provided ample light for Vincent to take note of the damage done. It was well past midnight, but visibility was sufficient for loading the waggon and preparing the horses for a quick departure. There was no time, nor inclination, to hunt down fresh game, raise a fire, and cook a meal. Though Ike Higgins asked about victuals and Rachel Hagers needed them more, nothing was done. In the hurly burly of leaving, food was an afterthought. A meal was to be found when fate permitted it to be found. Vincent had searched for something edible among the boulders and debris which had rolled down the mountainside and obliterated most of the Prophet's ring of stones. There was no trace of One-Eye's cooking fire, decapitated heads, or mutilated bodies. The mine entrance was buried under tons of rock—now, a forgotten memory. The ledge above it was no more. All creatures worth hunting had been scared away by its collapse. The enemy had been defeated, but hunger was not.

All that remained were three tall stones, which had been part of the ring; three empty iron cages sitting at jaunty angles in the weeds; two low sheds, and one large horse pen far from where the boulders fell. Mister Jarlman had suggested sacrificing one of Black Jake's penned stallions. However, the others voted him down. Slaughtering a beast, roasting its flesh, and consuming it would have taken too long. Besides, Bruder had advised Vincent and his men to take Spolden's steeds or turn them loose. Most of them were culled from the herd of wild horses that was a source of legend in Horse Pound Valley. Bruder, himself, had claimed a sorrel which he believed was Black Jake's preferred mount. He had it harnessed and in tow at his leaving.

Vincent studied the sorrel admiringly and wondered which ones Jimmy Hornbeck and Ansel Jarlman would fetch from the horse pen along with the team's own mounts and the bay Shires. He also wondered if they would find anything of value in the sheds. At least he did not have to wonder about Cut and Ike. They had drained the barrels of creek water and loaded the empty barrels back on the waggon. Now they were loading firearms and other equipment, which Vincent had no intention of returning to Forge Master Hoff. While Ike and Cut were tending to loading chores, Reverend Heaton was serving as audience to the Afric girl's plaints and wishes. He was also preparing her for leaving. Vincent feared neither one would be fit for too long a journey . . . so many things to worry about . . . so little time left to get away from this hellish place . . .

And where was Mister Jolly? He had asked Vincent for a waggon lantern in order to inspect the area where the cages sat. Vincent looked in that direction. The old gaoler was still at it. Earlier, Vincent had given him One-Eye's ring of keys, which he had stumbled upon at the cooking fire while retrieving Tom Ward's skull from the flames. Jolly thanked Vincent profusely for the keys and voiced interest in inspecting the cages. He wanted to examine the intricacy and craftsmanship of each contraption, but Vincent told him there was no time for such activity. Jolly confessed that he really wanted to locate the locks and match them with their keys. He was hoping they could be put to good use back in Amboy. They could substitute handsomely for what had been stolen from gaol. Vincent reluctantly allowed Jolly to go on his search. He knew the man would not give up until he had found all three locks. Jolly's search might take too long. Now, Vincent was regretting his decision to let the old gaoler go off on his own.

"Ain't you listenin' to a word I'm sayin'?" asked a perturbed Mister Bruder.

"Of course, of course," replied a startled young Wetherill, who was rubbing the uninjured side of his head with a gloved hand. "Congratulations on successfully completing your assignment, Mister Bruder. My men and I are glad to have played a small part . . ."

"T'was an accident, Wetherill," stressed the red-lipped Bruder, as he turned his horse, and the stallion in tow, to face the mule path. "An act of God, it shall be called—one which fell in our favor . . . nothin' more . . ."

"Wish it was as easy finding the murderer I've been searching for," contemplated Vincent. "My job's far from done."

"Can't help you there, Wetherill," disclosed Bruder. "Must return to Hibernia to file my report. However, I can tell you I don't believe those which'd claim your key suspect here has been eliminated. I suggest you lug your borrowed muskets down to the colliery, surprise any rogues remainin' there, and interrogate Mister Fagan. He's likely layin' on the floor in the Smultz cabin, dyin' from his wounds . . . better get down there quick, afore I report his demise.

I'd bet a shillin' or two that one of his devils is your murderer. Make Little Jake a deal—the bugger's name for information 'bout Sam Ford's trove. You've got nothin' to lose . . ."

With that said, the investor's agent tipped his wool hat, gave out an ingenuous laugh, spurred his horse, and broke for the climb up the westering mule path which snaked behind Horse Pound Mountain. He had explained earlier his intentions of avoiding the most direct route to the Hibernia forge. He wanted no part of running into the remnants of Spolden's minions or Fagan's gang. He intended to take a safe way down by skirting Dane's Lake and passing through Rockaway in order to get back to Lord Stirling's forge. Bruder had suggested to Reverend Heaton that he take the same way down when he was ready. Vincent wished he could do the same; however, the colliery lay in the opposite direction.

Vincent kept an eye on the self-assured agent until the man and his horses disappeared from sight. He envied Bruder as much as he disliked him. The man exuded great confidence and determination—always persuading others to do the dirty work, always receiving credit for the accomplishments of others. Bruder was a smooth manipulator, and he was always right. He was probably correct about the murderer being one of Fagan's hire. The challenge was finding the wounded General, and doing so without loss of life or limb. Vincent had come very close to getting killed right here. Facing such a prospect again did not appeal to him. The members of his team had voiced the same sentiment. However, they had come so far and were left with but one source of information. A visit to the colliery had to be made. They might learn nothing. They might face grave danger. Maybe it would be better to return immediately to Morris Town—take the safe way back— wait for a fourth corpse to be found. Perhaps, failure was the best option. He knew Karl Bruder would never consider it . . . neither would his sponsors. Vincent was glad he was not them.

Reverend Heaton decided he had had enough. He was not going to accompany Vincent any further. His primary responsibility now was to provide for the care and safety of Rachel Hagers. A short time after Karl Bruder vanished into the shadows of night, Heaton rode up to Vincent. He led no other horse. Rachel sat behind his saddle, holding tight with both arms at the preacher's waist. Two satchels, which had been judged unsuitable for lugging blackpowder up the mountain, were slung between the preacher and the slave. One satchel contained Heaton's souvenirs gathered from the adventure; the other, with holes poked in the canvas, held the rat-catcher. The dog whimpered in protest until Rachel uttered a few scolding words about being lucky to be alive. She saved soft words of gratitude for Vincent's ears. Rachel thanked him and his team for rescuing her. She vowed never to forget the pair of angels who woke her from her death sleep. She was convinced they had performed a miracle in bringing the rat-catcher back to life. She also confided to Vincent, as she had done to Reverend Heaton, that she was with child. Vincent wished her the best and reassured her that a fiddle-playing angel and a few other cherubs would be watching over her.

"Time for parting," interrupted Heaton sadly. "I must return the Princess to the Quakers. She does not want to be returned to her master. Rachel shall be welcomed as a sister by Amanda Sharp. God willing, Miss Amanda may gain a niece or nephew as well."

"Your decision is worthy of praise," said Vincent.

"I shall spare the Sharps all the details of the carnage here," continued Heaton. "I must dwell on the freeing of the two captives."

"That is wise," confided Vincent. "It complies with Mister Bruder's wishes."

"I was not thinking of that schemer's feelings on the matter," scoffed Heaton. "I wish to spare the Quakers. They are godly innocents—a passive folk who shun even the mention of violence. They will be glad to learn how Rachel was rescued by your two stalwarts and how one of them offered to buy her freedom."

"Cut is quite the gentleman when he chooses to be," Vincent noted. "I've a tale for Mister Morrell which will ensure Rachel's master never finds her. Cut will not have to lose his fortune to gain a slave's freedom. Old Morrell will fuss and fume over the double loss of a foreman and a servant. When he, and the rest of his ilk, finds out who the murderer is, the Fords will gladly pay for the man's losses."

"You are an optimist, Mister Wetherill," observed Heaton. "I wish you well in finding the culprit, and the best of luck in convincing the Fords to pay all expenses. You and your team shall be in my prayers for both endeavors."

"I am indebted to you, Reverend, for all you have done for us in the brief time of our acquaintance," affirmed Vincent. "You have gone out of your way to assist us against an evil man and his short-lived movement."

"I did so for selfish reasons—for my flock back on Schooley's Mountain," admitted Heaton humbly. "They will no longer fear the coming of Black Jake Spolden."

"I wish you God's speed in delivering poor Rachel to the Sharps," said Vincent, "and a safe return to your loved ones. May we meet again under more auspicious circumstances."

"I shall look forward to the event," responded Heaton with a smile. "On the occasion of your visit, please bring your father so he can avail himself of our healing springs. I shall be more than glad to serve as your contrite host."

"If and when we accept your invitation, I will be sure to . . . to bring a jug of iron water tonic," said Vincent half-seriously. "My father intends to start brewing the stuff soon as I deliver the barrels promised by Judge Cooper."

"Leave the tonic behind, Mister Wetherill," decided Heaton. "Keep it in your county. My flock of true Baptists has no use for Wetherill spirits. 'Tis the counsel and company of a true gentleman we crave and an opportunity to restore your father to good health. We need him to be fit to lead in the troubling years ahead."

"I shall consider the stipulations of your offer," concluded Vincent, as he raised his right arm and shook Heaton's hand vigorously.

"May God lead you to the murderer before he strikes again," said Heaton. "May his apprehension come at no cost of life or limb to the remaining members of your team."

With that said, the preacher gave a curt command to his horse and guided it slowly in the same direction Bruder had taken. Heaton intended to follow the westering mule path down to the Rockaway River and cross it to get to Mine Hill. He, also, wanted no part of outlaws plaguing the better roads. Vincent did not blame him. He wished he could lead his team along the same back way, but it was out of the question. It would have meant he had chosen failure. Vincent, and the men remaining, had to ride into the jaws of another hell. He was glad the preacher and the slave had decided to avoid such a fate.

Before Heaton and Rachel disappeared from sight, Jimmy Hornbeck and Ansel Jarlman returned from the horse pen with the mounts, the team of bay Shires, and a few spare steeds. They had set the rest free. Cut and Ike proceeded to hitch up Wetherill's dependable pair to the waggon. While Vincent was urging these men to hurry, Mister Jolly sidled up to the leader. The ring of keys and three locks, fastened to his belt, jangled and clicked with his every move.

"You're going to have to silence those treasures you've found, Mister Jolly," observed Vincent. "Where we are headed, we must dare not make a sound."

"I thought our little adventure was up, soon as the mine entrance was sealed," mumbled Jolly.

"Over by half," corrected Vincent. "We still have a murderer to bag."

"I thought Mister Jarlman has the culprit's head in his possession," Jolly argued. "He holds proof that the mystery of the murders 'round Morris Town has been solved."

"I wish you were correct, sir, but you are not," Vincent insisted. "Jarlman has the head of a kidnaper, not a killer. We have one last chance to catch the right man. We can't pass it up."

"Does it entail climbing another mountain?" beseeched Jolly with trepidation.

"No," Vincent chuckled, "but it may seem so . . ."

Before the grays of dawn appeared in the cloudless sky, Vincent's team reached a hunter's trail just north of the colliery. Jimmy Hornbeck, the only one who knew how close they were, suggested they turn off the mine road and proceed on foot. Nobody took exception but Ike, who joked about trying to keep up even though he was still without shoes. Mister Jolly was left behind again to guard the horses and waggon. He decided to sit in the vehicle, under the tallest tree, and wait for the others to return. Each man selected a musket from the waggon, save for Cut Hancock, who always preferred his own. The diminished team started following the hunter's trail east and then south. The full moon insisted on lighting the way. The trail appeared freshly widened, with occasional stumps poised to trip those who dared make their way in the pre-dawn darkness. The cedar pines were low, but cast deep shadows. Soon they gave way to stretches of runty scrub and marshy ooze. Hornbeck was in the lead, carrying an unlit waggon lantern. The men slashed through the damps until they came to dry, higher ground in a clearing dotted with dead collier stacks and empty arch pits. Where ricks of stacked wood remained, no smoke wafted from the flue holes. There was no cut wood being turned to charcoal here. The colliery's glory days were over. The place was dormant as a graveyard.

Jimmy Hornbeck picked his way through the maze of remains. The rest of the men followed silently behind him. The only sounds were the soft whisper of a morning breeze and the chirp and twitter of a few birds anticipating the approach of dawn. There was a solitary stand of cedars and birches up ahead. Hornbeck crept toward it. He knew the Smultz cabin sat just beyond the trees. None of the men paused there, for Vincent had them spread out and creeping closer to the cabin, tree to tree to tree. There was no light from candle or hearth at the two unshuttered windows. No smoke ascended from the slightly bowed chimney. No horses were tethered front or back, or in the fenced yard where the gate was missing. There was no sound of drunken, cursing men inside or out. No laughter. No snoring. The place seemed as dead as the collier's field behind it.

"We've snecked up on this place too late," whispered Hornbeck to young Wetherill. "Ain't a shab or sinner to be found here. This place holds a silence stranger than stones."

Vincent bit his lip. He did not want to believe the man was right. Maybe Little Jake Fagan had been left behind to die alone. Maybe the General had ordered his men to depart, strike out on their own, leave him to fate. Maybe his men had been scared off and Fagan was in no condition to follow them.

"Let's 'prove you right or wrong, Jimmy," said Vincent softly, as he stood up and strode toward the cabin door.

The rest of his men abandoned their cover and crept to the sides and rear of the small cabin. Their muskets were poised for the worst. So was Vincent's pistol. He kicked the door once and it exploded off its hinges. Panels of worm-eaten wood fell to the earthen floor. Vincent waited a moment before entering the foul-smelling place. A reek of blood, stale sweat, and old rust wafted from the place. There were other foul smells—vague, hard to define, and all horribly unpleasant.

Hornbeck stood right behind Vincent. He continued with his whispering: "No grand discoveries to be made here, Mister Wetherill . . . we better go . . ."

"Light the lantern, Jimmy," ordered Vincent in a low, sober voice. "We're not done here yet."

Hornbeck retreated from the cabin to find dry tinder and raise a starter flame with his strike stone. In two minute's time he was back at Vincent's side. The lantern wick was glowing strongly and providing ample light for inspecting the interior of the cabin. Jimmy handed the light source to Vincent and followed him.

The old Smultz cabin contained one large room. The center of the room was dominated by a table made of broad boards atop barrels, On either side of the table was a long bench. All sorts of clutter and debris lay on the table and on the floor. Holding the lantern up high, Vincent walked around the crude furniture. He took note of the scraps of food left on the boards and tried to figure how old they might be. Bugs had not gotten to them yet. He went over to the diminuitive hearth, poked at the dead cinders on the flat stones, touched a cold pot suspended from an iron hook, and dipped a gloved finger into the suspect liquid which half-filled the cooking vessel. He tasted it, but could not identify it. Vincent spit it out. He proceeded to check the corners of the room. At the base of each wall, beds of pine bows, leaves, and straw had been shaped. The impressions of where men had lain were in evidence. Blood stains, now black, painted the improvised bed nearest the hearth.

"This must be where Little Jake lay," observed Vincent, as he knelt by the remains of the bloodied bed. He had hopes of finding more clues, but there were none. Whoever had been in the cabin deserted it many hours ago.

Jimmy Hornbeck was not listening. He was sifting through the debris on the table boards. "Bring the lantern over here, Mister Wetherill. I think I've found something!"

Vincent rushed over and planted the light source in the center of the table. Where Jimmy had cleared space on the boards, letters and numbers could be seen. They had been carved neatly in the wood. Not one of them appeared to be a fresh sign. Each was darkly stained, but some were much darker than others, and barely readable.

Vincent read the darkest one out loud: "Devil 1—Wench 4 . . . what is the import of such names and numbers?"

Hornbeck had already deciphered them: "You know'd 'bout Fagan's agents as devils, 'cordin' to Mister Bruder 'n some others . . ."

"So, you're claiming this carving is a list of the General's agents?" asked Vincent.

"Sure as God's my judge," affirmed Hornbeck.

"I'll play your game, Jimmy," conceded Vincent, who had no better explanation, "but what is your take on the other word?"

"Simple enough, if you ever toiled at a colliery," answered Hornbeck crisply. "Them jobbers call their stacks of wood as wenches . . . often times givin' them pet names while stokin' their side holes . . ."

"Each of Fagan's agents has been assigned a rick," surmised Vincent, "but for what purpose?"

"My guess would be easy to prove if a map of this place was carved 'longside this here list," admitted Hornbeck, "but it ain't . . . no way to match up agent with wench . . ."

"And no way to figure which one on the list is the fellow we are looking for," decided Vincent.

"He's got to be one of 'em," added Hornbeck.

As the two men stood in silence, bent over the boards of the table and trying to make sense of devils and wenches, Ansel Jarlman and Ike Higgins marched in. Ike went directly to the hearth to inspect what was in the cooking pot. Jarlman took up a position by the back window. Cut had been left behind at the broken door. His purpose was to guard those who had gone inside.

Vincent gave orders to the pair who had entered the cabin: "Ike, raise a fire . . . the soup in the pot is rancid . . . toss it out and start anew. Mister Jarlman, go spell Mister Hancock, so he can fetch us some fresh kill for the hearth . . . make haste . . . we're hungry as hounds!"

The men jumped to their tasks. Vincent and Jimmy Hornbeck

went back to deciphering Fagan's code.

"I say we search the standing ricks one by one," decided Vincent, "and see what's been hid in any of them."

"Best to wait till the sun is up," advised Hornbeck, as a way of showing agreement. "Won't be long now . . ."

"Might waste too many hours in the doing," countered Vincent. "I say we start now."

"Your men'll work the quicker with their bellies full," suggested Hornbeck. "Let 'em break fast then turn 'em loose on the wenches. I'll go fetch some creek water in these empty jugs which'd Little Jake's men left behind."

"Can't argue with you, Jimmy," said Vincent resignedly, as he picked up two jugs and handed them to Hornbeck. "Be on your way."

In less than an hour's time, all the men had eaten the fresh kill Cut had bagged in the moonlight and Jimmy Hornbeck had caught with his hands at the nearby creek. The game had been roasted nicely by Ike over a handsome charwood fire. He had also prepared a birch bark tea in the boiling pot. The vessel had been cooled and passed around. Vincent made sure he praised Ike for his efforts. He thanked Cut and Jimmy for their contributions.

"Save the remains for Mister Jolly," instructed Vincent. "We shall bring such vittles to him after we're done here."

"I'll tuck the scraps in their skins 'n keep 'em in mein pouch," offered Cut.

Vincent nodded his approval. He then counseled with his men, at the rustic table, about the strategy he and Jimmy Hornbeck had come up with for carrying out a search of the collier stacks.

"We're looking for any evidence which reveals the identity of Dan Fagan's agent down in Morris Town—the one responsible for three murders," reviewed Vincent. "I'm thinking the General gave the orders and the man we want carried them out. That means the stipend for his slaying of Little Neb may be hidden in the stack Fagan assigned to him. The murderer probably has not had time to come up here and fetch his pay. So we'll fetch it for him . . ."

"May also mean instructions for the next job might be hidden in the same one," interrupted Hornbeck, "along with clues as to who this bloak actually is."

"Ain't gonna be no name sittin' in the right one," grumbled Ike, who drained the last of his tea from the pot, "'n there ain't gonna be none o' such you've been explainin'."

"Why do you doubt what we'll find?" asked Vincent.

"'Cause Tom Ward, the bastard who tricked me, said so hisself," divulged Ike adamantly. "Afore he got me drunk 'n hogtied me, he boasted o' knowin' the killer o' Jack Redmon 'n the buck fiddler . . ."

"Did he name the devil?" asked Jarlman.

"He was 'bout to," answered Ike, "but he pulls back his tongue 'n says I already met him twice . . ."

"Met him where and when?" asked Vincent urgently.

"I was so in me cups by then, I couldn't remember me own name much less anythin' else," confessed Ike.

"Since I was watching the bog lander the whole time he was on his medicine," Cut offered, "I'd be seeing the same character twice, now wouldn't I?"

"Yes you would," chimed Ike, "'cept when you was eyein' the ladies ev'rywhere we went . . . besides, the both o' us met many a scabber since leavin' Rattoon's . . ."

After a twitter of laughter over Ike's comment, Vincent cut to the chase: "I think our Mister Ward was talking about our time in Morris County, not before."

"Yup," mused Cut.

"Our crossin' at Book Town was the first time we saw mean-eyed Tom Ward, who was eyein' me up partic'lar like after I boasted o' me noble lineage," Ike contributed.

"The second time we ran into Morrell's foreman was at Cooper's kitchen house where he sat by his lonesome and ignored us," added Cut.

"So who besides Ward greeted us at the crossing, and who sat with you at the kitchen house?" prodded Vincent, as he leaned close to the lantern light and peered at Cut and Ike who sat across from him.

"Can't recall jus' yet," Ike admitted. "I was concentratin' on old Windy Burnet's jug 'n not much else at the kitchen house. I do 'member the Sheriff, gruff with us 'n askin' lots o' questions at the crossin' . . . Sheriff never showed hisself at the kitchen . . . 'n Windy weren't at the crossin' . . ."

"Two Constables was there at the crossin,'" Cut recollected, "'n one of the same came late to the kitchen house as I recall, but not the other."

"The Constable which showed," Hornbeck said, "came late."

"So we might have a suspect after all," sighed Vincent, as he pushed back from the table and stood up. He put his fists on the boards and demanded a name.

Ike hunched his shoulders and shook his head.

Cut did not hesitate: "Fairchild . . . met him before and after the bog lander disappeared with Ward . . . once when searching for Nettie's boy. He was sure sincere 'bout holding me for questioning . . . don't think he's the one we're looking for . . . don't know the name of the other Constable at the crossing . . ."

"He's a Burnet . . . related to Windy in some way," offered Ansel Jarlman. "He was guardin' me till Mister Jolly convinced the Sheriff to let me go . . . don't think either Burnet is able of murder."

Vincent stood up straight and slammed his fists together.

"Zachariah Fairchild, the Constable who crossed the road, is highly trusted by the elder Jacob Ford . . . could be our man."

"Mere speculation," chided Jarlman. "You've nothing to connect him with the murders. All you've got is the word of a dead kidnaper remembered by a full-drunk Irishman."

Ike jumped to his feet and reached across the table to get at Jarlman's throat.

Cut grabbed Ike with one hand and sat him down hard.

Ike was hurting, but not finished: "I knows what I knows 'n I tells it that way . . . Tom Ward told me somethin' worth tellin' . . . a villain had good reason to tell the truth at rare times . . ."

"I believe you, Ike," said Vincent, "but Mister Jarlman has a point. We've got to get the evidence which will lead us to the right man. Soon as we get back to Morris Town, we'll have to deal with the authorities. A few of our suspects are enforcers of the law. This will make our task exceeding tough."

"Can't set a trap without bait," muttered Jarlman, "legal or not."

"Let's go through with our search of the stacks," Vincent said. "The sun is up and bright as can be. We'll dismantle the ones still standing and see what we can find."

All the men left the table and followed Vincent out the door.

They were silent save for Ike, who was never at a loss for words:

"Mayhaps, I'll find a pair o' shoes fer me feets," he sang, "or hard coin to buy 'nother stout English pair."

Cut countered with what he thought would be the final word: "At the ricks, you'll be blackening your toes on char . . . it's all you'll find, bog lander."

"Bet I find more 'n you, cabbage head," retorted Ike.

"You got nothing to bet, but a broken mud spoon," chided Cut.

"All the luck I needs 'tis here," Ike declared, as he patted his shirt pocket where the piece of brass was hiding. "I ain't bettin' with such . . . I'm bettin' me reputation."

Cut roared with laughter. So did Jarlman and Hornbeck. Vincent did not. He knew Ike was the best at finding lost things.

In the span of two hours, all the standing ricks had been dismantled down to their frame poles. Even the ruined stacks had been checked. Nothing was found on most of the arch pit floors. An empty leather satchel was found at each of two locations. One was branded with a '2' and a '4'; the other, with a '3' and a '1'.

Hornbeck reviewed what each brand meant: "Fagan's agent number two was assigned to wench number four . . . agent three to wench number seven . . . what've we got left?"

Ike tugged on a heavy satchel he had dragged out of the arch pit farthest from the cabin. The others had ignored this rick because it was in near ruin. However, Ike had decided to dismantle what was left of it.

"Found a bag of rocks?" joked Cut, as Ike brought the satchel into the circle of arm-weary men.

"See fer yerself, cabbage head," said Ike. "Better 'n rocks 'n more than ye won at Powles Hook."

Vincent called out the numbers branded on the weighty satchel: "Five and thirteen." Then he turned the satchel on its side and let some of the gleaming coins spill out. "Ike's found a small treasure here, lads."

Ansel Jarlman snatched up a coin, bit it, and said, "Real coins of the realm." He held it up to the sun to inspect its marks. "No doubt about its worth."

Jimmy Hornbeck picked up one of the coins also. He stared at it hoping it would reveal more than just its worth. "This is reparation for a deed done well . . . or payment in advance for a deed yet done . . . or both by the size of the sack," estimated Hornbeck. "A good part of Fagan's own wealth was left here for someone who has yet to claim it. I say we put it back where Ike found it and wait for the devil to arrive . . . then we bag him."

"I ain't rebuildin' a stack," protested Ike, "'n I ain't givin' back me find."

Vincent agreed, but for other reasons: "We can't waste time waiting for one of Fagan's devils to come collect his due. The one we're after might commit another murder while we're in hiding up here. And how do we know devil number five is our man?"

"We don't," Hornbeck said, "but five and thirteen is all we got."

"Then let's use the numbers down in Morris Town," Vincent suggested.

"How do you mean?" asked Hornbeck, who was adamant about setting a trap at the colliery.

"Hear me out," Vincent said, as he waited for everybody to pay attention to his plan. "Let us assume this money is meant for our man. Fagan disappears, but before he abandons the colliery, he appoints another devil to assist number five with the next killing and to make sure agent five gets his coins. The devil entrusted with this mission must reach Morris Town before we do. He confronts all the suspects, mentions the number five and thirteen to each, and tells where he can be found. By that time, we'll be in hiding near the same place."

"This scheme's more foolish than your iron water ruse," groused Jarlman. "You almost got yourself kilt in that one. Who's bein' put in harm's way this time?"

"I was hoping you'd volunteer, Mister Jarlman," suggested Vincent.

"You've a better chance gettin' Mister Jolly to step for it," scoffed Jarlman, "'n you can't use the two mates you came with . . . the suspect will see through your trick."

"Leaves me," said Jimmy Hornbeck decisively.

"You've proved your worth beyond all expectations," said

Vincent. "Reverend Heaton was right about you, Jimmy. You are, indeed, a valiant man. I am proud to have you on my team, and doubly proud of you for volunteering to pose as Fagan's new devil."

"Every Harry has his price," Hornbeck proffered.

"What's yours, Jimmy?" asked Vincent.

"Half the coin in the satchel," declared Hornbeck, without any show of emotion, "after I trick the one I'm after with the same half."

Vincent expected Ike to explode again, but the Irishman did not; thus, Vincent lifted the satchel, turned it over, and let the coins spill to the ground. His intention was to count the coins and put half of them in one of the empty satchels, meant for Ike to keep. Vincent hesitated. A small piece of vellum fluttered from its hiding place at the bottom of the five-and-thirteen bag. Ike snatched it up and turned it over. He could not read the words written in blood on the other side. Ike handed it to Vincent and started scooping up the coins to be placed in the satchel intended for him.

Vincent read aloud the words on the piece of vellum: "Fords—Next—Bounty—Double."

23

BAGGING A DEVIL

• • • • • • • • • • • • • • • • •

—back to Judge Cooper's estate evening of Wednesday, September 29, 1773

The moon appeared, low and full, by the time Vincent and his diminished team of adventurers reached the fork in the road above Judge Cooper's estate. A different slave was there to greet them and make sure they meant no harm to his master. Vincent recognized this one as Buck, one of the searchers for little Neb.

"We return in peace, Buck," announced Vincent, with a gloved hand open and held high.

"Glad to be welcomin' you back, Mista Weth'rill, suh," said the slave, with no hesitation in his voice. He stood tall and lean in a loose-fitting, tattered shirt and patched trousers. He brandished a wooden rake for a weapon. No horse was in sight. He seemed glad to have someone to talk to.

"We've good news for your master," Vincent said.

"Judge Cooper's gonna like good news, sure 'nough," replied the sad-eyed slave.

"Don't tell me another murder's taken place?"

"Not yet, mista," cautioned the slave, "but folks 'round here is 'spectin' such any day now . . . any day . . ."

"Tell those folks my men witnessed the slaying of the killer, up north," lied Vincent with his best voice of conviction. "I want you to spread the word, Buck. There'll be no more murders by Tom Ward's hand."

The slave responded with a broad, beaming smile. "Old Nettie gonna like dat news . . . so'll my Masta Cooper. I'll be gettin' to da tellin' soon as my watch be o'er 'n my relief bring me a horse. I gets to spreadin' your good news, Mista Weth'rill, suh, right soon."

Buck gave a salute of sorts and Vincent reached to tip his tricorn.

He realized it was missing. Instead, he touched the bandage above his brow and gave the servant a full salute.

Vincent led his men down the road which passed closest to Cooper's manse. Ansel Jarlman and William Jolly rode behind him. The bay Shires, back under Cutlope Hancock's command, pulled a light waggon of empty barrels, weapons, and sundry supplies. Ike Higgins took up the rear. He was mounted on a purloined stallion rescued from the emptied horse pen up at the site of the Johnson Mine. Ike counted himself quite fortunate to have gained one of the Prophet's best steeds. He was also glad for the coins in the satchel slung over the withers of the horse. Half a fortune was better than no fortune at all . . . Good Mary was going to be exceeding proud.

Timothy Brown, the redemptioner from Dublin, opened the palladian door after Vincent had pounded the large brass knocker three times. Cooper's house servant held up a candle lantern and gaped at what he saw.

"My, my, Mister Wetherill," sputtered Brown, "you look much the worse for wear since last I saw you."

"I sure could use the shave I missed upon leaving," admitted Vincent cheerfully, "and someone to help redress the nick at my ear . . . other than such, I just need to rest my weary bones after an arduous trip up north and back."

Timothy Brown bowed to Vincent, then ushered him into the welcoming parlor. He was quick to indicate that the same guest room was waiting for the return of such a renowned gentleman. He promised he would check to see if steaming water, lather, blade, and spikenard were in place for Vincent when he was ready. He added a boast about his ability at dressing wounds and insisted on being the one to examine Vincent's injury.

"All well and good, and much appreciated, Timothy," said Vincent, "but I need to see Judge Cooper first. Please bring me to him now. I've important news to share. Then I must follow my team to the kitchen house to pay my respects to poor Nettie. After setting plans with my men, I shall return for a brief respite in the guest room. That is when I shall need you."

The house servant bowed low, turned on his heels, and led Vincent past the ornate table with blossom heads of dark gold, burnished orange, and deep burgundy in wide pewter bowls. The two men whisked through the spacious social room, where servants were busy changing candles in the chandeliers. The dimly lit blue-gray hallway, with its two small windows, contained no guard at the door to Judge Cooper's library study. Timothy Brown tapped the door once with delicate knuckles. Judge Cooper responded with his customary bombastic voice:

"Best be important, Timothy . . . I've no time for trifles . . . nor time wasters."

"Neither, sir," replied the house servant, as he opened the door and let young Wetherill brush past him.

The Judge, working at his desk, let out a gasp. He peered over his spectacles, dropped his quill, and slammed a ledger shut. He tried to stand and speak at the same time, but succeeded at neither.

"You'll need to sit, sir, for the news I bring from the northern hills," said Vincent firmly. "Best to keep your arse planted for what I have to say."

Cooper waved his servant out of the room, waited for the door to close, then spoke just above a whisper: "My poor lad, you look a sight . . . should I send for a doctor to treat that wound to your head?"

"A mere scratch," said Vincent, "and the least of what I have to tell you about. Your house servant has offered to redress the wound. Timothy has assured me that he is skilled in such things."

"He is very skilled in many things, Mister Wetherill," affirmed the Judge, "and a fiend when it comes to cleanliness. You are in good hands with him."

"Enough said about my scratch," said Vincent. "'Tis merely the result of an unlucky musket round, which led to much worse luck for certain parties, tracked down by my team."

Cooper leaned forward, placed his elbows on either side of the forgotten ledger, and steepled his stout fingers under his ample chin.

"Tell me everything, Mister Wetherill," begged the Judge. "Start at the beginning of your adventure and leave nothing out. I will make sure the Fords and certain other members of the Sons of Dawn are fully informed of your success."

"Successes," emphasized Vincent, as he stretched his legs, one at a time, and flexed his fingers by opening and closing his hands. The long ride down from the colliery had stiffened his limbs. He felt older than Mister Jolly.

"I am all ears," said the Judge, as he removed his spectacles slowly and placed them on the ledger. "Good news is hard to come by these days. However, I am glad to report that no murders occurred in your absence. We are holding here at three, nervously waiting for the next one. Wick's pork remains unfound . . . Morrell's foreman and slave are still missing . . ."

"Before I begin," interrupted Vincent, "would it be a bother to pour something for my parched throat . . . been a difficult journey down, with but a brief stop to rest the horses."

Cooper turned red-faced with embarrassment. He sighed heavily and sputtered, "My apologies for being such a rude host, but you surprised me so . . . forgot to offer you a glass of this fine Madeira I acquired recently." The Judge reached for the narrow-necked bottle on his desk and poured Vincent a near-full tulip glass of the fancy stuff. He held the expensive vessel up to the candlelight and pretended to look for flaws. Vincent got out of his chair to accept it. The Judge also offered sweet meats on a tray sitting next to the wine bottle.

"Many thanks," Vincent said, as he settled back into the plush chair and started sipping the wine and nibbling on the tasty fare. He found himself staring at the faded banner of the Sons of the Dawn Sword, as he quelled his hunger.

"Sorry I cannot offer you a bit of your father's precious brandy," confessed Cooper, "but it has been consumed . . . should have requested more barrels."

"The Madeira will do me just fine," said Vincent comfortably. "I will tell my father to send you a few more rundlets of his best brew as soon as I return to the plantation. I am sure his price shall be reasonable."

"Any price will be fine with me, Vincent," allowed the Judge, "for, you see, the one up here who likes it the most is my beautiful, young wife. Please make sure your father wastes no time in sending the next batch."

Vincent responded with a chortling laugh. It had been a long time since he had had a good laugh. It made him feel grand. So did the Madeira. He drained the glass, held it gently, and began his partially truthful tale:

"Things were uneventful till we reached the Hibernia forge. Rumors of trouble brewing were rampant up there. Mister Hoff, the Forge Master, was forming a vigilance group in anticipation of a possible raid by certain members of the Sons of the Sword. He invited my team to join his party and intercept the gang of villains before they could attack. Reverend Heaton, Cutlope Hancock, and myself decided to assist in Mister Hoff's plan."

"That man is a risk taker and a hot noggin," mused Cooper. "How did you find him?"

"Hard, for sure, but fair with his men," replied Vincent. "Hoff is unyielding when it comes to sticking to his plan, which proved to be near perfect."

"How do you mean?" implored the Judge.

Vincent proceeded to tell Cooper about what transpired at the Sign of the Raven.

"So you claim Dan Fagan was slain in the ambush?" pressed the Judge.

"Sure of it," Vincent said. "The General was hit twice. Cut's round must have finished the bastard."

"Good news for me and the Fords," sighed Cooper happily. "Tell me more."

Vincent told of the roundabout trek up to the Johnson Mine, the ruse employing the Judge's creek water, the escape of Ike Higgins and Rachel Hagers from iron cages, the courage of Reverend Heaton in confronting the Prophet, Jack Spolden, and the retreat of the Prophet's forces into the mine.

"So you claim this Spolden fellow never emerged from his hiding place?" pressed the Judge again.

"Sure of it," insisted Vincent. "The Prophet's fate was determined by blackpowder provided to my team by Hard Joe Hoff. The explosions and avalanche sealed the entrance to the mine . . . Spolden is no more."

"I trust the bodies of the slain are hiding well," beseeched Cooper without making eye contact with his new secret hero. "The Fords and I don't want the authorities stumbling upon them."

"All that remains in sight is the head of Tom Ward," said Vincent casually.

"What!" gasped Cooper, as he slapped his desk with a meaty hand and came close to knocking over his empty tulip glass. "You dispatched the murderer also?"

Vincent wanted to respond in the affirmative, for he enjoyed the game of fabrication which Karl Bruder had encouraged him to play. The more outlandish the stories about the slayings, the better. According to Bruder's way of thinking, the purpose was to confound interested parties as well as the authorities. Vincent agreed. He would reserve the truth for his father. The path of partial truths was for everyone else.

"Tom Ward was slain by the Prophet's hand before we arrived at the mine," Vincent explained. "Seems he and Spolden got into an argument over payments due for the kidnaping of my man and Morrell's servant. It appears Rachel Hagers escaped from Ward twice, and he caught her twice. So Ward wanted double for her. Spolden objected. Thus, Ward wanted out . . . did not want any part of the next assignment—capturing Lord Stirling."

"So you're telling me Jack Spolden was the one orchestrating the trouble down here," weighed the Judge, "and Tom Ward was his agent in carrying it out?"

"The Prophet preferred to call his agents angels," corrected Vincent.

"Ward weren't no angel," Cooper shot back with a fierce shake of his head.

"Well, he's dead as can be now," stressed Vincent, "and Ansel Jarlman has his head to bring back as proof to his boss, Verdine Elsworth. You and your gentleman friends won't have to worry about Tom Ward, alias Billy Walsh, ever again."

"Gruesome," muttered the Judge. "If I know Captain Elsworth, he will have the murderer's head limed and mounted, before Mister Morrell can lay claim to it."

"Doubt it much," opined Vincent. "I fetched Ward's skull out of a cooking fire myself . . . not much worth looking at."

"How do you know the skull belongs to Morrell's foreman?" Cooper asked with a frown of skepticism.

"The Prophet's cook told me so . . . told me himself," said

Vincent, with a bit of hesitation in his voice. He realized the Judge was poised to paint him in a corner. It was obvious the fate of Tom Ward was most important to Cooper. The Judge wanted to be completely sure Ward had been dispatched.

"The nob Mister Jarlman carries could be any dead lout's skull," brooded Cooper. "I need better proof than a rogue's word and a black skull."

"And I have such," announced Vincent confidently. After allowing a moment to gather his thoughts and assemble his lies in proper sequence, he continued, "The death of Tom Ward was witnessed by my own Ike Higgins and the Afric wench. Ike has returned with me and can vouch for what I say. Unfortunately, Morrell's slave disappeared after being set free from her cage. I fear she is gone for good . . ."

"I'm still not convinced," protested Cooper. "Your Mister Higgins is not much better than a rogue when he's sober, so I've been told, and worse than a rogue when he isn't . . . and a slave's testimony can never be trusted . . ."

"There is a mining agent who reported Ward's death to us, before we made it to the Johnson Mine," Vincent said. "This fellow infiltrated the Sons of the Sword. He gained the confidence of Jack Spolden and Dan Fagan. He was instrumental in bringing about the demise of both villains. He claims he was at the mine when Ward was beheaded by the Prophet."

"I'd like to meet this chap," said the Judge, smacking his lips loudly, "and so would the Fords."

"I know little about him," lied Vincent. "He wishes to remain anonymous in order to continue carrying out his clandestine efforts on behalf of certain investors in England. Hard Joe Hoff may know of his background, but I do not."

"Yet you trust his word on a sensitive matter," pursued the Judge.

"I saw him in action," said Vincent. "I saw him deal with my own men. The fellow means business. He gets done what has to get done . . . wastes no time in doing it. I trust what he says, and I trust what he said about the fate of Tom Ward."

"Then it's done," declared the Judge. He threw his hands up in a gesture of joy and acceptance of Vincent's news.

"Maybe, maybe not," inserted Vincent quickly.

"What do you mean?" asked Cooper, who allowed his hands to fall to his desk with a thud.

"Several of Jack Spolden's angels are still lurking about," claimed Vincent. "Several of Dan Fagan's so-called devils are here and there. Some of them do not know their leaders are gone. These rogues may be carrying out sinister assignments as we speak. They anticipate receiving large bounties if they are successful."

"You mentioned Lord Stirling as a possible target," the Judge remembered. "Who else is in danger?"

"Any man of wealth and any man who claims a title of nobility," whispered Vincent, "and any noblewoman for that matter."

"I thought it would be over for us," sighed Cooper, "with your news of Tom Ward's demise. I was about to pay the second installment of what the Fords had originally promised you and send you on your way with the barrels of iron water, which arrived this noon. Now, I'll have to ask you, Mister Wetherill, to remain till this ugly matter of angels and devils is taken care of. Please stay as my guest for as long as it takes. I will pay you double the half still owed."

"My wife and my father expect me home on the thirtieth at the latest," Vincent said. "I am already late in leaving here. I must go. Besides, I cannot hold my team together for another day. Ansel Jarlman must return to Powles Hook in the morning. William Jolly wants to return to Amboy as soon as possible. I'm afraid my Cut and Ike are more eager to leave than I am. That leaves you with Jimmy Hornbeck, who has been on loan to me by the Fords. He proved invaluable up north, and . . ."

"I need more than Jimmy," interrupted Cooper. "Ask me for anything and I will grant it, Mister Wetherill, even if you stay for one more day to organize things. Please, I'll offer you anything." The Judge reached under his desk and pulled out a small box, which he quickly unlocked. He extracted large Jersey bills of credit from it and placed them lovingly on his ledger. "None of these carry Stephen Skinner's signature . . . they're old and good . . ."

"Soon as I'm through bagging a devil," said Vincent reluctantly, "I will be on my way. I plan to succeed in less than a day if my strategy works out. The dark hours may be all I need . . . and a slack cooper's lidded barrel . . . a puncheon will do . . . if you can spare one . . ."

The Judge stared at Vincent quizzically. "A humble request, sir, and one easily fulfilled. Anything else?"

"Keep Sheriff Stiles away from me," Vincent requested. "He may have already gotten wind of my return. That means he will want to delay me—interrogate me and my men about Ward and all the rest. If I'm to bag the lone devil, whom I suspect is still operating down here, then I require no interference from authorities. Keep Stiles away from here till we are gone. Tell not one soul of our true purpose in returning here and remaining longer than expected. Tell those who want to know that we came for the iron water and left after our waggon was loaded."

"Consider it done, Mister Wetherill," promised the Judge. "I shall summon Sheriff Stiles to Jacob Ford's place for a meeting already scheduled for the morrow. I must attend it. Now the Sheriff must attend it. I'll send my overseer this evening to inform Stiles of, what I shall call, his mandatory obligation. Our meeting should keep the Sheriff preoccupied all day."

"Tell your overseer to advise the Sheriff to ride alone to your meeting," urged Vincent.

The Judge did not ask why. He didn't want to know. Cooper handed Vincent a fistful of bills and bid him a pleasant, restful evening.

Cooper's kitchen house was a flurry of late-hour activity. Nettie was at her hearth singing a happy tune and stirring a huge pot. The water was bubbly and boiling. It contained Cutlope Hancock's broad-cloth hunting coat. The horrible smell rising from it did not bother old Nettie. She was enjoying the chore as much as the news Ike Higgins had given her about the horrible death of Tom Ward. Balthazar was at her side, clinging to his mother—he had done so ever since being returned to Nettie. But he was smiling now—not about good news, which he could not understand, nor the song on Nettie's lips. He was being entertained by the pale, scarred Irishman in a tub nearby. Bale had helped a pair of slaves carry the huge metal vessel from the storage room and had helped fill the thing with boiling water from hearth pots. The tub was seldom used.

It was a rare sight to see a truly filthy person being forced into it against his will. But the victim had been held down and stripped by the fair-skinned man, whom Nettie called 'Missa Cut.' Then the sullied one had been tossed, screaming, into the tub by the same brute. After Cut departed to take his turn guarding the waggon, which had yet to be loaded with the barrels of iron water, Nettie's sister took charge at the tub. She was strong as Nettie and just as gruff. With one hand she held the Irishman down in the water. With the other she applied a brick of wood ash soap. This was followed by the application of a firm-bristled horse brush, which left the poor man's skin radiant red and nothing but curse words on his lips. When she was done, the fellow was allowed to soak. Nettie's sister spent the respite time preparing fresh bandages and salves for the Irishman's worst wounds. She determined that the man's old arm wound and both his feet needed her care the most. Bale wondered how his dear aunt was going to get the reluctant patient to cooperate. The boy could not bear to look at the old burn marks and fresh cuts on the fellow. He feared he would be called upon to help hold the man down once the ghostly fellow was lifted from the tub. Bale decided to cling even tighter to his mother and hide his eyes in the voluminous folds of her tattered dress.

The boy did not notice another white man fumbling with the latch on the Dutch door of the kitchen house. This pale one wore a dusty captain's jacket and had a stained bandage wrapped around his head. He called out Nettie's name. She turned to see who it was. She struck Bale on the head with her stirring spoon and motioned for him to let the man in. Her son did so in his usual shy and reluctant way. The handsome man entered; introduced himself; offered his condolences to Nettie over the loss of little Neb; repeated the news of the demise of Tom Ward, which she had already heard; and showed her a pair of well-worn ligoniers, which Judge Cooper had handed him to give to Ike Higgins.

Nettie bowed low, thanked Vincent for news she had already received, and pointed to her sister and the glistening head of the captive in the tub.

"Them buckle shoes looks a bit large for his feets, Missa Vincent," estimated Nettie, "but after my sis get done wrappin' his wounds on 'em, I'm guessin' them shoes'll fits jus' fine."

"Glad to see my Ike is getting the attention he deserves," Vincent replied. "You and your sister are angels, indeed."

"I'm thinkin' your man is guessin' my sis is a debble," assessed Nettie. "I'm thinkin' your man fears he's surrounded by debbles."

"He was recently surrounded by them," chuckled Vincent. "Yes, old Ike knows the difference between angels and devils. He will thank you when your sister is done with him and either of you brings him a hard drink."

"Gets plenty for the three of us, Missa Vincent," boasted Nettie, "'n more for the mens at their cards in the storage room . . . 'n vittles for all . . . includin' you."

Vincent tossed the shoes in the direction of the tub and called out to Ike that the footware was a gift from Judge Cooper.

Ike offered a none-too-pleased frown.

"Be sure to thank our host after these angels of mercy finish making you presentable," shouted Vincent playfully, as he selected a few items of food being kept warm on trays by the hearth stones.

Vincent's hasty repast was interrupted by another round of Ike's cursing. Nettie's sister shoved his head under water and held it there too long. Ike came up sputtering unintelligible things. Bale buried his head in his mother's gown once more. All was as expected in Cooper's kitchen house. In the midst of such mayhem, Vincent asked Nettie whom he might find in the storage room. She recollected that Constable Burnet came to snoop around, leave a message from the Sheriff, and stay long enough to partake of a bowl of rum. She mentioned Jarlman and Jolly without any show of emotion, then she hesitated because she could not remember the last man's name.

"I hope he is Mister Hornbeck, on loan from the Fords," prodded Vincent.

"Dat's him," exclaimed Nettie. "I calls him Missa Jimmy . . . seen him jus' a few times, so I knows little 'bout dat man . . . came here later 'n de rest of 'em, but ate more 'n any of 'em. Fix you a plate of de same vittles, Missa Vincent, if you'd like?"

Vincent thanked Nettie for her hospitality and confessed he had eaten his fill. He explained that he had important business to attend to. With that said, Vincent left Nettie to her coat-cleaning chore, scolded Ike for cursing at Nettie's sister, and entered the storage room.

The room was cluttered, dark, and cool. Three men hunkered over greasy cards at a small table which had been pulled close to the only window in the room. It was obvious supplies and foodstuffs had been pushed aside to accommodate the gaming table. Small barrels were employed as chairs. A squat candle, at the center of the table, provided meager light.

"Sorry to interrupt your fun, men," declared Vincent, "but I need to borrow Mister Hornbeck for a spell."

Jimmy got off his barrel quickly and headed for the doorway where Vincent was standing.

"I promise to bring him back soon," Vincent said.

Jarlman waved and went back to frowning at an obviously bad hand of cards. Jolly did the same, but felt it necessary to speak:

"When the wenches get the stink off Mister Higgins," wheezed Jolly, "he can sit in for Jimmy 'n take up his cards."

"Nope," advised Jarlman. "He'll rob you blind, William . . seen 'im in action down at the Hook . . . skinned two gamblers afore they knew their pouches was emptied by him. He's too slick for the likes of us."

"Too bad Constable Burnet could not stay," concluded Jolly.

"Let's play two ways till Jimmy gets back."

"Fine with me," Jarlman said. "Mister Hancock told Nettie to keep the Irishman out of this room . . . told her to give the man a jug of lightning and set him by the hearth to dry . . . 'n old Nettie listens to Mister Hancock real well. So we shouldn't have no problem."

Vincent and Jimmy Hornbeck left the two men to their cards and discussion of how best to deal with a superior gamesman if he happened to enter the storage room. Vincent led Hornbeck past the busy sisters and the soaking man, who was now the main topic of discussion in two rooms. They walked a fair distance from the kitchen house and found a bench outside Cooper's empty spring house. They sat there in the dark.

"Any luck?" asked Vincent.

"Same," responded Hornbeck.

"How so?"

"Soon as I made Morris Town, I stopped at the Haynes place to spread your good news."

"Who was there?" asked Vincent eagerly.

"Found Constable Fairchild 'n Henry Burnet there," said Hornbeck, "providin' the only audience for Windy Burnet, who was glad to invite me into his fun."

"Were you able to get a word in?" asked Vincent.

"Old Windy was sharin' his jug of thunder with the likes of me, but not the other two," admitted Hornbeck. "So I let him talk hisself out, 'n the others had nothin' to say. This left me with an invite to explain where I'd been 'n what I'd been up to."

"Did you tell them what we had discussed?" prodded Vincent.

"To the letter," said Hornbeck. "I started with the three of us—me, Jolly 'n Jarlman—goin' up to Hibernia to find you. I ended with us searchin' the abandoned colliery. In between, I told of Spolden 'n Fagan slippin' away from traps set, but learnin' of Tom Ward's demise. Mention of his name got a strong rise out of Windy 'n the Constable . . . not so much from Windy's brother."

"How about their reaction to the two numbers discovered at the colliery?" Vincent asked pointedly.

"Strange 'bout it," Hornbeck answered. "There was none. I tried 'em twice . . . the five I used in talkin' 'bout dice 'n cards layin' face up on the table in the colliery cabin . . . not a blink nor a frown . . . same result over usin' the thirteen for to explain how many wenches remained standin' at the colliery."

"Did you get to tell any of the other suspects the same account?" Vincent asked with a frown of discouragement.

"Ran into Solomon Burnet on my way here," said Hornbeck. "Told this Constable the same I told his blood kin . . . 'n told Cooper's overseer the same when I brought my horse to the stable here . . . never saw Sheriff Stiles."

"Did you get a reaction to the numbers from Solomon Burnet or Cooper's man?" pursued Vincent.

"None," continued Hornbeck, "'cept for when I mentioned Ward's fate, then it was a sigh of relief from both men. All them fellows think the killin' 'round here is at an end, since Ward is gone."

"One of them does not," mused Vincent, more to himself than to Hornbeck. "One of those fellows knows Tom Ward is not the killer . . . that one is the man we want . . . that one is the killer."

"You think the man we want will come lookin' for his pay?" Hornbeck queried.

"Depends on how well you set the trap, Jimmy," said Vincent, who then waited for the answer he expected to hear.

"To all of 'em I told of the same discovery," said Hornbeck.

"Good," coaxed Vincent, "and what was it you said?"

"The satchel of coins, found at the colliery, hides in your waggon. It'll stay right there, under guard 'round the clock, till you're ready to leave on the morrow. I boasted 'bout takin' my turn from midnight to four."

"Any reaction to all that?" prodded Vincent.

"None," said Hornbeck, "but both constables said Sheriff Stiles might be interested in counting what we'd found 'n interrogatin' all parties which did the findin' . . . 'n sure 'nough, Solomon Burnet dropped by later on his own at the kitchen house to tell us the Sheriff wants to question all of us 'bout our adventure."

"Good," exclaimed Vincent. "That means the killer will have to act before he figures we'll find the Sheriff or the Sheriff finds us."

"So you're sayin' the Sheriff ain't a suspect?"

"Slight chance, Jimmy," said Vincent. "If Stiles shows his face around here during the night, then he's not coming to interrogate us. He will have something quite sinister on his mind."

"I'm sayin' Stiles is not your man," insisted Hornbeck confidently. "I just know it."

"We'll find out, more than likely, during your turn at the waggon," warned Vincent. "Tell the others in the kitchen house of their assignments—Cut is half-the-way through his watch; your turn starts at midnight; Jarlman from four to dawn; Ike, if necessary, after that till we depart. Those not on their turn, including myself, will stay in hiding and wait a safe distance from the waggon."

"Agreed, Mister Wetherill," said Hornbeck crisply. He rose from the bench, attempted a quick bow, and started back to the kitchen house to inform the others.

Vincent watched him disappear into the darkness. What a valuable man, thought young Wetherill—the kind from low station who suddenly appears to make a difference in how things turn out. Jimmy Hornbeck was, indeed, an unexpected surprise—placing himself in danger repeatedly. And for what? A bit of praise. A bag of coins—probably more of Sam Ford's counterfeit. Not one man of power and influence would remember Jimmy's brave deeds, nor would any of them bother to reward him. Vincent knew the Fords would never care to know. Neither would Cooper. If all went well, none of the authorities would have a clue. Only Vincent would know the whole story. And, because of Jimmy Hornbeck, he felt confident his latest plan would succeed. He knew Reverend Heaton would not approve of his methods, and he felt Karl Bruder would insist that the plan would not work. Vincent was glad neither man was around to witness the wicked end in store for the murderer. They could not interfere this time.

Well past midnight the full moon started losing its battle against a gathering of clouds. Jimmy Hornbeck, with pistol in hand and a large knife at his belt, sat on the seat board of the Wetherill waggon. The vehicle was positioned in the middle of a neatly scythed yard, a fair distance from any barn. Next to the waggon stood barrels of iron water, yet to be loaded for transport back to the Wetherill plantation. Hornbeck spent his time peering beyond the barrels into the darkness framing the yard. He was looking for two things—any sign of someone approaching the waggon, and any indication that members of Mister Wetherill's team were actually at their hiding positions. Hornbeck saw neither. It bothered him. He wanted action. However, he wanted, most of all, to be sure there were members of Vincent's team ready to defend him. They were supposed to be hiding behind trees at the edge of the yard—too great a distance away to suit Jimmy. Trusting in others was not one of his strong suits. If he thought about it long enough, there were not many strengths or successes in the ledger of his life. As far as he was concerned, his page was filled with failures and dreams deferred. Bagging a devil on a night like this would be quite an accomplishment, even if he had promised Mister Wetherill to keep the outcome a secret. At least he could be a hero to himself . . .

Jimmy heard a click of metal against metal over by the barrels.

He turned his head to take a look, but the waggon blocked his view of most of the barrels. He quickly slipped from the seat board and made his way to the cluster of barrels behind the waggon. He found nothing but moon shadows. Jimmy started retracing his steps. He did not see a dark figure race from the other side of the waggon and slip up behind him. Suddenly, a mighty arm, encased in a coarse coat sleeve, snaked around Jimmy's neck and began to squeeze tightly. Hornbeck grabbed for the cloth on the arm, but only managed to get his hand cut by the broad knife his adversary wielded. Jimmy wanted to cry out but he could not. The pistol in his other hand was not primed, and, therefore, useless. In the next instant, a mighty hand grabbed his wrist and twisted his pistol and limb hard behind his back. He was spun around and brought down to his knees. His face was slammed against one of the full barrels. The last measure of punishment produced the ugly sound of a broken drum. Jimmy could not breathe. Whoever held him from behind was squeezing tighter and tighter. His head was yanked back again and smashed once more — this time on the lid of another barrel. It was in that instant, Hornbeck recalled the advice of Reverend Heaton. He dropped his pistol. With his bloody hand he grabbed at the duffel coat his adversary was wearing and pulled it down as hard as he could. With his good hand he found his knife, pulled it free of his belt, slumped to one knee, and plunged his blade into a boot that was not his.

"Damn you to hell!" cursed the strangler, as he lost his death grip around Hornbeck's neck. "Fagan's bounty is mine, you bastard! I'm the fifth devil, not you! I'm the avenger of the wrongful death of Davey Reynolds, not you! Where's my rightful pay?"

The death bringer was no longer in shadow. He held his blade high, allowing it to glint in the moonlight. It was obvious he intended to slash Jimmy with it. However, the man's foot was pinned to the hard ground by Hornbeck's well-planted blade, and the intended victim had crawled out of harm's way. Jimmy hid behind the large, empty puncheon. The man swiped at Hornbeck anyway. It was then he caught sight of several men approaching the waggon from various directions. He realized he was surrounded with no chance of escape.

"Damn you all," screamed Fagan's devil. "You'll never take me alive!"

Jimmy Hornbeck also spotted his protectors closing in slowly. He wanted to finish off the murderer before any of the others did. After all, the chiver almost killed him. By outland rights, Jimmy knew he was entitled to be the executioner. He pulled himself up quickly and leaned against the puncheon for support, while catching his breath. He realized he carried no weapon. It would have to be his bare hands against an expert's knife. What could be found quickly to even the odds?

The evil one in the dark duffel coat went down to one knee. He proceeded to tug at Jimmy's knife, which had pierced leather and flesh. He grunted and growled like a wounded beast as he attempted to pull the blade free from the ground. He succeeded, struggled to stand, and now stood with a knife in each hand—one clean and one sporting his own blood. He took one timid step toward his intended victim, but the pain in his pierced foot was too much to bear. He fell to one knee again, but kept swiping the air with the knives. His intention was to keep Hornbeck and the others at bay.

However, Jimmy had found a weapon. He lifted the large, empty barrel off the ground and staggered forward with it.

His adversary realized what Hornbeck intended to do. He opened his coat and plunged the bloody knife deep into his gut. He fell face down in the slick grass and the puncheon rolled over his body. It slammed against a barrel of iron water and came to a stop. Cooper's gift had withstood an arduous test—the hoops held and the staves did not crack. The dry barrel could still serve a purpose. The same could not be said for the man in the blue duffel coat.

Jimmy Hornbeck got to his attacker first. He rolled the man over just as Vincent and Cut came around the waggon. The cloud-beleagered moon provided enough light to identify the groaning man who was bleeding to death.

"Constable Fairchild," hissed Jimmy, as Vincent and Cut reached his side.

"Our murderer never crossed the road," added Vincent. "We should have known it was Fairchild, even before he slaughtered Little Neb."

"Yup," muttered Cut sadly. "We had two chances to figure him out."

"But it took three, and then some," concluded Vincent just as sadly. "Now we have to figure out what to do with the bastard."

"Bring Fairchild to the Sheriff," offered Mister Jolly, who was leaning against the rear of the waggon attempting to catch his breath.

"Can't do it," said Vincent. "'Tis Jimmy's blade which is buried in the man. Sheriff Stiles will accuse our Jimmy of stabbing his Constable. I suspect Fairchild had this in mind when he realized the game was up."

"We can bury him once'd he croaks," offered Jarlman, who stood next to Jolly by the waggon.

"Too much blood already spilled on this ground," observed Vincent. "Wherever we drag him, Jacob Ford's hounds would find Fairchild's carcass in hours, not days."

"Cage this black smiter 'n hang 'im from the nearest tree," contributed Ike angrily from his perch on the seat board of the waggon.

Vincent ignored the last suggestion and dismissed the other ones as impractical. He decided to stick to his original plan, which he was going to use if his team had captured the murderer alive.

"We have to make it look like Fairchild simply disappeared," announced Vincent. "I had intended on capturing this rogue, hiding him in the dry barrel, and, far from here, convincing him that a life at sea in the service of his King's Navy would be more desirable than torture and death."

"He's near dead already," gauged Jolly. "A doctor might still be able to save his arse, but I doubt it . . . kind of foolish at this point to cart a dying man to his freedom. Looks to me like he's got no days left . . . let's do the proper thing and turn the body over to the authorities."

"Mister Wetherill's right, though," countered Jarlman. "We can't leave Fairchild's carcass anywheres near here . . . gots to take him with us whether we likes it or not . . . sooner the better. Mister Hornbeck's knife did the killing, so his fate depends on how we handle this mess."

All the others, save for Mister Jolly, agreed with Jarlman. Thus, Vincent ordered his men to prepare for leaving. The dry barrel was placed in the waggon first. Fairchild was lifted up over the boards and sumarily stuffed into the puncheon. The lid was fixed in place. The barrels of iron water were then rolled into place on the waggon. Horses were fetched from Cooper's stable. Cut went to the kitchen house to fetch his valuables and his hunting coat. He also went to bid farewell to Nettie. Ike tagged along in order to thank Nettie's sister for all she had done for him.

The clean shaven and freshly bandaged Vincent Wetherill gave instructions to Jimmy Hornbeck to hasten back to the Ford mansion and be sure to claim he had returned hours earlier.

"Sleep in one of the barns, Jimmy," advised Vincent. "Claim you did not want to disturb anyone till dawn. Sheriff Stiles has been invited to the Fords. He will most likely want to interrogate you and ask if you have seen his missing Constable. He will ask how you came by those bruises on your face. I trust you know what to say?"

"A tale Mister Bruder would be proud of," said Jimmy, as he mounted his horse and checked the satchel of coins he had thrown over his saddle.

"Good enough then, my friend," Vincent said, as he patted the rump of Jimmy's horse. "You'll find a few bills of credit in that bag of coins of yours . . . spend them wisely."

Jimmy Hornbeck saluted young Wetherill and sped off to follow a little used road to the Fords. Vincent watched the good, loyal man until he disappeared into the darkness. He wondered what would have happened if Jimmy had not been on his team . . . he wondered often during the few remaining years of his life . . .

24

ALMOST HOME
. . . .
—from Long Ferry Tavern to Rattoon's and beyond
Thursday, September 30, into the wee hours of Friday,
October 1, 1773

"Where might your lads—Ichabod Higgins and Cutlope Hancock—be hidin'?" asked Big Tom Carnes, minehost of Long Ferry Tavern. He was employing his usual booming voice and directing his words towards his only guest at the far table of honor. He could barely be heard over the Thursday din raised by a crowd of thirsty patrons who were well into their afternoon cups.

"They split from Mister Jolly and me at Bottle Hill and followed Captain Elsworth's agent, who had to get back to Powles Hook," explained Vincent as loudly as he could. "My men have a small business matter to attend to at Snake Hill . . . a deposit of sorts. Soon as they're done, they will join me here."

Carnes grinned knowingly, but he did not follow up with another question. Perhaps he had not caught the full import of what young Wetherill had said or did not care to trifle over its significance. Vincent's clandestine business dealings did not interest him. No one dared question Big Tom about his secrets and he never pried secrets out of others. He always wanted to make his patrons feel at ease and upbeat. That made them want to come back. When Vincent first entered the tap room, the minehost's welcome had been a warm one. Carnes dropped what he was doing, rushed to the door to greet Vincent, and slapped him on the back with a large, greasy hand. He ushered Vincent over to his table of honor with much fanfare. This effort stirred the early crowd into uttering several halloos and hussahs as soon as Big Tom bellowed the Wetherill name. As soon as they sat down in the darkest shadows, Carnes ordered his youngest daughter, Rebecca, to bring food and drink for the one being treated as a returning hero. Even before the vittles and ale were placed on the boards in front of Vincent, the host had asked his only question.

"Cut and Ike should make it here before midnight," shouted Vincent. "I must wait till they arrive."

"The same upstairs room is waitin' for your weary bones, Mister Wetherill," said Carnes finally. "If old Cut don't get here till dawn, I promise things'll be quiet next door. You might remember the dibble-dabble from the last time you was here." Minehost gave a wink, took a generous gulp of his own house ale, and slammed his tankard down on the boards. "Now I'm not chargin' you for the room, nor the flounder and piss from Woden's horse. All I crave in return is a full and fairly honest account of what you've been up to since you last set foot in my humble establishment. Make it a lively tale and I might just reward you with one of my daughters for the evening."

Vincent blushed. He tried to concentrate on the tasty fare on his plate. He reached for his cup of ale and restored his composure by draining the vessel. The potent liquid raced down his throat and warmed his insides.

"Take your time, Mister Wetherill," blared Big Tom, as he signaled his youngest daughter to bring another round of ale for his parched and embarrassed guest. "A long tale needs lots of lubrication . . . if you catch my drift."

Carnes let out a hearty laugh, stood suddenly, and reached over the table. He gave Vincent another slap on the back. The guest wheezed and struggled to catch his breath. He rubbed his shoulder where minehost struck. When the second ale arrived, Vincent reached for it immediately. This time he sipped it slowly and avoided eye contact with Carnes and his unfortunately rough-cast daughter, who stood at her father's side until she was called back to business at the bar.

"'Becca has warmed to you, Mister Wetherill," announced Carnes proudly. "She's off work when the moon appears. After a tellin' of your little adventure and a fair nap, I encourage you to try the latch on the door of the room next to yours— the one your Cut is most familiar with . . . what say you?"

"I plan to tell you all about my successes up north with no favor asked in return," confided Vincent as soberly as he could. "I am a married man and less than a year into it, Mister Carnes. I plan to remain faithful for the rest of my life. Besides, my journey has left me dead tired. My nap may stretch beyond the arrival of Cut and Ike."

"Such a pity, Mister Wetherill," laughed Carnes, as he pounded the boards with his fist and made everything on it jump and rattle. "But an honorable pity just the same . . . and rare as your father's prize brandy. I see there is no way to bribe you. On with your tale afore I fall asleep myself and miss the arrival of your less-than-decent lads."

Vincent proceeded to tell Big Tom Carnes more than he told Judge Cooper. This version was closer to the truth, but still far from honest. In the process of weaving fact and fabrication, he made sure he praised Carnes for his dire prediction about the leader of the false rebellion. He stressed how dangerous the movement might have become if Spolden had lived. Vincent also emphasized the contributions made by William Jolly. By the time Vincent got to the mysterious disappearance of the Constable, who was found to have been an agent for one of the leaders of the Sons of the Sword, Carnes had drained his tankard. He was fidgeting with his black eye patch, attempting to give the appearance of being interested, and struggling to stay awake.

"What's left of the yarn you aspinnin'?" asked Big Tom finally.

"There is no more to tell," confessed Vincent with a yawn. "Now, I must find the proper room upstairs and catch a few winks before I keel over."

"Not so fast, Mister Wetherill," said Carnes, concluding his words with a loud belch. "My turn to catch you up on doin's 'round here and over at Radford's Landin' afore you climb my stairs . . . things you should know afore you head home."

"Perhaps it would be good to know what's going on before me and my men cross the Rariton," admitted Vincent reluctantly.

"Not much to report, so it will take little of your time," said Carnes, just as loud as when he greeted Vincent at the door. "The good news is 'bout Governor Willie comin' to 'bide in this fair city. 'Tis goin' to be good for business. The rumor is growin' strong. I've a bet on his bein' in Amboy afore the first snow . . . what say you?"

"I'm hoping the Governor gets settled here before November," offered Vincent. "I say so for my father's sake, If Franklin calls the General Assembly to convene this fall, as has been predicted, I would like to see the session held here. A trip to Amboy would be less strenuous than a trip to Burlington for my ailing father."

Big Tom Carnes slammed his table again. Everything on it shuddered. Vincent did too. "So be it then," bellowed minehost. "Bastard Willie shall be livin' here by next month. I'll be wagerin' on such!"

"What's the bad news?" Vincent shouted.

"All 'bout pig irons—the ones with the sword tattoos you mentioned in your tale," complained Carnes. "I got word last night of them rousers tearin' up Rattoon's establishment. Seems they're lookin' for your boy, Ichabod Higgins, who left Good Mary to fend for herself. Don't seem fair to me. I've been told this bad behavior's been goin' on for a few days. . . each gang of 'em which'd paid a visit ruined somethin' of worth in lookin' to get revenge on Ichabod. Seems the boys you rescued him from passed the word to other pig iron crews . . . seems they've all been highly embarrassed. Their honor, if they ever had a squib of it, was stained . . . their reputations smirched. They seek to polish their worth with Ichabod's hide. Now, you tell me in your tale of Mister Higgins bein' royalty. Them pig irons is sure goin' to be fumin' 'bout such a revelation. They may want to hang your noble bastard up on Swan Hill."

"Sounds like my men and I face a difficult reception when we reach the Landing," said Vincent.

"I've been thinkin' serious 'bout goin' over to that knock 'bout town myself, Mister Wetherill. I plan to straighten things out and even the score," contributed Carnes boldly. "Bad for business over here, if trouble's brewin' over there. Folks are afeared of travelin' 'cross to Radford's. From what I've learned, folks are preferrin' the crossin' upriver at Brunswick Town. I won't have any of my guests, comin' or goin', afeared of nothin'. Now you've reappeared, with Ichabod hisself bein' expected any hour now. My excuse for crossin' over has come. I'll be ready to depart soon as my oldest fair daughter takes over my chores. I'm goin' to send a boy to wake you, Mister Wetherill, when the time comes. We'll stifle the bad news together. I'm bringin' my mauleys and a blade just in case. What say you?"

Vincent liked the idea of Big Tom Carnes serving as an armed escort for the crossing to Radford's Landing. "One final adventure sounds good to me, Mister Carnes. I shall be honored to have you lead us into the fray." He forgot himself and reached over the table to shake minehost's hand. He regretted the move instantly.

Carnes beamed and squeezed Vincent's hand as gently as he could. As he did so, he said: "Anything else I can do for you, Mister Wetherill?"

Vincent winced in the midst of the excruciating handshake and blurted out his final request before escaping to a soft bed: "One thing your daughters might do for me . . ."

"And what, pray tell, may tickle your fancy?" asked Carnes too quickly and too loudly.

Vincent then confessed that he meant to keep his promise to his wife to purchase gifts for the women in his father's house—Abia, his wife, Fannie, and Sarah. However, he had failed to do so, for he had had no time or opportunity. He wondered if one or more of Big Tom's daughters might go to market and make a few lovely purchases for him while he was napping.

"I've got me some scrimshaws for your lonely women, Mister Wetherill," offered Carnes boldly with a laugh. "I say give 'em the scrims and they'll never be lonely no more . . . if you catch my drift."

"You are most kind, Mister Carnes," blushed Vincent, as he pulled out several bills of credit to cover the cost of the purchases he had requested, "but I was hoping your daughters might find some dainty things at the market square."

"Consider it done," trumpeted Carnes, as he slapped his table with the flat of his hand. "By the by, hide your ill-gotten pelf, my lad . . . save such for a bet on the exact day our Governor comes here to stay."

"I'd rather gamble on our chances against the pig irons at Rattoon's," countered Vincent with a chuckle.

Big Tom Carnes matched it with a mighty laugh and gave his guest some parting advice: "Never bet on a sure thing, my lad . . . 'tis Old Harry to pay if you lose."

❖

It was unusual for the ferryman to ply his vessel across the Raritan River after midnight, in a fog no less. However, Big Tom Carnes had requested, or more likely demanded, the late run. The ferryman dared not refuse the man. When Carnes spoke, folks listened; when he demanded, folks obeyed. Now the formidable mine-host was giving commands to a motley party consisting of a trio of homebound wayfarers, a quartet of robust tavern patrons, and one of his stalwart daughters. They were all armed and making no bones about itching for a fight. The ferryman and his apprentice were the only two on board who thought this late night escapade was foolish and a waste of time. The moon was supposed to be full and lighting the way. Instead, it was vague and brawling against the mist which hovered above the water. Finding Radford's docks would be a challenge. Luckily, the ferry boat carried a light load—the Wetherill waggon and four horses were tethered in place; the apprentice was busy freeing the mooring ropes; and the passengers were huddled around Carnes at the mid-boards. What could go wrong?

"As I see it," started Carnes, "we march up from the Landing . . . two abreast . . . swords and knives in view . . . a drinking song on our lips to scare off any shy-cocks and leave us the mean daddlers to contend with . . ."

"By rights, I should go first," declared Ike. "I've a grand song to be leadin' with . . . a ditty quite suited fer them pig irons."

"Your song I'll accept, Ichabod," said Carnes, "but you ain't leadin' us into the fray."

"Why ain't it me?" demanded Ike.

"'Cause you're royalty now and your heralds must march into Rattoon's first . . . for to clear the way and announce your triumphant return," Carnes explained. "So, 'tis me and your Cap'n here, Mister Wetherill, who will proceed first with fists and blades if necessary . . . then Cutlope and my fair 'Becca follow . . . then you waitin' outside with the four best brawlers in Amboy at your back."

"If I'm the noble gloak on this here worthy ship, how come I ain't givin' the orders?" groused Ike.

"'Cause you are a wise and cautious lord, indeed," Carnes offered. "You allow underlin's to do the dirty work and make it easy for you to seize the glory."

"As it should be," chimed one of the tavern patrons, followed by a chorus of chuckles from his companions.

"Right for the time being," added Vincent, "but changes are coming . . . a few more years, according to my father . . ."

"Then we have ample time," interjected Carnes with a laugh and a broad smile. "Plenty of time to do our wise lord's biddin.'"

"I approves o' yer plan, Gen'ral Carnes," declared Ike, with as strong a voice as he could muster, "but yer forgettin' one thing."

"What might that be?" rushed Carnes.

"A good Irish lord needs a strong drink afore followin' his best warriors into battle," stated Ike. "Where's mine?"

Cut produced his refilled flask of rum from one of the many pockets in his cleaned hunting coat. He handed it to Ike.

The Irishman took a generous swig. Then another. Cut grabbed the flask back, took a swig himself, and invited anyone else to take a turn. 'Becca was the only taker. She matched Ike's measure of consumption, then gave the flask back to its owner. The vessel was quickly returned to its hiding place before Ike could reach for it again.

In the time remaining to cross to Radford's Landing, Big Tom Carnes went over the details of his plan. The horses and waggon had to be led away to a safe place. The ferryman's apprentice was assigned to guard the steeds and vehicle until the two wayfarers returned for them. The ferryman was to wait for the five upstanding citizens of Perth Amboy to return from Rattoon's and take them back to their beloved city. If all went well, Ike Higgins would be the only one to remain at Rattoon's. The decision for any of the others to stay longer, if necessary, would be made by Tom Carnes. He had informed his followers of the possibility that they might have to stick around for a day or two. He also warned them that needless damage to property and injury to innocent bystanders would not be tolerated.

"We intend to scare the wits out of the trouble-makers," reiterated Carnes. "If a Constable shows his face, then we turn the tattooed luggers over to the law. What say you, Lord Ichabod?"

"Hope the Constable's late, as he was last time here," declared Ike with a noticeable slurring of his words. "Hope he don't never shows."

❖

The Landing dock was deserted when the late ferry from Amboy drifted in. It was moored without incident. The fog was thickening and the full moon was losing its battle against an onslaught of clouds. Big Tom Carnes ordered lanterns be lit for the climb up the hill to Rattoon's. His following complied and the loud march began. Ike started his ribald song and the rest joined in on the naughty chorus. 'Becca sang it as lustily as the men did.

The marchers met no opposition until they reached the hitch posts in the front yard of the Rattoon establishment. One of the iron posts had been pulled out of the ground. It was being swung menacingly by a pig iron brute, who was about to bludgeon a poor local that had already fallen to the ground. The song of the approaching marchers caused the aggressor to pause in what he was doing and glance over his shoulder. He was not alone. A hand of pig irons, all being entertained by their comrade's bullying, also turned to stare at the odd singing marchers. The pig irons showed no inclination to desist in what they were doing or step out of the way.

As Big Tom strode up to the wielder of the metal post, he barked out orders to the members of his party: "Keep to the singin', my loyal sons and daughters, whilst I plant a few scoundrels in sacred ground!"

The first to fall was the fellow with the iron post. He came charging at Carnes with intentions of crippling the much larger man with one blow. Big Tom had other ideas. He stepped out of harm's way and grabbed the post with both hands as it came arcing down. The pig iron lost hold of his weapon, tripped over Big Tom's foot, and fell face down in the dirt. Carnes dropped the iron post on the man's head and rendered him unconscious. Meanwhile, Vincent was holding off the five comrades of the fallen one. They were not impressed with his cutlass, and they did not step back. Likewise, when Big Tom's daughter stepped forward and brandished a throwing axe her father had used in the last war, the five pig irons started to laugh. However, when Cut charged and clubbed one of the five with the butt end of his gun, all of them scattered into the shadows. The fray in the yard was over before

Ike, and the four behind him, had a chance to participate in the initial fun. Their only contribution was the singing of more verses of Ike's randy song.

Big Tom Carnes, his daughter, and Cut stood over the remaining, lifeless pig iron, while Vincent, with a lantern in hand, bent down to inspect the man's tattoo.

"Sword in a ring," Vincent confirmed. "As we figured . . ."

"These six in the yard can't be all of 'em," growled Carnes. "The rest of 'em got to be inside."

Vincent stood upright and handed the lantern back to Big Tom's daughter. He addressed the man in charge: "Shouldn't we surround the place?"

"Our number ain't strong 'nough," assessed Carnes. "We're not 'bout sneakin' in no back way. I say the first four of us barge right in and take down the remains of these damn Sons of the Sword, or whatever you want to call 'em . . . keep Ichabod and my loyal four clean for the ceremony . . . keep 'em in the yard . . . ready, if needed, for to pounce on any tattooed bastard who flees Rattoon's."

Luckily, Ike did not hear all of Big Tom's latest plan.

Vincent stepped back to persuade the Irishman to go along with it. Ike stopped singing in order to listen to his boss. He raised no complaint. He agreed to wait until he was summoned to make his grand entrance.

Without further delay, Carnes and Vincent climbed the stone steps which led to the tavern entrance. Cut and 'Becca followed close behind. Big Tom took hold of the sagging oaken door and ripped it off its hinges. He tossed the thing aside and strode into what was left of the dimly lit main room of the Rattoon establishment. The place was a wreck—tables overturned; benches and chairs scattered and splintered; shards of broken glass, red ware, utensils, and artifacts strewn about on the blood-stained floor. Worst of all was the scene in the darkest corner of the room where Rat, the tavern keep on duty, sat alone. He was slumped over the boards of a table. His moaning drew the newcomers immediately to his location. 'Becca lifted her lantern and gasped at what she saw. The pig irons had beaten old Rat severely about his head. What was worse were his hands—they had been spread to the far ends of the table and pinned to the boards by knife blades buried deep in the wood.

"Set Mister Rat free!" ordered Carnes, quick as he could.

Cut and Vincent jumped to the task. They wrested the knives from the boards. This caused Rat to scream as mightily as he could. Vincent caught the poor man before he collapsed to the floor. Rat went back to moaning before 'Becca returned from the bar with strong liquor to splash on the keep's wounds.

After dousing the wounds, she served Rat a drink to chase away the pain.

"Where's the knot of rogues who did this to you, Rat?" asked Carnes with seething urgency.

"Game room in the back," rasped Rat behind clenched teeth. "They'll be takin' turns at Good Mary 'n Little Ned . . . at least six of 'em . . ."

Carnes waved his three companions in the direction of the source of muffled cursing and laughing. This time he put his shoulder to the flimsy door which was supposed to provide some privacy for gamblers and sporting men. The door exploded off its hinges. Four men, holding down a naked Mary Woods on the large gaming table, held mouths agape and feet frozen in place. The man astride Good Mary did not bother to look up from his endeavors. The pair of pig irons, struggling to keep hold of a shirtless little Ned in a corner of the room, let go of the boy and reached for their long knives. Cut was on them in an instant, slamming the butt of his musket-rifle into their faces. He dropped them before the blades could be pulled from their belts. Little Ned slipped under Cut's blows and ran to 'Becca's arms. Tears trickled from his eyes, but he did at cry.

At the same time, Big Tom grabbed the pig iron atop Good Mary and threw him against the two holders on his right. All three toppled to the floor. Vincent slashed at the other two with his cutlass. One of them fell back with a deep gash across his hand. The other—an ugly cut on his cheek. But these two managed to pull dirks from their belts. They started forward against young Wetherill. Carnes was busy pulling Good Mary off the gaming table. She pushed him away and crawled over to 'Becca and Little Ned. The minehost from Amboy turned his attention to Vincent's plight. He lifted the huge table on end and flipped it on top of the pair menacing Vincent. The weight of the table sent the knife-wielders crashing to the floor.

Big Tom wasted no time with formalities: "Daughter, take Good Mary up the stairs 'long with her Ned . . . make 'em presentable for the ceremony . . . for the triumphant return of the Earl of Ballynary!"

'Becca jumped to the detail and escorted the brave victims to the stairs.

"We must get these bastard pig irons to the main room and prepare 'em for the esteemed noble's return," instructed Carnes. "Four of 'em are out cold and three are too sore to rise. We must remove their stinking garments and bind 'em so they can't run. Hurry, lads, the Earl is not a patient man!"

When the chore was done and the bound men were dragged into the main room, they were forced to sit on the filthy floor by the hearth. Carnes sent Cut to bind and fetch the man who had been brained by the iron post. He also told Cut to alert Ike that the welcome ceremony was about to begin. Before Hancock returned with the lifeless pig iron, his boss had strengthened the blaze at the hearth with pieces of broken furniture. Big Tom told Vincent to leave his cutlass blade in the embers. Young Wetherill did so without questioning the move. Carnes placed a few of the knife blades, taken from the pig irons, in the fire. He did not explain his actions. It was obvious what he intended to do.

Shortly thereafter, Good Mary, with hair twisted into a semblance of order and dressed in her nicest blue-and-gray overgown, returned to participate in Big Tom's mad ceremony. A fully-clothed Little Ned clung to her side. Both were asking about the fate of Ike Higgins. Vincent assured them that the Irishman was in fine fettle, but had been delayed at the dock. Vincent claimed that Mister Higgins would be making his presence known any minute now. Good Mary was still concerned about her Ike and asked for the truth about his condition. Vincent reassured her that Ike was in better shape than when he left her. However, he gave no details. He was more concerned about Good Mary's condition, but he dared not ask. Like Little Ned, Ike's woman had not cried during her ordeal. She looked the same as she always did—corn blue eyes softened by sadness and difficult circumstance; shoulders stooped from too many years of toil; hands calloused and cut from having to claw her way through life. But she carried herself with a coarse dignity. Good Mary remained resolute to the core. There was no adversary fierce enough, or strong enough, to discourage her.

She was a survivor. Ike needed her for that reason—a compass so true, even in the worst of times. A man like Ike, who fell in and out of fortune too often, surely did not deserve Good Mary. But fate had brought them together and, soon, they would be reunited again.

Big Tom Carnes gave a sign that he was about to summon the returning noble. He stood guard over the subdued pig irons and instructed them to remain in place. His daughter was still tending to Rat's wounds. When Cut returned, both father and daughter started up the song Ike Higgins had taught them. Their voices were matched by the five men outside, who climbed the stairs and came tramping in.

"All rise!" bellowed Carnes. "The Earl of Ballynary has returned . . . triumphant in his campaign 'gainst the Sons of the Sword . . . 'gainst their various agents of evil!"

Big Tom poked and prodded his bruised and battered pig irons —made them genuflect to show respect when Ike strode into the main room. He strutted, proud as a peacock, around the room in order to show off his borrowed clothing and shoes. He gave the kneeling trouble-makers a furtive glance, then rushed over to Good Mary. The Irishman embraced her warmly. He plunked down the heavy satchel of hard-earned coins on the shaky table, which had been righted for Good Mary's use. He patted Little Ned on the head and told the boy to turn the satchel over. Good Mary's child obeyed and let the coins spill on to the boards. Cheers rang out in the destroyed room. Good Mary finally cried. She gave her man another hug, after struggling to stand.

"Don't know nothin' 'bout your fancy names for my Ike, nor do I know what your oak hearts has been up to," announced Good Mary. "But I do know what any noble 'n his loyal knights need the most at a time like this . . ."

"A steel nose drink!," exclaimed Ike.

"I'll see what's survived," declared Mary, as she limped to Rat's secret store of the best of Rattoon's brew. "A few rounds for all my handsome rescuers."

"Much as they want!" added Rat from his shadowed corner. "On the house . . . what's left of it."

"Enough of this friendly raillery," shouted Big Tom, as he forced his captives to turn and face the hearth. They obeyed while still remaining on their knees. He called for his Amboy brawlers to finish their drinks and assist him with the final chore. He invited Vincent and Cut to join the fun.

"What do you have in mind, Mister Carnes?" asked Vincent, as Good Mary brought him and Cut their first cups of corn whiskey.

"Nothin' for the squeamish," chuckled Carnes. "Long as the Constable in these parts stays away, I can finish what I started."

"He ain't comin' 'round," contributed Rat. "There's been worse trouble up river . . . Musgrove ain't comin' back till dawn."

"Good then," said Carnes. "We'll be done and gone by then."

"So what's in store?" asked a curious Vincent, who was now emboldened by a gulp of the liquid fire in his cup.

"These bastard pig irons need their tattoos removed," announced Big Tom. "Afore I lets 'em free, I have to make sure any trace of the Sons of the Sword is removed from their damn hides. They either agree, or we march 'em back down to the ferry. We'll tie 'em to their own pigs, take 'em with us to the deepest channel, and toss 'em over the side. What say you, my fallen knights?"

Mumbles and curses from the intended victims followed Big Tom's words.

"Glad to hear all you poor fish are in agreement with my methods," Carnes said. "Soon as I'm done with each of you, then you may leave . . . promisin' never to show your stinkin' heads at Rattoon's again. If you flinch from the fiery blade, then I'll keep you for drownin'. What say you, black ruffins?"

As heads nodded and mutterings of compliance were offered by the eight unlucky pig irons who had failed to avoid punishment, Carnes directed his brawlers and guests to unloosen the bindings on the captives. He prepared two of them, while his compatriots took care of one each. Big Tom took hold of the arm of his first victim, held it close to the hearth flames, grabbed the hilt of Vincent's cutlass, and pressed the heated blade on the flesh which held the onerous tattoo. The man cried out even before his flesh started to burn and bubble, but he did not flinch. Carnes let go of the man's trembling arm and left him to his whimpering. He placed the sword blade back in the flames and reached for the second man. Big Tom selected a broad knife and repeated the ruining process. The results were the same.

The four Amboy brawlers took their turns, as did Vincent and Cut. When they were done, no tattoo was recognizable.

Carnes allowed the punished men to dress in the clothes which had been used to bind them. As they did so, he inspected the damage done to each tattoo and gave them a warning about staying away from Rattoon's. Before he let them file out of the place, Big Tom gave final instructions:

"If I am summoned here again by the Earl of Ballynary, you louts, I intend to burn more than tattoos. All your hangin' parts will be fair game. Tell your brothers of my intentions . . . tell 'em to come in peace with hard coin, or don't come at all."

These words were followed by compliant mutterings and mumbles, but no curses. All wild horses in the room had been tamed . . . for the moment. As the scarred ones filed out, Ike started up his song again. Others joined in. Good Mary Woods laughed.

Dawn was breaking above the low and sluggish South River, as Vincent and Cut approached the Old Bridge near Spot's Woods. They had passed through the Barrens of Wickatunk without incident. With but two pole lanterns on the waggon and a well-rested dray team of bay Shires—Thor and Hercules—pulling a full load of barrels of iron water, the two men had still made good time. They had shown no fear in the worst dark stretches. No howling beast nor ghastly moon shadow scared them. Even the horses showed restraint. Man and beast had been through hell before leaving Rattoon's. The pair of south county men had been tempted and tested by depravity several times. They had triumphed over evil more times than not. They had been less than virtuous upon occasion—Cut moreso than Vincent. They had lied out of necessity—Vincent moreso than Cut. Their adventure had not made them better men. They were far from flawless heroes. However, they now possessed a heightened sense of confidence in facing adversity. All such ruminations about the import of each success and each shortcoming did not matter anymore. Leave that for others to determine. What really mattered was quite simple—Vincent and Cut were almost home.

"No rain coming," observed Vincent, as he studied the brightening sky and kept his Spanish barb at the pace of the dray team.

Cut did not respond. He was concentrating on stones and ruts leading to the bridge. He knew the weather would take care of itself. Neither he nor young Wetherill could do anything about it. Cut wished it would not rain until after a good night's sleep with his wife. She would certainly be in a frisky mood after he showed her the Spanish coins in his new pouch, some of which he found in the ruins at Rattoon's. Yes, Cut was glad for the lack of a pour. The road taking him home to his eager wife was rutty, but it was fast and dry. The way-going this time seemed the fairest and finest. All signs pointed to it being a bright autumn day. Cut was satisfied with the progress made so far and the prospects for what lay ahead. He had no reason to respond to young Wetherill's comment.

There was little traffic on the bridge, and there was no delay in crossing to the other side of the river. Vincent decided to stop and rest the horses for a spell. The two men were already a day late in getting back, so a few moments by the river bank would not matter much.

Cut pulled out his flask from his coat, took a swig, and passed it down to Vincent. Young Wetherill accepted it gladly and took a few sips before handing it back to its owner.

"Filled mein flask at Rattoom's when we was helping to straighten up the place," Cut commented, before taking another swig.

"Quite resourceful of you," praised Vincent.

"T'was Good Mary Woods who suggested I fill mein flask with the best rum in the house."

"That you did," grinned Vincent. "I'll testify to it."

"Yup," said Cut, "the best." He took another swig and returned the flask to its hiding place.

"What else did you gain from our little adventure?" asked Vincent, not anticipating much from the taciturn German.

"Enough gold for to purchase my own dray horse from Long

Bridge . . . and keep my wife happy for a winter," responded Cut. "No need to be asking for Thor or Hercules anymore."

"Anything else?" continued Vincent.

Cut thought awhile and then said: "Satisfaction in finding three bastards responsible for such evil . . . made me feel like I had some purpose in life . . . done some black things in the past, so helping to bring down Fagan, Spolden, 'n Fairchild balances the ledger, wouldn't you say?"

Vincent agreed with Cut. They had done the world a favor by ridding it of a few of the Devil's own minions. Their methods would be considered questionable by the authorities. However, those authorities would never know the truth. Vincent told Cut that John Wetherill would be the only man who would learn the truth.

"Your father ain't going to believe all which'd transpired up north," surmised Cut. "I still can't believe most of it, meinself."

"Just don't be prattling about our adventure to anyone," ordered Vincent, "especially your wife."

Cut laughed and replied: "She wouldn't believe a word of it anyways. I'll tell her of rescuing the Irishman from the Captain's barn 'n the successes in delivering the brandy 'n fetching the iron water . . . nothing else."

"Good," said Vincent with finality.

"Got one regret, though," added Cut.

"And what is that?" Vincent asked.

"We did all these good 'n not so good things in so few days," said Cut, "but we failed to come up with a name for our hunt club."

It was Vincent's turn to chuckle. He was surprised at Cut's seriousness about a subject he had given little thought to and, quite honestly, had forgotten about. "You're right, Cut," admitted Vincent. "Let's decide on a worthy secret name right now, and then complete our journey."

"Can't call ourselves the Sons of Dawn or the Sons of the Sword," said Cut dismissively.

"Already taken and wallowing in dark repute," added Vincent. "We need a name which represents our purpose in life . . . what we stand for . . . such as accomplishing dangerous chores most others shy from . . . and doing so in secret without fuss or feathers . . ."

"Rat-catchers," offered Cut. "A name suited for the likes of us . . . taken from what the Afric wench used for her dog, which'd I nursed back to life."

"I like your idea, Cut. After all, we were able to rid the world of a few rats," observed Vincent, who adjusted the new bandage Good Mary Woods had applied to his head wound. He got up from his crouch position at the river bank and mounted his Spanish barb. "However, let's refine it . . . make it more dignified."

"Fine with me," said Cut.

"Good ratters are we, my friend," declared Vincent, "but we have also been called knights—loyal thanes to the Earl of Ballynary."

"You've gone too far with this naming business," interrupted Cut, with a deep frown on his unshaven face. "I'll be no part of a name smelling of Ike Higgins, 'n you know it."

"That I do," laughed Vincent. "I simply wanted to know if you changed your mind about the gloak you snatched from death more than once."

"The bog lander saved you once," said Cut, "'n I saved his arse more 'n once . . . so what . . . your take on the fellow lies the same . . . so's mein feelings 'bout him. Besides, he ain't in our hunt club . . . so it must be Ratters . . . without the good."

"The South County Ratters fine with you?" concluded Vincent.

"Yup," said Cut.

EPILOGUE

· · · · · · · · ·

John Wetherill awoke well-rested. He had arrived in Burlington, the Provincial Capital of West Jersey, late in the afternoon on the second Tuesday of November, 1773. Boss, his most dependable drover had driven Wetherill's best coach and team down from the plantation near Cross Roads, and had made good time. The trip was long and tedious, but uneventful. By the time John made it to the Blue Anchor Inn, on the corner of High and Broad Streets, he was stiff and sore . . . and dead tired. After a light supper, Wetherill retired to his room. He retrieved a large flask of iron water from his travel satchel. John took a sip. He judged it tolerable. Fortunately, Fannie had added a few of her secret spices to the iron water before boiling it. Wetherill then located the medicine that Doctor Stites had given him, and chased it down with a few swigs of Fannie's bearable concoction. He felt better, but still tired. John did a bit of reading, but fell asleep earlier than he had anticipated. He dreamed of many victories—great and small.

One had him finding a young wife, almost as pretty as Little Abia. However, this one was taller and more mature. Wetherill never got the woman's name.

Boss came to wake his master way past dawn on a cool Wednesday that hinted at the winter coming. The slave raised the one window slightly, as per instructions from his master, and opened the curtains wide to allow the bright sunlight to invade the stuffy room. Boss then saw to his master's needs and helped dress the old man in an unrushed and efficient manner. John Wetherill approved of what he saw in the mirror. He felt like a new man and praised Boss for making him look like one.

Old John was ready and eager for the opening session of the General Assembly, called finally by Governor William Franklin. All gentlemen of the Council and all gentlemen of the Assembly had come to Burlington, prepared to tackle crucial matters which would, more than likely, be addressed at this often postponed session. Quite possibly, the final showdown between the Governor and the whiggish Assemblymen over Stephen Skinner's status as Treasurer of East Jersey was going to happen. Perhaps, cooler heads would prevail. Some sort of resolve might be reached. Skinner had to resign his position in order to stand trial for the Treasury robbery in sixty-eight. It might happen soon. It had to happen.

Wetherill was ready for anything—nicely recovered from his miseries; well-prepared with proposals and petitions well-written by his daughter-in-law; all salient facts and figures set to memory; and armed with heightened optimism about challenging the Governor and his allies over the viability of that snake, Stephen Skinner. Enough was enough. No more procrastination. The time had come to finally get rid of the proprietors' darling. Skinner had to go—one way or another. With him out of the way, the Assemblymen might gain the right to select the next Treasurer. The Governor had to be convinced of this. Old John felt he was up to the task—his health was much improved and his attitude was quite positive. It was about time . . .

First, however, John had to meet with certain Assemblymen prior to the Governor's noon speech marking the opening of the first session. The preparation and planning meeting had been arranged previously and Wetherill did not want to be late for it. He proceeded down the stairs to break the fast with peers who had chosen to partake of the fare at the Blue Anchor. John hoped the elder Jacob Ford, one of the Assemblymen representing Morris County, would be among the dining guests. Wetherill wanted a private moment with the stubborn man. He wanted to clear the air about some things—namely, making sure there were no untoward rumors, innuendoes, or outright lies about his son's activities at Hibernia, the Johnson Mine, and Judge Cooper's estate. More specifically, he wanted to make sure his son's name remained untarnished and in good standing in and around the iron hills—as spotless a reputation as it was in Middlesex County. John meant to allow Jacob his say on the matter, then correct any falsehoods and misconceptions if necessary. The elder Ford was supposed to be in attendance at the morning meal. However, when Wetherill entered the feasting room and looked about, he discovered that Jacob Ford was not present.

John was greeted warmly by the whig Assemblymen who had arrived before him. James Kinsey, the aggressive legislator from Burlington and leader of the movement to oust Skinner from office, invited Wetherill to sit next to him and share a trencher of caveached trout pickled in vinegar. John accepted the invitation, partook of the trout, as well as a large serving of corn meal and head cheese. He washed it all down with a mug of Newark cider. All the while, Mister Kinsey conducted a lengthy discussion of strategies to be employed this time around. Before all was said and done, toasts to their anticipated successes were completed with mugs of coffee held high. Not one tea drinker was to be found at this gathering.

Shortly before the final toast to the King, the elder Jacob Ford shuffled in, apologized for being late, and promised to be ready for the opening session. Kinsey reviewed the key points in his strategy for the benefit of the latecomer. The plan was to stall on supporting the Governor's anticipated request for stronger laws against counterfeiters of foreign coins, and to refuse to grant more monies to supply the King's troops. Such methods would continue as long as Skinner stayed in office. A new petition demanding that the Treasurer of East Jersey be removed from office would be presented to the Governor as early as possible. After some discussion on certain particulars and vocal approval from all in attendance, Kinsey excused himself and departed with most of the Assemblymen trailing him out.

John Wetherill took the opportunity to move over to the table in the corner where Jacob Ford sat alone. After an exchange of the usual gentleman's greetings, the elder Ford apologized for his failure to meet with the Middlesex Assemblyman earlier, as had been requested by the latter.

"A miserable journey down, John," complained Ford. "Made worse by difficulties crossing at the Rariton Landing and trouble managing the descent at the Devil's Featherbed."

"My drover took the lower road, Jacob, and managed such without incident," chided Wetherill cooly. "I attribute his success to his being an accomplished teamster. My Boss has had much experience on Lawrie's Road. He knows how to make a long trip bearable."

"Wish I could say the same for my boy and the King's Highway," grumbled Ford. "'Tis always circumstances getting in the way. If not foul weather, then 'tis something else. Things never turn out as they should, John . . . never."

"Perhaps that will all change at the twenty-second Assembly," mused Wetherill.

"Doubt it much," brooded Ford, who was obviously not in a good mood. "At least for me and my kind . . . got to this town late in the night . . . could find lodging only at Chisholm's Stage House . . . then overslept . . . rushed over here half awake and full of bad vapors. If Skinner dare show his face at Calling's Court House, I shall be the person who strangles him . . . the Governor too . . ."

"Have a coffee," suggested Wetherill.

"Hate the stuff," countered Ford. "What I crave is a pot of tea . . . a steaming pot of black boo-hee . . . too bad the bay pilots are up to refusing all tea ships . . . what a pity the captains have to return their fine bricks to Rotting Place."

"Seems a necessary pity at this juncture," empathized Wetherill. "Cider then?"

"Must be the hard kind, John," insisted Ford. "Your eight-year would do me just fine . . . wake me up in an instant. The house jack here is not held in high repute. Did you bring a flask of your own?"

Wetherill gave a polite laugh and said: "Wish I had done so, Jacob, for your sake as well as mine, but my doctor has denied me that pleasure. All I've brought from home is a flask of iron water . . . for medicinal purposes."

"Not interested in such foul stuff," Ford remarked with a sour face. "I assume the tainted liquid you speak of is the lesser part of the more than generous remuneration from Judge Cooper to your impulsive and haughty son."

John Wetherill flashed a look of startled surprise. He was amazed how easily the elder Ford had stumbled upon the topic of conversation old John wanted to bring up. The Middlesex Assemblyman kept his poise, looked askance, and chose his words well:

"I meant to talk to you in private about my son's comportment during his little adventure up in the hills of your county. Thank you for reminding me to do so. My purpose in sending Vincent, on what turned out to be such a dangerous exercise, was to give him an opportunity to show he had the makings to be a leader of men. In your estimation, Jacob, how did he measure up?"

"Lacking," quipped Ford quickly. "I found him lacking as a leader. He was worth as much as a compass in an iron mine. He was full of wild ideas and full of himself. I have reservations about your Vincent ever being a good leader. He is no son I would be proud of—not after hearing about all the foolish games he played and the time he wasted in accomplishing so little."

"He is not your younger Jacob Ford," inserted Wetherill. "I'll admit that . . . but he is no Dan Fagan either."

It was the elder Ford's turn to look startled. "You play with me, John," snapped Ford angrily. "I see your son has told you more than you should know."

Wetherill called a servant over to Ford's table and ordered two plain ciders. He paid for both with real coins. Ford did not bother to thank him. Things were taking an uncomfortable turn and Wetherill did not like it.

"Vincent has always been honest with me," said Wetherill, measuring his words carefully. "He told me everything about his escapade at the end of September. The way I see it, you Fords should be grateful for having a heavy burden lifted from the family's reputation. My Vincent accomplished more than expected by anyone. He performed exceedingly well under duress, lost only two worse-for-wear quarter horses in the process, and succeeded, even though he was hamstrung by those who sought to withhold crucial information from him."

The elder Ford squirmed, but he was not about to surrender to the truth. He decided on another path: "I can understand why a father would give a son more credit than he deserves, John. I would do so with my own Jacob. But, from what I have been told by more than one source, the coarse German fellow, Hancock, brought down that prodigal, Dan Fagan. The mad man, Jack Spolden, so I've been informed, dispatched the one responsible for the three murders 'round Morris Town. I also learned of some agent for royal investors taking credit for Spolden's demise. Besides all that, your son never located the monies connected to the Treasury robbery . . . never found any evidence which might clear Sam Ford's name. So that leaves your son with little to show for his efforts, other than unwarranted money gained from Judge Cooper and a few barrels of iron water. I must conclude that your son did not come close to proving himself a leader of men. Perhaps, in the future he will be sorely tested and come through for you. It did not happen this time 'round."

"Might the same thing be said for your sons?" Wetherill said. "None of them seem prepared for what may come."

"I disagree, John," countered Ford. "I can state, without wavering, that my son, Jacob, has already proved himself many times over. He is as ready and eager to fight for a just cause as we are. The other son, the one you insist on reminding me about, has never been acknowledged by me as my own. He prepared himself for a life of crime and succeeded. . . now he is dead."

"What if I told you your bastard son got away," posed Wetherill, "and is very much alive?"

"Damn you, John!" exclaimed Ford, loud enough to interest the few remaining patrons in the Blue Anchor. They looked up and stared at the man who raised his voice. "Stop playing with me. I take it back. Your son proved himself a fine organizer of men and a clever planner. Now cease and desist in ruining my day with falsehoods."

"What if I told you the Prophet, Jack Spolden, being the resourceful fellow he is, led those trapped in the Johnson Mine to safety by using a secret way out?" said Wetherill.

"You have no proof of either rogue getting away!" exclaimed Ford, just as loud as before.

"Nor do you have proof to the contrary," Wetherill said. "You have come to believe what you want to believe, Jacob, because it suits your needs."

"Next, you'll tell me Tom Ward, Morrell's foreman, is not the murderer of three innocents," stammered Ford.

"Indeed I will, for I am convinced he was falsely accused by those who sought a quick and convenient end to the matter."

"Nonsense," insisted Ford. "Everybody knows it was Ward who dispatched Jack Redmon, the buck fiddler, and Nettie's boy. He was out to get us Fords next, if he, by chance, had lived long enough to carry out his version of lex talionis."

"My son was determined to make sure that did not happen," said Wetherill calmly. "He succeeded in preventing the true murderer from striking again. You should at the least express a modicum of gratitude for my son's efforts. Vincent saved the Fords from bitter grief and horrible loss."

"That Spolden fellow dispatched the murderer," insisted Ford. "I cannot thank the so-called Prophet because he is now a trapped haint in a mineshaft. Your Vincent should not take credit for something he did not do. I think I should take back anything positive I may have said about your son."

"You are wavering, Jacob," sighed Vincent, while flashing a light grin. "This is so unlike you. Perhaps you may allow me one more opportunity to convince you that things are not as they seem."

"Try me," snickered Ford, as he took a sip of his cider.

"Please allow me one more question."

"What might that be, John?" hissed Ford.

"Whatever happened to the fellow you endorsed so strongly to be a Constable under Sheriff Stiles?" asked Wetherill. "Rumor has it this other bastard son of yours turned prodigal again and disappeared . . ."

Jacob Ford glowered at his peer, but he did not curse this time. A puzzled look crossed his chiseled face. Then he blinked, regained his composure, and responded crisply: "You wallow too long in rumors and lies, John. The lad you speak of is not from my loins. 'Tis none of your business who sired him. I took him under my wing as a favor to a distant relative of mine. Let's leave it at that. It is true that Zachariah Fairchild disappeared about the time your son returned to Judge Cooper's place, but there is no reason to connect him with the murders. Zachariah is a good man, but one with a troubled past . . . one sorely missed . . . but he has been replaced by a better man . . . one I recommended only last month."

"And who might the lucky fellow be?" Wetherill asked.

"The one true hero in all that transpired under the waxing harvest moon," preferred Ford. "My batter bull, Jimmy Hornbeck—he's the one who told me the truth about what took place in the iron hills. I am proud to say that Mister Hornbeck has been handsomely rewarded for his efforts."

"So his account of the events up north is what you accept then," prodded Wetherill.

"Yes," said Ford. "An account confirmed almost in its entirety by Judge Cooper, whom I trust as a brother."

"Then I must apologize for challenging your convictions on all this, Jacob," said Wetherill calmly. "I thank you for being so forthcoming with me on such an intemperate subject. I shall consider your version of events as closer to the truth than mine. My purpose in confronting you was to draw you out and make sure your account is close enough to pass as truth."

"My account is truth, John," said Ford. "No need to question me further. What's done is done. 'Tis best to forget the whole thing. You keep your secrets . . . I'll keep mine. We've more important things to attend to . . . hard work ahead . . . must throw ourselves into making things better for our sons and daughters."

"Agreed," said Wetherill, as he struggled to rise from his chair. "I have a feeling that the next rebellion will be far from the false one, which is now dead."

"With the Prophet out of the way," added Ford, rising with little difficulty and not bothering to drain his mug of inferior cider. "Our cause must, and will, gain a better chance of succeeding."

"Let us pray the Sons of the Sword never distract us again," concluded Wetherill.

"Unfortunately, there will always be distractions," predicted Ford.

Wetherill could not argue with his peer's wisdom. He said nothing more. The two Assemblymen donned their tricorns and heavy coats. They strolled out, shoulder to shoulder, into the cool, crisp November air. They headed directly up the street to the Court House for the opening session of the General Assembly. The words exchanged, as they slowly made their way, centered on the success of the harvest hunt, conducted by the Sons of Dawn, and the problems John Wetherill was having in preparing the iron water for brewing. Such were the idle concerns of two provincial gentlemen whose gravest matters and challenging decisions lay ahead. Neither man realized how difficult their situation would be in just a few years . . . neither man imagined losing a son to the cause for independency . . . in just a few years.

BACKGROUND NOTES

· ·

Iron Water, a Wetherill Mystery

Adventure Forge—In 1763, Samuel Ford, Jr., started the Hibernia Iron Works. It was located along the Whippany River in the hills of northern Morris County, four miles north of Rockaway, New Jersey. In 1765, he built the Adventure furnace at the site. Due to financial difficulties, Ford was forced to sell shares of the business to William Alexander, James Anderson, and Benjamin Cooper. The forge was operated successfully for many years thereafter.

Albermarle, Refugees of—In the mid-17th century, a group of Anabaptists in the Virginia colony were being harassed and tormented. Their belief in the denial of all ordination and their insistence that any true believer was worthy of preaching did not sit well with the Protestant establishment. A number of these victims of hatred and persecution crossed over to neighboring North Carolina. The majority of them settled in Albermarle County, which was named after George Menck, the first Duke of Albermarle and one of eight Lord Proprietors of the province of Carolina—hence, the use of 'Refugees of Albermarle' for the name of one of John Spolden's secret cells.

Alexander, William (aka: Lord Stirling)—This military hero of the Revolutionary War was born in the city of New York in 1726. He died in 1783. He was well-educated and proficient in mathematics and astronomy. Alexander was also a successful businessman. He married Sarah Livingston in 1747. She was the daughter of Philip Livingston and sister of Governor William Livingston. They had three children. Alexander sought the Earl of Stirling title in the late 1750's. This title had become dormant after the death of Henry Alexander, the 5th Earl of Stirling. William Alexander's father did not seek the title and, upon his death, the son lay claim to it. His claim was through the 'heir male collateral' since inheritance by proximity of blood was in doubt. However, the claim was settled in William's favor in a Scottish juried court in 1759. The next step, though ill-advised, was to petition the House of Lords to advance his claim, make it forever legal, and entitle him to vast land holdings in America. Unfortunately, the men called upon to testify William's right to the Stirling claim did not prove persuasive to the House of Lords. Thus, the claim to be the next Lord Stirling remained in limbo for years. This did not deter Alexander from using the title in America. With or without it, he became a wealthy and influential man. He invested heavily in mining and agricultural pursuits, such as viticulture and winemaking, and lived the life of a Scottish nobleman. That led to mounting debt and difficulty maintaining his affluent lifestyle. During this time he was building a grand estate in Basking Ridge(aka: Basker Ridge) in Bernards Township. Upon its completion, he sold his home in New York and moved to New Jersey. Throughout his life, William Alexander was a heavy drinker. Late in life he fell into poor health and was plagued by gout and rheumatism. His death in January of 1783 was just months before the official end of the war.

Allen's Town (aka: Allen Town)—This colonial community is located on the western boundary of Monmouth County, New Jersey. It borders Upper Freehold Township and Robbinsville Township. This town was named after Nathan Allen, who settled near York Road (pka: Main Street) in 1706. He operated three mills along Doctor's Creek. Allen's Town was a convenient stop for stage wagon passengers traveling to and from Philadelphia and New York on the Lower Road. The location was roughly halfway between Burlington and Perth Amboy.

Allstedt, Covenanters of—In the small town of Allstedt, in Saxony, Germany, in the early 16th century, Thomas Muntzer was appointed Preacher at St. John's Church. It was here he developed his radical Anabaptist stance against the Roman Catholic Church and Martin Luther. In his preachings in German, he accused both of being in league with "snakes" (priests) and "eels" (nobles). Such rogues and scoundrels had to be punished for grave transgressions and kept from "creaturely things." Thus, he formulated his "Allstedt Covenant" and encouraged his Covenanters to take up weapons and punish the evil ones. At this time he married a nun and had several of his books printed. By 1524, Muntzer was losing support in Allstedt and he had to slip out of town. He brought his message of the "Anabaptist Sword" elsewhere. The 18th century prophet, John Spolden, revived the name 'Covenanters of Allstedt' in naming one of his secret cells after them.

Alten—A hamlet on the banks of the Rockaway River, south of Hibernia, New Jersey, was named after the Alten family. This settlement was a section of old Whippany (aka: Whippenny) Township in Morris County. It no longer exists as a viable community.

Amboy (aka: Perth Amboy)—The name for this city in New Jersey evolved from the Lenape word—'ompoge,' which meant 'level ground.' It was combined with the English name 'New Perth' after it was settled in 1684, and named in honor of James Drummond, Earl of Perth, who was an associate of a company of Scottish proprietors. Perth Amboy served as the capital of East Jersey from 1684 until the union with West Jersey in 1702. From then on it served as an alternate capital, sharing honors with Burlington until the Revolutionary War.

Amboy Spaw—A mineral spring of popular repute was located near the road that served as a dividing line between Woodbridge and Perth Amboy. It came to be known as the Amboy Spaw in the 18th century. In the 1770's, according to the New Jersey Archives, a 'new and convenient bath' was erected there in the fashion of a German spaw (the German word for spa).

Anabaptist—This term refers to a member of certain Protestant sects that believe infant baptism to be invalid. Only true adult believers can be baptized. The term 'Anabaptist' literally translates to 're-baptized,' or 'adults baptizing each other.' Such a practice started in Europe in the early 1500's. At that time, as part of the radical Reformation, Anabaptists also advocated social and economic reforms starting with a complete separation of church and state. They sought to do away with tithing, usury, and military service. They also denied the viability of elaborate church bureaucracy. Instead, decision-making power rested with the entire congregation. No government or hierarchical church could coerce the people into thinking one way or another. The majority of Anabaptists believed that pacifism was the path to be taken. However, in the 16th century, there existed a faction of revolutionary Anabaptists who resorted to violence to achieve their goals. They were led by prophetic spiritualists, such as Thomas Muntzer, who saw the external world as impure and unjust. Church and state had to be purified by being destroyed. The millennial kingdom was imminent and the righteous had to take up the good sword of Gideon (aka: the obrigkeit) to free the poor and oppressed from the two swords of evil—the civil regnum and the ecclesiastical sacerdotium. In the process, both the Catholic hierarchy and reformation Protestant elite had to be overthrown in order for the apocalyptic revolution to succeed. After the failure of the radical Anabaptist at Munster, Anabaptists suffered much persecution. Several pacifist groups survived, however, and many migrated to other locations. Groups such as the Mennonites and the Amish settled in North America.

Anarchos of Zeno—Around 300 B.C., Zeno of Citium, the founder of Stoicism, gained inspiration from the Cynics—Diogenes of Sinope and Crates of Thebes—and developed his singular concept of the ideal utopian society. This was a critical response to coercive political institutions and the hierarchical social relationships of his day. Plato and Aristotle were not amused. Taking the premise set forth by Aristippus—"the wise should not give up liberty to the state"—, Zeno outlined a republic in the state of 'an archos,' meaning 'without rule.' There was no need for state structures. They were to be replaced by the moral law of the individual, following the instincts of sociability. The Anarchos of Zeno was acknowledged much later by thinkers such as Francois Rabelais, Etienne de La Boetie, Louis Armand, Edmund Burke, and William Godwin. In the New World, NativeAmericans were perceived by like-minded anarchists as prime examples of what Zeno had proposed. In reality, the Native American structure was far removed from the radical ideas of a number of German immigrants who came to the American colonies in the 18th century.

Aquakinunk—The Lenape Indians gave the name Aquakinunk, or Acquack-anonk, to an area along the Passaic River. The original meaning was 'a place in a rapid stream where fishing is done with a net,' or 'a place by the lamprey stream.' This area was first settled by Dutch traders in 1678. A township was formed by the British in 1693. It became part of Passaic County when the new county was created in 1837. It is now Clifton, New Jersey.

Arabian—Verdine Elsworth owned several racing stallions and regularly entered them in races at the Powles Hook oval in New Jersey. His most prized horse was 'Arabian,' which was named after the original English 'Arabian,' allegedly the best stallion of its time.

Arnold's Tavern—Jacob Arnold operated a tavern on the Morristown green, starting in 1760. He continued to operate his establishment throughout the Revolutionary War. His place served as George Washington's headquarters for a time during the early years of the war. Over time, ownership changed hands and the tavern was later called Freeman's, Hayden's, and Duncan's. The 20 Park Place site remains a landmark to this day.

Arthur Kull—This tidal strait and major navigational channel separates Staten Island from mainland New Jersey. It is more commonly referred to as the Arthur Kill. The name derives from the Dutch, 'Achter Kill,' which translates to 'back channel' or 'waterway behind the island.' A 'kille' refers to a riverbed, water channel, or stream. The British called it 'Cull Bay.' The Kill is ten miles long and connects Raritan Bay to Newark Bay.

Axum, Princess of—In ancient times, the Kingdom of Axum (or Aksum) in northeast Africa developed into a vital and thriving empire. This trading nation, in what is present day Ethiopia and Eritrea, flourished from 100-940 A.D. During the reign of Ezana (320-360 A.D.), the son of Ella Amida and Eofya, Christianity was adopted as the state religion. This kingdom was the alleged home of the Queen of Sheba and the final resting place of the Ark of the Covenant. Rachel Hager's claim to royalty, based on the tales her mother passed on to her, probably can be traced back to Ezana's ruling family.

Balcock, _____—This lesser-known criminal, operating in the northeast American colonies in the latter half of the 18th century, was remembered only by his surname. According to the NJ Archives, he had some connection with Samuel Ford and his counterfeiting operation.

Ballynary, Baron of—Ike Higgins was given this title, in mocking jest, by his associates. He claimed descent from Irish King Niall of Tara (c. 440 A.D.), since the patriarch of the O'Higgins noble clan, Sean Duff O'Higgins (c. 1600), wed a daughter of the O'Conor royal family of Ballin Tuber Castle in Connacht. The O'Conor clan claimed direct descendency from Niall of the Nine Hostages. Sean Duff O'Higgins was known as the Gaelic 'Baron of Bally-Nary'; thus, the title was 'assigned' to Ike Higgins.

Balthazar—This biblical name was given to one of the sons of Judge Daniel Cooper's slave cook. It was the name of one of the three Wise Men who traveled from the east to pay homage to the newborn Christ. In the ancient Phoenecian tongue, the name 'Balat-Shar-Usur' translates to 'Baal protects the King.'

Bannock Loaf—This flat, quick bread, usually large and round, was made from unleavened barley or oatmeal dough. It is probably Celtic in origin, but the name may come from the Latin, 'panicium,' meaning 'baked dough,' and 'panis,' meaning 'bread.' The Native Americans in the north also had a similar bread called 'muqpauraq.'

Banyan—This garment (also spelled 'banian') served as a lounging jacket or short dressing gown. It originated in India where its name comes from Gujarati—the 'vaniyo' was worn by merchants. Europeans referred to it as a morning gown, robe de chambre, or nightgown. It was loose-fitting, t-shaped or kimono-like, and made of cotton, linen, or silk. It was meant to be worn only in the home in Europe and North America, but occasionally it was used for informal street wear.

Barbadoes Neck—New Barbadoes Neck was the name applied to the peninsula between the lower Hackensack and Passaic Rivers. The Native Americans called this area 'Megh gectecock,' or 'where May-apples grow.' The Dutch called it 'Achter Col,' meaning 'rear mountain pass' or 'behind the ridge.' In the 1660's, the British took control of the area. Major William Sandford obtained a crown grant of 30,000 acres at this spot and named it New Barbadoes, after the island of his former home.

Barracks at Perth Amboy—The lodging for most of the British soldiers stationed in the capital of East Jersey was known as the 'Old Barracks.' During the French and Indian War, it was the largest such facility in the American colonies. It was located at the head of Barracks Street where troops paraded and drilled daily.

Barrett, _____—The original surname, claimed by the Prophet's reinsman and cook, was 'Barrett.' He never revealed his original first name. Instead, he favored the nick-name, 'One-Eye.' This was due to losing an eye in a fight. He was mistakenly called 'Mister Parrot.'

Baskeridge—The estate of William Alexander (aka: Lord Stirling) was located near the village of Baskeridge (pka: Basking Ridge, New Jersey}. This unincorporated community is located within Bernards Township in the Somerset Hills region of Somerset County. It was originally settled in the 1720's by British and Scottish people escaping religious persecution.

Batter Bull—Quite possibly this is a contrived expression related to a 'batman,' meaning an 'officer's servant,' from the French 'bat,' meaning 'pack saddle man.' Jacob Ford, Sr., used the expression to describe Jimmy Hornbeck as a 'faithful man known for his courage'—in other words, a 'bull of a batman' or 'batter bull.'

Bergen Meadows—This low, mostly flat, marshy area, now referred to as the Hackensack Meadowlands or Jersey Meadowlands, is located in North Jersey above where the Passaic and Hackensack Rivers flow into Newark Bay. The early Dutch settlers cleared the cedar forests from the area and used dikes to drain the land. Meadows of salt hay were created. One of the higher elevations in Bergen Meadows was Snake Hill (pka: Laurel Hill or Fraternity Rock), an outcropping of igneous rock, jutting 150 feet above the Meadowlands. Colonists avoided this site due to the number of black snakes found there.

Bier Right—The Law of the Bier was an ancient European custom of parading the one accused of murder past the victim. The accused was found guilty if, upon touching the deceased, the corpse bled or moved. If the corpse had no reaction, then the accused was considered innocent of the crime and set free. The Bier Right was occasionally employed in the early days of the North American colonies, but soon died out as a viable legal practice.

Black River—This tributary of the North Branch of the Raritan River in New Jersey is known as the Lamington River downstream of Pottersville. At James Eaton's house at Black River, several miles west of Morristown, there once was a starting point for a stage wagon run to Powles Hook.

Blue Anchor Inn—The Sign of the Blue Anchor on the south-west corner of High and Broad Streets in Burlington, New Jersey, may have been established before 1740. John Hider was the earliest known proprietor. This 'publick house' was noted for its food and drink, and a place for Whigs to meet and exchange ideas. It is not to be confused with other Blue Anchor taverns, such as the one in Philadelphia, Pennsylvania, and the one in Winslow Township, New Jersey.

Bog-Lander—In colonial times, a man from Ireland was often referred to as 'Bog-Lander,' or boglander, which described a person from the damp, misty island of large bogs.

Boo-Hee—This popular tea in colonial times was also called 'Black Boo-Hee.' It originated from the Wu-I Hills of the Fukian Province in China. The Bohea leaves were the larger, less-expensive ones lower down on the branch. They provided a distinctive, light smoky flavor. In the colonies, the Bohea brand was considered a high quality tea. The majority of tea destroyed in the 1770's during the protests in the American colonies was the Bohea kind.

Book Town—The location of this small village in New Jersey during colonial times was west of Horse Neck on the banks of the Passaic River, near the confluence with the Rockaway River. This area is now the northeastern section of East Hanover.

Boss—There was a slave named 'Boss' mentioned in John Wetherill's will. However, this was a mere youth in 1784. The one mentioned in the story may have been the father of the one cited in the will.

Bottle Hill—This small community in New Jersey during the British colonial period was located just south of Mor-

ristown and north of Springfield. It was established around 1715. In 1739, when Morris County was established, this community was split between Hanover Township and Morris Township. After several more changes, this community finally changed its name to Madison in 1834.

Boyd, _____—One of the counterfeiters, associated with the New England gang of Stephen Waterman, John Swan, and Noah Colton, was a man remembered only by his last name. His 'confession,' along with other such collaborative accounts, led to the apprehension of Samuel Ford and members of his gang of counterfeiters in 1773. This resulted in Ford being charged with the Treasury Robbery of 1768.

Brown, Timothy—One of Judge Cooper's house servants is a prototype character. He represents the numerous Redemptioners who came from Dublin, Ireland, in search of a better life. This one carries a color surname that was given to his ancestors by English conquerors during the early colonial period.

Bruder, Karl—This enigmatic character worked as an agent for the London-based American Iron Company. He served as a spy and trouble-shooter for certain investors in the business and reported directly to them. He was able to infiltrate the notorious Spolden/Fagan banditti organization, which was harassing mines and forges in northern Jersey. He was also successful in causing its demise.

Buck—One of Judge Cooper's stable slaves carried this name. It was a quite common name for an African male in servitude in colonial times. The name was usually reserved for a large, strong slave.

Budd, Barnaby—This Morris County doctor had his first name spelled several different ways in the archival sources—Barnabas, Bernardus, Bern, and Barny. He came from a well-respected Hanover Family, wed Phebe Wheeler, and set up a medical practice. He was related to Dr.

Stacy Budd, one of the founders of the New Jersey Medical Society. This put him in good standing in his community. He was able to acquire several landholdings and give the outward appearance of being well off. However, debts through bad business deals allowed him to be drawn into Samuel Ford's counterfeiting scheme. Budd got caught, along with other 'reputable' men in the community, and was scheduled to be executed in 1773. Due to some folks in high places vouching for his character and good reputation, Dr. Budd was granted a reprieve and his life was spared. He went on to serve as surgeon for General Wind's Brigade during the Revolutionary War, but three months into his military service he contracted putrid fever and died.

Budd, James—This Budd appears to have been no relation to Dr. Barnaby Budd. He was a career criminal and a member of a gang of counterfeiters who came from Rhode Island. He allegedly had some dealings with Samuel Ford in New York and New Jersey. His testimony, along with other members of the gang, connected Ford with the Treasury Robbery of 1768.

Burke's Idea—Foundational thinking that led to modern anarchism can be traced to the ruminations of Edmund Burke (1729-1797). His tract, published in 1756, entitled 'A Vindication of Natural Society' has been interpreted as an attempt to justify anarchism. What Burke was probably doing was making a deistic attempt to base religion on reason without reliance on revelation, tradition, or ecclesiastical authority. Burke was an Irish statesman, who was born in Dublin, moved to London, and was a member of the House of Commons. He aligned himself with the Whigs. He became a noted philosopher, political theorist, and author. His famous quotes included: "Those who don't know history are destined to repeat it" and "No one could make a greater mistake than he who did nothing because he could do only a little."

Burlington—In 1676, West Jersey proprietors purchased thirty miles of riverfront land from the Lenape Indians. English settlers, most of whom were Quakers, began settling there the following year. They named their chief settlement Burling's Town, allegedly after the English east coast town of Bridlington. The Jersey town was incorporated in 1693 and re-incorporated by Royal Charter in 1733. It served as the capital of West Jersey, starting in 1702. When West Jersey was combined with East Jersey, the colony still had two capitals. Burlington shared this status with Perth Amboy.

Burnet, Dan—The stage wagon captain, called 'Windy' by his friends and associates, operated his 'flying machine' from Morristown to Powles Hook at least once a week. His route started at the Haynes Tavern at sunrise, to Christopher Wood's Tavern in Hanover, to Ellis Cook's Tavern, to Munn's Tavern at Newark Mountain, and then to Powles Hook in one day. He would return early in the morning the next day and arrive at Morristown by nightfall. Burnet's nickname was earned from his propensity for spinning long-winded yarns rife with falsehoods and exaggerations.

Burnet, Henry—This man served as a stand-in tavern host at Haynes Inn in Morristown, New Jersey. Henry was related to Dan Burnet—probably his brother.

Burnet, Solomon—One of the Burnet brothers may have served as a Constable in Morristown, New Jersey. The name 'Solomon' was assigned to him in order to differentiate him from Dan and Henry.

Cabbage Head—One who was deemed a fool or inexperienced was often called a cabbage head in colonial times. The expression also referred to a person of German descent.

Campbell, Billy—An apprentice for Stephen Skinner, Treasurer of East Jersey under Governor William Franklin, was the first to discover the robbery of

Treasury monies at Skinner's mansion in Perth Amboy in 1768. His name was William Campbell, but he was commonly known as Billy. He appeared to give testimony about the robbery on July 25, 1768, before Chief Justice Smyth. Campbell was never accused of taking part in the robbery.

Carnes, Thomas—The minehost at the Landing Tavern and Inn in Perth Amboy, New Jersey, was popularly known as 'Big Tom' Carnes. He was the son of Richard Carnes (c 1706-1764) and a lifetime resident of the city. Due to his size and strength, he was feared and respected by all who knew him.

Carson Brothers—Charles and Joseph Carson both lived in the Cross Roads area of Middlesex County. They were neighbors of the Wetherills and the Hancocks. They were members of Vincent Wetherill's informal hunt club.

Castor Cap—This type of cap or hat was popular in the 17th and 18th centuries. It was originally made from beaver (genus—castor) fur. The spelling 'caster' was sometimes used.

Caveached—The pickling of fillet of mackeral and other kinds of fish in vinegar was referred to as 'caveached' in colonial times. The term comes from the Spanish 'escabeche,' meaning pickled.

Charlotteburg—In the 18th century, the furnace and forge on the west branch of the Pequannock River in Bergen County, New Jersey, were known as the Charlotteburg works. They were named after the wife of King George III, who was an important investor in American iron works. The man responsible for the outstanding production there was its superintendent, John Jacob Faesch. Charlotteburg, at the height of its production, was dependent on quality iron ore from the Hibernia mines, and, therefore, connected to Lord Stirling's holdings by royalties paid on tons of ore. The Charlotteburg complex burned down in 1776.

Chatham—The colonial village of Chatham, New Jersey, was established in 1710 by English settlers. The name was adopted in 1773. Chatham lies north of Springfield and south of Bottle Hill.

Chisholm's Stage House—Alexander Chisholm was the owner of a stage house in Burlington, New Jersey, in the 1770's. What was more recently called the Old Inn was previously called Chisholm's, or Chisolm's Stage House. This inn catered to stage wagon passengers on their way to either Philadelphia or points north, especially New York.

Colling's Court House—Francis Colling, or Collings, of Burlington, New Jersey, designed and built several structures there in the late 1600's. His most famous building was the hexagonal Quaker meeting house. He also built what was later used for the Burlington Court House. It was often referred to as Colling's Court House.

Collyrium Drops—A poultice for soothing eye irritation in colonial days was provided in the form of collyrium drops. The name comes from the Greek, 'kollurion.'

Colton, Noah—One of the notorious counterfeiters operating in New Jersey in the latter half of the 18th century was Noah Colton. He was captured, along with other partners in crime, on June 27, 1773. Upon being interrogated, he confessed to having knowledge of Samuel Ford's part in the East Jersey Treasury robbery.

Committees of Correspondence—The provisional patriot emergency governments established in response to negative aggressive policies by the British authorities in the thirteen American colonies were called Committees of Correspondence. They served as a viable network of communication for patriot leaders in the colonies. Committees were formed in major cities and regions of the provinces. The first originated in Boston, Massachusetts, in 1772.

It worked in conjunction with the Sons of Liberty. Instead of being secretive and resorting to force like the latter, the Committees of Correspondence sought to communicate openly, exchange information, and seek diplomatic solutions to problems. They sought to rally support for opposition against British policies and establish political union among the colonies. New Jersey was late to get organized, but eventually got theirs going prior to the outbreak of the war.

Cook, Ellis—The 'original blacksmith of Whippanong Township' turned to running the popular Cook's Tavern in the 1770's in Hanover, New Jersey. His place was a stop for stage wagons in Morris County, going to and from Powles Hook. Ellis (aka: Elias) Cook was born in 1731 and died in 1797. He was an ardent Whig and patriot activist who served on the Morris County Committee of Observation, the Provincial Council, and Committee of Safety. He later served as a Colonel in the Militia.

Cooper, Benjamin—One of the sons of Judge Daniel Cooper, of Morris County, got himself involved in the counterfeiting schemes of Samuel Ford in the 1770's. Benjamin was the third child of the union between Judge Cooper and his first wife, Grace Runyon. Benjamin's troubles began when he was a partner with Samuel Ford in the operation of the Hibernia Iron Works in the 1760's. This business venture soured and soon put the investors in the red. Ford turned to counterfeiting as a way to get out of debt. He lured several upstanding men into his scheme. They all had debts to pay. Benjamin Cooper was one of them. Eventually, he was arrested along with Dr. Budd, Samuel Haynes, and William Reynolds. They were brought to trial at a special court of Oyer & Terminer in early August of 1773. By August 14th, death sentences were handed down for all four. Lord Stirling and other men in high standing spoke in favor of Cooper, Budd, and Haynes, but not Reynolds. The three who received a punishment mitigation were respited until October 15, 1773.

Cooper's partial confession included testimony against Samuel Ford, implicating the leader of the counterfeiters in the Treasury Robbery of 1768. Cooper was eventually freed of all charges.

Cooper, Daniel—The father of Benjamin Cooper was born at sea in 1695. This Hollander came to America, settled in Piscataway, New Jersey, then moved to Long Hill on the southern edge of the Great Swamp in Morris County. Cooper wed Grace Runyon in 1726. She was related to Anne Susannah Runyon of Piscataway, who was the mother of John Wetherill. Daniel had several children by Grace, including sons Daniel, Jr., and Benjamin. Daniel, Jr., went on to serve as Sheriff in the 1760's. Benjamin was remembered as the son Daniel, Sr., had to sentence to be hung for being involved in Samuel Ford's counterfeiting scheme. After Grace Runyon died in 1755, Cooper married Jane Westbrook. After she passed away, Cooper married Grace Manning, Fannie Jones, Barbara Gibbs, and Hannah Martin in that order. Altogether, he may have sired at least eleven children and married six times. Daniel Cooper served as Justice of the Peace in the Passaic Valley from 1739 to 1759. He served as Judge in Morris County thereafter. He was known as 'a second Daniel come to judgment.' Cooper was feared by criminals of all stripes and highly respected amongst his peers.

Council, the—The upper house of the provincial government of New Jersey was called the Council. It was established in 1702, when the proprietors surrendered their right to govern in East and West Jersey. This occurred after the two Jerseys were united, under Queen Anne's rule, to form the Royal Colony of New Jersey. At this time, both the Council and the lower house Assembly were created. The twelve members of the Council were not elected but appointed by the British crown. Six were from East Jersey and six were from West Jersey. They could serve for life. The senior Councillor served as the President of the Council. The Council's powers included the appointing of judges, justices of the peace, and sheriffs. The members were the chief advisors to the Governor of the colony and usually like-minded on all matters of governance. In its final years, the Council was often at odds with the majority of members of the Assembly and the people who elected Assembly representatives. In 1776, the Royal Council was replaced by the New Jersey Legislative Council.

Court of Oyer and Terminer—The British Royal Commission conferred power to hear and determine criminal cases at home and in the colonies overseas. The term 'oyer' comes from the Anglo-French 'to hear,' and, likewise, 'terminer,' which means 'to determine.'

Cove, the—This water inlet on the east shoreline of Perth Amboy, New Jersey, served as a landing and docking point for small boats in the colonial years.

Cracknels—A light, curved biscuit, which was crisp on the outside and floury on the inside was referred to in Colonial times as a 'cracknel.' The name comes from the French 'craquelin.'

Cranberry—The village of Cranberry in the southern reaches of Middlesex County during colonial times is now known as the town of Cranbury. The original name has been attributed to the wild cranberries that grew in the area. The name was changed to its current spelling in 1869. This was a stage wagon stop on Lawrie's Road for those journeying between Perth Amboy and Burlington in colonial days.

Cross Roads—The unincorporated community of Dayton is located in South Brunswick Township, Middlesex County, New Jersey. In colonial times it was called Cross Roads, or Crossroads. Here is where Georges Road intersects with two other roads to make five corners (aka: Five Corners). On two of the corners were colonial landmarks—the Whitlock Inn and the Wetherill Tavern. The former is still standing.

Cyrus—This champion bay horse won several races for its owner, Verdine Elsworth of Powles Hook, in the 1770's. People who knew about sure bets in a horse race called this one 'a capital horse.'

Dane's Lake—An alternative name for Lake Denmark in Rockaway Township, Morris County, New Jersey, during colonial times was Dane's Lake. This body of water lies close to Picatinny Lake to the southwest and Green Pond to the northeast. A large swamp lies on the northern side of the lake.

Deutscher Bauernkrieg—The German term for the Great Peasants War in the early 16th century was 'Deutscher Bauern krieg.' This was a series of economic and religious revolts in 1524-25 that was supported by radical members of Protestant clergy. The revolts were opposed by central European nobility and the Roman Catholic Church. Martin Luther criticized the movement but took a middle course on peasant demands. Thomas Muntzer, one of the primary leaders of the radical Anabaptists sided with the peasants and provided a mystical and apocalyptic aspect to the movement. The revolts were eventually crushed because the peasants were militaristically unprepared to wage war. It is estimated that between 100,000 to 300,000 peasants lost their lives in this struggle.

Devil's Featherbed—Much of the low mountain area of Rocky Hill, on either side of the King's Highway (pka: Route 27) which separates Middlesex County from Somerset County in New Jersey, is strewn with rocks and boulders. The highest elevations of this land were referred to as the 'Devil's featherbed' in colonial times. This area is surrounded by South Brunswick Township on the east, Kingston to the south, and the Millstone River west and north.

Dickerson Mine—The largest mine in Mine Hill Township, Morris County, New Jersey, was in operation before and during the American Revolution. Before Jonathan Dickerson purchased it outright in 1779, it was known as the Suckasunny Mine and was owned by John Reading, then Joseph Kirkbridge and his descendants. Dickerson probably owned shares of several mines in the area and his name was applied in 1773 to one of them.

Dickerson's House—Captain Peter Dickerson operated a tavern in a house he purchased from Thomas Haynes in the 1770's. This Morristown, New Jersey, landmark was used as a stage wagon stop by the Burnet family at this time. Dickerson opened his establishment in October of 1773.

Dock Street Market—This historic mercantile center in Perth Amboy, New Jersey, included the general store and warehouse of Stephen Skinner. He operated a successful business there during the middle decades of the 18th century.

Duffel Coat—This garment was popular in cold weather in colonial times due to its ability to keep the wearer warm and dry. It was named after the Belgian town of Duffel, where it originated. The garment was made of a coarse woolen cloth with a thick nap. It came with a hood of heavy wool. It was fastened in the front by string loops over peg buttons. The spelling varied, such as duffle or duffil.

Durham Boat—This large wooden, flat-bottomed, double-ended vessel was used on interior waterways in North America in the middle of the 18th century. Its name came from the Durham Iron Works at Durham, Pennsylvania, where it was first used to haul freight on the Delaware River. A Durham boat could carry up to eighteen tons downstream.

East India Tea Company—The East India Company received its Royal Charter from Queen Elizabeth in 1600. The government held no shares in this company, and, therefore, had only indirect control. All shares were owned by wealthy merchants and aristocrats. The company developed a trade monopoly in Asia by opening trading posts as far away as Chi-

na. All went well, especially in the tea trade, until financial troubles in the 1770's led company directors to appeal to Parliament for financial exemptions. This led to the East India Company (aka: East India Tea Company) being exempt from tea import duties which colonial competitors still had to pay. The Tea Act of 1773 was followed by a boycott of tea by colonists in North America. The price of tea dropped and the East India Company continued to stagnate. Out of this came more attempts by Parliament to tax the colonists without their consent. This resulted in open rebellion and finally war.

East Jersey—The Province of East Jersey was established in 1674 as a distinct political division in accordance with the Quintipartite Deed. It was made up of four counties—Bergen, Essex, Middlesex, and Monmouth. In 1682, Perth Amboy was recognized as the capital of East Jersey. In 1702, the proprietors of East and West Jersey surrendered their right to govern to the Queen. In 1709, official acceptance of a merger was granted and East and West Jersey became the Province of New Jersey.

Elizabeth Town—This large colonial settlement became the city of Elizabeth in Union County, New Jersey, in 1855. It was founded by English settlers in 1664. It was named after the wife of Sir George Carteret, one of the original proprietors of the colony. The town served as the first capital of New Jersey.

Elsworth, Verdine—This wealthy entrepreneur of note left New York in 1768 to run the Ferry House at Powles Hook, New Jersey. He was successful in expanding business opportunities there and back in New York. He was also influential in making horse racing a popular event at Powles Hook. He was a business partner with Cornelius "Faddy" Van Vorst. They were involved in the construction of the tavern at Powles Hook and the racecourse oval. Expansion of transportation facilities to and from Powles Hook continued into the 1770's under the dynamic leadership of Elsworth and Van Vorst.

Fagan, Dan—The co-leader of the 'Sons of the Sword,' a violent gang of colonial terrorists, was also known as 'Little Jake' or 'the General.' Not much is known about this notorious leader of banditti who operated in the iron hills of northwestern Morris County in the 18th century. He may have been born in the late 1740's. He worked as a ditcher and woodcutter for Jacob Ford, Sr., first, and then Jacob Ford, Jr., second. Certain sources claim that he was an indentured Irish servant, while others claim he was connected somehow to the Ford family. In either case, Fagan ran away, accompanied by a pair of servants in 1767. The trio was rumored to have headed for the iron mines in search of work. Shortly thereafter he formed a gang of thieves, which he named after a local gentlemen's hunting club for which he had served as a hound tender. Fagan already had a nasty reputation before joining forces with Jack Spolden, the radical Anabaptist zealot.

Fahnrich—This title was given to Karl Bruder by Jack Spolden, the co-leader of the 'Sons of the Sword.' This German military rank is related to 'Fahnentrager,' which translates to 'flag bearer.' This is the equivalent in rank to the old Cornet, or the more contemporary Ensign.

Fairchild, Zachariah—There were a number of Fairchilds involved in law enforcement in Morris County in the decades prior to the American Revolution. Most of them were honest, contributing members of colonial society. The first was Sheriff Caleb Fairchild, who allowed John Pipes and his gang of counterfeiters to escape in the 1740's. His son, Phineas Fairchild, served as a Constable in Morris County in the 1770's along with Zachariah Fairchild, who may have been his brother. They were around when Samuel Ford's gang of counterfeiters was operating and eventually got caught. History repeated itself, when Ford and a few of his chums escaped from jail and were never recaptured.

Fannie—The cook for John Wetherill was also the mother of Sarah, Wetherill's house servant. Both mother and daughter remained on the Wetherill plantation until the master's death. There is a 'Fan' and her child mentioned in Wetherill's will, but the 'F' in the name may have been an 'S'.

Feldweibel—This German military rank was applied to the lower officers of each of Jack Spolden's secret cells. These were men charged with keeping the lowest members of each cell in line. A Feldweibel was the equivalent of an English Sergeant Major.

Ferry House Tavern—Cornelius "Faddy" Van Vorst had the Ferry House Tavern built at Powles Hook in order to accommodate his traveling patrons going to and from New York and various points in New Jersey. Verdine Elsworth, one of Van Vorst's partners was the proprietor of the tavern. He turned it into a popular gathering place for gamblers and merchants as well as the weary travelers from as far away as Philadelphia.

First River—In colonial times, another name for a major tributary of the Passaic River in North Jersey was the First River. It was later known as Mill Brook. It is the first main tributary closest to Newark Bay.

Five 'n Forty—This card game might have been a version of the Irish game, 'Spoil Five,' which evolved from the 17th century game called 'Maw.'

Flying Machine—The fastest form of public transportation in colonial times was nicknamed the 'flying machine.' It referred to the fastest of the regular stage wagon lines between New York and Philadelphia which cut the trip down from three days to two days. It was later applied to any fast stage wagon and team of horses.

Ford, Jacob, Jr.—The son of Jacob Ford, Sr., was born in 1738. He wed Theodosia Johnes, daughter of Rev. Timothy Johnes, in 1762. His father put him in charge of the family's iron mining and manufacturing business at Mount

Hope. Jacob Ford, Jr., and his wife lived in a stone mansion at the forge site and oversaw an operation which covered 2,000 acres. In 1772, he started construction of a Georgian style mansion east of the town center of Morristown and just south of the Whippany River on Piedmont Hill. Shortly thereafter, he moved to Morristown to look after his father's various business interests.

Jacob Ford, Sr.—The patriarch of the Ford family in Morristown, New Jersey, was born in Woodbridge in 1705. He wed Hannah Baldwin in 1724. Jacob was a shrewd businessman who became one of the most influential men in Morris County. He owned thousands of acres of land, was a successful merchant, tavern owner, and iron manufacturer. He was also a well-respected public servant who held the positions of Sheriff, Judge, and Assemblyman for Morris County.

Ford, Samuel—This son of Samuel Ford and Sarah Baldwin was born in 1735. He was a nephew of Jacob Ford, Sr. His first wife was Grace Kitchell, whom he wed in 1757. Sam Ford operated the Hibernia furnace, at first being successful, but soon failing to turn a profit. To pay off mounting debts, Ford turned to counterfeiting in the 1760's. To hone his skills in this illegal activity, he went to Ireland. While there he took another wife, who returned with him to the colonies. Upon discovering that Ford was already married, she returned to Ireland. In 1768, Ford was arrested in New York for forging and selling fake bills of credit. He was let go for lack of evidence. He went back to Ireland, and then to England, in 1771, to perfect his counterfeiting skills. Upon returning to New Jersey, he set up an even larger counterfeiting network which included several upstanding members of Morris County society. The secret location for his illegal operation was in the middle of the Hammock Farm swamp. Ford was eventually caught. His arrest and incarceration, along with several members of his gang, led to accusations that he was the mastermind behind the Treasury robbery of 1768. Sam Ford did not stick around to stand trial for the robbery or the counterfeiting activities. He and one of his partners in crime, John King, escaped from jail, hid out in former haunts north of Morristown, then headed west. The pair were joined by two other gang members near Juniata. Ford was rumored to have gotten to the Mississippi River and had made plans to head south to New Orleans. At this time, a bounty of several hundred pounds was raised for his capture. However, he continued to elude authorities. Sam Ford ended up in Virginia where he changed his name to Baldwin, married a third time, and worked as a silversmith. He was never brought to justice for the actual or alleged crimes he had been accused of committing. Popular opinion was that Ford played no role in the Treasury robbery. To some in Morris County, Ford was a hero of sorts, and remembered as very clever and highly skilled as a counterfeiter. Such admirers called him 'the honorary Treasurer of the Jerseys.'

Franklin, William—The illegitimate son of Ben Franklin was born around 1730. He served as the last colonial Governor of New Jersey, from 1763 to 1776. Throughout his tenure he remained steadfastly loyal to the King of England and eventually had a falling out with his father over the differences between patriot and loyalist stances which led to the American Revolution. William Franklin acquired his Tory leanings while studying law in London in the late 1750's. While there, he sired an illegitimate son, William Temple Franklin, in 1762. Later in the year, he wed Elizabeth Downes and moved to New Jersey the following year. When his father was in England in the 1770's, he took William's son under his wing and brought him back to Pennsylvania. Through Ben Franklin's lobbying for a high position in colonial government for his son, William was appointed Governor of New Jersey. During Franklin's governorship, things grew more and more contentious with various members of the Assembly. His staunch defense of the controversial Treasurer of East Jersey, Stephen Skinner, after the robbery of the

Treasury in 1768, was just one sore subject that festered for years. The situation culminated with Franklin's arrest in January of 1776. He was released in a prisoner exchange in 1778. He went to New York where he became a prime mover in the guerrilla war against patriots in New Jersey. In 1782, William Franklin sailed to England and never returned to New Jersey.

Gano, John—The Reverend John Gano was a Baptist minister who was born in 1727 and raised a Presbyterian in Hopewell, New Jersey. His father descended from Huguenots and his mother from English Baptists. Gano had a conversion experience when young and chose to follow the Baptist faith. During his ministry he travelled extensively throughout the colonies and developed a reputation as a dynamic evangelist. Legend has it that Gano baptized George Washington at Valley Forge during the American Revolution.

General Assembly—A bicameral legislative branch of government for East and West Jersey was established in 1702, when the Proprietors surrendered their right to govern to Queen Anne. The upper house was the Council. It was appointed by the Royal Governor to assist and advise him. The lower house was the General Assembly. Its members were elected by the colonists of New Jersey. This Assembly first consisted of twenty-four elected members, with two from Burlington and two from Perth Amboy, and ten at-large representatives from East Jersey and ten from West Jersey. In 1768, the number of Assemblymen jumped to thirty to include representation for Morris, Cumberland, and Sussex counties. The Governor retained the power to summon the General Assembly, dissolve it, and call for new elections.

George III—The King of Great Britain, George III of Hanover, was born in 1738. He reigned as monarch from 1760 to 1820. He favored a personal rule and a get-tough policy as far as the American colonies were concerned. The British defeat in the Revolutionary War made him very unpopular in England. He eventually went insane and the crown was held in regency from 1811 to 1820 by the Prince of Wales, who would become George IV.

Great Swamp, The—This vast area of marsh and bogland is located in southern Morris County, New Jersey. It is a remnant of a large glacial lake which extended thirty miles in length and ten miles wide, 15,000 years ago. The lake eventually drained via the altered route of the Passaic River. The area is now a wildlife refuge.

Grosse Hansen—This German term was popular among members of the lower class in the 16th century. It was used to describe the evil noble class. 'Gross Hansen' referred to the powerful magnates and bigwigs of the ruling families of the German states. These were the spiritual and temporal lords who held all the decision-making positions. The oppressed accused such individuals of being cruel and corrupt. They became the primary targets of the peasants and radical Protestants who revolted in the 16th century.

Gustine, Sam—One of the leaders of the counterfeiting gang from Newport, Rhode Island, was Samuel Gustine. He, along with James Budd and other members of the gang, were caught passing New York and New Jersey counterfeit in the summer of 1772. His confession and the confessions of others in this gang implicated counterfeiters in New York and New Jersey, including Samuel Ford and his gang.

Hackensack River—Native Americans called this river, in northern New Jersey, the 'Atchensehaky', or 'the river of many bends.' Europeans renamed it the Hackensack in the early 1600's. It is less than fifty miles in length, rising in southeastern New York and crossing into northern Bergen County, New Jersey, and emptying into the Meadowlands and Newark Bay at its confluence with the Passaic River.

Hacket's Town—This older, alternate spelling of what is now known as Hackettstown, New Jersey, was used in the 18th century. The community may have been named after Samuel Hackett, an early settler and large landowner there during its earliest days. Before that, it was called Helms Mills and, sometimes, Musconetcong. The station for the famous Schooley's Mountain springs was located here.

Hager, John—The person, once referred to as 'the wealthiest man around Schooley's Mountain,' was either Johannes Hager or his son, Captain John Hager. The Hagers were of German descent and among the original settlers in the German Valley area in New Jersey. The Hagers owned hundreds of acres on Schooley's Mountain and were instrumental in building the hotel associated with the famed healing springs in the area.

Hagers, Rachel—This character is based on two accounts in the New Jersey Archives from the early 1770's. Both accounts describe a female runaway slave. This particular Rachel was a mulatto whose father was allegedly John Hager, reputed to have been the wealthiest man on Schooley's Mountain. Rachel's mother claimed to have descended from African royalty and passed that claim to her daughter. After Mr. Hager re-married, his new wife insisted that he get rid of Rachel and her mother. He did so by selling both to Jacob Morrell of Chatham, New Jersey. Their new master was cruel to them. This resulted in Rachel blaming Morrell for her mother's untimely death. This caused her to run away when she gained the opportunity to do so. She took the Hager name as her own surname after adding an 's' to it.

Half-Jacks—This colonial slang term was applied to the multi-racial folk who inhabited lands in the Ramapo Mountain region on the border between New Jersey and New York. They may have been a mix of Native-American Lenape, free African Americans, and Dutch/German European Americans. They were often referred to as 'jacks-and-whites,' which evolved into the more modern exonym, 'Jackson Whites.' Most settlers in New Jersey assumed that these mountain folk were half-blacks (jacks) and half-whites—hence, the expression, 'Half-Jacks.'

Hancock, Cut—Gottlieb Hancock (or Hankok) was born in Germany in 1739 or 1740, but at one year old he was brought to New Jersey by his parents. They started a farm in or near Cranberry (pka: Cranbury). Locals had trouble with Gottlieb's name, and it evolved into 'Cutlope.' This eventually was shortened to the nickname, 'Cut.' Eventually, he took over his father's farm, expanded it, and remained good neighbors with the Carson brothers and the Wetherill family. He developed a close friendship with John Wetherill's son, Vincent, and served under him in the first year of the Revolutionary War.

Hanover—The township of Hanover lies just north of Morristown, New Jersey. It is considered one of the first European settlements in the northwestern part of the state. It was established in 1685 along the Whippany River, and grew to encompass most of Morris County. The Hanover name was adopted for the 'Whippenny' area in 1720. It was taken from the House of Hanover in Germany and meant to honor George I of Great Britain, who was of the House of Hanover. Over time the size of the Hanover in New Jersey was reduced and other municipalities were created as the County of Morris developed.

Hartwick Boys—This gang of criminals and troublemakers hailed from New Brunswick, New Jersey. At one time, they were suspected of robbing the East Jersey Treasury in 1768 in Perth Amboy. However, there was no evidence linking them to the crime.

Hasenclever, Peter—In the 1760's, Peter 'The Baron' Hasenclever recruited over 500 Germans to work in mines and at forges in northern and western New Jersey. He gained favor quickly with English notables who had invested heavily in American iron works. Hasenclever was able to work his way up the status ladder, but his spending on land purchases and iron works development led to allegations of mismanagement of other people's money. That, combined with a large number of German miners who ran away from the Ringwood mine, was cause enough to get Hasenclever discharged from his duties. He was bankrupt by 1770 and dead by 1774.

Haufen Gang—This German term is redundant in English. It refers to a heap or a pile; thus, a large amount, as in a group, a crowd, or a gang. Its sinister meaning carries with it the intent to do harm.

Haynes, Samuel—One of the well-respected citizens of Morris town, New Jersey, who was accused of passing counterfeit bills and being associated with the Sam Ford gang, was Samuel Haynes (or Haines). He operated a popular tavern out of his house. The place was a stop for stage wagon traffic to and from Powles Hook. In October of 1773, he sold both house and tavern to Captain Peter Dickerson. Shortly thereafter, he and his compatriots involved in the counterfeiting were exonerated.

Hazard—This dice game dates back to the 13th century and was probably Arabic in origin. The name comes from the Arabic expression, 'Al-Zahr,' which means 'to die.' The American game of craps evolved from the Hazard rolls of 'crabs,' which were 1 and 1, or 1 and 2.

Heaton, Samuel—This former Presbyterian from Wrentham, Massachusetts, migrated to New Jersey and established iron works near Mount Olive around 1735. He became a Baptist because his wife insisted that no passage in the Bible stated anything about infant baptism. Thus, Heaton became a member of the Schooley's Mountain Baptist Church in 1753. He served as the third pastor of this congregation from 1756 to 1760. He did itinerant preaching thereafter.

Hibernia—The Hibernia furnace and iron works was located four miles north of Rockaway in New Jersey. On land above John Johnston's 'Beach Glen' iron works, Sam Ford built a new furnace in 1765. He called his works, 'The Adventure.' This place was associated with the nearby village of Hibernia, which had been established in 1753. Ford's complex was often called the Hibernia furnace. When Sam Ford fell into financial difficulty, shares in the Hibernia works were sold to James Anderson and Benjamin Cooper. Ford kept a third of the shares for himself and his first wife, Grace. Further difficulties forced Ford to sell his remaining shares to Lord Stirling. Stirling became the sole owner in 1771.

Higgins, Ike—This character is based on a composite of low types who were mentioned fleetingly in the New Jersey Archives of the 1760's. One was Robert Ray whose hand was burned as punishment for a charge of manslaughter, just as Ichabod 'Ike' Higgins was. In an earlier account, a passer of counterfeit bills, John Higgins, was caught and hanged in 1761. His brother, Ichabod Higgins, was accused of being an accomplice and thrown in jail. However, he escaped and went to sea. From these coarse and humble origins, the riotous Ike Higgins was created.

Hoff, Charlie—The ne'er-do-well son of Hard Joe Hoff was named after Joe's brother, Charles Hoff, Jr. The brother succeeded Joe as manager at the Hibernia forge, but the son fell into a life of crime. He died young.

Hoff, Joseph—Joseph Hoff served as manager at the Hibernia furnace works in the 1770's. He hailed from Hunterdon County where his reputation as a strict boss preceded him, Those who worked under him gave him the nickname, 'Hard Joe.' He was actually a firm and fair manager who was respected more than feared. Certain sources have him as a brother-in-law of Benjamin Cooper. This may have been the connection that convinced Lord Stirling, owner of the Hibernia Iron works at the time, to hire Hard Joe.

Hoffmeister, William—A noted musician in the 1770's was 'Little Billy' Hoffmeister. He stood only thirty-seven inches tall. He endeared himself to folks in the Middlesex County area of New Jersey when he wed a woman living in New Brunswick at the time. She stood thirty-six inches tall.

Hopewell—This community evolved from a purchase of land by Daniel Coxe, a Royal British Governor of West Jersey in the late 17th century. Coxe transferred selling rights to Thomas Revell who recruited buyers of land and settlers on vast stretches of untamed wilderness. Revell's false claims of tame and fertile land led to disputes with the first families to settle there. Fifty of them filed a class action suit against Revell and the West Jersey Society. They lost and many of them moved away. In the early 1700's, some of the remaining settlers established a thriving Baptist church. Lumber mills became successful. Where forests were cleared, farms sprang up. They named their community Hopewell. The Hopewell Academy became another success which ensured Hopewell's survival.

Hornbeck, Jimmy—This Morristown local was hired as a body guard by Jacob Ford, Sr. He had been a former muler at the mines up north before getting down on his luck. His knowledge of explosives used in the mining process came in handy for dealing with some of Ford's enemies. His luck turned around after he had proved his worth to his superiors.

Horseneck—The Horseneck (aka: Horse Neck) tract in Essex County, New Jersey, developed into several modern municipalities—Caldwell, West Caldwell, North Caldwell, Fairfield, Verona, Cedar Grove, Essex Fells, and Roseland. In 1701, settlers purchased the Horseneck tract from the Lenape. This area included most of western Essex County from First Mountain to the Passaic River. It was first called Horse Neck.

Horse Pound Mountain—More than one mountain or hill in New Jersey carried this name, or some variation of the name, at one time or another. The one in this story is located in northwestern Morris County. It was once a source of quality iron in the 18th century. According to legend, the name derived from the wild horses that wintered in the valley at the foot of the mountain and migrated to higher ground for the rest of the year. This particular elevation was also referred to as Horse Pond Mountain.

Hull's Tavern—This popular public house in the 18th century was located in Perth Amboy, New Jersey. Mellick, in his Story of an Old Farm, mentions John Hull, the proprietor of this tavern.

Hutchins,_____—One of the counterfeiters of the 1770's, who claimed to have some connection to the Sam Ford gang, is only remembered by his last name in the New Jersey Archives. He was also associated with Stephen Waterman and John Swan, who were also counterfeiters.

Indian Queen Tavern—This high-class watering hole was located on Albany Street in New Brunswick, New Jersey, in the 18th century. It sat close to the waterfront and wooden bridge which spanned the Raritan River. The building was originally a house that was constructed in the early 1700's. It was enlarged and operated as a tavern inn throughout the years of the Revolution. During that time, several famous persons, such as Ben Franklin and John Adams, stayed the night there. The tavern was restored and still stands at Old Town Village in Piscataway.

Inn, The—What was commonly referred to simply as 'The Inn' was located in Cranberry (lka: Cranbury}, New Jersey. It was later called the Cranbury Inn and is still in operation. The inn itself is made from two inns that were in operation in the early 1700's. This location was a popular resting spot for wayfarers plying the Amboy/Burlington stage wagon route. During the early 1770's, Richard Handley may have been the innkeeper.

Inthill,_____—According to the New Jersey Archives, a Dr. Inthill had a practice in Morristown, New Jersey, in the early 1770's. However, his first name was not mentioned.

Irish 26th Regiment of Foot—This British military unit was one of five Royal Irish regiments. During the 1770's it was stationed in New York and New Jersey. Several months were spent at Perth Amboy during those years.

Jack—An alternative name for apple brandy in colonial times was apple jack, or simply 'jack.' It usually referred to a brandy of lesser quality and one not aged for a long time. In New Jersey, it was also called 'jersey lightning,' or 'blue lightning.' Regardless of what it was called, jack was inexpensive and extremely popular in the 18th century.

Jarlman, Ansel—This contrived character was usually referred to by superiors and peers alike as 'Anse.' The surname is derived from the Scandinavian 'jarl,' or 'of noble birth, but less than a king.' This status ranking was equivalent to the Old English 'eorl,' and later 'earl.' Ansel Jarlman, however, was far from being noble. He was more like a 'churl,' or 'a person of low birth' or 'one who is rude and ill-bred.' Churlman might have been a better name for him. Despite his deficiencies, Verdine Elsworth trusted Jarlman as a fetchman. Anse proved his worth to Vincent Wetherill in times of crisis.

Jileen—This Irish word for 'girl' was also spelled Jill(-een) or Gill(-een) in colonial times. It comes from the name Gillian, which means 'downy-haired' or 'soft haired, and youthful.' A Jileen usually referred to somebody's young sweetheart. On the negative side it substituted for wench or flirt.

Johannes Gold Piece—A popular coin in the 18th century was the Portuguese/Brazilian gold piece, known as a johannes, or simply a joe or jo. It was the equivalent of sixteen dollars in the colonies, and it was often found in counterfeit. Half-johannes were also popular.

Johnson Mine—In the 1760's the former Horse Pound Mine (aka: Beach Glen Mine) was owned and operated by John Johnson. It was located roughly four miles north of Rockaway beyond the meadows which were west of Hibernia. Samuel Ford owned land near the Johnson Mine. After the mine played out, it was referred to as the Old Johnson Mine and used as a hideout by outlaws and such.

Jolly, William—This man served as a gaoler in Perth Amboy, New Jersey, in the 1760's. Due to debt issues he was discharged under the act for relief. However, John Wetherill, who had befriended Jolly in the 1760's, helped him out with a generous loan. The former gaoler eventually returned on special assignment under the High Sheriff in Perth Amboy. He later joined Vincent Wetherill's investigative team, as a favor to Vincent's father and as a way to pay off the old loan.

Kemble's Thunder—Peter Kemble started his own brand of strong apple jack in the latter half of the 18th century. He hailed from the Mount Kemble area and sold his brew in places nearby. It was quite popular in Morristown, New Jersey, where locals called it 'Kemble's Thunder.'

Kersey—Verdine Elsworth, tavern owner and entrepreneur at Powles Hook, New Jersey, had a favorite house servant named Kersey. This slave was sharp-witted and well-spoken, but beyond that, little is known of him. His origins and fate remain unknown.

Kerssenbruck's History—Herman van Kerssenbruck (b. 1520-d. 1585), a noted German educator and historian, wrote the first account of the Munster Affair. His interpretation of the radical Anabaptist uprising was met with much controversy. It was translated from the German to Latin in 1771.

Kinchin—This derogatory slang term was used to describe a smallish man, a youth trained to steal, or one who robs or kidnaps children. It was a common expression in 18th century England, but used rarely in the American colonies. Hard Joe Hoff used it to scold his men and keep them in line.

King, John—This John King may have been the son of Constant King and Phebe Horton. He was born in 1742. King once served as a respected Justice of the Peace in Morris County, New Jersey, but he fell in with Sam Ford's gang of counterfeiters and eventually became Ford's trusted sidekick. Both were arrested in 1773 on counterfeiting charges and thrown into jail. However, they escaped, hid in the area for a short time, then fled west. The two were joined by Joseph Richardson of Pennsylvania and Thomas Budd, a loyal gang member, as they made for the Ohio River. They decided to split up after making plans to reunite, possibly in New Orleans. Richardson and Budd went one way and Ford and King another. Trackers never found them. King was described as 5' 8-9"; short and straight brown hair; full face with dark complexion; and using the name 'John Horton.'

King, Obediah—Little is known about this gaoler, who was mentioned briefly in the New Jersey Archives of 1773. He worked at the new jail in Perth Amboy around this time. King may have been born in 1730. His first name was also spelled 'Obadiah.'

King's Arms—There was more than one 'Sign of the King's Arms' in the American colonies (i.e. the King's Arms in Staten Island, owned by Anthony Waters). The one in Elizabeth Town (pka: Elizabeth, New Jersey) was formerly called 'The Old Nag's Head.' Captain Samuel Smith was the owner from 1771 to 1776. It was located between the courthouse and the river, next to the Old Mill. A tanyard enterprise was operating across the street on the river side.

King's Highway—The New Jersey portion of the King's Highway, which was laid out by order of Charles II of England, stretched along what is now called U. S. Route 206 and N. J. Route 27. The entire King's Highway in the 18th century was intended to connect Boston, Massachusetts, to Charleston, South Carolina.

Kinney, Tom—In the early 1770's, the High Sheriff of Morris County, New Jersey, was Tom Kinney (aka: Thomas Kenney). He was also involved in various business enterprises, including operation of a furnace and slitting mill along the Whippany River and co-owner of a general store in Morristown. He was probably the Thomas Kinney who was a Presbyterian of Scottish origins who was born in 1731 and died in 1793. He was known to be highly skilled in mineral assaying. He owned large tracts of land and tried his hand at several business ventures—many of which did not succeed. He was instrumental in getting iron masters and furnace and forge owners to meet to discuss pressing matters and prepare strategies for improving the industry.

Kinsey, James—This lawyer from Burlington, New Jersey, was born in 1731. He was a member of the General Assembly from 1772 to 1775, and a member of the Continental Congress from 1774 to 1775. He also served on the Committee of Correspondence for Burlington County during those two years. After the war, Kinsey served as Chief Justice of the New Jersey Supreme Court from 1789 until his death in 1803. During his years as an Assemblyman, he was recognized as a champion of legislative prerogatives. He led the movement in the legislature in favor of ousting Stephen Skinner from the position of Treasurer of East Jersey. He had accused Skinner of being responsible for the loss of the 'stolen' funds. Kinsey pushed for Skinner to pay up. Skinner did eventually resign, but a suit against him never went to trial. Kinsey, at least, gained a partial victory. As a staunch member of the Society of Friends, Kinsey abandoned political endeavors during the fighting of the Revolutionary War. He resumed his public service after peace had been restored.

Klompdraggers—This was a blanket term for various pacifist groups and sects that stood in the way of progress as defined by radicals and extremists in central Europe. Such pacifist elements included Culverites, Hussites, Adamites, Levellers, and most Anabaptists. The term was also spelled 'klompdaggers.'

Lawrence, John—The owner of Long Bridge (aka: Longbridge) Farm in the 1770's was John Lawrence, a wealthy entrepreneur and civil servant from Philadelphia, Pennsylvania. This Middlesex County, New Jersey, plantation was started in the 1730's by his father, Thomas Lawrence. This was an elite farming operation which featured extensive acreage and a large slave population. The farm passed to his son, John, when he died in 1754. The area where the farm had been located is now the Monmouth Junction area of South Brunswick Township.

Lawrie's Road—The main road between the old capitals of East and West Jersey was called Lawrie's Road (aka: the Lower Road). It ran from South Amboy to Cranbury and points south. The road was named after Gawen Lawrie, a 17th century Deputy Governor who resided in Perth Amboy. The road was in operation from the early 18th century. It was later called the Amboy Stage Road. Now it is called the Cranbury-South River Road.

Leutinger—The German equivalent to the English rank of Lieutenant in the 18th century was 'leutinger.' Jack Spolden used this rank for the mid-level officers in his new 'army.'

Lex Talionis—This is the Latin expression for the ancient principle of retaliation. It is the fancy term for 'eye-for-an-eye' justice. It is also known as 'law of talion,' or retributive justice. This form of punishment was created to prevent extreme punishments. It pre-dates biblical times. Basically it means that any punishment should correspond in degree and kind to the offense perpetuated by the wrongdoer. The punishment might range from the physical (eye-for-an-eye)

to the more modern suitable payment (100 pounds for the loss of an eye).

Leydon, John—John Buckholdt from Leyden was also known as John of Leyden (or Leiden), as well as John Leydon. His original name was also spelled Jan Beuckels or Bockelszoon. He was born in 1509 and died in 1536. He was co-leader, along with John Matthias of Haarlem, of the Anabaptist revolt in Munster, Germany in the 1530's. When Matthias was killed in 1534, Leydon took control. He attempted to establish his own 'Kingdom of God' in Munster and purged the city of 'unbelievers.' He attempted to establish a 'communism of goods and services' and sought to defend such a system by the sword. However, Leydon went too far when he introduced polygamy and crowned himself 'King of the New Jerusalem.' These efforts met with great opposition. In two years he was executed by those who opposed his ideas. His extremism led to the discrimination and persecution of all Anabaptist sects after his death. This eventually led to many Anabaptists migrating to North America. Leyden turned out to be an inspiration for Jack Spolden and his brand of revolution in America.

Ligoniers—These round-toed buckle shoes with low to moderate heels, short tongues, and latchets greater than an inch were popular in the 18th century. The name for a pair of them was derived from Fort Ligonier in southwest Pennsylvania during the French and Indian War. Ligoniers were a favorite of men who had fought in that confrontation and the popularity of such shoes spread in the final decades of the 18th century.

Lindsey Short Gown—This garment provided warmth and durability. It was also inexpensive. It was popular among the lower class and earned the nick-name, 'ugly dress.' It was popular in the colonies due to a shortage of finished wool. It was known as a 'linsey-woolsey' or 'wincky' in North America in the 18th century. The fabric is a coarse twill or plain-woven linen warp and a woolen weft. The name derives from 'lin,' which is an archaic word for flax and wool.

Little Jake—This was a nick-name for the banditti leader, Dan Fagan. He detested the name and what it stood for. No one dared utter this nick-name in his presence. The name reminded Fagan of his origins as the rumored bastard son of Jacob Ford, Sr. Fagan hated his alleged natural father and he hated the nick-name.

Long Ferry Tavern—This famous landmark on the waterfront of Perth Amboy, New Jersey, was a fixture in the city from 1684 to well into the 19th century. It was also referred to as the Landing Tavern, or simply the Landing. In the 1770's it was operated by Tom Carnes and his daughters. It became a social gathering place for Whigs during the years leading up to the American Revolution.

Long Hill—This southern region in the Passaic Valley in Morris County, New Jersey, was where Judge Daniel Cooper's estate was to be found. It is named after a ridge of the Watchung Mountains. The Great Swamp is located in this area.

Longbridge Farm—The Lawrence family of Philadelphia, Pennsylvania, used the Longbridge (or Long Bridge) Farm as their summer residence in the 18th century. The name was taken from the long bridge over the Lawrence Brook which feeds into the Raritan River. This was mainly a horse farm of handsome repute. It consisted of thousands of acres and operated year round. The farm also featured a large population of slaves—up to thirty or forty at its height. When the Lawrences were absent from the farm, the Wetherills helped oversee the operation.

Lord Corn—John Wetherill named one of his quarter horses 'Lord Corn.' This was a nick-name for Lord Cornbury—Edward Hyde, third Earl of Clarendon. He served as the Royal Governor of New York and New Jersey from 1701 to 1708. He was reputed to have been the worst governor ever appointed to an American colony by the British government.

He made taking bribes an art form and he was adept at plundering the public treasury. He was fond of cross-dressing—his excuse was that he liked to imitate Queen Anne. When Lord Cornbury showed up at his wife's funeral dressed as a woman, colonists had had enough, and complaints from them led the Queen to remove Cornbury from office. It is no wonder John Wetherill named his worst horse after Lord Cornbury.

Macaroni—A well-known bay race horse that was featured in several races at the Powles Hook oval in the 1770's was 'Macaroni.' This horse was got by 'Wildair,' son of Lord Godolphin's 'Old Cade', son of the famous 'Arabian.' The dam was 'Ariel,' out of 'Selema,' daughter of 'Old Spark' from the famed Tasker's farm in Maryland.

Mamzer—This slang term was used as a substitute for 'bastard' in the 18th century. It referred to one born of adultery or incest. The origins of the expression can be traced back to Old Testament times. Back then, one who had a parent born of adultery or incest was called a mamzer. The word was also used to refer to someone born of a Jewish father and non-Jewish mother. The root of mamzer meant 'spoiled' or 'corrupt,' with 'mum' meaning defect and 'zar' meaning strange or alien. The word can be found in Deuteronomy 23:3 and Zechariah 9:6.

Mansfield, Miners of—One of the secret cells organized by Jack Spolden was named after the discontented miners of Mansfield in Magdeburg, Germany. There was tension between the miners' guilds and the ruling class in that area in the 16th century. Things came to a head when Thomas Muntzer verbally attacked the Count of Mansfield and called for the slaying of the godless. Many miners then joined Muntzer's radical movement.

Martinet—A strict disciplinarian, usually a military officer, was called a martinet in the 18th century. The name comes from Jean Martinet, a French officer who used to severely discipline his men. His short, knotted whip came to be called a martinet.

Matthias, Jan—This leader of the radical Anabaptist movement was a follower of Melchior Hoffman in the early 1530's. After Hoffman's imprisonment in Strasbourg, Jan Matthias (also spelled Mattys, Matthijs, Mathijsz, Matthyssen, or Mathyszoon) a mere baker from Haarlem, rallied folks in the Low Countries to the radical Anabaptist movement. Other leaders reported to him from Munster on the teachings there of Bernhard Rothmann. Matthias was so impressed he declared Munster the 'New Jerusalem' and on January 5, 1534, sent disciples there to perform adult baptisms. Matthias eventually came to the city, had to defend it by force, and was killed in April.

Mauleys—Fists, or simply hands, were sometimes referred to as 'mauleys' in the late 18th century. It was used in describing a handshake or being employed in a fight where blows were struck by using the hands. The word might have come from the Romany 'mylier,' or certain striking tools called mauls.

McKnight,_____—The widow McKnight of Radford's Landing (lka: South Amboy, New Jersey) was the victim of a violent crime in 1773. A pair of runaway slaves was accused of the murder of the woman. They were captured and executed for the crime. This case was quite similar to the murder of Elizabeth Knight of Evesham whose skull was broken in two places. This incident occurred on May 22, 1772. Her murderer was found between Cooper's Ferry and Mount Holly, and, shortly thereafter, executed.

Meekers—This was a slang word used to describe Quakers in the 18th century. Such a pacifist religious group was known to be humble and meek—hence the descriptive substitute for the Quaker name.

Melchior, Peasants of—One of Jack Spolden's secret cells was named after an initiator of adult baptism in the early 16th century in the northern Low German area. Melchior Hoffman lent his name to what came to be known as 'Melchi-orite Anabaptism.' His teachings laid the foundation for the uprising in Munster in 1534-35. He predicted an apocalypse and declared his city of Strasbourg as the primary place of refuge at the end of the world. Word of Melchior's predictions spread to Munster and beyond, even to the Netherlands. His message was quite popular among the peasants who swelled the ranks of his following.

Millstone River—This forty-mile long tributary of the Raritan River in central New Jersey begins in western Monmouth County and flows north through southern Somerset County. The origin of its current name is somewhat speculative. Its original name was 'Mattawong,' which means 'hard to travel' in the Lenape language. One source for the English name of the river is from Scottish settlers who lived near the river. They named it after Millstone Hill, a landmark northwest of Aberdeen. Another source claims that a millstone was being transported across one of the river's bridges and it fell into the water and could not be retrieved. Hence, this river may have been named after that lost millstone. Another source was the quarry area north of Kingston from which millstones came. Still another source claims the place was first named 'Milestone' to indicate the distance from Princeton. Lastly, the stones for the first mill on the river may have provided its name.

Mine Hill—The village of Mine Hill, New Jersey, is located between Roxbury to the west and Dover to the east. In the 18th century the dominant industry in the area was mining. The Dickerson mine, owned by Mahlon Dickerson, was the most profitable operation there. Also in this area were successful farms along Quaker Church Road. One was the Quaker farm owned by the Sharp family.

Minehost—The title back in colonial times for a landlord or landlady of a pub or tavern was 'Minehost' (or Mine Host). It was an old German word which passed into English.

Mingo Tim—Dr. Budd of Hanover in Morris County, New Jersey, owned a slave who ran away in the 1760's. Details about this slave and what he wore and took with him were given in a posting as well as a reward for his return. This information was used to develop the character, Mingo Tim (aka: the Buck Fiddler), who ran away from Dr. Budd in 1773. There was an actual slave named Mingo (aka: Tim), who ran away from Samuel Ogden of Boonton, New Jersey. His description was posted in the New Jersey Archives in 1772 and 1773. This Mingo did play the violin.

Morrell, Jacob—The Morrell family came to the Morristown area from Newtown, Long Island, in the early 18th century. Thomas Morrell and his wife, Judith(?), had a son, Jacob, who was born in 1728. He became a well-to-do entrepreneur with large landholdings in the Chatham and Morristown area. He married four times—Abigail Ross, Nancy Pierson, Mary Horton, and Sarah Day. It has been claimed that George Washington stayed at the Morrell house on Main Street in August of 1781. The house still stands and is now a restaurant.

Morris, Joseph—Captain Joseph Morris was operating a stage wagon line from Black River, New Jersey, to Powles Hook in the 1770's, about the time he was accused of participating in Samuel Ford's counterfeiting ring. Through his connections with influential people he avoided harsh punishment for his crime. He had some business connection with Daniel Burnet at one time.

Mount Kemble—The 1,250-acre plantation of Peter Kemble, long-time member and once President of the Royal Council of the colony of New Jersey, was called Mount Kemble. Its owner purchased the land from Amos Strettell in 1751. The property was bound by the Passaic River to the south and Morristown to the north. Kemble was a staunch Tory. However, he was allowed to remain in his house during the Revolutionary War. Continental troops encamped on

his land and he maintained a friendship with George Washington throughout. His property was never confiscated.

Mud Spoon—This device, used by miners in colonial times, was also called a mudding spoon. It was made of brass or copper and some twenty inches long. The spoon-end was used to clean out rock dust from drilled holes in preparation for inserting explosives in the holes. There were inscribed lines at one-inch intervals along the length of the spoon handle to measure the depth of the hole and to determine the amount of blasting powder needed. The mud spoon was also used to remove the remains of a misfire.

Muhlhausen, Angels of—One of the strongholds of the radical Anabaptist movement in the early 16th century was Muhlhausen in Thuringia, Germany. The leaders there were Hans Romer, a furrier from Eisenach, and Ludwig Span from Ershausen. Thomas Muntzer was captured there, tortured, and put to death. Other leaders were imprisoned there—some died on the rack or by drowning, while others were eventually set free. The movement experienced a revival at Muhlhausen after the death of Georg, Duke of Saxony. It lasted beyond the middle of the 16th century. Jack Spolden used the name of this place for one of his secret cells.

Munster, Ravens of—Radical Anabaptists attempted to set up a communal sectarian government in Munster, the capital of Westphalia, in the 1530's. The Lutheran magistrates were deposed. Bernhard Knipperdalling was installed as Mayor of the city. Equality for all and the equal distribution of wealth was preached. Munster was declared the 'New Jerusalem.' A short time thereafter, the city was besieged by Franz Von Waldeck, the Bishop who had been expelled when the Anabaptists took control. One of the Anabaptist leaders, Jan Matthys, was killed leading a sally with thirty followers. John of Leiden took control. Starvation and disillusionment followed. The siege succeeded, the city fell, and the radical leaders were tortured and executed. Jack Spolden used the name of this place for one of his secret cells.

Muntzer, Thomas—This priest from Allstedt, Germany, became a leader of the Peasant Revolt in 1524-25 in Saxony. He attracted many radical Anabaptists by preaching in favor of full common language masses, lay communion, and hymnody. He maintained that the traditional clergy stood in the way of people's true expression of their piety to God. In order to reach the end of days, one had to return to the beginning of days. His enemies labelled him a 'Paedo-Baptist' because he did not promote re-baptism. Muntzer was accused of manipulating God's word to suit personal gains. Undaunted, Muntzer organized militant bands and marched to Muhlhausen. He led the fight against his enemies, lost, went into hiding, was captured and executed.

Musgrove, _____ —One of the law officers at Radford's Landing (pka: South Amboy, New Jersey), according to the New Jersey Archives, was Constable Musgrove in the 1770's. His first name was not given.

Musgrove Arabian, the—This famous English race horse was sire to several horses that were competing in the American colonies. Verdine Elsworth of Powles Hook, New Jersey, named one of his best horses after the Musgrove Arabian.

Musket-Rifle—Cut Hancock's weapon of choice may have been what was often called a 'musket-rifle' (aka: rifle-musket or rifled musket). It was a family heirloom passed down from father to son and an early prototype of the German rifle, which morphed into the Pennsylvania long rifle. Its main feature was the grooved barrel which spun lead balls for greater accuracy. Such a weapon was around since the beginning of the 18th century and first used along the frontier for hunting, fighting Indians, and later used in the French and Indian War and the Revolutionary War.

Nag's Head Inn—This tavern in Elizabeth Town (pka: Elizabeth, New Jersey) was in business under the name Nag's Head since 1763. James Johnson may have been the proprietor in the 1770s.

Nankeen Shirt—Such a garment was made from buff (a dull yellow) cotton cloth. It originally came from Nanking, China—hence, the name 'nankeen' for a popular shirt or jacket made from such cloth in colonial times.

Nanna—This was the nickname for John Wetherill's first wife, Ann(e). She bore five children—three girls and two boys. They were named Anne, Vincent, Sarah, John, and Rachel. Nanna was born around 1720. She was wed at a young age. The records are not clear as to when she passed away.

Neb—Little Neb was one of Nettie's boys. His full name was Nebuchadnezzar of biblical origin (King of Babylonia, 605-562 B.C.). The name was given to him by Judge Daniel Cooper who was Nettie's master.

Ned—Little Ned was Good Mary Woods mulatto child. He was a servant boy at Rattoon's Tavern in Radford's Landing (pka: South Amboy, New Jersey).

Nettie—The head cook for Judge Daniel Cooper was his slave, Nettie (aka: Net). She had two sons—Neb (Nebuchadnezzar) and Bale (Balthazar). Her sister also worked in Cooper's kitchen house.

New Bridge—This mill hamlet was located in New Jersey at the narrows of the Hackensack River. This location was originally called 'Aschatking,' which means in Lenape 'where the river narrows.' It lies ten miles above the head of Newark Bay. The later name came from the first draw-bridge at the narrows. It was raised in the 1740's. Much road traffic to and from the city of New York and points south used this bridge. The landing at New Bridge became the business hub for the upper Hackensack Valley.

New Brunswick—When European settlers first came up the Raritan River and settled in a swampy area in 1681, it was appropriately called Prigmore's Swamp. Later, when a ferry service was established there, it was called Inian's Ferry. In the early 1700's it became known as New Brunswick, Brunswick Town, or simply Brunswick. The name was borrowed from the German city of Braunschweig, in Lower Saxony, in honor of George, Duke of Brunswick-Luneburg and Elector of Hanover (the House of Hanover was also known as the House of Brunswick). This German noble became King George I of Great Britain (1660-1727). New Brunswick actually took its name from King George II, Duke of Brunswick-Luneburg. The town received its Royal Charter in 1730 and was incorporated as a town in 1736 and a city in 1784. It became a hub of transportation and commerce, and a rival of Perth Amboy. It was also the home of Queens College (lka: Rutgers University).

Newark—The town of Newark was founded in 1666 by Connecticut Puritans to avoid losing political power after the union of the New Haven and Connecticut colonies. The name 'New Ark' (from the New Ark of the Covenant) was decided upon rather than the less favored 'Milford.' The land along the Passaic River had been purchased from the Hackensack Indians by the Puritans. Their theocratic sway over the area lasted until 1746 when Episcopalians built a church there. Newark's rapid growth and status as a true city began in the early 19th century.

Newark Cider—In colonial days, in the opinion of many, the best apple cider in the world came from New Jersey. Newark cider was ranked among the best of its kind and preferred over cider from New England colonies. John Wetherill's cider, but especially his eight-year aged apple brandy, was considered as good, if not better, than anything coming out of Newark.

Niall of the Nine Hostages—One of the legendary prehistoric Irish kings was Niall Noigiallach, or Niall of the Nine Hostages. He allegedly reigned in the 4th-5th centuries A.D. He was the assumed progenitor of the O'Neill clan which dominated Ireland for the next four centuries. Niall had at least two wives and many sons—one of whom produced the O'Higgins line. Ike Higgins claimed to have descended from this line.

Obadiah—In the 18th and 19th centuries a Quaker was often referred to as an 'Obadiah.' At the time, this was a popular first name among those of the Quaker faith.

Obrigkeit—A rallying symbol for radical Anabaptists in the 16th century in central Europe was the avenging sword of the true authority. In German, this sword was known as the 'Obrigkeit.' There are biblical references to such a sword: "I will draw out my sword from its sheath, and I will cut off from you the righteous and the wicked"—Ezekiel 21:3. According to radical Anabaptist thinking, the 'two sword' concept, as expressed in Luke 22:38, was a papalist doctrine that was no longer viable. The 'civil regnum' and the 'ecclesiastical socerdatium' did not need to co-exist. Only the 'temporal regnum' (the Obrigkeit), mentioned in Romans 13:4, needed to exist. However, this one sword had to be used for the communal good—a new social order in which all were to be made equal.

Old Bridge—This township in Middlesex County, New Jersey, was originally incorporated as Madison Township. Before that it was part of South Amboy Township. The original name can be traced back to the first bridge which spanned the South River and was a vital link for sections of Lawrie's Road running from South Amboy to Cranbury. The first bridge was called the South River Bridge. Later, it was referred to as 'the Old Bridge.'

Old Harry—The Devil was often referred to as 'old,' since he was a primeval character. This adjective was followed by a variety of names—Ned, Nick, Roger, Scratch, Horny, Hob, Billy, Clootie, Gooseberry, Smoker, Serpent, and so on. When 'Harry' was used, it usually called to mind plundering and laying waste. To some it referred to Henry VIII, who was remembered for his cruel deeds. These folks saw the King as the Devil incarnate. He was occasionally referred to as 'Old Harrow,' 'Lord Harry,' or 'Old Harrington.'

One-Eye—This character served as a jack-of-all-trades for Jack Spolden, the Prophet of the Sons of the Sword. He was a skilled cook, waggoner, locksmith, and ironsmith. He was also called the 'Reinsman.' His original surname may have been Barrett. He claimed to have lost his eye in a brawl several years ago.

Ordinance of 1769—This law referred to the attempt by Royal authorities to prevent the selling of alcoholic beverages near or at mines and forges in the American colonies. It also stipulated that any public house which sold alcohol had to be a certain number of miles away from the mine or forge. This law was supposed to help cut down on the drunkenness of laborers in the iron industry. It did little to discourage such behavior.

Oznabrig Coat—Such a garment was made of coarse heavy linen which was originally made in Osnaburg, Germany. It was considered a low-status fabric and was used mainly to make sacking and work clothes. It came to be associated with poor man's cloth and servant's wear.

Palatines of Leyden—One of Jack Spolden's secret cells was named after the 'poor Palatines' who emigrated from the middle Rhine region of Germany in the 18th century. More specifically, Spolden meant to honor those Anabaptists from Leyden who were the descendants of the radicals that participated in the Peasant War of the 16th century. These German emigrants left their homeland to escape persecution. 13,000 of them got to England in 1709, but had difficulty integrating into British society. Many were sent to Ireland and the North American colonies. Most of them settled in the Hudson River Valley of New York in 1710.

Papiack Creek—This small body of water ran west to east above Perth Amboy at the location of present-day Woodbridge, New Jersey. It flowed into the Hudson River.

Parliament—The supreme legislative branch of the British government is called the Parliament. It is made up of the House of Lords and the House of Commons. Parliament developed from the Royal Council established by the Magna Carta in 1215. Over the centuries the English Parliament progressively limited the power of the monarchy. The supremacy of Parliament was settled in principle following the Glorious Revolution in 1688. From then on, all monarchs held limited executive authority. Parliament's relationship with the American colonies turned contentious after the French and Indian War. A series of laws passed by Parliament between 1763 and 1775, which regulated trade and taxes, caused tensions between colonists and imperial officials. Parliament's unwillingness to consider the Americans' complaints led to open rebellion and the Revolutionary War.

Paxton Boys—A vigilante group of Pennsylvania frontiersmen of Scotch-Irish descent attacked local Indians in 1763 near the Paxtang settlement. This group became known as the 'Paxton Boys.' In what was called the 'Conestoga Massacre,' twenty-one Susquehannock Indians were killed. At that time, Parson John Elder led the vigilantes and became the spokesperson for the right of settlers to defend themselves if government officials failed to do so. These officials declared that the Paxton Boys had committed murder and meant to bring the vigilantes to justice. Over two-hundred men marched into Philadelphia in January of 1764 to present their grievances. They claimed that the government was not protecting settlers on the frontier and that they had been falsely accused of murder. The Paxton Boys were met in Germantown by government leaders. These vigilantes agreed to disperse after Ben Franklin intervened and convinced them to cease and desist in their actions.

Peasant War—The German Peasant War, known as 'Deutscher Bauemkrieg' in German, was a widespread popular revolt in central Europe in 1524-1525. The conflict began with several insurrections in southwestern German states and Alsace. It spread quickly to central and eastern regions as well as Austria. The peasants were doomed from the start due to poor leadership, a lack of artillery and cavalry, and little military experience. What kept them going for a brief time was their desire for freedom and influence in a democratic structure in opposition to the traditional oppression by the nobles and church leaders. The tenets of their movement were to be found in the radical teachings of certain individuals, such as the Anabaptist leaders who favored a violent overthrow of church and state. The movement failed due to the strength of the aristocratic military. At least 100,000 peasants were slaughtered. Many survivors were fined. Very little was achieved.

Perth Amboy—The city of Perth Amboy is located at the mouth of the Raritan River and the Arthur Kill. It was settled by Scotch-Irish immigrants in 1683. It became a prime port because of its easily navigable harbor. In 1686, it became the capital of East Jersey. In 1718, Perth Amboy was officially incorporated as a city. Just prior to the Revolutionary War, Governor William Franklin moved from Burlington to Perth Amboy to establish residence there. At this time, British troops were stationed at the Barracks in Perth Amboy. The city remained the capital of New Jersey until 1776 when Franklin was arrested by Continental troops.

Pharo—This gambler's game is named after one of the playing cards in a special deck. The card is called the 'Phar aah' or 'Faro.' The name is derived from the French, 'Pharoan.'

Pharoah—Fannie, the slave cook for John Wetherill, was the mate of a field slave, named Pharoah.

Pinch-Beck Carved Buckles—An inexpensive accessory for certain boots and shoes was the pinch-beck carved buckle. Pinch-beck was an alloy of copper and zinc used as a cheap imitation of gold. It was called 'sham gold' in colonial times.

Pippins—These were varieties of dessert apples. The name for them comes from the Old French, 'pepin,' which meant 'seed.'

Pompians—An 18th century word for pumpkins was 'pompians.' The word comes from the Greek, 'pepon,' meaning large melon. The word was applied by colonists to the squash and pumpkins of the Native Americans. These were later cultivated by the colonists.

Powles Hook—A popular destination for stage wagon wayfarers in the 18th century was Powles Hook, New Jersey. This was originally called Michael Pauw's tract of land. Pauw's Hoeck, or Hook, referred to the point of land on the Hudson River waterfront, where Jersey City is now located. It is one mile across the river from Manhattan. In the 18th century, ferry service from Manhattan and Staten Island brought travelers across to Powles (aka: Paulus) Hook. Many used this as a departure point for journeys to New Brunswick, Princeton, Trenton, Philadelphia, and other points west and north.

Proprietors—In the early years of the Jersey colony, those gaining legal rights to large areas of land via royal charter were called proprietors. At that time, the proprietors gained full prerogatives to establish and run the colonial government and the manner of distributing the land. The proprietors held to this convention until 1702 when East Jersey and West Jersey were united under the rule of Queen Anne. New Jersey became a royal colony with an appointed governor having power over the proprietors.

Puncheon—In colonial times a puncheon was a large cask which contained from 70 to 120 gallons. The name refers to the amount the cask holds. The name derives from the Old French, 'poncon' or 'poincho

Quadrille—This four-handed card game is French in origin and an adaptation of the three-player game called hombre, or ombre. It is played with forty cards. The winner of the bidding selects a partner by calling a king. The game was quite popular in the 18th century until whist became more popular.

Quince—This pear-shaped astringent pome fruit originally came from a small deciduous Asian tree. It is the sole member of the genus cydonia in the family rosaceae. The fruit turns a bright golden-yellow when mature.

Radford's Landing—The ferry and landing across the Raritan River from Perth Amboy was originally called Radford's Landing, or Radford's Ferry. It was later called South Amboy (from the Lenape, 'ampoge,' meaning 'place shaped like a bowl'). Radford's Landing was in the south ward of Middlesex County and fourteen miles north of the Wetherill Plantation.

Randel's Tavern—This popular public house was located on the main street of Allentown, New Jersey. It was also referred to as the Lower Tavern during the 18th century.

Rariton Bay—The Raritan (fka: Rariton) River flows into the bay of the same name. The Rariton Bay is at the southern portion of lower New York Bay. It is named after the Native Americans who lived along the river. The name originally meant 'waterway beyond the island.' Dutch settlers adopted the name and gave it its colonial spelling.

Rariton Landing—A mile or two upstream from New Brunswick, New Jersey, in the 18th century, there was an inland port on the Piscataway side of the Rari-

tan (fka: Rariton) River. Sloops could ply the waters to this unincorporated community when the tide was in, making it the farthest upstream point on the river for ocean-going vessels. This shipping point for various raw materials was started in the early 18th century and lasted until the mid-19th century, when most of the port facilities were abandoned. It was also a receiving port for imported finished goods and a supply place for farmers in the upstream area. The development of the canal and railroad made New Brunswick the area's commercial center and doomed Raritan Landing to a sad fate.

Rariton River—One of the major waterways in New Jersey is the Raritan (fka: Rariton) River. Its watershed drains much of the upland low mountain area in the central part of the state. The river flows in two branches, north and south with many tributaries, and empties into the Raritan Bay and eventually the Atlantic Ocean. During the 18th century, the river served as an important transportation route for Native Americans and European settlers. The original meaning of the Lenape Indian word 'wawitan' or 'rarachons' may be 'forked river' or 'stream which overflows.'

Rattoon's Tavern—The owner of Rattoon's Tavern on Bordentown Avenue in South Amboy (fka: Radford's Landing), New Jersey, was John Rattoon—a resident of Perth Amboy and loyal to the King. However, he was known to service both sides once the conflict started. This was probably due to his inability to handle his debts. His close relatives, such as Thomas Rattoon, helped to run his businesses. This Thomas may have been the one commonly referred to as 'Rat.' He may have operated the tavern in South Amboy in the absence of John Rattoon.

Raven, Sign of the—This tavern was once located four miles north and west of the Hibernia iron works. It mysteriously burned down before Lord Stirling took control of the iron works. This was, allegedly, the place where Dan Fagan was born, since his mother was a serving maid there at that time. She perished in the fire, but Fagan did not. The ruins of the place, once a popular gathering spot for miners and forge workers, were used by Fagan's gang and Jack Spolden's cells as a secret meeting place.

Raway River—This waterway in central New Jersey is known today as Rahway River. It is a tributary of the Arthur Kill (fka: Arthur Kull) in the counties of Essex, Middlesex, and Union. The river is fed by the West Branch and East Branch in West Orange. In Rahway, the river receives waters from Robinson's Branch and South Branch then flows on to the Arthur Kill. The name for the river and town may have come from the Lenni-Lenape Chief, Rahwack.

Redemptioner—A 'temporary slave' in the 18th century was called a redemptioner or indentured servant. Such a person was bound to a number of years service, such as seven years, to a master who paid a ship captain for passage over. A redemptioner usually came from Germany, England, or Ireland. The purchaser of a redemptioner suffered great monetary loss if his servant ran away. This happened quite often in the American colonies.

Redmon, Jack—This character is based on a young man, named Redmon (or Reddon) who worked as a servant for Samuel Haines (or Haynes) of Morristown, New Jersey, in the 1770's. Redmon ran away in the spring of 1773. His description and what he was wearing was posted in the newspaper by his master. It is not known if Redmon was ever found. This man may be the 'older' brother of Jack Redmon, who appears in the prologue of the story.

Reinsman, the—This is another nickname for One-Eye.

Rescarrick, George—In 1686, George Rescarrick purchased 300 acres of land near the Millstone River and Cranberry Brook in central New Jersey. He came from Woodbridge and planned to build a house there and turn it into a house of entertainment for strangers and travelers. He moved to Cranberry (lka: Cranbury) in 1701. His inn (lka: Predmore's Inn) was located at the juncture of Laurie's Road (connecting Perth Amboy to Burlington) and the road to New Brunswick from Cranberry, which carried his name— George's Road or Rescarrick's Road.

Reynolds, David—For his role in Samuel Ford's counterfeiting operation, David Reynolds was the only man executed by hanging. The rest were freed or never caught. He was executed at a public hanging held in Morristown, New Jersey, on September 17, 1773. His accomplices—Dr. Barnaby Budd, Benjamin Cooper, and Samuel Haines (or Haynes) were accused of the same crime, but were respited and let go. They came from upstanding families in the community and were vouched for by influential people. Reynolds was not. He may have been a native of Ireland or may have been born in Pennsylvania. Before his execution, he may have been an innkeeper in Hackettstown, New Jersey. He became involved in the counterfeiting trade through a Mr. Rosecrans and Captain Joseph Richardson of Philadelphia, who had some association with the notorious Sam Ford gang. Reynolds got caught carrying plates and passing bogus money. Budd, Cooper, and Haynes were charged with simply passing counterfeit bills. These three also 'confessed' to knowing who took part in the robbery of the Treasury in 1768. Thus, Reynolds was singled out as the scapegoat for the counterfeiting operation, since the others either escaped or were spoken for and exonerated.

Rhode Hall—Some fifteen miles from South Amboy, New Jersey, along Laurie's Road in the 18th century, was a place named Rhode Hall. The main house there served as the 'half-way' resting stop for stage wagon passengers plying the route from Perth Amboy to Burlington. Rhode Hall lay north of Cranbury and east of Pigeon Swamp. The origin of the name may have come from an innkeeper named Rhodes who operated the public house. Another possibility is that David Williamson, a more recent owner of the establishment, came up with a proper English name for his place of business. Rhode Hall no longer exists but there is a Rhode Hall Road in the area.

Richardson, Joseph—One of the notorious counterfeiters of the 18th century in Pennsylvania and New Jersey was Captain Joseph Richardson. He was an associate of the infamous Doane Brothers of Pennsylvania and an associate of Samuel Ford of New Jersey. Richardson was successful in eluding authorities in both colonies, and joined Ford in escaping to the west. In the postings, Richardson was described as middle-aged, over six feet tall, and stout and active. There was a large bounty posted for his capture but that bounty was never paid.

Rockaway—This borough in Morris County was originally part of Rockaway Township and shares its name with the Rockaway River. The name comes from an English corruption of a Native American term which translates to 'place of sand,' 'creek between hills,' or 'difficult to cross.' The river is a tributary of the Passaic River. It rises in Sussex County and meanders through Morris County. After it joins the Whippany River, it merges with the Passaic River.

Rotting Place—This was a slang expression for a port in England from which tea was exported to the colonies. During the protests against East India tea by the American colonists, such shipments were refused and the ships were sent back to 'Rotting Place.'

Round Creek—This stream flowed into the Hudson River below Barbadoes Neck in New Jersey. It was located halfway between Elizabeth Town and Newark.

Rounders—This colonial ball game was a precursor to baseball. It was a child's game similar to town ball and was played in yards and flat fields where permitted. This bat-and-ball game originated with the English and Irish. It was called 'cluiche corr' in Ireland. A hard round object, usually encased in leather, was struck by a stout stick (held in one hand), and the hitter ran around four stick bases to score a run.

Rundlet—This small-sized barrel had no specific dimensions in colonial times. It could hold up to twenty gallons, but typically held less than twenty.

Runyon, Grace—Judge Daniel Cooper's first wife was related to John Wetherill. The latter's mother was Anne Susannah Runyon of Piscataway. Grace Runyon belonged to the same family. The first Runyon (fka: Rongnion) in the American colonies was Vincent from Portiers, France. He came to Elizabeth Town, New Jersey, around 1668. He wed Ann Boutcher that same year. They settled along the Raritan River by 1677 and had seven children. His son, Vincent, was the father of Anne Susannah Runyon, born in 1702. She married Thomas Wetherill (aka: Wetherly). One of their sons was John Wetherill of South Brunswick. Peter, another son of the original Vincent, was the father of Grace Runyon, who was born in 1706/07.

Russia Shirt—This poor man's apparel was mentioned occasionally in the New Jersey Archives in describing what a certain runaway servant was wearing when he fled. It was usually made from coarse linen and was white or yellow in color. It was loose fitting, quite long, and had a ring collar which was often embroidered.

Saggathy Coat—This type of garment was woven from wool in four-harness twill (two-up and two-down) with a white warp and a colored filling. It was usually given a high finish by calendering the worsted warp. The fabric was used more for curtains than for garments in the 18th century. The name is derived from the Latin, 'sagathi.'

Samson, Samuel—This name was used as an alias by Samuel Ford in order to keep his true identity from being discovered by authorities. His reputation as the most notorious counterfeiter in New Jersey in the latter half of the 18th century forced Ford to use assumed names in order to elude being captured.

Sarah—The daughter of Fannie, the cook at the Wetherill plantation, was named Sarah. She was a house servant for John Wetherill during the latter half of the 18th century. Sarah is mentioned in John Wetherill's will as the child of Fan, his negro wench. She is not to be confused with Wetherill's daughter of the same name and spelling.

Sargent, Sam—One of the barracks masters at Perth Amboy, New Jersey, in the latter half of the 18th century, was Sam Sargent. His name was spelled in the New Jersey Archives in various ways, including 'Serjant' and 'Sarjant.'

Sateen—This cotton fabric boasted a glossy surface meant to imitate satin and cost less than satin. It was quite popular in the 18th century and was used mostly in making garments, such as waistcoats.

Schooley's Mountain—This highland location provides the backdrop for German Valley (aka: Long Valley) and Fox Hill in Morris County, New Jersey. The area was a popular place in the summer due to the 'healing springs' emanating from deep down in Schooley's Mountain (aka: Schooler's Mountain), as far back as colonial times. This mountain rises six-hundred feet from its base to its top and sits 1,100 feet above sea level. The iron springs were discovered at the base of the mountain on the Hackettstown side by Culverites in 1734.

Schultheiss Marshals—Jack Spolden applied this name to the middling officers of his secret cells. Their main responsibility was to maintain order among the ranks and make sure initiates performed well during raids. In medieval times, the head of a German municipality was often called a 'schultheiss.' The word comes from 'schuld,' meaning 'find fault' and 'heiss,' meaning 'order around.'

Scion Branches—Shoots or branches from fruit bearing trees, which were used for grafting in colonial times were called 'scion' {aka: cion or sion) branches. The grafting of such branches was a favorite activity of John Wetherill at his plantation in Middlesex County, New Jersey.

Sharp, Abraham—The Elder Sharp owned a farm at Mine Hill in Morris County, New Jersey, in the latter half of the 18th century. He was a member of a large Quaker family, which included relatives involved in the Sharpsborough iron works and various mines in the area.

Sharp, Amanda—The oldest daughter of the Elder Sharp of Mine Hill, New Jersey, was Amanda Sharp. She befriended Rachel Hagers in her time of need.

Shattucks—In the 17th century, a Captain Shaddock brought Pomelo seeds from Indonesia to Jamaica. The name for the fruit produced became 'shaddock' or 'shattuck.' When it was crossed with the Jamaican sweet orange the result was the grapefruit.

Shires, Bay—Such draft horses, often geldings, were reddish brown in color with a black mane and tail. This tall breed usually stood over 17 hands high. This type has an enormous capacity for weight pulling and was popular in pulling brewery wagons. The breed was easy to handle. John Wetherill named his two bay Shires—Thor and Hercules.

Sippet Pudding—The name for this bread pudding came from the French 'sop', meaning 'piece of bread.' It was popular in the 18th century.

Skinner, Cortlandt—The most notable son of Rev. William Skinner and Elizabeth VanCortlandt Skinner was Cortlandt (or Cortland) Skinner. He studied law in Newark with David Ogden and went on to become one of the most influential public servants under Governor William Franklin. He was a member of the Board of Proprietors in 1752. He was also a member of the Governor's Council. In 1754, Cortlandt was appointed New Jersey's Attorney General. He also acted as Speaker of the Provincial Assembly between 1765 and 1770, and between 1772 and 1776. In the early 1770's he held the reputation of a man of integrity and ability. He was the brother of Stephen Skinner, Treasurer of East Jersey, and Thomas Skinner, High-Sheriff in Perth Amboy.

Skinner, Stephen—This younger brother of Cortlandt Skinner was a successful trader and merchant in Perth Amboy during the 1760's. He ran a popular general store in that city until 1767. In 1763, he was appointed Treasurer of East Jersey by Governor William Franklin. In the years that followed, the association between the conservative Governor and the tory Skinners strengthened. However, on July 22, 1768, the entire East Jersey Provincial Treasury of over 7,000 pounds was stolen from Stephen Skinner's house. Colonists blamed Skinner for being in on the robbery for his own gain. Others blamed him for being careless. Many called for him to resign or be dismissed. The Governor felt otherwise and defended Skinner until he finally resigned on February 23, 1774. The stolen funds were never recovered and the robbers were never caught. John Wetherill played an instrumental role in putting pressure on Skinner to resign and in getting legislation passed to ensure the security of Treasury funds. Thomas (Tom) Skinner, brother of Cortlandt and Stephen Skinner, was High-Sheriff at Perth Amboy, New Jersey, in the 1770's. He is mentioned several times in the New Jersey Archives.

Smith,_____—This counterfeiter from New York had some association with the Sam Ford gang of counterfeiters in New Jersey. His first name does not appear in the sources.

Smultz Cabin—One of the hideouts used by Samuel Ford in his attempt to elude the authorities, was the Smultz cabin. This abandoned colliery was located in the hills west of Hibernia, New Jersey, and south of Dane's Lake (aka: Lake Denmark). After Ford was done with the place, Dan Fagan's gang took it over and used the cabin as its headquarters.

Snake Hill—This promontory is located in the Meadowlands (aka: Bergen Meadows) in southern Secaucus, New Jersey. It is known currently as Laurel Hill, but in the 18th century it was known as Snake Hill. The early Dutch settlers called the high igneous intrusion 'Slangenburgh', which translated into English as 'Snakes Mountain.' Needless to say, it was a place where numerous snakes could be found.

Sons of Dawn—The revised and shortened name for the hunting club in the Morristown, New Jersey, was the Sons of Dawn. The name for this club was originally Sons of the Dawn Sword—a name given to the club at its inception by its most notable member, Lord Stirling. Over time, the long name was shortened to the more convenient Sons of Dawn. Many affluent and influential men in the area were members of the club—these included the Fords, the Coopers, and the Morrells.

South River—This tributary of the Raritan River flows through the south ward of Middlesex County. It forms at the confluence of Matchaponix Brook and Manalapan Brook. It joins the Raritan midway between New Brunswick and South Amboy. The river lends its name to the borough of South River.

South Ward—The southern portion of Middlesex County was known as the south ward in the 18th century. Its northern boundary was the Raritan River and it extended south to Princeton and Windsor. The southernmost part of the ward was included in the creation of Mercer County in the next century.

Spanish Barb—This breed of horse originated with he Berbers in North Africa. The agile African desert 'barb', as it was called, was brought to Spain during the Muslim occupation and was crossed with Spanish stock. From then on it was known as the Spanish barb. In the late 15th century, the conquistadors brought such a horse to the new world. By the 17th century, Native Americans had acquired such horses. Tribes, such as the Chickasaw, Choctaw, and Creek, favored them. Later, English settlers captured Indian horses of this kind and also Spanish strays. They were bred with various blood lines, including oriental-barbs, English race horses, and Irish blood lines. The result was the colonial Spanish barb and the colonial short horse.

Spanktown—One of the early names for Rahway, New Jersey, in colonial times, was Spanktown. The current name may have come from a local Indian chief's name, 'Rahwack.' Europeans began settling here in the latter decades of the 17th century. One of the first English names for the area was Spanktown. The origin of this name is one of legend— one settler physically reprimanded his wife, and, thus, rumors spread about the abuse. Some folks then started calling the place Spanktown.

Spolden, John—The spiritual leader of the Sons of the Sword was John Spolden (aka: Jack or Johnny Spolden). His followers referred to him as the 'Prophet.' His nickname among his detractors was 'Black Jake.' Spolden was born of Irish/German ancestry (c. 1750). He was a forge apprentice for Samuel Heaton at Schooley's Mountain from 1767 until the time he ran away, accompanied by two laborers on stolen horses. Heaton had unwittingly introduced young Spolden to certain religious texts—one of which provided inspiration for the creation of a revolutionary movement in north and west New Jersey. Spolden modeled his movement on the teachings and actions of the radical Anabaptist leaders of the 16th century. He created secret cells of banditti and sent them on pillaging raids in order to supply his movement

with booty and funds. In 1772, he started making incursions into Morris County. There, he and his followers met their match.

Spot's Woods—The current town of Spotswood was called 'Spot's Woods' in the 18th century. The first settlers came to the area in the late 17th century. James John Stone, from Scotland, named his new home 'Spotteswoode,' after the name of his old home. The settlement spread along Lawrie's Road in Middlesex County, New Jersey. Travelers from New York and Philadelphia occasionally stopped there. The place became known for its many mills which utilized waterways flowing there.

Springfield—This township is now located in Union County, New Jersey. It was first settled in the early 1700's by Dutch and English settlers who replaced the Unami Indians living there. The area was covered by dense forests and only one road cut through it, connecting Morristown to Elizabeth Town. This was an area of farms, mills, and lumbering activities.

Spruce Beer—The colonial beverage made from spruce buds, leaves, and twigs, along with sugar, water, and yeast, became quite popular in the 18th century in North America. The non-alcoholic form was first used by Native Americans as a winter beverage to cure scurvy. The European settlers preferred to use the tops and branches of red and black spruce in the alcoholic form, which was favored in the colonies.

Staten Island—Southwest of the city port of New York lies Staten Island. This borough is separated from New Jersey by the Arthur Kill and the Kill Van Kull. It is separated from the rest of New York by New York Bay. The Lenape Indians called this island 'Aque Honga Manacknong'' which translates to 'as far as the place of the bad woods.' Dutch settlers in the 16th century named the place 'Staaten Eylandt,' which meant 'States Island.' In the 17th century, under English rule, Staten Island became part of Richmond County. In the late 17th century, the British divided the island into four administrative districts which became the towns of Castleton, Northfield, Southfield, and Westfield. In the early 18th century, a county seat was established at Richmond Town.

Steel,_____ —This known criminal had some connection with the counterfeiting trade, and, hence, a probable connection with the Sam Ford gang. His first name is not mentioned in the sources.

Stingo—This word refers to a strong ale, or beer, that was popular in the 18th century. One of the leading brands of the beverage was 'Watney's Stingo-nips.' The origin of the word is speculative. It may have derived from 'sting,' meaning its bite, plus the Italianate ending 'o.'

Stiles, Jonathan—One of the Morris County sheriffs in the late 18th century was Jonathan Stiles. He was born in 1721. He served in the early 1770's and carried on the work of his father who had served as sheriff prior to his passing in 1758. Stiles was succeeded by Thomas Kinney in 1774. He is mentioned in the New Jersey Archives.

Stirling, Lord—(see Alexander, William)

Stites, Hezekiah—One of the prominent doctors in Middlesex County, New Jersey, during the latter half of the 18th century, was Dr. Hezekiah Stites of Cranbury (fka: Cranberry). He served as Secretary of the New Jersey Medical Society in 1775, according to the New Jersey Archives. His house was located on South Main Street in Cranbury.

Suppawn Pudding—This porridge made from cornmeal was also called hasty pudding, samp, or mush. It was either boiled in milk or water until it thickened. Such simple fare probably originated with the Native Americans and was introduced to European settlers by them. The Munsee Delaware Indians called it 'nsa-pa-n,' meaning 'soften by water.' The Dutch called it 'suppaen' or 'sapaen.' The English called it 'suppawn' or 'suppan.'

Swan Hill—One of the higher elevations associated with South Amboy, New Jersey, was Swan Hill. This was located near the south end of Broadway. Clay deposits there gave rise to a pottery and terracotta industry.

Swan, John—One of the notorious counterfeiters of the late 18th century in New Jersey was John Swan. He was captured by authorities in June of 1773. Shortly thereafter, he confessed to various crimes and implicated Samuel Ford in the Treasury robbery of 1768.

Tom Coward—One-Eye's nickname for Tom Ward was 'Tom Coward.' The nickname refers to one who is afraid to fight or come to the aid of those in peril.

Tom Doodle—This nickname was applied to Ike Higgins. 'Tom Doodle' refers to a simpleton. It was also spelled 'Tom-a-Doodle.'

Tower Hill—This promontory in Pennsylvania marked the dividing line between upper Makefield Township and Solebury Township. The land on which the hill sat was, at one time, owned by John Beamont. He lent his surname to the landmark. However, the place was also called Bowman's Hill. This name may have come from Thomas Bowman, an English merchant who plied the waters of the Delaware in the 17th century. Another possibility for the Bowman's Hill name was that it was named after John Bowman, who was a friend of Jonathan Pidcock, the first settler in the area. In the late 18th century the place became known as Tower Hill.

Trencher—This double-sized food plate was popular in the 18th century. It was used to serve food to more than one person. It also referred to a wooden board on which meat was carved and served. The name came from the French 'trenchour.'

Tricorn—This cocked hat was very popular in the 18th century. The brim was curled up to form three corners—hence the name, 'tricorn.' The purpose in doing so was to drain off raindrops.

Twenty-Second Assembly—Governor William Franklin called together his appointed Council and elected General Assembly in November of 1773. In his opening speech on November 12th, he announced that progress had been made in apprehending counterfeiters in Middlesex and Monmouth counties. Their confessions led to the discovery of Samuel Ford's gang and information connecting the leader of the gang to the Treasury robbery of 1768. Franklin announced that three members of the gang had been respited and one had been executed. The Governor recommended passage of stricter laws on counterfeiting. He also urged the Legislature to grant a fair supply for the King's troops stationed in New Jersey. Franklin also recommended that legislators enable him to offer rewards for apprehending Samuel Ford and the rest of his gang.

Twenty-Sixth Regiment of Foot—This Scotch-Irish regiment of British Regulars was known as such since 1751. It was first raised as the Cameronian Guard in 1689, and was led by Richard Cameron, a founder of the Presbyterian Sects Foundation. Each soldier was required to carry a bible. In 1689, it became the regiment of the Earl of Angus. While the regiment was stationed in Dublin, Ireland, it was called the Twenty-Sixth Regiment of Foot. In 1769, it was moved to the American colonies. One of the places the regiment was stationed at was Perth Amboy, New Jersey.

Van Vorst, Faddy—Cornelius "Faddy" Van Vorst was a wealthy entrepreneur in New Jersey and New York in the 18th century. He was a business partner with Verdine Elsworth at Powles Hook, where he built the popular mile-long oval race course at a site called Harsimus. He also ran a ferry service to and from New York.

Veal Town—The section of Bernards Township, formerly known as Veal Town or Vealtown, is presently called Bernardsville, New Jersey. It is located in the northernmost part of Somerset County, twelve miles south of Morristown. Much of the area was heavily forested and untamed in the 18th century.

Vellum—This fine parchment from treated calfskin was used for writing and binding books. It was popular in the 18th century. The word comes from the Old French, 'velin', which means 'manuscript written on calfskin.'

Walsh, Billy—Jacob Morrell's slave foreman was Tom Ward. His past was rather murky and rife with aliases. One name he used previously was Billy Walsh. He allegedly came from Ireland as a redemptioner in 1767. He served as an apprentice under Barrack Master, Sam Sargent, in Perth Amboy that year. He was introduced to thieving by soldiers from Dublin stationed with the 26th Regiment in Perth Amboy. He was caught stealing and given a choice of corporal punishment or joining up with the 26th. Walsh, instead, chose to run away. He ended up cleaning horse stalls at Powles Hook in 1769. From there he headed west to the mines, but got caught thieving in or near Black River. He was freed from jail by Jacob Morrell, who paid all fines and expenses, and hired him on. By this time he had dropped the Billy Walsh name and was using the Tom Ward name.

Ward, Tom—For background on this character, see 'Billy Walsh.' He led a double life by working as a slave foreman for Jacob Morrell of Morristown, New Jersey, and secretly as a special agent for Jack Spolden. For the latter, Ward was charged with finding any persons who claimed to have descended from royal blood. He was supposed to be handsomely paid for bringing such victims of kidnaping to Spolden to fulfill a prophecy which he did not care about or understand. In this odd way, Ward set about bettering himself so that he could leave his low station and miserable lifestyle behind. Things did not work out quite as he planned.

Watchungs, The—This mountain chain in New Jersey was formerly called the Blue Hills. They consist of three long ridges between 400 and 500 feet high in northern and western New Jersey. The original inhabitants, the Lenape, called these mountains 'Wach Links,' or 'high hills.'

Waterman, Stephen—This counterfeiter was apprehended in June of 1773 in New Jersey and incarcerated. During an interrogation, he confessed to knowing of Sam Ford's illegal activities. Waterman, along with John Swan, came from Rhode Island and had set up shop in Woodbridge, New Jersey, in 1772. They established a sham silver smith's trade, and started making and circulating counterfeit coin.

West Jersey—This distinct part of the province of New Jersey existed from 1674 to 1702. It was separated from East Jersey by the Keith Line and the Coxe/Barclay Line. Throughout its existence, Burlington served as the capital.

Westphalia—This region of northwestern Germany is located between the Weser River and the Low Countries. The city of Munster can be found there. In the 1530's Westphalia experienced the rebellion led by radical Anabaptists and their attempt to set up a communal sectarian government at Munster.

Wetherill, Abigail Lott—Vincent Wetherill's wife was fondly known as 'Little Abia.' They were wed in New Brunswick, New Jersey, on April 17, 1773. Their only child, Ann, was born in 1774. Abigail Lott was the daughter of Richard Lott and Letitia Phillips of Hopewell, New Jersey. She was rather young when she married and was reputed to be quite beautiful.

Wetherill, George—John Wetherill's younger brother was born circa 1720 and died 1804/5. His father, Thomas of Piscataway, New Jersey, left him over 200 acres of land at Drinking Brook Hollow in what later became known as South Brunswick Township in Middlesex County. George moved there and lived out his life on his estate, called 'The Brick-

yards.' He wed _____ (?) and raised at least four children—Thomas, Elizabeth, Ann, and Samuel. He was a leader in his community, serving as one of the first Freeholders for the South Ward, starting in 1773. George was involved directly or indirectly in several local business ventures, including 'The Brick Hole'—a clay excavation project, and the Cross Roads Inn (aka: the Wetherill Tavern) that was run by his son, Thomas. George was also involved with raising horses at the Longbridge Farm.

Wetherill, John—The most influential man in the old South Brunswick area in the late 18th century was John Wetherill. He owned a plantation southeast of Cross Roads (pka: Dayton), New Jersey, which consisted of more than 1,700 acres extending along Georges Road. He owned land in Pigeon (or Pidgeon) Swamp, which was used for culling timber. He had a profitable nursery of over 400 apple trees, of which a hundred were special grafted trees. Wetherill had at least seven slaves on his plantation. John was a prominent civil servant at county and state levels. He was elected to the colonial Assembly by voters in Middlesex County starting in 1749. He served several terms right up to the eve of the Revolution. He also served as Paymaster and Commissary Commissioner for the Jersey Blues in the 1750's. In 1774, he was appointed by the Assembly to the Committee of Correspondence. He was a member of the Provincial Congress in the summer of 1775 and at the start of 1776. He also attended the Provincial Convention in June of 1776. Throughout his political career he demonstrated whiggish and patriot tendencies. He was known for his penny-pinching ways. He resisted voting for expenditures of all kinds. He saw himself as the guardian of the public purse. He often challenged the excessive policies of proprietors, Parliament, Governor, and King. He gained the reputation of being a dissenter and was at one time called a rioter by his foes. John Wetherill was born in Piscataway, New Jersey, but the date of his birth is in question. Sources range from 1696 to 1720. His parents were Thomas Wetherill, a former militia Captain and church warden, and Anne Susannah Runyon, who could trace her ancestry back to French royalty. The Piscataway Wetherills may have come from Massachusetts, New Hampshire, or Burlington, New Jersey. Most likely, John's line may be traced back to the Piscataqua community in southeastern New Hampshire. The Wetherill (or Wetherell, Wetherly, Wetherby, etc.) line can be traced further back to England. The Piscataway and Burlington Wetherills probably all descend from Gyles Wetherill of County Durham. Under his father's tutelage, John was trained as a blacksmith, but he was destined for greater things after moving to the South Brunswick area where his father had given him several acres of land. He also acquired over 600 acres north of Cranbury Brook on which he tended to agricultural pursuits, married, and raised a family. Wetherill wed Hannah (often called Ann, as well as pet names—Nana or Nanny) Mount in 1744 (?). They had at least four children— John, Jr., Rachel, Sarah, and Vincent. It is not clear what church the family was affiliated with, but there is record of a John Wetherill, Warden of St. Peter's Episcopal Church in Spotswood, New Jersey, in the 1760's and the same person as Vestryman in the 1770's.

Wetherill, Thomas—This Wetherill was born in 1739. He was the son of George Wetherill and nephew to Assemblyman John Wetherill of South Brunswick, New Jersey. He wed Rachel FitzRandolph (1742-1829) and had at least five children by her. They were George, who died in childhood, Abigail, Rebecca, Sarah, and Ann. Thomas ran the Cross Roads Inn (lka: The Wines Hotel) in what is now known as Dayton, New Jersey. He also raised horses at Longbridge Farm and helped oversee that large plantation when the owner was absent. He inherited much land from his father as well as the 'Brickyards' estate along the Manaipon Brook near Cranbury, New Jersey.

Wetherill, Vincent—The second son of John Wetherill was born in 1749 or 1750. He wed Abigail Lott on April 17, 1773,

and had a daughter, Ann, by her in 1774. Vincent preferred to live in New Brunswick, New Jersey, rather than live on his father's plantation southeast of Cross Roads. Here, he helped run his father's business interests and became involved in patriot activities, which led to his joining the Middlesex County Militia and serving as Captain of a Company which saw action around New York City in 1776. He was captured and died in the Sugar House Prison that same year.

Wheat Sheaf Tavern—This popular watering hole was located along the King's Highway in present-day Linden, New Jersey, north of Rahway (fka: Spanktown) and south of Elizabeth (fka: Elizabethtown). It may have been constructed around 1745.

Whig—The origins of the Whig political group date back to the late 17th century when Shaftesbury's supporters opposed the succession of the future James II due to his Catholic sympathies. The Whigs helped organize the Glorious Revolution in 1688-9. They were dominant in the first half of the 18th century in British politics. The American Whigs opposed taxation by Parliament and various oppressive measures by King George during the years leading to the Revolutionary War. Whigs became synonamous with patriots and led the struggle for independency.

Whippanong River—The Whippany River, a tributary of the Rockaway River, has experienced many different spelling changes in its name over the centuries. The name has been spelled Whippanong, Whippannung, Whippenny, Whippeny, and, finally, Whippany. It is a Lenape name which means 'where willows grow.' The gentle and meandering waterway rises in Morris County in Mendham Township west of Morristown. It flows through Morristown and joins the Rockaway River in eastern Morris County.

Wick, Daniel—One of the prominent figures in the Morristown area was Daniel Wick. He developed land along the Passaic River with the help of his brothers. The family became prosperous. He was born in 1712 to John Wick and Temperance Barnes of Southampton, New York. Daniel and his wife, Jane, had at least five children.

Wickatunk, Barrens of—This wild and foreboding stretch of swamp and scrub land in Monmouth and Middlesex counties in New Jersey might be considered the northernmost extension of the Piney Woods. The name may have more than one meaning among Native Americans who at one time lived in the area. The Algonquian origin was 'wikwetung,' which means 'the finishing place.' Among the Lenape, 'wikwetunk' meant 'place of the house,' with 'wikwam' meaning 'house,' and 'onk' meaning 'place.'

Williamson's Inn—David Williamson operated a public house at Rhode Hall, New Jersey, in the late 18th century. According to the New Jersey Archives, this resting place for stage wagon travelers was called Williamson's Inn for several years. This stop was fifteen miles from South Amboy and a few miles north of Cranbury along Lawrie's Road. Williamson may have also come up with the name for Rhode Hall, which no longer exists as a community.

Wills, _____—This counterfeiter from Connecticut was apprehended in New Jersey in 1773. In the midst of his confession he mentioned the illegal activities of the Sam Ford gang. This information led to the apprehension of several members of the most notorious counterfeiters in New Jersey.

Wilton Coat—This lounging garment was popular in the 18th century. It was named after a town in Wiltshire, England, where linen was used on a jacquaro loom. The result was a garment with a velvety surface.

Wiston, William—This English theologian, historian, and mathematician was born in 1667 and died in 1752. He is best known for his translations of Antiquities of the Jews and The Works of Josephus in 1737. He also helped instigate the Longitude Act in 1714. He was mentored by Isaac Newton. He became an exponent of Arianism.

Wood Bridge—The present-day Woodbridge, New Jersey, may have been named for a wooden bridge which spanned the Rahway River in Middlesex County. The township of Woodbridge was settled in 1664 and was granted a charter by King Charles of England in 1669. The source of its name may also have come from honoring the Reverend John Woodbridge of Newbury, Massachusetts. This account favors the former possibility.

Woods, Good Mary—This character is based on a Mary Woods who ran away from her husband in 1771, according to an article in the New Jersey Archives. She left her home in Lancaster County, Pennsylvania, and headed for parts unknown. In this story, she and her son, Ned (or Little Ned), appear at Radford's Landing, under the employ of Mr. Rattoon. She was involved with Ike Higgins.

Wormwood—This bitter tasting medicine was recommended by a doctor summoned to treat Ike Higgins after the stable fire at Powles Hook, New Jersey. Wormwood is an aromatic perennial plant found in parts of Europe and Asia which yields an oil used in making absinthe. The medical term for wormwood is 'artemisia absinthium.' It was used to quell fevers and many ills in the 18th century.

Zwickau, Avengers of—Before the uprisings of peasants and farmers and craftsmen in 1524-25, there were three prophets from Zwickau in Saxony who led the radical reformation which provided an alternative to Martin Luther's movement. They were Nicholas Storch, Thomas Dreschel, and Markus Stubner. Their teachings led to the disturbance at Wittenberg in 1522, and provided inspiration for Thomas Muntzer to carry on a radical Anabaptist movement. The Zwickau prophets claimed that all revelations came from the Holy Spirit, not scripture. They opposed infant baptism. Most importantly, they preached that the end of days was near.